Herero Heroes

Books on Namibia
published by
James Currey
& Ohio University Press

Colin Leys & John S. Saul
Namibia's Liberation Struggle
The Two-Edged Sword

Edited by Patricia Hayes, Jeremy Silvester
Marion Wallace & Wolfram Hartmann
Namibia under South African Rule
Mobility & Containment 1915–46

Jan-Bart Gewald
Herero Heroes
A Socio-Political History of the
Herero of Namibia 1890–1923

Gretchen Bauer
Labor & Democracy in Namibia
1971–96

Herero Heroes

A Socio-Political History
of the Herero of Namibia
1890–1923

JAN-BART GEWALD
Research Fellow at Institute for African Studies,
University of Cologne

JAMES CURREY
OXFORD

DAVID PHILIP
CAPE TOWN

OHIO UNIVERSITY PRESS
ATHENS

James Currey Ltd
73 Botley Road
Oxford OX2 0BS

David Philip Publishers (Pty) Ltd
208 Werdmuller Centre
Newry Street
Claremont 7700
South Africa

Ohio University Press
Scott Quadrangle
Athens, Ohio 45701

1 2 3 4 5 03 02 01 00 99

British Library Cataloguing in Publication Data
Gewald, Jan-Bart
Herero heroes : a socio-political history of the Herero of
Namibia, 1890-1923
1.Herero (African people) - Namibia - History 2.Namibia -
History - 1884-1915 3.Namibia - History - Herero Revolt,
1904-1907 4.Namibia - History - 1915-1946
I.Title
968.8'1

ISBN 0–85255–754–X (James Currey Cloth)
ISBN 0–85255–749–3 (James Currey Paper)
ISBN 0–86486–387–X (David Philip Paper)

Library of Congress Cataloging-in-Publication Data Available

ISBN 0–8214–1256–6 (Ohio University Press Cloth)
ISBN 0–8214–1257–4 (Ohio University Press Paper)

Typeset in 10/11pt Plantin
by Nicholas Hardyman, Oxford

Contents

Studies that relate to the nature of German imperialism and the
development of totalitarian societies – Popular war histories –
Ethnographic studies

Introduction – *Ovatjimba* and missionary chiefs – Trade wars –
Building up the herds – The chieftains – Summing up

Introduction – German protection treaties – The coming of the
camel – Death by camel – In my father's house – The inheritance
– Murdered in peace – Windhoek, Windhoek is my death

Introduction – Manasse Tjisiseta and the Omaruru polity – The pillars
of independence – The SWACO affair – The ending of Omaruru's
independence – The ripping of Okombahe – Treaties – Treaty
enforcement – The centre cannot hold – Let loose the dogs of war –
Conclusion

Introduction – The introduction of rinderpest to Namibia –
Preventative measures – Kohlstock and Koch – The Etaneno affair
– Food, capital and patronage – Recouping their losses – The
balance – Conclusion

Maps, Photographs & Figures

MAPS

PHOTOGRAPHS

FIGURES

Preface

This book developed out of my doctoral thesis, 'Towards Redemption: A socio-political history of the Herero of Namibia between 1890 and 1923', which was defended in Leiden in 1996. As such it is in itself the product of a long history, and owes much to many people. To all those who have assisted me, some of whom are listed below, I am truly grateful.

In February 1986 I arrived in Leiden, a bewildered and stunned student who had refused to serve in the South West African Territorial Force, South Africa's proxy force in Namibia. In Leiden I soon discovered that my South African BA did not count for much, and that the powers that be were of the opinion that I should have to wait another eight months before I could even register, let alone study, as a first year history student. Thankfully Robert Ross, who was teaching in Leiden at the time, took me under his wing. With charming indifference to the formalities Robert allowed me to do course work.

The work that I completed under Robert's tutelage, in that first rather haphazard year in Leiden, brought stability and ensured that there was continuity with what I had been doing in South Africa; there, at Rhodes University in the eastern Cape, I had been a student of Julian Cobbing, and a member of the self-styled 'Mfecane Myth Marauders'. In effect, as a historian, I am a product of these two mentors. They taught me my craft, and I sincerely hope that in reading this, they will find echoes of their own skill and style. Without their awe-inspiring disregard for convention, this book, and my love for history, would never have come about.

After completing the compulsory undergraduate courses, some with such unintentionally ironic titles as *Vaderlandse Geschiedenis* (History of the fatherland), and after five months as an exchange student at the University of Ghana, Legon, I completed my MA in 1990 and began preparing my doctoral research.

In 1990 and early 1991 I was an exchange student at the Department of African Studies at the University of Cologne. This was made possible by the Erasmus exchange programme facilitated by Ridder Samsom. In Cologne, Mrs Kapuuo and Professor Möhlig taught me the rudiments of Herero language, grammar and structure. Without their input, my work would have been so much the poorer, and I am grateful to them for their assistance.

Between March 1991 and March 1995 I was lucky enough to find employment as an *Onderzoeker in Opleiding* (Researcher in Training) with the Netherlands Organization for the Advancement of Tropical Research (WOTRO). Under programme W 24-521, WOTRO funded most of the research that went to make up this book, and I am grateful to them for their assistance.

On and off between February 1991 and June 1996 the Leiden CNWS

Research School of Asian, African and Amerindian Studies provided me with the best office facilities imaginable. Added to this, the staff and fellow researchers at the CNWS ensured that going to work was fun. It is true to say that, without the CNWS, this book would never have been possible, let alone written, and I am therefore truly grateful to everybody associated with the school.

Research for this book was conducted in a number of archives. The first that I visited for the purposes of this book was that of the United Evangelical Mission in Wuppertal, Germany, which is very capably run by Barbara Faulenbach. Apart from introducing me to the handwritten scrawls of missionaries long gone, Barbara also taught me how to decipher the gothic Schrift in which most of the nineteenth- and early twentieth-century German documents are written. For this I am thankful.

In May 1991 and September 1996 I conducted research in the Federal State Archives in Potsdam, Germany. Apart from running a very tight show, and being in the midst of a complete removal to new quarters in 1996, the staff went out of their way to help me. For this I am grateful.

In Namibia I made use of the services of many institutions and people. I wish to thank the staff of the Namibian National Archives, the Estorff Reference Library, the National Museum library, the Namibian Scientific Society, the Evangelical Lutheran Church in Namibia, and the University of Namibia. In particular I wish to thank the late Brigitte Lau, whose caustic comments did much to ensure that this book was written, and who unfortunately never got to see more than the draft chapters of the thesis that preceded this book.

I wish to thank the president of the Republic of Botswana, for granting me permission to conduct research in Botswana. The staff of the University of Botswana, the National Institute for Research, the Botswana National Archives, the Botswana Scientific society, and the Botswana National Museum assisted me in every way possible. I am thankful to all of them for that.

I conducted a number of interviews in Namibia and Botswana. Many people went out of their way to take the time and trouble to listen to me, speak to me, and attempt to understand what it was that I was looking for. Not only did I truly enjoy my time with them, I also learnt an incredible amount about the manner in which people viewed their history. Their selfless assistance provided me with insights that I had never anticipated. I am indebted to all of them, and grateful for their assistance.

In South Africa I worked in the Cape Archives Depot in Cape Town and the Barlow Rand Archives in Johannesburg. In Zimbabwe I was permitted to spend some time going through the Zimbabwe National Archives. I wish to thank the staff of these institutions for their assistance.

A substantial part of the thesis that preceded this book was written between March 1995 and May 1996 in Téra, a small town in western Niger. I wish to thank the inhabitants of Téra, for introducing me to a new field of study, and for living up to the Prophet's adage that every stranger is to be approached as a believer.

Upon my return from Niger, I came to be employed as a historian within the Special Research Project 389, Arid Climate Adaptation and Cultural Innovation in Africa, of the German research foundation, attached to the University of Cologne. ACACIA has greatly facilitated my further research into Herero views of the past, and has kindly provided support during the revision of my thesis. I wish to thank my closest colleagues within the SFB 389, Heike Behrend and Inge Brinkman, for their company and inspiring insights, as well as their accommodating approach to my working style. In particular, in Cologne I wish to thank my office mate, Monika Feinen, for her excellent company, internet skills, and the maps that grace this book.

In Cologne Michael Bollig has not only been an exceptional colleague and exemplary house mate, he has also proved to be the most considerate birth attendant that anyone could wish for. It is a pleasure working with Michael and I treasure his friendship.

Within two months of my arrival in Holland in 1986, I was fortunate enough to meet Gertie Janssen. Gertie's insights and knowledge of the world have always been disturbingly incisive and stimulating. For the past twelve years, we have travelled and lived together. Without her presence this book would never have been written, and our daughter, Sieme, would never have been born. It is to Sieme and Gertie that I dedicate this book: nobody could wish for better company.

                                                                    Asmara, Eritrea

Introduction

In September 1995 in Windhoek, the capital city of the Republic of Namibia, Herero soldiers carrying German ranks and singing translated German hymns marched along Independence Avenue, previously known as *Kaiserstrasse*. The soldiers presented the visiting German Chancellor Helmut Kohl with a petition demanding the payment of war reparations to the 'Herero people'.[1] In essence, media coverage surrounding Kohl's visit encapsulated the image of Namibia as a former German colony where German is spoken, men and women get dressed in copies of German missionary and military clothing, and a terrible colonial war was fought. Though it is true that this concentration on Germany's role in Namibia, which extends into the academic fraternity, conveniently side-steps the horrors of the only recently ended South African occupation, it also overlooks the role of the Herero in determining their own history, and downgrades their position in the past to one of a group of people who were and are capable only of reacting to and in copy of external influences.

This book discusses the manner in which the Herero transformed and moulded their society between 1890, when Maharero Tjamuaha, the chieftain of Okahandja, died, and 1923, when his son Samuel Maharero died. During this period of time the Herero were devastated in a genocidal colonial war. Prior to, and after, the war Herero society appropriated, transformed and applied ideas, concepts and instruments, some of which were external in origin, to its own ends. The politics and society of the Herero prior to the Herero–German war, as well as the manner in which Herero society was able to overcome its destruction and reestablish itself in the aftermath of the war, form the subject-matter of this book. The central focus of this work is thus not the Herero–German war, but the manner in which Herero society operated in Namibia in the years of Samuel Maharero's reign, initially as chief of Okahandja and later as paramount chief of all of the Herero.[2]

[1] *Republikein* 28/8/95, pp. 1–2; 15/9/95, pp. 1–2; 20/9/95, pp. 1–2 & *Onze Wereld*, Dec. 95, p. 57.
[2] Earlier draft versions of this book contained an extra chapter on the history of the Herero in Botswana between 1890 and 1923. In the interests of continuity this chapter was later dropped. Parts of the dropped chapter were presented as a paper at the annual conference of the African Studies Association in Toronto 1994 as *Seeking to return? Herero exiles 1904–1923*.

It is hardly surprising that the deliberate policy of genocide which was practised by the Imperial German army against the Herero has had its impact upon those engaged in researching issues associated with Herero society and history. Between 1904 and 1908 there was a conscious attempt to eradicate all forms of opposition to the German colonial state in Namibia. Herero men, women and children were deliberately shot, raped, hanged, placed into camps and put to work as forced labourers. The South African invasion and subsequent occupation of Namibia in 1915 entailed an improvement in the living conditions of the country's black inhabitants. In the twentieth century research on Herero society and history has tended to concentrate on the Herero–German war and its impact on Herero society, and to shy away from dealing with the history of Herero society prior to the war, or in its immediate aftermath in the years prior to the death of Samuel Maharero in 1923.

Studies that have involved themselves with Herero society and the colonization of Namibia have tended to fall, broadly speaking, into three categories: (i) studies that relate to the nature of German imperialism and the development of totalitarian societies; (ii) popular war histories; and (iii) ethnographic studies. There are of course exceptions to this tendency, and these will be discussed at a later stage.

Studies that relate to the nature of German imperialism and the development of totalitarian societies

An example of the debate relating to the nature of German imperialism and the development of totalitarian society was that which was conducted by Horst Drechsler and Helmut Bley.[3] Though both provided insights into the nature of Imperial Germany and Herero society, both failed to expand upon the history of the Herero prior to, during and after the bloody conflict. In fact discussion as to the history of the Herero, their resistance and their reaction to colonization was subsumed in a discussion relating to the society and colonial policy of Imperial Germany. In recent years this debate has been reduced to the rather unfortunate business of debating numbers killed, and has continued to rage in ever more meaningless ways.[4] These works have all unsatisfactorily dealt with the history of those who were affected by German colonization, be it the precursor of Nazism or not, namely the Herero.

[3] Helmut Bley's *South-West Africa under German Rule 1894-1914* (London 1971) and Horst Drechsler's *'Let Us Die Fighting'* (Berlin 1966), were both history PhDs completed in Hamburg in 1968 and Berlin in 1966 respectively. Through the years these two works have provided inspiration not only for this work but for a number of other theses as well: Gilbert Isaac Schrank, *German South West Africa: Social and Economic Aspects of its History, 1884-1915* (New York University PhD 1974) & J.M. Bridgman, *The Revolt of the Hereros* (Berkeley 1981).

[4] The debate was given new impetus by the publication, shortly before the independence of Namibia, of Brigitte Lau's 'Uncertain Certainties: The Herero–German war of 1904', in *Mibagus*, No. 2 April 1989, pp. 4–8; a slightly reworked copy of this article was published in B. Lau, *History and Historiography*, edited by A. Heywood (Windhoek 1995) pp. 39–52. Lau's article elicited responses from Randolph Vigne and Henning Melber in *The South African Review of Books*, Feb./March 1990, June/July 1990, Aug./Oct. 1990; Tilman Dedering, 'The German–Herero-War of 1904: Revisionism of genocide or imaginary historiography?' in *The Journal of Southern African Studies*, Vol. 19, No. 1, 1993, pp. 80–8 and J.B. Gewald, 'The Great General of the Kaiser' in *Botswana Notes and Records*, Vol. 26 1994, pp. 67–76. Lau's article was followed by a series of articles and books which have sought to deny the genocide, or, at the very least, called for a revision

Popular war histories

Through the years a number of popular war histories of the Herero–German war have been written. Krüger has succinctly noted that the theme of the war between the Germans and the Herero appears to be 'continually rediscovered'.[5] As such, though the books and articles written by Pool, Nuhn and others provide us with a blow by blow account of the war, they give us little or no insight into the workings of Herero society at the time.[6] The archives of the *Schutztruppe* that operated in Namibia have disappeared; with the exception of Conrad Rust, who was given insight into the military files at the time, all of the other authors were therefore forced into being heavily dependent on secondary sources and the German military's own official war history.[7] Added to this these works have failed to explore or examine the position of the Herero in the war itself. Although these works are war histories, one will search in vain as to Herero command structures, strategies, tactics, aims or motivation for fighting in the war. Thus, unfortunately, they provide little insight into Herero society prior to, during or, for that matter, after 1904.

Ethnographic studies

The bulk of the material dealing with the Herero specifically has been of an ethnographic nature. Primarily anthropologists and ethnologists have been interested in Herero society for one of two reasons, the impact of the war on society, or the system of double descent that is practised in Herero society.

The ethnographic study of the Herero has a long history which started long before the Herero–German war. The travelogues of Frances Galton and Charles John Andersson, of the early 1850s, contained some material of ethnographic importance.[8] In the late 1860s the Windhoek-born theology student Josaphat Hahn, one of the sons of the Rhenish missionary, Carl Hugo Hahn, with whom Galton and Andersson had associated during their sojourn in Namibia,

of histories dealing with the war. See in this regard: Horst Kühne, 'Die Ausrottungsfeldzüge der "Kaiserlichen Schutztruppen in Afrika" und die sozialdemokratische Reichstagsfraktion', in *Militärgeschichte*, Band 18, 1979; Walter Nuhn, *Sturm über Südwest: Der Hereroaufstande von 1904 – Ein düsteres Kapitel der deutschen kolonialen Vergangenheit Namibias* (Koblenz 1989); Karla Poewe, *The Namibian Herero: A History of their Psychosocial Disintegration and Survival* (Lewiston & Queenston 1983); Gunter Spraul, 'Der "Völkermord" an den Herero: Untersuchungen zu einer neuen Kon-tinuitätsthese' in *Geschichte in Wissenschaft und Unterricht*, 1988/12, pp. 713–39; Gert Sudholt, *Die deutsche Eingeborenenpolitik in Südwestafrika. Von den Anfängen bis 1904*, Georg (Hildesheim, 1975).

[5] Gesine Krüger, *Kriegsbewältigung und Geschichtsbewusstsein. Zur Realität, Deutung und Verarbeitung des deutschen Kolonialkriegs 1904–1907*, PhD University of Hanover 1995, p. 2.

[6] Walter Nuhn, *Sturm über Südwest: Der Hereroaufstande von 1904 – Ein düsteres Kapitel der deutschen kolonialen Vergangenheit Namibias* (Koblenz 1989); Gerhardus Pool, *Die Herero-Opstand 1904–1907* (Cape Town 1979); Conrad Rust, *Krieg und Frieden im Hererolande: Aufzeichnungen aus dem Kriegsjahre 1904* (Berlin 1905).

[7] *Kämpfe der deutschen Truppen in Südwestafrika, bearbeitet nach Angaben der Kriegsgeschichtlichen Abteilung I des Großen Generalstabes* (Berlin 1906–8).

[8] C.J. Andersson, *Lake Ngami: or, exploration and discoveries during four years' wanderings in the wilds of South Western Africa* (London 1856) & F. Galton, *The Narrative of an Explorer in Tropical South Africa* (London 1853).

published two ethnographic articles on the Herero and Hereroland.[9] Throughout the remainder of the nineteenth century, as the Rhenish Mission sought to gain Herero converts, a series of articles appeared in the *Berichte der Rheinischen Missions-Gesellschaft*, some of which were of an ethnographic nature. The Rhenish missionaries regularly held conferences to discuss and administer the progress of their activities in Namibia. During the course of these conferences it was customary for some of the missionaries to present papers on subjects related to their work. Some of these papers, particularly those of Jakob Irle, were of a high quality and dealt specifically with Herero ethnology, but it was not until after the war had broken out that Irle published his work.[10] From then onwards the impact of the war has come to dominate all ethnographic research dealing with the Herero.

The double descent, or more correctly duolineal transmission, i.e. 'the utilization in one society of both patrilineal and matrilineal principles of affiliation resulting in two lineage systems cross-cutting each other', was and is practised by the Herero, and has resulted in a great deal of anthropological interest.[11] Though Jakob Irle had referred to the dual descent system, it was not until the completion of a doctoral thesis at the University of Leiden in 1933, that the full complexity of the system was worked out.[12] This complexity has provided inspiration for a series of dissertations and articles that have sought to come to terms with Herero descent systems.[13]

The majority of ethnographic findings dealing with the Herero has been concerned with the impact of the war on Herero society. Studies have ranged from those seeking to explain how Herero coped with living as refugees and ethnic minorities amongst the Tswana, through to those which have sought to discover the impact of the war on Herero social systems.[14] Associated with the

[9] Josaphat Hahn, 'Die Ovaherero', in *Zeitschrift der Gesellschaft für Erdkunde zu Berlin*, Verlag von Dietrich Reimer (Berlin 1869). Josaphat Hahn, 'Das Land der Ovahereró', in *Zeitschrift der Gesellschaft für Erdkunde zu Berlin*, 1868 pp. 194–243. At the same time Theophilus Hahn, who was no direct relative of Josaphat, published an article that also contained information on Namibia and the Herero: 'Ein Rassenkampf im nordwestlichen Theile der Cap-Region', in *Globus*, 14, 1869 pp. 270–1.

[10] Jakob Irle returned to Germany in 1903 and published his seminal book *Die Herero: Ein Beitrag zur Landes-, Volks- und Missionskunde* (Gütersloh 1906).

[11] Gordon D. Gibson, 'Double Descent and Its Correlates among the Herero of Ngamiland', in *American Anthropologist*, Vol. 58, No. 1, February 1956, p. 109.

[12] Hendrik Gerhardus Luttig, *The Religious System and Social Organisation of the Herero* (Utrecht 1933). Luttig's work on the Herero had important implications for the development of what became known as the 'Leiden School' in structural anthropology. The founder of this persuasion was Prof. Dr J.P.B. De Josselin De Jong who, in his inaugural lecture at the University of Leiden, singled out Luttig's work for having indicated the possibility of the existence of similar systems of descent in the Indonesian archipelago. J.P.B. De Josselin De Jong, *De Maleische Archipel als Ethnologisch Studieveld* (Leiden 1935) p. 2 fn. 3.

[13] Gordon D. Gibson, *The Social Organization of the Southwestern Bantu*, Unpublished DPhil Thesis, University of Chicago (Chicago 1952); Elhanan Hagolani, *Das Kulturmodell der Bantusprechenden Rindernomaden Südwestafrikas*, DPhil Thesis, Universität zu Köln (New York 1968); J.S. Malan, *Dubbele afkomsberekening by die Himba, 'n Herero-sprekende volk in Suidwes-Afrika*, Unpublished DLitt et Phil dissertation, Rand Afrikaans University (Johannesburg 1971); 'Double Descent among the Himba of South West Africa' in *Cimbebasia*, Ser. B. Vol. 2 No. 3, 1973 pp. 81–112; Carlos Laranjo Medeiros, *Vakwandu: History, Kinship and Systems of Production of an Herero People of South-West Angola* (Lisbon 1981); I. Schapera, *Notes on some Herero Genealogies* (Cape Town 1945) & F.R. Vivelo, *The Herero of Western Botswana* (New York 1977).

[14] Uri Almagor, 'Pastoral Identity and Reluctance to Change; the Mbanderu of Ngamiland', in *The Journal of African Law*, 24 (1980), 1, pp. 35–61; K. Alnaes, 'Oral Tradition and Identity; the Herero in Botswana', in *The Societies of Southern Africa in the 19th and 20th Centuries*, Vol. 11 (1981), pp. 15–23; 'Living with the past: the songs of the Herero in Botswana', in *Africa*, 59.3 (1989), pp. 267–99 & Vivelo, *Herero Botswana*.

latter has been the development of a series of studies which Krüger has correctly described as falling within '*einer Tradition der Pathologisierung*', a tradition of pathologization.[15] These have argued that on account of the war the Herero were and are physically as well as psychologically unfit. In the aftermath of the war, commentators dealing with the Herero asked whether the Herero were 'committing race suicide'[16] or argued that:

> The Herero no longer want to live. Even there where conditions are good for them, their birth rate has shrunk in an unbelievable manner.[17]

This tradition has been carried on into the present. An example of this is the work of the Canadian anthropologist Karla Poewe, who has sought to argue that, on account of the war, the Herero as a whole had become mentally unbalanced, and had remained so until the time of her research in the early 1980s.[18] Effectively these studies have done what the German colonial state so anxiously hoped for but failed to do: rob the Herero completely of independent action and thought.

On the whole the ethnographic works which deal with the Herero currently living in Botswana and Namibia stress the central role of the war in the creation of that which is alleged to characterize the present-day Herero. Though it is true that these works give some suggestion as to Herero society as it existed prior to the war, they fail to provide an adequate understanding of the causes of the war or Herero development before then. The same holds true for the recently completed doctoral thesis of Hendrickson, which, inspired by the earlier work of the Comaroffs amongst the Tswana, does have a historical component, in that it has sought to concentrate on the historical roots of Herero identity in the present.[19]

The only major work dealing with Herero society prior to 1890 is that written by the Rhenish missionary Heinrich Vedder: *South West Africa in early times, being the story of South West Africa up to the date of Maharero's death in 1890.*[20] Written more than sixty years ago, the book clearly reflected Vedder's ideas regarding the existence of superior and inferior races, unchanging 'tribes and nations', and the conflict-ridden nature of pre-colonial Namibia. Though Vedder had first-hand experience of the terrors of the Herero–German war, his work is graced by claims that the Herero were exterminated and enslaved prior to German colonization. His work was well critiqued by Brigitte Lau, who saw Vedder's 'nationalistic German nazi' *Weltanschauung* as having led to

[15] Krüger, *Kriegsbewältigung*, p. 7. Krüger coins the word *krankschreiben* (to write sick) to describe what happens in this ethnographic tradition, where illness is ascribed and attributed to people through the writing of others.
[16] W.P. Steenkamp, *Is the South-West African Herero Committing Race Suicide?* (Cape Town 1922).
[17] Viktor Lebzelter, *Eingeborenenkulturen in Südwest- und Südafrika* (Leipzig 1934) p. 182. JBG's translation.
[18] Karla Poewe, *The Namibian Herero.*
[19] Anne Alfhild Bell Hendrickson, *Historical Idioms of Identity: Representation among the Ovaherero in Southern Africa*, PhD Thesis (New York 1992); 'The "Long" Dress and the Construction of Herero Identities in Southern Africa' in *African Studies*, Vol. 53, No. 2, 1994, pp. 25–54.; 'Bodies and Flags: the Representation of Herero identity in colonial Namibia' in *Clothing and Difference: Embodied Identities in Colonial and Post-Colonial Africa* (Durham 1996); Hendrickson, *Women, Dolls and Herero Identity in Urban Namibia and Botswana*, paper presented at ASA conference Toronto 1994.
[20] Heinrich Vedder, *South West Africa in early times, being the story of South West Africa up to the date of Maharero's death in 1890* (London 1938), translation from German original of 1934.

the creation of a 'piece of work which in its essence is apologetic of colonial rule'.[21] Dealing with Vedder's work, Jill Kinahan came to the same conclusion and noted:

> Apart from his magpie interest in historical curiosities, Vedder's ideological preoccupations were to do with the racial history of the country. Thus, at the outset of the book, he is concerned with laying the basis for his point of view.[22]

Thus, though his work is more than sixty years old and marred by prejudice, Vedder did produce a considerable amount of information which, though it is sorely in need of a major overhaul, is still used as a benchmark in studies relating to Namibian and Herero society as a whole.[23]

The revision and restoration of written Namibian history commenced in the 1980s, with the publication of numerous works written or edited by Brigitte Lau. Along with Wolfgang Werner, Lau was a student at the University of Cape Town in South Africa where, under the tutorship of Professor Christopher Saunders, Namibian history and historiography became a hot subject for academic debate in the late 1970s. Starting in the early 1990s, as Namibia gained its independence, a number of historical theses dealing with Namibian history appeared, and many are still in the process of being written.[24] Of direct importance, within the context of this book, are the completed theses of Gesine Krüger and Wolfgang Werner, and the forthcoming thesis of Dag Henrichsen, all of which deal with aspects of Herero history.

In effect Dag Henrichsen's forthcoming thesis is an extensive revision of the material and subject-matter covered by Vedder. It covers the same time frame and geographical area dealt with by Vedder in his *South-West Africa in early times*. It, too, deals with the socio-political history of central Namibia in the nineteenth century up until the death of Maharero. Henrichsen's extremely detailed work is based not only on Vedder's own source material and archival research, but also on extensive oral historical fieldwork in Namibia. Henrichsen's work will provide historians with a fine description of central Namibia prior to the advent of an effective German colonial presence in the territory. In terms of chronology, this book picks up where Henrichsen's thesis ends.[25]

---

[21] Brigitte Lau, '"Thank God the Germans came": Vedder and Namibian historiography' in *Africa Seminar Collected Papers*, Centre for African Studies, University of Cape Town, Vol. 2, pp. 24–53, edited by K. Gottschalk and C. Saunders (Cape Town 1981) p. 28.

[22] Jill Kinahan, 'Heinrich Vedder's sources for his account of the exploration of the Namib coast' in *Cimbebasia*, 11, pp. 33–9, 1989.

[23] The most obvious examples of this are for instance the utilization of Vedder's work by representatives of the Dama community in Namibia to substantiate their land claims to much of central Namibia, and the reliance of the Kozonguisi commission on traditional leadership on Vedder's definition and description of Namibia's peoples. See: Jan-Bart Gewald, 'On being Damara between 1893 and 1993' in *Quellen zur Khoisan-Forschung/ Research in Khoisan Studies* (Cologne 1998).

[24] Jeremy Gale Silvester, *Black Pastoralists, White Farmers: The dynamics of land dispossession and labour recruitment in southern Namibia 1915–1955*, PhD School of Oriental and African Studies 1993; Patricia Hayes, *A History of the Ovambo of Namibia, ca. 1880–1930*, PhD Cambridge University 1992; Harri Siiskonen, *Trade and Socioeconomic Change in Ovamboland, 1850–1906* (Helsinki 1990); Marti Eirola, *The Ovambogefahr: The Ovamboland Reservation in the Making* (Jyväskylä 1992) & Frieda-Nela Williams, *Precolonial Communities in Southwestern Africa. A History of Ovambo Kingdoms 1600–1920* (Windhoek 1991).

[25] Dag Henrichsen, *Herrschaft und Identität im vorkolonialen Zentralnamibia. Das Damaraland im 19. Jahrhundert*, PhD University of Hamburg 1998.

Wolfgang Werner's thesis, *An economic and social history of the Herero of Namibia, 1915–1946,* focused on economic determinants in the reconstitution of Herero society in the aftermath of Imperial Germany's occupation of Namibia. Werner argued that 'by the outbreak of the First World War . . . virtually the entire population in the Police Zone [essentially the area south of Etosha] was proletarianized'.[26] Terence Ranger, in seeking to define an aspect of Zimbabwean history, coined the term 'self-peasantization', to refer to the concept of Africans becoming peasants to resist having to become labourers for the settler market.[27] Drawing on Ranger, Werner took the concept of 'self-peasantization' and sought to apply it to his study of Herero between 1915 and 1946. With its intense concentration on economic developments, particularly in the sector of settler agriculture, the thesis failed to adequately elaborate upon the development of social and political events in Herero society. To some extent the reliance on economic developments at the cost of social developments led, as Werner himself admitted, to a self-enforced limitation, which was only partly alleviated by the publication of an article on the *Truppenspieler*.[28] The bulk of Werner's thesis, as its title suggests, deals with a period of time that follows on from where this book stops.

The Herero–German war, the way in which Herero came to terms with the war, and how it influenced historical consciousness within Herero society, formed the subject of Gesine Krüger's doctoral dissertation, completed at the University of Hanover in 1995.[29] Krüger's work is principally concerned with the war, and the impact thereof on Herero thinking and society in the aftermath of the war. The extensive coverage that is given of the views of German soldiers at the time is complemented by Herero perspectives on the war as it has come to the fore in orature and ritual. It is the first piece of academic work that seriously attempts to come to terms with the position of Herero women in Namibian history; children and the mission at various stages in the aftermath of the war are also discussed. In seeking to describe and detail the manner in which Herero society coped with the war, Krüger abandoned the strict chronology of 'big man and event history' in favour of pursuing historical themes. Thus events that took place at various times between the war and 1945 are brought together, at the expense of an overview detailing the chronological development of Herero society and politics. Building upon the work of Dag Henrichsen, on watering places in pre-colonial Namibia as having formed the basis of a network that defined Herero territory and society, Krüger argues that it was following the funeral of Samuel Maharero in 1923 that, on the basis of *Orte der Erinnerung,* places of memory, Herero were able to reconstitute a network of points on the map of Namibia that mirrored the watering points that had bound and constituted the basis of Herero society prior to colonization,

[26] Wolfgang Werner, *An economic and social history of the Herero of Namibia, 1915–1946*, PhD University of Cape Town 1989, p. 69.
[27] Ranger developed this concept by enlarging upon the earlier work of Sharon Stichter, *Capitalism and African Responses* cited in Terence Ranger, *Peasant Consciousness and Guerilla War in Zimbabwe* (Harare 1985) pp. 26–31.
[28] Ibidem, p. 9. Wolfgang Werner, '"Playing Soldiers": The Truppenspieler Movement among the Herero of Namibia, 1915 to *ca.* 1945', in *Journal of Southern African Studies,* Vol. 16, No. 3, September 1990, pp. 485–502.
[29] Gesine Krüger, *Kriegsbewältigung und Geschichtsbewusstsein. Zur Realität, Deutung und Verarbeitung des deutschen Kolonialkriegs 1904–1907*, Ph.D. University of Hanover 1995.

and allowed for the symbolic reoccupation of their Hereroland.[30] In contrast to Krüger's work, this book, whilst also dealing with the reconstruction of Herero society, has as its cut-off point the funeral of Samuel Maharero in 1923.

This book, in distinction to the studies discussed above, covers the socio-political history of the Herero between 1890 and 1923: that is, it covers the history of Herero society prior to the war, and describes the manner in which this society was restructured and reestablished in the face of great adversity in the aftermath of the war. Though the bulk of this book is divided into seven chapters, it falls essentially into two halves. The first four chapters describe socio-political developments in Hereroland prior to the Herero–German war, and the remaining three chapters recount these developments in the aftermath of the war.

From the late 1860s onwards Herero society was transformed from a strongly decentralized transhumant pastoralist society into one which was strongly centralized and centred upon a number of specific urban centres. In this process Herero society appropriated, and transformed to its own needs, the political concepts and structures which it had drawn from outside sources. At the advent of German colonialism, Herero society was divided into five distinct chieftaincies which, though closely related in terms of kin, tended to compete with one another politically and economically. Following the death of the chieftain of Okahandja, Maharero Tjamuaha, in 1890, Imperial Germany became actively involved in central Namibian politics. Of the five Herero chieftains, only Samuel Maharero, the son of the deceased chief, was able to manipulate the Germans into supporting him in his struggle for political power which, though initially limited to Okahandja, eventually extended to all of Hereroland. In exchange for German military aid and political support Samuel Maharero sold the land, labour and cattle of his subjects. By the time the rinderpest epizootic struck central Namibia in 1897, Samuel Maharero had become the most powerful Herero chief that had ever existed.

Rinderpest, and the natural disasters that followed in its wake, led to the impoverishment and subsequent transformation of Herero society as a whole. Anxious to maintain their positions, the established chiefs were forced to change the manner in which they maintained power, and new elites, capable of making use of the changed circumstances, came to the fore. Rinderpest facilitated German colonization of central Namibia as Herero, who had been impoverished by the disease, and were now desperate for food, vaccines and medicines, were forced into positions of dependence upon the colonial state.

The Herero–German war, which broke out as a result of a series of misunderstandings, led to the destruction of Herero society in all its facets as it had existed prior to the war. The colonial legislation, passed in the aftermath of the war, sought to maintain the eternity of this condition. However, contrary to the hopes and expectations of those who had envisaged the final dissolution of the Herero, Herero society re-emerged. Beginning in the remaining years of German rule, the Herero re-organized their· society on the basis of the

---

[30] See Krüger, ch. 11; Dag Henrichsen, '"Ehi rOvaherero". Mündliche Überlieferungen von Herero zu ihrer Geschichte im vorkolonialen Namibia', in *Werkstatt Geschichte* No. 9: Afrika – Europa, Hamburg Dezember 1994; & Dag Henrichsen and Gesine Krüger, '"We have been captives long enough, we want to be free": Land, uniforms and politics in the history of Herero during the interwar period' in *Namibia Under South African Rule: Mobility & Containment, 1915–46*, ed. P. Hayes, M. Wallace, J. Silvester and W. Hartmann (Oxford 1998)

structures and beliefs existing in the German colonial army and Rhenish missionary activity. The South African invasion of Namibia, and the subsequent weakening of the colonial state, allowed the Herero to establish and maintain themselves with cattle in areas of their own choosing. The effective re-occupation of land by the Herero forced the colonial state, anxious to maintain the peace and cut costs, to come to terms with the existence of Herero society. The death and funeral of Samuel Maharero in 1923 was the catalyst that brought the disparate groups of Herero together to establish a single unitary Herero identity. It was only following the death of Samuel Maharero in 1923 that the colonial state, which had recently been granted Namibia as a mandated territory, sought to once again transform Herero society and rob it of its land.

This book, thus, describes the manner in which, between 1890 and 1923, the Herero of Namibia grappled to maintain and attain control over their freedom, and how, when they lost this, they reorganized to continue their struggle towards redemption.

1

For the Want of a Nation

Herero Polities on the Eve of Colonization

Introduction

In 1850, when the young Swedish adventurer Charles John Andersson first visited Hereroland, he was shocked to discover that, contrary to his expectations, the Herero, or Damara as they were referred to at the time, were far from being the subjects of a mighty African kingdom.[1] Instead, when first confronted with Herero society, which was at that stage strongly decentralized, Andersson believed that he was witnessing the demise of a once great and mighty race, which, for want of leadership and national unity, was now doomed to extinction.

> The Damaras were once, undoubtedly, a great nation; but, unlike others which gradually became more powerful by the union of a number of smaller tribes under the head of a single chief or king, they have dwindled into an endless number of petty tribes, ruled by as many chiefs.[2]

Little troubled by ideas as to his own stature, Andersson set about attempting to remould Herero society into something more in keeping with his own ideas regarding nations and kings. However, although Andersson drafted documents proclaiming his status as paramount chief of the Herero, Herero society changed

[1] Andersson accompanied the English tourist Francis Galton, who inspired by news of the newly 'discovered' Lake Ngami, had organized an expedition to south-western Africa. Galton and Andersson were well-educated products of their time, men intrigued and influenced by some of the more fashionable ideas current in learned circles in Europe in the mid-nineteenth century: the development of the human condition and nationalism. Francis Galton used his expedition experiences to develop the theory of eugenics. Charles John Andersson, on the other hand, developed delusions of grandeur. C.J. Andersson, *Lake Ngami: or, exploration and discoveries during four years' wanderings in the wilds of South Western Africa* (London 1856) & F. Galton, *The Narrative of an Explorer in Tropical South Africa* (London 1853).

[2] Charles John Andersson, *Lake Ngami* (London 1856) p. 217. To be sure, at the time of Andersson's and Galton's arrival in Namibia, a number of Herero had been attacked and impoverished by the raiders of Jonker Afrikaner. However, this in no way reflected the demise of what was an extremely decentralized pastoralist society. Andersson, as we will see further on, wanted to change this decentralization to his own advantage as a cattle trader seeking to subvert the controls imposed upon the export of cattle by Jonker Afrikaner.

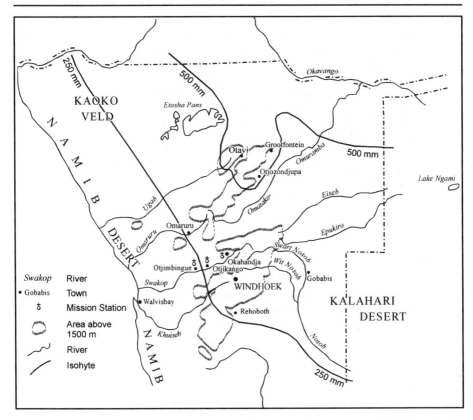

Map 1.1: Central Namibia showing heights above 1500 metres, and the 250 and 500 millimetre isohytes between which rainfall agriculture is not possible but pastoralism is.
Source: United Evangelical Mission archives, Wuppertal

in ways little anticipated by their self-styled commander in chief.[3] During the last third of the nineteenth century Herero society transformed itself from a strongly decentralized transhumant society into a strongly centralized society centred on specific urban centres independent of outside control. In doing this, the Herero appropriated terms, concepts and material goods from outside sources and transformed and applied them to their own ends. Far from remaining unaffected by the advance of the world system's frontier, Herero society transformed itself to be better equipped to reap its benefits, and thereby established societies hitherto unseen in central Namibia.

The Ovaherero, the people with whose history this book deals, lived predominantly on the highlands of what is now central Namibia. It is an area characterized by aridity and bounded by deserts; in the east by the Kalahari desert, in the west by the Namib desert, and in the south by these two deserts, where they meet to form the arid reaches of Namaqualand. With an erratic alternating cycle of droughts and rains, and an average rainfall of less than 500 mm, rainfall agriculture was well-nigh impossible on the central Namibian

---

[3] Charles John Andersson, *Trade and Politics in Central Namibia, 1860–1864,* edited by B. Lau (Windhoek 1989) p. 280.

Highlands.[4] Instead the inhabitants of central Namibia were primarily engaged in pastoralism, horticulture and hunter-gathering. Archaeological evidence indicates that by AD 1100 pastoralists, who were probably the Bantu-speaking ancestors of the Herero, had established themselves in the area.[5] These ancestors created a society characterized, as many African pastoralist societies were, by extreme social and political decentralization.[6] During the course of the nineteenth century, as an adaptation to the intrusion of the Cape colonial frontier into the area, a process of political centralization and social transformation took place within Herero society.[7]

In south-western Africa the people who speak dialects of the Bantu language Otjiherero have been glossed as Ovaherero, Ovambanderu, Ovahimba, Ovatjimba, Ovazemba and Vakwandu. Not only do these people speak dialects of a common language, but they also share a number of cultural elements that relate to social organization, preferred economy, cosmology, epistemology and spatio-political organization. Historically there have been three broad divisions within Otjiherero-speaking society: the Ovaherero, the Ovambanderu and the Ovahimba. These divisions, which appear to be historically true and significant, correlated roughly with environmental determinants and geographical distribution. Thus the Ovambanderu were a section of Otjiherero-speaking society engaged in pastoralism on the Sandveld of the Kalahari; the Ovaherero engaged in pastoralism on the Namibian highveld; and the Ovahimba engaged in pastoralism in the Kaokoveld. This book uses the term Herero, as a collective

[4] For further information on the central Namibian environment see: Antti Erkkilä and Harri Siiskonen, *Forestry in Namibia 1850–1990*, University of Joensuu (Joensuu 1992) pp. 19–24; H.J. Cooke, 'The Physical Environment of Botswana', in *Proceedings of the Symposium on Settlement in Botswana: the historical development of a human landscape*, edited by R. Renée Hitchcock and Mary R. Smith, Botswana Society (Gaborone 1982) pp. 1–12; and John Kinahan, *Pastoral Nomads of the Central Namib Desert: The People History Forgot*, Namibia Archaeological Trust, New Namibia Books (Windhoek 1990) pp. 2–6.

[5] For an overview of the movement of iron-age Bantu speakers in Africa see Jan Vansina, *Paths in the Rainforests: Towards a History of Political Tradition in Equatorial Africa*, The University of Wisconsin Press (Madison 1990). For an overview and discussion on the introduction of cattle to southern Africa see A.B. Smith, *Pastoralism in Africa: Origins and Development Ecology*, Witwatersrand University Press (Johannesburg 1992) particularly p. 84; James Denbow, 'A new look at the later prehistory of the Kalahari', in *Journal of African History*, 27 (1986), pp. 3–28.; J. Kinahan, *Pastoral Nomads of the Central Namib Desert: The People that History Forgot*, Namibia Archeological Trust and New Namibia Books (Windhoek 1991) pp. 67 & 149; H. Pager, *The Rock Paintings of the Upper Brandberg. Part 1: Amis Gorge*, Heinrich Barth Institute (Cologne 1989). Plate six of the site named 'Amis 6' has an excellent painting of a fat-tailed sheep. It must be borne in mind that there is a debate raging as to the introduction of pastoralism in south-western Africa which forms a backdrop to the 'Great Kalahari debate'. Archaeological findings are hotly contested and nowhere is this more clearly indicated than in an article by J.E. Yellen and A.S. Brooks, 'The Late Stone Age Archaeology in the /Xai /Xai Region: a response to Wilmsen', which appeared in *Botswana Notes and Records*, Vol. 22, Botswana Society (Gaborone 1990).

[6] John G. Galaty and Pierre Bonte, *Herders, Warriors, and Traders: Pastoralism in Africa*, Westview Press (Oxford, Boulder 1991).

[7] For a discussion on the expansion of the Cape colonial frontier see: M. Legassick, 'The Northern Frontier to 1820: The emergence of the Griqua people', in *The Shaping of South African Society, 1652–1820*, edited by Richard Elphick and Hermann Giliomee, Maskew Miller Longman (Cape Town 1984) pp. 243–90; N.G. Penn, 'The Frontier in the Western Cape, 1700–1740', in *Papers in the Prehistory of the Western Cape, South Africa*, edited by J. Parkington and M. Hall, BAR International Series 332 (Cape Town 1987) pp. 464–5; N.G. Penn 'Pastoralists and pastoralism in the northern Cape frontier zone during the eighteenth century' in *The South African Archaeological Society, Goodwin Series: Prehistoric Pastoralism in Southern Africa*, Vol. 5, June 1986, pp. 63–98. For a general discussion on the expansion and impact of the frontier see: R. Brian Ferguson, 'Tribal Warfare', in *Scientific American*, pp. 90–5, January 1992; *War in the Tribal Zone: Expanding States and Indigenous Warfare*, edited by R. Brian Ferguson and Neil L. Whitehead (Santa Fe 1992).

term to refer to all Otjiherero-speaking people, and uses the specific terms, Mbanderu, Himba and so forth, when the context demands it.[8]

A characteristic of pre-colonial Herero societies was their strong decentralization, a characteristic which was shared with the pastoralist societies of East Africa.[9] As we have already seen, this strong decentralization surprised observers in the nineteenth century.

> A common paramount they do not have and they do not appear to have ever been subject to one. Instead they exist divided in a multitude of bigger and smaller tribes of many hundred to thousands of souls. Every tribe is completely independent and stands in equality to the others.[10]

Prior to the latter second half of the nineteenth century no centralized leadership, beyond that of a patri-clan head, the *Omukuru*, who was seen to be the living embodiment of the clan's ancestor, existed amongst Herero groups. Association with a specific patri-clan head was by virtue of his stock wealth, personality, and both his secular and religious ability. This association was tempered by environmental circumstances as well as by the activities of the patri-clan head. If the *Omukuru* failed to provide either secular or religious services, or if he was seen as having wronged a follower, there was nothing to stop followers from voting with their feet and leaving. Allied to this was the transhumant pastoralism which was necessary for survival. *Ozonganda*, settlements under the leadership of an *Omukuru*, were arranged around ecologically advantageous points, and tended to shift with the changing seasons.[11] During the course of the nineteenth century this strong socio-political decentralization changed.

---

[8] For an introduction to Herero ethnology see Gordon D. Gibson, *The Social Organization of the Southwestern Bantu*, Unpublished DPhil Thesis, University of Chicago (Chicago 1952); J. Irle, *Die Herero* (Nendeln, Kraus reprint, 1973); H.G. Luttig, *The Religious System and Social Organisation of the Herero* (Utrecht 1933); K. Poewe, *The Namibian Herero* (Lewiston and Queenston 1983); I. Schapera, *Notes on some Herero Genealogies* (Cape Town 1945); T. Sundermeier and S. Kuvare. *Die Mbanderu; Studien zu ihrer Geschichte und Kultur* (St Augustin, 1977) & F.R. Vivelo, *The Herero of Western Botswana* (New York 1977).

[9] A.B. Smith, *Pastoralism in Africa: Origins and Development Ecology*, Witwatersrand University Press (Johannesburg 1992) p. 187.

[10] Josaphat Hahn, 'Die Ovaherero', in *Zeitschrift der Gesellschaft für Erdkunde zu Berlin*, Verlag von Dietrich Reimer (Berlin 1869) p. 253. JBG's translation.

[11] Vansina's discussion with regard to western Bantu political tradition correlates closely with the pre-colonial Herero political tradition. Jan Vansina, *Paths in the Rainforests: Towards a History of Political Tradition in Equatorial Africa*, The University of Wisconsin Press (Madison 1990) p. 35.

> Three interlocking social groups formed the framework of the ancestral society: the district, the village, and a large household establishment often called 'the house' or the 'hearth' . . . Their interrelations were quite flexible so that the system remained extremely decentralized. Each House freely chose which village its members wanted to belong to, and each village freely chose other villages as allies to make up a district. Over time the relative importance of the groups often shifted as one or another basic group gained in prominence at the expense of the others. At the extreme one group could be absorbed by another, as when a single House occupied an entire village or even a whole district. In a few cases the village or the district could even vanish . . .

> The loose nature of the system was enhanced by the fact that the House and the village were led by recognized leaders who achieved rather than inherited their status, but the district did not have a distinct leader. Leadership itself was a necessary institution, but who was to be leader was probably not institutionalized in the ancestral society. Men competed for leadership within each unit, and leaders of different units competed with each other, so as to increase their following at the expense of others. Competition was the counterpart of autonomy.

> In some languages leaders are referred to as 'great men', which recalls 'big men', the technical term in anthropology for such leaders.

Ovatjimba and missionary chiefs

The Herero were primarily pastoralists, though they did engage in horticulture
and hunter-gathering, and at times they were forced to rely totally on these
alternative forms of subsistence. In the 1830s large numbers of Herero relied
solely on hunter-gathering for their subsistence. This was due, not to
environmental determinants, but to the effects of prolonged forays on the part
of raiders seeking spoils to trade on the markets of the Cape colony.[12] Supreme
amongst these raiders were the Oorlam *Kapteins*, chiefs, Jonker Afrikaner and
Amraal Lambert.[13] Oorlam communities had emerged along the north-western
Cape colonial frontier in the late eighteenth century around the institution of
the Commando, and consisted of an amalgam of Khoi community remnants,
runaway slaves, Basters, Cape outlaws and others.[14] A contemporary succinctly
sketched the development of an Oorlam community when he stated that Klaas
Afrikaner:

> . . . collected a band of his people of his own race, runaway slaves and other
> desperadoes, and having by some means procured firearms, commenced a regular
> system of depredation upon the defenceless Namaquas and Korannas, plundering
> them of great numbers of their cattle which he exchanged again with some
> unprincipled colonists for further supplies of arms and ammunition.[15]

The polities were centred on the institution known as the Commando, which
consisted of a group of mounted armed men who engaged in hunting, raiding
and trading.[16] Herero pastoralists who had been robbed of their cattle either
became clients of the Oorlam *Kapteins*, or became *Ovatjimba*, people with no
means of subsistence beyond that of the *Tjimba*, the aardvark. They became
people forced to live as hunter-gatherers beyond the reach of their clan and
kin support structures. By the 1840s much of central Namibia was under the
control of Jonker Afrikaner and his Herero lieges Kahitjene and Tjamuaha. It
was at this stage that the first Rhenish missionaries, Hahn, Kleinschmidt and
Bam, arrived and settled in Windhoek, Jonker Afrikaner's settlement in central
Namibia.[17] However, the Rhenish missionaries engaged in such anti-social

---

[12] Spoils of the raid included cattle, people, hides, ivory and ostrich feathers.

[13] For further information on the life and times of Jonker Afrikaner see B. Lau, *Southern and Central Namibia in Jonker Afrikaner's Time*, Archeia (Windhoek 1987).

[14] The origins and meaning of the term Oorlam are quite contentious. Authors have suggested Malayan and/or pidgin Dutch sources. H. Bley, *South-West Africa under German Rule, 1894–1914* (London 1971) p. xxii, suggested that the term was derived from a Malay word meaning 'wide-awake'; Galton, *Explorer*, p. 68, suggested that 'Oerlam was a nickname given by Dutch colonists to the Hottentots that hung about their farms; it means a barren ewe – a creature good neither for breeding nor fattening, a worthless concern, one that gives trouble and yields no profit'. My input refers to the usage of the term Oorlam in Dutch, where it is taken to refer to a tot of alcohol commonly given to ship's crews. The first reference to Oorlam, in the southern African context, is as the personal name of the free burgher Kees Oorlam. Dr E.C. Godee Molsbergen, *Reizen in Zuid Afrika in de Hollandsche Tijd*, tweede deel, de Linschoten vereeniging (Den Haag 1916) p. 5.

[15] G. Thompson, *Travels and Adventures in Southern Africa* (London 1827) p. 291, quoted in Lau, *Jonker Afrikaner*, p. 20.

[16] For a fine overview of the development of the Commando polities in Namibia see B. Lau, 'Conflict and power in nineteenth-century Namibia', in *Journal of African History*, 27 (1986).

[17] Hahn and his companions were not the first European missionaries in central Namibia; they had been preceded by John Tindall, a Wesleyan missionary. B.A. Tindall (ed.), *The Journal of Joseph Tindall: Missionary in South West Africa 1839–55* (Cape Town 1959). Prior to the arrival of European missionaries there had been a string of African evangelists who had come up from the Cape, foremost amongst which was Jonker Afrikaner himself. Sir James Alexander, who was in central

practices that, in due course, they were drummed out of Windhoek.[18]

The missionaries, though nominally still subject to Jonker Afrikaner, trekked north and established themselves at Otjikango (Groß Barmen) and Otjimbingwe. Here they gathered around themselves a band of followers, which consisted primarily of *Ovatjimba*. The extent to which these followers came to hear the word of the Lord is debatable, particularly given that the first Herero conversion would only take place fifteen years after the missionaries had established themselves at Otjikango.[19] Contemporaries, missionaries and laymen alike, commented on this and noted that, though the *Ovatjimba* were indifferent to Christianity, 'a great number of the poorer classes were now living at the station'. The missionaries, conscious of the relationship that existed between their own relative wealth and the number of their followers, commented:

> We are not short of people. Unfortunately they do not long for the word of God. Out of the mass of heathens who surround us, no more than 80 come to the church services. Of all the children who abound here only about 20 to 30 attend school. Our audience in church and our school children are nearly all *poor* Herero.[20]

Furthermore they were well aware of the fact that:

> The wealthy Damaras [were] even more indifferent to spiritual matters than their poorer brethren; and if they happened to visit any of the stations, it was not for the purpose of learning the gospel preached, but . . . the hope of protection against their enemies, or with a view to business by bartering tobacco, iron ware, and so forth.[21]

The *Ovatjimba* gathered to the missionaries, as they would have to any other powerful chief or *Omuhona*, for the protection, support and possibilities which they provided. In this context it is interesting to note the impact of the Oorlam raids on the Herero language and political thinking. The Herero word *Omuhona*, which is currently glossed as chief, is a loan word derived from the Nama word /honkhoeb, meaning master.[22] Far from merely seeking to minister to a perceived

Namibia in the early 1830s referred to a man from South Africa's eastern cape named 'Magasee' (a name which betrayed his Malagasy slave origins), who travelled through southern Namibia as a Christian preacher. J. E. Alexander, *Expedition of Discovery into the Interior of Africa*, 2 volumes (London 1838) Vol. II, p. 33. For further detailed information on the initial European missionaries in Namibia see Carl Hugo Hahn, *Tagebücher 1837–1860; Diaries Parts I–V, A Missionary in Nama- and Damaraland*, edited and compiled by B. Lau (Windhoek 1985).

[18] Anti-social practices engaged in by the missionaries consisted of, amongst other things, the destruction of dagga (marihuana) plantations which belonged to the followers of Jonker Afrikaner (marihuana was and is one of the most important cash crops grown in southern Africa); the prohibition and active prevention of 'heathen' dances and ceremonies; the washing of sacred milk gourds (thereby ensuring that the cattle would become barren); and the refusal to extend beyond a token participation in the arms trade. Hahn, *Diaries* Part I: Hahn describes destroying plantations between February 1843 and February 1844: in Ai Gams itself pp. 112–113; Auchanas p. 142; Hunap p. 143; Khomas Hochland, Tsobis, Tinkas and beyond pp. 145–7; 'heathen' dances p. 131; arms trade p. 104 and washing of milk gourds p. 109.

[19] Heinrich Vedder, *Das Alte Südwestafrika: Südwestafrikas Geschichte bis zum Tode Mahareros 1890* (Windhoek 1981) p. 482.

[20] Vereinigten Evangelischen Missions Archiv (VEMA) 2.585, F.W. Kolbe, in Schmelens Erwartung, 3/6/1850, to mission directors. JBG's translation and emphasis.

[21] Andersson, *Lake Ngami*, pp. 102–3. See also VEMA, 1.581, J. Rath, in Walvisbay, 23/3/1845, to mission directors. In his letter Rath complained that the cattle herds of the Herero were preventing them from becoming interested in Christianity.

[22] R. Ohly, *The Destabilization of the Herero Language* (Windhoek 1987) p. 7.

religious need, the missionaries also supplied material commodities. These ranged from alms and protection through to arms and ammunition, alternative information sources and new forms of subsistence.[23] It was primarily in response to these 'worldly wants' that, within a short period of time, fairly substantial numbers of people gathered around, and settled with, the missionaries, who now effectively became *Ovahona*, in their own right.[24]

In due course, the mission stations, protected by the military, metaphysical and economic prowess of the missionary *Ovahona*, became beacons attracting those opposed to the established *Ovahona* of the the land. The advantages provided by eventual association with the missionaries were not lost upon those who had submitted and allied themselves to Jonker Afrikaner. In return for their allegiance and assistance, in the form of manual labour, herding, road building, the growing of tobacco and dagga, raiding, and tax and tribute collection, these chiefs, and their followers, were to some extent exempted from being raided. Furthermore they were rewarded for their allegiance with guns, raiding spoils and other goods.[25] In this way the Herero chiefs Kahitjene and Tjamuaha had built up substantial followings and great wealth. Those who failed to come to an arrangement with the Oorlam paramounts, but were still in possession of their herds, were forced to withdraw ever further into the Namibian interior. The surviving remnants of the communities raided became *Ovatjimba*, in so far as they were not captured, indentured or killed. Thus the missionary settlements continued to grow. In due course the missionary *Ovahona* came to provide an alternative to the authority of Jonker Afrikaner.

In 1842, Kahitjene had submitted to Jonker Afrikaner. In exchange for his allegiance, Jonker Afrikaner had provided Kahitjene with cattle. By 1847 Kahitjene had become remarkably wealthy and had acquired a large following. The images of independent and autonomous action, made possible through association with his own resident missionary, must have played upon Kahitjene's mind when he became the first vassal Herero chief who sought to withdraw from Jonker Afrikaner's control.

From 1843 onwards, Kahitjene had been in regular contact with the Rhenish missionaries. Immediately following his first meeting with the missionaries he had demanded a resident missionary of his own. Significantly the missionaries had rewarded Kahitjene's advances with presents of powder and lead. As Rhenish missionary, F.W. Kolbe, noted when he settled in Schmelen's Erwartung, Okahandja, in 1850:

> Shortly after we settled here, a number of poor Damara families came to live here. They were followed by others, so that at present there are already twenty of their houses here. Later Kahitjene, one of the biggest Ovaherero chiefs, who is very rich in cattle, also came and put up his huts here.[26]

[23] Lau, *Jonker Afrikaner*, pp. 76–83.
[24] Lau, *Jonker Afrikaner*, p. 108, uses the term 'missionary "chief"', but fails to develop the concept. C.H. Hahn, L. Fourie and H. Vedder, *The Native Tribes of South West Africa* (Cape Town 1928), p. 158, 'Hahn . . . gathered all sorts of poor and afflicted people round him, was recognised by the chiefs of the Hereros as being of equal rank with themselves . . .'
[25] In a letter from Jonker Afrikaner to C.H. Hahn, dated 21/3/1846, Afrikaner details how he provided Kahitjene and Tjamuaha (otherwise known as Weerlig and Kopervoet) with cattle after they had become destitute. Hahn, *Tagebücher*, p. 520.
[26] VEMA 2.585, F.W. Kolbe in Schmelens Erwartung, 3/6/1850, to mission directors. JBG's translation. See also VEMA 1.583 F.W. Kolbe, 'Kandambo was the first Ovatjimba who settled here with his two sons. He was soon followed by more families, so that at present with twenty houses we have the beginnings of a village'. JBG's translation.

Having broken free of Jonker's ambit, Kahitjene sought to capitalize on the promises contained in the presents of powder and lead, which the missionaries had presented him with prior to his switch in allegiance. However, in his meetings with Kolbe, which pleased Kahitjene little, it became clear that these had been mere inducements, and that the missionaries would be unable, and indeed were unwilling, to protect him and his followers from the depredations of Jonker Afrikaner. That the missionaries did not realize the danger Kahitjene was in is well illustrated by a conversation between missionary Kolbe and Kahitjene.

> He [Kahitjene] said that it was his intention to move to this place. I [Kolbe] replied that that was good and that the place was open to all Herero. Then he asked what I would think if he were to claim this place as his, would speak God's word and were to keep and drive others away. I replied that this could not be our intention. `We are preachers,' I continued, `and our endeavour is to tell all people God's word. We are not allowed to prohibit this place to anybody who comes with peaceful intentions. Added to this you have no right to prohibit this place to other chiefs, because this land is held in common by all. Live here but allow others the freedom to come and go as they like.' To which he replied that Jonker had set his sights on him and that HUKUMUNA, another Herero chief, would probably also come to fight with him.[27]

With rumours of an impending attack abounding, Kahitjene sought to find favour, and thus protection, with the missionaries. This he did through giving gifts, regularly attending Kolbe's church services and admonishing followers who dared to laugh during the sermons.[28] Kahitjene's perceptions, with regard to the Bible and the 'business' of evangelizing, are finely illuminated in Kolbe's diary:

> 7 July Sunday. Kahitjene sent a message that an ox had been slaughtered and therefore he couldn't come to church . . . A little later Kahitjene came. When I opened the Book, to read the text, he asked me to check in the Book whether or not Jonker Afrikaner was preparing to go to war. Thus I had to explain that God's word was not a magical word and that we were not soothsayers.[29]

The missionaries emphasized the importance of their work and the meta-physical nature of their mission through the use of symbols, such as the Bible, lectern, demeanour, facial expression and flags. Sermons that emphasized the all-encompassing nature of God, the unique qualities ascribed to the Bible, and the missionaries' particular connection to God, served merely to emphasize the spiritual nature of their activities, and their position as soothsayers. Kahitjene took the missionaries at their word and believed that they were imbued with particular qualities – qualities which he tried to turn to his own

---

[27] VEMA, 1.583, Kolbe in Schmelens Erwartung, 17/5/1850, to mission directors. JBG's translation.
[28] VEMA, 2.585, *Kolbe Tagebuch, gehalten auf Schmelens Erwartung*, 25/6/1850. Two years later Katjamuaha, who was at that stage under threat from Jonker, went to the extent of building an *Ondjuuo ya Mukuru*, 'house of God', so as to attract missionaries to his Onganda. Hahn, *Tagebücher*, p. 589.
[29] VEMA, 2.585, 7/7/1850. The prophetic function ascribed to the Bible was certainly not limited to Kahitjene. The sermons extolling the virtues and all-encompasing truth of God's word were not lost upon the Herero chief Kambazembi, who asked missionary Beiderbecke to check whether or not the rains would come. Dr N. Mossolow, *Waterberg: Beitrag zur Geschichte der Missions-station Otjozondjupa des Kambazembi-Stammes und des Hererolandes*, John Meinert (Windhoek 1980?) p. 9.

advantage. Thus in July 1850, Kahitjene asked Kolbe to check his Bible to see whether or not Jonker intended attacking him. Similarly, a short while later, it was with dread and foreboding that Kahitjene saw that a flag, which was emblazoned with a cross and which had been raised by Kolbe, blew in the direction of Jonker Afrikaner.[30]

It was indeed an ill wind that blew. Shortly thereafter Jonker Afrikaner's commando, of 350 men, 40 horses and 150 guns, sacked Okahandja.[31] Following the attack Jonker Afrikaner personally visited Okahandja to receive the allegiance of the survivors.[32] Kahitjene fled from Okahandja to the mission stations at Otjikango and Otjimbingwe. However, his fate had been sealed and following a dispute regarding cattle he found his death at the hands of his son.[33] The downfall of Kahitjene informs us as to the manner in which missionaries were perceived by the inhabitants of central Namibia. Unfortunately for Kahitjene, they were perceptions which his resident missionary could not hope to have fulfilled. Missionary Kolbe witnessed the attack on Okahandja, in which Kahitjene sought refuge in the church, and was thoroughly shocked by what he saw – his extensive subsequent reports conveyed the horror of the event. The ruthlessness of Jonker's attack, and Kolbe's reporting thereof, went a large way towards effecting a change in policy, on the part of the missionaries, with regard to Jonker Afrikaner. Henceforth the Rhenish missionary society was actively engaged in arming, sheltering and supporting those who were opposed to Jonker Afrikaner. In a nutshell, this meant supporting the *Ovatjimba* who had gathered to their mission stations.

Kahitjene's fall from power served as an example which ensured that, for the time being, the Herero chieftains allied to Jonker Afrikaner remained loyal. However, the raiding economy, upon which Jonker's hegemony was based, continued to supply a steady stream of people who settled at the mission stations. Here they consolidated the power and interests of the missionary chiefs.

Trade wars

Kahitjene could never have known about it, but, shortly after his death, he was to play a minor role in an English-language bestseller. The author of the bestseller was the trader, Charles John Andersson, the adventurer who had first come to southern Africa as an assistant to the tourist Francis Galton. Following various enterprises, Andersson chose to concentrate on the export of cattle to the markets of the Cape colony. It was in attempting to attain a monopoly in this trade that Andersson became allied to the missionary chieftains and embroiled in a war with the Nama chieftains of southern and central Namibia. In the end, the Nama chiefs were defeated and Andersson so seriously wounded that he had to give up the cattle trade. The Herero, however, through allying themselves to Andersson, carried off the spoils of war.

[30] VEMA, 2.585, 14/7/1850. Vedder in his *Südwestafrika*, p. 235, has Kahitjene interpreting the flag as indicating that the Jonker would not be attacking him.
[31] VEMA, 2.585, Okahandja Otjikango, 24.
[32] Francis Galton, *Explorer*, p. 66. Galton claims that Jonker arrived reeling drunk and demanding breakfast on the morning following the attack.
[33] Andersson, *Lake Ngami*, pp. 143, 144 and 149.

Photo 1.1: Charles John Andersson
Source: Namibian National Archives,
Windhoek

Photo 1.2: Chief Zeraua and his bodyguard, Okahandja 1876
Source: Namibian National Archives, Windhoek

From Hereroland cattle were exported overland, through the territories of the various southern Namibian Nama chieftains, to the Cape. Andersson attempted to gain sole control of the export of cattle from Hereroland to the Cape. At the same time, he tried to ensure the maintenance of profitable export routes to the Cape. That is, he sought to keep export costs, particularly passage, water and grazing taxes, down to a minimum. Previously the export of cattle overland to the Cape colony had been in the hands of traders allied to the various Nama chieftains, who straddled the route leading to the Colony. The Nama chieftains taxed these cattle drives and, through the quarantining of stock, sought to protect their own herds from the various cattle diseases which might be carried by the travelling herds.[34] During the late 1850s lungsickness had ravaged cattle herds elsewhere in southern Africa.[35] By 1860 there were reports of lungsickness amongst cattle in the Namibian interior. The Nama chieftains, anxious to prevent the contamination of their own herds, sought to prevent the passage of cattle through their territory. Though Andersson knew of the disease, he, in turn, needed to recoup his trading costs. Andersson's diary indicates the predicament he was in:

> Vero [another trader] and his friends are at Otjimbingwe. Hesitated sending his cattle by land this season on account of the lungsickness. I must and will risk that.[36]

In 1860 Andersson was able to convince Jonker Afrikaner and his 'Raad' to let his cattle through. In the following year Andersson, because his cattle were infected, did not ask for permission and drove his cattle through Jonker's territory. By way of warning, Andersson's party was attacked by an ally of Jonker Afrikaner, and in southern Namibia Andersson was forced to pay a fine of 100 sheep by another of Jonker's allies. Determined not to allow this to happen again, Andersson, upon arriving in the Cape, purchased two cannons and set about recruiting mercenaries. Following his return to central Namibia, Andersson, in alliance with the Rhenish missionaries and a number of like-minded traders, set about arming and training contingents of *Ovatjimba* at Otjimbingwe. Henceforth the mercenaries, euphemistically known as the 'Otjimbingwe British Volunteer Artillery', which in true Victorian style had its own motto, flag and song, were used to enforce the will of Andersson and his allies.[37]

Within this context it is important to note the development of the Zeraua chieftaincy at Otjimbingwe. Following Jonker's cattle raids, Zeraua and his followers had become impoverished; they had become *Ovatjimba*. Shortly before he died of syphilis, that most frontier of diseases, Zeraua, or 'Ou Willem' as he was known to the missionaries and traders alike, told a Cape colonial official how, following Jonker's raids, he had been able to reestablish himself.

> When the Namaquas overcame us, I stuck to my missionary, Mr. Rath. We were very much cast down in those days, and if I had an ox, it was a privilege accorded me by the Namaquas, through the influence of the Missionary. Petrus Swaartbooy

---

[34] See C.J. Andersson, *Trade and Politics in Central Namibia 1860–1864*, Charles John Andersson Papers, Vol. II, edited by B. Lau, Archeia (Windhoek 1989).
[35] See particularly, J.B. Peires, *The Dead Will Arise: Nongqawuse and the Great Xhosa Cattle-killing Movement 1856–7*, Ravan Press (Johannesburg 1989).
[36] Andersson, *1860–1864*, p. 16.
[37] Andersson, *1860–1864*, p. 31. A number of these recruits were from the former Kat river settlement. For references to the song, flag and motto see p. 281. On the invention of a specific Herero flag by Andersson see p. 111.

also assisted me. He brought me back 10 head of cattle. My people had to live on `Mietjes' [*uintjes*, small bulbs] and other herbs.

I wished to move into the Kaoko veldt, but I met Mr. Bassingthwaite, who persuaded me, as my people were broken down, to go and work with my people in the mines. I was asked to work in the mines by a second man, tall and thin, a third man who died, by Mr. Andersson and then by Mr. Hilder.[38]

Through his association with the Rhenish mission, the Swartboois, and the English copper-mining traders, Zeraua was able to recover from Jonker's raids. Throughout the 1850s Zeraua led a group of Herero copper miners associated with the 'Walvis Bay Mining Company'. From 1861 onwards, the group of men led by Zeraua came to form the basis of the Herero armed forces which fought along with the traders against the Afrikaners. In exchange for these services, Zeraua and his subjects acquired firearms.[39] The arming of the *Ovatjimba* by the traders, in return for their military loyalty, ensured a significant shift in the relations of power that existed at the mission stations. With firearms the *Ovatjimba* were no longer dependent on the missionaries for support. The granting of guns to the followers of Zeraua, and other trader associates, led directly to their later independence and move away from the direct control of the mission stations.

In 1861 both Jonker Afrikaner and his Herero vassal, Tjamuaha, died in Okahandja. They were succeeded by their sons Christian Afrikaner and Maharero. Shortly after their deaths, the *Ovatjimba*, subject to the missionary Chief Hahn, along with Herero and others employed by Andersson, became involved in various intrigues against Christian Afrikaner and his allies.[40]

It appears that intrigues commenced between the Damaras [Herero] at Otjimbingwe, and those in the service of the Afrikaners. Messengers were going backward and forward, and the next movement was that some of those Damaras were off with their masters' flocks and herds, and drove them into Otjimbingwe. The owners of the cattle came after them, on horseback, but the Damaras . . . protected by one Phillipus [Katjimune] . . . showed a bold front, and the Afrikaners, not having expected resistance in such form, returned.[41]

The intrigues were part of the build-up to what has become known as *Ovita vyongombonganga*, the war of the theft of the white brown-flecked cow. Christian Afrikaner was conscious of these activities. In lengthy letters he harangued those aiding and abetting the outbreak of war between '*die zwart en roe [sic] volk*', the black and the red people.[42] Writing to Andersson, Christian Afrikaner stated:

Furthermore, I must say that you wish to steal the land, even though you know that it has always belonged to us. Because you did not know how to get the land, you decided the following: `Let me instigate and support the Herero against the people'.

[38] *The Commissions of W.C. Palgrave: Special Emissary to South West Africa 1876–1885*. Edited and introduced by E.L.P. Stals (Cape Town 1991), Second Series No. 21 Van Riebeeck Society, p. 25. It is of interest to note here that the Kaokoveld is referred to as a possible safe haven.
[39] B. Lau (ed.), *The Matchless Copper Mine in 1857: Correspondence*, Charles John Andersson Papers, Vol. I (Windhoek 1987) & *Charles John Andersson: Trade and Politics in Central Namibia 1860–1864*, Charles John Andersson Papers, Vol. II (Windhoek 1989).
[40] A number of those involved in intrigues against the Afrikaners would later become hunters, traders and big men of renown in their own right within Herero society.
[41] Lau, *Jonker*, p. 129, quoting from CA GH 19/10, Chapman: 'Memo', 1865.
[42] See copies of letters of Christian Afrikaner to Andersson and Christian Afrikaner to Kleinschmidt, 4 June 1863, in Andersson, *1860–1864*, pp. 256–60.

So that they shall kill me and all my people. In this way you would get all the land. That is why you have strengthened these people with guns and powder.[43]

Finally, in 1863, following extensive lobbying by emissaries of 'ou Willem' Zeraua, Maharero, the man who had served in the commando that had annihilated Kahitjene's bid for autonomy twelve years previously, successfully did what Kahitjene had failed to do. Maharero, his followers and the cattle in their care, abandoned Christian Afrikaner.[44] Henceforth Maharero, the commando warrior who had raided and fought on behalf of the Afrikaners, operated in alliance with Andersson. In 1864, Maharero, along with the trader Green, one of Andersson's accomplices, attacked and destroyed the Afrikaner settlement in Windhoek. These attacks on the Afrikaners culminated in June 1864, when a combined *Ovatjimba*, Herero, mercenary and trader commando, of 3000 men, attacked and defeated the Afrikaners.[45]

For Andersson and the missionaries, it was to be a Pyrrhic victory. Andersson was badly wounded in the attack and soon left central Namibia as it was, not attempting further change. However, his armaments and intrigues had provided opportunities for a number of Herero to gain access to hitherto unknown forms of accumulation and power. The Herero who fought alongside the traders acquired substantial herds, and, perhaps more importantly, obtained large amounts of firearms. With the defeat of the Afrikaners, and the threat of raiding from the south severely diminished, Herero chiefs abandoned the sanctuary of the mission stations and started raiding north. Through his intrigues Andersson had sought to ensure the most cost-efficient form of cattle export to the Cape. On the other hand, for a number of Andersson's Herero and *Ovatjimba* allies, his intrigues offered opportunities which had hitherto not existed, opportunities which, when coupled to the radical weakening and eventual collapse of the Afrikaner polity, led to the development of highly centralized Herero chieftaincies. These chieftaincies came to exist independently of missionary and Afrikaner control. This was a new development. Henceforth the newly established Herero chieftaincies determined access to the outside world independently of missionary or Afrikaner involvement, even though they were in themselves a product of this involvement.

Elsewhere in African pastoralist societies the creative innovation of prophets, in 'colonizing vacant political niches' in response to political challenges and change, has been well documented.[46] In contrast to the Maasai, Turkana or Kalenjin prophets, Herero *Ombuke* (prophet) and, to a lesser extent, *Omurangere*

[43] Andersson, *1860–1864*, p. 57. JBG's translation.
[44] On Zeraua's role in convincing Maharero to abandon Christian Afrikaner, see Palgrave, *Commissions*, p. 26.
[45] For further details regarding the battles, see Lau, *Jonker*, pp. 119–41 & Andersson, *1860–1864*, pp. 236–48.
[46] In this context I am thinking particularly of the political transformations that took place in Maasai, Turkana and Nandi societies, which allowed for the further aggressive expansion and centralization of these societies, but also of the incorporative role of the Nuer prophet Ngundeng Bong in the aftermath of aggressive expansion. See Richard D. Waller, 'Kidongoi's Kin: Prophecy & Power in Maasailand'; David M. Anderson, 'Visions of the Vanquished: Prophets & Colonialism in Kenya's Western Highlands' & Douglas H. Johnson, 'The Prophet Ngundeng & the Battle of Pading: Prophecy, Symbolism & Historical Evidence', in David M. Anderson & Douglas H. Johnson (eds), *Revealing Prophets* (London 1995). For specific references to Turkana society, which in its expansion mirrored Herero expansion following 1863, see John Lamphear, *The Scattering Time: Turkana Responses to Colonial Rule* (Oxford 1992) & 'The People of the Grey Bull: The origin and expansion of the Turkana', in *JAH*, 1988, Vol. 29, No. 1, pp. 27–39.

(one engaged in religious activity) were unable to transform and expand their positions to respond to the challenge of Oorlam expansion in the first half of the nineteenth century. Instead, Herero society appropriated the terms and structures existing in Oorlam society to further the centralization of what had hitherto been a stateless society. Prior to 1863 the people who spoke dialects of the Bantu language that would later become standardized as Otjiherero lived in stateless societies, or were the subjects of missionary and Oorlam chiefs. The term *Ombuke* was used to denote a prophet and is derived from the Proto-Bantu *-búki*, doctor, which is derived from *-búk-*, divine. Similarly the term *Omurangere*, used to denote somebody engaged in religious practice, was also derived from the Proto-Bantu *-dàng-*, teach. In contrast to other African pastoralist societies, where prophets were able to transform their role into a more centralizing political authority, and where terms referring to prophets were recast to refer to and encompass the new forms of political leadership, Herero society appropriated new terms to define new positions and structures that had hitherto not existed. The Herero words referring to chief, *Omuhona*, and law, *Ovetta*, are derived from Nama and Cape Dutch, the languages of the Oorlam polities that controlled central Namibia in the first half of the nineteenth century. Similarly words that were already current in Otjiherero underwent shifts in meaning. Thus the meaning of the word *Otjira*, council, derived from Proto-Bantu *-nda*, village, clan, appears to have shifted slightly from gathering of wealthy men, to a meaning equivalent to the Dutch *raad*, which was used by the Oorlams to refer to a chief's council.[47] The terms of Oorlam political structures were appropriated and superimposed upon Herero society by Herero political leaders, most of whom had served 'internships' as Oorlam lieges prior to establishing their own political followings independent of Oorlam control. An exception to the rule, as far as prophets are concerned, was the Ovambanderu leader, Kahimemua, who was credited as being an *Ombuke*. Kahimemua alone of all the Herero chiefs that emerged in the second half of the nineteenth century was credited with mantic as well as political power. Why this should be so needs to be researched, but could lie in the apparent historical depth ascribed to Ovambanderu supernatural powers.

Building up the herds

Within a year of the defeat of the Afrikaners, the majority of the Herero living at the mission stations in Otjimbingwe and Otjikango had withdrawn into the Namibian hinterland. Here the Herero set about reestablishing themselves as pastoralists. Apart from the herds taken from Afrikaner control in 1863 and 1864, the Herero also reacquired the cattle which they had pawned to the Ovambo kingdoms or stashed in the Kaokoveld, the only area which had not been ravaged by the Afrikaner raids. Furthermore, through a series of raids, the Herero acquired substantial herds of cattle. Between 1863 and 1871 Herero commandos, making use of the unstable nature of Namaland, raided far and wide into Namaland. The expansion of the Herero herds, coupled with their newly acquired firearms, led to and allowed Herero conquest of new territory, particularly in the Otavi Grootfontein area. Here Damara cattle herders were

---

[47] With thanks to S. Elders and Prof. T. Schadeberg for information regarding the derivation of Proto-Bantu words.

dispossessed of their cattle and land. At the same time Herero hunters used their hunting skills to acquire cattle from traders such as Eriksson who in turn procured cattle from the Ovambo.[48] Ivory and other hunting spoils, acquired by Herero hunters and dependants, were traded in return for Ovambo cattle.

Throughout the 1860s and 1870s Herero were loath to trade their cattle though they were willing to trade the spoils of the hunt. As the Herero cattle herds continued to expand, so too did the demand for herding labour. In what the missionaries described as a pagan reaction, the remaining Herero and *Ovatjimba* occupying the mission stations withdrew into central Hereroland.[49] In 1870 and 1871, as Afrikaner hegemony collapsed in southern Namibia, there was a major movement of Herero and Banderu, who had been living in Namaland, northwards into the Herero heartland. These migrants, by being members of the Herero cultural setting, were, on the basis of kinship – inferred or otherwise – incorporated into the newly emerging Herero pastoralist society. Here they were employed in the herding of the ever-expanding Herero herds.

The chieftains

It had been 'Ou Willem' Zeraua, in alliance with other mission Herero, who had convinced Maharero to abandon his alliance with the Afrikaners in 1863. As Zeraua later put it:

> . . . I went and brought Kamaherero out of the mountain [Osona] and down to my place . . . before the Namaqua commando came against us.[50]

Following the war, in which the forces of Christian Afrikaner were defeated, 'Ou Willem' Zeraua deserted his missionary mentors and established himself, in 1868, as an independent chieftain in Omaruru. Previously Omaruru had served as a horticultural settlement for the mission station in Otjimbingwe. However, by 1870 it had developed into the main regional trading centre on the route between Ovamboland and Walvisbay. Following his death, Zeraua was succeeded by his nephew, Tjaherani. Described by the missionaries as a 'hard drinking heathen', Tjaherani died shortly afterwards and was succeeded by his half-brother, Manasse Tjisiseta, who, as a school teacher and church deacon, was the firm choice of the mission.[51] During the first years of his reign, Manasse extended his polity's control over the trade routes that led from Omaruru to Ovamboland and southern Angola. In doing this his polity came into an extended series of conflicts with the Swartbois and Boer trekkers, who also sought to control these routes. As a result of these conflicts Manasse developed a standing army, modelled on Andersson's 'Otjimbingwe British

---

[48] W.G. Clarence Smith and R. Moorsom, 'Underdevelopment and class formation in Ovamboland, 1845–1915', in *Journal of African History*, XVI, 3 (1975) pp. 365–81. Describes how the impact particularly of the 'cape' trade led to the underdevelopment of the Ovambo kingdoms. They note that by the 1860s Cape traders, who were more highly capitalized, began to supplant the Portuguese traders. The terms of trade led to intensified internal taxation to meet the shortfall of cattle export. 'And there are clear signs of this process at work among the Kwambi, a southern Ovambo people, as early as the 1870s.' p. 375.

[49] Lau, *Jonker*, page 140. *BRMG* 1869, 275ff; *BRMG* 1868, 243-7.

[50] *Palgrave*, p. 26.

[51] Archives of the Evangelical Lutheran Church in Namibia (ELCIN), Windhoek, V Chroniken 23.1, Omaruru.

Photo 1.3: Maharero Tjamuaha and Riarua (sitting),
and Wilhelm Maharero (standing), Okahandja 1876
Source: Namibian National Archives, Windhoek

Volunteer Artillery', and armed with a cannon. At the advent of German
colonialism, Manasse Tjisiseta's polity, centred on Omaruru, was undoubtedly
the strongest and most cosmopolitan of all the Herero polities in the territory.[52]

In 1851 the horticultural settlement at Otjozondjupa was abandoned
following raids by Kahitjene.[53] Following Kahitjene's demise, Tjamuaha began
stocking his herds on the veld around Otjozondjupa.[54] After 1863, Tjamuaha's
son, Maharero, used Otjozondjupa as a cattle post and horticultural centre.
Two men, Krüger and Kambazembi, oversaw the running of Maharero's
operations in the Otjozondjupa region. Krüger, a Baster who had previously
been armed as a hunter by Andersson, lived in Otjozondjupa with a large
following of Nama and Damara horticulturalists and hunters.[55] On the extensive
grasslands to the west of Otjozondjupa Kambazembi grazed immense herds

[52] In the 1870s Andersson's successors, Green and Eriksson, had established themselves in
Omaruru. When Palgrave visited the centre in 1876 he found an international gathering of
Angolans, Americans, Finns, Swedes, Germans, Englishmen, Cape colonials and various
representatives of other African polities in the region.
[53] See Andersson, *Lake Ngami*, pp. 153 and 154. Hahn, *Tagebücher*, p. 396, '19/12/1848 Jonker
reports having been to Otjozondjupa and that it is a settlement with gardens where large numbers
of rich Nama and Damara live'.
[54] Hahn, *Tagebücher*, p. 590. Ibid. p. 1127, mentions that Tjamuaha's cattle raided from the
Ovambo were stored at Otjozondjupa.
[55] Mossolow, *Waterberg*, pp. 5 and 9; Krüger later went back to Griqualand leaving his son Wilhelm
behind.

of cattle. At the advent of German colonialism Kambazembi was the richest of all the Herero *Ovahona*.

Significantly, the Ovambanderu *Omuhona* Kahimemua was circumcised in *ojomandjembere*, the year of the gun, 1850.

> As a youth Kahimemua had on several occasions accompanied the Nama chief [Amraal Lambert known as Mbarandu] on his journeys, indeed had been his constant travelling companion. He therefore had no difficulties with the Nama. He was trusted by the Nama chief, but equally by his own people since he was all the time secretly doing everything in his power to supply the Mbanderu with weapons, that is guns and ammunition, so that they might one day make war against the Nama.[56]

In the early 1860s, Amraal Lambert's polity was shattered by the twin impact of lungsickness, which devastated the Nama cattle herds, and smallpox, which decimated the Nama settlement at Gobabis. Coupled to these natural reverses was the collapse of the southern trade network following the disintegration of Afrikaner hegemony in central Namibia. When this occurred, Kahimemua along with other Banderu *Ovahona* took 'their' cattle herds and withdrew their allegiance to the Nama.[57] Following his withdrawal from Amraal Lambert's political ambit, Kahimemua settled close to and associated with Maharero. By the early 1880s Kahimemua's close association with Maharero had paid off, to the extent that Kahimemua and his followers were able to successfuly challenge and trek into territory which at that stage was nominally under Nama control.[58] At the advent of German colonialism Kahimemua's Ovambanderu straddled the trade routes that led from Walvisbay to Lake Ngami in the interior.

In 1861, following the deaths of Tjamuaha and Jonker Afrikaner, Maharero had withdrawn his allegiance to Christian Afrikaner. Following the battles of 1864, Maharero had settled in Okahandja. By 1876 Okahandja was a bustling trade centre where Maharero had a brick house built 'as a mark of a great man and . . . only to store his European belongings'.[59] Maharero's sons Wilhelm and Samuel were being trained for the wider world. The brothers, along with other Herero 'royals', attended the mission school in Otjimbingwe, and, along with Asser Riarua, the son of Maharero's military commander, they visited Cape Town. However, already during the 1870s, Okahandja, as a trading centre, was being eclipsed in importance by Omaruru. Increasingly trade from the Cape to Ovamboland passed via Walvisbay and Omaruru, and bypassed the overland trade via Namaland and Okahandja. Trade via Okahandja came to a complete standstill in 1880, when, following a grazing dispute, war broke out between Maharero and a number of Nama and Oorlam chieftains. These chieftains would soon come to be allied under the leadership of Hendrik Witbooi.

Summing up

Following 1864, Herero hunters and traders came to act as middlemen operating between the Ovambo kingdoms and the Cape. The Herero were able

---

[56] Sundermeier, *Mbanderu*, Windhoek 1986, p. 10.
[57] Chief Apona, who was the most important of these big men, remained allied to Lambert for at least another three years. Sundermeier, *Mbanderu*, p. 13.
[58] *Ojorutjindo*, the year of migration, 1883. See Sundermeier, *Mbanderu*, p. 20.
[59] Gerhard Pool, *Samuel Maharero* (Windhoek 1991) p. 48.

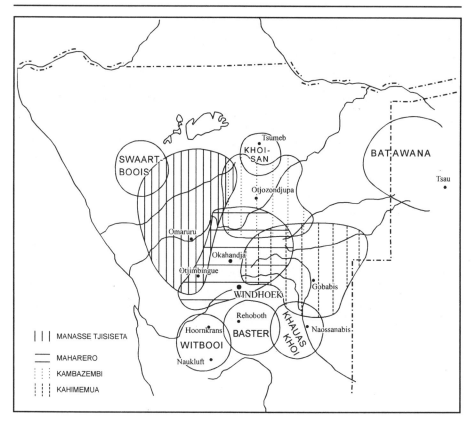

Map 1.2: Central Namibia showing areas under the control of the four principal Herero chiefs at the advent of German colonialism in 1884 '

to tax the trade routes which led to Ovamboland. It is in this context that new regional trade centres, such as Omaruru and Okahandja, developed. These replaced the old and eclipsed centres of Otjimbingwe and Windhoek, both of which had been major trading entrepôts under the control of the missionaries and the Afrikaners respectively. In essence the frontier had moved north, no longer were the Nama polities the direct middlemen between the Cape and the north.

By 1876 the Herero of central Namibia were living in what can only be described as an age of plenty, an age which led a Cape colonial official to comment:

> Long intercourse with white people has developed singularly few wants amongst them . . . More than three-fourths of the Damaras [Herero] are without a single want that the trader can gratify that would compel them to part with a sheep or a goat from a herd of thousands; and the wants of the other fourth are limited to a little powder, and lead, and a little clothing . . .[60]

However, it would be wrong to infer from this, as some have, that 'the . . .

[60] Commissioner Palgrave quoted in Lau, *Jonker*, p. 146.

social change observed in the whole of Namaland subsequent to the Oorlam migrations/invasions was not paralleled in Hereroland'.[61] Though the influx of European goods was closely controlled and the 'structures of underdevelopment' were not apparent, it must be borne in mind that the Herero chieftaincies, after 1840, were a product of and an adaptation to the impact of the 'Cape' frontier. Indeed all the major Herero chiefs who reigned during the Herero golden age of the 1870s were products of this frontier and its trade. The new chieftaincies were all closely related, not only in kinship terms, but in that they were products of the same shaping force. The skills and contacts acquired through association with the frontier were applied to create and maintain a new form of centralized Herero polity. From being a society characterized by an endless series of loosely linked kinship groups centred around patri-clan heads, Herero society became a society characterized by strongly centralized chieftaincies centred upon specific geographical areas.

Herero political structures at the advent of colonization were far from static. Indeed, those which appeared static to observers were in themselves the products of appropriated and inherited structures and systems, which the Herero had transformed to their own ends. The seemingly static nature of Herero socio-political institutions belied a never-ending transformation and appropriation of outside influences. It was a system of flux which carried on into the period in which Imperial Germany sought to colonize Hereroland.

[61] Ibid., p. 145.

2
The Herero Succession Dispute
1890–94

Introduction

In 1890 Maharero Tjamuaha, the once mighty chief of Okahandja, died a broken man. In the four years that followed his death, central Hereroland was racked by the ensuing succession dispute, and ravaged by the attacks of Hendrik Witbooi, the Nama chieftain who had risen to power in the south. Out of this mêlée Samuel Maharero, Maharero Tjamuaha's son, who at the time of his father's death had no customary rights to the chieftaincy of Okahandja, manipulated the incoming German colonial forces into supporting him in his successful bid for the chieftaincy of Okahandja.

Though it is of central importance to the further development of Herero history, comparatively few authors have seriously dealt with the Herero succession dispute of 1890–94. Generally those dealing with the succession have mentioned that Samuel Maharero succeeded his father but have failed to delve into the machinations by which Samuel sought to attain his father's position, inheritance and wealth. The fact that Samuel Maharero's rights to his father's *Oruzuo* inheritance were extremely tenuous, and that he was in no way entitled to an aspect of Maharero's *Eanda* inheritance is overlooked by most authors. On the whole authors have tended to emphasize German perceptions of the inheritance dispute and have failed to take into account Herero beliefs and perceptions with regard to kinship structures and inheritance. An exception is the recent work of G. Pool which seeks to deal with the succession dispute with reference to the *Eanda* and *Oruzuo* rights of the various contenders.[1] However Pool's work, too, fails to deal effectively with Samuel's creative use and manipulation of German beliefs with regard to succession and inheritance. In his work Helmut Bley refers to *Eanda* and *Oruzuo* in passing and notes that the Germans recognized Samuel Maharero as paramount chief, but that:

It would be wong, however, to see in this more than a passive interest in confirming

---

[1] G. Pool, *Samuel Maharero* (Windhoek 1991) pp. 77–84.

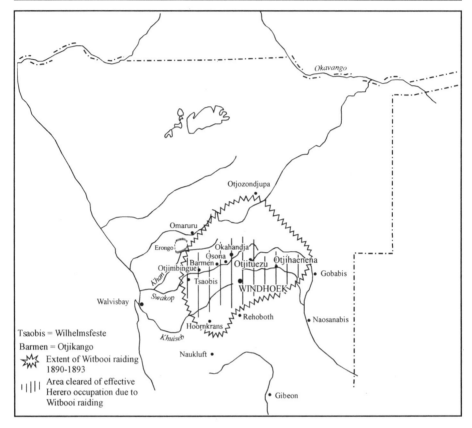

Map 2.1: Central Namibia showing area cleared of effective Herero occupation due to Witbooi raiding, 1890–93

an internal decision of the tribe, for the Germans did not have at their disposal the power to intervene in so hotly disputed an issue.[2]

This chapter, as will be seen, argues that it was precisely because Samuel Maharero was able to mobilize German support and the power at their disposal that he was able to triumph in 'so hotly disputed an issue'.

German protection treaties

Though German missionaries had begun operating in central Namibia in the early 1840s, formal German government interest in the territory, when compared to the other colonial powers at the time, only came at a rather late stage.[3] In the late 1860s, following the failure of C.J. Andersson's endeavours,

---

[2] Bley, *South-West Africa*, p. 18.
[3] Compared to the other colonial powers at the turn of the century, Germany only became interested in attaining colonies at a rather late stage. Why this should be so, and Germany's conversion to the 'Imperial mission', is covered in H.L. Wesseling, *Verdeel en Heers: De Deling van Afrika, 1880–1914* (Amsterdam 1992) pp. 137–47.

the Rhenish mission had petitioned the Prussian government for protection. Caught in the struggle for German unification and the impending Franco-Prussian war, the missionary request was turned down. As a result, throughout the 1870s central Namibia fell firmly within the Cape Colony's, if not the British Empire's, sphere of influence. Indeed, during the 1870s, William Coates Palgrave was dispatched to administer the territory as the Cape Colony's special commissioner, and in 1878 Britain took formal possession of Walvisbay and its immediate environs.[4] If the Rhenish missionaries had hoped for further British involvement in the territory, their hopes were dashed by British defeats elsewhere in southern Africa. Though the British eventually won the Anglo-Zulu war, and exacted revenge for their drubbing in the first Anglo-Boer war, the débâcle of defeat at the hands of African forces, in Isandhlwana in 1879 and Majuba in 1881, ensured that British Imperial interest in the colonial venture in southern Africa was temporarily reduced to a minimum.

In early 1884 the Imperial German government granted protectorate status to lands acquired in southern Namibia by a Bremen merchant by means which it knew to be fraudulent.[5] In August of 1884, Imperial Germany expanded the area under its protection, when it annexed the Namibian coast, with the exception of Walvisbay, from the Orange river in the south to the Cunene river in the north.[6] Germany's claims to the coast were recognized at the Berlin conference in late 1884.[7] In order that claims to the hinterland be recognized, treaties had to be concluded with the territory's inhabitants. To this end, in September 1885 three German officials, Imperial Commissioner Dr Heinrich Ernst Göring, Chancellor Nels and police chief Goldammer, were landed at Walvisbay.[8] Operating out of Otjimbingwe, and assisted by the Rhenish missionaries, the German officials sought to conclude 'protection' treaties with the territory's inhabitants.

In 1885 the forces of the Nama Chief Hendrik Witbooi regularly attacked and raided Okahandja and its cattle posts. In the aftermath of one such raid, Maharero, the Herero chief of Okahandja, and his councillors were persuaded into signing a protection treaty with Imperial Germany. Unfortunately for the Herero, Germany saw the treaty solely as a further substantiation of its claims to German South West Africa. The three German officials, who constituted all of Germany's official presence in the territory, could not seriously have been expected to protect Maharero and his subjects from the debilitating attacks of Hendrik Witbooi and his commandos.[9] It took three years of unremitting

[4] For further information see The Commissions of W.C. Palgrave Special Emissary to South West Africa 1876–1885, edited and introduced by E.L.P. Stals, Second Series No. 21, Van Riebeeck Society (Cape Town 1991).
[5] Bundesarchiv Potsdam (BAP), Reichs Kolonial Amt (RKA) 2100.
[6] Wesseling, Verdeel en Heers, p. 355.
[7] Bley, South-West Africa, p. xxv.
[8] Drechsler, Fighting, p. 31. Heinrich Göring was the father of the Nazi Air Marshall Hermann Göring.
[9] According to international law the three Germans, Göring, Nels and von Goldammer represented Imperial Germany in her newly established South West African Protectorate. Note here the true background to the protection treaty. Negotiations started on 18 October closed on 21 October 1885; the missionaries played a central role in the negotiations. 'The majority of the Chiefs had already left Okahandja before the commencement of negotiations.' The German negotiators told Maharero that he didn't need all his advisers to sign the treaty as he himself 'as paramount chief had the right to sign a treaty, that affected the whole country, even without the presence of the other chiefs'. Dr Göring noted that missionary Diehl and Pastor Buttner convinced Maharero,

warfare and vague promises of British protection before Maharero and his councillors decided to annul their treaty with Germany. The three German officials were summoned to Okahandja, charged with having failed to fulfil their treaty obligations, and ordered to leave the country. To all intents and purposes Imperial Germany's colonial involvement in south-western Africa was at an end.[10]

The Rhenish missionaries had been extensively involved in Germany's short-lived colonial adventure. Through selling houses and properties to the German officials and through mediating on their behalf, the missionaries had severely compromised themselves in the eyes of the Herero. Consequently, a month after the expulsion of the officials, Maharero and his council ordered the closure of the mission church in Okahandja and summoned the missionaries resident in Hereroland to Okahandja. Here they charged the missionaries with being *Ovazepe* (people of murder), conspiring with the colonial officals, desecrating and exhuming Herero graves, establishing trade routes that bypassed Oka-handja, and, perhaps most importantly, assisting chiefs opposed to Maharero's authority.[11] Following lengthy discussions, the missionaries were permitted to remain in the territory, but the bonds of trust and friendship that had existed beforehand had been destroyed. Henceforth missionaries were consciously excluded from all *Otjira*, council meetings. Though the missionaries publicly lamented their previous actions, privately they thought and acted differently. Epitomizing this two-faced sham, Brincker, the then head of the Herero mission, wrote the following letter to the German foreign office:

> . . . Kamaherero is a negro chief who offers anyone who is prepared to pay him, even a Turk, concessions and rights on paper. Which on the following day he will cheekily nullify and provide the same on paper to another. To conclude treaties with Kamaharero is as good as concluding treaties with a small child . . .
>
> Morally Damaraland belongs to the German fatherland as our Rhenish mission, and it alone, has spent thousands on this. Here lie the graves of her fallen missionaries . . .
>
> Damaraland cannot be held by treaties and chiefs, but by explicitly presented European power [*etablierte europäische Macht*] in the form of a detachment of at least 400 men and at least 2 artillery batteries.[12]

even though Göring had his doubts [meinen Bedenken] that Maharero had the right to sign on behalf of all of Hereroland. BAP, RKA 2100, *Abschrift A 3281 p. iV Marz 1886 Rehoboth den 21 November 1885*. See *BRMG* 1886 p. 47, for report on missionaries bandaging Herero wounded and the activities of the German officials which included the firing of rockets and the placing of German flags on Maharero's house.

[10] BAP, RKA 2100, *Das Herero-land 1885–1891*.

[11] Evangelical Lutheran Church in Namibia (ELCIN), I 1.21 *1888–1890 Besondere Angelegenheiten*, Briefwechsel zwischen Maharero u. den Missionaren Diehl u. Eich sowie Schreiben der Konferenz an die Gemeinden über die Vorgänge in Okahandja 1888. ELCIN I 1.3 1873–1905 *Protokolbuch der Konferenzen in Hereroland*, Bericht über die Verhandlungen zwischen der Herero Konferenz und Maharero gehalten zu Okahandja am 17–18 Dec 1888.

[12] BAP, RKA 2105, H. Brincker as superintendent of the Rhenish mission in Damaraland, 13/3/89, to Reichskanzler Bismarck. Brincker's remarks regarding Germany's moral obligation towards Damaraland also referred to the extensive relations that existed between the Rhenish mission and the Kaiser, going back to the King of Prussia. German missionary societies emerged from a wave of pietism that had come about as a reaction to the secularizing modernism of the French revolution, and were therefore politically acceptable to the establishment. See Elizabeth Elbourne and Robert Ross, 'Combatting Spiritual and Social Bondage: Early missions in the Cape Colony', in Richard Elphick and Rodney Davenport (eds), *A History of Christianity in Southern Africa* (Cape Town, Berkeley and Oxford 1998).

Photo 2.1: Samuel Maharero
Source: United Evangelical Mission archives,
Wuppertal

The coming of the camel

At the time of the German expulsion, there were four major Herero chieftains in central Namibia. These chiefs were Manasse Tjisiseta of Omaruru, Maharero Tjamuaha of Okahandja, Kambazembi of Otjozondjupa, and the Ovambanderu chief Kahimemua Nguvauva at Otjihaenena. These four men were the chiefs of four highly centralized polities which together made up a loosely structured confederacy in which Maharero was nominally the most important. The four main chiefs cooperated on issues of mutual importance and strengthened alliances through marriage and tribute. In much the same way that the rings of the symbol of the Olympic games overlap one another, Herero spheres of chiefly influence overlapped one another. Thus the sub-chief Zacharias Zeraua of Otjimbingwe was under the authority of both Manasse Tjisiseta of Omaruru and Maharero Tjamuaha of Okahandja.[13] At the same time all three chiefs were interrelated through ties of marriage and descent. Thus, in the event of trouble in Otjimbingwe, Zacharias Zeraua could and did call upon the strength and support of both the Okahandja and the Omaruru chieftaincies.

Three months prior to the expulsion, Kaiser Wilhelm II had succeeded his father as heir to the throne of Imperial Germany. Kaiser Wilhelm II was a man with an ego easily bruised, and in later years he would sanction the sending of

[13] Zacharias Zeraua was one of four sons of 'Ou Willem' Zeraua, the Herero chief who had risen to power through supplying labour and soldiers to the traders and missionaries. Zacharias Zeraua's sister Albertine was married to Manasse Tjisiseta of Omaruru. He was a firm Christian believer who attempted to remain neutral during the Herero–German war. He was the sole pre-war chief to survive the war in Namibia, where he was settled in Windhoek. In March 1915 he died in Otjimbingwe.

massive contingents of German soldiers to GSWA to defend Germany's interests; however, in this instance an expeditionary force consisting of an officer, twenty-one soldiers and a camel would have to suffice. Advised as to what to wear by the Rhenish missionary director, dressed in the latest in exploratory fashion and sporting 'Bowie knives', the force landed at Walvisbay in June 1889.[14]

Captain Curt von Francois, the man who led the German expeditionary force along with his brother Hugo, was a professional soldier but a lousy diplomat.[15] Within two months of his arrival, Francois had so irritated and exasperated the inhabitants of the territory that he and his troops were forced to withdraw to Tsaobis, a waterhole on the edge of the desert on the waggon trail that led from Otjimbingwe to Walvisbay. In withdrawing to Tsaobis Francois demonstrated his military skills:

> For my purposes Tsaobis was ideally situated. Here the two main thoroughfares over Salem and Tinkas, which pass south of the Swakop from Walvisbay to Otjimbingwe, meet. All the heavily loaded waggons, which are intended for Otjimbingwe, have to pass Tsaobis . . . The favourable waterhole, the good grazing, the accessibility attract the traffic. Because of this it was easy to police the traffic to the coast. The buildings of the station, which I christened Wilhelmsfeste, occupied a dominating position, and with 18 men I could confidently anticipate any attack from the Herero.[16]

Prior to withdrawing to Tsaobis, Francois and his troops had visited Otjimbingwe and Omaruru. In both centres they had been rebuffed by the Herero, ignored by the traders and shunned by the Rhenish missionaries. Now ensconced in his fort, Wilhelmsfeste at Tsaobis, Francois exacted his revenge. He decreed that henceforth arms could no longer be imported into the territory. Waggon trains coming up from the coast were stopped and searched. All arms and ammunition found were confiscated and, in the case of waggons belonging to Robert Lewis, a man believed to be conspiring with the Herero against the Germans, all goods were impounded and personal letters opened.[17]

At the time of Francois's arrival, the Herero were engaged in a war against the forces of Hendrik Witbooi. As Hendrik Witbooi controlled the trade routes leading southwards to the Cape, the Herero were forced to rely on the waggon trails that led from the interior via Tsaobis to the coast for their supply of arms and ammunition. Alarmed at Francois's occupation of Tsaobis and his subsequent ban on armament imports, the Herero chiefs, Maharero, of

---

[14] BAP, RKA 2103–2105 *Aufstand der Hereros 3 Bänder* & RKA 2106–2110 *Entsendung einer bewaffneten Expedition gegen die Hereros unter Führung des Hauptmanns von Francois. 5 Bander; Marz 1889–Sept 1892.* The Germans entered GSWA through subterfuge and a minor diplomatic row ensued between Great Britain and Imperial Germany. The German soldiers were disguised as a scientific expedition. Accompanied by a camel, they set out from Liverpool, where they had lodged at the 'Northwestern hotel'. The 'scientific expedition' travelled, on board an English Castle liner, to Walvisbay where it disembarked. By marching to and fro and engaging in assorted martial pursuits, on what was after all British territory, the newly landed troop greatly disturbed the Cape Colony's resident magistrate in Walvisbay.

As regards fashion see, C. von Francois, *Deutsch Südwestafrika* (Berlin 1899) p. 34.

[15] He and his brothers, Albert and Hugo, were members of a Huguenot family that had served the Prussian kings since the late seventeenth century. The military skills of the von Francois family, which had served to provide them with sanctuary in Prussia, served to isolate von Francois from the Herero.

[16] C. von Francois, *DSWA*, p. 50. JBG's translation.

[17] BAP, RKA 1574, Official Statement of claims sent by the British foreign office on behalf of R. Lewis to German foreign office, 12/3/90.

Okahandja, and Manasse Tjisiseta, of Omaruru, sent footmen and mounted troops to Zacharias Zeraua in Otjimbingwe. Samuel Maharero accompanied his father's soldiers to Otjimbingwe and was joined there by Manasse Tjisiseta, who had come down personally to oversee events in Otjimbingwe.[18]

As a first step Samuel Maharero wrote to the commander of German forces in Hereroland, Curt von Francois, and demanded that he and his troops withdraw from the territory:

> If you did not come with warlike intentions, then I ask you . . . to return to Germany. I ask you once again to pay heed to what I say, do not needlessly spend your money but rather go home. If you do not want to listen to my words then please declare so openly and tell me directly that you are at war with us.[19]

Francois's answer was blunt and to the point. As his brother Hugo later noted:

> We referred them to the prohibition on the import of ammunition and explained that our actions were to be seen as reprisals for the hospitality which we had received when we left Otjimbingwe.[20]

Seeking an explanation for the situation, Samuel Maharero wrote to the English magistrate in Walvisbay:

> . . . I ask you as magistrate you are the chief man and suppposed to be wise and you must tell me the truth what have I done to the Germans? I know I make war with the Hottentots but I don't think they (the Germans) are of the same family . . .
>
> The first time the Germans came to my father and asked for a protectorate. My father said no I will not allow a German protectorate. My father said to them I want an English Protectorate. So my father called Mr. Lewis and told him he must go to Town [Cape Town] and get an English Protectorate. Also he must tell Queen Victoria so. That is the reason why the Germans are now stopping my guns and Ammunition, because I have given my country to the English.[21]

Faced with an arms blockade and with impending attacks by Hendrik Witbooi, the Herero chiefs sought in turn to impose a blockade on Tsaobis.[22] Traders and missionaries, operating out of Otjimbingwe, were prohibited from having any dealings with the German force in Tsaobis. Consequently when Francois ordered some pre-fabricated corrugated iron buildings from the trader H. Kleinschmidt, both Zacharias Zeraua and Samuel Maharero, wrote to the trader informing him that the buildings were not to be transported anywhere in Hereroland with the exception of Walvisbay.[23] Similarly missionaries in

---

[18] BAP, RKA 2107, Brincker in Otjimbingwe, 17/9/89, to German consul Cape Town & Nels in Tsaobis, 15/9/89, to Auswertiges Amt.

[19] BAP, RKA 2107, S. Maharero in Otjimbingwe, 18/8/89, to C. von Francois. Hugo von Francois printed a rather mangled version of this letter in his book, *Nama und Damara* (Magdeburg 1895) p. 112.

[20] Hugo von Francois, *Nama und Damara* (Magdeburg 1895) p. 112.

[21] Cape Archives Depot (CAD), Native Affairs (NA), *Letters received from Damaraland and Walfish Bay, 285–293*, Office of the RM W Bay 26/8/89 to NA in Cape Town, enclosed is a translation of a letter written by Samuel Maharero in Otjimbingwe 16/8/89. The resident magistrate was convinced that the Germans would be expelled from the territory and that the settlement in Walvisbay would also come under attack, he therefore asked for a detachment of soldiers and a maxim gun.

[22] BAP, RKA 2107, Letter Brincker in Otjimbingwe, 17/9/89, to German Consul in Cape Town, indicates Manasse's involvement.

[23] BAP, RKA 2107, folio 77, Samuel Maharero and Zacharias in Otjimbingwe, 21/8/89, to H. Kleinschmidt.

Otjimbingwe were prohibited from travelling to Tsaobis to minister to the German troops.[24] However, this in no way affected Francois, who, through maintaining control of Tsaobis, was able to resupply and provision his troops with goods, confiscated or otherwise, which had been transported directly from Walvisbay, en route to the interior via Tsaobis.

The longer Francois maintained his blockade, the more the Herero needed arms and ammunition. The longer the Herero forces remained in Otjimbingwe, the more they and the other unprotected Herero settlements became vulnerable to an attack by the forces of Hendrik Witbooi. In the end, the Herero were forced to back down, salvage what they could and attempt to resolve the situation peacefully. Of the chiefs present in Otjimbingwe, Manasse Tjisiseta was the one least affected by Francois's blockade. Waggons laden with arms and ammunition, intended for Omaruru and coming from the coast, could and did bypass the blockade in Tsaobis.[25] Assured of a continued supply of arms, and faced with the threat posed by the forces of Hendrik Witbooi, a threat which far outweighed that posed at the time by the Germans in Tsaobis, Manasse Tjisiseta forced the hand of the other chiefs by being the first to withdraw, with his forces, from Otjimbingwe. The united Herero front collapsed. Following Manasse Tjisiseta's withdrawal, Samuel Maharero wrote to the Christian Herero community in Otjimbingwe and ordered them not to undertake any action against Francois.[26] Samuel Maharero's father, Maharero Tjamuaha, anxious to dismiss Francois's presence as an affair existing solely between Germany and Great Britain, which therefore need not affect him, wrote to Francois:

> For me there is no difference between you and the English; I hate and love neither (i.e. we are equally disposed to either party), however I do not want to be drawn into the conflicts of you and the English.[27]

Zacharias Zeraua, as a good Christian, went one step further and wrote a formal apology and asked for a pardon.[28]

In the end the immediate threat posed by Hendrik Witbooi's forces appeared to nullify the immediate threat posed by Francois and his men in Tsaobis. The threat posed by Hendrik Witbooi prevented the Herero from maintaining a unified front against Francois, let alone undertaking a joint attack on his small party. Thus Manasse Tjisiseta withdrew back to Omaruru, Samuel Maharero returned to Okahandja and Zacharias Zeraua stayed in Otjimbingwe. All three prepared for the attacks and raids of Hendrik Witbooi's commandos. The rich cattle owners abandoned the settlements and the poor and the Christians, who generally provided for themselves through riverbed agriculture, remained and prepared to weather the storm. The superintendent of the Rhenish mission in Hereroland, Brincker, in referring to Hendrik Witbooi's impending attacks, once again showed his true feelings, when he noted that the attacks would be the best for the Herero as:

---

[24] *Berichte der Rheinischen Mission-Gesellschaft (BRMG)*, 1890, p. 247.
[25] C. von Francois, *DSWA*, p. 53. Mentions the arrest of Tatlow, one of Manasse's traders, with a waggon of armaments in the vicinity of the Swakop river in December 1889.
[26] BAP, RKA 2107, Brincker in Otjimbingwe, 17/9/89, to German Consul in Cape Town, referring to letter written by Samuel Maharero to the Christian Herero community in Otjimbingwe.
[27] BAP, RKA 2107, Maharero Tjamuaha in Okahandja, *ca.* 23/8/89, to von Francois.
[28] BAP, RKA 2107, Zacharias Zeraua in Otjimbingwe, 3/9/89, to Nels.

The younger generation is so cheeky and conceited that it is hardly bearable. I believe that when the Hereros are properly beaten [*unter die Knute kommen*] they will become truly nice chaps, then they will learn to pay more attention to their missionaries. With love and generosity we have dealt with them long enough . . .[29]

Suggestive of the extreme frustration felt by many Herero at the time is an incident that occurred in Otjimbingwe in late 1889. On Christmas Eve 1889 three Christian Herero, Elia, Josua and the school teacher Heinrich, bought three bottles of brandy.[30] When the three bottles had been consumed Heinrich was sent out to purchase more alcohol; however, the store keeper Hutton refused to serve him. A fight started and: 'the drunken schoolmaster crying in anger shouted: "Leave me, I cannot do otherwise, I must kill all the whites."'[31]

Death by camel

In the face of Witbooi's impending attacks, the chance, which had existed, of expelling Francois and his small force from Hereroland passed. Safely ensconced in Tsaobis and with the threat of a Herero attack removed, Francois requested reinforcements and in January of 1890 these men arrived.[32] During January and February of 1890 Hendrik Witbooi's commandos, operating out of their base at Hoornkrans, raided Herero cattle posts between Otjimbingwe, Omaruru, and to the south of Otjikango.[33] Manasse Tjisiseta and Zacharias Zeraua attempted to ensure the safety of their followers by ordering them to move closer to the mission stations, or to withdraw into the Erongo mountains. However, this was to be to no avail. The Herero forces were severely beaten and were unable to prevent Witbooi's commandos from striking seemingly at will. For the Herero, the newly arrived German 'protectorate force' was anything but a protection force. Instead they observed how the Germans stood by and watched as Witbooi's commandos raided and escorted their captured Herero cattle herds past Tsaobis. That Hendrik Witbooi felt that he had nothing to fear is well illustrated by the fact that, at one stage, he asked the Germans for permission to water his captured herds at Tsaobis.[34]

---

[29] BAP, RKA 2107, Brincker in Otjimbingwe, 17/9/89, to RKA.

[30] Note here that Elia and Josua were joint signatories to the letter of 14/8/1889 addressed to von Francois at Tsaobis.

[31] *BRMG*, 1890, p. 246.

[32] In November 1889 an Imperial Guardsman, A. Henker, stationed in Potsdam, the residential seat of the German Kaisers, was so attracted by the prospect of a new uniform, that he volunteered for service in Imperial Germany's new South West African Protectorate. On the day prior to his departure, Henker and his fellow volunteers were inspected by the Kaiser in the gardens of the royal palace, Sansouci. Following the inspection, a number of the volunteers, hoping to become better acquainted with their destination, attended a theatre production at the Viktoria Theatre, in Potsdam. Here they saw an '. . . African production, *Stanley in Afrika*' with which:

We were very pleased, what with the beautiful jungle and plentiful water. But when we later landed in Sandwich harbour we were most put out.

The volunteers were met at Sandwich harbour by Lt Hugo von Francois, who had served in the jungles of 'Stanley's Africa'. Francois led his new reinforcements across the sand dunes and gravel plains of the Namib desert to Wilhelmsfeste at Tsaobis. Namibian National Archives Windhoek (NNAW), Acc.547, A. Henker, 1890–1904.

[33] ELCIN, I.1.3. Konferenz Synode 1890.

[34] See ELCIN, V. Missionschroniken Omaruru and Otjimbingwe, 1890, as well as NNAW, Acc.547.

Photo 2.2: Hendrik Witbooi
Source: Namibian National Archives,
Windhoek

Following Francois's withdrawal to Tsaobis, a number of Herero had argued that once Francois was reinforced he would sally forth against the Herero. Francois's cordial relations with Hendrik Witbooi seemed to substantiate this line of argument. Thus when in March 1890 the newly reinforced German troops, under the command of Lt Hugo von Francois, marched to Otjimbingwe, they found the settlement deserted by all but its European inhabitants. From Otjimbingwe Francois travelled on to Okahandja, the residence of Maharero Tjamuaha.[35]

At the time of Francois's arrival in Okahandja, most of the Herero chiefs of southern and central Hereroland had gathered to discuss and organize a response to the attacks of Hendrik Witbooi.[36] Francois was aware of the import of these discussions and did all in his power to impress upon his Herero audience the military prowess and power of Germany. During all of his stay in Okahandja, Francois presented himself and his men as a powerful military force and an ally to be coveted in the war against Hendrik Witbooi. Much like the 'Grand old Duke of York', Francois marched his men to and fro, displayed his camel, gave rifle and gymnastic displays and conducted mock attacks.[37] Francois was successful in his approach, and Maharero came to regard Francois as a gun for hire. Following a single meeting, in which Maharero demanded

[35] ELCIN, V. Missionschronik Omaruru, 1889:

> . . . it is expected that once he gets extra troops he will attack Otjimbingwe, if this happens Manasse cannot remain neutral as they belong to the clan of Zeraua.

H. von Francois, *Nama und Damara*, p. 118.
[36] Unfortunately the sources, which could have given us more insight into these discussions, namely the ELCIN Chroniken for Okahandja, are missing.
[37] H. von Francois, *Nama und Damara*, p. 122.

whether it was normal for Germans to be armed in the presence of others, Maharero left all further dealings with Francois to his military commander, Riarua.[38] Francois's demand for a patch of land for the establishment of a military garrison was turned down, but it was decided to meet again in the near future.

Two months later, in May 1890, the Francois brothers, Curt and Hugo, accompanied by camels and virtually all the German troops in the territory, escorted the Imperial Commissioner Dr H. Göring, on his return to Okahandja, less than two years after his expulsion. Once again, Okahandja was in readiness for an anticipated Witbooi attack. Once again, besides Maharero, the most powerful Herero chiefs, Manasse Tjisiseta of Omaruru, Kambazembi of Otjozondjupa and the Mbanderu chief Kahimemua, had gathered in Okahandja to determine a strategy against the attacks of Hendrik Witbooi. Following the arrival of the German force, the German officials were invited to Maharero's brick house to take part in the discussions and to explain exactly what it was that they could do for the Herero. Manasse Tjisiseta started the talks by stating that a number of the chieftains were unsure as to whether or not they were under German or English protection, and demanded that they be provided with a clear answer. Göring replied that the Herero were under German protection, whereupon Manasse Tjisiseta emphasized Germany's moral duty to provide the Herero with concrete protection.[39] Though Göring promised to do this, it is indeed indicative that, less than a month later, Göring travelled to Cape Town and left southern Africa for good.[40] As a result of these discussions, the protection treaty, which had been rejected by the Herero two years previously, was reinstated.[41]

Besides Manasse Tjisiseta, at least one other man realized the full import of Maharero's decision to reinstate the German protection treaty, this was Maharero's sworn enemy and opponent, Hendrik Witbooi. Upon hearing of Maharero's decision, Hendrik Witbooi wrote to Maharero. The letter is a fine example of Hendrik Witbooi's letter-writing and betrays his deep religious beliefs and incisive political understanding of the time. The following rather lengthy extract is taken from Witbooi's caustic though prophetic letter to Maharero:

> To you paramount of Damaraland I today write this letter, because I have received a letter from Dr. Göring [Imperial Commissioner], and I have gathered major things from this letter, and these things have shown me the necessity of saying something to you. I have heard and understood from Dr. Göring's letter, that you have placed yourself in German protection, and that hereby Göring has acquired influence and full right to order something and to enforce these orders over our country's affairs, and also in our war, which has existed from long past between us, thus I am suprised and I am greatly offended [neem U grootelyks Kwalyk] because you call yourself the paramount of Damaraland, and this is true, because this dry country has but two names, Damaraland and Namaland, that is to say that Damaraland belongs solely to the Herero nation, and that is an independent kingdom on its territory, and Namaqualand, that belongs solely to the red coloured nations, and those are also independent kingdoms, and this is also what is said of the countries of the white

[38] Ibid., p. 124.
[39] BAP, RKA 1574, Göring in Okahandja, 22/5/90, to RKA.
[40] Dr Göring left southern Africa and became the German government's representative in Haiti.
[41] H. von Francois, Nama und Damara, p. 125.

people in Germany, and England and so forth, as the countries of the present, and those are countries on the water, and those are also independent Kingdoms, and all the different peoples have their own leaders, and every leader has his own people and country, over which he alone orders and governs, that no other person or captain has the right, to order him in power, and to order, to do like that, and not to do like that, because every chief on this world, is only a caretaker [*plaatsbekleeder*] of our all mighty God, and is only responsible to the great God, the king of kings, and Lord of Lords, for whom we all, who live under the heavens shall bend their knees, and from him alone seek help, advice, and power, and protection, and support, in all these heavy circumstances of this life, because he alone gives generously to all who pray to him for this.

But dear Captain! you have accepted another government, and submitted yourself to that government, to be protected by a human government, from all dangers, the first, and the nearest, against me, in this war, which exists from long past between us, to be protected from this and helped, by the German government, but dear captain! do you know, what you have done, and for whom you have done this, that which you have done, or have other people convinced you, or have you done this out of your own independent enlightened mind? Maybe you only saw me standing before you, in your heart, and in all your life, as a hindrance, and as a stone of repulsion [*steen des aanstoots*], therefore you accepted this other powerful government, to destroy me with this mighty man, this is possibly your intention, why you did this, but it is very difficult, to say and to know, that you will certainly succeed, or not, but it appears to me, you did not consider enough what the implications were on your side, for your country, your people, and your descendants, and also not for your leadership rights, and you believe that you shall retain all these things of your independent leadership, after you have destroyed me, if you succeed, as you believe you will, but dear captain! It will eventually cause you much remorse, and you shall eternally bear remorse, for having placed your land and government into the hands of the white people . . .

I know D[r]. Göring and you, you are of different nations, and you are from time long past not good and true friends with one another, but you have concluded this friendship, solely to destroy me, just like Herod and Pilate, so that they could remove the lord Jesus, they hid and downplayed their differences . . .[42]

Hendrik Witbooi's words were indeed prophetic. On 7 July 1890, little more than a month after the reinstatement of German protection, Witbooi commandos attacked Herero cattle posts at Otjituesu, south-east of Okahandja. Maharero appealed to the Germans for help, but no help was forthcoming. In response to Maharero's appeals, the Germans replied that: '. . . help could not now be supplied, as the troops had instructions not to get involved in "native" affairs.'[43]

In early September Witbooi's commandos once again raided deep into Hereroland. Cattle posts in the foothills of the Erongo mountains were attacked and the settlement of Otjimbingwe was overrun by Witbooi's forces. Here the German officials and traders actually drank coffee with Hendrik Witbooi during a lull in his assault on the town.[44] Once again, German soldiers stationed at Tsaobis watched Hendrik's commandos pass by escorting rustled cattle and wounded comrades.

For the Herero, German protection was a sham. Maharero, his closest

[42] ELCIN, V. *Politischen Briefe etc. 1879–1892*. Hendrik Witbooi in Hornkraans, 30/5/90, to 'Wel geliefde Kapitein Maharero Tsamaua!'. JBG's translation.
[43] H. von Francois, *Nama und Damara*, p. 129.
[44] Ibid., p. 130.

followers and the poor were all that were left in Okahandja. His former prowess as the mightiest of the Herero chiefs had shrivelled. His attempted alliance with the Germans had failed. The arrival of the Germans with their camels in Okahandja had not provided Maharero with the long-expected remedy against Witbooi's attacks. Instead, if one chooses to believe Herero traditions, the arrival of the camels spelt disaster for Maharero. At some stage during Francois's stay in Okahandja, a camel, a hornless animal and therefore taboo for Maharero's *Oruzuo* or patri-clan, defiled Maharero's *Okuruo*, holy fire. It was due to this poisoning that, the traditions contend, Maharero died.[45]

In my father's house

On 7 October 1890 Chief Maharero Tjamuaha died of dysentery in Okahandja. His mattress, blankets, clothes, shoes and hat were laid in his grave, and a number of thorns were placed upon his body.[46] The thorns were meant to ensure that Maharero's enemies would be like the thorns in the veld, stabbing and injuring one another.[47] In part they may also have influenced the nature of the ensuing succession dispute. The death of Maharero Tjamuaha brought about a power vacuum in the centre of Hereroland, into which a number of men were drawn, struggling to inherit what they claimed was their rightful share of Maharero's estate. In this tussle the various candidates relied upon all possible forms of support. Samuel Maharero, however, went one step further. He alone successfully solicited the support and power of Germany, the new player on the ballfield.

Immediately following the death of Maharero Tjamuaha, the succession dispute and the struggle for claimed inheritance broke out. The prime contenders in this struggle were all men, and all were directly related to Maharero in terms of the dual descent and inheritance system which Herero culture utilized. In Herero culture, men inherited and traced their descent patrilineally and matrilineally. Herero society was built up out of clans, which were arranged according to patrilineal (*Oruzuo*) and matrilineal (*Eanda*) descent. The between twenty and thirty-six *Otuzuo*, patrilineal, clans and six to nine *Omaanda*, matrilineal, clans were in turn associated with specific taboos which related primarily to cattle and sheep. Indicative of the preferred essentially pastoralist mode of subsistence was the linkage that existed between stock and the double descent system and its concomitant taboos. Cattle colour and horn shape vary extensively, and the two variables were used to determine the epistemological impact of cattle. That is, horn and colour variability determined whether or not a cow was to be considered taboo for specific *Otuzuo*. *Eanda* cattle were inherited matrilineally and could be used for trading purposes. *Oruzuo* cattle were inherited patrilineally and, as they were considered to be imbued with magico-religious properties, could not be used for trade or exchange.[48] There were four men who could, and did, lay claim to

---

[45] G. Pool, *Samuel Maharero* (Windhoek 1991) pp. 72–74

[46] BAP, RKA 2100, Nels in Otjimbingwe, 11/11/90, to RKA. & ELCIN, V. Chroniken Otjimbingwe 1890. Lists as cause of death 'Brechruhr'.

[47] *BRMG* 1891, p. 85.

[48] For further information on Herero ethnology and anthropology see: Uri Almagor, 'Pastoral Identity and Reluctance to Change: the Mbanderu of Ngamiland' in *Journal of African Law*, 1980, Vol. 24(1), pp. 35–61; Eduard Dannert, *Zum Rechte der Herero insbesondere über ihr Familien- und*

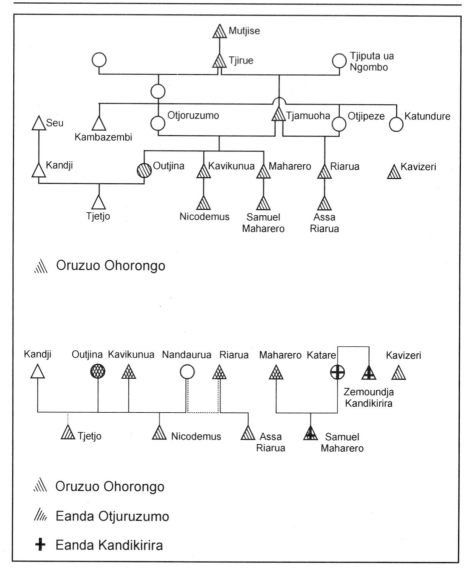

*Figure 2.1: Kinship diagrams indicating decendants of Mutjise, and those entitled to
Maharero's* Eanda *and* Oruzuo *inheritance*

Maharero's patrilineal, or *Oruzuo*, inheritance. These men were his son Samuel
Maharero, his brother through a different mother Riarua, his adopted brother

Erbrecht (Berlin 1906); Gordon D. Gibson, *The Social Organization of the Southwestern Bantu*,
Unpublished DPhil Thesis, University of Chicago (Chicago 1952); Josaphat Hahn, `Die
Ovaherero', in *Zeitschrift der Gesellschaft für Erdkunde zu Berlin*, Verlag von Dietrich Reimer (Berlin
1869); J. Irle, *Die Herero. Ein Beitrag zur Landes-, Volks- und Missionskunde* (Gütersloh 1906);
Hendrik Gerhardus Luttig, *The Religious System and Social Organisation of the Herero*, Published
PhD Thesis, University of Leiden (Utrecht 1933); I. Schapera, *Notes on some Herero Genealogies*
(Cape Town 1945); Heinrich Vedder, 'The Herero', in *The Native Tribes of South West Africa*,
compiled by C. Hahn, L. Fourie and H. Vedder (Cape Town 1928).

Kaviseri and his brother's son Nicodemus Kavikunua. Two men had a legal right to and contested Maharero's matrilineal, or *Eanda*, inheritance. These men were Maharero's sister's son, Tjetjo, and Riarua, the son of his father and his mother's sister. It will be noticed that Riarua had a right to, and laid a claim to, both Maharero's *Eanda* and *Oruzuo* inheritance.

In late 1890 the remaining Herero chieftains travelled to Okahandja to discuss and arbitrate on Maharero's succession and inheritance. Initially it appeared as if the theory and practice of Herero inheritance were one and the same. A look at the kinship diagram indicates that in terms of the *Oruzuo* inheritance, Samuel Maharero, Riarua, Nikodemus Kavikunua and Kaviseri were contenders. Maharero's wives, *Okuruo* (holy fire), arms and chiefly position were considered part of the *Oruzuo* inheritance. As far as Maharero's wives and *Okuruo* were concerned, both Samuel Maharero and Nicodemus Kavikunua were immediately disqualified as they were nominally Christians. Being Christians, they were not permitted to inherit and administer an *Okuruo*, as this would have entailed ministering to the ancestors and thus, in the eyes of the missionaries, the demonic practice of ancestor worship. Furthermore, being Christians as well as being the sons of Maharero and his brother, Kavikunua, neither of them was permitted to marry Maharero's wives. Riarua did not contest his rights to either Maharero's widows or *Okuruo*, choosing instead to concentrate on other aspects of the inheritance. Instead, Maharero's adopted brother, Kaviseri, married Maharero's widows and inherited his *Okuruo*. Kaviseri was content with this and waived his rights to all further aspects of the inheritance. During his half-brother's life, Riarua had been Maharero's closest confidant and the widely respected supreme military commander of Maharero's forces; not surprisingly, therefore, he inherited Maharero's arms.

As regards the issue as to who was to inherit the chieftaincy of Okahandja, Riarua, Nicodemus Kavikunua and Samuel Maharero were serious contenders. The eldest patrilineal heir to Tjamuaha was Kavikunua. However Kavikunua had died and his brother Maharero had become Tjamuaha's heir. The inheritance had thus passed to Maharero. Strictly speaking therefore, in terms of the *Oruzuo* inheritance system, Kavikunua's son, Nicodemus, was to be the immediate heir to Maharero. However, a number of years previously Nicodemus Kavikunua had left Okahandja and lost his immediate support base, following an affair with Samuel's wife.[49] Added to this Nicodemus's mother, Nandaurua, had married Riarua, following the death of her first husband Kavikunua. Riarua was therefore Nicodemus Kavikunua's step-father. Though Nicodemus travelled to Okahandja to take part in the deliberations, he was unable to muster enough support amongst the Herero for his claims to the chieftaincy of Okahandja. Instead his stepfather, Riarua, as the eldest living male heir to Tjamuaha, came to be recognized by the Herero as Maharero's heir to the chieftaincy of Okahandja. For his part, Samuel Maharero, being a nominal Christian, received the support of the missionaries and the Christian Herero resident in Okahandja.[50]

In terms of the Herero matrilineal descent system or *Eanda*, Maharero's sister's son, Tjetjo, was entitled to, and was the sole contender for, Maharero's material goods. These consisted primarily of what remained of Maharero's cattle

---

[49] J. Irle, *Die Herero*, p. 217.
[50] BAP, RKA 2100, Nels in Otjimbingwe, 11/11/90. *BRMG*, 1891, pp. 85–86.

*Photo 2.3: Riaru, commander in chief to
Maharero Tjamuaha*
Source: Namibian National Archives,
Windhoek

herds, in so far as they had not been appropriated by the commandos of Hendrik
Witbooi. Strictly speaking, Samuel Maharero was not entitled to any part of
the *Eanda* inheritance. However, and this was more in keeping with his status
as a Christian, he did inherit his father's brick house. Maharero's house, which
had been built to store trade goods, was strictly speaking part of the *Eanda*
inheritance. It was situated in the Christian quarter of Okahandja. Samuel
Maharero received this house primarily because none of his rivals had any need
for it. Neither Kaviseri nor Riarua, who lived in Okahandja, were Christians.
Tjetjo, who by virtue of his *Eanda* inheritance rights, had a right to Maharero's
house did not live in Okahandja, and Nicodemus, though a Christian, also
did not live in Okahandja. Instead he had left and sought support amongst the
Ovambanderu chieftains in the east.

The Herero chieftains visiting Okahandja soon reached their verdicts and,
all in all, by the time they abandoned Okahandja in early 1891 in the face of
imminent attacks by Hendrik Witbooi, the apportionment of Maharero's
inheritance had been determined. Riarua, Kaviseri and Tjetjo, as one would
have expected, had carried off the bulk and the most important effects of the
inheritance. Samuel Maharero had won the right to live in his father's house
and enjoyed the support of the missionaries and the Christians, which, when
compared to the *Okuruo*, arms, cattle herds and chiefly recognition, which had
been inherited by his rivals, was rather insignificant. Living in a town constantly
threatened by Witbooi raids, the supply of arms, such as that which Riarua
had inherited, was far more significant than the support of impoverished
Christians and missionaries. As the chieftains hastily left Okahandja, Samuel
Maharero cast around for support with which to expand his meagre inheritance.

There were essentially two sources of support to which Samuel Maharero
now turned. One was rooted in his existence as a Herero, and the other was
rooted in his existence as a Christian associated with the mission and all that
this entailed.

In terms of Herero culture a man inherited his wordly goods matrilineally, through his *Eanda*. Thus Tjetjo, and not Samuel Maharero, had inherited the cattle herds of Maharero. In life a man called upon his mother's brother for material support. In the case of Samuel Maharero his mother's brother was a rich man named Simoni Zemoundia Kandirikirira. Very little is known about this man, apart from the fact that he was the father of teachers and evangelists closely associated with Samuel Maharero.[51] His support was essential to Samuel Maharero. Immediately following Maharero's death, Zemoundia supported Samuel Maharero with cattle and was closely associated with Samuel in his visits to German officials in Windhoek.[52] It is an indication as to the power and import of Zemoundia's support, that it was only following Zemoundia's death that Riarua and his allies dared to openly oppose Samuel Maharero.

As a Christian, Samuel Maharero was able to access support networks otherwise closed to his rivals. Thus Samuel Maharero was supported as a candidate of the Rhenish missionaries in his bid for the chieftaincy of Okahandja. His elder brother, Wilhelm, had been the mission's hope for the future, but, unfortunately for them, Wilhelm had been killed in battle in 1880. Samuel Maharero had attended mission school, and, though not a star pupil, he was literate and this was a skill which he used to his full advantage. Samuel Maharero was well acquainted with the system of inheritance that existed in Germany, whereby a man's eldest son inherited his father's property. Indeed, it had been on this basis that the missionaries had sought to groom the sons of Maharero Tjamuaha, Samuel and Wilhelm. Now following the death of his father, Samuel Maharero sought to cash in on the claims made by the missionaries. Within two weeks of Maharero's death, at exactly the same time that messages were being sent out to the remaining Herero chieftains to come to Okahandja, Samuel Maharero wrote to Curt von Francois seeking his assistance and urging him to come to Okahandja.[53] Francois failed to come to Okahandja and for the duration of the chieftains' visit to Okahandja he kept his distance. Commenting on Samuel Maharero's advances, Francois wrote:

> With great eagerness he sought information from me, in anticipation of his crowning, as to how Kings were proclaimed with us.[54]

In the end Samuel Maharero's persistence paid off. In August of 1891, in response to Samuel Maharero's letters, Curt von Francois sent his brother Hugo von Francois to Okahandja to inform Samuel Maharero that the Imperial German government had recognized him as the paramount chief of the Herero.[55]

Thus Samuel Maharero was recognized by the Germans as paramount chief of the Herero. But, at this stage, this recognition was worth very little in terms of actual wealth and power. Added to this, German recognition did not immediately imply German assistance. This much is made clear in Hugo von Francois's account of a meeting with Samuel Maharero in late 1891:

[51] See for instance the appearance of preacher Elia Kandirikira at Samuel Maharero's deathbed in 1923. NNAW, ACC 200.
[52] BAP, RKA 2081, Kohler in Windhoek, 24/12/93. Reports on a visit by Samuel Maharero to Windhoek accompanied by his brothers and Zemoundia Kandikirira.
[53] BAP, RKA 2109, Letter Samuel Maharero in Okahandja, 21/10/90, to von Francois.
[54] C. von Francois, *DSWA*, p. 78.
[55] Ibid., p. 147. H. von Francois, *Nama und Damara*, p. 144.

After some preliminary questions he requested the protection of the government against uncooperative chiefs, apparently so as to cover his back. He did not want to carry responsibility for all the problems in the Herero territories. Regardless of this admittance of weakness he requested our permission to improve his income through taxation. He wished to tax every trader operating in Hereroland 100 mark for water and grazing, whereas previously money had been paid to the single owners thereof. It goes without saying that this Testimonium paupertatis could not be covered by the government.[56]

Samuel Maharero had effectively become the paramount chief of a people who refused to recognize him, and of territories which were either beyond his control, or under constant threat of Witbooi attack. As long as this was the case, there was very little challenge to his position, but, once the threat of Hendrik Witbooi had been removed, it was a different matter altogether.

The inheritance

The chieftains who scuttled out of Okahandja in early 1891 left primarily because, in terms of Maharero's inheritance, there was not much to be had in Okahandja, and, added to this, there was the ever-present threat of a raid by Hendrik Witbooi, which would have made dilly-dallying in Okahandja at best unsafe.

There were three interrelated reasons as to why, by the time of Maharero's death, southern Hereroland had become such a dismal and unhealthy place. The first related to the fulfilment by Hendrik Witbooi of his promise to 'smite' Maharero Tjamuaha.[57] The second related to the economic decline of Okahandja and Otjimbingwe, which was aggravated by Witbooi's attacks. The third related to the natural disasters of famine and disease, which in turn were exacerbated by Hendrik Witbooi's attacks and the region's economic decline.

Between 1889 and 1891, Hendrik Witbooi's commandos raided, seemingly at will, throughout southern and central Hereroland. In 1890 alone, nearly fifty Herero cattle posts, situated between Omaruru, Okahandja and Otjimbingwe, were raided on three separate occasions in January, July and September. Added to this, the Herero quarter in Otjimbingwe was burnt to the ground and the settlement's cornfields destroyed.[58] The attacks continued unabated into the following year, with further raids in which approximately 3000 cattle and 1000 small stock were captured.[59] In early 1891 Herero communities in the far north, around Otjozondjupa, were being directly affected by the raiding.[60] In the face of these attacks Herero were forced to abandon southern Hereroland. As has been seen, followers were ordered to withdraw into the mountains or, in the interests of security, to congregate around settlements further to the north.[61] By early 1891 the Herero had been expelled from their former grazing areas between the Khan and the Swakop

[56] H. von Francois, *Nama und Damara*, p. 144.
[57] *The Hendrik Witbooi Papers*, edited and translated by Eben Maasdorp (Windhoek 1991) p. 65.
[58] ELCIN, V. Chroniken 1890, Otjimbingwe and Omaruru. The raiders took with them no less than 5000 large stock, 1000 small stock, twenty horses, a waggon, a cart and further unspecified goods.
[59] ELCIN, V. Chroniken Omaruru, 1891.
[60] BAP, RKA 2109, Curt von Francois, 5/3/1891, to AA.
[61] ELCIN, V. Chroniken Omaruru, 1891.

rivers.[62] Herero chiefs sought to stem the onslaught and retain their rights to the land by ordering their Christian followers to occupy the settlements under attack. Thus in the case of Otjimbingwe, Manasse Tjisiseta of Omaruru ordered his Christian followers to Otjimbingwe, 'to strengthen this important post, so that it doesn't fall into the hands of Hendrik Witbooi'.[63] But it was all to no avail. Herero continued to abandon southern Hereroland up until such time that the threat of Hendrik Witbooi had been neutralized.[64]

Through a policy of scorched earth, Hendrik Witbooi cleared southern Hereroland of its Herero inhabitants. Witbooi conquered the land and by right of conquest he claimed Otjimbingwe as his. In a letter to the European inhabitants of the settlement Hendrik Witbooi made this clear:

> You of all people are well acquainted with the law of conquest. And you know that I defeated the Herero at Otjimbingwe. You know that it is only because they fled into your houses . . . that I turned around on that occasion.
> Now I ask you . . . are the Herero still there? and if they are still there, on whose behest? If it is at your urging, I ask you now, sirs, let them go, for it is my land; I conquered it.[65]

The second factor affecting the dismal condition of Maharero's legacy was the complete and utter economic malaise in which southern Hereroland found itself at the time of his death. In the face of Witbooi's withering attacks Herero cattle stocks had been depleted or driven away to other regions of the territory. Maharero's once mighty herds, in so far as they had not been captured by Witbooi, were dispersed throughout the northern reaches of his territory and amongst his allies. Though his cattle may have been in safe hands, and cattle trading on his mind, Maharero was forced to turn his attention elsewhere in the face of Witbooi's assault. Added to this, the settlements of Okahandja and Otjimbingwe, which had blossomed as trading centres in the 1870s, had been superseded in importance by Omaruru, which lay across the most direct route from Walvisbay to Ovamboland. During the 1880s, whilst central Namibia had been in conflict, traders had shifted their attention northwards to Ovamboland and southern Angola.[66] This market soon supplanted that of central Namibia. Associated with the development of the Ovamboland trade was the establishment, from 1884 onwards, of trade routes, which totally bypassed Hereroland. Instead these routes led from Ovamboland directly through the Kalahari to Kimberley and the Witwatersrand.[67] In the face of economic gloom it was to these brighter lights that many were drawn. As a contemporary noted:

> Many Herero have trekked away . . . all profit is gone. The few known trading stores are nearly empty. Several Herero have taken work on the English mines.[68]

---

[62] ELCIN, V. Chroniken, 1888–90 Omaruru and Otjimbingwe. Also BAP, RKA 2109 Hugo Francois in Windhoek, 5/3/91, reports a locust plague between Windhoek and Okahandja. Curt von Francois, 5/3/91, reports Witbooi wars affecting north-eastern Hereroland.
[63] BRMG, 1892 p. 304.
[64] ELCIN, V. Chroniken Otjimbingwe 1892.
[65] The Hendrik Witbooi Papers, p. 57.
[66] See in this regard the career of Axel Eriksson who between 1869 and about 1882 operated out of Omaruru. After 1884 Eriksson established himself in Ovamboland and totally bypassed central Namibia.
[67] For a discussion of the development of trade routes from the Cunene to Kimberley and the Rand, see Harri Siiskonen, Trade and Socioeconomic Change in Ovamboland, 1850–1906, Studio Historica 35 (Helsinki 1990) pp. 158–61.
[68] BRMG, 1891, pp. 12–13.

In the wake of economic decline and war came famine and disease. In 1890 and 1891 southern Hereroland was struck by famine. This was the result of both human and natural agency. Due to Witbooi raiding, Herero livestock had been driven off and cornfields deliberately destroyed. Added to this, drought, flooding and, particularly in 1891, locust swarms initiated a famine which further weakened the inhabitants of southern Hereroland. In 1890 the region was struck by chickenpox, to be followed in the following year by smallpox.[69] Though attempts were made to quarantine the sick, nothing could be done to prevent the famished from inadvertently spreading the disease, as they begged and scavenged from post to post for food.[70]

In the aftermath of the Tsaobis affair, when Francois had forced the Herero to stand down, it was clear that the Herero were in no state to repel settlers should they choose to move onto and occupy tracts of land in southern Hereroland. Added to this, in the face of Witbooi attacks, Herero were unable and unwilling to prevent settlers from settling on tracts of land which were to all intents and purposes unoccupied. Another aspect was that Herero chiefs, such as Samuel Maharero and Zacharias Zeraua, were willing to sell tracts of land, often in areas which had fallen from, or were beyond, their control, in exchange for much needed trade goods with which they could then extend their patronage and improve their positions. This was particularly true of Samuel Maharero, who, in the first four years following the death of his father, was effectively broke. The German government, which was anxious to lessen the cost of its colonial venture, sold concessions to land companies for extensive tracts of land in Namibia, and encouraged settlers to move to Namibia.[71] Thus in 1892 the German government granted land, earmarked for settlement by homesteaders in the Windhoek area, to the Deutschen Kolonialgesellschaft. Settlement terms were very generous. Each homesteader was granted three to four Morgen of irrigable land and grazing rights to further land. After five years' ownership, the land reverted to the settler who, in turn, had to pay a small fee for water and grazing rights and was obliged to build a house and grow crops. Attempts were made to attract settlers from Germany and the German community in the Transvaal, Cape and Natal.[72] Though prospects in the newly established Charterland of Cecil John Rhodes seemed far better, a number of Boers and Germans, who had settled in the Cape and the Transvaal, were prepared to move to the newly established German colony. Amongst these was the trader Ludwig, who, as well as leading vigilante posses, established an inn with a beer garden and bowling alley in Klein Windhoek.[73] Other settlers at the time were the Voigts brothers, who had operated as traders in the Transvaal and Chile, and the trader Fritz Wecke, who had also been a trader in the Transvaal. In September 1892 these men established the Wecke and Voigts company, which still exists today.[74] At first settlers consisted primarily of traders, Boers and small homesteaders who settled in the fertile Klein Windhoek river valley. Though the land companies were granted concessions, actual occupation of the lands by German settlers did not take place until much later.

[69] *BRMG*, 1890, p. 244.

[70] ELCIN, V. Mission chroniken Otjimbingwe, 1891.

[71] For concession company claims to Namibia see, Drechsler, *Fighting*, pp. 45–53.

[72] Otto von Weber, *Geschichte des Schutzgebietes Deutsch-Südwest-Afrika*, second edition (Windhoek 1979), pp. 82–3.

[73] Weber, *Geschichte*, p. 83.

[74] H.E. Lenssen, *Chronik von Deutsch-Südwestafrika* (Windhoek 1994) pp. 43–4.

Initially, settlers who occupied lands in southern Hereroland were spared by the raiders of Hendrik Witbooi, who were anxious not to antagonize the settlers and the German forces. In due course the distinction between settlers and soldiers ceased to exist as decommissioned *Schutztruppen* often chose to settle in Hereroland.[75]

Even prior to the death of Maharero, the Herero confederacy, which had come into being around his leadership, had begun to crumble as its constituent chieftains withdrew. Maharero was very conscious of this process and it had formed the basis of his complaints vis-a-vis the missionaries in 1888.[76] By the time Maharero died, most of the influential Herero chieftains had withdrawn out of central Namibia. Following his death, the Herero chiefs, who had already been slipping out of the confederacy, now did so completely and left Samuel Maharero to weather the attacks of Hendrik Witbooi in Okahandja. Though Herero leaders had travelled to Okahandja in late 1890, to help decide on the division of the spoils of inheritance, they had soon withdrawn in the face of Hendrik Witbooi's attacks. The result was that only the missionaries, the Christians, the traders and the poorest Herero remained in southern Hereroland. Samuel Maharero, as a poor Christian, remained in Okahandja. This then was Maharero's legacy. The fact that Samuel Maharero was recognized by his fellow paupers and the Germans as a chief did not overly bother his rivals. For they knew that the area that Samuel Maharero claimed to be the chief of was either in constant danger of being raided, or at best beyond his effective control. As long as the threat of Witbooi remained, and the German presence was insignificant, whatever Samuel Maharero claimed and did was of no real import to the remaining Herero chiefs.

Murdered in peace[77]

Central to developments in Herero society in the late nineteenth century were the activities of Hendrik Witbooi. It is therefore necessary to discuss Hendrik Witbooi and the relationship that developed between him, Samuel Maharero and the Herero in general.

Originally a carpenter by training and a church deacon by choice, it had been following a near escape from death, at the hands of the Herero in August 1880, that Hendrik Witbooi had become a divinely inspired prophet and the paramount chief of northern Namaqualand. He later recounted how, returning home following his escape, a voice had spoken to him. The voice had told him that the time had been *fulfilled*, that the way had been *opened* and that a heavy *task* had been laid upon him: 'These three words started my whole mission.'[78] At this stage Witbooi had lived in Gibeon, a settlement in southern Namibia,

---

[75] Weber, *Geschichte*, p. 268.

[76] See, ELCIN, I 1.3 *Bericht über die Verhandlungen Dec. 1888*, where Maharero accused the missionaries of strengthening his fellow chiefs at the expense of weakening himself. This was done by, amongst other things, opening and rerouting hitherto closed trade routes, setting up mission stations in the interior; and, perhaps most importantly, making and assisting the other Herero chiefs become increasingly more independent of Maharero.

[77] JBG's translation of 'in vrede vermoord' which was written on a note addressed to Missionary Eich, at Otjiseva, by the Witbooi schoolmaster, Samuel, following the ambush of the Witbooi trek at Osona on 15 October 1885. *BRMG*, 1886, p. 44.

[78] *Witbooi Papers*, p. 33. Witbooi's prophecy was indeed fulfilled.

which had been founded by his grandfather, Kido Witbooi. Kido had named the settlement in memory of the biblical Gibeon, where God had made the sun stand still for a day so that Joshua could defeat his enemies. Kido, Hendrik had believed, only meant to pause for a while in Gibeon, before trekking on. In accordance with his revelation and in the belief that he had been fulfilling his grandfather's aims, Hendrik Witbooi had voiced his intention to trek north. As to where he had intended trekking to, Hendrik Witbooi had noted:

> That I do not know yet, with my trekking I am only continuing the great work started by my Grandfather, who in his trek northwards, to a very good land, only rested for a while in Gibeon.[79]

In 1884, Witbooi had travelled north to Okahandja to ask for permission to trek through Maharero's territory.[80] Permission had been granted and, during the course of 1884, Maharero had twice confirmed this. In the following year, Hendrik Witbooi, taking with him the cream of Gibeon society, had set off with a trek of no less than 600 followers.[81] Trekking north, to the promised 'very good land', people had flocked to join Witbooi's following. A contemporary had noted:

> It is a colourful collective mass of people, about 600; apart from the Gibeonites there are also Veldschoendragers, Kol with some of his people, some of the Red nation, the Janian people [the surviving followers of Jan Jonker Afrikaner] and then all kinds of leaderless people, even blind, lame and cripples.[82]

On 13 October 1885 Witbooi had written to Maharero thanking him for his assistance and permission to trek through his territory.[83] However, it was not to be. Two days later, a Herero commando had ambushed the Witbooi trek at Osona, approximately twenty kilometres to the south of Okahandja. In the attack, Witbooi had lost two of his own sons, twenty-four followers, a number of horses and all of the trek's waggons and provisions; added to this twenty-two men had been wounded.[84] As the refugees had withdrawn past Otjiseva, missionary Eich had received a note. It had said simply, 'In peace we were murdered.'[85]

Hendrik Witbooi had been betrayed, and this betrayal was to colour all of his further dealings with the Herero, particularly Samuel Maharero, whom he believed had led the assault. Henceforth Hendrik Witbooi was to be at war with the Herero. In a letter to Maharero, Witbooi had written:

> Well you know that I arrived in peace, but you deceived me. You wanted to lure me

---

[79] *BRMG*, 1886, p. 42.

[80] This was not unique; following the destruction of the Zwartbooi community at Rehoboth in 1863, the Zwartboois had been granted permission to settle on Hereroland to the north of Omaruru.

[81] *BRMG*, 1886, pp. 36–45. As missionary Rust of Gibeon put it:

> *Hier hat sich die Gemeinde nun fast ganz aufgelöst, höchstens werden vielleicht noch 40–50 Gemeindeglieder vorhanden sein.*

[82] Missionary Eich in Otjiseva, 14/10/85, in *BRMG*, 1886, p. 40.

[83] *Witbooi Papers*, p. 6.

[84] Missionary Eich in *BRMG*, 1886, p. 43, referred to forty Nama dead, 130 horses, all their oxen, two waggons, four carts. The Herero who had fired from both sides on the Nama lost thirty men and had eighty wounded. Missionary Rust in *BRMG*, 1886, p. 46 noted that Hendrik's second son Jeremias and his fourth son Salomo were killed.

[85] BRMG, 1886, p. 44.

into your Kraal and then kill me without warning. I defended myself as best I might. You know how the day went. I had to retire because I ran out of ammunition. You did not defeat me, as well you know. At no point were my men giving way. But I ran out of ammunition, so I left.

Now I am once again prepared for war, and soon I shall again meet you at the same place. So sit there and wait for me! With your talk of truce you had bound my hands; now your treachery has loosened the bonds. As before, I have again cast open the gates of war. You shall get war from all sides. I tell you that openly. You know that I had closed those gates when I accepted peace. But then you tried to murder me through cunning.

Truly, now the Lord shall judge between us!

I close, and am, offended and betrayed,

Hendrik Witbooi[86]

Significantly the attack had taken place in 1885 at precisely the same time that German officials and missionaries had been in Okahandja attempting to convince Maharero and his councillors to sign a protection treaty with Imperial Germany. Indeed the missionaries and the officials had sought to impress Maharero of their intentions by bandaging wounded Herero.[87] Immediately after the ambush, Maharero had completed his negotiations and signed the treaty. These events did not go unnoticed by Hendrik Witbooi, who in a letter had warned Maharero: '. . . preserve the land too, so that I do not have to claim it from foreign hands'.[88]

Following his defeat Hendrik Witbooi had returned to southern Namibia. Here, he had consolidated his position and in due course he had recovered sufficiently to begin exacting his revenge. In 1888, on three separate occasions, his commandos had raided Otjimbingwe, and cattleposts between Otjimbingwe and Okahandja. With the cattle captured Witbooi had financed his arms purchases.[89] In late 1888 Hendrik Witbooi and his followers, having gained control over most of southern Namibia, had moved north into the Khomas Hochland and established themselves at the mountain fortress of Hoornkrans. In 1889, in exchange for concessions sold to the newly floated Great Namaqualand Exploration company, Witbooi had received two waggons fully loaded with ammunition.[90]

Well-armed, and with an ever-larger following, Hendrik Witbooi had fulfilled the threats of his earlier letters:

You have deceived me in the name of God. Maharero, recall the words we exchanged under the camelthorn at our first meeting. You then said that if you broke the peace I should destroy you with cold hands; and if I should break the peace you would destroy me with cold hands, seeking me out among all my warriors. The Lord heard these words come from your mouth.[91]

Throughout 1890, Witbooi had sought out Maharero and his followers.

---

[86] *Witbooi Papers*, p. 7.
[87] G. Pool, *Samuel Maharero*, p. 62.
[88] Witbooi to Maharero, 30/10/85, in *Witbooi Papers*, p. 8.
[89] *BRMG*, 1888, pp. 366–8.
[90] *BRMG*, 1891, p. 23. See also interview between Hugo von Francois and Hendrik. When Robert Duncan, the man who had brokered the deal and who was married into Witbooi society, was later arrested by the Germans; Rhodes's role in the affair became apparent when Witbooi wrote to Rhodes asking for him to intercede on Duncan's behalf.
[91] Hendrik Witbooi in /Ga-os, 30/10/1885, to Maharero, in *Witbooi Papers*, pp. 8–9.

Maharero's power had waned. Maharero's allies had withdrawn from central Namibia, and isolated him in Okahandja. In a desperate attempt at turning the tide, Maharero had sought to reinstitute his protection treaty with the Germans, only to be greeted by Hendrik's caustic letters and prophetic words. Even with German protection, Hendrik's debilitating raids had continued unrelenting, and in due course, as Hendrik Witbooi had written to Samuel Maharero:

> I smote your father because of his unrighteous practices, and while I was smiting him, God Himself smote him with death.[92]

Hendrik Witbooi had attempted to make use of the power vacuum that existed in southern Hereroland following Maharero's death. As we have seen, Hendrik's commandos had struck whilst the iron was hot. Less than three months after Maharero's death, whilst the Herero chieftains had gathered in Okahandja to discuss Maharero's inheritance, Witbooi's commandos had raided throughout southern Hereroland. Not surprisingly, as soon as the inheritance had been divided, the chiefs, and their followers, in so far as they had not done so already, had withdrawn from Okahandja and left southern Hereroland. However, there was to be no reprieve for the Herero. Hendrik Witbooi believed that it had been Samuel Maharero who had led the attack on his ill-fated trek at Osona in 1885.[93] Witbooi commandos had continued to raid Herero positions throughout 1891 and 1892. However, being a man of God as well as a man who had realized the futility of war, Hendrik Witbooi did initiate a lengthy correspondence with Samuel Maharero.[94] Finally, following a series of puerile replies by Samuel, an exasperated Hendrik Witbooi had harangued Samuel:

> Surely you can distinguish between what is just and true and what is unjust. So if the works of your father appalled you because you felt them to be unjust, but you were powerless to stop them, or to stand aside, today you have that power, and the right to act and speak according to your own choice and vision. For I believe that

---

[92] Hendrik Witbooi, 27/7/91, to Samuel Maharero, in *Witbooi Papers*, p. 65.
[93] Diary entry Hendrik Witbooi for 27 June 1890, in *Witbooi Papers*, p. 48.
[94] Hendrik's first letter was addressed to his 'dear Herero children'. Shortly thereafter Samuel replied in a cynical letter addressed to his 'dear Nama children' and signed, though he was as yet not recognized by anyone except the Christians and missionaries as such, as 'your Captain'. As always Hendrik's reply was direct and to the point:

> I have received your letter, but am dissatisfied by your answer . . . You replied neither to my question nor to my intention, but jestingly turned my own words around. You answered with nothing of your own but with my words. Where I had said Herero children, you said Nama children, and so on with all the rest. When I used the term Herero children I meant: Now that old Maharero has died, you and the whole Herero nation are orphans, for I have not yet heard that a new chief has been appointed. It is only now through your own letter, that I learn that you are Captain. Here at Hoornkrans, on the other hand, there are no children in that sense, for I am Captain and Father, and I am alive. So it is not children that speak to you, but I the captain alone. So answer me dear Samuel, as Captain – for you claim to be the captain – answer with your own plans for your own time.

What followed was a series of letters, in which Samuel consistently referred to himself as Captain, and attempted tit for tat gains by signing off as follows: 'You did not greet me, but I shall close this letter with greetings.' It is of interest to note how important titles were seen as being, by the various protagonists. Thus Francois wrote to Hendrik Witbooi lambasting him for having failed to use the correct form of address. This is perhaps best reflected in a letter by Hendrik Witbooi to the resident magistrate in Walvisbay, cleverly asking for information as to what the correct form of address would be for Francois.

man is a being capable of change. He can gain insight all at once, and turn.[95]

The moment of Samuel Maharero's insight and conversion, which Witbooi had hoped for, came in April of 1892. In the previous month Assa Riarua, a close friend of Samuel Maharero, had travelled to Windhoek, where he had asked for and received freedom of passage, from the Germans, for a Herero commando which was to attack Hendrik Witbooi at his base at Hoornkrans. In April of 1892, the Herero commando attacked Hoornkrans and, though driven off by Witbooi, the commando was able to capture a substantial amount of cattle. As the Herero withdrew, German settlers, under the command of Ludwig, of beer garden and bowling alley fame, organized a posse and attacked the returning and unsuspecting Herero. Two Herero were killed, a number wounded and a substantial amount of their captured cattle driven off. In Windhoek German colonial officials passionately hoped that the Herero had not recognized Ludwig and that they were under the impression that they had been attacked by Witbooi forces.[96] However, the Herero were not fooled. Indeed Samuel Maharero asked the German Kaiser to take action against his officials for failing to take action against Ludwig:

> In this year 1892, on the 8th of April I sent my soldiers [*Oorlog*] to Hendrik [Witbooi] at Hoornkrans. When my soldiers turned round, the Germans of Windhoek shot two of my men, even though they were innocent. The man who shot my people is a known man his name is Ludwich. There were witnesses, a whiteman whose name is Laas, and a Baster whose name is Samuel van Wijk. When I heard about this incident I wrote to the German *Regering Asseser* Köhler. Until today Köhler has failed to answer me.[97]

Needless to say, following this incident, Samuel's faith in German protection was a little shaky. Added to this, German demands, that Samuel Maharero compensate a trader who had been raided by his *Oruzuo* rival Nicodemus Kavikunua, merely served to enhance this doubt.[98]

Shortly after the Herero attack on Hoornkrans, Hendrik Witbooi and Samuel Maharero entered into negotiations. The negotiations were a success. The two men had come to realize that the German presence in their territory posed a greater threat to them than their mutual differences. The danger posed to them by the Germans was the loss of land to settlers, who were being encouraged and supported by the German administration. It was on the basis of this realization that Witbooi and Samuel Maharero buried their hatchets and

[95] Hendrik Witbooi in Hoornkrans, 31/7/91, to Samuel Maharero, in *Witbooi Papers*, p. 65.
[96] BAP, RKA 2110, Kohler in Windhoek, 12/4/91, to RKA.
[97] BAP, RKA 2081, Samuel Maharero in Okahandja, 19/3/93, to 'Zijn Hoog Ed. Majesteit de Keiser van Deutsland te Berlin'. JBG's translation.
[98] In October 1891, following a raid by Hendrik Witbooi, an Ovambanderu commando under the command of Nicodemus Kavikunua, attacked and robbed the trader Duncan Robertson, who had been travelling to the Cape Colony with traded cattle. Nicodemus Kavikunua was one of Samuel Maharero's rivals to the chieftainship of Okahandja who, having failed in his bid, had travelled eastwards to settle amongst the Ovambanderu of Kahimemua. After the raid Mr Duncan Robertson, an accomplice of Robert Lewis, complained to the German authorities. Shortly thereafter *Regierungs Assessor*, Köhler, wrote to Samuel Maharero, reported on Nicodemus's attack on the English trader Robertson, and demanded that, even though the attack had been carried out by Nicodemus, the goods were to be returned to Robertson.
    BAP, RKA 2081, Köhler in Windhoek, 30/11/91, to Samuel Maharero.
    BAP, RKA 2081, Newspaper clipping taken from *Cape Times* 30/12/1891.

concluded their peace agreement.[99] Referring to the Germans, Witbooi noted in a letter to the British magistrate in Walvisbay:

> They have given land which I won from the Herero to the Boers, having declared it 'no-mans-land'. They have also given farms on my land to people to whom I had not sold or given it.[100]

At peace with one another, Hendrik Witbooi and Samuel Maharero now cooperated with one another to prevent further settlement of the lands they claimed as theirs. Thus in late 1892, Samuel Maharero wrote to Hendrik Witbooi:

> . . . I must go to the two rivers Nosob and Tsoaxoub. These two rivers are now deserted because of the war, and there are those who want to seize our land from us. So let us first settle the two rivers now that we are at peace. The actual concluding and consolidating is merely a formality.
>
> The most urgent task for me just now is to ensure that all of our land is occupied by our nation, and that we push this powerful and strong nation back from our country with energy and force, lest we lose it by default . . .
>
> I have also heard that the Boers are intending to trek into our land. So be good and do not permit them passage through your land here, nor allow them to settle there. Use all your powers to keep them out, and do not wait until they have overrun you.[101]

Samuel Maharero and Hendrik Witbooi's alliance seriously threatened to derail Germany's attempts at colonizing the territory. In the face of this united opposition, the German military force in Windhoek, under the command of Curt von Francois, undertook unprecedented action. On the morning of 12 April 1893 German troops, guided to their goal by crowing cocks, surrounded and attacked Hoornkrans. In the aftermath of the attack, a badly shaken Hendrik Witbooi wrote:

> . . . I knew of no war which would shoot me, therefore I was completely at peace and unsuspecting with my men, therefore the few guns we had were not carried in slings on our bodies but everything had been put away into the chests. In this condition the *Hoofman* [von Francois] shot us early in the morning as we still lay unsuspectingly asleep, I left with all my men, without offering them resistance, in this way the *Hoofman* captured our place, and destroyed the place in the most terrible manner, as I had never imagined from a white civilised nation, which knows the laws and conduct of war, but he robbed me, and small children, which still lay at their mother's breast, and bigger children and women and children he shot them dead, and many corpses, which he had already shot dead, he placed in the grass

[99] H. von Francois, *Nama und Damara*, p. 153, '*Wie sehr die Boern von den Eingeborenen gehaßt wurden . . . geht daraus hervor, daß angesichts der gemeinsamen Gefahr Witbooi und Samuel Maharero die Kriegsart begruben und auf Rehoboth Frieden schlossen.*'

[100] Hendrik Witbooi in Hoornkrans, 17/11/92, to Magistrate in Walvisbay, in *Witbooi Papers*, pp. 111–12. In an earlier letter to the magistrate Witbooi referred to the Berlin Conference:

> I have heard that the British and the German Governments held a large meeting to decide who should make Protection treaties with the chiefs of which country in Africa; and that you the British let the Germans have this land. But you stipulated at the meeting that no chief shall be forced. If a leader is willing, and understands what it means to accept Protection well and good; but if another is not willing to, and does not understand why he should need Protection, he cannot be coerced. That was the agreement reached at your meeting, which was endorsed by all those present. (*Witbooi Papers*, pp. 88–9.)

[101] Samuel Maharero in Okahandja, 1/11/92, to Hendrik Witbooi, in *Witbooi Papers*, p. 106.

houses which he lit and burnt the bodies to ash. Sadly and terrifyingly the *Hoofman* did his work in disgraceful war.[102]

In all, according to Witbooi's own account, ten men and seventy-five women and children were killed. The remaining women were captured and taken to Windhoek.

Windhoek, Windhoek is my death

In March of 1893, Samuel Maharero, secure in the knowledge of Hendrik Witbooi's support, wrote letters to the German Kaiser condemning German colonialism. Five months later Samuel Maharero visited Windhoek, the seat of the German colonial government, to seek the self-same Kaiser's aid and protection. This apparent paradox can be explained only when one bears in mind what had happened to Samuel's erstwhile opponent and ally Hendrik Witbooi. With his attack, in April 1893, Francois had effectively eliminated the importance of Hendrik Witbooi's support for, and recognition of, Samuel Maharero as a Herero chief. Inadvertently, he had also unleashed a guerrilla war upon his own forces, which would keep German troops tied up for the coming two years. This meant the temporary removal of the threats posed by the Germans and Hendrik Witbooi to the Herero chieftains opposed to Samuel Maharero. Therefore, it was precisely when the threat of Hendrik Witbooi's raids had been neutralized, and southern Hereroland had once again become attractive to Herero chieftains, that Samuel Maharero came under threat from the remaining Herero claimants to the Okahandja throne. They seized their chance and openly challenged Samuel Maharero's chieftainship. Those Herero chiefs who, in the face of Witbooi attacks, had withdrawn northwards and eastwards, returned to assert their authority to lands and people now claimed by Samuel Maharero. It was under these conditions that Samuel Maharero eventually found himself forced to seek an alliance with Imperial Germany.

In March of 1893 Samuel Maharero, secure in the knowledge of his alliance with Hendrik Witbooi, and alarmed at the prospect of Boer settlers settling in central Namibia, wrote to the German Kaiser in Berlin. In his letter, Samuel Maharero asserted his rights of sole governance to Hereroland, and contested the right of the Kaiser to meddle in the affairs of his country. Indeed, Samuel Maharero went so far as to call into doubt the validity of the *Schutzvertrag* between Germany and the Herero. Referring to the occupation of Windhoek by German troops, Samuel wrote:

> From that day onwards I saw that the friendship which my father first heard was not friendship, but was my father's death and my death . . . Windhoek, Windhoek is my death.[103]

---

[102] ELCIN, *Politische Briefe etc. 1876–1893*, Letter Hendrik Witbooi at 'Hoornkrans den 18 April 1893' to Kapt. H. van Wijk. JBG's translation.

[103] BAP, RKA 2081, Samuel Maharero in Okahandja, 19/3/93, to 'Hoog Ed Majesteit de Keiser van Deutsland te Berlin'. JBG's translation.

H. von Francois, *Nama und Damara*, p. 153, refers to the activities of Graf Joachim Spiel, who, on behalf of the 'Siedlungs Gesellschaft', attempted to induce Boer and German settlers to settle in central Namibia.

Missionaries of the RMG were also alarmed at the prospect of Boer settlers, *'Für die beabsichtigte Besiedelung des nördlichen Teiles des Landes haben sich fast nur holländische Buren gemeldet, deren kommen aber für unsere Missionsarbeit wohl kaum sehr erwünscht sein würde'*. BRMG, 1893, p. 168.

Shortly thereafter Francois attacked Hendrik Witbooi at Hoornkrans. This did not immediately affect Samuel Maharero's position. As late as July 1893 Samuel was still unchallenged by the rival Herero chiefs. In that month German forces, who had been attacked by Witbooi commandos and had sought the assistance of Herero in Otjimbingwe, were greeted with malicious laughter. The Herero refused to come to the assistance of the Germans and told them that, as their chief, Samuel Maharero, was now at peace with Hendrik Witbooi, they refused to participate in the struggle against Witbooi.[104]

The ineffectiveness of German attacks on Witbooi did not go unnoticed and rumours abounded as to the defeat of German troops at the hands of Witbooi's forces. As the missionary chronicles for Omaruru reported:

> The exploits of the Schutztruppe are followed closely and rumours of the defeat or destruction of the Schutztruppe are eagerly believed and spread.[105]

The German troops were held to a stalemate by Witbooi's commandos, and this influenced the thinking of all observers. As both sides were ensnarled in a protracted guerilla war, Herero opposed to Samuel Maharero seized their chance and began to agitate against him.

By December of 1893 Samuel Maharero, along with his closest supporters, had taken to travelling to Windhoek, not only to drink tea, eat butter snaps, and listen to *Lieder* being played by Francois's wife, but also to solicit the support of the Germans against his opponents in Okahandja.[106] Seeking an alliance against his fears, it was not Francois's newly laid-out garden that impressed Samuel Maharero, but rather a cannon which, as Francois noted: 'I twice had loaded with blank cartridges and fired'.[107]

The opposition to Samuel was headed by Riarua, whom the missionaries referred to as 'Samuel's heathen uncle'.[108] Riarua, who had been recognized by all but the Christians, the missionaries and the Germans as chief, challenged Samuel Maharero's claim to the position of chief of Okahandja. Riarua was supported in his challenge by his stepson Nicodemus Kavikunua, who was another of Samuel's *Oruzuo* rivals.[109] In April of 1894, Riarua's forces, in alliance with those of Tjetjo, raided cattleposts belonging to Samuel Maharero.[110] Samuel Maherero's ally, Hendrik Witbooi, and his potential ally Germany were at each other's throats and were unable to come to his aid. Added to this, his mother's brother Zemoundya Kandikirira, the man who, in terms of his *Eanda*, was pledged to support Samuel Maharero, was sick and dying.

In June 1894, the barely suppressed opposition to Samuel Maharero's position finally broke out into open attack. Riarua's forces drove Samuel

---

[104] *BRMG*, 1893, p. 358. It is interesting to note that at this stage Otjimbingwe considered itself to be under the authority of Samuel.

[105] ELCIN, RMG, Chroniken Omaruru 1894.

[106] H. von Francois, *Nama und Damara*, pp. 179 and 188. BAP, RKA 2081, Köhler in Windhoek, 24/12/93, to RKA, details a visit by Samuel Maharero to Windhoek, accompanied by 1. Andreas Maharero, Samuel's brother; 2. Zemoundia Kandikirira, Samuel's mother's brother; 3. Johannes Mupcana; 4. Johannes Ngoimuo; 5. Barnabas Katjirongo; 6. Silas Kamuvatu (3–6 are cousins of Samuel); 7. Josaphat Kamatoto; 8. Wilhelm Kaumunika; 9. Gotthard Kambepahua (7–9 are nephews of Samuel) 10. Christian Mupurua, cousin of Johannes Mupurua and 11. Assa Riarua, cousin of Samuel Maharero.

[107] BAP, RKA 2081, C. von Francois in Windhoek, 26/12/94, to foreign affairs.

[108] *BRMG*, 1894, p. 103.

[109] BAP, RKA 2081, C. von Francois in Windhoek, 26/12/93, to RKA.

[110] NNAW, ZBU 2027, W II d 12 Tjetjo.

Maharero and his followers out of Okahandja.[111] It was to the power that comes through the barrel of a German cannon that Samuel Maharero now attached his destiny. Like Noah stranded on Mount Ararat, Samuel Maharero and his followers were ensconced on a hilltop at Osona, twenty kilometres to the south of Okahandja. From this perch Samuel Maharero, in appealing for help, released neither raven nor dove to collect an olive twig; rather, Samuel Maherero chose confrontation by calling on the Germans to come in force.[112]

The newly arrived *Landeshauptmann*, Theodor Leutwein, was delighted with Samuel Maharero's request.[113] Well aware of the fact that, as he put it, 'in terms of Herero customs', Nicodemus Kavikunua had been the rightful heir to Maharero, Leutwein noted with, what can only be described as being great candour, '. . . it is obviously more convenient for us to deal with a politically divided [zerrissenen] Herero nation, than with a closed and unified one'.[114] Anxious to seize the initiative, Leutwein promised Samuel Maharero that he would come to his aid: 'Such a beneficial opportunity, at influencing Herero affairs, was not soon again to be expected.'[115]

Stranded on an isolated hilltop, surrounded by a clean field of fire and with the Imperial German flag fluttering above them, Samuel's 300 followers, huddled within a densely packed palisade of thorn bushes, and waited for the German cavalry to arrive.[116] When the German troops approached Osona they were impressed by the sight of the Imperial German flag fluttering in the wind above Samuel's laager and by the sound of Christian hymns that wafted down on the breeze to meet them. One can well imagine that their impression was further improved when they were met by Samuel's veld-cornet and commander in chief, Assa Riarua, who, dressed in a uniform of the German Kaiser's French Guard regiment, told them that Samuel would be joining them as soon as he had finished conducting a field church service.[117]

Leutwein's forces set up camp next to Samuel's laager, and a message was sent to Riarua in Okahandja ordering him to come to Leutwein's camp to parley. Riarua sent a message that on the grounds of sickness he was indisposed and was thus unable to attend. Hereupon Leutwein ordered his forces into Okahandja. Riding eight abreast the German troops cantered into Okahandja. Whilst the majority of the troops rode to the north-eastern, non-Christian, section of town, where Riarua's house was to be found, a cannon was unlimbered in front of missionary Viehe's house in the south-western, Christian, section of town. At Riarua's house the German troops were met by forty to fifty men, about half of whom were armed with guns, who informed them that Riarua was not present. After searching in vain for Riarua, Leutwein ordered Lt Troost to demonstrate the cannon's fire-power. Shortly thereafter Riarua

[111] BAP, RKA 2100 & NNAW, ZBU 2027.
[112] NNAW, ZBU 2027, Samuel Maharero at Osona, 20/6/94, to Leutwein.
[113] Major Theodor Leutwein arrived in Namibia in December 1893 to take over as *Landeshauptmann* from von Francois. In 1898 he became Governor of GSWA. Prior to his appointment in Namibia he had been a lecturer at the military staff college in Freiburg, an aspect of his past that comes to the fore in his correspondence.
[114] BAP, RKA 2100, Leutwein in Windhoek, 17/6/94, to RKA.
[115] Theodor Leutwein, *Elf Jahre Gouverneur in Deutsch-Südwestafrika* (Berlin 1906) p. 60. JBG's translation. See also, NNAW, ZBU 2027, Leutwein in Windhoek, 17/6/94, to Samuel Maharero.
[116] NNAW, ZBU 2027, Leutwein in Windhoek, 24/6/94, to Samuel Maharero. Leutwein promised to come to Samuel's assistance with thirty men and a cannon.
[117] BAP, RKA 2100, Von Lindequist in Windhoek, 24/7/94, to RKA.

sent a messenger, and later came in person, to indicate his willingness to negotiate.[118]

Having taken Okahandja, Leutwein was joined by Samuel Maharero who, at the head of eighty mounted soldiers, set up camp next to the German encampment in Okahandja. As one of the Germans noted nostalgically: 'For the first time German soldiers and Hereros camped together as allies.'[119]

On the following day negotiations started. In the face of German fire-power Riarua found himself having to give up all of his rightful inheritance to the usurper Samuel Maharero. On the basis of his being the eldest patrilineal heir, Samuel Maharero had been able to convince the Germans as to the validity of his claims, to his father's throne and inheritance. The Germans whom Samuel Maharero had been unable to convince, such as Theodor Leutwein, chose to ignore the implications of this in the interests of the further extension of German power. Added to this, Samuel's claims, as the eldest son, a position accepted in German law, did provide the legal excuse Leutwein sought for further German intervention. Through his use of the Germans Samuel Maharero was able to cut through all the conventions associated with the *Oruzuo* and *Eanda* inheritance. Effectively Samuel was able to step beyond the bounds of Herero society, yet directly influence those who continued to be confined within it. Riarua found himself humiliated. His nephew, backed up by German firepower, forced him to rescind all his claims to Maharero's inheritance. Samuel Maharero had found the power to force Riarua to agree to the following points:

1. All the decisions regarding Maharero's inheritance were to be left to Samuel Maharero.
2. Riarua was prohibited from using his status in Herero society in such a way that could bring Samuel Maharero into discredit.
3. The cattleposts which had been in the possession of Kamaherero and which after his death had passed to Riarua and his supporters were to be transferred to Samuel Maharero.
4. The ammunition which had been in the possession of Kamaherero was to be transferred to the possession of Samuel Maharero, who transferred it to the care of the military station which [in exchange for German involvement] was to be established, although it would temporarily be stored in the house of traders Wecke & Voigts.[120]

In a single swoop Samuel Maharero had completely undermined the power of his opponents, ensured for himself substantial wealth and acquired the power with which to maintain his new status as chief of the Herero. Herero norms regarding the inheritance and succession of chiefs were overturned.

Faced with the incredible show of force it is not surprising that Riarua was prepared to negotiate.[121] What does at first appear surprising is that Riarua was prepared to accept the incredibly harsh settlement drawn up by Samuel

[118] BAP, RKA 2100, Von Lindequist in Windhoek, 24/7/94, to RKA.
[119] BAP, RKA 2100.
[120] Leutwein, *Elf Jahre*, p. 23. JBG's translation.
[121] Referring to the cannon used Leutwein noted:

Vor diesem hatten die Eingeborenen eine geradezu wahnsinnige Angst, während sie heutzutage das Feuer ganzer Batterien aushalten. Der Mensch gewöhnt sich eben an alles. (*Elf Jahre*, p. 23)

Maharero and Leutwein. For in effect the settlement totally disempowered Riarua, and reduced his position to that of a man at the mercy of Samuel Maharero. There is only one possible explanantion for Riarua's willingness to negotiate. When Riarua agreed to negotiate, and indicated his willingness to abide by stringent and humiliating conditions laid down, he had the intimidating precedent of the recently executed Andreas Lambert firmly in mind. Less than four months previously, in a manner uncannily similar to Leutwein's current raid on Okahandja, German troops had occupied Naosonobis, the main Khauas Khoi settlement. Here, in a single day, Leutwein had charged, tried, convicted and executed Andreas Lambert, the chief of the Khauas Khoi, and Lambert had been a firm ally of Nicodemus Kavikunua, Riarua's stepson.[122]

Given that Samuel Maharero now owed his position to the power of German cannons, it was only to be expected that Leutwein exacted a heavy price from him. In exchange for German assistance, and continued German protection, Samuel Maharero agreed to the establishment of a German garrison in Okahandja. As Leutwein noted: 'Hereby the capital of Hereroland was placed truly within the power sphere of the protectorate.'[123] Added to this, and in keeping with his new position as chief of the Herero, Samuel Maharero agreed to refund cattle which his erstwhile opponent, Nicodemus Kavikunua, who had now become his subject, had taken from traders in 1891. Furthermore Samuel Maharero committed himself to future talks on the determination of a definite southern boundary to Hereroland, and the delimitation of further land for German settlers.[124]

Looking back at the Herero succession dispute of 1890–94, we can see that initially Samuel Maharero had no legitimate claims, in terms of Herero culture, to his father's inheritance or power. It was only in terms of inheritance based upon primogeniture, a concept alien to Herero society at the time, that Samuel Maharero could claim rights to any of his father's inheritance. Samuel Maharero was able to capitalize upon missionary and German beliefs in the validity of primogeniture in terms of inheritance, and transform this into active support for his position. As the eldest patrilineal heir of Maharero Tjamuaha, he was able to convince the missionaries and the German forces as to the validity of his claims to his father's inheritance and position. The missionaries and German forces in the territory sought to support Samuel Maharero for their own ends, but they legitimized their support on the basis of what they believed was the only correct form of inheritance. Samuel Maharero's skill lay in being able to convert what was initially mere recognition on the part of the missionaries and Germans into active support for his position as heir to his father. He was able to transform his position from that of a recognized minority Christian leader in Okahandja, to that of chief of Okahandja. Initially Samuel Maharero's opponents could choose to ignore him, for effectively he had inherited nothing but the support of a minor section of Okahandja society and posed no real

---

[122] On the morning of 17 March 1893 Leutwein, accompanied by Schutztruppe, Batswana auxiliaries and a cannon, galloped into Naosonobis, which was the settlement of Andreas Lambert, chief of the Khauas Khoi. Leutwein established his camp in the centre of the settlement and after two days had Andreas Lambert executed for murder and theft, and replaced by his brother Eduard Lambert as chief of the Khauas Khoi. Leutwein, *Elf Jahre*, pp. 23–7.

[123] Leutwein, *Elf Jahre*, p. 61. JBG's translation.

[124] BAP, RKA 2100.

threat to any of his opponents. Riarua had inherited the bulk of Maharero Tjamuaha's inheritance and evidently expected to govern the Okahandja Herero. Riarua did not anticipate that German recognition and presence would become of crucial importance, and he underestimated Samuel Maharero's ability to come to an arrangement with Hendrik Witbooi. The German forces present in the territory had similarly not expected Samuel Maharero to come to an arrangement with Hendrik Witbooi. Once Hendrik Witbooi had been attacked at Hoornkrans, it became clear to the Herero and Witboois alike that the German forces were a force to be reckoned with. Too late Riarua realized that Samuel Maharero's solicitation of German support could be of crucial importance. Thus while German forces were ensnarled in a protracted guerilla war with Witbooi forces, Riarua and his allies sought to eliminate the threat posed to their position by Samuel Maharero. Samuel Maharero was driven out of Okahandja and appeared ready to make his last stand. But, through the effective use of his skills, as a Christian well-versed in missionary thought and rhetoric, and as a skilled diplomat who had long associated with the Germans, Samuel Maharero was able to convince the German forces in the territory to come down in support of his position. Samuel Maharero was not able to convince all the Germans that Riarua had cheated him of his inheritance, but it was a lie that Leutwein was prepared to accept in the interests of the further extension of German power in the territory.

3

Samuel Maharero as Paramount Chief
1894–6

Introduction

Between 1894 and 1896 Samuel Maharero, at the expense of other Herero chiefs, and through the skilful utilization of the threat of German fire-power, extended the power and extent of his initially tenuous position, as chief of Okahandja, to that of paramount chief of all of Hereroland. This extension of power came at a price, for which Samuel Maharero paid with the land, labour and cattle of his subjects. As there was but a finite amount of these goods, this policy held within it the seeds of its own destruction. As supplies of available cattle, labour and land, with which Samuel Maharero purchased German support, ran low, the outbreak of the Ovambanderu Khauas Khoi war only temporarily alleviated German settler demand by effectively liberating Mbanderu cattle, labour and land for resale by Samuel Maharero and his allies.

The interdependence of the Germans and Samuel Maharero is an aspect of Namibian history that has been referred to before by historians, most notably Helmut Bley, who has seen this as an integral part of what he termed 'Leutwein's Political System'.[1] Bley extensively analysed the system of control and governance which the German governor Theodor Leutwein set up in an attempt to successfully colonize Namibia. Bley argued that it was when this system, which was largely based on the power of Leutwein's personality, collapsed that the Herero–German war broke out. A drawback to such an analysis of this period of Namibian history is that it presents Theodor Leutwein as the prime initiator of action. The Herero, and the Nama, are seen as being acted upon and as participants in a set and plot devised by Theodor Leutwein. Though it is true that Theodor Leutwein was a consummate politician, it is equally true that individual Herero leaders also had good reasons for participating in alliances and treaty-building with German colonial officials. Thus the discussion of this interdependence, as it is presented here, differs from previous handlings of the topic in that it concentrates on attempting to analyse Herero motivations for wishing to participate in this relationship.

[1] Bley, *South-West Africa*, pp. 3–70.

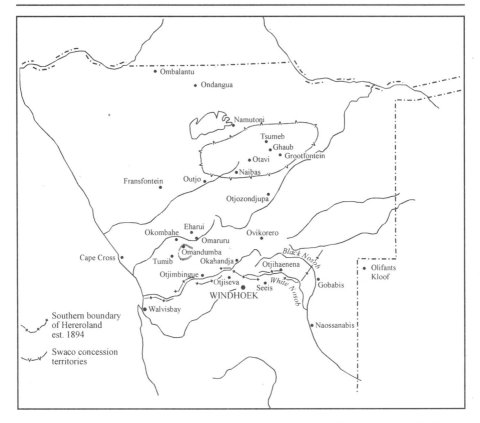

Map 3.1: Central Namibia 1894–6, indicating the increased confinement and delimitation of Herero lands

Manasse Tjisiseta and the Omaruru polity

Following the death of Maharero Tjamuaha of Okahandja in 1890, Manasse Tjisiseta of Omaruru was the most powerful Herero chief in south-western Africa. Even prior to the death of Maharero, Manasse and his following in Omaruru had acquired and retained a great degree of autonomy vis-a-vis Okahandja, and extended the territories under their control. During the 1870s Omaruru had grown as a settlement catering for the trade passing from Walvisbay northwards to Ovamboland. By 1880 Omaruru had become the second largest settlement in Hereroland and its leadership followed a political course which was largely independent of that of Maharero and his councillors in Okahandja.

Indicative of Omaruru's independence and unique regional interests were its extensive dealings with the Swartbooi Oorlam polity centred on Fransfontein to the north of Omaruru. Throughout the 1870s and 1880s the Swartboois and the Herero of Omaruru were involved in a struggle for control of the trade routes that led northwards from Omaruru through to the south-western

Ovambo kingdoms and south-western Angola.[2] A direct result of the polity's incessant skirmishing with Swartbooi commandos and Hendrik Witbooi's raiding commandos was that Manasse's forces were of necessity well-armed and well-organized. This was possible only through the maintenance of well-established trading links with the Cape Colony. The success of these links is indicated by the fact that at one stage Manasse's forces even had access to a cannon.[3] The eventual success of Manasse's forces vis-a-vis the Swartboois was due to his polity's ability to maintain what was in effect a standing army.[4] Apart from good trading links, for arms and ammunition, this implied good discipline and, as all armies march on their stomachs, a sufficient food surplus with which to feed the soldiers operating out of Omaruru. On this basis, Manasse Tjisiseta and his followers were able to maintain a polity independent of Maharero Tjamuaha and his councillors in Okahandja. In the late 1880s, following the arrival of German colonial forces in central Namibia, Manasse Tjisiseta and his councillors in Omaruru sought to maintain their political independence.

In 1888 Maharero Tjamuaha of Okahandja annulled his treaty with Imperial Germany, expelled Dr Göring and his assistants, and signed a new treaty with the English trader Robert Lewis. Shortly thereafter Lewis travelled to Omaruru where he tried to persuade Manasse to agree to sign a similar treaty. Manasse Tjisiseta politely refused to sign and dismissed Lewis saying, 'Treaties can only be concluded between rulers, people and people, but not between a people and a trader.' When Lewis persisted and urged Manasse to follow Maharero's example, Manasse let it be known that 'he had no intention of becoming the servant of Lewis and that he would prefer to remain chief in his own area'.[5]

For the German colonial authorities, Manasse's rebuttal of Lewis created the impression, eagerly emphasized by missionaries of the Rhenish missionary society who sorely wanted increased German involvement in the territory, that

[2] Following their expulsion from Rehoboth, in 1863, the Swartboois had moved into north-western Namibia around the settlement of Fransfontein. From this base the Swartboois had developed a hunting and raiding economy that stretched northwards into southern Angola. During the late 1870s trekboers had begun moving into the areas directly to the east of Fransfontein and had established the republic of 'Upingtonia'. The Trekboers and the Swartboois, sharing a similar economy, came into conflict with one another. Manasse had allied himself with the Trekboers and up until 1888 Swartbooi commandos and Herero commandos had clashed with one another. The establishment of friendly relations with the Swartboois, in 1888, led to the strengthening of trading and hunting links with areas to the north of the Kunene river in southern Angola. Up to this day one of the drifts on the Kunene carries the name Swartbooi's drift.
For an introduction to the long and convoluted history of interaction between the Zerauas and the Swartboois, and for more information on the Swartboois in general see, *The Commissions of W.C. Palgrave Special Emissary to South West Africa 1876–1885*, edited and introduced by E.L.P. Stals, Second Series No. 21, Van Riebeeck Society (Cape Town 1991).
[3] ELCIN, V. Chroniken, Omaruru 1888.
[4] Without a doubt referring to Manasse Tjisiseta's forces as a standing army is asking for trouble. Without wishing to conjure visions of massed marching by uniformly uniformed men, it is true that Manasse could rely on a group of men who were permanently present as soldiers. Throughout the period under discussion Manasse could rely on and had access to the military might of a group of men who were stationed in and around Omaruru for the sole purpose of supplying Omaruru with military force. Though there is as yet no direct proof of Manasse maintaining a standing army, there is circumstantial evidence in the maintenance of extensive tracts of agricultural lands, the reference by Manasse's signposts to soldiers, and the infamous Christie case, which is discussed further in this chapter. Clearly the military aspects of Omaruru history need to be further researched.
[5] ELCIN, V. Chroniken, Omaruru 1888. Lewis's further demand that he be recognized as being in charge of the whites in Omaruru was also turned down.

Manasse and his councillors were prepared to accept German protectorate status. On the basis of these ill-informed reports Curt von Francois visited Omaruru in 1889.[6] Not surprisingly Francois's overtures were turned down and, apart from a short visit by Francois, whilst on an intelligence mission in 1891, Manasse Tjisiseta and his councillors in Omaruru were left well alone to do as they felt best[7] much to the chagrin of the Rhenish missionaries who were left to lament the 'abandonment' of Omaruru by Germany.[8]

The pillars of independence

The pillars of independence upon which Manasse Tjisiseta and his polity in Omaruru based their sovereignty were fourfold. Broadly speaking they consisted of taxation, agricultural production, labour export and land allocation. Through these activities and with the monies generated thereby, arms were bought, soldiers fed and trade routes maintained. In short these independent sources of wealth ensured that Manasse Tjisiseta and his polity were able to attain and maintain a measure of independence vis-a-vis Okahandja. It was an independence which the polity struggled to maintain as Imperial Germany sought to colonize Hereroland.

One of the prime pillars upon which Omaruru's independence was based was the polity's export of indentured labour to the Cape Colony in exchange for trade goods and arms. It was a business which, particularly during periods of ecological crisis, ensured a steady income. Building upon contacts established during the missions of W.C. Palgrave, the special emissary of the Cape Colony to Damaraland, Manasse Tjisiseta and his councillors supervised the export of Berg Damara labour via Walvisbay to the labour-hungry farms of the western Cape.[9]

Throughout the second half of the nineteenth century, people described as Berg Damara were exported to the Cape Colony and elsewhere. In the early 1860s Johan van Reenen, whose ancestors had been slave traders in Namibia, petitioned the Cape administration recommending the introduction of Damara labour into the Colony.[10] Following the first three commissions of W.C. Palgrave, the Cape colonial government ordered Palgrave to:

> . . . direct [his] attention towards obtaining a supply of labour for the Colony by inducing Berg Damaras to emigrate to the Colony for the purpose of entering into contracts of service with the Government or with private individuals or companies.[11]

Mr James Murray, a former gaoler at Durban Village, in the Cape Colony, was

---

[6] BAP, RKA 2107, C. von Francois in Usakos, 28/7/89, to RKA.

[7] BAP, RKA 2109, H. von Francois, 6/1/91, to RKA.

[8] ELCIN, V. Chroniken, Omaruru 1894.

[9] Berg Damara as a separate ethnicity came into being in the nineteenth century and came to include Nama/Dama-speaking people who were as dark-skinned as the majority of the Herero but were not in possession of cattle, but lived as horticulturalists and hunter-gatherers. For a detailed overview on the development of Damara ethnicity, see J.B. Gewald, 'On being Damara between 1893 and 1993', presented at the Khoisan studies conference, Tutzing 11–14 July 1994, forthcoming in *Quellen zur Khoisan-Forschung/Research in Khoisan Studies* (Cologne 1998).

[10] Cape Archives Depot (CAD), Colonial Office (CO) 4127 Memorial Jh Van Renen. Recommending Introduction of Negroes from Damaraland. 1862.

[11] Stals, *Commissions Palgrave*, p. xxvii.

Photo 3.1: (From left to right) Leutwein, Johannes Maharero or Michael Tjisiseta, Kleinschmidt, Manasse Tjisiseta, Samuel Maharero, Omaruru 1895
Source: Namibian National Archives, Windhoek

appointed as labour agent, 'for collecting Berg Damaras', and sent to Walvisbay in late 1879.[12]

Immediately following the arrival of Murray in Walvisbay, a steady stream of indentured labour began flowing towards Cape Town. In two trips, in February and May 1880, the schooner *Louis Alfred*, employed by the Cape colonial government, shipped at least seventy-three indentured labourers to Cape Town.[13] It is clear that the prolonged drought, which not only limited the availability of *veldkos* but also reduced pasturage for Berg Damara stock and thus also the possibility of Berg Damara herding for others, as well as the continuing dispossession of Berg Damara territory by both Herero and Nama encroachment, led to the creation of an ever-growing number of impoverished people. The reports, almost without exception, refer to the Berg Damara as being 'all in a most deplorable condition'.[14] Indicative of their desperate position, Berg Damaras came to Palgrave's camp to 'be taken to Cape Town . . . [and] to know the conditions on which Berg Damaras are taken to the Cape'.[15]

In Cape Town the Berg Damara were placed into the Native Affairs Department's 'Native Depot' on New Market Street, which had previously been used to house the captured 'prize slaves', after which they were distributed as

[12] Ibid., p. 308.
[13] CAD, NA 1138, Palgrave 14/2/81 & 3/5/81.
[14] CAD, NA 1138, Palgrave, 20/3/80.
[15] CAD, NA 1138, Palgrave, 25/3/80.

labourers amongst the farmers of the western Cape.[16] The number of Berg
Damara exported to the Cape Colony were, given the population densities at
the time, extensive. For a while, Berg Damaras even established cohesive exile
communities. The Rhenish missionary Kronlein, who had previously worked
in Namaland and thus spoke Nama Dama, reported that he had a congregation
of eighty to ninety Berg Damaras at Wynberg.[17]

How were the Berg Damara induced to emigrate? Intermediaries operating
on behalf of Mr Murray, known only as Narib, Schoonraad and Pampoen, were
sent into the interior to induce Berg Damaras to come to Cape Town.[18] Traders
operating out of Walvisbay were also urged to participate in the collection of
Berg Damara. In a memorandum to the Cape Colony's Public Works
Department the Colony's special emissary, Palgrave, wrote:

> The establishment in Damaraland for the collection of Berg Damaras consists of a
> depot at Walwich Bay for their reception, and agents, one at Otjimbingwe and one
> at Rehoboth for collecting and forwarding to the coast.
>
> All traders are invited to collect Berg Damaras and those who have done so have
> been paid sums varying from five to ten shillings for each Berg Damara, male or
> female, old enough to be educated to a master.[19]

The traders were undoubtedly succesful recruiters; indeed as Palgrave noted:

> Out of the 51 adults I am now sending up not one has been obtained by the Labour
> agent; all having either come here themselves, or been brought by traders with whom
> he had no communication.[20]

Be that as it may, the collection of Berg Damaras was essentially seen as a
process of capture. Thus journal entries read as follows: 'Samuel Gertze has
got no Berg Damaras yet, but is sending out some of his people.'[21] Or elsewhere,
'Mr Murray returned from Otjimbingwe with one waggon, bringing 18 Berg
Damaras. He had 49 but the rest made off. Schoonraad is following with
more.'[22] Added to this was the fact that the traders were not as strictly bound
to the niceties of Cape colonial law, particularly as regarded arms trade to the
interior.[23] Apart from cups of rice and bags of maize meal, Rhenish missionaries,
operating in central Namibia at the time, reported that 'Bergdamra' were also
exchanged for waggonloads of arms and ammunition.[24]

It is clear that arms and ammunition, extremely lucrative goods in the central
Namibian context of the time, were a great draw card for the Herero chiefs.

---

[16] CAD, PWD 2/70, Native Depot Office, Cape Town, 6/4/81, to the Assistant commissioner
Cape Town.

> Sir I have the honour to report the death in Depot yesterday morning of one Berg Damara
> man named 'Zaligen' he arrived ill from Damaraland some time back, and was sent to the
> new somerset hospital, from whence he returned of his own accord . . . the immediate cause
> of his death was consumption, G.H. Stevens Contracting and pass officer.

[17] BAP, RKA 2080, General Consul in Cape Town, 7/4/91, to RKA.

[18] CAD, PWD2/70, Resident Magistrate, Musgrave, in Walvisbay, 5/1/81, to PWD.

[19] CAD, PWD 2/70, Palgrave, *Memorandum on the Collection of Berg Damaras in the vicinity of
Walwich Bay*, 22/1/81, to PWD.

[20] CAD, PWD 2/70, Resident Magistrate Musgrave in Walvisbay, 5/1/81, to PWD.

[21] CAD, NA 1138, Palgrave, 28/3/80.

[22] CAD, NA 1138, Palgrave, 3/5/1880.

[23] See particularly CAD, NA 291, Resident Magistrate in Walvisbay, 6/1/83, to NA.

[24] Vereinigte Evangelische Missions Archiv, Wuppertal, (VEMA) 1.594, Brincker in Otjimbingwe,
24/6/82 and 21/9/82, to Wuppertal.

Manasse's predecessor, Tjaherani, in monopolizing control over the export of Berg Damara labour from the interior of the country, had led mounted Herero commandos in attacks on labour recruiters operating independently of his control. In January of 1883, one such commando led by Tjaherani attacked, dispersed, captured and killed a number of Berg Damara, who had been gathered together into holding camps, by Mr H. Rydin, an agent of the Ohlsen company operating out of Cape Town.[25] From 1884 onwards the Berg Damara being offered for export to the Cape were being drawn exclusively from areas that fell under the control of Manasse Tjisiseta.[26]

Throughout the 1880s, as the mines of Kimberley (and after 1884 the mines of the Witwatersrand) consumed all available labour, farms in the western Cape were understandably short of labour. The Public Works Department of the Cape Colony sought ways to alleviate this labour shortage and attempted to increase the import of labour from central Namibia.[27] The resident magistrate in Walvisbay, John Cleverley, noted that substantial amounts of money would be necessary if he were to induce the Herero not to 'put a stop to the efflux of their Helots'.[28] Furthermore Cleverley recommended that labour agents, equipped with waggons, be sent into the interior and that they be paid £1 per head of recruited labour.[29] Cleverley's request was granted when in 1891, a full seven years after the official establishment of the German protectorate of South West Africa, the department of Native Affairs of the Cape Colony provided the Public Works Department with £300, 'for the transport and maintenance of Damara Labourers from Walfish Bay'.[30]

In 1891, whilst on an intelligence-gathering mission, Hugo von Francois reported that the British magistrate at Walvisbay had travelled to the settlement of Okombahe to recruit labour for the Cape.[31] It is highly unlikely that the magistrate of Walvisbay ever visited Okombahe. More probable is that labour agents, working for the firm of Messrs Webster & Co., had been to Okombahe.[32] But, be that as it may, it is clear that, even following the arrival of German troops in central Namibia, Manasse maintained strong links with traders operating out of the Cape Colony and that one of Manasse's prime sources of income was the export of Berg Damara labour.

Another pillar upon which Omaruru's independence was based was the polity's ability to feed itself and produce a surplus with which to feed its standing army. This food surplus did not consist solely of dairy products and collected veld foods, but also consisted in large part of cultivated grains and

[25] CAD, NA 291 *Letters received from Damaraland and Walfish Bay*, Resident Magistrate in Walwich Bay, 6/1/83, to Native Affairs. Interestingly Ohlsson, who had worked in Namibia as one of Erickkson's hunters, established a brewery in Cape Town and the rights to his name for commercial beer were bought up by South African Breweries in 1982. Ohlsson is now sold as a light beer in South Africa.

[26] CAD, NA 293, Manifest of the *Nautilus* for 21/11/1890 lists all the Berg Damara being exported as having come from Omaruru.

[27] CAD, PWD 2/8/20 *Aided Immigration. Introduction of Natives from Damaraland and St Helena.*

[28] CAD, NA 293 *Letters received from Damaraland and Walfish Bay*, Resident Magistrate in Walfish Bay, 20/10/90, to the Under Secretary for Native Affairs Cape Town.

[29] CAD, NA 293, Resident Magistrate in Walvisbay, 20/11/90, to NA.

[30] CAD, PWD 2/8/20, Office of the Secretary for Native Affairs Cape Town, 8/7/91.

[31] BAP, RKA 2080, H. von Francois in Otjimbingwe, 15/5/91, to RKA. Von Francois also reported that papers bearing the seals of the Cape Colony and the magistrate of Walvisbay had been found in Omaruru.

[32] This company had been recommended by Cleverley to the Cape colonial authorities.

vegetables. Omaruru was initially settled by Zeraua in 1868 precisely because it was one of the few areas in central Hereroland where agricultural production was possible. Various crops were grown in and around Omaruru. These included tobacco and calabashes, both of which featured prominently in inter-regional trade, as well as wheat, sorghum, millet, beans, onions and other foodstuffs. The agricultural potential of the Omaruru polity was further enhanced by the inclusion of the settlement of Okombahe within its sphere of influence in 1873.

The settlement of Okombahe was another of those few in central Namibia that could support a limited degree of horticulture. At the time of German colonization, it was occupied by both Herero pastoralists and Berg Damara horticulturalists, under the administration of Manasse's cousin, Daniel Kariko. Throughout the 1870s and early 1880s, as Herero pastoralists expanded their control over central Namibia, Berg Damara refugees, robbed of their pasturage, trekked to Okombahe and attempted to settle there.[33] Through Daniel Kariko, Manasse sought to maintain strict control over the Berg Damaras settled in Okombahe.[34] By his own account Manasse received a yearly tribute in agricultural produce to the value of no less than 1200 marks from the settlement's Berg Damara inhabitants. Added to this, Okombahe not only supplied Manasse's polity with agricultural produce, it also provided the polity with a population of labour, which, if the need arose, could be exported to the Cape in exchange for trade goods and arms.

A further source of income and basis for Manasse's independence was his polity's ability to levy tax on his subjects and on those visiting and make using of its resources.[35] Omaruru straddled the lucrative trade routes that led from Walvisbay northwards to the Ovambo kingdoms. This overland trade had to pass through Omaruru and provided Manasse with an opportunity to generate capital.[36] Travellers entering Omaruru were greeted by the following printed notice, written in English and Dutch:

> Notice is hereby given, that any person or persons passing this beacon, waggons, carts, cattle or horses, without permission of my soldiers, will be fined the sum of £5 sterling. Chief Manasseh.[37]

[33] Effectively, since the early 1860s, the newly established Herero chieftaincies, along with their allies, clients, and those whom they had tolerated, had expanded into the central and north-western regions of Hereroland at the expense of less strongly organised groups, such as the Damara. In the 1870s the Swartboois, former Herero clients living to the north of Omaruru, came into conflict with Boers from the newly established republic of 'Upingtonia' who were allied to Manasse. As a consequence, until 1888 there were numerous occasions on which Swartbooi and Herero commandos loyal to Manasse clashed with one another. A direct result of this unsettled nature of warfare was that Berg Damara, not immediately allied to one of the warring factions, were forced to flee.

[34] ELCIN, V. Chroniken, Omaruru 1887. Thus, for instance, when in 1887 there was imminent threat of Swartbooi attack, Manasse ordered the Berg Damaras to abandon Okombahe and to move closer to Omaruru. The relationship between the Swartboois and the Herero of Omaruru is something that is badly in need of further research. The conflict between the two dealt with trade and raids to the north into southern Angola, and could have dealt with issues relating to the control of exportable labour.

[35] BAP, RKA 2109, C. von Francois in Otjimbingwe, ?/5/91, to RKA.

[36] From the 1870s onwards Omaruru became the most important trading centre in Namibia. By the 1880s transactions conducted in and around Omaruru were highly monetarized, and evidence indicates that the Herero sought to acquire money precisely because of its versatility. One way of doing this was by taxing traders passing through the settlement, and demanding payment in cash.

[37] BAP, RKA 1482, *Berichte des Mr Matthew Rogers an die South West Africa Company. 1892–1893.* According to the missionaries the waggon tax was imposed by Manasse following the

Manasse's soldiers collected a tax of 10 shillings per waggon in exchange for water and grazing rights. Failure to pay tax led to a fine of £5 and the possible confiscation of waggon and goods.[38] The tax collected undoubtedly went some way towards paying for the upkeep of Manasse's soldiers, though, as with most soldiers in charge of roadblocks, they tended to overstep their mark and levy charges of their own. The Rhenish missionaries resident in Omaruru wrote irate letters to Manasse demanding that they be exempted from the tax, on the grounds that they were residents of Omaruru, and that the soldiers be ordered to refrain for demanding bribes. The missionary chronicles report that the missionaries were given written documents, by Manasse's council, which freed them from tax obligations. Unfortunately for the missionaries, not all of Manasse's soldiers were literate and every so often the missionaries were still asked to pay up.[39]

Apart from generating income through holding jurisdiction over grazing and water rights, Manasse's council also administered corn prices, alcohol consumption, mining claims and land rights. In exchange for an agreed price or tax, and an undertaking to accept the authority of Manasse and his council, white settlers were permitted to establish trading stores or canteens in Omaruru. On the same grounds white settlers could also be issued with land and/or mineral rights, within the territory of the polity. Amongst those who were prepared to accept Manasse's authority were Boer trekkers who broke away from the trader and trekker Will Worthington Jordan and his newly formed republic of Upingtonia in 1886.[40] In exchange for their allegiance and a yearly rent these people were granted land by Manasse.[41] Though the allocation of land to settlers provided his polity with money, in the long run it was this policy which led to the undoing of Manasse's independence. Amongst those who applied for land was an English trader, named Christie. As with the other applicants, Christie acknowledged Manasse's authority. But when Christie, who had killed another man in a drunken brawl, was shot whilst being arrested by Manasse's soldiers, it provided justification for German involvement in the affairs of the Omaruru polity and the termination of its independence.

The SWACO affair

The independence of the Omaruru polity, vis-a-vis the Germans and the Okahandja Herero, the geographical extent of the polity's regional influence, and the foundation upon which this independence was based are all well

maltreatment, by German soldiers, of members of a Herero delegation which had travelled to Windhoek. ELCIN, V. Chroniken, Omaruru 1891. In dire financial straits, in the first two years after his father's death, Samuel Maharero attempted to follow Manasse's example but was prevented from doing so by the German authorities. H. von Francois, *Nama und Damara*, p. 190.
[38] BAP, RKA 1480, Copeland, 26/11/92, to SWACO.
[39] ELCIN, V. Chroniken, Omaruru 1891.
[40] In the late 1870s the *Dorslandtrekkers* left the western Transvaal for south-western Angola. In 1884 a number of these trekkers moved out of Angola onto land between Grootfontein and Outjo allegedly bought by Jordan from the Ndonga king Kampingana. This led to conflict with the Herero chiefs who also laid claim to the area. Jordan was murdered a short while later whilst on a trip to southern Angola.
[41] BAP, RKA 1574, Du Plessis at Grootfontein, 20/10/85, to Manasse Tjisiseta.

illustrated by the events surrounding the South West Africa Company (SWACO) affair of 1892.

Shortly after the founding of the German South West African Protectorate, the Imperial German government, unable to entice enough capital from the German market, floated the SWACO with capital drawn from the London stock exchange. The newly founded company was granted extensive mineral and mining rights to areas of northern Namibia. However, when a SWACO expedition was sent to Namibia, to proceed with prospecting and surveying, it became clear that Germany's authority did not extend much beyond its military forts at Tsaobis and Windhoek, and certainly not up to Omaruru. Though German forces, stationed in central Namibia, had been instructed to escort the SWACO expedition, they were prevented from doing so by Herero opposition. Indeed the expedition was permitted to proceed only after Manasse and his councillors had been convincingly lied to, by the expedition members who claimed that the expedition had nothing whatsoever to do with the German government.

Two of the mining engineers, Rogers and Copeland, who accompanied the SWACO expedition, made extensive reports of the trip which provide us with a number of insights into the manner in which Omaruru was able to maintain its regional independence.[42] Thus after having paid their grazing and water tax, the expedition was escorted into Omaruru by a mounted contingent of Manasse's soldiers, led past extensive fields of maize, wheat and tobacco, and allocated a place to stay in the vicinity of Manasse's quarters. During their stay in Omaruru the expedition members were constantly watched and reports of their activities were brought before the Omaruru council. Finally the expedition spokesmen were led, by mounted and armed horsemen, to a thatched enclosure for their meeting with Manasse and his councillors.[43]

With great candour Rogers noted: 'The reason and common sense evinced by the Chief was a matter of surprise to most of us.'[44] Copeland, also evidently impressed by what he saw and heard, described in clear terms parts of the expedition's first meeting with Manasse and his councillors.

> Manasse and his Raad continually ask if we were involved with the Germans . . . and I knew if he got in any way to understand that we were with the Germans, we would go no further. This is *our* country! We are *owners* of it! We do not want war! We are for peace. We have been cheated many times before; but now our eyes are opened, and when once you could buy our land with a bottle of whisky or a suit of clothes, that time is all gone by.[45]

Fellow expedition member, Rogers, in a letter to Bulow and Duft, German officials who were to have accompanied the expedition, reported similarly on the expedition's meeting with Manasse and his councillors in Omaruru. Rogers noted that the councillors would only allow them to proceed:

> . . . as an English company from London acknowledging their [the Herero] right as owners of the country through which we will pass and accepting the protection of

[42] BAP, RKA 1480, *Expeditionen der South West Africa Company, vom 17 September 1892 bis 15 Mai 1893* & RKA 1482, *Berichte des Matthew Rogers an die South West Africa Company. 1892–1893.*
[43] BAP, RKA 1482, Rogers report for 21/11/92.
[44] Ibid.
[45] BAP, RKA 1480, G.H. Copeland in Omaruru, 26/11/92, to the SWACO.

the chief Manasse while in his country. Under these conditions we will be allowed to proceed but on no other; if we refuse to accept them they have ordered us to return immediately to Walfischbay.[46]

The expedition members understood Manasse's message and drew their own conclusions; it was clear that they would not be able to proceed if they were to be accompanied by German colonial officials. Therefore Rogers continued his letter by noting that:

> the feeling in the Raad and of the natives generally appears to be very bitter against the German authority and we think that it might be desirable for your party to remain in the background for the present and to allow our party to proceed alone to Otavi and to complete our mission.[47]

Unquestionably intimidated by such a show of independence and power, Rogers was, in his concluding remarks to his company directors, as always, forthright:

> . . . I do not believe that the company had any knowledge of the state of affairs in the country, had it known it would never have sent the expedition without a thorough briefing . . . it is not possible to do any work here without the protection of an armed force.[48]

Copeland was similarly impressed, and his concluding words to the SWACO directors are even more illuminating in what they had to say about Samuel Maharero and his allies:

> . . . I would not try to treat with Samuel Maherero at all; the Germans say that they have so compromised him, that he will not dare to interfere. But this Manasse is an educated man, and cannot be fooled; he is, in fact, very intelligent, and the Germans say a far more agreeable man than his brother chief.[49]

The reports of Rogers and Copeland, apart from giving an indication of Omaruru's independence, also provide us with an indication as to the basis upon which this independence was built: the ability to levy tax and the ability to provide foodstuffs.

---

[46] BAP, RKA 1480, Rogers in Omaruru, 23/11/92, to Duft and von Bulow.
[47] Ibid.
[48] BAP, RKA 1482, Rogers in Omaruru, 21/11/92, to SWACO. Rogers' reports are extremely illuminating and give us extensive insights into conditions in the Otjiwarongo and Tsumeb area. The unfortunate man was clearly intimidated by the opposition evinced by his presence and particularly his association with the Germans.

> July 29 1893. The recent raid on Henry Whitboi and the reported murderous onslaught on the defenceless women and children by the German soldiery have increased rather than allay their fears.
> We are looked on by some as being purely and simply Germans, and our coming here is simply a dodge for a vantage ground for a further attack from the north, by others as being accessory with the Germans, and by most as being in sympathy with them as against the native races. In vain we endeavour to show them our peaceable intentions, and that we are simply here for observations, enquiry, and mineralogical examination. They say our stores, provisions, and associations betray our nationality. Our guns and our ammunition are German, and if we were not German we should not be able to get ammunition from them.

[49] BAP, RKA 1480, Letter G.H. Copeland in Omaruru, 26/11/92, to the SWACO.

The ending of Omaruru's independence

The Francois brothers, following two short visits, had left Omaruru well alone
during the rest of their stay in central Namibia.[50] The missionaries noted:

> From Omaruru so many complaints had come to Windhoek, that *hauptmann* and
> *leutnant* von Francois, who had until then been the representatives of the government
> in the country, had broken off all contact with Omaruru. Their successors Major
> Leutwein and Assessor von Lindequist dealt differently, as they did with everything,
> with the people of Omaruru.[51]

Leutwein was a master diplomat; nowhere was this more apparent than in his
early correspondence with Manasse, where each of his letters was perfectly
timed to gain maximum advantage. Initially Leutwein refrained from writing
to Manasse and let Lindequist intimidate Manasse with threats of German
military might. Letters dealing with subjects as diverse as lungsickness or the
establishment of liquor stores contained references to Germany's, and by
implication Leutwein's, military might:

> . . . thank you for your letter . . . unfortunately Leutwein who was very pleased to
> hear from you was unable to come as he had to collect nine new soldiers . . . after
> this he will advance immediately on Hendrik, after the war he will come to you
> immediately.[52]

Significantly, Leutwein only began to correspond directly with Manasse upon
his return from Naosonobis, where he had arrested, charged, tried and
summarily executed the Khauas Khoi chief, Andreas Lambert. In an opening
paragraph Leutwein demanded whether Manasse intended keeping to the
conditions laid down in the *Schutzvertrag*. Not surprisingly Manasse answered
that he intended keeping to the treaty.[53] Leutwein next wrote to Manasse
immediately after he had had Samuel Maharero installed as paramount chief
of the Herero. Once again Leutwein advised Manasse to keep to the
Schutzvertrag. Once again Manasse confirmed that he intended keeping to the
treaty.[54] Even so German officials still refrained from visiting Omaruru. It was
not until August of 1894, when Lieutenant Hartmann, as official representative
of the SWACO, visited Omaruru, that direct face-to-face contacts between the
Herero in Omaruru and the German authorities were reopened. Hartmann,
who was ostensibly not connected to the German authorities, submitted to
Leutwein a lengthy and illuminating report:

> I have had a two hour long meeting with Manasse, who greets you and states that
> he badly wants you to visit him. I told him that Omaruru had not been as good as
> what the Germans would have wanted but that whites had also been 'mischief
> makers'. Furthermore I could calm him and inform him that those whom he could
> endure least of all, Major and Lieutenant von Francois, have left the protectorate

[50] In 1890 von Francois's soldiers raped a woman at Omburu, one of the settlements allied to
Omaruru. This may well explain why German troops steered clear of Omaruru until 1894. *BRMG*,
1895 p. 85.
[51] ELCIN, V. Chroniken, Omaruru 1894.
[52] NNAW, WII d 10, von Lindequist in Otjimbingwe, 2/7/94, to Manasse. See also ZBU WII d
10, von Lindequist in Windhoek, 5/11/94, to Manasse.
[53] NNAW, ZBU, WII d 10, Manasse in Omaruru, 13 & 16/6/94, to Leutwein.
[54] NNAW, ZBU, WII d 10, Manasse in Omaruru, 18/7/94, to Leutwein in reply to Leutwein's
letter of Okahandja, 28/6/94.

for ever, and that a new Major has been appointed to lead the German protectorate.[55]

During the course of the meeting Manasse had asked Hartmann why the Germans had decided to come to the assistance of Samuel Maharero during the Okahandja succession dispute. Hartmann's answer did little to calm Manasse's nerves. The Germans had decided to help Samuel Maharero 'precisely because Samuel, as chief, did not possess enough authority with his great men. The new master [Herr] helped Samuel because in Germany the first law is: obey authority.'[56] After which Hartmann noted: 'The fear that Manasse appears to have is that he is to be punished, repressed or placed under Samuel.'[57]

In the light of the above, Hartmann's conclusion that Manasse would be happy to accept a garrison, even though Hartmann had not brought up the matter, must be seen as more than a little optimistic. On a lighter note, the letter ended with sound advice as to where best to stay:

> ... in the house of missionary trader Pyrainen, this is preferable as Mr Tatlow and his store keeper Schwartz are continually drunk. Though Mrs Erickson has a boarding house, where you would be able to get good meals, it would be preferable to stay in the house of the missionary as this will also increase his standing.[58]

In early September 1894, on the day that Hendrik Witbooi, the man who had posed the greatest threat to Manasse's interests, sued for peace with the Germans, Lindequist assured Manasse that Germany intended strengthening the power of the 'big chiefs' (großen Häuptlinge) and that to facilitate this a German garrison would have to be established in Omaruru. Germany's intention, according to Lindequist, was merely the establishment of peace, tranquillity and order in the country; this Germany would seek to achieve by peaceful means. As Witbooi and his followers were being banished to southern Namibia, Lindequist went over the terms of the Schutzvertrag and received further commitments from Manasse that he would adhere to the treaty.[59] In terms of German intentions Lindequist's visit to Omaruru was an unrivalled success. This is clearly reflected in the correspondence between Manasse and Lindequist. Yet in amongst the queries of Manasse, who suffered from suppurating ulcers, regarding medicated creams, 'can one smear with the medicine I have?', lay the more sinister undertones of power: 'What you wrote about the Christian peace that was concluded between Major [Leutwein] and Hendrik Witbooi, I have understood well', to which the reply was '. . . glad to see you have become a peaceful friend of the German state again'.[60]

Finally a situation presented itself which provided Leutwein with the excuse he had been waiting for to justify his direct involvement in the affairs of the Omaruru polity. In September of 1894, a drunken Englishman, named Christie, shot and killed a Baster, named Buijs, after he had insulted Christie's

[55] NNAW, ZBU, WII d 10, Hartmann in Omaruru, 15/8/94, to Leutwein.
[56] Ibid.
[57] Ibid.
[58] Ibid.
[59] BAP, RKA 2150, von Lindequist in Omaruru, 12/9/94, to RKA & BRMG 1895 p. 74. Regarding Witbooi see Leutwein, Elf Jahre, pp. 54–8.
[60] Regarding medicated creams see NNAW, ZBU WII d 10, Manasse in Omaruru, 19/10/94, to Lindequist. Regarding peace treaty see Manasse in Omaruru, 19/10/94, to Lindequist. Regarding 'peaceful friend' see Lindequist in Windhoek, 5/11/94, to Manasse.

companion Dr Sinclair, a former ship's doctor who had fallen on hard times. Dr Sinclair and Christie, the brother-in-law of Tatlow, a tavern keeper and trader in Omaruru, lived at Oukhas, along the Khan river, on a farm which they had acquired on loan, in exchange for their professed loyalty to Manasse and his council in Omaruru. Immediately following the murder Dr Sinclair and Christie had hurried to the German fort in Otjimbingwe, to report that Christie had shot Buijs in self-defence. Christie and Dr Sinclair were cautioned to remain in the territory and to be present at the next magisterial sitting in Otjimbingwe. Even so, the two abandoned Oukhas and following a trip to Windhoek they holed up in the Otjipatera mountains.[61]

Manasse considered Oukhas to be within his polity's sphere of influence, and obviously so too did Dr Sinclair and Christie, as had it been to Manasse and his council that they had applied for permission to settle at Oukhas.[62] By abandoning Oukhas and by informing the German authorities in Otjimbingwe of the case, Christie and Dr Sinclair had attempted to extricate themselves both physically and legally from Manasse's authority. Immediately following the shooting of Buijs, Manasse wrote to both the British magistrate in Walvisbay and the German authorities in Windhoek asking for information:

> A little thing has happened in my country, a bastard man was shot near this [sic], he was shot without any reason, he was shot just like a woman. Those men who shot this man did not let me know that they had shot him, and what they had shot him for. I heard these men went to Windhoek with a load & they came there to you, please let me know in what way you have settled with these men, for this thing which they have done.[63]

In reply Manasse received a short note from the German authorities stating that they could disclose no information, but that the case would be investigated.[64]

Before the killing of Buijs, Lindequist had visited Omaruru and informed Manasse that once Hendrik Witbooi had been defeated Leutwein intended travelling to Omaruru.[65] In anticipation of Leutwein's long-awaited visit to Omaruru, Manasse, who had received little more than a rather wishy-washy reply to his queries on the Buijs case, sought to apprehend Christie and Dr Sinclair, so that the two men could be tried during Leutwein's visit. Twice Manasse's soldiers were sent out to capture Christie and Dr Sinclair. Though the first party failed to find them in early November 1894, Manasse's second party discovered the two Englishmen, at a cattlepost in the Otjipatera mountains. Manasse's soldiers, who were later tried and convicted for murder, claimed that, as they had approached, Christie had gone for his gun and they had been forced to shoot him in self-defence. Having killed Christie, Manasse's soldiers looted the campsite and took all the Englishmen's possessions except the cattle which they suspected of having lungsickness.[66]

Leutwein, who since June 1894 had declared that it was his intention to visit Omaruru, was en route to Omaruru, in early November, when he first

[61] *BRMG* 1895, pp. 75–7.
[62] *BRMG* 1895, p. 77.
[63] NNAW, ZBU, WII d 10, Manasse in Omaruru, 30/10/94, to Leutwein.
[64] NNAW, ZBU, WII d 10, von Lindequist in Windhoek, 8/11/94, to Manasse.
[65] BAP, RKA 2150, von Lindequist in Omaruru, 12/9/94, to RKA.
[66] ELCIN, V. Chroniken, Omaruru 1894; *BRMG* 1895, pp. 75–7.

received reports of the killing of Christie. Leutwein immediately halted in Otjimbingwe and, believing that Manasse had gathered between 800 to 1000 soldiers at Omaruru, waited for further reinforcements, and for the depletion of food stocks in Omaruru.[67] From Otjimbingwe Leutwein wrote:

> I wonder if I should still come to Omaruru as I do not know if you are still my friend. You have written a letter to Otjimbingwe which I don't find very friendly . . . In terms of article 4 of the *Schutzvertrag*, which was drawn up between us, the [Christie] case fell within my jurisdiction. I would have punished him, however on the 5th of this month ten of your men came and shot him down, tied up Sinclair and all the goods of the two were taken away. This is against the *Schutzvertrag* whereas I have been handling in keeping with the *Schutzvertrag*.[68]

Effectively, the killing of Christie had provided Leutwein with a golden opportunity with which to browbeat Manasse, and to claim that like Andreas Lambert, whom Leutwein had executed at Naosonobis, Manasse had broken the terms of the *Schutzvertrag*. With ill-concealed menace Leutwein ended his letter to Manasse by reminding him that it was he who had defeated Hendrik Witbooi.[69] With the examples of Riarua, Lambert, Witbooi, Leutwein's letter, and missionary Bernsmann's predictions of German wrath on his mind, it is hardly surprising that Manasse did his utmost to appease Leutwein:

> Dear *Landeshauptmann* why are you not coming? I have heard that you are very unhappy about a letter that I am alleged to have written to Hanemann [a German official] in Otjimbingwe however I do not recall having written such a letter. I did write one letter to Otjimbingwe asking for Cootze Danta [a Berg Damara] to come to Omaruru. I feel guilty of the death of Christie who was killed by my people I do not however have any intention of ending our treaty as Christie was killed when my people went to fetch him. Truly truly I would never break this *Schutzvertrag*![70]

Before proceeding from Otjimbingwe Leutwein summoned Zacharias Zeraua and Samuel Maharero to accompany him to Omaruru. As Leutwein noted: 'I was able to interest him in the case by telling him that now his position as paramount chief could also be made to count in Omaruru. This temptation he could not resist, particularly so, as Manasse had never recognised him.'[71]

Following reports on the massing of German forces, Manasse, fearing an attack by Leutwein, abandoned his *Onganda*, which lay half an hour to the south of Omaruru, on the road to Otjimbingwe whence Leutwein's attack was expected to come, and moved into the house of his late uncle, Zeraua, next to the house of his chief councillor Mutate, in the Christian section of the town.[72] On 23 November Leutwein's scouts rode into Omaruru. Missionary Bernsmann and Manasse sought to convince the scouts that the Herero had no intention

---

[67] Leutwein's estimates regarding the size of the Omaruru militia vary from source to source, from 800 (*Elf Jahre*, p. 62) to 1000 in his official correspondence, BAP, RKA 2150, Leutwein in Otjimbingwe, 11/12/94, to RKA. Missionary sources make no mention whatsoever of increased troop activity in Omaruru prior to the arrival of Leutwein, and it is probable that the inflated figures used by Leutwein were such because he was attempting to impress upon the RKA the need for more troops.
[68] NNAW, ZBU, WII d 10, Leutwein in Otjimbingwe, 8/11/94, to Manasse.
[69] NNAW, ZBU, WII d 10, Leutwein in Otjimbingwe, 8/11/94, to Manasse.
[70] NNAW, ZBU WII d 10, Manasse in Omaruru, 13/11/94, to Leutwein.
[71] Leutwein, *Elf Jahre*, p. 62.
[72] *BRMG* 1895, p. 77.

of fighting. At dawn three days later Leutwein and his forces marched into Omaruru:

> At the head rode three trumpeters playing a fanfare. At the church they formed up on the left hand side of the road, whilst the Major [Leutwein] together with the Assessor [von Lindequist] and the assistant medical officer Dr Schöppwinkel formed up opposite to them. The procession paraded in between them to the sound of the trumpeters raucous [*schmetternden*] fanfare. First to pass by were 60 to 70 horsemen, under the command of Lieutenant Eggers, immediately followed by the mounted Herero, who had accompanied the Major, amongst whom [were] Samuel Maharero and Zacharias Zeraua; they too attempted to sit at attention and keep their eyes right. The parade halted at brother Piirainens house. Then followed about 40 soldiers on foot under the command of Lieutenant Volkmann and immediately behind them a number of Herero and Berg Damara on foot from Otjimbingwe; their parade march wasn't too successful. Then followed a cannon with ammunition waggons drawn by nearly a thousand oxen, and with that the parade march, which made my old soldier's heart beat faster, passed by. 4 waggons, still followed . . .[73]

With the exception of Manasse, and a few of his Christian followers, very few Herero were present to watch the parade. Manasse's reliance on the missionaries may have done something to appease Leutwein and keep German occupation at bay, but in the short term this policy appeared to have backfired completely. The German forces surrounded the Christian quarter of Omaruru and established themselves in the missionary buildings. The missionaries, who in the past had lamented the lack of interest of the colonial government in the affairs of Omaruru, now did all they could to ensure the establishment of a colonial presence in Omaruru. The cannon was unlimbered near to Piirainen's garden wall, Dannert's smithy was converted into a jail, and Bernsmann vacated his bedroom and study in anticipation of their becoming the court room and the basis of the new German military station.[74]

On the very next day court proceedings began. Seven young men were charged with the murder of Christie. In what was missionary Bernsmann's former sitting-room sentence was passed. Ndaja, the only accused not present, was sentenced in absentia to two years' imprisonment with twenty-five lashes to be applied every three months during the course of his incarceration. Kauzeesa, son of the former chief Tjaherani and nephew of Manasse, was sentenced to eight years' imprisonment with hard labour. Karuhere was sentenced to death. The remaining four were sentenced to seven months' imprisonment.[75] Anxious to impress upon the inhabitants of Omaruru the gravity of his intentions, Leutwein ordered that, following the passing of sentence, the convicted Herero, Kauzeesa and Karuhere, be tied to a tree with the cannon aimed at them. Of the two, Karuhere was able to break free, but was wounded as he ran to Manasse's quarters.[76]

Unfortunately for Karuhere the relations of power that had existed in Omaruru had changed to such an extent that Manasse now found himself unable to provide the sanctuary which Karuhere could have anticipated from his *Omuhona*. All of the actions undertaken by Leutwein had indicated his

---

[73] *BRMG* 1895, p. 80. As the *BRMG* footnote states, 'Brother Bernsmann fought in the expedition against France in 1870/71.'
[74] *BRMG* 1895, p. 80.
[75] BAP, RKA 2150, Leutwein in Omaruru, 11/12/94, to RKA; *BRMG* 1895 pp. 81–3.
[76] *BRMG* 1895, p. 82.

willingness to attack Manasse. Manasse was well aware of this and sought by all manner of means to appease Leutwein's demands. It was on these grounds that Manasse had Karuhere promptly handed over into the custody of Samuel Maharero and Zacharias Zeraua. That Karuhere was handed over into the custody of Samuel Maharero and not to the Germans is in itself interesting. In doing this Manasse did exactly what Leutwein would have wanted him to do. By this act Manasse indicated to Leutwein that he was willing to submit to Samuel Maharero and therefore ultimately to Leutwein's authority. Commenting on the fact that during the court proceedings four of the accused were handed over into the custody of Samuel Maharero, Leutwein had written, 'This measure served his standing amongst his tribal colleagues.'[77] At the same time though, in the eyes of the Herero, Leutwein's actions had served to further embroil Samuel Maharero in German activities. Similarly, by handing Karuhere over to Samuel Maharero, Manasse implicated Samuel Maharero in Karuhere's later execution and, perhaps more importantly, he had cleared himself of complicity with the Germans, whilst in the eyes of the Germans he had now given the appearance that he was indeed subservient to the new paramount chief Samuel Maharero. In exchange for peace Karuhere was the blood offer demanded and exacted by Leutwein; all that Manasse could do was to request that Karuhere not be executed in Omaruru. Two days later Karuhere and Kauzeesa were led out of Omaruru in a covered waggon. Karuhere was executed outside Omaruru at a distance of about half an hour's ride from the settlement.[78]

The trial was more than the mere conclusion of a murder case. It was, as Leutwein, succinct as always, put it, 'more important to politically exploit the Captain's inconvenient [*übel*] position'.[79] And this he certainly did. Making use of Manasse's 'inconvenient position' Leutwein sought to cripple the power and influence of Manasse and his polity in Hereroland. To achieve this objective Leutwein employed a three-pronged offensive that tackled the issues of land, labour and governance. In exchange for peace, Manasse's life, and continued independence vis-a-vis Samuel Maharero, Leutwein had Omaruru garrisoned, and, through the delineation of boundaries, cut off from its main sources of independent wealth. The richest of these independent sources of wealth was the settlement of Okombahe.

The ripping of Okombahe

Okombahe lies approximately sixty kilometres west of Omaruru along the Omaruru river. Between 1870 and 1894 it developed into the second largest settlement in western Hereroland with twenty brick houses and 150 *pontoks*. The settlement was populated primarily by Berg Damara horticulturalists and Herero pastoralists.[80] In 1894 Okombahe was under the chieftainship of Daniel Kariko, who was subservient to his uncle Manasse Tjisiseta of Omaruru. In terms of the labour and tribute it generated, Okombahe was vital to the continued independence of the Omaruru polity. Leutwein sought to terminate

[77] BAP, RKA 2150, Leutwein in Windhoek, 11/12/94, to RKA.
[78] *BRMG* 1895, p. 84.
[79] Leutwein, *Elf Jahre*, p. 63.
[80] BAP, RKA 2108, Francois in Wilhelmsfeste, 6/1/91, to RKA.

this independence and thus extracted Okombahe from the control of Manasse and his council.

When in 1889 Curt von Francois had ensconced himself in Tsaobis, he had employed Berg Damara, from Otjimbingwe, as labourers. These people came to feature prominently in Francois's book *Nama und Damara*. In his book and elsewhere Francois expanded upon the theme of the Berg Damaras as a subject race of the Herero. In a similar vein, and drawing parallels with ancient Greece, Cleverley, the English magistrate in Walvisbay, referred to the Berg Damara as the 'Helots of the Herero'.[81] Both the German and English authorities believed that the Berg Damara were a distinct subject race of the Herero, and were anxious to tap their labour. At least until 1891 Okombahe, through the mediation of Manasse, continued to supply the magistrate in Walvisbay with labour.[82] Francois's intelligence report on Namibia, written following his return to Germany in mid-1891, devoted a major section to the settlement of Okombahe and the feasibility of tapping its labour reserves.[83] Elsewhere his brother Hugo von Francois concluded:

> This nation no longer has a future; but its labour power is a not to be underestimated factor in the social development of the protectorate.[84]

The report formed part of Theodor Leutwein's background reading prior to his enshipment to Namibia. Undoubtedly Leutwein's thinking, regarding the alleged 'enslavement' of Berg Damaras by Herero, was influenced by the report and this is clearly reflected in Leutwein's correspondence.[85]

Following the arrival of the Francois brothers in the territory, a close association developed between the German military and the Berg Damaras. Ever since the establishment, with the aid of Berg Damara labour, of Wilhelmsfeste at Tsaobis, the German forces employed Berg Damaras as labourers, in the building of their forts, the tending of their gardens, the herding of their stock, and labour in general. Employment with the *Schutztruppe* provided opportunities for a large number of people at the bottom of the social ladder. The relationship that developed between the German forces and those classified as Berg Damaras was obviously not a one-sided one. Apart from benefiting from one another's presence, each side also developed ideas vis-a-vis the nature of the other's social structure and being. The manner in which the German presence could be exploited to their own advantage was an issue that not only occupied the minds of the Herero chiefs, but also the minds of a number of Berg Damara, some of whom saw in the presence of the Germans more than merely increased employment opportunities.

In July of 1894 Cornelius Goraseb, a baptized Berg Damara *Otjira* member of Okombahe who had been associated with the Francois brothers and had assisted in the recruitment of labour for both the German and Cape colonial authorities, travelled to Windhoek. Here, in an audience with Major Leutwein, he stated that in Okombahe the Berg Damara were being oppressed by the Herero and that they wanted to be freed from this oppression.[86] Goraseb's visit

[81] CAD NA Letters received from Damaraland and Walfish Bay, 293 Resident Magistrate Walfish Bay 1889-91, Walfish Bay 20/10/1890 to the Under Secretary for Native Affairs Cape Town.
[82] BAP, RKA 2080 Francois in Otjimbingwe, 15/5/91, to AA.
[83] BAP, RKA 2080, Report Francois in Berlin, 5/8/91, folio 119-75.
[84] H. von Francois, *Nama und Damara*, p. 77. JBG's translation.
[85] BAP, RKA 2150, Leutwein in Windhoek, 11/12/94, to RKA.
[86] Leutwein, *Elf Jahre*, p. 64.

to Windhoek is remarkable in that it provided the basis for the establishment of a new ethnically based polity in the territory.[87] For Leutwein, already influenced by his readings of the Francois brothers and others, saw in Goraseb the solution to two major problems that were troubling his administration at the time, the supply of labour and the submission of Manasse Tjisiseta. Thus when he travelled to Omaruru, on account of the Christie affair, Leutwein was accompanied by Cornelius Goraseb whom he was determined to use to undermine the position and power of Manasse Tjisiseta. One way of doing this was by withdrawing Okombahe from out of Manasse's control and placing it under the control of Cornelius Goraseb, who, needless to say, was more amenable to German control. Thus in return for peace Manasse and his council found themselves forced to agree to the following:

> In accordance with the wishes of Major Leutwein and as proof of his friendly and loyal intentions, Captain Manasse relinquishes into the control of his majesty the German Kaiser, the place Okombahe along with as much grazing land as is necessary for the inhabitants' present number of stock.[88]

Cornelius Goraseb, for his part, was installed as the first paramount chief of Okombahe, for which, in turn he was contractually bound to supply the colonial state with as much labour as the state deemed necessary.[89] Following the signing of the treaty Leutwein noted that Okombahe was the only place where the Damara had been:

> . . . consolidated into a political unit. However even here they had been vassals, of a particular type, strongly oppressed by the Herero. Now that the Damara have moved directly under German authority, we have not only won and gained access to a tribe of workers, we have also ensured that the basis for the complete emancipation of all berg-dammaras as a nation from their previous oppressors has been laid, so that in time they will be treated equally, as the third independent tribe next to the Hereros and Namaquas.[90]

The removal of Okombahe from out of the control of Manasse Tjisiseta and his councillors deprived them of labour and the products of this labour, both of which were used for the maintenance of a standing army, and to control followers through patronage. Furthermore the establishment of a centre within Manasse's area of influence and independent of Manasse's control created a major destabilizing factor in Omaruru politics. Though Herero living in Okombahe had been placed under the control of Daniel Kariko, they were, in due course, forced to leave. This resulted in instability as displaced Herero sought to maintain their rights to land, cattle and water. Added to this, Okombahe now provided a safe haven, within his area of influence, for Manasse's opponents.

Apart from forcing Manasse Tjisiseta and his councillors to part with Okombahe, Leutwein determined the territorial boundaries of the Omaruru polity and ensured that Manasse and his councillors agreed to the establishment

---

[87] See J.B. Gewald, *The Creation of Damaraland, The Creation of a new Ethnicity?*, paper presented at the 'Ethnicity and Nationalism in Southern Africa Conference', held in Grahamstown, South Africa in April 1993.
[88] BAP, RKA 2150, Copy of treaty regarding Okombahe signed 30 November 1894.
[89] BAP, RKA 2150, Leutwein in Windhoek, 11/12/94, to RKA, & ELCIN, VII 22.1 *Okombahe Schriftstucke*, 30/11/94.
[90] BAP, RKA 2150, Leutwein in Windhoek, 11/12/94, to RKA. JBG's translation.

of a permanent German garrison in Omaruru. Following the trial of the executioners of Christie, Leutwein had presented Manasse, Zacharias Zeraua and Samuel Maharero with a map, which he had drawn, which showed their respective territories.[91] Leutwein later admitted that he had left it deliberately vague, so that the respective Herero chieftains would vie for the colonial state's favour with regard to boundary disputes.[92] Furthermore, on the basis of these discussions and in return for continued independence vis-a-vis Samuel Maharero, Manasse agreed to relinquish his claim to Otjimbingwe. Given Manasse's intensive attempts to maintain his influence in the settlement, particularly in the face of numerous Witbooi attacks, this further curtailment of Manasse's power is a fine indicator as to the extent of Leutwein's. Otjimbingwe was now placed under the chieftainship of Zeraua, who was in turn placed under Samuel Maharero.[93]

With the signing of treaties and the effective limitation of Manasse Tjisiseta's power, Leutwein left Omaruru, leaving behind a garrison of twenty-five men and a cannon.[94] Effectively Theodor Leutwein had forced Manasse Tjisiseta into submission, and placed Omaruru firmly within the sphere of German colonial control. Missionary Bernsmann was aware of the predicament Manasse Tjisiseta had been faced with: to acquiesce to German demands or to fight. With this in mind he wrote the following:

> When I consider the course of all the events I must conclude that God has passed judgement and that the two bad murders were turned to good. Through these the major was forced to apply great force in Omaruru, and this was good for the inhabitants who still believed that all the German soldiers were dead, this because they had been told so a thousand times before. The Major, had he come with the thirty men he had originally intended coming with, would have failed to impress and without the pressure, brought to bear upon Manasse and his people by the murder of Christie, he would scarcely have achieved so quickly and so easily that which he achieved with the new treaties, which I, in my opinion, consider good and useful. Samuel Maharero would not have come, if the Major had not called him to come because of the murder of Christie, and the important treaty, regarding the borders, would not have been concluded, or at least not signed that quickly. And whether Manasse would have immediately relinquished Okombahe, if he had been more free internally, I must doubt seriously. It cannot be denied that Manasse and the Omaruru Herero are depressed, but I hope, the depression will be good for them; they deserved it.[95]

Bernsmann's text clearly indicates the changed balance of power in central Namibia. Until Hendrik Witbooi had been effectively neutralized, the German forces were not perceived as being of much importance. However the German victory over Hendrik Witbooi, even if it was largely political, ensured that Germany had become a force to be reckoned with in central Namibia. In the end it was Leutwein's threat of war which had forced Manasse to accept the stringent conditions imposed.

[91] ELCIN, V. Chroniken Omaruru, 1894. BAP, RKA 2150, Leutwein in Windhoek, 11/12/94, to AA.
[92] Leutwein, *Elf Jahre*, p. 64.
[93] BAP, RKA 2150, Leutwein in Windhoek, 11/12/94, to RKA.
[94] ELCIN, V. Chroniken, Omaruru 1894. The four men who had been sentenced to seven months' labour for the death of Christie were used to build the new fort.
[95] *BRMG* 1895, p. 85.

Treaties

In late 1894 Major Leutwein and Samuel Maharero had curtailed the independence of Manasse Tjisiseta and countered his influence and power in central Namibian politics. The threat of German fire-power had ensured that Manasse Tjisiseta had accepted Samuel Maharero's jurisdiction and position as paramount chief of the Herero. Having subjugated Manasse, Samuel Maharero and Major Leutwein sought to further strengthen their positions and extend their influence and power. This they did through concluding a string of treaties with a number of previously independent Herero chieftains who were henceforth placed within the ambit of Samuel Maharero's and ultimately Germany's control. Leutwein, who was under pressure to clear sufficient lands for the settlers, sought to ensure that the lands previously cleared of Herero by Witbooi raiders were reserved for German settlement. To do this the boundaries of Hereroland had to be determined and enforced. In the space of a year, between early 1895 and early 1896, Samuel Maharero and Leutwein, accompanied by contingents of soldiers supported by German cannons, travelled throughout Hereroland, and delivered judgement, concluded treaties, installed chieftains, and, through the delineation of boundaries, circumscribed and decided upon the borders of Hereroland and thus the extent of Samuel Maharero's jurisdiction.

Nicodemus Kavikunua
The first to be graced by the presence of Samuel Maharero and Theodor Leutwein was Nicodemus Kavikunua, Samuel Maharero's *Oruzuo* rival and defeated opponent in the Okahandja succession dispute. In the build-up to the succession dispute, Nicodemus Kavikunua had attempted, as his rival Samuel Maharero had done, to woo the Germans into supporting him in the struggle for the chieftaincy of Okahandja. Much as Samuel Maharero had done, Nicodemus Kavikunua had regularly travelled to Windhoek and held extensive talks with the German authorities aimed at ensuring their support for his claims to the Okahandja chieftaincy. In private Theodor Leutwein was quite prepared to accept Nicodemus Kavikunua's claims to the chieftaincy, yet in public Leutwein was only prepared to accept Nicodemus's status as an independent chieftain.[96] Leutwein believed that it was more beneficial for the German colonial state to have to deal with a politically divided society than with a closed unitary one.[97]

Following Samuel Maharero's expulsion from Okahandja in July 1894, Leutwein had summoned Nicodemus Kavikunua to appear before him in Okahandja. Then, accompanied by cavalry and cannons, he had ridden to the assistance of Samuel Maharero, who, having fled Okahandja, was ensconced on his hilltop at Osona. During the course of Samuel Maharero's installation as paramount chief, Nicodemus Kavikunua failed to appear and thereby effectively ruined his fragile relationship with Theodor Leutwein. Nicodemus, who wisely enough had been awaiting developments from afar in Otjivango, later stated that he had failed to appear, as he had been afraid that Leutwein would have had him shot, in much the same way as Leutwein had had the

96 BAP, RKA 2100, Leutwein in Windhoek, 17/6/94, to RKA.
97 BAP, RKA 2100, Leutwein in Windhoek, 17/6/94, to RKA. JBG's translation.

*Photo 3.2: Chief Nicodemus Kavikunua
surrounded by German soldiers shortly
before his execution in Okahandja 1896*
Source: Namibian National Archives,
Windhoek

Khauas Khoi chief, Andreas Lambert, shot at Naosonobis a few months
earlier.[98] However, once it had become clear that Leutwein had not once again
resorted to summary executions, Nicodemus did come to Okahandja. He
arrived the morning after the two opposing Okahandja camps had held peace
celebrations fuelled by German alcohol. Given the undoubtedly hung-over
condition of the German negotiators and the inhabitants of Okahandja in
general, it is not suprising that Nicodemus's arrival was treated coolly and that
his requests and claims were turned down. Leutwein, who in assisting Samuel
Maharero had achieved a victory in Okahandja, clearly did not find it difficult
to rebuff Nicodemus's claims to the position of paramount chief. Instead
Nicodemus was told by Leutwein to accept the Kaiser's will and that if he did
this he would be made captain over his own lands, much as had occurred with
Zacharias Zeraua of Otjimbingwe.[99] Similarly, Nicodemus's complaints
regarding the establishment of settlers, shops and military stations in his
territory were rejected. Instead Nicodemus Kavikunua, who had attempted to
court the Germans in much the same way as Samuel had, found himself the
victim of the selfsame treaties he had signed whilst attempting to acquire
German assistance for his claims to the Herero paramountcy.[100] As Lindequist
smugly noted: 'Nicodemus had signed the Windhoek protocols and there was
not much that he could do.'[101]

Following his defeat in the Okahandja succession dispute, Nicodemus
Kavikunua lived at Otjihaenena along the White Nossob river among the
Ovambanderu of the chieftain Kahimemua Nguvauva. Even so Nicodemus
Kavikunua and his followers were not beyond the reach of Samuel Maharero
and his allies. In return for his installation as paramount chief of the Herero,

[98] BAP, RKA 2100, Lindequist in Windhoek, 19/1/95, to RKA.
[99] BAP, RKA 2100, Lindequist in Okahandja, 24/7/94, to RKA.
[100] BAP, RKA 2100, Lindequist in Windhoek, 24/7/94, to RKA.
[101] Ibid. JBG's translation.

Samuel Maharero had taken to the signing of a series of agreements and treaties, which dealt with land, water and boundary rights of people nominally under his control as paramount chief of the Herero.[102] During early 1895 German forces, assisted by Herero appointed by Samuel Maharero, began to enforce the signed treaty boundaries of southern Hereroland. Obviously people who had previously never been subject to the chiefs of Okahandja, let alone Samuel Maharero, resisted being moved. Writing about people living between Windhoek and Korras, Lindequist laconically reported:

> Here the cattle chaps [*Viehgasten*] only withdrew when the Major dragged the cannon through the settlement and threatened to shoot if they did not follow.[103]

Not surprisingly there was a lot of opposition to these activities, and, even with a cannon, the forced removals were not a one-way affair. Indeed, shortly after the incident described above, whilst Lindequist was involved in further forced removals 'in Omatame on the White Nossob . . . the *Unterkapitän* Nicodemus [Kavikunua] along with approximately 100 well armed and battle hardened [*kriegsgewohnten*] people arrived to greet me and talk about the border'.[104] Euphemisms aside, Lindequist and his boundary party were effectively taken into custody by Nicodemus Kavikunua and his followers, and taken to Otjihaenena. Force had been met by force.[105] Backed by armed might Nicodemus was able to ensure that talks were held in Otjihaenena and that a number of aspects, particularly regarding the boundary, as delineated by Samuel Maharero and the Germans, were renegotiated. Though Nicodemus Kavikunua was unable to prevent the fountains at Seeis, the brackish waters of which were of crucial importance to Herero cattle herds, from falling into German settler hands, he was able, in this instance, to force an agreement regarding water rights along the Nossob river. It was the ability of Nicodemus Kavikunua to wield true power independently of the nominally paramount Samuel Maharero that forced the Germans to reconsider their policies in eastern Hereroland. He alone, of all the Herero chiefs, was able to mobilize sufficient military might with which to intimidate the Germans. Following this incident it became clear that new arrangements had to be reached with regard to Nicodemus and the eastern Herero.

Determined to exact his revenge, Leutwein wrote to Samuel Maharero, in early May 1895, notifying him of his intention to travel to Nicodemus Kavikunua in Otjihaenena. Resolved not to suffer the fate of Lindequist's boundary commission, Leutwein informed Samuel Maharero that he would be taking along fifty men and a cannon, and requested that Samuel accompany him with about thirty men, 'also with something prominent, so that I alone do not have to hit too much'.[106] At the same time Leutwein wrote to Nicodemus Kavikunua and the remaining eastern chiefs, Kahimemua, Kajata, Omambo

---

[102] Regarding the southern boundary of Hereroland as determined by Samuel Maharero and Imperial Germany, see BAP, RKA 2100, *Vertrag mit Samuel Maharero betr. Festsetzung der Südgrenze des Herero Landes*, 11/7/94 & Leutwein in Windhoek, 13/12/94, to RKA regarding further southern boundary treaty signed 6/12/94.

[103] BAP, RKA 2100, von Lindequist in Windhoek, 19/1/95, to RKA.

[104] BAP, RKA 2100, von Lindequist in Windhoek, 19/1/95, to RKA. JBG's translation.

[105] Leutwein, *Elf Jahre*, p. 68.

[106] NNAW, ZBU 2027, WII, d. 9, Leutwein in Windhoek, 3/4/95, to Samuel Maharero. JBG's translation.

and Tjetjo, informing them that he intended paying them a friendly visit.[107]
Nicodemus Kavikunua's answer to Leutwein bespoke confidence:

> I have received your letter. I am now at the werft of Kahimemua. I have called Tyetyo
> and Omumba; so that we can all be here together to discuss that which bothers you.
> We are all here Kahimemua, Nicodemus, Muambo, Konangati, Tjetyoo, Mbararatyo
> and Kajyata. We await you all here.
> I am Nicodemus Tjamuaha Captain of the Herero.[108]

It is of interest to note that Nicodemus Kavikunua signed his letter as 'Captain
of the Herero' and with the name Tjamuaha, which was the name of his and
Samuel Maharero's grandfather. It is clear that, following the events at
Otjihaenena, Nicodemus felt himself to be in a strong position and, secure
with the evident support of the eastern chiefs, he sought to emphasize to
Leutwein the importance of his position and person. That is, he was, and was
considered by others to be such, still the rightful heir of Maharero, the son of
Tjamuaha.

After having bolstered his forces Leutwein set off with two cannon, fifty
German soldiers and approximately 200 Herero auxiliaries.[109] At the time
Lindequist wrote that the 'main aim of the expedition is to demonstrate to the
eastern Herero and the nearly completely heathen tribe, the Ovambandjeru
once and for all German power and German soldiers'.[110] Given the size of the
German force approaching, it was hardly suprising that Nicodemus Kavikunua
and Kahimemua Nguvauva believed that they were about to be attacked. With
this in mind Otjihaenena, which lay along the White Nossob river, was
abandoned and defensive positions were taken up in the hills surrounding the
settlement on the northern bank of the river. In turn the incoming German
forces took up defensive positions on the southern bank of the river. It was a
stalemate. The German forces failed to overawe the Herero. The Herero position
of strength, and concomitantly Leutwein's desire to achieve a negotiated peace,
is indicated by the fact that negotiations were held in the Herero camp, not
the German camp as had been the case on all previous occasions. Added to
this Leutwein, Lindequist, Samuel Maharero and their aides, in going to the
Herero camp to commence negotiations, had to slog, under the eyes of
approximately 300 Ovambanderu and Herero riflemen, through the hot white
sands of the dry White Nossob river bed, which formed the frontline between
the two camps.[111]

The negotiations lasted for two days. The main topic of discussion was the
issue of the paramount chieftaincy and the extent of this position's authority.
Anxious to avert a costly war, and in keeping with his ideas regarding a
preference for a divided Herero society, Leutwein agreed to give in to and

---

[107] NNAW, ZBU 2027, WII, d. 9, Leutwein in Windhoek, 11/5/95, to Kahimeua, Kaiyata and
Omambo. & WII, d. 14 Leutwein in Windhoek, 26/4/95, to Nicodemus.
[108] NNAW, ZBU 2027, WII d. 14, Nicodemus Tyamuaha in Otjihaenena, 12/5/95, to Leutwein.
JBG's translation.
[109] Leutwein, Elf Jahre, pp. 74–5.
[110] BAP, RKA 2100, von Lindequist in Windhoek, 24/5/95, to RKA.
[111] BAP, RKA 2100, von Lindequist in Windhoek, 24/5/95, to RKA & Leutwein, Elf Jahre, p. 78.
It is interesting to note that later, when writing for a different audience, and seeking then to
convince them of the correctness of his actions, in his published account Leutwein downplayed
the occasion and even claimed that the Ovambanderu and Herero abandoned their positions,
whilst both his and von Lindequist's letters written from the field disprove this.

appease a number of Nicodemus Kavikunua's demands. As a result the negotiations were a success for Nicodemus Kavikunua, as well as the Germans, but a setback for Samuel Maharero and Kahimemua Nguvauva. Leutwein's advocated tactics of divide and rule appeared to work well for the Germans. Most of the animosity and distrust of the Herero leaders present at the discussions was directed towards Samuel Maharero, as opposed to the German government who directly supported Samuel Maharero.[112] In return for territorial concessions Nicodemus Kavikunua was recognized as chief of the eastern Herero, independent of Samuel Maharero; furthermore, the various Herero chiefs living along the Nossob – Mambo, Kajata, Kanangati, Baradjo, and the Ovambanderu under Kahimemua – were all placed under the chieftainship of Nicodemus Kavikunua.[113] Tjetjo, family member of both Samuel Maharero and Nicodemus Kavikunua and *Eanda* heir to the chieftaincy of Okahandja, was recognized as a sub-chief and placed directly under Samuel Maharero.[114] As Theodor Leutwein later noted, Nicodemus Kavikunua had, by the signing of the treaties, been transformed from being 'merely a possessor of large herds of stock into a true chief with lands and subjects'.[115] At the same time Leutwein had effectively sought to deny the existence of a separate Ovambanderu identity by placing them and their chieftain, Kahimemua, directly under the control of Nicodemus – a move that continues to have its impact in the present.

Though not as successful as Samuel Maharero in his pursuit of the paramountcy of the Herero, Nicodemus Kavikunua was, in his use of the German colonial state, able, in the short term, to retain a far greater level of independence. Until open war broke out between supporters of Nicodemus Kavikunua and the *Schutztruppe*, Nicodemus Kavikunua was able to retain a large degree of independence vis-a-vis the German authorities. Indeed it was not until Nicodemus Kavikunua and his supporters had been defeated in battle that the eastern districts were opened to German settlement.[116]

Tjetjo Kandji

Tjetjo Kandji, who lived at Ovikorero, north-east of Okahandja on what is now the farm Harmonie, was a grandson of Tjamuaha, a nephew of Maharero, and a cousin of Nicodemus Kavikunua and Samuel Maharero. He was thus a close family member of Samuel Maharero, and, though not a claimant to the chieftainship of Okahandja, he did inherit most of Maharero Tjamuaha's *Eanda* inheritance. Consequently Tjetjo was a rich man, this in contradistinction to his cousin Samuel Maharero who, though later installed as chief of Okahandja, initially only inherited a brick house from his father's *Eanda* inheritance.

As we have seen, in early 1894 Tjetjo and his 'elder brother' Riarua, Maharero's former commander in chief, united in action against their impoverished family member, Samuel Maharero.[117] As a result, in June 1894,

---

[112] BAP, RKA 2100, von Lindequist in Windhoek, 24/5/95, to RKA.
[113] BAP, RKA 2100, *14/6/95 Vertragsabschluss zwischen Nicodemus und Leutwein*. This was followed by a further protocol 3/7/95 which determined the southern boundaries in eastern Hereroland.
[114] BAP, RKA 2100, Lindequist in Windhoek, 24/5/95, to RKA and Leutwein in Aais, 14/6/95, to RKA.
[115] Leutwein, *Elf Jahre*, p. 77.
[116] NNAW, ZBU 2028, Treaty signed at Aais 15/6/95.
[117] In a letter Tjetjo refers to Riarua as his elder brother. NNAW, ZBU 2027, WII d 12, Tjetjo in Ovikokorero, 6/7/94, to Leutwein. It would appear that things came to a head in early 1894,

Photo 3.3: Chief Tjetjo Kandji in black jacket and his son Traugott Tjetjo on the light horse, possibly in 1895 during boundary discussions
Source: United Evangelical Mission archives, Wuppertal

Samuel Maharero and his followers had been forced to forsake Okahandja for a fortified hilltop at Osona. In much the same way as Nicodemus Kavikunua had done, Tjetjo sought to push his advantage and contacted Major Leutwein, asking him to mediate in his conflict with the usurper Samuel Maharero.[118] At this stage Leutwein had not, as yet, made any firm decisions as to the manner in which the Okahandja chieftainship debate was to be resolved. Consequently Leutwein wrote back in a conciliatory manner, informing Tjetjo that he would willingly negotiate in Tjetjo's conflict with Samuel Maharero.[119] However within six days of this letter Leutwein, accompanied by troops and cannon, had travelled to Okahandja and taken up his position with regard to the Okahandja chieftainship. Leutwein installed Samuel Maharero as paramount chief, not only of Okahandja but of all of Hereroland. Consequently Leutwein's next letter to Tjetjo was written in a completely different manner. Whereas Leutwein had previously referred to Samuel Maharero solely by name, Leutwein now referred to Samuel Maharero as Tjetjo's paramount and lambasted Tjetjo for not having

following the death of Zemoundja Kandirikirira, the brother of Samuel's mother, who had supported Samuel during his struggle for the Okahandja chieftaincy. Tjetjo believed himself to be one of Zemoundja's *Oruzuo* heirs and as such had acquired his five wives and *Oruzuo* cattle. NNAW, ZBU 2027, WII d 12, Eduard Oyamuaha in Okahandja, 10/7/94, to Samuel Maharero; Kaiserliche Distriktschef Eggers in Okahandja, 8/9/94, to Tjetjo & Tjetjo Kandji in Ovikorero, 10/9/94, to Leutwein[?].
[118] NNAW, ZBU 2027 WII d 12, Leutwein in Windhoek, 20/6/94, to Tjetjo, refers to a letter brought by Tjetjo's messenger Johannes Waterboer asking Leutwein to intercede.
[119] Ibid.

obeyed Samuel Maharero's orders.[120] Referring to the course of events in Okahandja Leutwein wrote:

> Riarua has, as it should be, submitted himself to his master, the paramount chief Samuel Maharero, who in turn has forgiven him for his trespasses and has once again granted him his friendship. I hope that I will be able to end the conflict between you and your paramount in a similar manner.[121]

Having decided to back Samuel Maharero, Leutwein embarked upon an aggressive approach to Tjetjo. In letters to Samuel Maharero, Leutwein repeatedly urged him to participate in a campaign against Tjetjo: '. . . let me know if our campaign against Tjetjo is still necessary. So that I will know how many of my people I will need to take along . . . I do not believe it necessary to shoot Tjetjo.'[122] Tjetjo was undoubtedly informed as to the contents of Leutwein's letters and there is no reason to suppose that Tjetjo dismissed them as mere bluff. For one thing Samuel Maharero certainly did not see Leutwein's threats as mere bluff, and this is best reflected in his own words:

> Tjetjo tells me he will come when called. I have told Riarua that he has to fetch Tjetjo when you arrive in Okahandja from Omaruru. Instead of the war, which we wished to wage upon him, I would rather that we wait and see whether or not he will submit himself to me. I ask you, as paramount chief, to deal with him first in peace.[123]

It is well worth noting the irony of the situation and Samuel Maharero's intended snub of Riarua, in ordering him to fetch Tjetjo. By so doing Samuel Maharero emphasized Riarua's subservience to himself, and thus to Leutwein the success of his policy with regard to the paramountcy.

Tjetjo's correspondence indicates that he believed that an attack was imminent, and as such he consistently attempted to defuse the situation by emphasizing his peaceful intentions and urging the German authorities to negotiate with him.[124] Tjetjo's overtures were rebuffed. Instead he received replies which emphasized Leutwein's military activities and prowess:

> I am glad to hear that you are well, I do not doubt that you will keep the peace with Samuel Maharero. Leutwein, with many soldiers from Germany, is at present involved in war against Hendrik Witbooi after which he will visit you.[125]

This aggressive German approach was exacerbated when in late 1894 Samuel Maharero was able to convince the German authorities that Tjetjo had stolen a substantial amount of property from the recently deceased Zemoundja Kandikirira. This man was Samuel Maharero's maternal uncle, and therefore his prime sponsor. Following Kandikirira's death, Samuel Maharero was entitled to his *Eanda* inheritance, and Tjetjo Kandji was entitled to Kandikirira's *Oruzuo* inheritance. At the time of the death of Maharero Tjamuaha, Samuel Maharero had initially inherited nothing but his father's house, whilst Tjetjo

---

[120] NNAW, ZBU 2027, WII d 12, Leutwein in Okahandja, 26/6/94, to Tjetjo.
[121] Ibid.
[122] NNAW, ZBU 2027, WII d 9, Leutwein in Windhoek, 27/10/94, to Samuel Maharero.
[123] NNAW, ZBU 2027, WII d 9, Samuel Maharero in Okahandja, 27/10/94, to Leutwein. JBG's translation.
[124] NNAW, ZBU 2027, WII d 12, Tjetjo Kandji in Ovikorero, 6/7/94 & 10/9/94, to Leutwein.
[125] NNAW, ZBU 2027, WII d 12, von Lindequist in Windhoek, 14/8/94, to Tjetjo, JBG's translation. See also von Lindequist in Windhoek, 14/7/94, to Tjetjo; Eggers in Okahandja, 8/9/94, to Tjetjo and Leutwein in Okorukambe, 10/12/94, to Tjetjo.

Kandji, by virtue of his rights to the *Eanda* inheritance, had inherited Maharero Tjamuaha's cattle herds. Now Samuel Maharero exacted his revenge. Although he had absolutely no rights to the *Oruzuo* inheritance of Semoundja Kandirikira, which had rightfully been inherited by Tjetjo Kandji, Samuel Maharero, through the judicious use of the German forces present, was able to obtain Semoundja's *Oruzuo* inheritance, which had already been allocated to Tjetjo Kandji. Without referring to the issue of inheritance, Samuel Maharero convinced the German authorities that the *Oruzuo* cattle and wives of Kandikirira, who in terms of the inheritance had passed to Tjetjo, had been stolen by Tjetjo. In effect Tjetjo was charged with having stolen two cattleposts and abducted five women. Not suprisingly Lt Eggers, *kaiserlicher Distriktschef*, stationed in Okahandja, summoned Tjetjo to Otjimbinde and wrote the following to Tjetjo:

> To my great surprise I have heard that you have illegally taken from Zemundya and other people of Okandyoze 5 women and 2 posts of cattle. I must urge you to desist from this idea, if you want to keep the friendship of the Major.[126]

To some extent we can glean from Tjetjo's answer his fear and his frustration in attempting to explain the intricacies of *Oruzuo* inheritance:

> . . . I ask you which women have I robbed, because are not the ones that are here my children, and upon their father's death they came here, that is why they came here . . . What should I have done otherwise? As regards the cattleposts, ask the people yourself how they came here . . . As regards Otjombinde, where you tell me I should wait for the Major . . . If I travel to Otjombinde I will write to you so that you will know exactly. That which could make me move to Otjombinde was precisely that which I fear and wonder about, namely the accusations.[127]

With the examples of the fate of Lambert, Witbooi, Riarua and Manasse before him, it is not suprising that Tjetjo failed to keep his appointment with Leutwein in Otjimbinde or later in Okahandja.[128]

In early 1895, prior to embarking upon his trip to Nicodemus Kavikunua in Otjihaenena, Leutwein wrote to Samuel Maharero: 'My dear Samuel . . . let me know whether it is still necessary for us to go to war together against Tjetjo.'[129] At some stage between late 1894 and mid-1895 Samuel Maharero and Tjetjo came to some form of agreement, which resulted in Samuel Maharero feeling strong enough to call off the threat of war. It is likely that the agreement reached was one whereby Tjetjo bought Samuel Maherero's peace by handing over Semoundja Kandikirira's *Oruzuo* cattle herds to Samuel Maharero. Indicative of the changed relations between Samuel Maharero and Tjetjo were the negotiations at Otjihaenena in mid-1895 where Tjetjo fell within Samuel Maharero's camp and was given recognition as an independent chief under Samuel Maharero.[130]

---

[126] NNAW, ZBU 2027 WII d 12, Eggers in Okahandja, 8/9/94, to Tjetjo.

[127] NNAW, ZBU 2027, WII d 12, Tjetjo in Ovikorero, 10/9/94, to Leutwein[?].

[128] NNAW, ZBU 2027, W II d 12, Leutwein in Okorukambe, 10/12/94, to Tjetjo & BAP, RKA 2100, Leutwein in Okahandja, 13/12/94, to RKA.

[129] NNAW, ZBU 2027 WII d 9, Leutwein in Windhoek, 3/4/95, to Samuel Maharero. JBG's translation.

[130] BAP, RKA 2100, Lindequist in Windhoek, 24/5/95, to RKA & Leutwein in Aais, 14/6/95, to RKA.

Kambazembi and the northern chiefs

By May 1895, all those chiefs who had posed a threat to Samuel Maharero's newly acquired position as paramount chief of the Herero had been effectively contained and neutralized. Step by step Samuel Maharero and Theodor Leutwein had frustrated the attempts of the chiefs, Riarua, Manasse Tjisiseta, Nicodemus Kavikunua and Tjetjo Kandji, to jeopardize Samuel's position. In central Hereroland not a single chief remained who could seriously endanger Samuel's position. However, in northern Hereroland one chief remained, and, even though he had been largely beyond the course of events in central Hereroland, he did have the wealth and influence, to affect, if he had wanted to, the course of events in central Hereroland. The name of this fabulously rich chief was Kambazembi, who lived north of Okahandja in the area of Otjozondjupa near the Waterberg.[131] Caught up by the course of events in central Hereroland, Kambazembi and the remaining northern chiefs had remained largely beyond the interest of Samuel Maharero and Theodor Leutwein. It was not until the second half of 1895 that Samuel Maharero and Leutwein could undertake action and actually embark upon a trip to the northern chiefs.

Already in the 1870s Kambazembi was reported to be a rich man. In 1877 he was reported to have had no less than 12,000 followers and 60 to 70 *Ozonganda*, homesteads.[132] These figures fluctuated with the changing seasons, Francois reported fifteen years later that Kambazembi had 2320 followers and 23 *Ozonganda*.[133] Either way Kambazembi is remembered as being a generous patron who provided cattle, with which to reestablish herds, to many impoverished Hereros, particularly during the many cattle raids of the various Nama chieftains.[134] During the numerous raids by Hendrik Witbooi's commandos in the 1880s, cattle which belonged to Maharero and other southern Herero chiefs were given over into the care of Kambazembi's cattle herds. As such Kambazembi was an incredibly rich man and is remembered as such. Hugo von Francois who visited Kambazembi at Okamaye in December 1890 described Kambazembi's *Ozonganda* as follows:

> It was beautifully sited in the shade of a small forest. A piece of land 600 by 300 metres was enclosed by thorn bushes. In the middle there was a small kraal of about 300 metres in length for calves and small stock. Along the inner borders of the enclosure lay the huts of the 32 wives of the chief with behind them, in the corners of the enclosure the huts of the slaves [*Sklaven*] and on one of the longer sides the hut of the Chief.[135]

---

[131] BAP, RKA 2100, Leutwein in Okahandja, 13/12/95, to RKA.

[132] BAP, RKA 2101, Typed document entitled *Zur Frage der Nordgrenze des Herero-landes*.

[133] BAP, RKA 2080, *Rapportage von Südwest-Afrika*, Francois, 15/8/91, to auswertiges Amt Kolonialabtheilung Berlin.

[134] See *Warriors, Leaders, Sages and Outcasts in the Namibian Past*, edited by A. Heywood, B. Lau and R. Ohly (Windhoek 1992) pp. 152–3.

[135] H. von Francois, *Nama und Dama*, p. 134. The reference to slaves by Hugo von Francois is intriguing. Did Francois mean *Ovatjimba*, Damara, or Khoi-san dependents, or did he really mean slaves. This may well have been possible, given Kambazembi's close links with both traders and hunters from around Lake Ngami and the Kruger family who were also involved in the slave trade. The recent work by B. Morton indicates that in the nineteenth century there was a substantial amount of slave trading in north-western Botswana. To what extent this slave trade extended into Namibia is as yet unknown. Von Francois's remarks might indicate that slavery was present in Kambazembi's area of jurisdiction in the late nineteenth century.

Following the death of Maharero, Kambazembi initially supported Samuel Maharero's claim to the chieftaincy of Okahandja.[136] This is far from surprising given that Kambazembi had so many of Maharero's cattle in his care which, had one of Samuel Maharero's more powerful rivals become chief, he would have had to return. Initially Samuel Maharero was in no position to pose any threat to Kambazembi's position; indeed he travelled to Kambazembi seeking his assistance in the Okahandja chieftaincy dispute in early 1891. However, by late 1894, with Samuel Maharero and Leutwein working in alliance, the balance of power had changed.

In late 1894 having neutralized Manasse Tjisiseta, Leutwein wrote to Kambazembi and informed him of his intention to visit and warned: 'We have signed a treaty with Maharero and this applies to you too though all the reports I have received until now only speak well of you.'[137] In April 1895 Leutwein contacted Samuel Maharero and asked him to accompany him on his intended visit to Kambazembi.[138] However, this intended visit was cut short by the events of Otjihaenena in May of 1895. As a result of the negotiations at Otjihaenena, between Nicodemus Kavikunua, Kahimemua Nguvauva and Tjetjo Kandji on the one hand and Samuel Maharero and Theodor Leutwein on the other, a number of major decisions regarding land, boundary and chieftaincy rights were taken. Kambazembi felt that he was being bypassed. Throughout June of 1895 Kambazembi sought contact with Samuel Maharero and Leutwein.[139] Eventually Kambazembi sent one of his sons to Windhoek asking Leutwein to visit him.[140] Leutwein let it be known that he intended coming in peace, though he advised Samuel to make sure that he took along as large a contingent of horsemen as possible.[141]

In early August 1895 Leutwein set off from Windhoek on what was to be a round trip of the German colony's northern marches to the south of the Etosha pan. Indicative of Theodor Leutwein's skills as a careful statesman is the fact that the trip commenced only after Manasse Tjisiseta had been successfully lured to Windhoek with the promise of medical treatment.[142] At Okahandja Leutwein was joined by Samuel Maharero. On their approach to the Waterberg they were met by Kambazembi's two eldest sons Kainjumjua and Salatiel who escorted them to their father's settlement.[143] From the moment of their arrival Kambazembi sought to downplay his political power and position. Instead Kambazembi claimed that he was only a 'king of the cattle' and that he had no political ambitions beyond that. Kambazembi's willingness to forgo any political claims to either Samuel's position or to areas to the north of Otjozondjupa, which were nominally under the control of the SWACO, but had not been determined yet, meant that the 'koning van die Beeste' and his people were left largely undisturbed by Leutwein and Samuel Maharero.[144] As a result of Kambazembi's foresight he was left in peace and Samuel Maharero, as

[136] BAP, RKA 2100, H. von Francois in Walvisbay, 10/2/91, to RKA.
[137] NNAW, ZBU 2027 WII d 11, Leutwein in Okahandja, 5/12/94, to Kambazembi. JBG's translation.
[138] NNAW, ZBU 2027 WII d 9, Leutwein in Windhoek, 3/4/95, to Samuel Maharero.
[139] ELCIN, *I Konferenzen und Synoden, I 1.3 1873–1905 Protokollbuch der Konferenzen in Hereroland.*
[140] NNAW, ZBU 2027 WII d 11, Leutwein in Windhoek, 1/7/95, to Kambazembi.
[141] NNAW, ZBU 2027, WII d 9, Samuel Maharero in Okahandja, 17/7/95, to Leutwein.
[142] BAP, RKA 2150, Das Gebiet von Omaruru, Leutwein in Windhoek, 30/7/95, to RKA.
[143] BAP, RKA 2100, Von Lindequist in Windhoek, 24/8/95, to RKA.
[144] Leutwein, *Elf Jahre*, pp. 80–2.

paramount chief of the Herero, was able, two weeks later, to sign a series of far-reaching boundary agreements with the SWACO. These agreements, which determined the northern boundary of Herero territory, as well as allocated land and mineral rights to the SWACO, were signed on 21 August 1895 in Grootfontein.[145]

From Grootfontein Leutwein and Samuel Maharero continued their trip through to Tsumeb and Otavi. Leutwein noted that in this area there were no Herero to be found and that this was due to the activities of Bushmen who lived in this area. The mines of Otavi were long known to have been under the control of Bushmen. Those seeking copper were forced to pay tribute to the Bushmen who controlled the mines.[146] An indication of Bushman power in the area can to some extent be gleaned from the fact that at both Naidas and Ghaub treaties were signed with Bushman chiefs.[147]

From Naidas through to Outjo, Leutwein and Samuel Maharero, assisted by no less than eighty mounted German troopers, enforced the newly concluded northern boundary agreements. All Herero encampments found living to the north of the newly concluded boundary were ordered to move south, into 'Herero territory'.[148] At Outjo Leutwein concluded further boundary agreements with the Topnaar and Swartbooi chiefs of Fransfontein before travelling on to Omaruru.[149] A direct result of this trip was that Leutwein decided to establish a military post at Outjo, on the western trade route leading from Omaruru to Omabalantu and from there to Mossamedes.[150] Thereby Hereroland's last independent outlet to the wider world was cut off. Furthermore, as Leutwein noted, Samuel's position as paramount chief of the Herero had been emphasized: 'the escort of 80 German mounted men does a lot to increase the stature of the *Oberhäuptling* Samuel Maharero'.[151]

Upon the completion of their round trip Samuel Maharero and Leutwein had signed a string of treaties which effectively delineated the boundaries of Hereroland and the specific areas of authority within this territory. It was when Leutwein assisted by Samuel Maharero, under pressure of the land companies and the incoming settlers, attempted to enforce these new boundaries that conflict broke out. Between 1896 and 1897 various Herero chieftains sought to shrug off the ever-encroaching net which Leutwein and Samuel had thrown upon them. The manner in which this took place and the effects that this had will form the following section of this chapter.

Treaty enforcement

Signing treaties was one thing; enforcing them another. The territories which

[145] BAP, RKA 2100, Leutwein in Grootfontein, 29/8/95, to RKA & Leutwein, *Elf Jahre*, pp. 81–7.
[146] Chapter three of R. Gordon, *The Bushmen Myth: the Making of a Namibian Underclass*, (Boulder, San Francisco, Oxford 1992), entitled 'Bushman Copper and Autonomy', has a fine discussion of Bushman control of copper mines in the Otavi district.
[147] BAP, RKA 2100 Leutwein in Otjimbingwe, 19/10/95, to RKA, reports installing in Ghaub '. . . Herero bastard Jak Krueger as captain of the Berg Damara and bushmen as well as the Bushman Aribib at Naidas'. See also Leutwein, *Elf Jahre*, p. 88.
[148] Leutwein, *Elf Jahre*, p. 88.
[149] BAP, RKA 2100, Leutwein in Otjimbingwe, 12/10/95, to RKA.
[150] Ibid.
[151] Ibid., JBG's translation.

were now formally outside Herero control had not been vacated by their Herero inhabitants. Thus, they could not be opened to German settlers until the Herero had been driven off the lands which were now no longer officially in their possession. However, it was when German authorities, working in alliance with Herero allies, sought to enforce the various conditions stipulated in the assorted boundary treaties that disagreements surfaced and armed conflict broke out between the German authorities and their allies on the one hand, and the various Herero groups on the other hand.

Not surprisingly, as the conditions of the various boundary treaties were enforced, and the Herero were forced into ever closer confinement, the population pressure of Herero and their stock in the territories nominally still in their possession increased. As the noose of treaties tightened, and access to water, grazing, game and lands became ever more contested, tension rose. Apart from resulting in increased pressure on natural resources, the forced removals of Herero stock into ever smaller areas meant that infectious stock diseases would soon be able to run riot. With nowhere to turn to, the effective quarantining of stock became impossible.

Even before the outbreak of armed conflict in March 1896, tensions rose continually during 1894 and 1895, as Samuel Maharero asserted new-found authority. As the paramount chief of the Herero, Samuel Maharero claimed jurisdiction over people and territories never before controlled by the chiefs of Okahandja. The new-found subjects of Samuel Maharero found themselves in a position where they no longer had recall to their own chiefs. Added to this, due to the newly delineated boundaries of Hereroland, it was no longer possible for disaffected subjects, as they had done in the past, to 'vote with their feet' and abandon Samuel Maharero for another chief. The impact of the changed balance of power that had come about in Hereroland is well illustrated in the case of the Omaruru sub-chiefs, Katarre and Daniel Kariko. The men were sub-chiefs of Manasse Tjisiseta of Omaruru. Due to the changed circumstances that had come about in the course of 1895, the two men were no longer able to seek redress from their chief Manasse Tjisiseta, who had been cowed in late 1894.

Katarre

In late 1895 Samuel Maharero and Major Leutwein, accompanied by cannon and cavalry, delineated and sought to enforce the northern frontier of Hereroland. Apart from fulfilling the wishes of the land companies, the German authorities had their own agenda for seeking to enforce this boundary. In keeping with Leutwein's policy of divide and rule, Leutwein was anxious to prevent contact, and thus the development of an alliance between the Herero chieftains of Hereroland and the Ovambo kingdoms that lay to their north. An added aspect was that the German administration wanted to gain control of the trade leading to and from the north. To this end a military fort was established at Outjo, along the main western trading route that led from Omaruru to the Ovambo kingdoms.

The settlement of Katarre, one of the sub-chiefs of Manasse Tjisiseta of Omaruru, straddled the trade route that led from Omaruru to Ovamboland. Acting on reports supplied by Francois and missionary Rautanen, a man who particularly feared an alliance between Kambonde, the king of the Ondonga kingdom in Ovamboland, and the Herero chief Katarre, Leutwein sought to subjugate Katarre. In his official dispatches Leutwein noted that he wanted to punish Katarre because he was 'the swindler of all white traders and travellers'.[152] As such, Katarre was charged with having stolen a chest belonging to the Cape trader Jan Lambert, and, though he protested his innocence, Katarre was found guilty, fined eighteen cattle, and all of his firearms were confiscated.[153] Katarre, believing himself to still be subject to his chief Manasse Tjisiseta, lodged a protest with him in Omaruru. Manasse Tjisiseta, in keeping with his role as Katarre's *Omuhona*, sought to defend his subject. In a letter to Leutwein, Manasse Tjisiseta supported Katarre's claims of innocence and wrote, 'from all that I have heard about the man who stole the chest I must conclude that everything that Katarre has told you about the chest is true'.[154] In answer, Leutwein deliberately snubbed Manasse Tjisiseta by referring to the affair in a postscript to a letter wherein he had harangued Manasse Tjisiseta for failing to move his subjects back from the northern Hereroland boundary. Leutwein's postscript deliberately emphasized Manasse Tjisiseta's subservience to Samuel Maharero:

> Regarding the confiscation of Katarre's weapons. As you were not present in Pallafontein I requested the paramount chief to take over your position and duties. This I did so that the Herero could see that the confiscation of weapons occurred in keeping with law and custom.[155]

Daniel Kariko

As noted earlier, in November of 1894 the settlement of Okombahe, and the lands immediately surrounding it, was removed from the control of chief Manasse Tjisiseta of Omaruru. During the rains Herero pastoralists living in Okombahe tended to leave their permanent water sources and trek to pastures with temporary water sources which were accessible only during the rainy seasons. Berg Damara horticulturalists, who lived in symbiosis with the Herero pastoralists at Okombahe, remained at the permanent water sources to tend to their gardens. For a variety of reasons a number of these Berg Damara horticulturalists saw themselves as the subjects of rich Herero pastoralists. This symbiotic relationship was one which the German authorities found untenable. In terms of German thinking at the time, the Berg Damara were a subjected and enslaved people. A people that needed to be freed from their enslavement so that they could develop as a counter – naturally allied to the Germans – to Herero and Nama power. Furthermore, once freed from perceived Herero enslavement they could supply the labour so desperately sought after by the incoming German authorities and settlers. It was on the basis of this thinking, along with the pure *realpolitik* of Leutwein, which sought to weaken Manasse Tjisiseta and Herero power as a whole, that led to Leutwein's insistence that Okombahe be removed from the control of Manasse Tjisiseta of Omaruru. In exchange for agreeing to supply labour to the German colonial authorities, Cornelius Goraseb of Okombahe was installed as the first paramount chief of the Berg Damara. At the same time Daniel Kariko, a cousin of Manasse Tjisiseta of Omaruru, who had been in charge of the settlement prior to November 1894,

---

[152] BAP, RKA 2101, Leutwein in Windhoek, 25/12/95, to RKA. JBG's translation.
[153] NNAW, ZBU 2027, WII d 10, Leutwein in Outjo, 9/9/96, to Manasse.
[154] NNAW, ZBU 2027, W II d 10, Manasse in Omaruru, 16/9/96 & 26/9/96, to Leutwein. JBG's translation.
[155] NNAW, ZBU 2027, W II d 10, Leutwein in Okombahe, 2/10/96, to Manasse. JBG's translation.

was ousted as chief of the whole settlement and was henceforth only permitted jurisdiction over the Herero population resident in Okombahe.[156]

By January 1895, German officials, operating out of the newly established military garrison in Omaruru, had begun voicing their dislike of Daniel Kariko. Thus *Leutnant* Volkmann, who travelled to Okombahe in December 1894, described his meeting with Daniel Kariko, in a letter to Leutwein, as follows:

> I could immediately see that the captain Daniel Karriko, who was a blown-up frog with a big mouth in everything and who suppressed the Berg Damaras severely, was in no way suited to govern together with Cornelius and that the struggles/strife would not be resolved. I told him therefore that he could no longer be the captain of Okombahe, but that he was only captain of the Herero in Okombahe. Furthermore that your excellency [*Eurer Hochwohlgeborenen*] had given the place for use to Cornelius.[157]

A few months later in early 1895, once the rains had begun and the garrison fort completed, *Leutnant* Volkmann, who had been left in charge of the German garrison in Omaruru, travelled throughout the areas now officially under his jurisdiction. Volkmann reported that the Hereros had left their gardens in charge of their Berg Damara servants. This was a situation which he found untenable and which he resolved to alter. Henceforth the gardens, lands and resident Berg Damaras were removed from Herero, and thus Daniel Kariko's jurisdiction, and placed under the direct jurisdiction of the German authorities.[158] Not surprisingly Daniel Kariko's relationship with the German authorities was not improved by this affair. However, Volkmann's dislike of Daniel Kariko was soon to increase even more.

In late July of 1895, Manasse Tjisiseta arrived in Windhoek for medical treatment. As a gesture of his goodwill, Manasse Tjisiseta brought along fourteen Berg Damaras whom he handed over to the colonial authorities for labour purposes.[159] Needless to say, the Germans, who were desperately short of labour, were pleased with the gift. However, for Daniel Kariko, Manasse's gift of Berg Damara labourers had totally different implications.

Prior to travelling to Windhoek, Manasse had pondered on how to placate the Germans. The events of November 1894, when Herero prisoners were used as labourers, and Okombahe had been granted autonomy in exchange for labour, had emphasized to Manasse Tjisiseta and his council the German hunger and need for labour. This was further underscored when Lindequist wrote the following to Manasse:

> My dear captain I have one more request to make to you, you promised . . . Volkmann [the German officer in charge of the garrison in Omaruru] a number of Berg Damaras as Labour for Windhoek. Volkmann has told me that once the ones that had been brought together by you, were brought to him they ran away. Here they receive good food and also money. As we need them badly, I ask you, to send along, as quickly as possible, about 20 energetic labourers, failing which you can bring them along when you come here yourself.[160]

[156] BAP, RKA 2150, Treaty regarding Okombahe of 30/11/94.
[157] NNAW, ZBU 2027, Volkmann in Omaruru, 1/1/95, to Leutwein. JBG's translation.
[158] BAP, RKA 2150, Volkmann in Omaruru, 5/3/95, to RKA.
[159] BAP, RKA 2150, Leutwein in Windhoek, 30/7/95, to RKA.
[160] NNAW, ZBU 2027, WII d 10, von Lindequist in Windhoek, 27/6/95, to Manasse. JBG's translation.

With this in mind Manasse Tjisiseta ordered the Herero chief in charge of Okombahe, Daniel Kariko, to raid for Berg Damara labour. Kariko's activities did not pass the Germans unnoticed. In an official statement, entitled, *Report on what was done by the Herero to the Berg Damaras in the Bockberge*, Sergeant Herz reported his findings as follows:

> On 11/7 the Berg Damara Richard told me that at the Bockberge stock had been slaughtered and stolen by Hereros . . . I rode to Bockberge where I was met by *voorman* [foreman] Kurirab and other aged men 20–22 in all. After I had warned them to tell the truth Kurirab began to tell as follows: Daniel Kariko was present in Omaruru (day undetermined) Manasse spoke to Daniel, 'I am now going to Windhoek, the *Herr Major* [Leutwein] will ask me as to the labourers, therefore I will send you to the Bockberge so that soon some [labourers] will come.' Daniel arrived in Bangibloed (Otjipane) and sent 3 of his and 7 of Saul's own people under the leadership of the old Joseph (the last named being a councillor of Daniel [Kariko]) with the order to capture and collect many of our young men and bring them to him. All 10 Herero were armed with firearms, and arrived at one of our cattleposts, which was situated halfway between here and Ameib. The post people [servants at the cattlepost] gave them their *Unkis* [small field bulbs] and milk as a sign of friendship. Five of the Hereros went into the veld and drove the stock onto the post. Without asking the post people they slaughtered 2 *karpater* [sheep] drank honey beer and then burnt down the werft (about 20 pontoks). All the blankets and skins which the post people possessed, as well as 10 big pots of honey beer, valued at 150 mark were taken away or robbed by the flames. Approximately 100 small stock and all the living beings which were to be found at the post, were taken along. Then they arrived at the second post (day unknown) where they slaughtered three sheep, burnt down the werft, honey beer to the value of 45 mark and tobacco valued at 24 mark was taken . . . the firearms of the post people were taken.
>   . . . Joseph took 8 labourers from here, these had been collected at the cattleposts.[161]

Although Kurirab was shot at twice during the course of the three-day raid, he followed and confronted the leader of the raid, Joseph, who was one of Daniel Kariko's councillors. Having presented Joseph with a sheep, Kurirab was able to gain an audience with Joseph and Daniel Kariko: 'Upon my complaints he [Kariko] answered me: ". . . It is all the fault of Manasse and the *Herr Major*."'[162]

The writings of *Leutnant* Volkmann, the German officer in charge of the garrison in Omaruru, indicate that he knew full well what the background was to Daniel Kariko's labour raid: 'When the *Kaiserliches Landeshauptmannschaft* wrote to Manasse directing him to send labourers he ordered Daniel [Kariko] to gather these together.'[163] Even though the raid had been initiated in response to German demands for labour, Volkmann pressed charges of murder against Kariko.[164] Charged with murder, Daniel Kariko failed to appear in Omaruru when summoned. Instead, in a gesture extremely illustrative of Herero perceptions regarding the colonial authorities, Kariko sought to appease the Germans by presenting Leutwein with a further fourteen labourers.

Herrn Major Leutwein in Windhoek . . . This is to inform you that I am sending you

---

[161] NNAW, ZBU 2027 WII d 10, *19/7/95 Station Okombahe Bericht über Sachen welche von Hereros an BDs im Bockberge verübt wurden.* JBG's translation.
[162] NNAW, ZBU 2027, W II d 10, *Bericht über Sachen welche von Hereros an Bergdamaras im Bockberge verübt wurden.* JBG's translation.
[163] NNAW, ZBU 2027, W II d 10, Volkmann in Omaruru, 6/8/95, to Leutwein. JBG's translation.
[164] Ibid.

14 of my people who until now have worked for me. I only have these people, I have
no more. I will lend them to you to help on the roads but please return them when
you have finished with them. When their work is completed write me a letter
informing me that you are sending them back to me, furthermore write to me how
much money they have earned. As I have told you previously in Omaruru these are
my very own servants [*Knechte*], who are in my service, and are not people such as
the bergdamaras at Okombahe who have been freed. Finally I ask of you to please
look after these people well.[165]

The colonial state was seen as a labour-hungry institution, which indeed it
was.[166]

Not only had Daniel Kariko been placed in charge of Okombahe by Manasse
Tjisiseta of Omaruru, he also claimed and possessed rights to a number of
cattleposts and settlements in the Bockberge, Erongo mountains. As had been
the case with Okombahe it was believed that once Herero control of these
settlements and cattleposts had been lifted, then Berg Damaras would be freed
to labour for German colonial interests. In a report entitled, *Report on the
availability of labour from Okombahe*, Volkmann reported on the availability of
labour in the Bockberge:

> In the Backberge [*sic*] (Erongo mountains) a number of Bergdamara werften are to
> be found, of which Omandumba is the biggest. It is situated on a big plateau in the
> mountains east of the road Okambahe to Ameib and a number of hours east of
> Tumeb. In the mountains a number of scattered Bergdamaras live wild, for which
> the Hereros have great fear. They are bothered by no one. Omandumba has a fairly
> well stocked small stock population and in the mountains even a number of cattle
> posts.
>
> Daniel Kariko, a chief who Manasse had originally placed in charge of Okombahe,
> has during the course of time enserfed and repressed the Berg Damaras who possess
> stock. He has declared that the land belongs to him, all the stock is his possession
> and the people are his servants [*Knechten*]. As Daniel is an extremly authoritative
> [*gewalttätiger*] person nobody has previously dared to voice disagreement with him.
>
> In order to maintain the appearance of rights to these Berg Damaras, Daniel has
> given some numbers of stock into the care of these people.[167]

Volkmann concluded his report by recommending that Omandumba be placed
under the control of Manasse Tjisiseta: 'Daniel Kariko no longer has anything
to say there. The Berg Damaras stay living there as people of Cornelius
[Goraseb] the Hereros are warned to live with them in peace. Possibly the place
can be declared a neutral area.'[168] Consequently Daniel Kariko was ordered to
relinquish all his authority in the Bockberge to Manasse Tjisiseta and Cornelius
Goraseb.

It is clear that the German authorities saw Daniel Kariko primarily in terms
of labour, and specifically as a blockage to the effective supply of labour. Added
to this, the German authorities sought to 'tidy up' the ethnic map of
Hereroland. Herero were to be placed under Herero, Berg Damara under Berg
Damara and all of them were to be under the ultimate authority of the Germans.
In line with this thinking and in flagrant violation of the Okombahe protocols

---

[165] NNAW, ZBU 2027, W II d 10, Daniel Kariko in Okombahe, 12/7/91, to Leutwein. JBG's
translation.
[166] See particularly, NNAW, ZBU 2027, Volkmann in Omaruru, 12/5/95, to Leutwein.
[167] NNAW, ZBU 2027, WII d 10, Volkmann in Omaruru, 6/8/95, to Leutwein. JBG's translation.
[168] Ibid.

of November 1894, Leutwein proclaimed that Daniel Kariko no longer had any say whatsoever in Okombahe, and all the Herero living there had to leave the settlement immediately.[169]

Through the activities of Leutwein, Volkmann and Manasse Tjisiseta, Daniel Kariko was dispossessed of the settlements and lands associated with Okombahe and Omandumba, and thus of land which could be used for patronage and as a source of exploitable and exportable Berg Damara labour. Anxious to retain a measure of independence, Daniel Kariko sought to strengthen his northern flank and retain his independent access to ammunition. To do this, Daniel Kariko trekked north, in late 1895, and entered into negotiations with Kambonde the king of the southern Ovambo kingdom of Ondonga. Apart from seeking permission for his followers to withdraw into and settle upon the territory of Kambonde, Kariko also sought to secure an independent and dependable source of arms and ammunition.[170] Since 1884, when the trader Eriksson had abandoned Omaruru and established himself in Mossamedes, the Ovambo kingdoms, which were in direct contact with the Angolan harbour of Mossamedes, had become the main source of arms for the northern Herero chieftains.[171] The wells at Namutoni, on the southern fringes of the Etosha pan, formed one of the main centres in this trade. Apart from Daniel Kariko and his allies, the sons of Kambazembi also utilized their links with the Ovambo kingdoms for arms trading.[172] Daniel Kariko was successful in his negotiations with Kambonde. Missionary Schaar, stationed at Okombahe, reported that all the Herero formerly living at Okombahe were trekking north in late 1895 and early 1896.[173] It is probable that the Herero, referred to by Leutwein in a letter of complaint to Manasse for having transgressed across the northern boundaries of Hereroland near Namutoni in 1896, were these selfsame followers of Daniel Kariko trekking north.[174]

Apart from trading and negotiating with the Ovambo kingdoms, Daniel Kariko, in an effort to strengthen his position further, reestablished his contacts with a section of the Swartboois at Fransfontein and Sesfontein.[175] Until 1885 the Swartboois had been at war with the Herero of Omaruru. Following peace negotiations, in which Daniel Kariko played a central role, the Swartboois had concentrated on and developed links with groups living in north-western Namibia and southern Angola.[176] It was these links that Daniel Kariko, in

[169] BAP, RKA 2101, Leutwein in Windhoek, 25/12/95, to RKA & Leutwein, *Elf Jahre*, p. 91.

[170] NNAW, ZBU 437, D. IV. C. 4, Hartmann in Otavi, 8/12/95, to Leutwein.

[171] For a detailed overview of the shift in trade away from Omaruru to Walvisbay and the Cape towards Mossamedes, the Kalahari and the Transvaal, see Harri Siiskonen, *Trade and Socioeconomic Change in Ovamboland, 1850–1906, Studia Historica* 35 (Helsinki 1990) pp. 158–63.

[172] NNAW, ZBU 437, D. IV. c. 4, Volkmann in Omaruru, 27/4/96, to Leutwein. This arms trade was well established by the 1860s and presumably led in part to the considerable wealth of Kambazembi.

[173] *BRMG* 1896, p. 132.

[174] NNAW, ZBU 2027 W II d 10, Leutwein in Okombahe, 2/10/96, to Manasse.

[175] NNAW, ZBU 437, D. IV. c. 4, Hartmann in Otavi, 8/12/95, to Leutwein & Volkmann in Omaruru, 27/4/96, to Leutwein.

[176] Particularly well situated to supply Daniel Kariko with armaments was Vita Tom. He had moved into southern Angola after Omaruru had gone into economic decline in the early 1880s. In southern Angola Vita Tom had set himself up as a war-lord engaged and employed successively by the Boer community and Portuguese authorities in warfare against the Ovakwanyama and Ongandjera, Ovambo kingdoms. For a fine overview of the life and times of Kaptein Oorlog see E.L.P. Stals and A. Otto-Reiner, *Oorlog en Vrede aan die Kunene; Die verhaal van Kaptein Vita Tom 1863–1937*, (Windhoek 1990).

seeking to secure his northern flank, sought to tap into and expand.

Apart from seeking friendship, refuge and armaments from communities along his northern frontier, Daniel Kariko also sought to secure the friendship, assistance and armaments of Cape colonial business interests and through them ultimately of Great Britain. One of the ways in which Daniel Kariko sought to do this was through the supply of Berg Damara labour and slaughter stock to the Damaraland Guano Company, which had a company base at Cape Cross on the Atlantic coast.[177] Here, since the 1840s, and at other places all along the coast, centuries of accumulated guano had been scraped off the rocks and shipped throughout the world as fertilizer. Conditions in the guano camps along the coast were harsh, and it was with difficulty that people could be induced to work there. In exchange for trade goods, news of the world and armaments, Daniel Kariko provided the Damaraland Guano Company with much needed labour and slaughter stock. In May 1896, Daniel Kariko and eight of his councillors rode out of the Namib desert and into the small settlement at Cape Cross. Mounted upon riding oxen, the men were dressed in military-style fatigues, and on their upper left arms they wore armbands of red, white and blue. The German non-commissioned officer Bahr, who had recently been stationed in Cape Cross, later wrote:

> When I remarked that instead of the black [which would have made up the German colours] they were wearing a blue band, they [the Herero] replied that they were English colours . . . Accompanied by an Englishman they visited the Guano camps [*Guanolagern*]. They also visited the schooner *Alert* which was lying here at anchor.
> . . . I believe that the only reason for their coming here was to acquire ammunition. The Hereros wish to return later with the English trader Labather [Sabata].[178]

Kariko followed up his call to Cape Cross with a visit to Okombahe, the settlement which had only recently been taken from his control. One of the German soldiers stationed in Okombahe later reported that when he inquired as to the armbands being worn Kariko replied: 'I should know better than he did, he [Kariko] was now an English subject.'[179]

Little more than a month later Daniel Kariko, ten of his councillors and a herd of slaughter cattle revisited Cape Cross, and Bahr reported the following:

> . . . they had come to trade slaughter stock. They wanted weapons in exchange, as Elers [employee of Damaraland Guano Company] did not want to give any [*sic*]. As Elers told me he badly wanted to buy the slaughter stock. I therefore allowed the request.[180]

Bahr's words indicate that as late as 1896 Daniel Kariko could, and still did, rely on his contacts at Cape Cross for the import of arms and ammunition, and that German authorities were in effect powerless to do anything about this. The German authorities had long suspected that Daniel Kariko was acquiring arms via the Cape, and had repeatedly accused the British Magistrate in

---

[177] NNAW, ZBU 436, D. IV. c. 1, Resident Magistrate Cleverley in Walvisbay, 7/6/96, to Leutwein.
[178] NNAW, ZBU 437, Bahr in Cape Cross, 12/5/96, to *Kaiserliche Distriktskommando* in Otjimbingwe. JBG's translation.
[179] NNAW, ZBU 437, Statement Carl Richard Dähnel taken down in Omaruru, 19/8/96. JBG's translation.
[180] NNAW, ZBU 437, *Abschrift aus dem Berichte des Feldwebels Bohr vom 2 Juli 1896. J. N. 40.* JBG's translation.

Walvisbay of complicity in the smuggle of arms to Daniel Kariko.[181] However, it was not until they had gained a measure of control in the affairs of the Omaruru polity that they were able to undertake any action against Daniel Kariko.

In much the same way that he had exploited Samuel Maharero's differences with his subjects, so Theodor Leutwein sought to exploit Manasse Tjisiseta's differences with Daniel Kariko. Following the Christie affair, Manasse Tjisiseta, in return for peace, had been forced to rescind his control over the Berg Damara population of Okombahe, and in so doing had effectively cast his sub-chief Daniel Kariko adrift. In the two years following the Christie affair, Theodor Leutwein used the issue of the Berg Damara population of the Omaruru polity as a chisel with which, bit by bit, parts of the polity were removed from Manasse Tjisiseta's control. For each of the Omaruru polity's alleged infringements of German rule, Daniel Kariko became the 'fall guy' – the blood offer which was expected in exchange for peace and the continued existence of Manasse Tjisiseta as an independent chief. Effectively Theodor Leutwein exploited Manasse Tjisiseta's power and desire for peace to be able to get at and undermine Daniel Kariko.

Once news of Daniel Kariko's visits to Cape Cross became known in Windhoek, orders for his immediate arrest were issued.[182] A factor influencing this decision, and allowing for its feasibility, was that, at the time of his visits to Cape Cross, Daniel Kariko had withdrawn himself and his followers from Manasse Tjisiseta's authority. Indeed it was Manasse Tjisiseta who, anxious to improve his standing with the Germans, first informed the German authorities as to Daniel Kariko's whereabouts, his military status, and requested his arrest.[183] The German authorities, anxious to further the split that had emerged between Manasse Tjisiseta and Daniel Kariko, acceded to Manasse Tjisiseta's request on condition that he supplied soldiers to accompany the German troops sent out to capture Daniel Kariko.[184] In the past Manasse Tjisiseta had ordered Daniel Kariko to comply with German demands; now he went one step further by setting up a trap for the arrest of Daniel Kariko by summoning him for talks to Omaruru.[185] Daniel Kariko did not suspect that Manasse Tjisiseta would take part in a scheme to have him arrested. Indeed, he welcomed the opportunity to talk about his position and requested that Volkmann and Cornelius Goraseb be present at the talks. However, he was saddened by Manasse Tjisiseta's attitude towards him and felt that he was being unfairly persecuted, and, in responding to Manasse Tjisiseta's summons, he signed his letter with *Karambua*, meaning the persecuted one.[186]

Daniel Kariko was betrayed by Manasse Tjisiseta. In response to his chief's call Daniel Kariko travelled to Omaruru, where he was promptly arrested, incarcerated and charged with high treason. The court martial, which was held following his arrest, found Daniel Kariko guilty of high treason and sentenced

---

[181] BAP, RKA 2101, Leutwein in Windhoek, 25/12/95, to RKA & extremely cheesed-off letter in NNAW, ZBU 436, Cleverley in Walvisbay, 7/6/96, to Leutwein.
[182] NNAW, ZBU 437, Volkmann in Omaruru, 17/6/96, to Leutwein.
[183] Ibid.
[184] NNAW, ZBU 437, postscript by Leutwein, 25/6/96, appended to letter sent by Volkmann in Omaruru, 17/6/96, to Leutwein.
[185] NNAW, ZBU 2027, Leutwein in Windhoek, 6/3/96, to Manasse & ZBU 437, Daniel Kariko in Eharni, 26/6/96, to Manasse.
[186] NNAW, ZBU 437, Daniel Kariko in Eharni, 26/6/96, to Manasse. JBG's translation.

him. Due to Manasse Tjisiseta's intervention Kariko's life was spared. However, he was sentenced to a two-year jail sentence, later converted into banishment to Eharui, and all his firearms were confiscated. Furthermore Daniel Kariko was prevented from exercising any authority in the settlements, Eharui, Sorris Sorris and Cape Cross, all of which had previously been under his control. Half of the cattle taken as payment of fines were transferred to Manasse Tjisiseta as chief of Omaruru.[187] Following his banishment, Daniel Kariko wrote once more to his erstwhile protector and chief, Manasse Tjisiseta. Kariko knew exactly what his position had become, and in his own bitter words he wrote:

> I have nothing to write except to greet you . . . I fear for myself while I am as a sacrifice, I mean I am dead, I have moved on, and I am truly dead, I am far away, my heart has moved far away, I fear you. When you say you [Daniel Kariko] are still in existence, then you mean your mother Kamaija and Gerhard and my Berg Damara Kumeb. It refers to them when you say I still have a younger brother and a werft even though you sold them to the Germans. I fear to be sold, I would/will [?] go and die there where the sun goes down. Will you now kill me yourself or will you send your emissaries to kill me[?] So I wait as your younger brother praying, in this instance to tell you; If you kill me, then do not do this as an act of your authority [on behalf of your leadership]. Do not send the very first people at hand, because you are lazy or so that you can say of those to be killed that they were not killed by you. To kill me send Gerhard and Philemon or will you have the bravery to face those, who know you to be the killer, who ask you 'Why did you kill Daniel?', to know that you killed a child of your mother.
> . . . Enough.
> The sacrifice greets you I am Daniel Kariko.[188]

Less than a year later Daniel Kariko escaped to Walvisbay.[189]

The centre cannot hold

Between his installation as paramount chief of the Herero in July 1894 and the outbreak of war in March 1896, Samuel Maharero extended his power and influence throughout all of Hereroland. In effect he became the most powerful Herero chief that had ever existed. However, his power, which was based primarily on his ability to manipulate the threat of German military firepower, came at a cost, which Herero, most of whom had but recently found themselves to be the subjects of Samuel Maharero, had to bear.

Following his installation as paramount chief in 1894, Samuel Maharero, in return for German aid, had agreed, not only to the establishment of the first of many German garrisons in what had now become his territory, but also, more importantly, to the first of many boundary agreements that delineated the southern boundary of Hereroland.[190] Aside from delineating territory to

---

[187] NNAW, ZBU 437, See court martial of Daniel Kariko. It is of interest to note that B. Tembo, who was used as Translator in the trial, was the son of Tembo, a freed slave from the Mozambique coast who had come to Namibia as an employee of C.J. Andersson. After 1894 B. Tembo became the personal servant of Major Franke and later gave evidence for the 'Blue Book', *Report on the Natives of South West Africa and Their Treatment by Germany* (London 1918).

[188] NNAW, ZBU 437, Daniel Kariko in Eharui, 4/9/96, to Manasse. JBG's translation.

[189] NNAW, ZBU 2027, Manasse in Omaruru, 9/8/97, to Leutwein.

[190] BAP, RKA 2100, von Lindequist in Windhoek, 11/7/94, to RKA; and later RKA 2100, Leutwein in Windhoek, 13/12/94, to RKA.

be handed over to settler and German control, Samuel Maharero, by agreeing to these boundary treaties, also asserted his rights and claims to territories never before controlled by the chiefs of Okahandja.[191] Anxious to retain German support, and attain wealth and power, Samuel Maharero actively assisted in the enforcement of the treaty conditions, even though this consisted primarily of the expulsion of Herero from their lands. Samuel Maharero seconded his troops, councillors and even his own sons to the German boundary patrols which determined and enforced the newly established southern boundaries of Hereroland, and, at times, Samuel Maharero was not beyond becoming personally involved in the expulsions.[192] Apart from expelling Herero from territories, Samuel Maharero extended his powers of patronage by ordering his own favoured sub-chiefs and followers into territories which had now officially become his.[193] From November 1895 onwards, all Herero cattle impounded, for alleged boundary transgressions, were publicly auctioned, whereafter the proceeds were split between the German authorities and Samuel Maharero.[194] The traumatic nature of this measure, can be garnered from the fact that, when this occurred for the first time, Samuel Maharero's son and nephew, who were volunteers in the German army, broke down in tears and immediately requested that they be released from further duty in the German army.[195] Needless to say these activities inflamed passions amongst all those who were not allied to Samuel Maharero.

As the newly delineated boundaries were enforced and the expulsions continued, Herero attempted to escape the ever encroaching boundaries and withdraw away from the German threat of dispossession. There was but one way in which they could move, northwards ever deeper into the newly delineated Hereroland. German authorities were aware of this migration, and it was something they had hoped for, as Leutwein noted:

> It is certain that throughout Hereroland a certain spirit [*Gahrung*] has emerged. The people see themselves and their means of existence as being under threat from all sides, and they no longer know where to turn to with their enormous cattle herds.[196]

Leutwein expressed the hope that once the population pressure became acute, the Herero would be forced to sell their huge herds to the European settlers.[197] However, this was not the case and travellers began reporting the effects of overgrazing as the Herero herds were forced into an ever-increasing small area.[198]

---

[191] See boundary treaties in BAP, RKA 2100, 11/7/94 southern boundary; 13/12/94 southern boundary adjustment; 26/2/95 & 3/7/95 Boundaries & 29/8/95 northern Boundary.

[192] BAP, RKA 2100, von Lindequist in Windhoek, 19/1/95, to RKA, refers to Herero councillors Assa Riarua, Julius, Paulus, Christian, Friedrich Maharero, Hugo and Wilhelm accompanying the boundary commission of 1895. Leutwein, *Elf Jahre*, p. 92. On Samuel Maharero's personal involvement in the expulsions see NNAW, ZBU 2027, Samuel Maharero in Okahandja, 31/8/94, to Leutwein.

[193] *BRMG* 1895, p. 71 mentions that the chiefs Kanagati, Kajata and Mbataera, who were allies of Samuel Maharero and who had been settled around Otjosazu were moved, under orders of Samuel, into the eastern border areas of Hereroland.

[194] BAP, RKA 2100, *Hauptmann* Muller in Windhoek, 19/11/95.

[195] Leuwtein, *Elf Jahre*, p. 92.

[196] BAP, RKA 2101, Leutwein in Windhoek, 25/12/95, to RKA. JBG's translation.

[197] BAP, RKA 2100, Leutwein in Windhoek, 3/7/95, to RKA.

[198] BAP, RKA 2100, Leutwein at Grootfontein, 24/8/95.

In late 1895, the Ovambo king of Ondonga, Kambonde, let it be known
that a number of Herero had come to see him, complaining that Samuel
Maharero had become the servant of Leutwein.[199] Large numbers of Herero
felt that they no longer had recourse to authority, apart from that sanctioned
by Samuel Maharero and his German allies. In line with this, Rhenish
missionaries reported that large numbers of Herero no longer stayed at the
mission stations out of fear for the new colonial regulations.[200] This sense of
powerlessness was not confined merely to the common Herero. Chief
Kahimemua Nguvauva of the Ovambanderu wrote bitter letters to Theodor
Leutwein declaring his rights to land, water, people and leadership, and
demanding that his authority should be recognized. Particularly galling, for
Kahimemua, was that he had received no recognition, in the form of land rights,
from Theodor Leutwein, for the fact that he had stood alone in the wars against
Hendrik Witbooi, whereas Nicodemus Kavikunua had received extensive land
rights and had even been appointed as his superior:

> I place my troubles before you, I travelled faraway with *Kaptein* Maharero [Samuel's
> father], all people had fled and had left him in the lurch during the days of the wars,
> I however stood by him in his need. [Standing] Next to him I was assailed by 10
> wars and I did not abandon the land while he fled, until we made peace with Hendrik
> Witbooi. And I thought then for my efforts you would give me a small bit of land, in
> exchange for the troubles which I experienced. I have had more troubles than any
> of those whom you have granted land. Therefore I ask of you dear sir that you make
> known where my debts to you lie, whether I owe either you or Samuel, why you
> refuse to grant me part of the land.
>
> You gave land to Zacharias in Otjimbingwe, Kambazembi you gave land, you gave
> land to Manasse, and you gave to Nikodemus the land which was actually meant
> for me. I in turn have spilt my blood for nought.
>
> I think that you alone have a good heart, that you will see the troubles that I have
> suffered, however I know that all the land here belongs to you and Samuel . . . I beg
> of you that I be granted rights to the lands between Otjihaenena and Epako [Gobabis]
> in the name of you and Samuel.[201]

Unfortunately for Kahimemua, and the majority of other Herero who, in
seeking justice, petitioned Leutwein, it was part of Leutwein's avowed policy
of divide and rule that prevented him from acceding to their demands. Not
surprisingly this condition could not last indefinitely and in March of 1896 it
broke.

Let loose the dogs of war

In early 1896, Major Leutwein, commander of the German forces and governor
of German South West Africa, wrote to his superiors in Berlin stating that he
believed that the chances that peace would be maintained in the territory were
slim.[202] In the previous two years, German forces and their Herero allies had
expelled Herero and their stock from areas lying beyond the boundaries of the

[199] BAP, RKA 2101, Leutwein in Windhoek, 25/12/95, to RKA.
[200] *BRMG* 1895, p. 71.
[201] NNAW, ZBU 2028, W II d 14, Kahimemua Munjuku in Otjihanena, 3/3/96, to Leutwein.
JBG's translation.
[202] BAP, RKA 2100, Leutwein in Windhoek, 29/1/96, to RKA.

newly demarcated Hereroland, and forced them into the ever more crowded areas of central Hereroland. Not surprisingly this boundary enforcement and forced removal had led to tension and open armed conflict was often only narrowly averted. In March of 1896 armed conflict did break out. Within two short bloody months, hundreds of Herero, Banderu and Khauas Khoi were killed and two chiefs executed. The following section looks at the events leading up to the Ovambanderu Khauas Khoi war of 1896.

The Otjihaenena boundary commission incident of January 1895, when Lindequist and his commission had, to all intents and purposes, been arrested and taken to Otjihaenena by the forces of Nicodemus Kavikunua, had led to the renegotiation of parts of the boundary agreement in favour of Nicodemus Kavikunua.[203] In follow-up negotiations Nicodemus was appointed as an independent chief and as Samuel Maharero's representative in eastern Hereroland.[204] At the same time the German authorities established a garrison at Gobabis and a military post at Olifantskloof, ostensibly to control the trade to and from the Bechuanaland Protectorate.[205]

In September 1895 German troops, operating out of Gobabis under the command of *Leutnant* Lampe and assisted by the soldiers of Samuel Maharero and the son and soldiers of Nicodemus Kavikunua, arrested a number of Tswana Rolong traders at Olifantskloof.[206] Even though he was being assisted by the soldiers of Samuel Maharero and Nicodemus Kavikunua, Lampe believed that whilst returning to Gobabis he was to be ambushed by Herero and Mbanderu forces. No attack took place, and apart from an argument regarding rights to the captured firearms, Lampe and his prisoners arrived unscathed in Gobabis. However, this did not prevent him from sending off a rather panicky missive to his superiors in Windhoek.[207] In response to this *Hauptmann* von Sack, accompanied by forty mounted men and a cannon, was despatched to Gobabis. Sack arrived in Gobabis spoiling for a fight and left the inhabitants of Gobabis in no doubt as to his intentions:

> . . . [when] asked why I had brought along a cannon, I replied, that the function of the cannon was to punish all the tribes that transgressed the German laws and did not keep to the treaties.[208]

Strengthened by the arrival of Sack and his reinforcements, Lampe reopened boundary discussions with Nicodemus Kavikunua. During the course of three days of negotiations, Nicodemus Kavikunua agreed to further boundary adjustments and reiterated that he intending sticking to the treaties he had signed. As a token of his sincerity Nicodemus handed his son, Hosea, over into the care of the German authorities.[209] Though followers of the Ova-mbanderu chief, Kahimemua Nguvauva, were present during the course of the negotiations, Kahimemua himself was not present. Indeed, Nicodemus

---

[203] BAP, RKA 2100, von Lindequist in Windhoek, 19/1/95, to RKA.
[204] BAP, RKA2100, Treaty concluded between Nicodemus Kavikunua and Leutwein, 14/6/95.
[205] Ibid.
[206] Later, following lengthy negotiations between Germany the Cape and the Bechuanaland Protectorate, it would become apparent that Olifantskloof lay within British territory. But, for the time being, the traders, who were led by a man named Muzikuma (?), were arrested, on charges of arms smuggling, and escorted to Gobabis.
[207] BAP, RKA 2100, Lampe in Gobabis, 2/9/95, to Leutwein.
[208] BAP, RKA 2100, Hauptmann von Sack in Gobabis, 8/10/95, to Leutwein. JBG's translation.
[209] BAP, RKA 2100, Von Sack in Gobabis, 8/10/95, to Leutwein.

Kavikunua complained that, even though, in terms of the German treaties and agreements, Kahimemua had been placed under his authority and was therefore his subject, Kahimemua had left Otjihaenena without informing him.[210] Though Nicodemus Kavikunua was clearly intimidated by Sack's show of force, he was anxious to maintain his alliance with the Germans and Samuel Maharero, if only for the benefits that this alliance had brought him. However, Nicodemus Kavikunua's decision to continue his association with Samuel Maharero and the Germans served to isolate him not only from his erstwhile benefactor, Kahimemua Nguvauva and the Khauas Khoi, but also from his own followers. Herero interpreters, who had accompanied Sack on his mission to Gobabis, reported that, at the close of the negotiations in Gobabis, Nicodemus Kavikunua had lost the support of a large section of the Mbanderu, Herero and Khauas Khoi councillors present in Gobabis at the time.[211]

In itself, Kahimemua's break with Nicodemus Kavikunua, who had clearly allied himself with Samuel Maharero and the Germans, was not surprising, for in south-eastern Hereroland it had primarily been Kahimemua's people who had suffered from the forced expulsions.[212] The involvement of the soldiers of Samuel Maharero, since early 1895, and of Nicodemus Kavikunua, from July 1895 onwards, alongside German troops in the forced removals associated with the boundary enforcement, did not do much to ensure the maintenance of cordial relations between Kahimemua Nguvauva on the one hand and Nicodemus Kavikunua and Samuel Maharero on the other.

After two years of forced removals, tensions within Herero society were at breaking point, even amongst the direct followers of Samuel Maharero. Though Herero soldiers operated alongside German troops in the boundary patrols, this did not mean that they remained unconcerned by what was happening. In August of 1895 Herero troops, under the command of Riarua's son Assa, operating alongside German troops in a boundary patrol led by Lindequist, refused to obey orders and even went to the extent of raising their firearms against their German patrol members.[213] These tensions were exacerbated following the conclusion of treaties, in late 1895, by which Herero cattle impounded south of the Hereroland boundary were to be sold by public auction, and the proceeds to be equally divided between the German authorities and Samuel Maharero.[214] In due course, in November of 1895, *Hauptmann* Müller raided Herero cattleposts to the south of Okahandja and confiscated no less than 236 cattle and 176 small stock.[215] The cattle were auctioned for 3500 marks and Samuel Maharero received approximately 1500 marks.[216] The cattle raid was clearly intended to weaken Samuel Maharero's position within his own society and make him more dependent on German assistance and support. For, in this instance, the cattle taken belonged to some of Samuel Maharero's closest advisers and followers, Johannes Tjamuaha and Barnabas,

[210] BAP, RKA 2100, Von Sack in Gobabis, 8/10/95, to Leutwein.
[211] Ibid.
[212] See particularly BAP, RKA 2100, von Lindequist in Windhoek, 19/1/95, to Leutwein.
[213] NNAW, ZBU 2027, W II d. 9, Leutwein in Outjo, 17/9/95, to von Lindequist.
[214] Leutwein, *Elf Jahre*, p. 92.
[215] NNAW, ZBU 2027, W II d. 9, Mueller in Windhoek, 17/11/95, to Leutwein & BAP, RKA 2100, Leutwein in Windhoek, 19/11/95, to RKA.
[216] NNAW, ZBU 2027, W II d. 9, Mueller in Windhoek, 17/11/95, to Leutwein, mentions that the cattle were auctioned for 3500 marks & BAP, RKA 2101, Leutwein in Windhoek, 29/1/96, to RKA. Mentions that cattle impounded brought up 2950 marks.

both councillors of Samuel Maharero, and Paulus Kanaimba, Liccus and Nathienel, all of whom were firm supporters of Samuel Maharero.[217] Indicative of Samuel Maharero's powerlessness vis-a-vis the Germans was that, even though he complained to Leutwein, he was unable to do anything other than accept his share of the proceeds of the auctioned cattle.[218] Opposition to Samuel Maharero in Okahandja and elsewhere increased. Added to this, his position was not strengthened by the blanket dismissals with which the German authorities greeted his complaints. An example of this was Leutwein's reaction to Samuel Maharero's following letter:

> Dear sir, I received your letter regarding the impoundment of the cattle. After receiving your letter I left Okahandja to ensure that all posts were to the north of the border. There are still some posts beyond the border, please don't impound them as I have sent people to make sure that they withdraw as quickly as possible. I have done this in accordance with our agreement and have brought the posts to Otjizeva. As there is no water and no grass I do not know where I should turn to with them. As until now I still do not know where it has been determined that the border should be therefore I have brought the cattle here. As the border is as yet undetermined, if I were to send the cattleposts to Otjitugu [?] they would also be impounded. Therefore I request of you that these affairs be sorted out as soon as possible so that I will be able to find place for my wealth.
>
> I have thankfully received the letter in which you referred to one of your men shooting at one of my men. However these people, the traders as well as your soldiers have very often hurt me with small things, which are not important and need not concern you. Whilst trading these people repress my people, so too do your soldiers.
>
> The soldier who shot at my man was not drunk he only wanted to kill my man so that he could take his horse.
>
> These are my complaints, investigate them before you dismiss them.[219]

Theodor Leutwein did not even bother to answer Samuel Maharero's letter, let alone investigate his complaints. Instead, he sent the letter on to missionary Viehe, stationed in Okahandja, with a subscripted scrawl ordering Viehe to give Samuel Maharero a geography lesson.[220]

Samuel Maharero's precarious position was further exacerbated by his growing dependency, in the absence of confiscated cattle, on land with which he could settle his extensive trading debts.[221] Typical of the traders associated with Samuel Maharero was Ludwig Conradt, who instituted court proceedings against Samuel Maharero and his councillor Assa Riarua for debts valued at 13,200 marks. As with other prospective settlers and land speculators, Ludwig Conradt let it be known that he was willing to accept payment from Samuel Maharero in either land or cattle.[222] Samuel Maharero's position as paramount chief of the Herero had allowed him to repay his debts through the allocation of land as farms to traders; however, more often than not these farms were in territories previously beyond the control of the Herero chiefs of Oka-handja.[223] Not surprisingly Samuel Maharero's involvement in land sales, land

[217] NNAW, ZBU 2027 W II d. 9, Mueller, ibid.
[218] NNAW, ZBU 2027, W II d. 9, Samuel Maharero in Okahandja, 26/11/95, to Leutwein.
[219] NNAW, ZBU 2027, Samuel Maharero in Otjiseva, 12/12/95, to Leutwein. JBG's translation.
[220] In due course Viehe replied that he had done as ordered. NNAW, ZBU 2027, WII d. 9, Viehe in Okahandja, 23/12/95, to Leutwein.
[221] NNAW, ZBU 2027, W II d. 9, Samuel Maharero in Okahandja, 26/11/95, to Leutwein.
[222] NNAW, ZBU 2027 W II d.9, Ludwig Conradt in Rehoboth, 20/2/96, to Leutwein.
[223] NNAW, ZBU 2027, W II d 14, Samuel Maharero in Okahandja, 11/1/96, to Leutwein, in which he refers to having sold a farm to a trader in the Grootfontein district.

dispossession and cattle theft did very little to endear him to his subjects, particularly so when his very own councillors and family members were the ones slighted. By early 1896 Samuel Maharero's power base, purchased and based upon land sales and cattle dispossession, had become increasingly tenuous and troubled to the extent that Riarua started reasserting his leadership position. Added to this, conflict increased between Herero and settlers moving into territories recently purchased or allocated as farms. In early 1896 the number of German patrols operating between Windhoek and Gobabis, that is, precisely those territories recently cleared of Khauas Khoi, Herero and Banderu, were stepped up.[224] These events, along with the tales based on the evidence of traders operating in Hereroland, and German reports on the illegal importation and stocking of arms and ammunition, led to settlers becoming increasingly willing to believe that a war was imminent.[225]

In late 1895 and early 1896, German settlers held stormy meetings in Windhoek calling for the immediate dismissal and replacement of Theodor Leutwein with a more forceful colonialist.[226] Settler representative Carl Weiss submitted petitions to the Imperial German government complaining about Leutwein's all too mild an *Eingeborenenpolitik*, in particular with regard to the Herero.[227] Alarmed by what was happening amongst the settlers in Windhoek and elsewhere, Samuel Maharero asked Leutwein to travel to Okahandja to discuss the issues related to the southern boundary and in particular the settlement of Seeis.[228] It is clear that Leutwein was also alarmed by the attitudes expressed by the settlers. However, in contrast to the settlers, of whom Leutwein did not hold a high opinion, he believed that in the long term it was impossible to merely force the Herero off lands claimed by the settlers. Instead, if the colonial settlement of Namibia was to succeed, it was necessary that Samuel Maharero be supported in his position as paramount chief, for it was only through working with him that further boundary incidents could be avoided. With this in mind and anxious to avoid a war, Leutwein agreed to Samuel's request and called for a meeting to be held with all the Herero chiefs in Okahandja in early 1896.[229]

When Leutwein rode towards Okahandja, in January 1896, the sincerity of Nicodemus Kavikunua's willingness to cooperate, and perhaps more importantly to be seen to be cooperating with the German forces and Samuel Maharero, was emphasized once again. As Leutwein approached Okahandja, which was decked out for the occasion in bunting in the colours of the German flag, Nicodemus Kavikunua and Samuel Maharero, accompanied by twenty uniformed Herero carrying German flags, rode out to meet him.[230] All the major chiefs, with the exception of Kambazembi, Manasse Tjisiseta and Tjetjo, were

---

[224] BAP, RKA 2101, Leutwein in Windhoek, 29/1/96, to RKA.
[225] For reports regarding the illegal importation of arms into the territory, see BAP, RKA 2101, Lombard in Grootfontein, 20/1/96, to Leutwein. For war scare, see BAP, RKA 2101, Leutwein in Windhoek, 29/1/96, to RKA.
[226] BAP, RKA 2101, Leutwein in Windhoek, 29/1/96, to RKA.
[227] BAP, RKA 2101, Weiss in Windhoek, 7/2/96, to RKA. About a month later Samuel Maharero wrote a letter to the German Kaiser requesting that Leutwein be kept in the territory. BAP, RKA 2101, Samuel Maharero in Otjimbingwe, 18/3/96, to Kaiser.
[228] RKA, BAP 2101, Samuel Maharero in Okahandja, 23/1/96, to Leutwein.
[229] BAP, RKA 2101, Leutwein in Windhoek, 29/1/96, to RKA. To be on the safe side, Leutwein also wrote to Germany and requested an extra 400 troops, four cannons and officers.
[230] BAP, RKA 2101, Leutwein in Windhoek, 29/1/96, to RKA.

present in Okahandja to discuss the issues relating to the southern boundary. Leutwein opened and set the agenda for the talks by stating that there were two issues which needed to be clarified if peace were to be maintained in the territory: what was to be the southern boundary of Hereroland, and what was to be the punishment for those who transgressed the boundary. After twenty-four hours of deliberation the assembled Herero chiefs submitted their views on paper. In response to Herero suggestions, Leutwein agreed to the boundary being temporarily shifted south, this so as to allow Herero cattle access to the brackish waters at Seeis. However, of far more importance was that Leutwein, a master in the art of divide and rule, was anxious to prevent the build-up of a unified Herero front against him. He therefore refused to accede to Nicodemus Kavikunua's request, that he be permitted to settle in Gobabis, even though Nicodemus Kavikunua had done all he could possibly have done to indicate his willingness to cooperate with Samuel Maharero and Leutwein. At the time Leutwein wrote:

> . . . the relationship between these two chiefs [Nicodemus Kavikunua and Samuel Maharero], which has until now been one of animosity, appears, of late, to have improved. Nikodemus stubbornly requested that he together with his councillors and herds of oxen be permitted to settle at Gobabis. Referring to our treaty I just as stubbornly turned down his request. Gobabis is of such strategic and commercial importance, that I would never relinquish this place.[231]

In doing this, Leutwein effectively turned Nicodemus Kavikunua against him. Nicodemus Kavikunua, who had been rejected by most of his followers for cooperating with Samuel Maharero and the Germans, had nowhere to turn to. The gamble that Nicodemus had taken, in cooperating with Samuel Maharero and Leutwein, had not been successful. Instead Nicodemus Kavikunua found himself consigned to exist in limbo until the events of war overtook him.

Leutwein and the Herero chiefs had held their meeting in Okahandja, in an attempt to alleviate the tensions that, on account of the forced removals and cattle dispossession, had built up in the territory. Though there were some minor temporary adjustments to the boundaries, it had become clear at the conclusion of the meeting that there was to be no substantial let-up in the dispossession of land and the enforcement of boundaries. With settler and Herero tensions running high, it was no real surprise when, in late March 1896, war broke out in Gobabis. In three battles, Herero, Banderu and Khauas Khoi forces, who had initiated action against the German garrison in Gobabis, were defeated by combined Herero, Nama, Tswana and German forces under German command.[232]

As the hostilities wound down, Nicodemus Kavikunua travelled to Okahandja to plead his innocence. In Okahandja he stayed in the house of his step-brother Assa Riarua, who guaranteed that Nicodemus would not leave Okahandja.[233] Kahimemua Nguvauva was captured at Kalkfontein and taken to Okahandja.[234] Though he protested his innocence, Nicodemus was arrested shortly before Kahimemua was brought into Okahandja. The two men were

---

[231] Ibid. JBG's translation.
[232] NNAW, ZBU 436, D IV c.1 Band 1. *Feldzug gegen die Hereros und die Khauas Hottentotten 1896 Band 1.*
[233] NNAW, ZBU 436, Schwabe in Okahandja, 16/5/96, to Leutwein.
[234] Ibid.

charged with high treason, found guilty and sentenced to death. On 12 June 1896 Samuel Maharero, who in late April 1896 had written to Leutwein pleading Nicodemus Kavikunua's innocence, now refused to pardon his erstwhile *Oruzuo* rival and openly spoke out endorsing the forthcoming execution of Nicodemus Kavikunua.[235] After a few sips of wine Nicodemus Kavikunua and Kahimemua Nguvauva were bound and taken by ox-cart to a spot outside Okahandja. Nicodemus Kavikunua was tied to a tree and shot, whereafter Kahimemua Nguvauva was similarly killed by firing squad.[236] The followers of Nicodemus Kavikunua and Kahimemua Nguvauva, in so far as they had not been killed, fled into the Bechuanaland Protectorate or were placed under the chiefs loyal to Samuel Maharero. The Khauas Khoi ceased to exist as a political entity. In a policy of genocide all Khauas Khoi survivors were captured and taken to Windhoek where they were placed in a concentration camp, and used as forced labour by the German colonial state.[237]

Conclusion

Between his installation as paramount chief of the Herero in 1894 and the outbreak of the Ovambanderu Khauas-Khoi war of 1896, Samuel Maharero, through the shrewd manipulation of German colonial power, consolidated and extended his power. In the symbiotic relationship that developed between Samuel Maharero and Theodor Leutwein, Samuel Maharero used, and came to rely on, Leutwein's power to extend his own power. Similarly Major Leutwein was dependent on Samuel Maherero, and, albeit to a lesser extent, Manasse Tjisiseta, to extend his own power and to add an air of legitimacy to his colonization. One by one Herero chieftains opposed to Samuel Maharero were forced to submit to him in the face of German fire-power. In exchange for the services rendered by the Germans, Samuel Maharero signed treaties pertaining to the rights and properties of people who had never before been under his jurisdiction. Land, newly acquired by Samuel, was either sold off to German settlers or signed away in a series of boundary adjustments instigated by Theodor Leutwein. Through the conclusion of these treaties Herero chieftains were placed within the ambit of Samuel Maharero's and ultimately Germany's control. Furthermore the newly delineated boundaries led to the encirclement of Hereroland and the encroachment by German settlers and land companies on former Herero lands. Between 1894 and 1896 Samuel Maharero supplied troops to delineate and enforce the southern boundary, assisted in the expulsion of people from their ancestral lands, settled his own followers on land now officially in his control and in return for payment assisted in the enforced sale of his subjects' cattle. In effect, Samuel Maharero used the territories and cattle of people who had recently become his subjects, as patronage for his supporters and as payment of his debt to the Germans. Needless to say these activities inflamed passions amongst all those who were not allied to Samuel Maharero.

It was when soldiers, operating under the authority of Samuel Maharero and Germany, sought to enforce the conditions laid down in the various treaties

[235] NNAW, ZBU 436, Samuel Maharero in Okahandja, 22/4/96, to Leutwein.
[236] NNAW, ZBU 437, Statement by Kahimemua.
[237] NNAW, ZBU 436, D IV c.1, *Band 1–2 Feldzug gegen die Hereros und die Khauas Hottentotten 1896* & ZBU 2030 W. II d. 23, which contains lists of captured Khauas Khoi.

that tension and later conflict broke out. More and more people and their livestock were forced off their former lands and into the ever more crowded areas of the newly delineated Hereroland. In an effort to reduce the strains that had been brought to bear on their people, Herero chiefs sought to come to agreements with the German authorities, independently of Samuel Maharero, and sought to renegotiate boundary delimitations, it was all to no avail.

In a sense, the Ovambanderu Khauas-Khoi war, which broke out in 1896, only temporarily relieved the land pressures existing within Hereroland. As a result of the war large tracts of Herero territory were cleared for German settlement and large amounts of Herero stock captured and distributed amongst German settlers. However, the war did nothing to change the fundamental process of land dispossession which was taking place in the territory. The land clearances which continued unabated following the war led to continued overcrowding in the territories allocated to the Herero. This inadvertent overcrowding was to have dire implications for Herero stock when rinderpest struck in the year following the Ovambanderu Khauas-Khoi war.

4
The Curse of Kahimemua
1897–1903

Introduction

In June 1896 the Ovambanderu chief, Kahimemua Nguvauva, was executed by a German firing squad in Okahandja. Prior to his death, Kahimemua singled out his tormentors, cursed them and cursed the land as a whole:

> . . . when my knee dislocates the men with whom I have eaten the blood of sheep are all going to die. When my hair comes off my head there will be a rinderpest epizootic (*Omutjise uo Pesa*) and those cows that I have milked are going to die. When my pancreas falls off and bursts I will make friends fight.[1]

Less than a year later, Kahimemua's prophecies came to pass. The rinderpest epizootic decimated Herero cattle herds, led to the reorganization of Herero society as new elites capable of profiting from the changed circumstances came to the fore, and facilitated German colonization of the territory as Herero, desperate for food, vaccines and medicines, were forced into a position of dependence vis-a-vis the colonial state and the settlers.

The impact of rinderpest on the Herero has been discussed before elsewhere. Contemporary Jakob Irle and the historians Helmut Bley and Horst Drechsler have devoted a number of pages to the epizootic's impact on Herero society.[2] In essence this chapter builds and expands upon the arguments of these authors. It differs from previous accounts in that it is more detailed, attempts to assess the impact of secondary epidemics and famines on the Herero, and seeks to chart the rise of new social forces in the aftermath of the disasters that befell Herero society.

---

[1] Interview conducted with Mr Tjitunga in Gaborone 14/12/92. Transcribed in BB1, pp. 31–32. For published accounts of oral histories on this topic see Heywood, Lau and Ohly (eds), *Warriors, Leaders, Sages and Outcasts in the Namibian Past* (Windhoek 1992) and Sundermeier and Kuvare, *The Mbanderu: Their history until 1914 as told to Theo Sundermeier in 1966 by Heinrich Tjituka, Heinrich Hengari, Albert Kajovi, Heinrich Kavari, Paul Katjivikua, Ernst Ketjipotu*, translated from German by Annemarie Heywood and annotated by Brigitte Lau (Windhoek 1986).
[2] Irle, *Die Herero*, pp. 301–3; Bley, *South West Africa*, pp. 124–9 & Drechsler, *Fighting*, pp. 97–8.

The introduction of rinderpest to Namibia

> When we arrived 28 oxen had already died. They lay scattered around. All the sick animals – ca. 10 – were presented, we saw a gruesome image. The tall, sometimes gigantic beasts in a pitiful state; deeply socket sunk washed out eyes, matted [*gesträubte*] hair, palpitating flanks, stumbling gait; a disgusting stinking bloody black slime emptying from their behind. We are immediately agreed that here we are dealing with the pest and have two of the animals shot.[3]

Rinderpest was introduced to the African continent at some stage in the late 1880s. By 1892 the disease had reached the territory of present-day Zambia, where it was held up for a while by the Zambesi river, which it eventually crossed in 1896.[4] By July of 1896, the German authorities in Namibia, alerted to the approach of the disease, had begun taking measures to prevent it spreading into the territory.[5] In October 1896 there were reports of an outbreak of the disease around Lake Ngami in the Bechuanaland Protectorate.[6] Lake Ngami was connected by trade routes to western Namibia and was an important centre for traders operating out of the territory. Though measures were taken and the trade routes immediately closed, it was virtually impossible to prevent the spread of the disease. The disease was unwittingly introduced to the territory by infected trek oxen operating along the extensive trans-Kalahari trade routes, and by game, particularly by eland and kudu, whose rotting cadavers infected the cattle herds of Tjetjo Kandji and traders operating amongst his people in eastern Hereroland.[7] The measures taken were too late to prevent the spread of the disease, and this was exacerbated by the fact that those expected to enforce the trade ban were themselves often involved in trading. This is aptly illustrated by the activities of *Hauptmann* Franke. To supplement his military

---

[3] NNAW, ACC 560, Franke's Tagebuch, 24/5/97. JBG's translation.
For a similar view from elsewhere in southern Africa:

> Experience soon guides the eye and ear, and the broken-winded cough and the discharge of tears from angry-looking eyes are at once noticed. As the disease runs on, the animal becomes disinclined to rise from the ground – some of the the beasts may be constipated, passing hard pellets of yellow-grey clay – but most will be affected by a watery and foetid diarrhoea, often tinged with blood. The temperature is very high, and the breathing laboured . . . ropey saliva hangs round the mouth and nostrils . . . As the temperature falls, the animal becomes semi-comatose and weaker; muscles quiver incessantly, moaning and gulping increase, and about six days after the attack commences the beast dies.

C. Ballard, 'The repercussions of Rinderpest: Cattle plague and peasant decline in colonial Natal' in *The International Journal of African Historical Studies*, 19, 3 (1986) quoting from *Natal Witness*, 6 May 1896. Franke's descriptions echoed the reports of veterinary services throughout Africa at the time. In East Africa the disease was described as '. . . an acute contagious virus disease of ruminants and swine, characterised by diarrhoea, nasal and lacrimal discharge and by ulceration of the mucous membrane of the mouth'. H. Kjekshus, *Ecology Control and Economic Development in East African History: The Case of Tanganyika, 1850–1950* (London 1977), p. 126 quoting from the EAAJ 1939 (5):57. In South Africa the disease was described as 'a specific malignant and highly contagious fever characterised by acute inflammation of the mucous surfaces, affecting cattle, game, and, in a minor form, sheep'. Charles van Onselen, 'Reactions to Rinderpest in South Africa 1896–97', in *Journal of African History* XIII 3(1972), pp. 473–88, quoting from Colonial Veterinary Surgeon, Cape of Good Hope, *Special Report on Rinderpest in South Africa March 1896–February 1897*, p. 32.
[4] Van Onselen, *JAH* 1972, pp. 473–88.
[5] BAP, RKA 2101, Leutwein in Windhoek, 20/7/96, to AA.
[6] BAP, RKA 2083, Leutwein in Spitzkoppie, 7/10/96, to AA.
[7] Otto von Weber, *Geschichte des Schutzgebietes Deutsch-Südwest-Afrika* (Windhoek 1979) p. 75.

income, Franke indulged in a number of activities which ranged from labour recruitment to horse and cattle trading. Writing in his diary entry, for 13 October 1896, Franke referred not only to his worries regarding the rinderpest reports, but also to buying twelve horses at £16 each which had been driven from the Transvaal through the Kalahari, and thus along routes already infected by the disease, to Namibia.[8]

Though the disease had already entered the territory by late 1896, definite reports on the outbreak of rinderpest in Namibia only reached Windhoek in April of 1897. The first herds to be struck by the disease were those of the followers of Tjetjo Kandji, who lived in eastern Namibia. Given the density of traffic on specific trade routes, the disease spread incredibly rapidly. Due to environmental circumstances ox-waggon trains were forced to pass along very specific routes. The mission chronicles for Otjimbingwe, in detailing conditions along the route to Walvisbay, provide us with a graphic indication as to the density of traffic on some of the waggon trails.

> It was a gruesome road. It was covered with ox bones. A couple of weeks ago the Finns [missionaries who had begun operating in Ovamboland in 1870] with 5 waggons lost 82 oxen. The road could not be otherwise, as in one year 880 consignments were transported inland, of these over 500 passed Otjimbingwe. During the past year 10000–12000 oxen passed Otjimbingwe as draught animals.[9]

Even before news detailing the infection of Tjetjo's herds had reached Windhoek, the disease had already been carried into the settlement by traders operating along the Skaap river.[10] The spread of the disease was further facilitated by the displacement and relocation of substantial numbers of people and cattle, into the already densely populated areas of southern Hereroland between 1890 and 1896. Due to war and land clearances, particularly in eastern and southern Hereroland, Herero settlements had been forced to relocate to the already densely populated areas of what had been newly designated as Hereroland. This packing together of people and cattle ensured that there was virtually no tract of land that was not utilized. Thus when the disease struck, the possibilities of quarantining were severely limited; consequently the disease spread like wildfire.[11] Within six months of its introduction to Hereroland, at least two-thirds of the cattle in the territory had been killed by the disease. Some communities lost 95 per cent of their cattle.[12]

Preventative measures

Once it had become clear that the rinderpest would not be kept at bay by the Zambesi river, authorities throughout southern Africa sought to undertake action, initially to stop the spread of the disease and later to attempt to limit the damage caused by the disease. Already in July 1896, when rinderpest had

[8] NNAW, ACC 560, Tagebuch Franke, 13/10/96.
[9] ELCIN, V. Chroniken, Otjimbingwe 1895.
[10] Leutwein, Elf Jahre, p. 126.
[11] For an overview of the clearances following the Ovambanderu Khauas-Khoi war see BAP, RKA 1489, Militarisches Einschreiten der Schutztruppe; 20 Juli 1896 – 2 Februar 1898.
[12] Horst Drechsler, Let us Die Fighting, p. 98, quoting from Irle, Die Herero, p. 301, who reported that barely 5 per cent survived. Gerhard Pool, Samuel Maharero, p. 165, has figures of 97 per cent of cattle being killed.

barely crossed the Zambesi, the German authorities had begun planning for
an eventual outbreak in Namibia. All garrisons were strengthened and ordered
to secure enough stocks to ensure that they could exist for two years without
being resupplied, and extra troops were dispatched to the eastern frontier,
ostensibly to seal the territory's borders.[13]

When it became clear that the disease would not bypass Namibia, the
German authorities sought to introduce a 20-km quarantine corridor on the
northern and eastern borders of Hereroland. However, there were insufficient
troops to enforce the quarantine, and those soldiers who were employed were
generally inexperienced, or, particularly in the northern districts, sick with
malaria. Added to this, the incubation period that existed between infection
and the first outwardly visible symptoms of the disease resulted in many people
continuing to transport cattle under the false impression that they were
healthy.[14] The impossibility of enforcing a quarantine zone is well illustrated
by the case of Estorff who, with less than thirty soldiers at his disposal, sought
to enforce a quarantine zone, extending four days' travel north and east of
Omaruru, along the most important trade routes to Ovamboland and Angola.
According to Estorff's orders, traders were to be allowed to take goods to
Ovamboland but were not allowed to return until after the rinderpest had
passed. Those accused of failing to report outbreaks of the disease were to be
arrested and fined. However, more often than not, those expected to report
were themselves involved in long-distance ox-waggon trade. At times this
included the troops themselves. Indeed rinderpest first broke out in
Grootfontein in the cattleposts of the German troops. The disease had been
introduced to Grootfontein by trek oxen, used to resupply the garrison, from
Windhoek, where many had died without diagnosis.[15] It was an unworkable
situation and in due course the disease was reported to be rife along all the
trade routes from the north.[16]

Associated with the policy of attempting to implement an effective quarantine
of Namibia was the policy of culling all cattle herds believed to have been
infected by the disease.[17] Apart from the fact that there were instances where
German soldiers and settlers acted of their own accord in killing Herero cattle,
the killing of what was to all intents and purposes healthy stock had a
fundamental impact on Herero society. This fundamental breakdown in what
was after all a world dependent on the ownership of living cattle herds was
exacerbated when young Herero men, most of whom were too young to be
stock owners in their own right, were employed, and paid an ox a day, to assist
in the slaughter of cattle.[18] Whole herds were slaughtered in a vain effort to
prevent the disease from spreading.[19]

As the sheer scale of the epidemic became apparent, a number of Herero
men were employed to assist in combating the disease. Chiefs supplied young

[13] BAP, RKA 2101, Leutwein in Windhoek, 20/7/96, to AA, mentions sending 100 reinforcements
to the eastern districts to strengthen the garrison in Gobabis and to ensure the sealing of the
border against the rinderpest.
[14] Weber, *Geschichte*, p. 75. ELCIN, V. Chroniken, Omaruru 1897.
[15] ELCIN, V. Chroniken, Omaruru 1897.
[16] NNAW, ZBU 2027, WII D 10, Bensen in Omaruru, 2/8/97, to Leutwein.
[17] ELCIN, V. Chroniken, Omaruru 1897.
[18] *BRMG*, 1897, p. 323.
[19] Ibid.

men to assist in the enforcement of the quarantine and vaccination campaigns.[20] Prior to their direct employment by the German forces in their fight against the disease, Herero had undertaken action of their own accord. Once news of the rinderpest became widespread, large numbers of Herero attempted to quarantine their cattle herds by trekking away from the areas worst affected. Previously densely populated settlements such as Otjimbingwe, Otjosazu and Omaruru were all but abandoned, as people left the settlements in droves and attempted to drive their cattle herds away from the worst-affected areas.[21] Unfortunately for them, their search for safe havens failed. Due to the forced removals and land dispossessions of the previous years, population pressures in southern Hereroland had increased prior to outbreak of the disease, and this facilitated the spread of the disease when it struck.[22]

Apart from merely attempting to ensure the effective isolation of their stock from the epidemic, Herero also sought to employ medicines which would ensure the well-being of their cattle. During the latter half of 1897 an Omubanderu man was reported to be living along the Omuramba Omutako, one of Namibia's least accessible areas and thus an area initially spared by the scourge. It was believed that he, through the utilization and application of various roots, was capable, not only of preventing the infection of healthy cattle, but also of curing cattle already afflicted by the disease.[23] Be that as it may missionary reports noted that:

> The heathens and a number of baptised sought their refuge in roots that grow in this land and gave these to their beasts, however it was all in vain.[24]

Kohlstock and Koch

After having crossed the Zambesi river, rinderpest devastated the cattle herds of Charterland, present-day Zimbabwe, which had recently been appropriated by Cecil John Rhodes's British South Africa Company. The BSAC lost a tremendous amount of money as a result of the rinderpest, and Rhodes, who until the Jameson Raid had been prime minister of the Cape, was anxious to prevent a repeat of this happening in the Cape Colony. Consequently a telegram was sent from Cape Town to Berlin in October of 1896: 'Cape government very desirous that doctor Koch should come to investigate rinderpest would he accept and come out immediately no difficulty as to terms.'[25] Within two

[20] NNAW, ZBU 2027, WII D 10, Manasse in Omaruru, 28/8/97, to Leutwein.

[21] *BRMG*, 1897, p. 304 reports on people leaving for the field.

[22] NNAW, ZBU 2027 WII D 10, Leutwein in Windhoek, 15/9/96, to Manasse.

[23] Missionary Eich of Otjozondjupa quoted in Mossolow, *Waterberg*, p. 20.

Ovambanderu are well known in Herero orature as being well versed in medicines and, to some extent, the occult. In the light of this it is of course interesting to note that in 1897 people believed that the curse of the rinderpest, now ascribed to the powers of the executed Mbanderu chief Kahimemua, could be cured by an Omubanderu. Bearing Michael Taussig's, *Shamanism, Colonialism, and the Wild Man: A Study in Terror and Healing* (Chicago 1986, 1987), in mind it is probable that this relates more to the marginalized position of the Ovambanderu.

[24] *BRMG*, 1897 p. 323.

[25] BAP, RKA 6089, Consul in Cape Town, 22/10/96, to AA. Robert Koch was a German physician with a very distinguished career. He was one of the founders of the science of bacteriology, and discovered the tubercle bacillus and the cholera bacillus. He conducted research on a variety of diseases, amongst others, leprosy, bubonic plague, surra, malaria and rinderpest. He was awarded the Nobel prize for physiology or medicine in 1905.

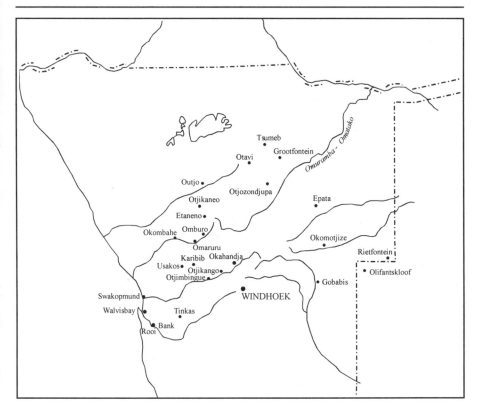

Map 4.1: The spread of rinderpest in central Namibia, 1897

months of receiving these summons, Prof. Dr Koch and his assistant Dr Kohlstock travelled to the Cape and installed themselves in a laboratory owned by De Beers, one of Rhodes's companies, in Kimberley, Rhodes's personal fiefdom.[26] Though Koch and Kohlstock succeeded in producing a rather rough and ready vaccine, the disease could not be curtailed. A contemporary report concluded that the results of the serum developed in Kimberley were 'sometimes good, sometimes bad'.[27]

During the course of their activities in Kimberley, Koch and Kohlstock were summoned to Namibia by the German government. In February 1897 Koch wrote to Windhoek informing them of his intention to send Kohlstock to Namibia and that:

> . . . I have succeeded in developing a vaccine against rinderpest. I believe that this prophylaxis can also be used in South West Africa and that with the help of this the threatening danger to the colony can be averted with little difficulty.[28]

[26] For a detailed overview of the activities of Koch and Kohlstock in southern Africa see BAP, RKA 6089. *Entsendung des Geh. Med. Raths Prof. Dr Koch und das Stabarztes Dr Kohlstock nach Südafrika. Oktober 1896 – 10 Juli 1897.*
[27] Van Onselen, *JAH*, 1972 p. 483, quoting from E.P. Herald 12/7/1897. Rhodes cannot have been too pleased with the results of Koch's activities when game on his private estates in Cape Town were killed by rinderpest less than a year after Koch and Kohlstock's arrival in South Africa.
[28] BAP, RKA 6089, Koch in Kimberley 28/2/97 to AA.

However Kohlstock kept procrastinating, and sent a string of letters to the authorities, both in Windhoek and Berlin, in which he sought to explain his delay. In March Kohlstock wrote that serum trials had not worked out but that this should be no problem as Namibia was still *rinderpestfrei*, a comment which not surprisingly elicited the clerical comment, 'barely!', in the margin.[29] By early March the doctors Koch and Kohlstock had perfected their serum.[30] Two weeks later Kohlstock wrote to report that Koch had left for Bombay and that he himself intended travelling to Namibia before the end of April.[31] In late April Kohlstock wrote from Cape Town that he was unable to proceed to Namibia as the injections which he had ordered had not arrived, and that he was therefore returning to Kimberley allegedly to conduct further research.[32] By this time rinderpest was raging in the eastern and northern districts of Namibia. Eventually in late May, when Kohlstock was officially ordered by Governor Leutwein to Namibia, he left for the territory.[33] By the time that Kohlstock arrived in Namibia, in late May 1897, rinderpest had already reached deep into the Namib desert, and Kohlstock could see for himself the effects of his procrastination, with cattle deaths at Anawood and Wilhelmsfeste along the trade route leading from the coast to the interior.[34]

Following Kohlstock's arrival in Hereroland in June 1897, a systematic inoculation programme started.[35] The Namibia colonial authorities ordered all cattle to be inoculated. To acquire the gall necessary for vaccinating purposes, every stock owner, depending on the amount of cattle possessed, had to donate one or more of his cattle. These were then purposefully infected with the disease, whereafter their gall was then used to inoculate healthy cattle against the disease. Not surprisingly the enforced donation of cattle, for inoculation purposes, was not greeted with much enthusiasm, particularly so, as lack of experience and the generally chaotic manner in which cattle were inoculated resulted in wildly varying success rates. This is well illustrated by what happened to the cattle herds belonging to missionaries Dannert and Bernsman. The herds were inoculated by Dr Langheld. Of Bernsmann's herd of thirteen, a mere four survived, whilst all of Dannert's herd of twenty survived.[36]

As in South Africa, Koch and Kohlstock's method of vaccination was a somewhat uncertain affair. In Otjosazu in a period of six weeks no less than 2000 cattle, of the 3000 cattle vaccinated, died.[37] In Otjimbingwe, of the 6178 cattle vaccinated with gall vaccine, 2731 cattle (43 per cent), died, whilst a mere six head of cattle of the 1394 cattle vaccinated with a blood vaccine died.[38] Rhenish missionary Eich, who was stationed at Otjozondjupa near the Waterberg, reported that at Hamakari, cattle started dying of the disease only after having been vaccinated against it. At the Waterberg the eventual tallies

[29] BAP, RKA 6089, Kohlstock in Kimberley, 6/3/97, to AA.
[30] BAP, RKA 6089, Koch in Kimerley, 10/3/97, to AA.
[31] BAP, RKA 6089, Kohlstock in Kimberley, 27/3/97, to AA.
[32] BAP, RKA 6089, Kohlstock in Cape Town, 25/4/97, to AA.
[33] BAP, RKA 6089, Pauli in Cape Town, 19/5/97, to AA.
[34] BAP, RKA 6089, Kohlstock in Windhoek, 28/5/97, to AA.
[35] Leutwein, *Elf Jahre*, p. 126.
[36] ELCIN, V. Chroniken, Omaruru 1897.
[37] Irle, *Die Herero*, p. 301.
[38] BAP, RKA 6090, Dirrling in Otjimbingwe, 15/8/97, to AA. This contradicted clinical trials conducted by Koch and Kohlstock which had concluded that the gall vaccine was more effective than the blood vaccine.

were that 50 per cent of the vaccinated and 95 per cent of the unvaccinated herds died. Small wonder that Eich concluded:

> The Herero have completely lost all faith in the inoculation program and refuse to allow further inoculations to be conducted.[39]

German colonial reports make ample mention of Herero refusing to participate in vaccination campaigns. It was a refusal to participate which was engendered in part by the unreliability of the gall and blood vaccines. Another major factor in limiting Herero participation in the vaccination campaigns was the apparently inconsistent and erratic manner by which cattle were selected for purposeful infection, for the production of gall and blood vaccine which was then used elswhere. Not surprisingly people were unwilling to donate cattle, in the sure knowledge that they would be infected and die terrible deaths, to ensure the creation of vaccine which was then used to protect cattle elsewhere. Added to this was the fact that in a number of cases vaccinators, who can at best be described as having been over-zealous, confiscated cattle for the production of vaccine regardless of the size of the stock owner's herd, and then used the vaccine on the herds of totally different stock owners. The enforced vaccination and donation of cattle, for the purpose of vaccine production, was a policy open to abuse. A fine example of all of these events, abuse and mis-understandings was the Etaneno affair.

The Etaneno affair

The independence of Herero society, which had already been substantially curtailed by the activities of Samuel Maharero and Leutwein, was to be even further curtailed by events originating out of the rinderpest. Apart from the impoverishment of Herero society, and the development of dependence by the society on outside sources for food, employment and so forth, there was a further direct curtailment of Herero independence which arrived in the guise of veterinary assistance. Under the mantle of aid and assistance in combating the disease, German colonial forces were given substantial and far-reaching powers with which to interfere in the affairs of Herero society. Powers which, but for the disease, would never have been willingly relinquished to Germany. The Etaneno affair provides us with some insight into the far-reaching nature of this involvement in the guise of aid.

In August of 1897, Dr Langheld, accompanied by a vaccinating team, of ten German soldiers and ten Herero soldiers loyal to Manasse Tjisiseta of Omaruru, arrived in the settlement of Etaneno in north-western Hereroland. Here the vaccinating team found between 300 and 400 cattle, many of which were already sick. According to Langheld's later account, he ordered the Herero headman of Etaneno, a man named Karukammo, to vaccinate his stock. However, according to Langheld, the headman refused to cooperate and Langheld therefore had him placed under guard. Langheld's account of events in Etaneno differs substantially from those of two of the Herero soldiers who served on the vaccinating team. According to the accounts of Jonathan Hans and Katougonua, Langheld had ridden to Etaneno not to vaccinate, but for

---

[39] Mossolow, *Waterberg*, p. 20.

the express purpose of acquiring gall with which to vaccinate cattle in Otjikango. According to Jonathan Hans, Langheld demanded that Karukammo, the headman of Etaneno, supply cattle for the production of gall vaccine for use on the cattle of the Onganda of Kahorouga, the son of Kawajo in Otjikango.[40] Jonathan Hans gave the following rendition of what the headman Karukammo told Langheld:

> I have no more oxen, to which Langheld replied, here are enough, I said no those I will not give away, Langheld then grabbed my arm and said come inside the house, there you can think about the issue, I repeated my case and didn't want to enter the house. Langheld then ordered his men to take up arms, the Herero seeing this ran to their arms, Langheld released me and walked towards the crowd, Katakatjura aimed his rifle. Then things quietened down the Herero thought that Langheld wanted to have me shot.[41]

Jonathan Hans's statement was backed up by Katougonua, another of Manasse's soldiers serving on the vaccinating team. Katougonua reported that in answer to Langheld's demand for cattle, Karukammo replied:

> I have no more oxen. When I initially gave 8 oxen away, the *Herr Stabarzt* [Langheld] rode to Otjimbingwe and squandered the gall away. Langheld then grabbed my arm and told me to come into the house where I was to think the issue over. I entered the doorway . . . I wanted to run away, Langheld held me and told his soldiers, take your guns and stand guard at the door, so that the man cannot run away.[42]

Needless to say Langheld had a totally different view of the the situation. For his part Langheld intimated that the events in Etaneno had been prearranged as an attack on German authority consequently he described the course of events as follows:

> I asked him [Karukammo] if he wanted his cattle vaccinated. He continually kept evading the question. Thereupon I told him that he should discuss the issue with his people in a hut, and I called the 10 men [troopers] whom I had with me, to arms and told them to set up a [Guard]post at the door. At this moment a number of people, nearly 60, jumped up and ran away, whilst loudly shouting their displeasure. They gathered at a distance of about 600 meters and, now nearly all armed with firearms, they began advancing back. I must accept that the rifles were already lying in wait in the immediate vicinity. In a short time the whole place was crawling [*wimmelte*] with people, there were about 200 men and 100 women, who, whilst shouting threateningly, advanced upon our hut. Their armaments consisted of approximately 40 breachloading rifles and about 50 muskets, the remainder were armed with lances, bows and kirri's.[43]

When the Herero saw what had happened, Katjipikuara – a man whom Manasse Tjisiseta had appointed as foreman to the quarantine line at Etaneno – shouted: 'Do not allow this man to be killed, take your guns and let us shoot.'[44] One of the Herero soldiers, possibly Katjipikuara, later told Langheld that, though

[40] There is more than one place named Otjikango, the most famous of which is the missionary settlement also known as Groß Barmen. In this instance the Otjikango referred to lay NW of Etaneno.
[41] BAP, RKA 6090, Protocol, Omaruru 13/10/97, of Herero Jonathan Hans.
[42] BAP, RKA 6090, Protocol, Omaruru 13/10/97, of Katougonua.
[43] BAP, RKA 6090, Langheld in Otjikango, 26/8/97, to von Estorff.
[44] BAP, RKA 6090, Protocol Katougonua.

they were good friends of the German soldiers, 'they were also Ovaherero and would not countenance that one of their brethren be harmed. They belonged to Manasse of Omaruru who was a good friend of the *Landeshauptmann* and if Langheld had problems with them they should go to Omaruru to discuss this with them.'[45] It was however primarily through the intercedence of this Herero soldier that bloodshed was averted, in that he was able to convince Langheld to release Karukammo.[46]

Obviously similar incidents, where gall was taken from the culled cattle of one herd to vaccinate the cattle of another herd, occurred elsewhere in Namibia. Partly as a result of the Etaneno incident, Kawayo (also known as Gaweyo or Kawaio), who had recently been heavily fined on charges of theft by Leutwein, refused to allow his cattle to be vaccinated.[47] Furthermore there was also the issue of certain chiefs claiming cattleposts as theirs and giving vaccinating teams permission to cull cattle therein for gall. That is, chiefs donated cattle which belonged to their subjects or others to vaccinating teams in exchange for the immunization of their own herds. It is probable that as a result of these incidents the vaccinating teams were instructed to be a trifle more diplomatic in their activities. That this was not always the case, and that abuse continued, is best indicated by a letter written by an officer in charge of a vaccinating team in north-western Namibia:

> . . . I dispute that Reitner and Jacob Wimmer received orders from me to take oxen to be shot for gall, against the will of the Herero Captain . . . All gall, which was used to inoculate the stock of Banjo, was taken from a cattlepost between Okan and Otjombonde, of which Kapitan Banjo told me personally that the cattle there were his and that he gave me permission to shoot the same. When I was nearly finished with vaccinating at Banjo I rode via Epano to Etonneno, to set up a vaccinating station. In Epano the captain refused to allow me to shoot his sick cattle, I didn't shoot any and rode to Etonneno, where I spent the night. I was again called to Epano where I shot three sick oxen but their gall was unsuitable.[48]

Even with the extensive vaccination campaign, cattle continued to die in droves. Cattle became worthless. Cattle prices plummeted. In 1897 missionaries reported that one could buy 'enormous oxen' for no more than a few marks.[49] Indicative of the worthlessness of cattle is the fact that Herero youth, most of whom had never owned their own stock before, employed as assistants to the vaccinating teams, were paid an ox a day for their assistance.[50] Cattle continued to die. The eastern chiefs Tjetjo, Kukuri and Omambo retained a mere 5 per cent of their herds.[51] The cattle cadavers lay scattered around the settlements, in the cattleposts and along trade routes of Namibia, and as they started to rot, the scavengers being sated, the air of the territory was filled with the cloying smell of putrefying flesh.[52]

[45] BAP, RKA 6090, Langheld in Omaruru, 26/8/97, to Estorff.
[46] BAP, RKA 6090, Langheld. When Governor Leutwein got to hear about the affair he blamed Langheld, but in good colonial tradition the Herero soldiers were singled out as scapegoats.
[47] BAP, RKA 6090, Langheld in Omaruru, 28/11/97, to Leutwein.
[48] BAP, RKA 6090, Graf von Bethany in Franzfontein, 29/10/97, to the *Kaiserliche Bezirkshauptmannschaft* Otjuo.
[49] ELCIN, V. Chroniken, Omaruru 1897.
[50] *BRMG*, 1897, p. 323.
[51] Irle, *Die Herero*, p. 301.
[52] ELCIN, V. Chroniken, Omaruru 1897.

Food, capital and patronage

The most immediate result of the rinderpest was that whole herds of cattle were exterminated, and this, in one swoop, deprived the majority of the Herero of their livelihood, food and source of patronage. Effectively in the space of a few months Herero society was completely bankrupted and the Herero transformed into paupers.

As pastoralists, the majority of Herero were almost entirely dependent on the food products of cattle. Herero cattle were utilized primarily for the production of cultured milk, *Omaere*, which was a staple food resource. As a food resource the products of cattle slaughter, meat and fat, were only of secondary importance. The consumption of meat products was further limited by the *Oruzuo* and *Eanda* taboo systems. In general, cattle were slaughtered only for ritual purposes or for the purpose of culling.

The meat of cattle killed by rinderpest could be dried or eaten with no ill effects to the consumer. However the sheer mass of cattle cadavers meant that people could not process them for food. Therefore the cadavers started rotting and had to be burnt or buried. Due to deforestation, particularly in the vicinity of permanent settlements, such as the mission stations, there was not enough wood available with which to burn the cattle cadavers. As a result, the cadavers had to be buried. The hard rocky soils of central Namibia generally meant that the bodies came to be buried in the soft sandy riverbeds that ran through the centre of most of the permanent settlements. Unfortunately as a result of this, the wells which had been dug in the riverbeds came to be contaminated by the decomposing body fluids of the buried cadavers.[53] Later, when hunger became extreme, people disinterred the cadavers for the marrow which was to be found in the bones of the decomposed carcasses.[54] Due to drinking contaminated water and eating inadequate or strange foods the health of people was substantially weakened. This was exacerbated by the outbreak of diseases amongst the weakened cattle and sheep that had survived the rinderpest. These diseases were referred to by the Rhenish missionaries as *Terasfieber*, *Blutseuche* and lungsickness. At the same time diseases, primarily related to insufficient nutrition, also broke out amongst the inhabitants of Hereroland.

The epidemic, which appears to have been a cocktail of diseases, struck between March and August 1898 and was particularly destructive as it infected water, milk and meat.[55] The diseases referred to included scurvy, typhoid and a form of malaria.[56] It is probable that forms of anthrax, induced by eating rotten flesh, were also prevalent.[57] The missionary chronicles of Omaruru, one such settlement struck by typhoid, give a clear and graphic description of the terrible conditions prevalent at the time:

> In the beginning of the year, typhoid broke out throughout the land, so that the year 1898 brought even more need and sorrow than the year 1897. People got sick and were dead or alive by the end of the week, primarily people between 20 and 50 years old. Some of the werften in the field died out completely, the corpses were

[53] ELCIN, V. Chroniken, Otjimbingwe and Omaruru 1897.
[54] ELCIN, V. Chroniken, Otjimbingwe 1897.
[55] Irle, *Die Herero*, p. 302.
[56] Weber, *Geschichte*, p. 76. Irle, *Die Herero*, p. 301.
[57] For this information I wish to thank veterinary epidemiologist Dr Klaus Depner and veterinary virologist Dr Katie Depner, both formerly of the Namibian state veterinary services.

then found unburied in the pontoks [huts]. In Omaruru itself there were days when 6–7 people died in a day. It was not possible to find people to help in burying people so children had to help in carrying their own parents to the graveyard. Elders Joel and Barnabas died and the wives of elders Asa and Ferdinand and teacher Elisa died. In the space of a few months 56 deaths had to be filled into the death-register, this was a loss of 12 per cent of the community. Amongst the heathens, where food and living conditions are generally much worse, than amongst the Christians, the percentage of deaths was much higher. Amongst those who survived the typhoid fever a serious lower body affliction developed, this apparently developed due to an imbalance in the patient caused by typhoid and which generally manifested itself in the form of intestinal abscesses.[58]

The settlement of Otjimbingwe appears to have been particularly hard hit. Missionaries blamed the outbreak of the human epidemic on the disinterment, by starving people looking for marrow, of cattle carcasses, and reported that, '90 per cent of the people were sick, the death knells sounded all the time. In some pontoks up to 12 were dead or dying.'[59] Approximately 10 per cent of the settlement's total population died as a result of the disease.[60] Missionary Irle, who was based at Otjosazu, reported that during the course of four weeks at Otjosazu and Okatumba approximately 450 people died and in total an estimated 10,000 lives were taken during the plague of 1898.[61]

> No house no werft was spared, whole Werften died out. Added to which the famine amongst the natives was appalling, many died due to starvation [*Entkräftung*]. Often there was nobody left to bury the dead. Our youngest daughter also died – as a result of drinking pestilent milk.[62]

The epidemic was confined to the settlements found along courses of the Swakop, Okahandja and Nossob rivers, and not further north.[63] That is, along precisely the most densely populated areas in Hereroland at the time. It was here that people, who had historically been dispossessed of their cattle, had sought to make a living out of riverbed agriculture. It was in these selfsame areas that people, only recently dispossessed of their cattle and land by war, relocation and rinderpest between 1890 and 1896, now too sought to make a living out of engaging in riverbed agriculture. The massive loss of life, and the extent of the epidemic amongst the populace of Hereroland, had a further debilitating impact in that labour, necessary for the production of food and thus the continuance of life, was lost.

When the Rhenish missionaries first arrived in central Hereroland, in the early 1840s, they found a number of communities engaged in horticulture and small-scale agriculture, albeit in forms that they did not approve of – marijuana grown in round fields. The missionaries, who needed sedentary flocks to preach to, established mission stations at sites where riverbed agriculture could be conducted, which would then preclude a migratory mode of living. In the past, with the added protection of missionary firearms, and the attractions of Cape trade goods, the mission stations had soon become a refuge for large numbers

[58] ELCIN, V. Chroniken, Omaruru 1898.
[59] ELCIN, V. Chroniken, Otjimbingwe 1897.
[60] ELCIN, V. Chroniken Otjimbingwe 1897, 200 people died at Otjimbingwe alone. Of the Christians 72 died out of *ca.* 800 people.
[61] Irle, *Die Herero*, p. 302.
[62] Ibid.
[63] For the distribution of the epidemic see Irle, *Die Herero*, p. 301.

of impoverished people. A number of these people, as the subjects of the missionary *Ovahona* had sought to make a living for themselves on the basis of riverbed agriculture. Following the rinderpest, people who had been robbed of their cattle by the epidemic, also sought to make a living on the basis of riverbed agriculture. Unfortunately for them, most of the prime agricultural areas in central Hereroland had already been occupied. Elsewhere in southern Africa, following the rinderpest, there was also a substantial shortage of available agricultural land and in this regard central Namibia was certainly no exception.[64]

At Omaruru and Otjimbingwe a struggle for agricultural land ensued after the rinderpest. At both stations Herero, who had previously lived in the field as pastoralists, came to the stations to grow crops on the agricultural lands hitherto claimed by the mission station Herero.[65] Some Herero found employment in carting dung from the now abandoned cattleposts in the *veld*, for use as fertilizer on the fields and for sale to those engaged in agriculture. The carting in of manure was limited to those few who still possessed draught oxen, and was by nature a lucrative business. The profitability of this business and the extent of people's desperation can partially be gathered from the fact that there were cases of people stealing manure from kraals, partly because it had become too expensive to buy. Traditionally built Herero houses were demolished so that the manure and sand mixture used to cement the walls could be utilized in the newly established gardens and cornfields.[66] However even if Herero managed to get access to seed, fertilizer and a patch of agricultural land, there was always the danger that they would never get to eat the produce of their agricultural endeavours. The crops were continually threatened by the possibility of flood, drought, birds, locusts, trampling, thieves, debt collectors and famished relatives.

By virtue of Hereroland's arid climate, agriculture could only be conducted in riverbeds. This, however, brought with it the ever-present danger that a newly sown or shortly to be harvested crop could be washed away in a matter of seconds by flash floods. As bad as too much rain was the problem of too little rain, drought. Between 1899 and 1902 central Namibia was racked by a drought so bad that wells dried up, *veldkos* became exhausted, and cattle-owning people moved away to other areas, taking with them the manure and milk necessary for survival. Those who possessed nothing sought employment along the railway or moved to the new town and mining centres of Karibib, Windhoek and Tsumeb. Though the rainy seasons of both 1901 and 1902 started with good rains, the rains stopped early and those crops that did sprout were soon consumed by locust swarms.[67] Famine stalked the land, to the extent that impoverished Berg Damaras, deprived of their main staple field food, *uintjes* (small bulbs), found sustenance in the *voetgangers* (locust larvae) which were to be found in droves behind the Epako mountains.[68]

A further threat to agricultural production was the role played by the traders.

[64] Van Onselen, *JAH*, p. 486.
[65] ELCIN, V. Chroniken, Otjimbingwe and Omaruru 1898–1902.
[66] ELCIN, V. Chroniken, Otjimbingwe 1897.
[67] ELCIN, V. Chroniken, Omaruru and Otjimbingwe 1899–1902. Throughout the 1890s locust plagues afflicted much of southern Africa, see E.A. Walker, *A History of Southern Africa* (London 1965), p. 459. Pool, *Maharero*, p. 165.
[68] ELCIN, V. Chroniken, Omaruru 1900.

In Otjimbingwe in early 1902 a number of people, some of whom had previously been living in the fields for a long time, came to the station and started engaging in agriculture production. However, towards the middle of 1902 there was a massive move of Herero away from the station. This move away was due in part to the continuing drought. However, the main reason for this move was a statement issued by the colonial *Distriktsamt*, that all debts to the traders in Otjimbingwe had to be paid within two months. Not surprisingly people abandoned the settlement, and their fields, as they trekked from cattlepost to cattlepost, seeking to evade the debt collectors or vainly attempting to collect the stock with which to pay off their debts.[69] The predicament of Herero in central Hereroland at the time is well illustrated in the following discussion:

Missionary: 'Why do you get yourself into debt?'
Herero: 'The Halbichs and Redeckers give us no or very little credit, that [credit] we can only get over there in the other stores, and we have to live, there is no more work and the transport business is finished, so what else should we do?'
M: 'Make gardens!'
H: 'But the gardenlands are already occupied, and then at night the cattle break in, or thieves steal all our harvest, or so many starving people, who want to eat with us, come to our werft that for all our efforts we have nothing left . . . If we bring cattle there is not enough grazing and anyway the traders will take the cattle.'[70]

Driven into debt, no longer able to subsist on the produce of the fields, let alone the produce of their gardens, fields and former herds, substantial numbers of Herero were increasingly forced to abandon their homelands and take up employment as wage labourers on the newly created settler farms of Namibia and in the mines and towns of southern Africa as a whole.

As noted earlier the most immediate result of the rinderpest was that whole herds of cattle were exterminated. Not only were the majority of Herero in Namibia at the time almost entirely dependent on the food products of cattle, a substantial number of them were also dependent on the labour power of cattle for the production of capital. A substantial number of influential Herero owned ox-waggons and earned their living through transport riding. With the rinderpest this form of income generation became severely curtailed to those few fortunates whose oxen had survived the epizootic. A number of chiefs and influential Herero were engaged in freight riding, among them Manasse Tjisiseta of Omaruru who in July 1897 sent an urgent appeal to Leutwein for vaccination: '. . . I wanted to engage in transport riding, so as to acquire money, however the disease has closed the road and I can thus not ride.'[71]

Unable to transport goods on their own terms, and, more particularly, being cut off from a substantial form of independent income generation, the chiefs ran into difficulties as regards patronage and the loyalty of their own subjects.

[69] ELCIN, V.Chroniken, Otjimbingwe 1902.
[70] Ibid.
[71] NNAW, ZBU 2027, Manasse in Omaruru, 3/6/97, to Leutwein. Added to this was the fact that Manasse had hoped to send his two sons to Germany; however, due to the rinderpest he no longer had sufficient money for this. NNAW, ZBU 2027, Halbich in Otjimbingwe, 14/3/97, to Leutwein. Halbich turns down Leutwein's appeal for money to send Michael Tjisiseta to Germany instead he urges Manasse to save up.

Already substantially weakened by the activities of Samuel Maharero and Leutwein, chiefs found their power being further eroded by the fact that they were unable to cater for the needs of their subjects. They, as *Ovahona*, were unable to fulfil their obligations as the protector of their subjects in times of need. The chiefs simply had no cattle left with which they could allow their subjects to reestablish themselves.

Obviously the loss of draught animals struck not only the Herero, but everybody engaged in ox transport or dependent on it.[72] As a consequence the price of trade goods soared. There were incidents of racketeering. In the year following the rinderpest, when human disease ran rampant, this form of trading was not confined to bulk goods, such as rice and maize, but was extended to the sale of medicines.[73] Apart from racketeering, traders, hoping to get rich quickly, took to extending credit in the hope of acquiring land.[74] Be that as it may, following rinderpest, increasingly large numbers of Herero, commoners and royals, were driven into debt with the traders. Not all of these debts were necessarily solely the product of the rinderpest. For instance, cattle were forcefully taken from Ovambanderu to repay the debts allegedly incurred by Kahimemua, prior to his execution and thus prior to the outbreak of rinderpest. There was also the issue of drinking debts. As the missionary chronicles for Omaruru put it:

> For the people and the land it is to be mourned that the intelligent and reasonable Manasse was followed up by his son Michael. He is addicted to liquor and sins of the flesh. Nearly all the baptismal candidates of his werft stay far away from the lessons. Together with his people he is said to have incurred drinking debts of 1700 Marks within a period of three months.[75]

Though it is true that Michael Tjisiseta incurred massive drinking debts within an incredibly short period of time, it must be borne in mind that he had but recently ascended to the chieftaincy of Omaruru. Unlike Manasse, who at the time of his ascendancy, could depend on the wealth generated by his cattle herds, labour export, taxation and Berg Damara serfs to purchase and reward the loyalty of his subjects, Michael inherited a chieftaincy cut off from virtually all forms of income generation. Instead Michael had to rely on the distribution of alcohol, bought on credit from the traders, to ensure the loyalty of his subjects.

Recouping their losses

Deprived of their wealth in cattle, weakened by the activities of Samuel Maharero and Leutwein, and driven ever further into debt, the Herero chiefs attempted to recoup their losses through raiding, exporting labour and selling land. In the unstable conditions that emerged, established *Ovahona* often found

---

[72] Missionary Eich, of Otjozondjupa, was forced to curtail his building programme as there were no more draught animals and as a consequence he was unable to transport building materials from Grootfontein to his mission station at Otjozondjupa. Dr N. Mossolow, *Waterberg: Beitrag zur Geschichte der Missionsstation Otjozondjupa, des Kambazembi-Stammes und des Hererolandes* (Windhoek 1980?) p. 20.

[73] Irle, *Die Herero*, p. 301.

[74] ELCIN, V. Chroniken, Otjimbingwe 1902 and V. Chroniken, Omaruru 1900.

[75] ELCIN, V. Chroniken, Omaruru 1900.

their followers appropriated by new elites who emerged in the wake of the decline of the *ancien régime*. These new elites, who built upon their alliances with German colonists and/or Samuel Maharero, were particularly active in eastern Hereroland.

Raiding

> It is possible that the intense tribal raiding that the Germans experienced in the first years of their stay in East Africa – and to which they reacted so violently – was the direct consequence of economic losses suffered initially through the rinderpest.[76]

Though the above passage refers specifically to eastern, and not south-western, Africa, Kjekshus's statement is particularly relevant here, because, had a traveller happened to visit eastern Hereroland in the late 1890s, he would have been similarly struck by images of seemingly never-ending 'intense tribal raiding'. In the remaining years of the nineteenth century, Herero councillors allied to Samuel Maharero were engaged in extensive raiding in eastern Hereroland, particularly amongst the followers of Tjetjo.[77] These raids began prior to the outbreak of the rinderpest, as Samuel Maharero established himself following his ascension to the paramountcy. With the rinderpest, raiding intensified. It is in this raiding that we see most clearly the emergence of new power elites in Hereroland. With the Okahandja succession dispute of 1890–94, the Herero elites that had been established by Maharero and Zeraua, in the fallout of Afrikaner hegemony in the late 1860s, were effectively pushed aside by the emergence of the usurper Samuel Maharero as paramount chief of the Herero. This process of change in Herero politics was continued and intensified in the aftermath of the rinderpest. It is at this time that young men such as Willy Cain and Kajata, who traditionally had no rights to power by virtue of their descent in the structures established by Maharero and Zeraua, through their association with Samuel Maharero and the colonial state came to emerge as the new Herero *Ovahona*, with large followings of both cattle and people.

In the years immediately prior to the rinderpest, Samuel Maharero and forces loyal to him had engaged in raiding in the guise of boundary enforcement or as reprisal for alleged transgressions against his authority. With the outbreak of the Ovambanderu Khauas-Khoi war, a year prior to the outbreak of rinderpest, the followers of Samuel Maharero were effectively given free rein to raid at will in the eastern districts of Hereroland. The cattleposts of chiefs allied to Kahimemua or Nicodemus Kavikunua were raided throughout the war and in the months thereafter. One such chief, Kahikaeta, who was allied to Kahimemua, received orders to surrender unconditionally, at precisely the same time that Herero troops loyal to Samuel raided no less than 1200 cattle and fourteen guns from him.[78] German forces also engaged in these officially sanctioned raids. By early 1897 forces under the command of Major Mueller had taken no less than 6000 cattle from the Ovambanderu, and cleared the district of all of its Khauas Khoi inhabitants.[79]

A prime victim of these officially sanctioned raids was Tjetjo Kandji, the

---

[76] Kjekshus, *Ecology*, p. 131.

[77] NNAW, ZBU 2027, WII d.9. Contains extensive correspondence regarding Kajata's raiding on behalf of Samuel Maharero.

[78] BAP, RKA 1489, Leutwein in Okahandja, 8/6/96, to AA.

[79] BAP, RKA 1489, Mueller in Gobabis, 10/2/97, to Leutwein.

man who had dared to cross Samuel Maharero following the death of Samuel's uncle and benefactor, Semoundja Kandikirira. After hostilities had begun in eastern Hereroland, Tjetjo wrote to Leutwein in a vain attempt to avert disaster:

> . . . thank you for your letter which was also sent to Wilhelm and Barnabas, I will keep to the treaty . . . my posts are far away so the cheekiness of my youths is theirs, if the cattle are shot I will turn to you and Samuel.[80]

Although Leutwein replied to Tjetjo advising him to move his posts until the end of the war, Tjetjo's claims of neutrality were not accepted. Thus in early 1897 Tjetjo's werft was ordered to pay 300 cattle as compensation for involvement in the war. The cattle were collected from Tjetjo by Willy Cain, the son of one of Maharero's trader accomplices, John Cain.[81] Significantly upon the arrival of a first batch of 190 cattle, they were immediately handed over to traders in Okahandja.[82] Apparently these cattle were not sufficient to pay off Samuel Maharero's debts, for in the margin of a letter reporting the incident, Leutwein scribbled: 'Following discussion with SM a further 1200 head of cattle is to be paid as compensation for war.'[83]

Samuel Maharero's theft of cattle, and Leutwein's willingness to sanction this theft, was given a gloss of legality, when Samuel Maharero declared in a police report, drawn up in the presence of the traders Albert Voigts and Ziegler, that on the orders of Leutwein all Herero involved in the war against the Germans had to pay fines.[84] Samuel continued his police report by noting that, as the sons of Tjetjo had fought alongside Nicodemus – an allegation for which there was no proof – Tjetjo had to pay a fine. Samuel Maharero claimed that Tjetjo had written to him, significantly in a letter allegedly also read by the trader Voigts, that he intended paying Samuel 1700 oxen.[85] All in all it has been estimated that, on the grounds of compensation, in total approximately 12,000 cattle were confiscated following the Ovambanderu war.[86] This was, however, not enough to pay off Samuel's extensive debts, which merely increased with the outbreak of the rinderpest.

Following the rinderpest, forces loyal to Samuel Maharero continued raiding Herero who were alleged to be against him. In early 1898 Herero horsemen and foot soldiers, under the command of one of Samuel Maharero's councillors, Kajata, moved into territory claimed by Tjetjo along the upper black Nossob. Here they plundered the *Werften* and raided what remained of the cattle and small stock of Tjetjo's followers.[87]

> Even at old Joseph's, near Gobabis, fleeing Herero have arrived, who claim that their small stock has been taken from them by the horsemen of Kajata and that one of their big men has either been captured or killed.[88]

In essence these raids were a continuum of the move and expansion into the

[80] BAP, RKA 1488, Tjetyoo Kandyii at Okondyezu, 17/4/96, to Leutwein.
[81] Cain was murdered by Lieutenant Prince Prosper von Arenberg in 1899. On the grounds of 'tropical frenzy' von Arenberg was pardoned. Drechsler, *Fighting*, pp. 134–5.
[82] NNAW, ZBU 2028, W II d 12, Held at Okandjezu, 6/3/96, to Leutwein.
[83] NNAW, ZBU 2028, W II d 12, Leutwein writing in the margin of Held in Okandjezu, 6/3/97, to Leutwein.
[84] NNAW, ZBU 2028, W II d 12, Protocol Okahandja, 29/3/97, Samuel Maharero.
[85] Ibid.
[86] Drechsler, *Fighting*, p. 94.
[87] NNAW, ZBU 2027, W II d 9, the *Bezirkisamt* in Gobabis, 11/1/98, to Lindequist.
[88] NNAW, ZBU 2027, WII d 9, Leutwein in Windhoek, 15/1/98, to Samuel Maharero.

eastern districts, by forces loyal to Samuel Maharero, which had begun
following Samuel's rise to power and installation as paramount chief in 1894.[89]

Survivors clearly saw the alliance that existed between Samuel Maharero
and Leutwein, and reported that Kajata had been sent out under orders of
Samuel Maharero to collect cattle for the German government. The German
authorities, who in other instances had aided and abetted Samuel in his cattle
theft, considered this as going to far. Governor Leutwein wrote to Samuel and
complained that, though Kajata claimed to be raiding on behalf of the
government, this could never be the case, and concluded his letter by ordering
Samuel to command Kajata and his troops to stop what they were doing and
to withdraw from the area.[90] In reply to Leutwein's letter Samuel protested his
innocence and stated that he had only ordered Kajata to guarantee that the
Herero, living in the eastern districts, did not cross over into the Bechuanaland
Protectorate. Samuel concluded his letter as follows: 'If cattle have been
confiscated this has been without my prior knowledge.'[91]

In essence both Samuel Maharero and Leutwein were lying. In response to
Kajata's raiding, Tjetjo complained to the German officers Reiss and Heldt,
and asked them to intercede and to prevent further raids.[92] Following Tjetjo's
request, the German authorities ordered Samuel Maharero to prohibit any
further raiding by Kajata.[93] Yet at exactly the same time that this correspondence
was going on, one of the officers, Reiss, to whom Tjetjo had complained,
submitted a report of his activities in the eastern districts.

> To report that the native patrols – Willy's people – sent out between Okomotjize
> and Oliphantskloof have visited all the *Bandjeru Werften* . . . When the patrol arrived
> at the *Werft*, the chaps [*Kerls*] started shouting, 'those are Willy Cain's people, those
> are Germans we must kill them.' . . . As punishment we took the stock from 3 werften,
> 10 cows and 27 small stock.[94]

Six months later, in August 1898, Reiss described how he participated in
another raid.

> I rode with 10 horsemen, Willy Cain with 13 of his people, [and] Traugott Tjetjo
> [the son of Tjetjo Kandji] with 3 men. We travelled in the night from Olifantskloof
> to the Big pan, where we arrived after the moon had set. At this time the Hereros,
> due to the great cold, go to bed and I wished to surprise the werften with no prior
> warning.[95]

In this raid five *Werften* were dismantled and between 150 and 200 Banderu
were disarmed and placed under the control of Traugott Tjetjo. A few months
later these Banderu were placed under Willy Cain.[96]

Raiding, conducted in the guise of fines for alleged transgressions, as well
as raiding with no gloss of legitimation, continued throughout the remaining
years of the nineteenth century. This raiding took place primarily so as to offset

---

[89] See previous chapter and *BRMG* 1895, p. 71 for references to Kanangati Hoveka, Kajata and
Mbataera moving into the eastern districts at the command of Samuel Maharero.
[90] NNAW, ZBU 2027, WII d 9, Band 2, Leutwein in Windhoek, 15/1/98, to Samuel Maharero.
[91] NNAW, ZBU 2027, WII d 9, Band 2, Samuel Maharero in Okahandja, 23/1/98, to Leutwein.
[92] NNAW, ZBU 2028, W II d 12, Tjetjoo Kandjii in Otjihaenena, ?/1/98, to Leutwein.
[93] NNAW, ZBU 2028, W II d 12, von Lindequist at Okondjesu to Tjetjo.
[94] NNAW, ZBU 2028, W II d 14, Band 2, Reiss in Epukiro, 3/2/98, to *Kaiserliche Landeshauptmannschaft.*
[95] NNAW, ZBU 2028, W II d 14, Reiss in Oas, 4/8/98, to *Kaiserliche Landeshauptmannschaft.*
[96] NNAW, ZBU 2028, W II d 14, Reiss in Oas, 16/8/98, to *Kaiserliche Landeshauptmannschaft.*

the lack of capital which had resulted from the rinderpest, and to repay debts to traders.[97] A report written by Lieutenant Streitwolf, a German officer instructed to prevent further raiding, provides a clear insight into the situation:

> . . . activities undertaken with regard to the plundering by the sub-captains living along the Black Nossob. 1.) Once again I have most sternly warned Samuel and his big men to desist from these attacks. 2.) I have travelled to Otjosazu Otjoniati, Otjituesu, Omunjeriti, Okatumba, Otjihenena, . . .
>
> The chiefs assured me that they had only collected cattle with which to satisfy the demands of the Boer Swart, of Epukiro, who had demanded the payment of oxen owed to him as war reparation [*Strafochsen*], and another case so as to pay off debts owed to the trader Wiese. The driving together of cattle by the chiefs is therefore only partly as a result of the egotistical [*eigerose*] activities of the traders. This is backed up by Lang [Rhenish missionary] who accompanied me on a trip to the Nossob. Salesman Albert Voigts denies that any of his employees demanded stock from the captains.[98]

Contemporary reports make abundantly clear that the raids conducted by Kanangati Hoveka, Willy Cain and Kajata, in eastern Hereroland, were conducted to acquire cattle with which to pay off debts to the traders, Albert Voigts, Ziegler, Wiese and Swart.[99]

The Ovambanderu war coupled with the rinderpest allowed for the expansion of Samuel Maharero's authority into eastern Hereroland, an area hitherto closed to the authority of the chiefs of Okahandja. The move into the eastern districts provided Samuel Maharero with substantial tracts of land, cattle and people, with which he could in turn purchase and maintain the loyalty of his subjects. These eastern territories were brought into his ambit by allied raiders dependent upon him for their position. The men engaged in this raiding, on behalf of Samuel Maharero, acquired small stock, cattle, guns, followers and in some instances people. In short they became the new power elites of the territory.

Labour

> For the building of the railway line from Swakopmund to Windhoek, which will start this year, a large number of people, christians and heathens, have also been recruited here and will be sent to Swakopmund. Large numbers of Ovambo, also recruited as labour for the railwayline, passed [the station]. From the other stations labourers have also been sent there. Manasse gave the people the former school teacher Asser Mutjinde as their foreman.[100]

A further way in which the chiefs recouped their capital losses was through the trade in labour. As mentioned earlier, the newly developing German colonial state was desperately short of labour and consequently it sought to alleviate this shortage by paying commission to Herero chiefs who supplied labour to the colonial state, and by importing labour from Ovamboland, at that stage still beyond German control. As Tjetjo, who was trying to reestablish his power, implored: 'Give me the money of my people which are with you, give it to my

[97] NNAW, ZBU 2027, WII D 9, Streitwolf in Okahandja, 25/7/99, to Leutwein.
[98] Ibid.
[99] NNAW, ZBU 2027, WII D 9, Statement by missionary Lang of Otjihaenena in Okahandja, 29/6/99. For Voigts and Ziegler, see NNAW, ZBU 2028, W II d 12, Protocol Samuel Maharero. Swart and Wiese, see NNAW, ZBU 2027, W II d 9, Streitwolf in Okahandja 25/7/99 to Leutwein [?].
[100] ELCIN, V. Chroniken, Omaruru 1897.

messenger.'[101] Both Herero and Ovambo chiefs appointed headmen who accompanied the labour gangs to their places of employment. This was done not only to ensure that the monies paid were returned to the chief, but also to ensure that an eye could be kept on conditions of employment. It was following reports to Tjetjo by Jacob, one such foreman appointed by Tjetjo, that Tjetjo withdrew his labourers from German service, at which Lindequist was forced to write to Tjetjo requesting that he continue to send labourers. Lindequist concluded his letter as follows:

> Why do the people in this country always tell so many stories and lies about the government, who gives them their food, so that they can be sated and do not hunger? If you have now heard the truth from Jacob, regarding the manner in which my people treated your people here in Windhoek and you have seen how well things are with them, then send even more people as labour to me, as you promised me previously.[102]

Though it is clear that the labourers referred to were still largely free to desert when conditions warranted it, the same cannot be said for all of the labourers supplied. It has already been noted that in early 1898 Willy Cain took part in a number of officially sanctioned labour raids on Banderu settlements in eastern Hereroland. Following requests from Willy Cain, the German commanding officer, Reiss, placed the inhabitants of these Banderu *Werften*, which they had raided together, into the care of Willy Cain, who in turn now supplied a number of these Banderu as labourers on six-month contracts to the colonial state.[103]

Land sales
Rinderpest cleared the land of cattle, pastures were abandoned as cattle died and pastoralists were forced to move to other areas to survive. Following the rinderpest, Herero chiefs took to selling large tracts of land, some of it in the middle of their territories.[104] Prior to the rinderpest Samuel Maharero, in attempting to shore up his position through the payments of cash and liquor, had already taken to selling land, initially often beyond the domains of Okahandja.[105] After the rinderpest, Samuel Maharero was joined in this activity by Michael Tjisiseta and Salatiel Kambazembi who also sought to rid themselves of their debts and acquire funds with which to purchase and maintain the loyalty of their subjects.[106] For their part, the traders, in attempting to live up to their ideals of becoming settler farmers, sought to acquire land and sold goods on credit with land given as mortgage. The missionary chronicles of Omaruru provide a fine illustration of this process.

> . . . the traders speculate primarily on the acquisition of farms, of which Michael has already sold a substantial amount. The missionary has repeatedly warned him of the suicidal implications of his dealings, however without success. In this way Michael has already sold the whole of the right bank of the Omaruru river from 8 kilometres below until 3 kilometres above Omburo, so that the mission station Omburo has lost half of its grazing grounds. Furthermore downstream he has already sold the farm Ovimbara, which, however, is necessary for the survival of Omaruru. By this selling of farms the chief now often acquires money in his hand and one can

[101] NNAW, ZBU 2028, W II d 12, Tjetjo, 23/7/00, to Leutwein.
[102] NNAW, ZBU 2028, W II d 12, von Lindequist in Windhoek, early 1898, to Tjetjo.
[103] NNAW, ZBU 2028, W II d 14, Reiss in Epukiro, 16/8/98 and 27/8/98, to Leutwein.
[104] Leutwein quoted in Drechsler, *Fighting*, p. 113.
[105] See particularly Samuel's land sales in the Otjiwarongo district.
[106] Pool, *Maharero*, pp. 166ff for a discussion on land sales and debt.

usually notice when a further payment has been made. Then the young folk ride around the place like wildmen until deep at night so that one cannot but feel sorry for the poor horses.[107]

Movement

Thus far we have only touched, in passing, on a further consequence of the rinderpest, that of the extensive social and geographical mobility and movement of Herero rinderpest survivors. To escape raiding, debt collecting, hungry relatives, hunger, new legislation, evictions, forced labour and disease, many Herero survivors abandoned their ancestral homes and sought a brighter future elsewhere.[108] Those who still owned cattle but were not allied to the new power elite that had emerged around Samuel Maharero attempted to escape, with their herds, eastwards into the comparative sanctuary of the Bechuanaland Protectorate, or northwards to the Ovambo kingdoms and the Kaokoveld.

During the early nineteenth century following a succession dispute in the Bamangwato polity in what is now south-eastern Botswana, Tawana, the eldest son, but not the heir to Mathiba, the *Kgosi* of the Bamangwato, trekked north together with his followers, and established the Batawana kingdom, with control over Lake Ngami and the Okavango delta in what is now north-western Botswana. In full control of the trade leading to and from this wealthy area, the Batawana became the most powerful society on the eastern flank of the Herero. Herero traders and hunters, wishing to continue operating in the northern Kalahari, had to pay tribute to the Batawana. Both Banderu and Herero traditions record that, at some stage during the nineteenth century, reciprocal sanctuary agreements were reached with Sekgoma Letsholathebe, the then *Kgosi* of the Batawana.[109] Already prior to the death of Maharero, Herero had begun abandoning Hereroland, which at that stage was in turmoil as a result of the war with Hendrik Witbooi, and exchanging it for the relative peace of Batawana rule in Ngamiland in the Bechuanaland Protectorate. This movement increased as Mbanderu refugees fled the war of 1896, and it continued after the rinderpest through to 1904 and beyond. The Herero who trekked into the Bechuanaland Protectorate could, broadly speaking, be divided into two categories, those with cattle and those without cattle. Those with cattle tended to settle just beyond the Namibia boundary, near to Olifantskloof, on the outer reaches or just beyond the reach of Batawana authority and tribute collection. A number of those who entered the Bechuanaland Protectorate without cattle found employment on the Boer farms, which had recently been established in the Ghanzi area, whilst the majority of them trekked on to Tsau and Ngamiland proper.[110] Substantial numbers of Herero, with or without

---

[107] ELCIN, V. Chroniken, Omaruru 1900.
[108] For moves as a result of raiding see NNAW, ZBU 2027, W II d 9, Streitwolf in Okahandja, 25/7/99, to Leutwein; Samuel Maharero in Okahandja, 23/1/98, to Leutwein & ZBU 2028, W II d 14, Band 2, Reiss in Epukiro, 3/2/98, to *Kaiserliche Landeshauptmannschaft*. For people moving due to demands of debtors and hungry relatives see ELCIN, V. Chroniken, Otjimbingwe 1902.
[109] Josaphat Hahn, 'Die Ovaherero' in *Zeitschrift der Gesellschaft für Erdkunde zu Berlin*, 1869, p. 244. Refers to Batawana traders in Okahandja in 1868 to trade and to conclude agreements with Maharero. It is possible that this meeting came to be the basis of the mutual refuge agreement that existed between the Batawana and the Herero and Mbanderu.
[110] BNA, HC.145/1, Resident Commissioner in Mafeking, 15/12/97, to High Commissioner. In late 1897 British colonial officials, operating in the Ghanzi district of the BP, were at a loss with what to do with over 200 Herero who had moved into the area and had taken to squatting on the farms newly allocated to Trekboers, who had been brought in by the BSAC of Cecil John Rhodes.

cattle, also trekked northwards into the Kaokoveld and Ovamboland beyond German control.[111]

Both the German colonial authorities and the Hereros allied to them were anxious to regain control over the people and flocks who had withdrawn from their control, and to prevent a further exodus. In early 1898 German patrols travelled throughout the eastern districts of Hereroland urging Kajata, and other Herero chiefs allied to Samuel Maharero, to desist from raiding the remaining settlements of Tjetjo and the Mbanderu, and to assist in preventing these settlements from crossing over into the Bechuanaland Protectorate.[112] Somewhat paradoxically, at the same time patrols of German and Herero soldiers were also engaged in raiding these selfsame settlements.[113] At times these patrols even crossed the boundary into the Bechuanaland Protectorate to raid *Werften* which had sought sanctuary in British territory.[114] Indeed German officers even asked for permission to raid *Werften* lying beyond Rietfontein within British territory. In one instance it had already been decided beforehand to whom the prisoners, who still needed to be captured, were to be allocated.[115] Not surprisingly Pr Lt Reiss, who along with Cain and Kajata, had profited from the captured stock and people, was able to lie and conclude:

> ... except for a few armed insurgents, the German area has been cleaned [*gesäubert*] ... the big Banderu trek, which exited via Epata a year ago has completely perished of thirst, up to the last child and last piece of stock.[116]

Elsewhere in the territory, following the rinderpest, an ethnic swap appeared to be taking place at settlements as Herero increasingly sought to move out to the field whilst Damara increasingly came in from the field.

> It was as if the Bergdamara had grown tired of living in the field whilst in turn the Herero increasingly removed their *Werften* to the outer veld particularly to Oyjiuua.[117]

This apparent reversal was probably increased as impoverished Herero of the settlements were employed as herders for those who still had some stock. Thus Herero, whose herds had been decimated, no longer had a need for Berg Damara herders. The need for herders was henceforth primarily fulfilled along lines of ethnic solidarity. That is, Herero with stock appeared to be more inclined to employ impoverished Herero. At the same time it was clear that this was also part of the process whereby Herero left the settlements to escape debts and German laws.

One of the suggestions considered by the Bechuanaland Protectorate administration was that, 'It might be possible to settle these Demaras as cotters or bijwooners with such boers as may require them.' BNA, HC.145/1, Lt Scholefield in Tsau ?, 8/12/97 to RC.
[111] For instance ELCIN, V. Chroniken, Omaruru 1901 makes mention of people with cattle moving away to other areas. Given Omaruru's northern orientation it is probable that these people and herds travelled to the lands of the Ndonga kings and the Kaokoveld chiefs.
[112] NNAW, ZBU 2027, W II d 9, Streitwolf in Okahandja, 25/7/99, to Leutwein.
[113] NNAW, ZBU 2028, W II d 14, Reiss in Epukiro, 3/2/98, to *Kaiserliche Landeshauptmannschaft*.
[114] NNAW, ZBU 2028, W II d 14 Band 2, Reiss in Epukiro, 4/8/98, to *Kaiserliche Landeshauptmannschaft*.
[115] NNAW, ZBU 2028, W II d 14 Band 2, Reiss in Epukiro, 16/8/98 & 27/8/98, to Leutwein. A few weeks later these unfortunates were placed into the hands of Willy Cain who in turn sent them out on six-month contracts to the German colonial state.
[116] NNAW, ZBU 2028, W II d 14 Band 2, Reiss in Epukiro, 4/8/98, to *Kaiserliche Landeshauptmannschaft*.
[117] ELCIN, V. Chroniken, Otjimbingwe 1899.

For some it is the police, with their freedom curbing and punishment mandating proclamations, who became the cause for leaving the Station and withdrawing into the field.[118]

The movement of Herero away from the stations was exacerbated by the drought. Eventually the only Herero who remained on the station were those with continued access to gardens.[119]

Not surprisingly, a result of this movement was that the Rhenish missionaries increasingly lost control of their spiritual flocks. This loss of souls galled the missionaries. An extreme example of this is provided by the missionary chronicles for Otjimbingwe. Here the missionaries lauded the economic decline of Otjimbingwe, which had resulted from the development of the railway-line from Swakopmund to Windhoek. Otjimbingwe, as a thoroughfare for goods and materials, ceased to be a place of importance, and with the decrease in Otjimbingwe's economic importance the missionaries hoped that Herero would return to congregate at the settlement to escape from the disliked regime of the German government.[120] In this it is interesting to note that the missionaries were attempting to reassert, or rather regain, their central role of importance to Herero society. That is, they attempted to reassert their ascendancy over a large section of Herero society, which had been lost with the coming of the German colonial state.

People trekking away from the settlements sought to gain access to unsettled lands, particularly for those without cattle, lands which to some extent could be farmed. In some districts impoverished Herero were moved, with the assistance of the German authorities, to other districts, where there was the possibility of conducting agriculture or living as *bijwoners* with Trekboers and newly settled German settlers. In 1898 on the advice of *Distriktschef* Dr Kuhn a number of Herero families, consisting of thirty to forty men, twenty women and fifteen children, trekked from the Omaruru area to Grootfontein, 'as their cattle had died of the pest and they would otherwise have died of hunger'.[121]

Conversely though, the German authorities were also clearly worried by the increased mobility of Herero who were no longer encumbered by their cattle herds. This led to the belief that the Herero were more inclined to war, as, having lost everything already, they now no longer had anything to lose.[122] As a consequence of this fear the German authorities attempted to gain a measure of control on the movement of Herero. This was particularly the case at Outjo, where the *Distriktschef* Franke prohibited the movement of Herero without officially sanctioned business in the district.[123] In the activities of Franke, seeking to limit the movement of Herero, and the missionaries, seeking to ensure Herero access to land free from colonial intervention, we see the beginnings of what would later become the *Reservationsfrage*, reservation question.

Referred to in passing above was the movement of Herero into wage labour. Initially this move was out of pure necesssity, though it soon became a way in

[118] ELCIN, V. Chroniken, Omaruru 1902. JBG's translation.
[119] ELCIN, V. Chroniken, Otjimbingwe 1900.
[120] ELCIN, V. Chroniken, Otjimbingwe 1899.
[121] ELCIN, V. Chroniken, Grootfontein 1898. Apart from the Herero there were also about 20 Bushmen and 20 Berg Damaras.
[122] NNAW, ZBU 2027, WII D 11, Volkmann at Waterberg, 27/2/01, to Leutwein.
[123] ELCIN, V. Chroniken, Omaruru 1900.

which to finance re-stocking. However, as has been noted for other parts of the subcontinent, large numbers of people who tried to reinvest in cattle herds were forced to make a permanent move off the land and become wage labourers.[124] This proletarianization also occurred in central Namibia, where 'those without possessions moved to other areas, with their children to Karibib or to the railway so as to be able to support themselves'.[125]

Herero found employment assisting in the construction of the railway-line, for which funding was provided by the German state following rinderpest, from Swakopmund to Windhoek.[126] Herero men found extensive employment with the German colonial authorities, where they were primarily employed in assisting in the building of military garrisons. Herero women and children were employed in what are now referred to as 'work for food' programmes. In Otjimbingwe, a mission station which had been totally denuded of all its trees forty years earlier, women and children brought wood to the missionaries in exchange for milk and rice.[127] Large numbers of Herero women were employed as washerwomen by the German troops. The missionaries, however, were not overly impressed by this form of employment: '. . . women doing the washing of the soldiers. This last form of employment also forms an ample source of many moral dangers [sittlicher Gefahren].'[128] Employment was also found in the mines run by the SWACO in northern Namibia:

> Dr Hartmann of the SWACO and English miners passed to the north for the copper. The native labourers, who are not being kept in custody in Outjo and who will receive 3 Mark per month, will probably trek to the copper mines.[129]

With the ending of the Anglo-Boer war in South Africa, the newly reopened gold mines of the Transvaal and diamond mines of Kimberley once again began devouring labour. Herero rinderpest survivors were also recruited for these mines.[130]

The balance

Rinderpest broke the economic basis of Herero society. The established political structures of Herero society, which had already been significantly transformed by the activities of Leutwein and Samuel Maharero, were further altered by the disease. Herero lands were lost for ever and a substantial number of Herero were transformed from pastoralists into proletarians. Effectively within the space of a few months Herero society was completely transformed from being an independent autonomous whole into a series of dependent and splintered parts.

On the level of the colonial state the new intrusive forms of governance

[124] Van Onselen, JAH, p. 486.
[125] ELCIN, V. Chroniken, Otjimbingwe 1901.
[126] In Bechuanaland, too, the railway to Rhodesia was built, in part, by 'rinderpest labour'. Van Onselen, JAH, p. 486 quoting from A.J. Wills, An Introduction to the History of Central Africa, p. 159.
[127] ELCIN, V. Chroniken, Otjimbingwe 1902.
[128] ELCIN, V. Chroniken, Omaruru 1899.
[129] ELCIN, V. Chroniken, Omaruru 1900.
[130] J.-B. Gewald, The Road of the Man called Love and the Sack of Sero (Boston 1993) ASA annual conference paper.

increased their control over central Namibia. Following rinderpest, massive displays of power, as had been demonstrated in mid-1896 by Leutwein in Omaruru with 300 soldiers, 100 auxiliaries and two cannons, were no longer necessary.[131] Omaruru's power, and along with it the polities of Kahimemua, Tjetjo and Kambazembi, had been broken. In their stead the colonial state asserted its authority and control of social and economic life.

Whilst the epidemic was raging through the country, the colonial state had begun increasing its control through the allocation of vaccine. Those who had access to the colonial state, or who were allied to the Germans, received vaccine. The Etaneno affair indicated that those with friendly relations with the Germans could expect their herds to be vaccinated. Those with less cordial relations to the colonial state and its agents could expect their cattle to be slaughtered to provide gall vaccine for the herds of those Herero who were well connected to the colonial state. However, those with herds which had been vaccinated were soon to discover that this vaccination was not without its costs. A tax had to be paid in cattle for the vaccinations administered. This was not something people took lightly. When Estorff travelled the eastern districts to round up cattle as vaccination taxes, he was accompanied by no less than seventy mounted men and a cannon.[132] The colonial state was thorough in its tax collection. Following the Etaneno affair, where cattle were culled for vaccine for other people's herds, German officers came to collect vaccination tax from the headman at Etaneno.[133] In instances where Herero cattle owners were unable to pay, grazing land was taken in lieu of cattle.[134]

Dealing with another part of southern Africa devastated by rinderpest, Shula Marks noted the observation of the Natal administration 'that the destruction of African cattle gave the colony a most favourable opportunity for delimiting African lands which had thus been vacated'.[135] The same held true for Namibia. Even prior to the arrival of the disease in the territory, the threat of rinderpest was used to further the ends of the colonial state in the clearance of land for land companies and settlers. Indeed in late 1896 Leutwein explicitly used the threat of rinderpest against Manasse Tjisiseta of Omaruru to ensure that the cattleposts of his subjects were withdrawn from the lands allocated to and appropriated by the SWACO.[136] Following the rinderpest the Herero chiefs took to selling extensive tracts of land in an effort to recoup losses suffered. In effect, this meant that the colonial state found itself in a position where it had the power to decide on and allocate land without anything but the slightest of consultations with the Herero chiefs. In effect, the colonial state claimed ultimate authority over all land allocation. This is best reflected in discussions relating to the allocation of reserve lands to the territory's autochthonous populace.[137]

---

[131] ELCIN, V. Chroniken, Omaruru 1896.

[132] Mossolow, *Waterberg*, p. 22.

[133] NNAW, ZBU 2027, WII D 10 Band 2, von Lindequist in Windhoek, 16/4/98, to Omaruru *Kaiserliche Distrikts Kommando*.

[134] Drechsler, *Fighting*, p. 98.

[135] S. Marks, *Reluctant Rebellion* (Oxford 1970), p. 130, cited in van Onselen, *JAH*, p. 487.

[136] NNAW, ZBU 2027, WII D 10, Leutwein in Windhoek, 2/10/96, to Manasse.

[137] See ELCIN, V. Chroniken, Omaruru 1901. NNAW, ZBU 2032, *Berlin 16/2/02 Bericht betreffend Schaffung von Reservaten für Eingeborenen im Hererolande*, written by Volkmann at the request of the foreign office.

By the late 1890s, Rhenish missionaries, alarmed by the extensive Herero land sales and consequent loss of land, had begun petitioning the colonial state to allocate reserves of inalienable land to the Rhenish mission and to the Herero living there. In their petitions the missionaries argued that either the Herero be given extensive tracts of land, so as to allow them to reestablish themselves as pastoralists, or that extremely fertile lands be allocated to the Herero, so that they could build upon their new-found existence as agriculturalists.[138] On the issue of reserve allocations, apart from petitions from the Rhenish missionary society, the colonial state also garnered information from its own representatives. On the whole these representatives were not in favour of allocating inalienable tracts of land to the Herero. In a report written at the request of the *Auswärtiges Amt*, as part of the discussion initiated by the Rhenish Mission Society, Lieutenant Volkmann wrote:

> According to my opinion there is at this moment in time absolutely no necessity for there to be a general regulation regarding the reservation question.
>
> As a result of the rinderpest the stock of the Herero has been decimated for years to come, added to this during the last couple of years the population has decreased, as a result of diseases, to such an extent that at this moment approximately half of the 'dependable' waterholes in northern Hereroland are uninhabited.

Volkmann concluded his report by noting that he was totally against the establishment of reserves, primarily because it would then become necessary for permission to be asked before one could build roads, dams and railways.[139]

For Theodor Leutwein, who was governor of German South West Africa at the time, the most important result of the rinderpest was that it led to the construction of the railway-line between Swakopmund and Windhoek.[140] Already in 1896 Leutwein had requested funds from the German government for the construction of a railway-line between Swakopmund and Windhoek.[141] In the years immediately following the establishment of a German protectorate, there was a dramatic increase in the amount of freight transport. This led to serious environmental degradation which in turn limited the extent to which ox-drawn freight transport could expand. However, it was not until rinderpest had halted all forms of bovine freight transport that funds were finally granted.[142]

The increased mobility that came about as a result of the railway construction had a threefold impact upon Herero society. The most immediate impact was that the train totally undercut all previous forms of freight transport in the territory. This primarily affected those Herero who were engaged in *Frachtfahren*, particularly the chiefs who saw their power and income reduced even further.[143] The second impact was that new centres, such as Karibib and Usakos, came to acquire regional importance whilst Otjimbingwe declined in

---

[138] ELCIN, V. Chroniken, Omaruru 1901. NNAW, ZBU 2032, ZBU 3032, WII e1, *Eingeborenenreservate und Lokationen 'generalia', Band 1 & WII e2 Eingeborenen Reservate und Lokationen specilia, Band 1.*

[139] NNAW, ZBU 2032, *Berlin 16/2/02 Bericht betreffend schaffung von Reservaten fur Eingeborenen im Hererolande,* Volkmann & Report by *Distriktschef Oberleutenant* Kuhn of 1/3/02.

[140] Leutwein, *Elf Jahre,* p. 132.

[141] BAP, RKA 2101, Leutwein in Windhoek, 20/7/96, to AA, calls for the establishment of railway-line.

[142] Weber, *Geschichte,* p. 77.

[143] ELCIN, V. Chroniken, Otjimbingwe 1899.

importance as the railway bypassed the settlement.[144] The third factor, which in due course would have dire consequences for Herero society, was that German troops could henceforth be easily transported and resupplied.

In building the railway, initially from Swakopmund to Windhoek and later from Usakos to Otavi, the German colonial state acquired extensive control over labourers who, had they not worked, would have died of starvation. In late 1897, following the maltreatment of labourers sent to work on the railway, Manasse Tjisiseta of Omaruru wrote to the German authorities:

> From here I have nothing to tell you; except the famine that oppresses us we are still well . . . Last time you were here you came to ask for labour for the railway, I replied yes and no. The no I based on the fear I had for my willing workers for the mistreatment and difficulties, you said that you would protect the Herero against these problems, and I said that I would support the issue, when you left I gathered the other chiefs and sent 160 people, however that which I feared has now come to pass. The people are now fleeing from Swakopmund they fear the hard treatment and that they do not receive enough food for the heavy work that they have to do.[145]

The death of Manasse and the subsequent accession of his son Michael is a fine indicator as to the extent to which the colonial state was able to increase its presence in Omaruru, which had hitherto had a strong anti-German reputation. It is inconceivable that, prior to the rinderpest, the *Otjira* of Omaruru would have permitted the German authorities to decide upon Manasse's successor. However, this did occur, primarily because the colonial state had the power to sanction and legalize the land sales of *Otjira* members, who now indulged in these transactions in an effort to accumulate capital following the rinderpest. The extent of this dependency was emphasized when in 1899 an extra contingent of soldiers was introduced into the town without a murmur of discontent.[146]

The impact of rinderpest was also felt in the ways in which Herero made sense of the world around them. Ideas regarding the causes and effects of disasters are created and transformed within a field of public discussion and reflect generally accepted beliefs and prejudices. During the late 1980s Zimbabwean friends of mine jokingly changed the acronym AIDS into an 'American Induced Disease to Stop Sex'. In doing this they reflected the generally accepted idea that AIDS was but another in a long line of western donor attempts at reducing the Zimbabwean birth rate. Similarly whilst conducting fieldwork, informants would tell me that the rinderpest had been induced by Kahimemua Nguvauva or that the disease had been created by the Germans. As in other parts of Africa, people believed that rinderpest had been engineered by whites; indeed there was a 'universal suspicion that the whole rinderpest enterprise was a sinister device to impoverish Africans in order to coerce them into the white man's services'.[147] The various observers at the time had varying ideas as to the causes of the disease, and in effect the extent of

---

[144] The missionaries cheered this development as they believed that Otjimbingwe could now form a centre away from German interest and influence in which the Herero could be exposed to the Good Word. ELCIN, V. Chroniken, Otjimbingwe 1899.

[145] NNAW, ZBU 2027, WII d 10, Manasse in Omaruru, 23/11/97, to Leutwein.

[146] ELCIN, V. Chroniken, Omaruru 1899, mentions that at mid-year an extra contingent of soldiers was introduced into the town.

[147] Pule Phoofolo, 'Epidemics and Revolutions' in *Past and Present*, p. 134.

their reflections on the topic are an indication as to the stupendous impact the disease had on society as a whole.

Commentators have noted that the Herero in German South West Africa, devastated by the loss of their cattle, were placed at the mercy of the missionaries. As a consequence of convenience or conviction, they went to the mission stations. Throughout the land there were, as another commentator has put it, 'signs of a general movement towards conversion, which the missionaries saw as a blessing concealed in the disaster'.[148] Though this may generally speaking be true, the specifics of the situation indicate that this conversion was part of a process. The case of events at the mission station Otjimbingwe, which lay along the main coastal ox-waggon route, illustrates this point well. At first missionaries at the mission station in Otjimbingwe were ecstatic at the appearance of rinderpest, as they believed that the initially selective impact of the disease had vindicated their belief in Jesus Christ and his teachings. When the disease approached the settlement, Herero herds were withdrawn from the station and dispersed to the many cattleposts in the field. As a consequence the disease initially appeared to have spared the settlement, particularly as a mere 6 per cent of the inoculated cattle died. Enthusiastic in their apparent deliverance the missionaries reported that people were saying that the disease had spared Otjimbingwe as its inhabitants had prayed to God. However, this deliverance was of but short duration. A few weeks later the disease ravaged the cattle herds of Otjimbingwe in the same way as it had decimated herds elsewhere in the territory. However, the missionaries saw this yet again as a message from God.

> . . . what was more important was that the whole populace had received a deep impression of the punishing hand of God [züchtigenden Hand Gottes] and that the punishments of the Lord brought about the necessary respect for his justice.[149]

These ideas were also shared by sections of the colonial authorities. The rinderpest was a blessing in disguise; the Herero would now be converted.[150] There was indeed a major move to the missions by large numbers of Herero. Those who argue cynically that the sole reason for Herero conversion was to gather material benefits from the missions are unaware of the extreme rigour with which mission Christianity had to be lived. Becoming a Christian did not merely entail claiming a belief in a Christian God; it required a complete change of lifestyle. Missionary reports of church services at the time illustrate this point.

> The serious Christians seek their refuge in prayer. The evening hours of prayer in the church and on Sundays after the services are well attended. I note here that the hours of prayer were an initiative that emerged completely out of the people's own wishes.[151]

[148] H. Bley, South West Africa under German Rule (London 1971) p. 123.
[149] ELCIN, V. Chroniken, Otjimbingwe 1897.
[150] ELCIN, V. Chroniken, Omaruru 1897.

> In a conversation with the missionaries he [von Estorff] said, that he hoped that this period of crisis would become a blessed period for missionary work. He himself had requested that the Landeshauptmannschaft in Windhoek ask our Missionary society or more missionaries, as he was convinced that the Herero people would now turn to Christianity and that this period should not be allowed to pass by unused.

> JBG's translation.

[151] BRMG, 1897, p. 324.

Added to this was the fact that the missionaries were at times well aware of their own position within Hereroland society. They were cynical enough to realize that not all their converts were true believers. Indeed they said as much in their reports and they did not shy away from using material inducements to attract and convert souls. However, the truth was that:

> . . . the gifts of charity by the Missionary community in the homeland, which consisted of rice and meal for the starving did not fail in their impact on the Herero. Heathendom broke down. Offers to the dead were no longer made. The holy sacrificial oxen had been torn away by the storm: the death laments grew silent; polygamous marriages were as good as totally dissolved through death.[152]

It was not merely the fact that Herero cattle, as food and capital, were destroyed. Herero cattle formed the underpinning of their society. Through the death of their cattle, Herero society was plunged into a fundamental crisis, a crisis that tore asunder many of the social boundaries and beliefs that people had shared prior to the rinderpest. One particularly fundamental boundary that collapsed was that which existed between generations. The rinderpest tore asunder the age sets and generational boundaries that had limited access to cattle:

> The youth, who have to assist in the vaccination, receive an ox for every day that they work; this was their salary; and with this they danced and sang.[153]

Young, uninitiated youths were granted permission to cull cattle, irrespective of the taboos which existed within Herero society. Herero youths, too young to own cattle, were paid cattle to kill cattle which were ostensibly healthy. Society was turned upside-down, old values no longer appeared to be relevant, and Herero society, in attempting to come to grips with what was happening, changed.

At the level of the settlers, the most important impact of the rinderpest was that they gained access to land which had hitherto been inaccessible. The German punitive measures against those who were accused of having 'revolted' in 1896, together with the rinderpest, depleted the cattle herds along the White Nossob river and the Seeis river to such an extent that large parts of Hereroland were left open and ungrazed.[154] Due to Herero land sales large numbers of settlers were now able to claim and move onto lands previously owned by Herero.[155] Another factor was that, as a result of the rinderpest, cattle ranching now became a viable option for settler farmers. Following the rinderpest cattle prices rose to three times their pre-rinderpest level and: 'It was only now, with the Herero out of competition that the rearing of cattle became a profitable business.'[156]

Conclusion

Kevin Shillington has written on the southern Tswana:

> Rinderpest . . . helped to accelerate that process which the natural limitations of the

---

152 Irle, *Die Herero*, p. 303.
153 *BRMG*, 1897, p. 323.
154 Pool, *Maharero*, p. 165.
155 ELCIN, V. Chroniken, Omaruru 1897. Due to sale of land to the SWACO many Boers trekked to Omaruru and Otjimbingwe.
156 Drechsler, *Fighting*, p. 98.

ecology combined with the coercive policies of colonization had done so much to promote in the preceding decades.[157]

In a sense this was also the case with Herero society. Rinderpest and colonization were processes that fed into and off one another. Due to the activities of Theodor Leutwein and Samuel Maharero, people and cattle had been pushed together onto ever smaller areas of land. Not only had this led to a heavy burden being placed on limited and scarce environmental resources, it had also facilitated the spread and impact of rinderpest when the disease struck. Added to this, Samuel Maharero and Theodor Leutwein had, prior to rinderpest, substantially weakened the position of the remaining Herero chiefs; with the rinderpest the power of these chiefs was further reduced, as they lost the means to control the loyalty of their followers. The economic devastation that rinderpest wrought upon Herero society ensured that the society became hopelessly indebted, which in turn led to further labour export, land sales and continued dispossession.

As a result of the rinderpest epidemic there was a major break in Herero society as it existed before and in the aftermath of the disease. Rinderpest finalized the breakdown in authority of the chiefs who had already been weakened and encapsulated by the activities of Theodor Leutwein and Samuel Maharero. In the aftermath of the epidemic, as Samuel Maharero sought to recoup his losses, new Herero elites allied to Samuel Maharero emerged. Men such as Willy Cain and Kajata, who overshadowed and defeated Tjetjo Kandjii in eastern Hereroland.

Herero were forced to seek new forms of economic subsistence. Herero commoners were forced into wage labour or indentureship, within their own territories and in other countries. Herero chiefs took to selling large tracts of land to traders and land companies, whereby further stretches of Herero territory were opened to settler occupation and thus further Herero dispossession.

Socially rinderpest transformed Herero society. Age boundaries were broken as young uninitiated men acquired cattle, power and wealth independently of their elders. At the same time systems of patronage that had existed were either transformed or destroyed. Unable to provide cattle, chiefs sought to bind their subjects to them through the allocation of alcohol – something that had happened before, but now with the absence of cattle this form of patronage increased. It was, however, a form of patronage that entailed further dependence on traders as land was exchanged for cash and goods. Associated with these changes, institutionalized conventional forms of looking at the world appeared to have failed to deal with the awesome power of rinderpest. In attempting to come to terms with what had happened a substantial number of people turned to the missionaries for religious assistance.

Rinderpest did not merely kill cattle; it was the death knell of an independent Herero society as a whole. Following rinderpest, Herero society lost its land, people and cattle, and sank ever further into debt. It became dependent on the goodwill of the colonial state for its very existence. It became dependent on the colonial state for land, in the form of reserves, and food, in the form of employment, on the traders and settlers for credit and employment, and on

---

[157] Kevin Shillington, *The Colonisation of the Southern Tswana, 1870–1900* (Johannesburg 1985), p. 113.

the mission for religious guidance. By 1904, Herero society was a series of scattered groupings centred on urban centres subject to German garrisons and their associated chiefs. Effectively Herero society had lost its independence and the German colonial state was victorious.

5
Ovita Ovia Zürn
Zürn's War
1904–8

Introduction

On 12 January 1904 the Herero–German war broke out. When the war finally ended in 1908, Herero society, as it had existed prior to 1904, had been completely destroyed.[1] The surviving Herero were deprived of their chiefs, prohibited from owning land and cattle, and prevented from practising their own religion. The war was not the result of a premeditated insurrection against German colonial governance. Instead the war resulted from a series of misunderstandings, in which war became the inevitable result of panic, on the part of a German colonial official, and the self-fulfilling prophecy of Herero war that existed within the mind of settler paranoia. Due to German short-sightedness, and conflicts within the German military and administration, opportunities to come to a negotiated settlement with the Herero were consistently ignored in favour of a needlessly protracted genocidal war.

Undoubtedly 'the socio-political offensive of the German settler society after the rinderpest, and the process of regeneration of the Herero society and their herds around 1900 produced a very tense situation'.[2] But, for war to break

---

[1] The dating, 1904–8, may at first seem rather unusual. Military operations against the Herero 'officially' ceased in 1906 and were ended by 'imperial decree' against the Nama in 1907. However the incarceration of Herero POWs only officially ended in April 1908. NNAW, BWI 406, *Windhoek 3 April 1908 Durch Verfügung des Kaiserlichen Gouvernements vom 26 Marz 1908 ist die Kriegsgefangenschaft der Hereros mit dem 1 April 1908 aufgehoben.* Operations were carried on against the Nama even into Botswana in 1908. Wulf D. Haacke, 'The Kalahari Expedition March 1908. The Forgotten Story of the Final Battle of the Nama War', in *Botswana Notes and Records*, Vol. 24, 1992, pp. 1–18. Between 1904 and 1911 German patrols were active in the *Omaheke* Sandveld against Herero. BAP, RKA 1492, *Einschreiten der Polizeitruppe in SWA vom 22 April 1911 bis 9 August 1911.* The case of the Herero Kandiapu, who was to be deported to Cameroon and died whilst in police custody in Swakopmund, is a case in point. NNAW, BSW 74, Windhoek, 9/8/1911, Deportation order for Kandiapu on the grounds that he had participated in an armed band in the *Omaheke* Sandveld. Hostilities against the aboriginal inhabitants of Namibia were still in progress in 1915 when Namibia was occupied by troops of the Union of South Africa. See in this case particularly the work done by Robert Gordon on social banditry in north-western Namibia in *The Bushman Myth: the Making of a Namibian Underclass* (Boulder, San Francisco, Oxford 1992).

[2] Comment contained in thesis referee's letter, May 1996.

out, triggers were needed to initiate the outbreak, and these can be found in individual fears and guilt complexes, in given places and times, and given individuals in very specific misunderstandings. It is this that this chapter seeks to bring to the fore.

The causes of war

Angered by the loss of their lands to settler farmers and land-companies, the Herero initiated a premeditated, carefully planned and centrally led country-wide insurrection against German colonial rule. That, at least, is what the majority of commentators dealing with the Herero–German war have sought to argue.[3] An exception was the historian, Helmut Bley, who refined this line of argument and showed that:

> In 1903 the Herero did not suffer from any acute shortage of land and there was no deliberate German political initiative and no particular acceleration of the land question.[4]

Instead, he argued that the war was not so much caused by the loss of land, as by Herero perceptions that this was about to happen:

> The Africans believed that German expansion would never stop, and that the German government would not honour its protection treaties. The negotiations for native reserves were seen as a preliminary to a general expropriation of the tribes, or were interpreted as such by the head-men who were resolved on declaring war. Their actual losses of land were less significant than the fact that the Herero head-men felt the position and future of their tribe to be threatened.[5]

I, for my part, argue that the origins of the war are to be found in the interpretations and perceptions of the German settlers and missionaries, rather than in those of the Herero. It was these German interpretations and per-ceptions of Herero society which in effect ensured that in the end the Herero–German war became a self-fulfilling prophecy. Typical of this mode of thinking was a German officer, *Leutnant* Zürn, who, troubled by his conscience and his perceptions of what was happening in Herero society, panicked, over-reacted and effectively initiated the Herero–German war. The following section details the build-up to the war and analyses the direct causes of the war.

It was not the Herero chiefs, but the missionaries operating in Hereroland, who were opposed to the sale of land. In order to be able to conduct their vocation, the missionaries needed stations which had enough land to support stable concentrations of settled sedentary followers, and which formed permanent centres within specific pastoral ranges. Thus the missionaries were consistently opposed to the sale of land associated with their stations, for fear that their resident Christian followers would be forced to move away from the stations. Already at the start of German colonial involvement in Hereroland, they had sought to ensure that the lands associated with their stations were

[3] See amongst others, C. Rust, *Krieg und Frieden im Hererolande: Aufzeichnungen aus dem Kriegsjahre 1904* (Berlin 1905) pp. 3–4; G. Pool, *Samuel Maharero* (Windhoek 1991) p. 201 & W. Nuhn, *Sturm über Südwest* (Koblenz 1989) p. 53.
[4] Bley, *South West Africa*, pp. 133–4.
[5] Ibid.

Photo 5.1: The German military fort in Okahandja
Source: Namibian National Archives, Windhoek

reserved for inalienable Herero occupation.[6] Indeed the oft-quoted letter, allegedly written by Kajata in 1901 and used as proof of Herero chiefly opposition to the further sale of land to settlers, was actually drawn up and written by missionary Lang.[7]

For their part the Herero chiefs continued to sell their land, and in amounts that often startled European observers.[8] Prior to the rinderpest, Herero chiefs had sold land to supplement their income. In the aftermath of the rinderpest, the sale of land by chiefs was essential if they were to retain their position and recoup their losses. Thus Herero chiefs, deprived of their cattle herds, had taken to selling extensive tracts of land. The sale of Herero land to land-companies and traders was not as pressing as it may seem. The companies bought the land to speculate with and were in no position to enforce the removal of Herero from the lands which had been bought. Indeed, following the war, Rohrbach noted that one of the war's benefits had been the eviction of company lands, a task that would otherwise have proved difficult.[9] Furthermore, though the traders bought land to farm on, Herero cattle herds had not built up to a level that led to competition for land.

It was on the issue of what would happen in the long term, when it was envisaged that Herero cattle numbers would return to pre-rinderpest levels, that Leutwein and the missionaries were in agreement. As has been noted elsewhere:

> In his [Leutwein's] judgement, the Herero did not realise that they were undermining their whole economy by selling land instead of cattle, the means of production rather

---

[6] For missionary opposition to the sale of Herero land see ELCIN, I 1.14, *1889–1904 Gouvernement Korrespondenz (Gesetze, Zoll, Reservate) (Dokumente II), Briefe an Gouvernement, Amtstellen und Beamte 1891–1904. & I 1.3 1873–1905 Protokollbuch der Konferenzen im Hereroland.*
[7] Rohrbach, Paul, *Kolonialwirtschaft*, pp. 330–1.
[8] Indeed Bley, *South West Africa*, p. 136, cites the case of colonial official Rohrbach seeking to convince Samuel Maharero, contrary to his wishes, that at least 25 per cent of his land should become a reserve of unsaleable land. See Leutwein, *Elf Jahre*, p. 276 for Leutwein's expressed opposition to the sale of Herero land.
[9] Bley, *South West Africa*, p. 134.

than the products themselves, nor that their grazing-land was only temporarily unused. If they managed to raise fresh herds, they would simply take back the land which they had sold in their traditional manner – by force – a process which would have very obvious political consequences. The army would have to protect land purchased by the Europeans, particularly that which was not yet occupied, or was kept back speculatively 'in mortmain'.[10]

Frightened, not by the costs of enforcing land clearances, but by the cessation of their activities, which would result from the inevitable land clearances, the missionaries petitioned the German government for the establishment of Herero reserves.[11] The missionary lobbying, in combination with Leutwein's own insights, led to Leutwein introducing measures which sought to curb the sale of Herero lands to traders, and led to the establishment of reserves of inalienable Herero land. To do this Leutwein passed legislation that operated on two levels: firstly, new credit regulations which would prevent traders from being paid or claiming debts in the form of land, and, secondly, the creation of reserves of inalienable Herero land. During the course of 1903, discussions began with Herero chiefs regarding the establishment of reserves, and the new credit legislation came into effect.[12]

Those opposed to Leutwein's new legislation were the settler farmers, traders and the *Schutztruppe* who hoped to settle in the territory following their military service. In 1899 Leutwein had also attempted to introduce credit regulations, but, following a howl of settler protest, these had been turned down by the Imperial German government.[13] Now, in 1903, Leutwein ignored their indignant yelps and ensured their undying opposition when his actions effectively cut them off from cheap land and their envisaged dream of living as a colonial landed gentry.

> One way to become an independent farmer was by trading . . . most farmers in the area of the Herero uprising became farmers this way. A few years of trading were sufficient to gain enough cattle from the natives. The 10,000 hectares of grazing land necessary for a farm were often acquired in a similar way.[14]

The settlers felt cheated of their rightful prize. The Herero chiefs were quite willing to sell land. Following the rinderpest there was no land pressure, and in any case land companies didn't enforce dispossession. In 1902 settlers could expect to pay land companies between one and five marks per hectare of land, whilst the government charged thirty pfennig to one mark fifty, and Herero land could be bought for between fifty pfennig and one mark.[15] Land-companies, which had acquired land to speculate with, were loath to sell and only sold land at highly inflated prices. The settlers were therefore dependent on Herero chiefs or on the government for the purchase of land. With Leutwein's credit regulations and reserve policy, the possibility of obtaining cheap land appeared to have been placed beyond the reach of the aspirant settlers. Leutwein knew that his moves did little to endear him to the

---

[10] Ibid., pp. 135–6.
[11] NNAW, ZBU 2032, WII e1, *Eingeborenenreservate und Lokationen 'generalia', Band 1.*
[12] For a discussion on the introduction of this new legislation see Bley, *South West Africa*, pp. 133–4.
[13] Leutwein, *Elf Jahre*, p. 269 & pp. 559–68.
[14] G. Schrank, *German South West Africa: Social and Economic Aspects of its History, 1884–1915*, New York University, PhD, 1974, pp. 132–3, citing Rohrbach, *Kolonialwirtschaft*, p. 320.
[15] Schrank, *South West Africa*, p. 129.

ever-increasing settler population, of whom he noted that they:

> ... were inclined, with their inborn feeling of belonging to a superior race, to appear as members of a conquering army, even though we had conquered nothing. The majority of settlers had no knowledge of the protection treaties signed with the Herero.[16]

However, undaunted, Leutwein attempted to continue to administer the territory.

The attitudes of the settlers were shared by the majority of the aspirant settlers who served as soldiers and officers under Leutwein. With the exception of a few officers associated with Estorff, Leutwein knew himself to be opposed in his policies by his officers united around Franke. The reports of *Oberleutnant* Kuhn, *Premierleutnant* Volkmann and others made no bones about their opposition to Leutwein's policies and new legislation. Whilst on leave in Germany, Volkmann, asked to comment on the feasibility of establishing reservations, wrote: 'There is absolutely no reason why at the present time there should be a general regulation of the reservation question in Hereroland.'[17] Yet these were the very same men who were expected to enforce and negotiate the boundaries of the newly to be established reservations – a policy which they opposed and felt was at the expense of the settlers. Paul Leutwein, the son of the governor, provided some indication as to the 'gung-ho' attitude existent among reservists, troops and white settlers at the time.

> The company of Franke marched into Windhoek on 31 December 1903. On the same day there was a celebration in *Kasino Sylvester*. Here there were a large amount of Farmers whose farms lay in the Herero area. These were generally opposed to the ruling that White farms could no longer be enlarged at the cost of the Herero. All believed that the time had now come to change this ruling in favour of the whites. Not one thought of any danger. I can still see before me how, in a fiery speech, one of the oldest *Afrikaner* [settler], the *Hauptmann* v. Francois called for a general *razzia* against the Herero.[18]

It was in this alcohol-fuelled atmosphere that men such as Okahandja's *Distriktschef Leutnant* Zürn sought to implement and carry out the legislation passed by their supreme commander, Theodor Leutwein.

The tensions that existed in the minds of settler society in GSWA were exacerbated in October of 1903, when the colonial government became involved in a war against the Bondelswarts chieftaincy in the south of the territory. Following a series of defeats, Governor Leutwein assumed direct command of the operations, trekked south to the conflict and withdrew most of the colonial troops from central and northern GSWA.[19] To counteract the effects of this troop displacement, there was a general mobilization of all German forces in GSWA in late December of 1903.[20] Only those reservists associated with the maintenance of the railway between Windhoek and Swakopmund were excused from service.[21]

---

[16] Leutwein cited in Bley, *South West Africa*, pp. 139–40.
[17] NNAW, ZBU 2032, WII e4, *Bericht betreffend Schaffung von Reservaten für Eingeborenen im Hererolande*, Volkmann in Berlin, 16/2/02.
[18] Paul Leutwein cited in Nuhn, *Sturm*, p. 52.
[19] Pool, *Samuel Maharero*, pp. 196–7.
[20] Kol. Blatt. p. 207, Bericht des Kaiserlichen Gouvernements vom 20 Januar 1904.
[21] Otto von Weber, *Geschichte des Schutzgebietes Deutsch-Südwest-Afrika* (Windhoek 1979) Second edition, pp. 126–7.

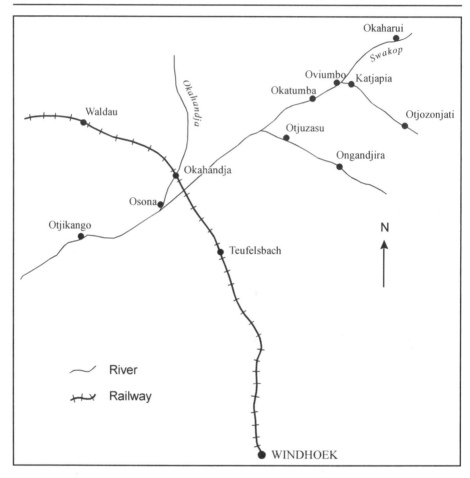

Map 5.1: Schematic map of central Namibia in the first stages of the Herero–German war

Left behind in Okahandja and charged with implementing a reserve policy for which he felt little sympathy, *Distriktschef Leutnant* Zürn determined the boundaries of what, it was envisaged, would become the Okahandja and Waterberg reserves. Zürn was not particularly happy in his place of employment, but he was anxious to make a career for himself. Indeed, at exactly the same time that he was finalizing the reserve treaties, he was also applying to the governor for a transfer out of his position in Okahandja. Not yet thirty years of age, and after a mere two years in service, he requested that Leutwein appoint him as the replacement of *Hauptmann* Franke, who had just marched through Okahandja en route to the war in the south, as temporary *Bezirksamtmann* in Omaruru.[22]

The Okahandja reserve was determined against the wishes of the Okahandja councillors associated with Assa Riarua, who wished to see more land

[22] BAP, RKA 2021, Zürn in Okahandja, 29/12/03, to the Governor.

reserved.[23] Missionary Diehl commented that in the first instance the Herero rejected the boundaries drawn by Zürn as the territory allocated to them was: '(i) too small; (ii) located in a part of the country more or less unfamiliar to most of them; and (iii) left much to be desired in terms of grazing land'.[24] However, as Diehl continued:

> Zürn summoned the Headmen again to bring the matter to a close. They were, however, sorely disappointed to hear that Herr Zürn was still insisting on the borders as originally defined by him. Indignant, they refused to sign on the dotted line. Herr Zürn thereupon dismissed them in what they said was a rather rude fashion, observing that he could well do without their signatures as Samuel would be prepared to sign in their place and that would be quite sufficient.[25]

Thus, after more than a little cajoling on the part of Zürn, the boundaries of the Okahandja reserve were decided upon. As another contemporary observer, Paul Rohrbach, noted:

> A number of witnesses have stressed that during discussions with Herero councillors in the fort of Okahandja the *Distriktschef von Okahandja* [Zürn], the same official, whom Samuel claimed wanted to kill him, used threats [*Drohmittel*] to ensure their acceptance of a smaller reserve for Okahandja. This happened after the Governor had already left for the South.[26]

However forceful he may have been, Zürn had at least gone through the pretence of having had discussions with the Okahandja councillors before determining the boundaries of the reserve that was to be assigned to them. In the case of the inhabitants of the Waterberg, Zürn dropped all pretence of engaging in discussion and did not even bother to consult the heirs of the late Kambazembi, who had died earlier in the month.[27] Instead, Zürn determined the boundaries of the Waterberg reserve on his own account, and forged the signatures of David Kambazembi, Salatiel Kambazembi, Theurtheus and Gabriel of the Waterberg, and Ouandja of Otjikururume on the treaty.[28] Having appended the forged signatures to the document Zürn claimed that, 'In my presence [the document had been] agreed to and signed', which was a blatant lie.[29] Indeed the Herero delegation, en route from the Waterberg for boundary discussions in Okahandja, was ordered to turn back as the boundaries of their reserve had already been determined.[30] Zürn's blatant disregard for the rights of the Herero and sympathy for the settlers opposed to Leutwein's reserve policy are well illustrated by his actions with regard to the Waterberg and Okahandja reserves. Nevertheless, on 8 December 1903 *Leutnant* Zürn, having failed to

[23] BAP, PTS 2115, Leutwein in Okahandja, 2/6/04, to Kolonial Abteilung AA.
[24] Diehl cited in Drechsler, *Fighting*, p. 116.
[25] Ibid.
[26] Rohrbach, *Kolonialwirtschaft*, p. 338.
[27] Lenssen, *Chronik*, p. 120.
[28] NNAW, ZBU 2032, Treaty between Zürn and Herero chiefs, September 1903, folio 98–9. Zürn placed crosses at the end of the document and then subscripted them with the text 'signature of the Kaptein David in Waterberg' and so on for all the Waterberg councillors. None of the Waterberg councillors were present in Okahandja when Zürn appended their signatures to the treaty that threatened to disown them of a substantial part of their territory. Some of the councillors had enjoyed some missionary education, particularly Salatiel and David Kambazembi, and could thus write their own names. That the Herero chiefs of the Waterberg were not present when the treaties were signed see: Pool, *Samuel Maharero*, p. 186 fn. 48 & *Opstand*, pp. 48–50.
[29] NNAW, ZBU 2032, reverse 99.
[30] Leutwein, *Elf Jahre*, p. 277.

consult the Waterberg Herero and having cajoled the Okahandja Herero into acceptance, announced the boundaries of the Okahandja and the Waterberg Herero reserves.[31]

It was in this aggressive atmosphere of crude disregard for Herero rights, on the part of the settlers and their *Schutztruppe* allies, that rumours of an impending Herero uprising started. By late 1903 these rumours were persistent and widespread. So credible were these rumours in the eyes of the settlers, that they went to the extent of attempting to entrap their servants into 'betraying' the impending revolt.[32] Though the Herero consistently denied wanting to start a war, there appears to have been a belief, on the part of the settlers, that the Herero would undertake some form of action against colonial rule. The fear of the settlers was enhanced by events in the south of the territory where the Bondleswarts were proving to be more than a walk-over. The withdrawal of troops from central Namibia, as well as the general mobilization of all German reservists, merely served to emphasize to the settlers that war was imminent. It was in this climate of general distrust that the settlers, now mobilized reservists, and soldiers like Zürn, left in charge of Hereroland, dealt with and interpreted the events that led up to the war.

Beginning in early January 1904, German officers and settlers showered one another with rumours and reports on the envisaged Herero insurrection. Meetings held between German officials and Herero chiefs consistently referred to and dealt with the rumours of war. On 6 January Traugott Tjetjo and Lt Streitwolf held a meeting in the Gobabis district to discuss the shooting of alleged Herero cattle thieves by a settler named Bulack.[33] Streitwolf reported that he did not believe that war was imminent.[34] On the same day, at the Waterberg, Sergeant Rademacher and the Rev. Eich, acting on the reports of Frau Sonnenberg, whose husband had been drafted, spoke to David Kambazembi on the growing indebtedness of Herero buying goods on credit irrespective of the price. Sonnenberg believed that the Herero were buying goods in preparation for war. However, David Kambazembi emphasized that the Herero had no intention of starting a war, and both Rademacher and Eich reported that war was unlikely. Instead Rademacher reported that a large number of the late Kambazembi's councillors had travelled to chief Ouandja at Otjikururume, a settlement where the late Kambazembi had lived prior to moving to the Waterberg.[35] Eich believed that it was possible that the Herero had heard rumours of the Bondelswarts war in the south and that this may have made them unsure of the continuance of trade supplies, as traders, as was the case with Sonnenberg, would be called up to fight in the South.[36] Furthermore, there was a rumour that some Herero would be called up to join the German forces in the war against the Bondelswarts, and Herero had begun buying goods in anticipation of this mobilization.[37] Another factor may simply

---

[31] Ibid. & Pool, *Opstand*, pp. 48–9.

[32] Rust, *Krieg*, p. 5. The settler Conrad Rust, laid traps for his servants in a vain endeavour to discover when war was due. He describes in detail how at Christmas 1903 he arranged a mass at which he hoped to entrap his servants into betraying the impending revolt.

[33] Nuhn, *Stürm*, pp. 51–3.

[34] Pool, *Opstand*, p. 58, fn. 8.

[35] BAP, RKA 2111, Copy of letter by Rademacher at the Waterberg, 6 January 1904, to the Kaiserliche Distriktsamt Okahandja. Includes a letter sent by missionary Eich to Rademacher on the same day.

[36] Kol. Blatt. 1904, p.211, Eich at Waterberg, 6/1/04, to Zürn.

[37] Kol. Blatt. 1904, p. 210.

have been that, in the absence of the late Kambazembi's councillors, who could have kept an eye on their subjects, Herero had begun buying goods. Or as Eich put it, some Herero took part 'Because buying is so nice'.[38]

On Saturday 9 January 1904 Rademacher's patrol arrived in Okahandja from the Waterberg. Acting on the patrol's observations, Lt Zürn reported to Windhoek that he did not believe anything untoward was happening, but that it would be advisable to strengthen the *Schutztruppe* station at the Waterberg with a few extra men.[39] On the same day the trader Jakobs arrived in Okahandja and reported that he had passed large numbers of Herero travelling towards the settlement from the Waterberg.[40] In normal circumstances, this report need not have worried Zürn, as both Rademacher and Eich had already reported that the councillors of the late Kambazembi were travelling towards Okahandja and even Zürn himself referred to their coming in his own report.[41]

On the following day, Sunday 10 January, nothing untoward happened. However, in the night of the tenth, trader Alex Niet arrived in Okahandja and caused panic in settler circles, with his report that 300 armed Herero were going to attack the town on the following day.[42] Zürn ordered all the settlers living in the area to immediately come into the fort at Okahandja, and sent out a patrol to investigate.[43] The Herero, when questioned by the patrol, reported that they had come to Okahandja from the Waterberg so that, in assembly with the 'Councillors and the paramount chief Samuel Maharero, deliberations could be held to determine the inheritance of a number of chiefly positions'.[44] The men from the Waterberg had every reason to be in Okahandja. Kambazembi had died in September and his heirs, having begun dividing his inheritance, had come to Okahandja to seek the guidance and sanction of Samuel Maharero. For Zürn, however, the arrival of the delegation from the Waterberg was something completely different. For here, now in the capital of Hereroland, a delegation of men had arrived whose signatures he had forged on a document that would remove the rights of these men to land which they believed was theirs. Added to this were the thoughts of Missionary Wandres who wrote:

> Zürn's cowardice . . . had its basis in his bad conscience. He had dealt with the inhabitants of Okahandja, particularly Samuel, in a very brusque manner. Herr Gathemann will confirm that in his presence he [Zürn] shouted at Samuel: '*Halte das Maul, du Schwein!*' [hold your mouth, you pig!]. One day Zürn told brother Diehl, in the presence of brother Meier, 'When a native comes and complains, then I wallop [*haue*] him a couple of times behind the ears'.[45]

[38] Kol. Blatt. 1904, p. 211.

[39] BAP, RKA 2111, Copy of letter by Zürn in Okahandja, 9/1/04, to governor; see also Kol. Blatt. 1904, p. 210.

[40] Rust, *Krieg*, p. 131.

[41] Kol. Blatt. 1904, p. 210.

[42] Pool, *Opstand*, p. 66. Pool's reference is based on Niet's deposition of 29/4/07, in which he claimed compensation for services rendered. Unfortunately no other reference backs up this assertion of 1907, i.e. three years after the event, that 2000 Herero were advancing on Okahandja. It is probable that the amount never exceeded 300. Pool and others following him (Nuhn) report that on the night a further 300 armed Hereros headed towards Osona. Pool's reference is based on *BRMG*, 1904, p. 115, but probably refers to the same Hereros referred to originally by Niet.

[43] Pool, *Opstand*, p. 66.

[44] *BRMG*, 1904, p. 115.

[45] VEMA, RMG 1623 c Personalakten Wandres Carl, Band 3 1900–1905, Wandres in Windhoek, 29/6/04, to the mission directors in Wuppertal. Interestingly, Wandres's report on Zürn echoes

The fears that Zürn entertained were increased as German traders and settlers, complying with his own orders, sought shelter from the anticipated revolt in his fort. One can well imagine that the tales and reports, brought in by the settlers and traders, who had been ordered to shelter in the fort by reservists and soldiers who were convinced that war was about to break out, did little to sooth Zürn's fears. Influenced and infected by the rumours and tall tales of the reservists, frightened traders and settlers, Zürn became convinced that the revolt had started. Trapped in a spiral in which everything he did served to convince him of the validity of his belief, Zürn panicked and towards 1 a.m. on the morning of the eleventh he telephoned Windhoek and reported that the Herero were approaching, that he believed that a revolt was imminent, and that he needed reinforcements.[46] A few hours later Zürn sent the following telegram:

> Samuel and many councillors [at] Osona, believe following Native reports revolt very possible. Patrol sent to Osona, have 26 men at station with volunteers, based on the amount who marched through there must be approximately 200 Hereros at Osona. Zürn.[47]

In the morning, Monday, 11 January, the provisional governor Richter summoned *Bergrat* Duft and reported, on the basis of Zürn's panicky missives, that at Okahandja 'the Hereros had gathered in suspiciously large numbers and were probably planning a revolt against the Germans'.[48] The Germans now believed that the revolt was a reality and following discussions it was decided that Duft should travel to Okahandja to negotiate with Samuel Maharero and his councillors, and seek to prevent the revolt. Accompanied by eighteen soldiers, Duft set off by train to Okahandja. The Germans, convinced that the war had already begun and that the railway bridges had been sabotaged, ordered a train to patrol the line from Okahandja towards Teufelsbach, in the direction of Windhoek. Anxious to ensure that the train would get through and that extra reinforcements could be brought into the settlement, the soldiers travelled hidden and out of sight to observers on the last stretch of the line between Teufelsbach and Okahandja.[49] For all their panic and subterfuge, the train arrived in Okahandja at 2.30 p.m. without an incident.

When Duft and the reinforcements arrived in Okahandja, the settlement was in a state of heightened nervousness. Zürn had ordered all reservists to the fort and, by having the battlements manned by armed guards, had increased

the words of another, who 35 years later wrote of a settler farmer:
> 'When I get a new boy,' he said, 'the first thing I do is walk over to him and twist his ear.'
> With a terrible thumb and forefinger he showed me how he walked across to a new black labourer, took hold of the man's ear, and screwed it around.
> 'But doesn't that humiliate them?' I asked.
> 'Sometimes I make them cry.'
> 'Don't they ever try to hit back?'
> 'Sometimes a Herrero [sic] will. They've too damn much cheek; two words for every one of yours.'

Negley Farson, *Behind God's Back*, Sixteenth impression (London and New York 1941) p. 7.
[46] BAP, RKA 2111 Telegram, Bülow in Windhoek, 11/1/04, to RKA.
[47] BAP, RKA 2111, Copy of Telegram Zürn in Okahandja, 11/1/04, to Richter. Zürn sent telegram at 7.15 a.m. arrived 8.05 a.m.
[48] Kol. Blatt. 1904, p. 215. Windhoek 17 January 1904, *Tagesbericht Bergrats* Duft.
[49] Kol. Blatt. 1904, p. 216 & Rust, *Krieg*, p. 6.

the military preparedness of the fort.[50] Duft was informed that a meeting had been arranged with Ouandja of Otjikururume, and that Samuel Maharero was not in the settlement. Believing that Zürn wanted to have him killed, Samuel Maharero had withdrawn from Okahandja to Osona, which lay twenty kilometres to the south along the Swakop river, where he had joined Assa Riarua who was sick.[51] The misgivings and apprehension felt by Samuel Maharero were shared by the Herero who had agreed to meet Duft; they refused to come to the fort. Instead, at 5 p.m., after the Herero delegation had ascertained that the Germans were unarmed, Duft, Zürn and the missionary Diehl met Ouandja, and a number of Herero councillors from the Waterberg and Okahandja, on the path that led from the fort to the Herero location. Duft described the meeting as follows:

> In a sincere manner Ouandja reported that Samuel was in the field collecting debts and the like, but that he was expected. Likewise we were told that Assa Riarua was very sick.[52]

Thus the two most important Herero men of the Okahandja chieftaincy, Samuel Maharero and his adviser Assa Riarua, the two men whom Zürn had harangued and cajolled into signing reservation treaties, were absent and indisposed. As regards the Herero who had arrived from the Waterberg on the previous day, the Herero delegation confirmed that they had come to Okahandja to settle the inheritance of the late chief Kambazembi.[53] This confirmed discussions held earlier on in the day by the Rev. Diehl and the Herero.[54] In rounding off the discussion, Duft warned the Herero delegation that the Herero ought to do nothing to endanger the peace. In response, the Herero urged the Germans to refrain from sending out patrols as they distressed the people, and in any case 'They the whites had nothing to fear from . . . the natives.'[55]

> Of their own accord the natives referred to the protection treaty, and the negotiations were closed in complete peace and a new meeting was arranged for the following morning. The missionary Diehl, when asked as to his opinion of the negotiations, noted that there were no grounds to mistrust the Natives.[56]

Diehl's opinion was thrown to the wind. Even as the German delegation walked back to the fort, Duft and Zürn dismissed the idea that the Herero did not intend to wage a war. Instead, 'We [Duft and Zürn] and the white inhabitants of Okahandja believed that the statements of the Natives were fabricated.'[57]

If there was an element of alarm amongst the Germans, then this, too, primarily through the actions of the Germans, was transmitted to the Herero

[50] Kol. Blatt. 1904, p. 216. In a letter to Leutwein, Samuel Maharero referred specifically to German soldiers being hidden in chests and occupying the battlements, *Moskanze* (derived from the Dutch Schans, fortification) of Okahandja fort, prior to the outbreak of the war. ELCIN, I 1.19 A., Samuel Maharero at Otjozonjati, 6/3/04, to Leutwein.

[51] ELCIN, I 1.19 A., Samuel Maharero at Otjozonjati, 6/3/04, to Leutwein. *BRMG*, 1904, p. 117. Substantiated by Immanuel Hoveka. Zürn's aggressive attitude towards Samuel Maharero is also substantiated by missionary Wandres. VEMA Personalakten 1623, Wandres in Windhoek, 29/6/04, to the mission directors in Wuppertal.

[52] Kol. Blatt. 1904, p. 216.

[53] Kol. Blatt. 1904, p. 216.

[54] *BRMG*, 1904, p. 115.

[55] Ibid., p. 116.

[56] Kol. Blatt. 1904, p. 216.

[57] Ibid.

living in the settlement. Samuel Maharero and Assa Riarua had withdrawn from Okahandja, for fear of what Zürn might do. As a Herero informed Diehl, earlier in the day, '. . . you must see that we do not understand why there are so many German patrols and why have all the whites fled into the fort?'[58] The Herero could see that the Germans were preparing for war, but did not understand why. Samuel Maharero believed that Zürn wanted to have him killed and that the German patrols were being sent out for this purpose.[59]

Following the meeting, and the agreement to meet the next morning, members of the Herero delegation rode the twenty kilometres to Osona, to report back to Samuel Maharero and his council in hiding on the day's events in Okahandja and the meeting. Back in the fort, Duft telephoned Richter in Windhoek and also reported on the day's events. At this stage, no hostile action on the part of the Herero had taken place. Yet Zürn telegraphed Swakopmund and requested that the German naval cruiser *Habicht*, which was in the vicinity of Cape Town, land a company of marines as reinforcements. All the remaining settlers were ordered to enter the fort or to spend the night in the railway station. Further orders were issued to reinforce the fort in anticipation of attack.[60] Finally, against the express wishes of the Herero negotiating team, as darkness fell on 11 January at least two further mounted patrols were sent out. One of the patrols succeeded in confiscating a number of unregistered Herero rifles and returned unscathed. The second patrol, sent to warn settlers on the outlying farms and order them to the fort, left at 5.30 p.m. and disappeared.[61]

Ensconced in their fort, the German settlers, traders and soldiers once again expanded upon one another's fears. The frayed nerves of the fort's inhabitants were hardly soothed when, during supper, a prisoner was shot and killed as he sought to escape from the fort.[62] Shortly thereafter the trader Leinhos confirmed everybody's fears, when he reported that he had received information, from a Herero woman, which indicated that the Herero movements were directed against the whites.[63] At this stage Zürn telegraphed Windhoek and requested that a machine gun and further reinforcements be brought up by rail from Windhoek.[64] For all their fears, the night of the eleventh to the twelfth passed quietly; indeed Dr Maaß, after having travelled through Herero territory, arrived unscathed from Karibib and reported nothing untoward.[65]

At daybreak on the morning of Tuesday 12 January the traders, who had spent the night in the fort or the railway station, headed back to their homes and stores in Okahandja. Missionary Meyer, who had spent the night in the mission station, walked across to the Herero location.[66] Lt Griebel, a

[58] *BRMG*, 1904, p. 115.
[59] ELCIN, I 1.19 A., Samuel Maharero at Otjozonjati, 6/3/04, to Leutwein.
[60] BAP, RKA 2111, *Generalkonsul* in Cape Town, 12/1/04, to AA, asks for Habicht to be sent to Swakopmund at the request of the Swakopmund *Bezirkshauptmann*. Pool, *Opstand*, p. 67 & Kol. Blatt. 1904, p. 216.
[61] Kol. Blatt. 1904, p. 216. It is possible that this patrol, which left at the same time that the Herero delegation was on its way to report to Samuel Maharero in Osona, followed the Herero en route to Osona and were subsequently killed. This patrol may be the one referred to in Samuel's letter; if this is the case, then it is hardly surprising that Samuel Maharero failed to pitch up in Okahandja on the following morning.
[62] Rust, *Krieg*, p. 8.
[63] Kol. Blatt. 1904, p. 216.
[64] Ibid.
[65] Kol. Blatt. 1904, pp. 216 & 217.
[66] *BRMG*, 1904, p. 115.

representative of the *Otavibahngesellschaft* [Otavi railway company], who had arrived a few days previously, with the intention of recruiting Herero labourers for the Otavi railway, left the fort and wandered to the Herero location and Samuel Maharero's *Werft*.[67] *Bergrat* Duft and Dr Maaß, who had an appointment with the Herero delegation later in the morning, walked to the Wecke and Voigts' store, which was run by Mr Störmer, and visited the garden, which was situated close to the graves of Tjamuaha and Maharero, and then strolled on towards the Herero location and the prearranged meeting with the Okahandja and Waterberg councillors. As they walked towards the location, they were met by missionary Meyer who, in an unconscious pastiche of true colonial melodrama, declared 'the natives are restful'.[68]

On the previous day Duft, Zürn and the settlers had expressed the belief that the expressed peaceful intentions of the Herero were mere fabrication.[69] Yet until this stage, as they were walking towards their prearranged meeting, nothing whatsoever had occurred which justified the German's fears. Indeed missionary Meyer's words served only to emphasize that nothing untoward was happening. However, as they passed the house of the Herero church elder, Johannes, Duft claimed that Johannes told them not to proceed any further. More specifically, the Germans concluded from the man's *facial expression* that they shouldn't proceed as the war had started. The Germans substantiated this fear for themselves, when they saw a large number of armed Herero at Samuel's *Werft* and a large number of armed Herero moving past the buildings of trader Denker and *Gastwirt* Dickmann towards the house of the Herero councillor Barnabas. Alarmed, Duft and Maaß turned back towards the fort. As they walked back, they were joined by Lt Griebel, who was at that moment returning from the Herero location. Griebel made absolutely no mention of war preparations and like missionary Meyer appears to have been unconcerned.[70] Griebel, who had arrived in the previous week, was a labour recruiter. He had been to the Herero location in the hope of holding meetings with Samuel and his councillors for the supply of labour to the *Otavibahngesellschaft*. Having failed to find Samuel, he had turned back to the fort. Significantly, after the war started, Samuel stated that the Germans had waged war against him because he hadn't been willing to supply them with labour, whereas he had been willing to supply the labour recruiters of the mines of the Witwatersrand with men.[71]

Back in the fort Duft and Maaß reported what had happened. Zürn believed that the long-awaited revolt had started and immediately telephoned the trader Denker, ordering him and *Gastwirt* Dickmann to come back to the fort at once.[72] Shortly thereafter, in response to Zürn's telephone call, Denker, accompanied by his wife and a child of the Dickmanns, arrived at the fort. Denker reported that he had told the Dickmanns, who were in the company of a Miss Müller, to come to the fort; however they had chosen to remain.

---

[67] Kol. Blatt. 1904, p. 217.
[68] Ibid.
[69] Kol. Blatt. 1904, p. 216.
[70] Kol. Blatt. 1904, p. 217.
[71] Botswana National Archives (BNA), RC.11/1, *Correspondence regarding Hereros (and flight to Ngamiland after rebellion in German South West Africa)*. Samuel Maharero in Mogopa, 28/9/04, to Resident Magistrate.
[72] Kol. Blatt. 1904, p. 217.

Shortly thereafter shooting started.[73] In the fort the Germans opened fire on Herero in the vicinity of the fort. Lt Zürn and *Bergrat* Duft sent a telegram to Berlin reporting that the long-anticipated uprising had begun. Effectively the Herero–German war had started.[74]

At 11 a.m. Miss Müller arrived in the fort and reported the deaths of Mr and Mrs Dickmann and settler Kuntze.[75] A few hours later a troop train armed with a machine gun entered the outskirts of Okahandja on the line from Windhoek. At this stage none of the bridges or sections of the track leading into Okahandja had been destroyed. However, just beyond the first houses of the settlement, near to Denker's store, the track had been sabotaged and the front waggon derailed.[76] Following a heavy firefight and a failed sally from the fort the train was forced to withdraw.[77] By the following day the Herero were prepared and the railway-line had been sabotaged at a number of places along a 5-km stretch to the south of the settlement. As a result the second attempt by train also failed.[78] A third attempt to lift the siege by train took place from within Okahandja on 20 January, but failed.[79]

Throughout the day on 12 January shooting continued. The missionary house came under heavy fire, not from the Herero, but from the fort. The missionaries, it is clear, had nothing to fear from the Herero, instead they feared their countrymen in the fort. Towards evening, missionary Diehl was reduced to carrying a white flag to the fort, with a request that the troops desist from shooting at the mission buildings. In the evening, under the cover of darkness, the various trading stores were looted and a number of them torched. Under the cover of darkness, and thus safe from German rifle fire, missionary Meyer and the son of missionary Diehl walked from the mission house to the Herero location. Samuel Maharero and Assa Riarua were not present.[80]

It is clear that the outbreak of the war hinges around what the Germans made of what it was that the Herero church elder Johannes may or may not have said to Duft. Duft's *Tagesbericht* clearly demonstrates that he did not understand what Johannes said, and that it was on the basis of Johannes's facial expression that they decided to turn back. In later accounts detailing the development of the war, Johannes's meeting with Duft has been transformed into a dialogue, in which Johannes explicitly warned Duft in *Otjiherero* to turn back.[81] Given that Duft and Maaß did not speak *Otjiherero*, their interpretation of whatever it was that Johannes may or may not have said is open to discussion. But, accepting that Johannes did tell them to turn back, there is no reason to assume that this was on account of a war breaking out. One perfectly plausible explanation as to why Johannes should have wanted to tell the Germans to

---

[73] Ibid.

[74] Pool, *Opstand*, p. 69.

[75] *BRMG* 1904, p. 116.

[76] Rust, *Krieg*, p. 153.

[77] Reichskolonialamt, *Die Kämpfe der deutschen Truppen in Südwestafrika. Auf Grund amtlichen Materials bearbeitet von der Kriegsgeschichtlichen Abteilung I des Großen Generalstabes. Erster Band. Der Feldzug gegen die Hereros* (Berlin 1906), p. 30.

[78] Rust, *Krieg*, pp. 154–6. A careful reading of Rust's text indicates that a number of soldiers were left behind as the train withdrew.

[79] Pool, *Opstand*, p. 77. It is of interest to note that these failed attempts to lift the siege by train were referred to by Maharero in his letter to Hermanus van Wijk.

[80] *BRMG*, 1904, p. 117.

[81] Rust, *Krieg*, p. 8; Pool, *Samuel Maharero*, p. 207; Nuhn, *Sturm*, p. 57.

Photo 5.2: The destroyed trading store of Wecke & Voigts in Okahandja shortly after the outbreak of the Herero–German war
Source: Namibian National Archives, Windhoek

return to their fort is that the meeting could not take place because on the previous evening the Herero delegation had travelled to Osona, where Samuel Maharero and his councillors had taken refuge, and had not yet returned to Okahandja. Uninformed as to what it was that their councillors had decided, the Herero were simply not ready to begin discussions.

Osona, a place where Samuel Maharero had on previous occasions sought refuge, lies approximately twenty kilometres to the south of Okahandja. The events of the night of the eleventh to the twelfth will have occurred as follows. Following the meeting, which ended between 5.30 and 6 p.m., on the evening of the eleventh, Herero emissaries travelled to Osona to report back to Samuel and his councillors on the meeting. Given that the Herero delegation had to discuss amongst themselves who would travel to Osona and exactly what it was that the emissaries would inform Samuel and his councillors of, the emissaries only left Okahandja at 6.30 p.m. at the earliest. The emissaries reached Osona at some time between 8.30 and 10.00 p.m., depending on whether they walked or trotted their horses. After having had a meal and refreshments, the emissaries began reporting back to Samuel Maharero and his councillors on the day's events and the meeting with Duft, Zürn and missionary Meyer. Hereafter discussions ensued and continued until late into the night. At daybreak, on the following morning, 12 January, the Herero emissaries waited until Samuel Maharero and his councillors had finished consulting their ancestors or saying their Christian prayers. Then, as their horses were being fetched from the veld, the emissaries had breakfast and once again went through the discussions of the previous night. Finally together with Samuel and his councillors they went through exactly what it was that they were expected to tell the German delegation in the forthcoming meeting. Accepting that events sketched in the scenes above are correct, and there is nothing to show that they aren't, the Herero emissaries could only have left

Osona for Okahandja at 8 a.m. at the earliest. By 9.30 a.m., the earliest time by which the emissaries could have returned to Okahandja, the war had already started. Johannes told Duft and his delegation to turn back on the morning of the twelfth, not because war was about to break out, but because the emissaries had not yet returned from Osona, and as such the meeting could not begin.

The absence of Samuel Maharero, Assa Riarua and Theodor Leutwein from Okahandja, at the moment that shooting started, coupled with Zürn's panic, were the two major factors that allowed an incident to lead to the outbreak of war. If either Leutwein or Samuel and Assa Riarua had been present in Okahandja at the time, it is likely that the shooting in Okahandja would have remained but an incident, and the war would have come to an early end. Unfortunately though, Samuel Maharero was scared of Zürn whom he believed wanted to kill him. Samuel was therefore not prepared to remain in Okahandja. Equally unfortunate was the fact that Theodor Leutwein was away fighting a war in southern Namibia; otherwise he might have been able to play a greater role in restraining his junior officer Zürn.[82]

Missionary Wandres reported *Bergrat* Duft as saying: 'If Zürn had not been in Okahandja, then the issue would not have developed in the manner that it did.'[83] Indeed, following the outbreak of the war, Zürn was recalled to Germany. Upon his return the possibilities of instituting court martial proceedings against him, for having instigated the war, were investigated. Fortunately for Zürn, he was never court martialled and the investigations regarding his role in the outbreak of the war were quashed as the war caught the Kaiser's and public imagination and Leutwein was ignominiously removed from office to be replaced by von Trotha.[84]

The letters

Four letters, allegedly written by Samuel Maharero prior to the outbreak of the war, are used to prove that the Herero–German war resulted from a carefully planned and premeditated insurrection against German colonialism. The letters purportedly show that Samuel Maharero, in the days immediately prior to the outbreak of the war, called the Herero to war, and called upon the leaders of the Rehoboth Basters and the Witboois to join the Herero – 'let us die fighting' – in their struggle against the Germans.[85]

Central to the proof that there was a premeditated insurrection initiated by

[82] For Leutwein's dislike of Zürn, see Bley, *South West Africa*, p. 134. Leutwein told missionaries Wandres, Hamann and Meier:

> Samuel wrote to me, that Zürn and the traders were guilty of having caused the outbreak of the revolt. I did not think that Zürn could have been so brave, [Ich hätte nicht gedacht, daß Zürn so tapperich gewesen sei] . . .

VEMA, Personalakten 1623, Wandres, Windhoek 29 June 1904.
[83] VEMA 1623, Wandres in Windhoek, 29/6/04, to mission directors in Wuppertal.
[84] BAP, RKA 2021, Personalakten, Ralf Zürn, *Aus Amt Betr. beschuldigung gegen Zürn Schuld an Hereroaufstand*.
[85] The phrase 'let us die fighting' which Samuel Maharero included in a letter to Hendrik Witbooi was taken by Horst Drechsler as the title of his book. Drechsler was a conscientious historian; though he believed that the letter was written prior to the outbreak of the war, he did note in his footnote 52 of chapter III that the versions of the letter which he had found were incomplete and that the opening passage was missing.

Samuel Maharero is the letter attributed to Samuel's hand and dated 11 January 1904, that is, on the day prior to the outbreak of the war.

> To all the chiefs of my land. I am the paramount chief of the Herero, Samuel Maharero.
> I have issued an order, a straight word, meant for all my people, that they should *no longer* lay their hands on the following: namely Englishmen, Basters, Bergdamaras, Namas, Boers; we do not lay our hands on these. Do not do this. I have sworn an oath to this, that this case does not become open, also not to the missionaries. Enough. I am the paramount chief S. Maharero, Okahandja.[86]

All commentators who have written on the war state that this was Samuel Maharero's order to his subjects to rise up in revolt against the Germans.[87]

Writing under orders of the *alte Afrikaner*, settler *Hauptmann* von Francois, Conrad Rust, himself an *alte Afrikaner* wrote the book, *Krieg und Frieden im Hererolande*. The book was issued free of charge to all the members of the German *Reichstag* as they met to discuss the compensation that was to be paid to German settlers following the war in GSWA.[88] Rust referred to the letter, in his book, as 'Samuel Maharero's Manifesto' and stated that it had been issued on 11 January 1904, and that it was an order to war.[89] He did not, however, provide his readers with a copy of the manifesto. Theodor Leutwein, writing after the war in an attempt to exonerate himself from blame for the outbreak of the war, referred to the letter as 'The order of the paramount chief to revolt' and quoted it in full but attached no date to it.[90] The historian Gerhardus Pool referred to the letter as a directive to revolt and wrote, 'This order was unmistakably aimed at the German population and was interpreted as such by the Hereros.'[91]

But what were the origins of the letter, how did this crucial bit of evidence fall into German hands, and was the letter really an order to revolt? At no stage does the letter urge anyone to attack anybody. Instead, accepting the translation as correct, it commands Herero not to lay their hands on specific groups of people, and not to tell anybody, not even the missionaries. It was this last clause, calling upon Herero to maintain secrecy and not to tell anyone, not even the missionaries, that led to the letter becoming public.

From the very beginning of the war, German settlers and a number of officials believed that the missionaries had aided and abetted the Herero in their insurrection, and had failed to provide warning of the revolt. At the outbreak of the war, as a result of this settler mistrust, the mission house in Okahandja became one of the prime targets for German marksmen ensconced in the fort. The missionaries had more to fear from German bullets than they did from Herero assault. Missionary Diehl, in a letter to his relatives, provided a clear description of this episode:

---

[86] ELCIN, I 1.19 A. *Verschiedene Briefe von u. an Samuel Maharero u. a. Herero 1887–1904*. The letters dealt with in the text are included in these files and are accompanied by German translations. JBG'S translation from the German text.

[87] O. Hintrager, *Südwestafrika in der deutschen Zeit* (München 1955) p. 45; Bley, *South-West Africa*, p. 142; Drechsler, *Fighting*, p. 143; Weber, *Geschichte*, p. 125; G. Pool, *Opstand*, p. 62 & *Maharero*, p. 202.

[88] Rust, *Krieg*, pp. v–xi.

[89] Ibid., p. 4.

[90] Leutwein, *Elf Jahre*, p. 467.

[91] Pool, *Samuel Maharero*, p. 202.

We have not been molested in the least by our Herero. They did not fire a single shot at our house. We had nothing to fear from them. It was safe for us to pace up and down the area in front of the house that was within the range of their rifles. Things were different on the opposite side where our German fellow countrymen were firing away. We could venture there only at the risk of our lives, although the house was well outside the line of fire and no shot was ever fired from there or nearby . . . One bullet penetrated my study, embedding itself in the wall above the desk . . . If I had been sitting there, as I had the day before at this time of day, I would now be a dead man. The bullet would have gone straight through my head.[92]

Following a series of ever more vociferous attacks in the press, both in Germany and in GSWA, the Rhenish Missionary Society launched a counter-offensive.[93] In a biting commentary, in which he lambasted the 'sharpshooters' of Okahandja fort for having used the windows of the mission house for target practice, the inspector of the Rhenish Missionary Society, P. Hausleiter, introduced the May edition of the Rhenish missionary reports with the claim that they contained proof that the missionaries were innocent and beyond blame.[94] The proof was provided in the form of a lengthy quotation taken from a letter written by missionary Brockmann. The letter consisted of two parts; the first dealt with the settler and military distrust of the missionaries, and the second provided the proof of missionary innocence and loyalty to the German cause. Brockmann's letter began with a description of how he and fellow missionary Diehl greeted Governor Leutwein, when he arrived in Okahandja in the second half of February 1904, following his return from the battlefront in southern Namibia:

The Governor greeted us in a friendly manner by shaking our hands and said to brother Diehl: 'What on earth have your confessional children done?' There was of course no time for further discussions; but yesterday [19/2/04] we were already invited to visit him. I was not present and brother Diehl alone went to the station. The Governor expressed his surprise that even the missionaries had had no prior indication that the revolt would take place.[95]

The surprise expressed by Leutwein, as well as his clearly articulated belief that the missionaries ought to have known what their 'confessional children' were up to, was shared by the German settler community. They for their part believed that the missionaries, who were not to be trusted anyway, had known about the outbreak of the war beforehand. With Leutwein's statements it became clear to the missionaries that they were in danger of losing the support of Leutwein, whose support was essential if they were to carry on with their activities in the territory. But help was at hand, and Brockmann continued his letter:

Yesterday evening a Herero letter fell into our hands, which had been written by Samuel Maharero to his councillors on 11 January, that is, a day before the outbreak of hostilities. From this one can see to what lengths the people went to make sure [wie sehr den Leuten darum zu tun war] that even we missionaries did not get to hear anything about their evil intentions . . . With this letter all evil allegations, such as,

[92] Diehl cited in Drechsler, Fighting, chapter 3, fn. 39.
[93] For example it was claimed by the Deutsch Südwest Afrikanischen Zeitung, 9/2/04, that shots had been fired on the German military from within the missionary house in Okahandja. BRMG, 1904, p. 149.
[94] BRMG, 1904, pp. 141–4.
[95] Ibid., pp. 147–8. JBG's translation.

that we knew about the case before hand, can be refuted by us. The Lord be thanked
that he has now deflected all the false suspicions away from us.[96]

For the future of missionary endeavour in the territory, the letter could not
have arrived at a more fortuitous time. It arrived precisely when the
missionaries, who were already under extensive pressure from the German
settlers and military, were confronted with the beginnings of expressed doubts
by Governor Leutwein, a man who hitherto had consistently supported the
mission. The letter served not only to free the missionaries from suspicion but
also served to further implicate Samuel Maharero in the revolt. However, as
has been stated earlier, the letter can in no way be construed as a call to arms.
Instead it is a document that clearly calls upon Herero not to continue harming
non-combatants and if it was written by Samuel Maharero it was issued after
fighting had begun. It was this aspect of the letter that prevented Rust, even
though he referred to it as 'Samuel's Manifesto', from including the letter in
his text. Leutwein, in following Rust, did refer to it as an order to revolt but
neglected to date the letter presented in his text.

Leutwein's failure to date the letter may have been for the following reasons.
The archives of the Evangelical Lutheran Church in Namibia contain the
correspondence and administration of the Rhenish Missionary Society. In a
file entitled *Letters to and from Maharero 1887–1904*, the letter, ascribed to
Samuel Maharero, has been found written in Otjiherero. Inspection of the letter
shows that it was not written in Samuel's handwriting, nor is it signed by
Samuel's hand, furthermore the letter has been dated in a German manner;
that is, '11 d. Jan'. In a later letter to the German colonial office, Governor
Leutwein, in providing evidence as to the origins of the war, referred to four
other letters ascribed to Samuel Maharero and noted, 'The originals were not
signed by the paramount chief, whose handwriting is known to me.'[97] Of the
four letters described by Leutwein one was presented without dating and
opening sentences, and another was demonstrably postdated.[98] It is possible
that Leutwein was aware of the German dating on the letter referred to by Rust
as 'Samuel's Manifesto', and that he therefore left it out of his published work.

In summing up. The letter, dated 11 January 1904, ascribed to Samuel
Maharero, was first made public by the missionaries in the second half of
February 1904, and has been referred to by all commentators following Rust
as Samuel's call to war. I accept that the letter was written by Samuel or that
it was written on Samuel's orders. However, I contend that the letter was not
written a day before the outbreak of the war and it was certainly not written as
an order to revolt. Instead, the origins of the letter may be described in the
following manner. At the outbreak of the war a number of non-combatants
were killed by Herero soldiers. Samuel Maharero was well aware of the
damaging effects that this had on one's public relations, and, if he was not
aware of this already, the missionaries and Christian Herero would most
certainly have emphasized this point.[99] Following the first initially chaotic weeks

---

[96] Ibid.
[97] NNAW, ZBU 450, p.92, Leutwein in Windhoek, 14/3/04, to Colonial department.
[98] Reference to Samuel Maharero's letter of 21/1/04 to H. van Wijk.
[99] See particularly the letters of Witbooi on the outrage experienced when non-combatants were
killed. ELCIN, *Politische Briefe etc. 1876–1893*, Letter Hendrik Witbooi at 'Hoornkrans den 18
April 1893' to Kapt. H. van Wijk. Similarly see Kolbe recording Jonker's raids on Kahitjene.
VEMA, 2.585, Okahandja Otjikango, 24.

of war, Samuel Maharero and his councillors were able to take stock of what had happened. I contend that it was in this period of stand-off that Samuel Maharero issued the directive calling upon his followers to '*no longer lay their hands*' on non-combatants. The German dating was later added to the letter by the missionaries, who may well have believed that it was a call to arms, but were far more interested in finding proof with which to prove their innocence. In other words in early February, possibly the eleventh, Samuel Maharero issued a directive to his followers that henceforth non-combatants were not to come to any harm. The missionaries, seeking to prove their innocence, seized upon this letter, which in no way can be construed as a call to war, as proof of their innocence and probably added the date.

Following the outbreak of the war, the German government instituted a commission of inquiry into the causes of the war. As part of the commission's evidence four letters ascribed to Samuel Maharero were submitted.[100] One of the letters submitted to the commission was a letter addressed to the Baster Captain Hermanus van Wijk in Rehoboth. The copy of the letter handed in to the commission was dated as having been written on 2 January 1904. In Leutwein's later published account of the war the letter was left undated and Leutwein noted that it had not been dated.[101] Part of the letter which was submitted to the commission as proof of Samuel's premeditated planning read as follows: 'Here in Okahandja we have fought three times with the machines and I won.'[102]

In the text submitted to the commission, brackets had been placed after 'machines' and the words, 'probably with rifles 88' (which were standard German issue at the time), included. However, Samuel Maharero used the word 'machines' not because he was unable to articulate the word 'rifles'. Rather the word referred to the three failed attempts by German armoured trains to lift the siege of Okahandja. The term 'Maschine', was current at the time, and referred to trains.[103] Why then was the term incorrectly translated in the commission's report? Primarily because, if it had been translated correctly, it would have implied that the letter was written at some stage after 20 January, that is when the third battle between the Herero and the Germans in armoured trains had taken place. This would in effect have meant admitting that the letter had been written after the war had broken out. The third failed attempt by the Germans took place on Wednesday 20 January 1904.[104] Samuel Maharero's letter could only have been written after this event had taken place, that is around 21 January, nine days after the outbreak of war.[105] The original letter which has been found in the Namibian national archives is indeed dated 21 January 1904.[106] The letter can therefore not be used as proof of a premeditated insurrection on the part of the Herero.

[100] NNAW, ZBU 450, Leutwein in Windhoek, 14/3/04, to Colonial department.

[101] Leutwein, *Elf Jahre*, p. 469.

[102] NNAW, ZBU 450, p. 94.

[103] For the use of the word *Maschine*, see Rust's description of the disastrous second German attempt to enter Okahandja on 14 January 1904. Rust, *Krieg*, p. 154–6.

[104] Kol. Blatt. 1904, p. 218.

[105] It is interesting that Pool, in his first book *Die Herero-Opstand* (Cape Town 1979) p. 64, has the dating as 21 January 1904. In his later work, *Samuel Maharero* (Windhoek 1991) p. 204, Pool has the dating as 2 January 1904 and concludes that the dating must be incorrect. The original letter is to be found in the Namibian national archives in Windhoek and shows the dating to be 21/1/04.

[106] NNAW, ZBU 451 D. IV. 1.2. With thanks to D. Henrichsen for sending the photocopies to me.

A further letter, allegedly written by Samuel Maharero as a call to war, was submitted to the commission. This letter was directed to Hendrik Witbooi. However, the letterhead and introductory paragraphs were not included, and are not to be found on the original archive copies. There is thus no way in which this letter can be used to prove that it was sent out prior to the outbreak of the war as part of a 'national' mobilization campaign. Given that this letter was intercepted by Hermanus van Wijk and handed over to the German colonial authorities along with the letter that Samuel Maharero had written to him, it is probable that this letter was also written around 20 January. Samuel Maharero's letters, to Hermanus van Wijk and Hendrik Witbooi, were undoubtedly two of a number of similar missives sent to various chiefs in the territory, calling upon them to support Samuel Maharero in the war against Imperial Germany.[107]

The inevitability of war: Otjimbingwe

Though the war was not the result of a premeditated plan drawn up by the Herero chieftains, once it had begun, the remaining Herero chieftaincies were drawn into the war. Through a combination of German and Herero mistrust, suspicion and revenge, the tide of war flowed across the country and engulfed the whole of Hereroland. There was no preplanned insurrection, and the remaining Herero chiefs were clearly shocked and surprised at the outbreak of war. Men such as Michael Tjisiseta in Omaruru, when informed that war had broken out between Samuel Maharero and the Germans, noted:

> I don't believe in this thing. Samuel Maharero can surely not make war on the Germans alone. And he has not, as yet, informed us of any intention to do so.[108]

Yet war did break out, and the sheer inevitability of the outbreak of war, even in those centres where Hereros protested their innocence, peaceful intentions and civilized Christian lifestyle, is well illustrated by events in Otjimbingwe. Here during a period of two weeks following the outbreak of war, the Herero were slowly but surely forced into a war which they did not want and which was not of their choosing. Primarily due to German military short-sightedness, Herero settlements which could have been spared from the horrors of war became engulfed in war. In much the same way that Ouandjo and the Herero delegation in Okahandja had protested their peaceful intentions up until the bullets had begun flying, so for two weeks Zacharias Zeraua and his followers desperately sought to keep the peace in Otjimbingwe. It was all to no avail. The case of events in Otjimbingwe provides a microcosm of events throughout Hereroland at the time.

> In Otjimbingwe a Herero captain named Zacharias had his throne; however only a small part of his tribe, mostly Christians, lived permanently at the settlement, the remaining people lived scattered at the cattleposts in the outback [*Ausenfelde*]. Between the Herero and most of the whites of the settlement (approximately 30) there existed since ages a good understanding; the two main families H. and K.

---

[107] The Ndonga King Kambonde and Chief Nehale also received a letter from Samuel Maharero on 24 January 1904. Marti Eirola, *The Ovambogefahr: the Ovamboland Reservation in the Making* (Rovaniemi 1992) p. 165.
[108] Pool, *Samuel Maharero*, p. 206.

Photo 5.3: The buildings of the Hälbich family compound, which was transformed into a fort shortly before war broke out in Otjimbingwe
Source: T. Leutwein, *Elf Jahre*, (Berlin 1906), p. 370

belonged to the old missionary colonists who had been brought into the land forty years ago by the missionary Hahn.[109]

In this manner the missionary chronicles for the settlement of Otjimbingwe introduce their account of 1904 and the outbreak of the war in the settlement. The settlement is situated at the confluence of the Omusema and Swakop rivers. The Omusema, which flows into the Swakop from the north, divides the settlement into three sections. In 1904, the north-eastern section was referred to as *Die Overkant*, the other side, where the military station, a couple of trade stores and the houses of the settlement's white inhabitants were to be found. In the north-west the church, the mission buildings, the school, the houses of missionary trader families, Hälbich and Kleinschmidt, and the houses of the settlement's various non-Herero inhabitants; to the south of the Swakop, the houses of the settlement's Herero inhabitants were to be found.

Crucial to the outbreak of the war were settler perceptions of Herero intentions. The same held true for Otjimbingwe where settlers received a string of ever more alarming messages. Whereas on 11 January the white inhabitants of the settlement had gathered to celebrate a wedding at the quarters of the Hälbich family, where 'It was a gay day and the natives [had] also received their share of the party spirit.'[110] In the evening, as the party broke up, the ever-present settler fears, of what the Herero were up to, were increased when a messenger galloped into the settlement from Karibib, bringing news that an unusually large number of Hereros had gathered at Okahandja with intentions that were clearly not peaceful. At this stage, with the exception of Zürn's panicky missives, nothing untoward had happened. Yet these reports and fears were expanded upon on the following morning, when two further couriers arrived from Windhoek, with reports, based on Zürn's observations, that 300 mounted and armed Herero had gathered at an hour's distance from Okahandja, Samuel Maharero and his councillors had left Okahandja and the garrison in Okahandja was to be reinforced by a cannon and forty men. Upon receiving this news, missionary Olpp called upon Zacharias, in his 'roomy brick house', and asked him to convene a meeting with his councillors, church elders and the Basters.[111] By the time the meeting was held in the early afternoon, reports started trickling into the settlement of events in Okahandja. At the meeting Olpp and the quantity surveyor and reservist *Leutnant* Von Frankenburg, who had been left

[109] ELCIN, V. Ortschroniken, Otjimbingwe 1904, pp. 129–30.
[110] ELCIN, V. Ortschroniken, Otjimbingwe 1904, p. 130.
[111] Ibid., pp. 130–31.

in charge of the German forces at the settlement, informed the twenty Herero and six Basters of what had happened at Okahandja:

> I reminded them of their longstanding peaceful nature [*alte Friedfertigkeit*] and appealed to their reasoning which would inform them that Germany's power would immediately suppress every revolt, whereafter the natives would lose their land and freedom. Therefore they should be wary of making common cause with those of Okahandja and not to descend into rottenness with them.[112]

Anxious to avert disaster, and with absolutely no intention of wanting war to break out in their settlement, Zacharias and his councillors declared their peaceful intentions and wrote a letter to the governor declaring their loyalty.[113] For their part the Germans continued to strengthen and fortify their position. On the following morning ten reservists accompanied by four waggons loaded with food and ammunition arrived in Otjimbingwe.[114]

During the following days refugees and settlers, who had abandoned their farms at the behest of the German military patrols sent out to urge the settlers to move into the settlements, began straggling into Otjimbingwe. These refugees brought in reports of dead settlers and burnt farms. Yet the Herero at Otjimbingwe continued to express their loyalty to the German colonial administration. Indeed, when it was reported that a cattlepost belonging to the trader Redecker had been robbed, Zacharias immediately sent out a commando to recapture the rustled cattle.[115] A day later, following this show of loyalty, all Otjimbingwe Herero were prohibited from carrying weapons whilst at the settlement.[116]

Herero displays of loyalty were to no avail. On Sunday 17 January, as had happened in Okahandja, where the settlers had believed that an attack was imminent, the soldiers abandoned their fort and the settlers abandoned their houses and stores at *Die Overkant* and occupied the complex of buildings that made up the lodgings of the missionary trader Hälbich family. The Hälbich family buildings were situated in the north-western section of the settlement adjacent to the house of Zacharias Zeraua. The move took place whilst Herero parishioners, who were too scared to move into the confined space of the missionary church, held their Sunday service out in the open next to their chief's house.[117] As Herero hymns wafted over them, the German soldiers carted their supplies, arms and ammunition into the Hälbich building complex and transformed it into an impenetrable fortress. As the missionaries preached peace and goodwill to mankind, wooden stakes were driven into the ground surrounding the Hälbich buildings, where they served as range markers with barbed wire strung between them. As Herero parishioners prayed, soldiers paced out their future fields of fire, the windows of the Hälbich complex were barricaded, gunports were knocked into walls, the wind pump transformed into an observation post, and a barrier of thornbushes erected. Henceforth no whites, with the exception of the missionaries, were permitted to be outside the confines of the fortification.[118]

---

[112] Ibid.
[113] *BRMG*, 1904, p. 123.
[114] ELCIN, V. Ortschroniken, Otjimbingwe 1904, p. 133.
[115] Ibid., p. 135.
[116] Ibid.
[117] Ibid., p. 139.
[118] Ibid.

Needless to say, in the face of such concerted settler war efforts, tensions within the Herero population of Otjimbingwe ran high. Rumours spread that Hendrik Witbooi, at this stage an ally of the Germans and a renowned opponent of Otjimbingwe in the past, was advancing on Otjimbingwe to attack the settlement.[119] Herero reports started coming in from Okahandja which stated that the whites were killing all Herero, and though the missionary dismissed these reports they were soon backed up by Herero reports coming in from Karibib.[120] In the face of all of this Zacharias Zeraua continued to order his councillors and church elders to maintain the peace.[121] These were not merely words spoken for the benefit of the missionaries and the German settlers. Two days after the whites had abandoned their houses and stores at *Die Overkant*, some cattle were rustled and the store belonging to trader Kronewitter was broken into. Zacharias reported the crimes and saw to it that the goods were returned on the same day.[122] Similarly on 20 January, eight days after the outbreak of war in Okahandja, Zacharias reported to Frankenburg that a Herero from Otjimbingwe had murdered an English trader. Zacharias went on to express his regret that his authority had not prevented the killing, but that he would see to it that the killer was apprehended.[123]

The Herero of Otjimbingwe clearly demonstrated their peaceful intentions and loyalty to the colonial administration. For their part the Germans did little to alleviate the fears of the Herero. Instead, in exchange for their displays of loyalty, they were consistently mistrusted by the Germans present in Otjimbingwe. Added to this, the Herero received a continual stream of reports of what had been happening elsewhere in Hereroland.

> The Herero expressed their fear that the men of the cruiser Habicht, who had recently arrived in Karibib, would come this way to exact revenge for the murder of the English trader. Considering all things it appears to me that the Herero now have a greater fear that the Germans will hit out at them, than that we could expect anything like that from them.[124]

The fear of the Otjimbingwe Herero, as expressed by missionary Olpp, was in no way misplaced. The marines landed by the *Habicht* deserved their fearful reputation. That much is made clear by their own accounts. After having been landed in Swakopmund, the marines, who had dyed their uniforms with coffee and tobacco, set off by train, accompanied by two machine guns and two revolving cannons.[125] All the 'blacks' whom they found at the railway stations were captured and sent back under guard to Swakopmund, where they were placed as prisoners on board the *Woermann* steamship lying at anchor there, this to cut off any contact with their tribe.[126] Apart from capturing people, the marines had arrived in Karibib without incident. The published text of one of these marines, G. Auer, makes for gruesome reading and even the most

[119] Ibid., p. 136.
[120] Ibid., p. 139. On 18 January Olpp received information regarding the return of Leutwein from the south and the landing of the troops of the ship Habicht in Swakopmund.
[121] Ibid., p. 141.
[122] Ibid.
[123] Ibid., p. 142.
[124] Ibid. JBG's translation.
[125] G. Auer, *In Südwestafrika gegen die Hereros: Nach den Kriegs-Tagebüchern des Obermatrosen G. Auer*, bearbeitet von M. Unterbeck, Zweite Auflage (Berlin 1911), p. 30.
[126] Auer, *Gegen die Hereros*, p. 31. These captured Herero were then sold to Alex Hewitt and shipped off to the mines of the Transvaal.

Photo 5.4: Herero men who had been stripped of their clothes and lynched
Source: C. Rust, *Krieg und Frieden im Hererolande, Aufzeichnungen aus dem Kriegsjahre 1904*,
(Berlin 1905), p. 196

conciliatory reading of the text makes it clear that the troops were told that
men, women and children were to be slaughtered.[127] Stationed in Karibib, Auer
expressed his disgruntlement at not being able to capture any 'blacks'.[128] When
they did capture prisoners the following happened:

> The prisoners were immediately subjected to an extensive interrogation whereby
> they betrayed one another. In this way we captured a number of the murderers, who
> were sentenced to death and hung from the nearest tree as a warning example for
> their tribal comrades [Stammesgenossen]; these criminals were not worth a shot of
> powder.[129]

The Herero in Otjimbingwe received written reports of these atrocities. The
Herero believed that they too were to be attacked and slaughtered. The extent
of their fear is well illustrated by the course of events on 21 January. Shortly
after midnight, two young Herero boys stumbled into Otjimbingwe from
Karibib and reported, 'now all the Herero are being killed by the Whites' and
that the *Distriktschef* (Franke) was advancing on Otjimbingwe. The Herero
immediately abandoned the settlement.[130] Missionary Olpp spent most of the
night searching for his scattered flock, who had fled to a kopje about five
kilometres up the Swakop river. Olpp later wrote,

> . . . according to the letter, which they received in the night, all the Natives of Karibib

[127] Ibid., p. 34.
[128] Ibid., p. 37.
[129] Ibid., p. 46.
[130] ELCIN, V. Ortschroniken, Otjimbingwe 1904, p. 143.

were locked up in a courtyard whereafter they were slaughtered. Particularly the sons of the families H and R [Hälbich and Redeker], that is the best friends of the Hereros, were engaged in this bloody work.[131]

After lengthy discussions Olpp was able to convince Zacharias to return to Otjimbingwe, though he kept away from the German stronghold and the women and children remained outside the settlement. Apart from young Herero men playing chess in front of Zacharias's house two days passed without incident.[132]

In the end war did break out. And, as in Okahandja, cooler heads, which could have averted the outbreak, were absent. On the morning of 23 January, Olpp looked out of his window and saw how Herr Kronewitter and his wife walked to their house at *Die Overkant* which had recently been burgled. An evidently angry missionary Olpp later noted that 'in the face of my warning he dares to [cross over] unarmed!' At this stage Zacharias was not at the settlement. Olpp sent off a message to Zacharias and hurried to the German fortifications. Shortly thereafter a Baster church elder burst in to report that Kronewitter had been killed. As Olpp hurried back to his house the German soldiers opened fire on the Herero settlement.[133] Frau Kronewitter made it to Olpp's house and reported:

> Her husband had intended repairing the broken windows of their house. Suddenly ten young Hereros had appeared. They had demanded tobacco from her husband. When he replied that they had already stolen it, they had torn him from his ladder and worked him over with their *Kirris* [clubs] so that he soon lay streaming blood. She had sought to protect her husband, had pleaded, had praised, then an unknown heathen Herero had aimed at her. At this moment the councillor Nikanor had interceded by knocking the flintlock away and shouting: 'Is this not our old Frau Kronewitter?, she is not to be harmed.' She had clutched at him and he protected her whilst he led her away from the scene of the tragedy to my house.[134]

The following day being Sunday, Olpp asked his Herero parishioners to respect the Sabbath. These restrictions did not apply to the German reservists. For them the war had broken out and the Herero were to be driven off. Allegedly in the interests of a clean field of fire, they burnt a number of Herero houses and demolished Zacharias's brick house with dynamite. Nearly two weeks after the outbreak of war in Okahandja, war had eventually broken out in Otjimbingwe. On the day of the Kaiser's birthday the Herero raised a German flag in the abandoned German fort at *Die Overkant*. Thereafter they torched the buildings and abandoned the settlement completely. Less than a year later Zacharias was captured and tried. In his trial it was noted that, 'Zacharias did not issue any order to make war. The cattle, which his people had stolen in the beginning, he had returned to the whites, particularly Redecker.'[135] Nevertheless, for most of the settlers and soldiers under arms, Herero, whether Christian or otherwise, were Herero and therefore they were guilty. The *Habicht* Marine Auer, who was later stationed in Otjimbingwe, was an eloquent exponent of this position:

---

[131] Ibid., p. 144. That the reported lynchings did take place was later confirmed by governor Theodor Leutwein. Nuhn, *Sturm*, pp. 81–2 & p. 183.
[132] ELCIN, V. Ortschroniken, Otjimbingwe 1904, p. 145.
[133] Ibid.
[134] Ibid., p. 146. JBG's translation.
[135] NNAW, STR 1. 1.a.5., folio 8, Aussage des Zacharias 10.1.05. JBG's translation.

Otjimbingwe . . . the captured Blacks we laid in heavy chains and kept them under secure guard, drew upon them for all forms of work. A number of prisoners claimed to have no knowledge of a Herero revolt and to have no malicious intentions towards us, naturally these were all lies with which they sought to escape punishment.[136]

Failed negotiations

The Herero had not anticipated the outbreak of the war, and were quite unprepared for it. Far from seeking to press their initial overwhelming military advantage, the Herero sought to withdraw from central Namibia and await the return of cooler minds and the beginning of negotiations. Unfortunately for them, negotiations were not allowed to succeed.

Three days after the outbreak of shooting in Okahandja, Samuel Maharero abandoned the settlement and withdrew along the Swakop river towards Okaharui. Herero military activities at the time were hardly those of an army seeking to expel an invader. Instead, the Herero withdrew and sought to regroup and assess what had happened and what was to be done. Thus in late January, in the vicinity of Ongandjira, Samuel Maharero wrote to the other Herero chiefs and asked them to come to him. For their part, the Germans, after the settlements had been cleared of Herero, also regrouped and sought to discover what was going on. On 11 February, nearly a month after the outbreak of the war, Leutwein, having travelled from Port Nolloth, arrived in Swakopmund where he was met by two of his subordinates. An indication as to Leutwein's optimistic mood is indicated by his opening words: 'It is not as bad as all that. If I were now to go to Okahandja I would let Samuel come to me, and you would see, the revolt has ended.'[137]

Anxious to come to a quick negotiated settlement, Leutwein, upon his arrival in Okahandja, dispatched a letter to Samuel Maharero in which he asked Samuel as to the causes of the war.[138] In early March Samuel replied from Otjozonjati, a small settlement along the Swakop river. In his letter Samuel clearly outlined what he saw as the causes of the war.

Otjozonjati 6/3/1904, To the Kaiser's representative Gouverneur Leutwein, I have received your letter, and I have understood everything well, that you wrote to me and my councillors. I and my councillors answer you in the following manner. The outbreak of this war was not initiated by me in this year, rather it was begun by the whites. How many Hereros have the whites, particularly the traders, killed? Both by guns and by locking them up in the prisons. And each time I have brought these cases to Windhoek [*Otjomuise*] the blood of my people always had to pay. Cattle to the amount of 50 to 15 head. Many of the traders have exacerbated the difficulties by shifting their debts onto my people. And when something like this occurred you shot us. And began making my people pay and to drive away their cattle, and the people had to pay up to 1 pound if they robbed 2–3 cows.[139] These things have led to the outbreak of war in this country. And now in this year, when the whites saw that you had friendly intentions and love towards us, they began to say to us 'Your beloved Gouverneur, who loves you, has gone to a serious war and has been killed,

---

[136] Auer, *Gegen die Hereros*, p. 101.
[137] Nuhn, *Sturm*, p. 107.
[138] Leutwein, *Elf Jahre*, p. 511.
[139] Reference to the pound fees that had to be paid by Herero following the impoundment of 'stray' Herero cattle.

and because he has died, so you too will die. Then added to this they then killed two Hereros of Tjetjo, until also *Leutnant* Zürn began killing my people in prison, up to 10 men. They claim that they died due to disease, however they were killed by their captors [*ovaungurise*]. Finally *Leutnant* Zürn began to mistreat me and to look for a reason with which to destroy me [*ndji zepere*]. And it happened that he said the people of Kambazembi and Ouandja are busy with war. And it happened that he called me to him to ask me and I told him directly that this was not the case. But he did not believe me. And finally at dawn [11 January] he added soldiers to the fort [*moskanza*] which he hid in chests [*movikesa*] and called me, but if I had come they would have shot [*jahe*] me. Because I realized this I fled. Then *Leutnant* Zürn sent people of the gun on my path to follow me and shoot me [*ovandu nozandjembo okandjijaha*] this incensed me and consequently I killed the whites which had damaged us, because my death was ordered. This I heard from a white man present here named M. von Michaelis.[140] This is how the war began. It was initiated by the traders and *Leutnant* Zürn [*via utua i ovarande na Leutnant Zürn*]. I indicate how the war started, It is not mine. Question the traders and *Leutnant* Zürn as to their war, when they have told you then we can talk about it. The present war is that of Zürn. [*Nambano ovita ovia Zürn*] These are my words, I am the chief Samuel Maharero.[141]

Samuel Maharero's letter described in detail the run up to the war and directly implicated Zürn and the trader settlers in the outbreak of the war. It clearly showed how, in the absence of Leutwein, Zürn and his acolytes had operated beyond their jurisdiction and effectively brought about a war. However, once it became known to the settlers that Leutwein had corresponded with Samuel, it was leaked to the press.[142] In the jingoistic atmosphere that had developed, the settlers found themselves supported by none other than the Kaiser himself. Leutwein was instantly ordered by Berlin to desist from entering into any form of negotiation. Instead he was ordered to immediately engage in an offensive against the Herero. Leutwein's prophetic words, written in defence of his actions, were dismissed; 'In colonial issues there must always be a diplomat standing next to a leader. The rebels must know that their route back is still open, one that does not always lead to death.'[143]

As negotiations were broken off, and a German offensive planned, the Herero and their herds tried to gather to Samuel Maharero at Ongandjira, north-east of Okahandja. On the night of 28 March the followers of Zacharias Zeraua of Otjimbingwe crossed the railway-line between Okahandja and Windhoek.[144] Two days later they reached Samuel's encampment at Ongandjira. At approximately the same time Michael Tjisiseta, and his followers from Omaruru, arrived, and six days later, on 6 April, they were joined by David Kambazembi and his followers.[145] The missionary Eich met Samuel Maharero at Oviumbo in early April. Eich later reported that there were an estimated

[140] Von Michaelis had an unsavoury reputation and was disliked by Leutwein. Pool, *Samuel Maharero*, p. 194, & Rohrbach, *Kolonialwirtschaft*, p. 333.

[141] ELCIN, I 1.19 A. *Verschiedene Briefe von u a Samuel Maharero u a Herero 1887–1904*. Letter written in Otjiherero on Rhenish missionary society paper dated Otjozonjati, 6 III 04, signed by Samuel Maharero. The letter is not in Samuel's handwriting and it is probably a copy. Another copy in German exists. The Herero text has been used in this instance. JBG's translation. Another version of this letter was first published by Rohrbach, *Kolonialwirtschaft*, p. 338.

[142] Leutwein, *Elf Jahre*, p. 511.

[143] Leutwein cited in Nuhn, *Sturm*, p. 112. JBG's translation.

[144] Nuhn, *Sturm*, p. 122.

[145] Pool, *Samuel Maharero*, p. 225.

20,000 Herero in the area and that besides Samuel the chiefs, Michael Tjisiseta, Ouandja, Assa Riarua and David Kambazembi, were present. Furthermore Eich reported that in the laagers Baster gunsmiths were engaged in repairing Herero rifles.[146] Though not referred to by Eich, the chiefs Tjetjo, Zacharias, Traugott Tjetjo and Kajata must also have been in the vicinity.

In accordance with his orders from Berlin, Governor Leutwein regrouped his forces and advanced on the Herero chiefs and their followers. On 9 April German forces fought a day-long battle with Herero forces at Ongandjira. Though the Herero had dug trenches and erected a kilometre-long barricade of thorn bushes, they were unable, in the face of German artillery, to hold their positions. The Herero retreated eastwards and four days later they clashed once again with the Germans at Oviumbo. This time, however, the two sides were more evenly matched and after a day of fighting the opponents withdrew.[147] Following the battles of Ongandjira and Oviumbo the Herero began trekking northwards towards the Waterberg, which they reached towards the end of July. For his part Governor Leutwein, having failed to defeat the Herero, was relieved of his command and replaced by the German Kaiser's own candidate, Lieutenant-General Lothar von Trotha.[148]

Leutwein strongly believed in a negotiated end to the war, all the more so now that his ordered offensive had failed to bring about the crushing victory so desired by the Kaiser and his settlers. Earlier Leutwein had written:

> . . . I do not concur with those fanatics who want to see the Herero destroyed altogether. Apart from the fact that a people of 60,000 or 70,000 is not so easy to annihilate, I would consider such a move a grave mistake from an economic point of view. We need the Herero as cattle breeders, though on a small scale, and especially as labourers. It will be quite sufficient if they are politically dead.[149]

In keeping with these sentiments, Leutwein, shortly before the arrival of the Kaiser's candidate, Trotha, had one last attempt at a negotiated settlement. On 30 May 1904, the following proclamation, printed in Otjiherero, was distributed to the Herero by 100 couriers:

> Hereros! You well know that after you have risen against you protector, the German Kaiser, nothing else awaits you but a fight to the death. Until then I cannot stop the war. However you can stop the war, by coming over to me, handing in your guns and ammunition, and receiving your expected punishment.
>
> However it is well known to me that a lot of you carry no guilt for the many evil affairs that have happened. And these can safely come to me; their lives will be spared. However no mercy will I show to those who have murdered whites and robbed their homes. These will be placed before a court and must receive the value of their guilt. You others however, who have no such guilt upon themselves, be clever and no longer connect your fate with that of the guilty ones. Leave them and save your life! This I say as representative of your paramount lord, the German Kaiser.
> Okahandja, 30 May 1904 (Sgd. Leutwein)[150]

Leutwein, as always a stickler for correct procedure, sent a copy of the proclamation to Berlin accompanied by a letter in which he justified his actions.

---

[146] Ibid., p. 226.
[147] Ibid., pp. 232–9.
[148] See Bley, *South West Africa*, pp. 158–63, for a discussion on the appointment of von Trotha.
[149] Leutwein cited in Drechsler, *Fighting*, p. 148.
[150] Nuhn, *Sturm*, pp. 197–8.

Leutwein noted that it would be impossible to encircle all the Herero at the Waterberg and force them to surrender; a number would escape and continue the war. He concluded his letter by stating that he had offered the Herero a chance of surrender in an attempt to curtail the war.[151] Reaction from Berlin was swift and immediate; Leutwein was ordered to refrain from any further interference in German military policy.[152] Summoned to a meeting with Trotha, Leutwein asked him to 'conduct the war in such a way as to preserve the Herero nation'. Trotha refused and informed Leutwein that he would 'conduct the war as he saw fit'.[153] Henceforth a negotiated peace was out of the question.

The war

Counter to Leutwein's wish to negotiate, Imperial Germany had decided to continue the war; there was, however, no way that the Herero could know this. After the Battle of Oviumbo there was a four-month period of relative calm, as German troops were withdrawn and regrouped. Far from pressing their advantage, as one would have expected from the initiators of a carefully planned insurrection against German colonialism, the Herero did nothing.

The Herero expected that the negotiations initiated by Leutwein would continue. There were historical precedents for this train of thought. In the past Leutwein had reached negotiated settlements, even following extensive engagements and German losses. The examples of the negotiated settlements with Hendrik Witbooi in 1894 and the Bondelswarts in early 1904 were clear cases that supported this line of thinking. Following a military stand-off, as had happened at Oviumbo, the Herero believed that Leutwein would now come to a negotiated settlement with them. Indeed Leutwein's declaration of 30 May indicated that this was Leutwein's wish. However, negotiations were cut short at the orders of Berlin and Trotha. Henceforth, all attempts by Herero chiefs to negotiate were dismissed. When, in response to Leutwein's proclamation of 30 May, Salatiel Kambazembi sought to negotiate a surrender, Trotha noted 'That will hardly help him; fought together, caught together, hanged together.'[154]

During the four months of phoney war, in which the Herero undertook no offensive actions against the Germans, the Herero had not an inkling as to what was going to happen. The Herero did not even attempt to sabotage the German telegraph lines, let alone disrupt the over-extended German supply lines. Indeed, five days prior to what would be the deciding battle in the war, the battle at Hamakari, Herero soldiers were still ordered to refrain from engaging German patrols.[155] Instead between April and August the Herero retreated northwards towards the plains between the Omuramba Omatako and the Waterberg. In the Herero laagers church services continued to be held by the Rhenish Mission evangelists Julius (Okahandja), Christian (Otjiruse), Elifas (Otjimbingwe), Elifas (Otjosazu), Josaphat, Komatoto and Johannes (Okahandja).[156] English traders such as Wallace and Cain, who had been a

[151] Ibid., p. 198.
[152] Pool, *Samuel Maharero*, p. 247.
[153] Bley, *South West Africa*, p. 162.
[154] Von Trotha cited in Pool, *Samuel Maharero*, p. 249.
[155] Ibid., p. 254.
[156] Rust, *Krieg*, p. 135.

councillor of Maharero, lived and moved with the Herero laagers for approximately five months.[157] Basters who had worked on the mines, and others such as Hendrik Cloete, were employed as gunsmiths and in repairing saddles.[158] Firearms and ammunition were brought to the Herero from Ovamboland and from South Africa.[159] Though settlers claimed that the Herero were engaged in cannibalism, the Herero depended for their nourishment on their cattle herds, which had recovered somewhat in the seven years following rinderpest and were still largely unaffected by the war, their maize fields along the Nossob river, their links with the Ovambo, and collected field foods.[160]

For their part the Germans, under the new command of Trotha, sought to engineer a crushing defeat of the Herero. To this end, all possible negotiations with the Herero were to be avoided. German forces, under the new command of Trotha, were ordered not to engage in battle with the Herero. Instead they were ordered to regroup and ensure that, through encirclement, the Herero did not leave the vicinity of the Waterberg.[161] Finally when he believed that enough reinforcements had been brought into the country, Trotha, in keeping with Moltke's principles of separate deployment and encirclement, sent out his armies to encircle and annihilate the Herero at the Waterberg. Or, as he put it in his own words:

> My initial plan for the operation, which I always adhered to, was to encircle the masses of Hereros at Waterberg, and to annihilate these masses with a simultaneous blow, then to establish various stations to hunt down and disarm the splinter groups who escaped, later to lay hands on the captains by putting prize money on their heads and finally to sentence them to death.[162]

In early August, Trotha issued battle orders to his troops. On 11 August the battle of Hamakari at the Waterberg took place. The Herero were defeated and fled in a south-easterly direction into the dry desert sands of the Kalahari, known to the Herero as the *Omaheke*.[163] Trotha's troops pursued the Herero ever deeper into the *Omaheke*. On 16 and 26 August Trotha issued orders which, by placing a cordon along the waterholes, cut off all escape routes to the west, south and north-east, and effectively forced the fleeing Herero to move further into the inhospitable stretches of the *Omaheke*.[164] On 21 August, Trotha placed a price of 5000 marks on the head of Samuel Maharero, and 1000 marks on the head of any Herero headman.[165] In a series of follow-up skirmishes, during August and September, the German troops pursued the fleeing Herero. In early

[157] Ibid., pp. 132–5.
[158] Pool, *Samuel Maharero*, p. 226. & Rust, *Krieg*, p. 136.
[159] CAD, AG 1931, *Blouboeke en Wetboeke in Verband met Damaraland en Walfisch Bay 1880–1906.* Governor Sir W.F. Hely-Hutchinson in Cape Town, 17/5/05, to Mr Lyttelton. Pool, *Samuel Maharero*, p. 226, has reports of waggons laden with firearms coming down from Ovamboland.
[160] For cannibalism see Rust, *Krieg*, p. 133. For maize fields see same p. 137. As regards Herero cattle herds, these had certainly not attained the numbers that they had before the rinderpest. However, these herds, small as they may have been, were at this stage of the war still largely intact, and as yet largely unaffected by the war.
[161] Pool, *Opstand*, pp. 210–11.
[162] Von Trotha's diaries cited in Pool, *Samuel Maharero*, p. 251.
[163] Pool, *Opstand*, pp. 219–40. *Omaheke* is the Otjiherero name for the sandveld area east of the Waterberg.
[164] Pool, *Opstand*, p. 245ff.
[165] Pool, *Samuel Maharero*, p. 269.

Photo 5.5: German troops watering their horses at the waterholes of Hamakari shortly after the battle of the Waterberg, 11 August 1904
Source: Namibian National Archives, Windhoek

September, German troops attacked the rearguard of the bulk of the Herero at Ovinaua-Naua near the Eiseb river.

> After a battle of one hour the pursuit began. The artillery moved as one detachment and fired into the thick rows of the fleeing enemy, which attempted to cover its withdrawal by setting ablaze the grass behind it.[166]

Troops under the command of Estorff prevented the Herero from fleeing southwards and forced them north-eastwards into the *Omaheke*.[167] Cornered by the desert and the German patrols the Herero chiefs and their followers congregated along the Eiseb river.

Around 1 October 1904, General Lothar von Trotha, who was actively taking part in the pursuit, and his retinue had reached the waterhole, Osombo-Windimbe. During the afternoon of the following day, Sunday 2 October 1904, after the holding of a field service, General von Trotha, addressed his officers.[168] In his address Trotha declared that the war against the Herero would be continued in all earnestness, and read out the following proclamation:

> I the great General of the German troops send this letter to the Herero people.
> The Herero are no longer German subjects. They have murdered and stolen, they have cut off the ears, noses and other body parts of wounded soldiers, now out of cowardice they no longer wish to fight. I say to the people anyone who delivers a captain will receive 1000 Mark, whoever delivers Samuel will receive 5000 Mark. The Herero people must however leave the land. If the populace does not do this I will force them with the *Groot Rohr* [cannon]. Within the German borders every Herero, with or without a gun, with or without cattle, will be shot. I will no longer

---

[168] Rust, *Krieg*, p. 384.

accept women and children, I will drive them back to their people or I will let them be shot at.
These are my words to the Herero people.
The great General of the mighty German Kaiser.[169]

At dawn the following morning, Herero prisoners who had been sentenced to death by a field court martial were hung in the presence of about thirty Herero prisoners, women and children amongst them. After the hanging, Trotha's proclamation was read out to the prisoners in Otjiherero. Printed copies of the text in Otjiherero were distributed amongst the Herero prisoners. The prisoners were then turned loose and driven out into the *Omaheke*.[170] Trotha described the day's events in his diary as follows:

> Before my departure yesterday I ordered the warriors captured recently to be court-martialled and hanged and all women and children who sought shelter here to be driven back into the sandveld, handing them a copy of the proclamation drawn up in Othiherero [*sic*].[171]

Of late a number of authors have sought to deny or at least downplay the existence and implications of Trotha's proclamation, which has become known as the *Vernichtungsbefehl*.[172] However, Trotha's own words, in his diary and elsewhere, indicate that he knew full well what his proclamation entailed. On the day that the proclamation in Otjiherero was handed to the prisoners at the hanging in Osombo-Windimbe, Trotha wrote in a letter:

> Now I have to ask myself *how* to end the war with the Hereros. The views of the Governor and also a few old Africa hands [*alte Afrikaner*] on the one hand, and my views on the other, differ completely. The first wanted to negotiate for some time already and regard the Herero nation as necessary labour material for the future development of the country. I believe that the nation as such should be annihilated, or, if this was not possible by tactical measures, have to be expelled from the country by operative means and further detailed treatment. This will be possible if the water-holes from Grootfontein to Gobabis are occupied. The constant movement of our troops will enable us to find the small groups of the nation who have moved back westwards and destroy them gradually . . .
> My intimate knowledge of many central African tribes (Bantu and others) has everywhere convinced me of the necessity that the Negro does not respect treaties but only brute force . . .
> I find it most appropriate that the nation perishes instead of infecting our soldiers and diminishing their supplies of water and food. Apart from that, mildness on my side would only be interpreted as weakness by the other side. They have to perish in the Sandveld or try to cross the Bechuanaland border.[173]

---

[166] Over a hundred Herero were killed whilst one German was wounded. Rust, *Krieg*, p. 382. JBG's translation.
[167] Pool, *Opstand*, p. 249.
[169] NNAW, ZBU D.1.a Band 3 - 4, leaf 165. With thanks to Mr W. Hillebrecht for finding it at such short notice. JBG's translation.
[170] Rust, *Krieg*, p. 386 & Nuhn, *Stürm*, p. 282.
[171] Drechsler, *Fighting*, p. 161
[172] Brigitte Lau, 'Uncertain Certainties: The Herero–German war of 1904', in *Mibagus*, No. 2, April 1989, pp. 4–8.; Karla Poewe, *The Namibian Herero: A History of their Psychosocial Disintegration and Survival*, Edwin Mellen Press (Lewiston and Queenston 1983); Gunter Spraul, 'Der "Völkermord" an den Herero: Untersuchungen zu einer neuen Kontinuitätsthese' in *Geschichte in Wissenschaft und Unterricht*, 1988/12, pp. 713–39, & Gert Sudholt, *Die deutsche Eingeborenenpolitik in Südwestafrika. Von den Anfängen bis 1904*, Georg Olms verlag (Hildesheim, 1975).
[173] Pool, *Samuel Maharero*, pp. 272–4

At a later stage Trotha enthused:

> The exercise of violence with crass terrorism and even with gruesomeness was and
> is my policy. I destroy the African tribes with streams of blood and streams of money.
> Only following this cleansing can something new emerge, which will remain.[174]

German contemporaries of Trotha also understood full well what the general
meant. In September of 1904, a month after the battle at Hamakari, Major
Ludwig von Estorff had urged Trotha to enter into negotiations with the Herero.
At that stage Trotha had answered: 'No, my friend, I will have nothing of that,
only that we have to start all over again. We will fight for as long as possible.
Basta!'.[175] From 1904 and through into 1905 Estorff, along with the divisions
of v.d. Heyde and Mühlenfels, '. . . had the thankless task of chasing after the
refugees in the Sandveld and preventing their return'.[176] Estorff's own words
describe clearly what he did and what the intentions were of his commanding
officer, Trotha:

> . . . I followed their spoor and found numerous wells which presented a terrifying
> sight. Cattle which had died of thirst lay scattered around the wells. These cattle
> had reached the wells but there had not been enough time to water them. The Herero
> fled ahead of us into the Sandveld. Again and again this terrible scene kept repeating
> itself. With feverish energy the men had worked at opening the wells, however the
> water became ever sparser, and wells evermore rare. They fled from one well to the
> next and lost virtually all their cattle and a large number of their people. The people
> shrunk into small remnants who continually fell into our hands [unsere Gewalt kamen],
> sections of the people escaped now and later through the Sandveld into English
> territory [present-day Botswana]. It was a policy which was equally gruesome as
> senseless, to hammer the people so much, we could have still saved many of them
> and their rich herds, if we had pardoned and taken them up again, they had been
> punished enough. I suggested this to General von Trotha but he wanted their total
> extermination.[177]

The policy of extermination was one which had been embarked upon by Trotha
for some time prior to Osombo-Windembe. Major Stuhlmann, describes in
his diary entry, for 11 August 1904, a scene from the battle of Hamakari on
that day. Stuhlmann muses on the horrors of war and of a wounded Herero
child lying next to his cannon:

> . . . the little worm had flung his arm around the wheel of the cannon, which had
> possibly destroyed his other family members . . . we had been explicitly told
> beforehand, that this dealt with the extermination of a whole tribe, nothing living
> was to be spared.[178]

Stuhlmann's diary describes how on the following day they marched through
what had been the Herero encampments at Hamakari. All around them lay
the evidence of the hasty Herero retreat; scattered household goods and
children, with staring eyes, abandoned and sitting at smouldering camp fires.

---

[174] Horst Kühne, 'Die Ausrottungsfeldzüge der "Kaiserlichen Schutztruppen in Afrika" und die
sozialdemokratische Reichstagsfraktion', in Militärgeschichte, Band 18, 1979. p. 211. JBG's
translation.

[175] Pool, Samuel Maharero, p. 270.

[176] Ludwig von Estorff, Wanderungen und Kämpfe in Südwestafrika, Ostafrika und Südafrika: 1894–
1910 (Windhoek 1979) p. 117. JBG's translation.

[177] Ibid., pp. 116–17. JBG's translation.

[178] NNAW, Acc. 109, p. 49. JBG's translation.

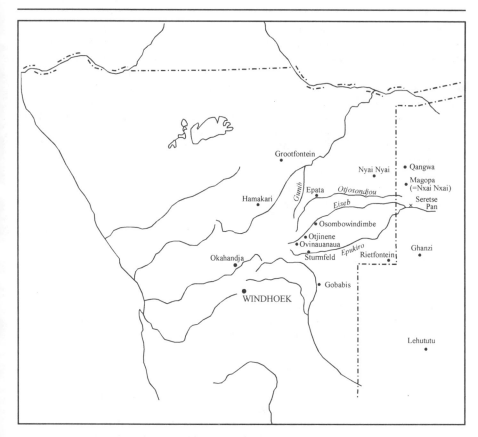

Map 5.2: Map showing Herero flight after the battle at the Waterberg

As they moved on they came across milling cattle, goats and sheep, doomed to die, as the herds had been shot by the German troops. In his diary Stuhlmann mused on how easy it would have been to save this livestock, as water and pasture were amply available. But, as he noted in his diary, '. . . the orders were an extermination war waged on the Herero with no turning back'.[179]

Herero movements in the aftermath of the Waterberg

German military deployment forced the defeated Herero to flee south-eastwards ever deeper into the *Omaheke*. Though Herero sought to congregate around the few waterholes that bordered the desert, they were systematically driven from these by German patrols, and forced to attempt to cross the *Omaheke* and reach the relative safety of the Bechuanaland Protectorate. Very little is known as to the movement of people and the development of events in Herero society in the immediate aftermath of the battle at the Waterberg. What follows is an attempt at plotting the course of a number of Herero chieftains and their followers in the *Omaheke*.

[179] NNAW, Acc. 109, p. 50. JBG's translation.

Following the battle at the Waterberg on 11 August 1904, the Herero were forced to flee into the *Omaheke*. The majority of the chiefs and their followers survived the actual battle at the Waterberg. But, cut off from water and their cattle, the majority of the Herero died as they tried to struggle through the desert. By early September the Herero had congregated along the Eiseb river, which bisects the *Omaheke* and leads to the Botswana border. Zacharias Zeraua, the erstwhile chief of Otjimbingwe, who was later captured and interrogated, reported that the chiefs Banjo (Otjombonde),[180] Salatiel Kambazembi (Waterberg), Ouandja (Otjikarurume), Kajata (Otjihaenena), Michael Tjisiseta (Omaruru), Mutate (Omaruru), Kainjonna (son of Kambazembi otherwise known as David), Katjahingi, Assa Riarua and Samuel Maharero had gathered, at Osombo Onjatu – a waterhole otherwise known significantly enough as Omkeer – along the Eiseb river.[181] The chiefs Mambo and Tjetjo were also on the Eiseb river but at the waterholes Otjinena and Epata. By circumstance and not by choosing, the Herero chiefs and their followers were forced to congregate along the dry water course of the Eiseb river. Here, the Herero, desperate for water, dug pits, some of which were up to twelve metres in depth. Here, too, at what was effectively the sole major source of water in the desert, the surviving Herero were found and attacked by the troops of Estorff. Following Estorff's attack, the Herero were forced to flee once again.

On 9 September Estorff's forces attacked Owinaua Naua, dislodging the chiefs Tjetjo and Mambo and forcing them to flee eastwards in the direction of the Bechuanaland Protectorate. Neither of the two chiefs reached the border. Tjetjo died of thirst near to a waterhole named Oruaromunjo and Mambo apparently died of exhaustion whilst following Tjetjo's party.[182] Samuel Maharero, encamped in the Eiseb at Osombo Onjata, fled as soon as he received reports of the attack at Ovinaua Naua.[183] With four waggons, his councillors and nearest associates Samuel fled downstream. However, due to the absence of water, Samuel and his party were soon forced to abandon their waggons and most of Samuel's non-mounted followers were forced to turn back. Only those followers of Samuel Maharero who were fortunate enough to be mounted eventually reached Njai Njai in the Bechuanaland Protectorate. Samuel Maharero's nephew, Willy Maharero, was also forced to turn back, though Willy's messengers did manage to make it to Njai Njai and return. Upon their return they reported that, due to thirst and salty water, most of Samuel Maharero's cattle and horses had died and that all of his party were sick.[184] Willy Maharero remained in the vicinity of Sturmfeld and later crossed into Bechuanaland via Rietfontein in early 1905.[185]

When Samuel Maharero fled Osombo Onjata, Salatiel Kambazembi and

[180] Zacharias listed Banjo, though a later reader of the report, probably von Estorff, noted in the margin that Banjo had died.

[181] NNAW, Str.1.a.5, reverse folio 8.

[182] NNAW, Str.1.a.5, folio 9 and reverse.

[183] Zacharias reported that Samuel fled when the first shots were fired at Osombo-Windimbe, that is on 29 September. This is unlikely as Samuel sent a letter to Sekgoma Letsholathebe dated Njai Njai 28 September. In his evidence Zacharias noted that the distance between Omkeer and Njai Njai was about 8 days. NNAW, Str.1.a.5 reverse folio 9. In his first interrogation of 10 January 1905, Zacharias stated that Samuel Maharero fled with Ouanja, Kajata, Michael, Mutate, David (Kainjonja, Kambazembei's son), Katjahingi and Assa.

[184] NNAW, Str.1.a.5, folio 9.

[185] Willy had originally intended surrendering to the Germans but changed his mind following the Ombakaha affair. Drechsler, *Fighting*, chapter III, fn. 120.

Zacharias Zeraua fled to Osombo Onguti, four days' travel to the north-west. However, there was insufficient water there and they lost most of their cattle and a number of followers due to the thirst. Therefore Salatiel trekked on to Otjikoko in the Omuramba Otjosondjou and from there on to Ovamboland where, along with forty women and thirty men, he was granted refuge by the Ndonga chief Nehale.[186] Zacharias sought to turn back to Osombo Onjata and remained to the east of the waterhole on the Eiseb river before surrendering to German forces in early 1905.

According to the evidence supplied by Zacharias Zeraua, following his capture in early 1905, he, Mutate and his cousin, Michael Tjisiseta, had not been directly involved in the battle at Hamakari on 11 August. Instead, during the battle at the Waterberg, they had been at Otjikaru; 'no white soldiers came there'.[187] However, after the battle, as they sought to join Samuel's party, Michael's party ran into Estorff's troops on 15 August and Omaruru church elder Asa Kaijombo was killed.[188] Following the attacks at Ovinaua Naua, Michael's party appears to have split up into three sections, two of which reached the Bechuanaland Protectorate, and a third which remained in GSWA. In early 1905 a party of Herero, who owed allegiance to Michael Tjisiseta, were found south of Ghanzi on the trade route towards Vryburg at Lehututu.[189] As with these people, Michael Tjisiseta also made it to Bechuanaland but instead of heading southwards from Olifantskloof towards Vrijburg, Michael travelled north to Tsau, the capital of the Batawana.[190] Michael remained in Tsau for a short period of time before he turned back to Hereroland. Lieutenant Streitwolf reported that when he visited Tsau in August 1905, 'The Herero eagerly enquired after Michael, kaptein of Omaruru, who had left Tsau for German territory.'[191]

Back in Hereroland Michael dispatched a nineteen-man patrol, led by Asser Mutjinde and Gerhard Afrika, to Walvisbay, with instructions to buy arms and ammunition. The patrol made it safely to British territory, but were disarmed and interned upon their arrival in Walvisbay.[192] According to Asser Mutjinde's son, the patrol also escorted an English trader, who had been with them in the Omaheke, to safety in Walvisbay.[193] At some stage during 1905 Michael Tjisiseta left Tsau and attempted to make the same journey, that is traversing GSWA from east to west. Michael succeeded in this endeavour and on 8 December 1905 Michael, his brother, Hugo, and eight followers were interned in Walvisbay.[194] In January 1906, Michael led more than 130 prisoners in a break-out from the concentration camp in Swakopmund. On 29 January Michael

---

[186] NNAW, Str.1.a.5, folio 9. & Eirola, *Ovambogefahr*, p. 181. H.E. Lenssen travelled to Nehale for Herero and labourers. H.E. Lenssen, *Chronik von Deutsch-Südwestafrika* (Windhoek 1994) p. 172.

[187] NNAW, Str.1.a.5, reverse folio 9.

[188] ELCIN, V. Ortschroniken, Omaruru 1904, folio 298.

[189] BNA, RC 11/1, Acting Magistrate [Merry?] in Tsau Ngamiland, 3/4/05, to resident Commissioner in Mafeking.

[190] BNA, RC 11/1, RC in Mafeking, 26/4/05, to HC.

[191] Drechsler, *Fighting*, Chapter III, fn. 139.

[192] ELCIN, V. Ortschroniken, Omaruru, 1904, folio 298.

[193] K. Schlosser, 'Die Herero in Britisch-Betschuanaland-Protektorat und ein Besuch in einer ihrer Siedlungen Ncwe-le-tau', in *Zeitschrift für Ethnologie*, Vol. 80 (Berlin 1955), pp. 200–58, p. 209.

[194] Ibid., p. 209.

and a party of 198 Herero embarked in Walvisbay and were shipped to Cape Town and the mines of the Witwatersrand.[195] In return for the supply of mine labourers from amongst his followers Michael was permitted to live on a farm near Johannesburg. Michael never returned to Omaruru, but died in exile in Krugersdorp.[196] Following the Second World War a number of his descendants and followers left South Africa and settled in the Gabane area in south-eastern Botswana.[197]

Following his internment in Walvisbay, Asser Mutjinde was shipped to South Africa, probably to Port Nolloth. In 1905 Asser wrote to the missionaries in Omaruru from Nababes in Namaqualand, northern Cape. Mutjinde reported that together with about 250 Herero he was working in the copper mines of Nababes. Furthermore Mutjinde reported that they had erected a school, were engaged in baptismal churches and had become affiliated to the Rhenish Mission community in Concordia.[198] In 1908, when the Wankie colliery in Rhodesia was extremely short of labour, labour recruiters desperately sought labour throughout southern Africa. It is possible that members of Asser Mutjinde's exiled Herero community were being referred to when the general manager of the Wankie colliery wrote the following:

> We received an offer from an independent labour agent in Vryburg to supply us with any quantity of 6 and 9 month natives at 25/- per head . . . In the meantime I have wired the agent in Vryburg to send us 100 natives.[199]

Once war had broken out, a sizeable number of Herero fled northwards to the kingdoms of Ovamboland; these numbers increased substantially following the battle at the Waterberg. In the months of the phoney war, prior to the battle at the Waterberg, Herero traded cattle for grain and firearms with traders from the Ovambo kingdoms. With the exception of the Ndonga king, Nehale, the Ovambo kings refrained from attempting to intervene directly in the Herero–German conflict.[200] As the war turned against the Herero they made use of the trading contacts and long association with the Ovambo kingdoms to seek sanctuary. Amongst those Herero who sought sanctuary in Ovamboland was Daniel Kariko, the erstwhile chief of Okombahe.[201] Daniel and his followers sought refuge with the Ongandjera king Tshaanika, who in later years was reported to have Herero men attached to his court as 'Secretaries of War'.[202] Previously Kariko had sought refuge with his followers in Walvisbay.[203] At a later stage Daniel Kariko travelled to the Transvaal, probably via the trans-Kalahari cattle trade route pioneered by Erikkson.[204] At the outbreak of the

---

[195] *Deutsche Kolonialzeitung* (Berlin 1906), p. 61.
[196] Schlosser, *Ethnologie*, p. 210.
[197] On 17 December 1992 Mrs Brown (a.k.a. Vinderine Kavi Muvangua) of Gabane, Botswana, confirmed that her father Huko Tjisiseta (Hugo Tjisiseta Michael's brother) had travelled from Omaruru by sea to Kimberley and Johannesburg. Gewald, Fieldnotes book 1, December 1992.
[198] ELCIN, V. Ortschroniken, Omaruru 1905, folio 321.
[199] Zimbabwe National Archives, A 11 2/8/22, Wankie Mine Labour, General Manager Wankie mine in Wankie, 8/6/08, to his honour the administrator Salisbury.
[200] Eirola, *Ovambogefahr*, pp. 165–77.
[201] Drechsler, *Fighting*, p. 167.
[202] Eirola, *Ovambogefahr*, pp. 181 & 184.
[203] NNAW, ZBU 2027B, reports on Kariko in 1900 with 500 men in Walvisbay.
[204] After an initial period of acceptance in the the Ovambo kingdoms large numbers of Herero moved onwards towards Angola and the Kaokoveld. Eirola, *Ovambogefahr*, pp. 180–5.

First World War Daniel Kariko was employed either as a 'boss boy' or native policeman at a mine of the Witwatersrand Deep Ltd (later to become Western Deep Levels). Together with Lucas Kamangoti, Daniel Kariko was seconded by the mine as a scout to the Union Defence Force prior to its invasion of Namibia. Following his return to Namibia, in 1915, Daniel Kariko was employed in the office of the military magistrate in Omaruru.[205]

In later years the opium addict, mystic, naturalist and manic depressive Afrikaner writer Eugene N. Marais met Samuel Maharero and his followers in Groenfontein in the Transvaal, South Africa. Here Samuel and his few remaining followers were caught in a catch-22 situation of being permitted to live on land on condition that they supplied labour to the mines and farms of the Anglo-French company. When recovering from bouts of depression Eugene Marais visited his friend and confidant Gustav Preller whose farm lay near to Groenfontein. Marais was most impressed with the Herero refugees whom he described as black Afrikaners.

> Most of them could read and write – High-Dutch was the normal 'School language' and a form of Afrikaans the 'learned' language of speech. All wore European clothes; many lived in built houses and farmed as Afrikaners did.[206]

Marais spent many an afternoon chatting with the ageing and ailing Herero chief and his confidant, the preacher-teacher Julius Kauraisa. It was on the basis of these conversations that Eugene Marais later wrote up Samuel's account of *Die woestynvlug van die Herero's*.[207]

Following the attack at Ovinaua Naua, Samuel Maharero and a few of his closest followers had fled along the Eiseb. After eight days of travel they finally reached the pans at Nyae Nyae.[208] The area around Nyae Nyae fell within the usufruct range of the Batawana polity. Consequently Samuel Maharero wrote and sent the following letter to Sekgoma Letsholathebe, the *Kgosi* of the Batawana:

> Nyainyai (Mogopa) 28 Sept 1904 . . . I am in the Batawanas country. I am writing to tell you that I have been fighting with the Germans in my country, the Germans were my friends, they made me suffer so much by the manner in which they troubled me that I fought with them. The beginning of the trouble was that I gave the English some boys to work at Johannesburg. This is the reason that they fought with me. An Englishman called Juda [Hewitt] knows this he was the man who came to get the boys. I have been fighting for eight months and my ammunition is finished. As I have come into your country at Magopa I ask help from Queen Victoria. In olden times my father was friendly with the English government and on this account I come to the English government for succour and request permission to live in their country. I now ask you to have mercy on me and help me in my heavy trouble, please reply to me. This is my prayer to you that I may follow those of my people who have

---

[205] NNAW, NAW 4, Subfile Native Affairs Native Police, *Herero Police previously employed by the Wit Deep Ltd*.

[206] Eugene N. Marais, *Sketse uit die Lewe van Mens en Dier*, Kaapstad 1928, p. 3. JBG's translation. With thanks to R. Gordon for the reference and G. Krüger for the photocopy.

[207] Marais, *Sketse*, p. 3.

[208] Nyai Nyai has as many spellings as it has exact locations. Properly speaking Nyai Nyai refers to a series of waters lying between Tsumkwe and Gam on the Namibian Botswana border. Zacharias Zeraua indicated in his statement that Nyai Nyai lay eight days' travel from Ovinaua Naua. Samuel's letter to Sekgoma indicates that he had arrived in Magopa, which today lies in Botswana just across the border from Gam in Namibia.

gone before me till I get there. If you allow me I will leave here at once. Sir I ask you to answer me as soon as possible.

I send my best greetings I am the chief of the Damaras Samuel Maharero.[209]

From Nyae Nyae (Magopa) Samuel Maharero and his followers travelled north to Qangwa.[210] Here they were met by one of Sekgoma's confidants, his father's former secretary, Samuel Sheppard, who handed him the following letter:

Banwato, October 17, 1904. I am your friend that likes [you] I say if you are fighting with the German, do not fight with the hole [sic] country. Sir, if you see that you are beaten you are to come here like Kahada [Kahaka], Kwenengo, and Kicodemus [Nicodemus]. Come under me and the English. I ask you not to take any care of fighting, because you will have nowhere to go to. The English are your friends. I am your friend too. With greetings Sekgoma Letsholathebe.[211]

Henceforth Samuel and his small party of followers were in the unenviable position of being refugees with nothing to offer but their labour. After a short period of time in the Tswana capital, Tsau, Samuel and his followers were moved on to Makalamabedi on the Botletle. Here 'Matabele' Wilson, a trader and labour recruiter for the British South Africa Company found Samuel and his party in late 1905.

Conversation with these people reveals the fact that they consider the protection afforded by the British flag is not all they thought it would be. For a time, they were supplied with a bag of mealies per diem by the Protectorate Government, but they are not allowed firearms of any sort, and now the supply of mealies has been cut off. The Bechuanas employ a number of them as servants – for a paltry dole per day and a handful or two of kafir corn. When the writer saw them, they were suffering not a little from hunger. The Bechuanas resent the presence of these refugees in their midst, the Kafir doctors are predicting that murrain will visit the cattle as a result of their presence.[212]

The labour recruiters sought to induce Samuel to supply labour to the South African mines. With nothing left, Samuel Maharero attempted to survive by making use of the contact referred to in his asylum application as Juda. Juda, as the British official who read Samuel's letter had correctly jotted down in the margin, referred to a labour recruiter for the South African mines, Mr Alex Hewitt. Hewitt was employed by the Witwatersrand Native Labour Agency (WNLA) which had been set up to recruit labour throughout southern and central Africa for the mines of South Africa.[213] In later years Samuel Maharero wrote what had happened:

[209] BNA, RC.11/1, Correspondence regarding Hereros (and flight to Ngamiland after rebellion in German South West Africa). Samuel Maharero in Mogopa 28/9/04 to Resident Magistrate. This is a translation of an original letter written in Otjiherero to Sekgoma Letsholathebe. Another copy of the letter addressed to Sekgoma is to be found in the CAD, AG 1931.
[210] BNA, RC 10/18, Williams at Tsau, 6/9/04, to RC. Xangwa, Qangwa, is a small settlement along the Kama river. Herero pastoralist settlements surround it and the area is referred to as Magopa. In the 1960s anthropological research on the Dobe !Kung was conducted at Magopa, Xangwa and Dobe.
[211] CAD, AG 1931, Mervyn G. Williams in Johannesburg, 8/2/05, to imperial secretary.
[212] 'In Bechuanaland; Words by an Eye-witness', 19 May 1906, in The Bulawayo Chronicle, edited by Barry Morton, Bloomington Indiana.
[213] For more on Alex Hewitt see J.B. Gewald, The Road of the Man called Love and the Sack of Sero: The export of Herero labour to the South African Rand, 1890–1914, Paper presented on Saturday 4/12/1993 at the 'Politics and Labor in Namibia' session of the 1993 Annual Meeting of the African Studies Association held in Boston.

After I had fought the Germans in my own country, I sought refuge under the Government, and the Latter received me and prevented my enemies from pursuing me. And after the Government had received me, a white man named Jund [Hewitt] came to me at Tsau, Lake N'gami, and said to me 'I have been sent by the Government to you, the Government has given you ground on which you and your people will build'. But, Chief, this was an untruth, he was only getting me into trouble, he was referring to ground owned by Companies. And after I had left with him he took me to the Transvaal and told me that it was a country of contracts and that I must send my people to work on contract at the Mines. Thereupon I began to send men to work on contract, and they died in large numbers.[214]

Following the battle at the Waterberg, although substantial numbers of Hereros fled eastwards and northwards into Bechuanaland and Ovamboland, the majority of the Herero were confined to the *Omaheke.* A number of Herero were able to slip through the German cordon and head westwards back into central Namibia.[215] There were also groups of Herero who had never left central Namibia, but had managed to remain living undetected in the more inhospitable regions of territory. German military patrols regularly came across traces of these groups and as late as 1907 detachments eagerly requested permission to shoot at them. Primarily these groups of free Herero were to be found in the Khomas Hochland mountains and along the course of the Khuiseb river. These Herero were in contact with Walvisbay and traded rustled cattle and horses for goods in Walvisbay. In 1908 a German patrol, which had chanced upon tracks in the lower Khuiseb, followed a Herero party along the Khuiseb deep into the Khomas Hochland mountains. The Herero party was eventually attacked in the mountains overlooking Windhoek.[216]

One such party which had remained in the mountains and had kept its distance from the fighting was that led by Andreas Maharero, Samuel's younger brother. Andreas was in contact with Walvisbay and wrote the following letter to the magistrate there:

Kansberg den 9.5.1905
To the *Omuhona* of Walvisbay magistrate.
It is I Andreas Maharero who wrote this letter to get permission from you and ask whether you will help me or not. I have got my people and weak ones. And I also have cattle and small cows and small horses. Tell me whether we will get some place if you accept us. I do not want to continue with the peace with the Germans, because my brother is also not here and I do not trust the peace of this people and I want to go to the colony of the English there where my brother was.

Please give the answer to the same man who brought the letter. Let him try to come back quickly.

Can you please tell me where my brother is? Because you are the one who knows where he is. This is the end.

A last word: I would like some tobacco and coffee. This is the last and I greet you, the great *Omuhona* of Walvisbay.

It is I Andreas Maharero the younger brother of Samuel Maharero.[217]

[214] NNAW, South West African Administration (SWAA) 2085, 460/25 Maharero volume 1, copy of letter from Samuel Maharero to Resident Commissioner, 25 February 1920. That Hewitt consciously lied to Samuel Maharero is substantiated by the writings of A. Loton Ridger, who accompanied Hewitt on his trip to the Herero. A. Loton Ridger, *A Wanderer's Trail: Being a faithful record of travel in many lands* (New York 1914), pp. 282–9.
[215] NNAW, Str.1. 1.a.5.
[216] NNAW, ZBU 459, folio 148, *Meldung,* Windhoek 10/2/08.
[217] CAD, File No. 1/WLB 4/1/21/1 Private individuals. With thanks to Dag Henrichsen for alerting me to this letter and to him and Louis von Hasbad for the rough translation.

Seeking to end the war

In an atmosphere where Trotha's proclamation had in effect been the mere legal sanctioning of that which, as the numerous diaries of the *Schutztruppen* show, had already been commonplace, a negotiated settlement with the Herero seemed remote.[218] In effect the Herero, defeated in battle, were given no other option but war. In these conditions negotiations and a return to peace could not take place. In late 1905 Willy Maharero told Lieutenant Streitwolf, who had been sent into Bechuanaland on an intelligence mission, that he had intended surrendering to the Germans in January. But that he had changed his mind and fled to Bechuanaland when he heard what had happened at Ombakaha.[219] Here little more than three weeks after the issuing of Trotha's *Vernichtungsbefehl Oberleutnant* von Beesten lured a number of Hereros into an ambush. Under the pretext of wanting to engage in negotiations with the Herero captains, Beesten persuaded eleven Herero headmen, led by Joel Kavizeri of Okahandja and Saul of Otjenga, to enter unarmed into a German camp. Whilst the Germans surrounded the approximately seventy Herero who remained outside the camp, Beesten allowed the 'negotiations' to break down and in the words of Beesten:

> . . . I gave orders to open fire. For a brief period of time the enemy vigorously returned the fire, but then careered down the hillside, pursued by our shells and bullets, to come to a halt at a distance of approximately 300 metres. In the meantime the kapteins and headmen had tried to escape and had all been killed within a radius of 10 to 300 metres . . . About 12 noon the remainder of the enemy withdrew. As far as I know, no one escaped unscathed . . . There were no casualties on our side.[220]

Though incidents like the above occurred on a daily basis they did little to end the war. The examples of Michael Tjisiseta and Andreas Maharero clearly indicate that German forces were unable, however much they and their commanders may have wanted, to drive all the Herero from the territory. The incident at Ombakaha emphasized to the Germans once again that though the Herero were defeated they would have to come to some form of arrangement with the Herero which went beyond merely attempting to annihilate all of them.

Zacharias

Pressure to end the war eventually came from within Germany itself. Alarmed

---

[218] The diary entries of *Schutztruppen* H.F.R. Knoke provide some indication as to indiscriminate slaughter that was going on and was commonplace. NNAW, ACC.538, pp. 73ff.
> 8/7/04 Of the 5 captured Herero 4 have been hung. The 5th is used for labour purposes.
> 9/7/04 Our prisoner has a noose around his neck which is then attached to the saddle of a horse. The particular Witbooi ensures that things do not become too comfortable for him.
> 16/8/04 A captured Herero female [Hereroweib] was, after she had been given supplies, set free. However the bitterness of the people is great. The female had barely left the encampment when two shots were fired. A sign that this one had also left its life.
> 7/10/04 As last night we had noticed a number of fires in our vicinity, we looked for spoor this morning, which, after a bit of searching we found. We junior officers galloped ahead, our men followed on foot. We took the *werft* shot down part of the inhabitants, the remainder we took along as prisoners.

[219] Drechsler, *Fighting*, ch. III, fn. 120.
[220] BAP, RKA 2089, p. 105. Also cited in Drechsler, *Fighting*, ch. II, fn. 119. For a published account see Pool, *Opstand*, p. 256.

by what was happening in Namibia, particularly following the publication of the *Vernichtungsbefehl* and *Schutztruppen* letters in the German press, the Rhenish Missionary Society, the German social democratic party and other groups urged the Kaiser and his government to accept the surrender of the Herero. Events on the ground had shown that, though the Herero had been militarily defeated, it was impossible to destroy them all, added to which, all attempts to do so led to a hostile reception in Germany itself. However, even when the possibility of an honourable negotiated settlement was forced upon Trotha and his sympathizers, Trotha ensured that Herero interests were disregarded. One of the Herero chiefs who attempted to surrender was Zacharias Zeraua of Otjimbingwe. A detailed account of his surrender and subsequent fate provides an indication as to the manner in which Herero concerns were simply disregarded and promises broken.

At quarter past ten on the morning of 9 December 1904, the following telegram was sent from Berlin to General Lothar von Trotha in Namibia:

> His royal Highness the King and Kaiser wishes to grant mercy to all those Herero who surrender voluntarily and orders that, apart from the incontrovertibly guilty and the leaders, their lives be granted. You are to make this known to the Herero in a suitable manner. You are to accept the good services offered by the evangelical mission to care for the initial accommodation of the surrendering Hereros.[221]

Immediately thereafter, Estorff who was at that stage stationed at Ovinaua Naua on the Eiseb river, was ordered to inform the Herero that, if they gave up their weapons and surrendered, then their lives would be spared.[222] Discharged from seeking to enforce the containment of the Herero in the *Omaheke*, Estorff issued a proclamation to 'the Herero people'. The Herero were called upon to surrender, in exchange for which Estorff promised to spare their lives and resettle them in the areas they had originally come from:

> I speak the truth, I do not lie. I will send you there where you previously were, some to Otjimbingwe, some others to Waterberg or also to Omaruru or to Okahandja. [At this point Trotha, who later saw the proclamation, scrawled *unerhört*, unheard of, in the margin] I will issue letters to you so that nothing will happen to you on the road or at the settlements.[223]

Estorff's proclamation was the first genuine attempt by the Germans to negotiate with the Herero since Leutwein had been relieved of his command for attempting to do the same. Clearly the Herero had long looked forward to an end to the war. Estorff's offer met with a positive response and in due course he received a reply from the councillors of Zacharias Zeraua, Victor Metirapu, (Gerhard) Jephta Marritta, Nehemia Katjipitua, Kahapa Metirapu and Katjiheive Mbakuru, all formerly of Otjimbingwe. Zacharias Zeraua himself didn't reply, but he must have known of this letter, which was probably written with his consent. It must be remembered that at this stage Zacharias, as a chief, still had a price on his head. Added to this Trotha's promise of immediate

---

[221] NNAW, Str. 1. 1.a.5, folio 1. Interestingly this file is one of only four archival files of the *Schutztruppe* in Namibia to have survived. A possible reason for this is that the files were destroyed by the retreating German forces in 1915 when the Union troops invaded Namibia. This line of reasoning is backed up by the fact *Zu vernichten 1915* [To be destroyed 1915] has been scrawled across folio 1 in red ink.

[222] NNAW, Str. 1 1.a.5, folio 2. Telegram from von Trotha in Windhoek 9/12/04 to von Estorff.

[223] NNAW, Str. 1 1.a.5, folio 4. Proclamation to the Herero People 12/12/04 von Estorff.

summary execution and Beesten's betrayal at Ombakaha formed a sombre background to anyone wishing to surrender. Not surprisingly Zacharias failed to make his presence immediately known to the Germans. For their part, Zeraua's councillors thanked Estorff for his proclamation and wrote: 'We, who live in the field, have received the paper of peace, however we do not believe that it is peace. Your word of peace is good, however we recently heard of the events at Ombakaha.'[224] They continued by noting that they and their followers had no interest in continuing the war, but were afraid that if they surrendered they would all be killed as had happened 'in Ombakaha and Okahandja'.[225] Estorff replied immediately, that the events at Ombakaha had made him angry and sad, but that this would not happen again.[226] Encouraged by Estorff's letter, Zacharias now dared to show himself. In an extremely cautious and God-fearing reply, in which he sought to emphasize his peaceful past and intentions, Zacharias wrote:

> We have received the letter of peace and we are very happy. We are very happy that God has touched the Kaiser's heart to make peace with us, this makes us extremely joyful. We have accepted the peace . . . I have accepted the peace as have all my councillors. Our people have, as God's people, all been joyful. With regard to the Kaiser's letter I wish to call all the people together. At present I cannot come as my people have been scattered; they have extreme hunger. Peace is made by all the people. In all truth my heart is intent on peace, along with my councillors, my people and I we are all in peace. Soon I will also tell Samuel Maharero's people and along with the people in the vicinity I will attempt to seek the peace.
>
> I will write as to whether or not these people want peace with you or not. I will soon tell you, you must wait for the answer . . . As far as the weapons are concerned I have one with powder [muzzle loader] and not a 88 [Schutztruppe standard issue] . . .
>
> I come in peace in God's name. I am the great ruler of Otjimbingwe, I Zacharias along with my councillors. I joyfully anticipate your letter.[227]

During the course of three weeks Estorff and Zacharias negotiated Zacharias's surrender. Initially through the exchange of letters, and finally in face-to-face talks between Viktor Metirapu and Estorff, Zacharias and his followers were seduced into surrender. Zacharias was informed that henceforth no Herero would be allowed to own firearms and that all the cattle of the Herero would now belong to the Germans.[228] When Estorff threatened to continue the war, if Zacharias failed to surrender, Zacharias let it be known that he was having difficulty gathering all his people and more importantly that he was being pressurized by Willy Maharero not to come to a negotiated settlement with the Germans. Some members of Zacharias's party were also against the negotiations. At one stage Zacharias appended a letter with a message known solely to Viktor Metirapu. In it Zacharias urged Estorff to ensure that his cattle and horses were well guarded as Willy Maharero intended attacking Estorff. Zacharias ended his secret message of betrayal with the words, 'Do not let the other people see these words, instead communicate solely via Victor.'[229]

---

[224] Ibid., Victor Metirapu *et al.* to von Estorff, reverse folio 4.
[225] Ibid. Note the emphasis on events in Okahandja.
[226] NNAW, Str.1. 1.a.5, folio 5. Von Estorff in Ovinaua Naua, 18/12/04, to Victor Metirapu.
[227] Ibid., Zacharias to von Estorff, folio 5.
[228] NNAW, Str. 1 1.a.5, Von Estorff in Ovinaua Naua, 23/12/04, to Zacharias.
[229] NNAW, Str. 1 1.a.5, Zacharias in Omahua, 27/12/04, to von Estorff.

Eventually Zacharias and his followers began moving along the Eiseb river towards Estorff at Owinaua Naua.

> I wish to inform you that I am now at Epata. The people can only come along slowly as they are very thin.
> I would once again like to have news from you, so that I can be informed of all events. It is the pure truth that I have accepted the peace, the peace that the Kaiser made. In God's name. I greet you on behalf of all my people.[230]

After observing Sunday in the field, Zacharias and his people marched into captivity on Monday 9 January 1905.[231] Estorff wrote to Trotha and recommended that Zacharias Zeraua and his followers be sent back to Otjimbingwe. Trotha had different ideas and in the margin of Estorff's letter he scrawled: 'No way, Zacharias is to be investigated for the murders, none to Otjimbingwe; to the missionaries, the men are to go to the troops for labour.'[232] All through Estorff's letter Trotha vented his anger with sarcastic comments. When Estorff recommended that some Herero may be suited for labour, Trotha scrawled 'All! are suited,' or that it would be no problem to employ them for food, he scribbled 'Also that! generous belief.'[233] Estorff's promise to the Banderu councillor, Nicolaus, that he and his followers would be settled near Gobabis was greeted by Trotha with, 'You have nothing to promise!'[234] Trotha ended his marginal tirade with the following words:

> Are these then the circumstances in which the end of this unheard of revolt is to be achieved, that now with our promises we have to beg for peace? This position is the cause of the revolt. Tr.[235]

Under no circumstances was Zacharias to be permitted to return to Otjimbingwe. Instead in captivity Zacharias was immediately interrogated and charged with instigating the murder of white settlers.[236] In court Zacharias stated under oath:

> Before the beginning of the war I did not hold meetings with the captains in Okahandja, therefore I knew nothing of an impending war. I also did not receive a letter from Samuel that he wanted to make war.[237]

The camps

A direct result of the war was, as Leutwein had foreseen and feared, a shortage of labour. To alleviate this shortage, forced labour camps were established. Between 1904 and 1908, Herero, who were captured by German forces, were incarcerated in forced labour camps across the country, and made to work on civilian and military projects. There are those who have argued that: 'There is

[230] Ibid., Zacharias in Epata, 4/1/05, to von Estorff.
[231] Ibid., Zacharias in Oyjinene, 8/1/05, to von Estorff. The letter indicates that Zacharias, as a true Christian, observed the Sunday.
[232] NNAW, Str.1 1.a.5, von Estorff to the northern military command, January 1905, reverse folio 10.
[233] Ibid., folio 11.
[234] Ibid., folio 12.
[235] Ibid., reverse 12.
[236] NNAW, Str. 1 1.a.5, folio 13–22. These are the papers dealing with the trial of Zacharias Zeraua.
[237] Ibid., Okahandja 22/2/05, trial of Zacharias, folio 17.

absolutely no evidence . . . that the Herero perished or were used on a large scale as "slave labourers".'[238] What follows is a dry description of the history of the camps. In the following chapter the impact of the camps on Herero society will be discussed.

Prior to the battle of Hamakari at the Waterberg, German commanders received requests from labour-hungry settlers for the allocation of Herero prisoners of war, large numbers of which, it was anticipated, would be made. With the expulsion of the Herero from central Namibia, the perceived Herero threat had diminished and, at the same time, a dire labour shortage had developed in the colony's settler economy. As the war approached its climax, the settler economy, which serviced the German military presence, started picking up again and the demand for labour increased. From the very beginning of hostilities, the German army had employed prisoners of war as forced labour. As it was anticipated that the German army would make a large number of prisoners of war, it was hardly surprising that settlers applied to its commanders for labour:

> According to reports, large numbers of Herero have already been captured in the battles at the Waterberg. Bearing in mind that the containment and maintenance of large numbers of prisoners in Damaraland [Central Namibia] is likely to be bound up with major difficulties, the *Gibeoner Schurf und Handelsgesellschaft* has submitted an application that of these prisoners they be immediately granted ca. 50–100 Men as mine workers . . . It is perhaps advisable that the Herero be chained together in groups of about ten men before transported south.[239]

As the Herero–German war wound down in northern and central Namibia and the Nama–German war developed in the southern reaches of the country, the military and settler demands for labour, and the concomitant shortage of labour, developed continually. However, as a direct result of the German military's successes, most of the Herero were confined to the dry regions of the *Omaheke*, and could thus not be approached for labour purposes. With this in mind the German *Reichskanzler* recommended that missionaries be asked to encourage the Herero to surrender and that those Herero who surrendered were 'to be placed in concentration camps [*Konzentrationslagern*] in various parts of the country where, under guard, they could then be used for labour'.[240] With the effective containment of the Herero survivors, missionaries of the Rhenish Missionary Society and their assistants were sent into the *Omaheke* to lure the survivors out and into the newly established camps. In anticipation of the new prisoners, a number of holding camps were set up in Omburo, Otjosazu, Otjihaenena and later Otjozongombe.[241] Given the circumstances, the missionaries were extremely successful in their endeavours. Large numbers of Hereros, starved, pursued and hunted like animals, were enticed out of the desert. The captives were placed in holding camps, from whence they were then redistributed to smaller camps all around the country.

[238] B. Lau, 'Uncertain Certainties', p. 5. One short look at any of the German colonial government files entitled *Kriegsgefangene* (prisoners of war), stored in the Namibian National Archives in Windhoek, will disprove these claims.
[239] NNAW, ZBU 454, Kaiserliches Bezirksamt Gibeon, 18/8/04 an das Kaiserliche Gouvernement. JBG's translation.
[240] NNAW, ZBU 454 DIV 1.3. Band 1, Telegramm des Reichskanzlers an das Gouvernement, eingegangen am 14 Januar 1905.
[241] ELCIN, V. Ortschroniken, Omaruru 1905 & II. 9.1,7, *Privatbrief von Missionar J. Bohm aus der Aufstandszeit 1904 ff aus Walfischbay.*

From the very beginning of the war, settlers and colonial businesses demanded captured Herero for labour purposes. The army, which was also desperately short of labour, was loath to let its monopoly go and it was not until 1905 that, following lengthy discussions, it was decided that civilians and civilian businesses would also be permitted to use captured Herero for labour purposes.[242] Henceforth civilians could apply to the military for labour. Once the military needs had been fulfilled, captured labour was to be made available to civilians:

> The district authorities will determine the number of prisoners required for labour purposes and will inform the military authorities [*Etappenkommando*] accordingly. Bearing in mind the number of prisoners available, the military authorities will allocate, to the district authorities, prisoners, who will then be allocated to the individual applicants according to their importance and need . . . As prisoners they are not to be paid for their labour.[243]

Civilians could collect their daily allotments from the various camps, whilst large civilian companies, such as the Woermann shipping company, maintained their own camps.[244]

Herero prisoners of war were used as labour by both military and civilian enterprises for a wide range of activities. Prisoners were put to work in civilian companies, ranging from laundries to transport contractors, breweries and shipping companies.[245] Various military units used their prisoners, often children, primarily for the maintenance and care of their stock. This entailed the construction of cattle kraals, the pumping of water, and the cutting of grass for fodder and herding.[246] The German colonial civil administration used its Herero, and later Nama prisoners of war, for the building of railway-lines between Usakos and Otavi and later between Lüderitz and Keetmanshoop.[247] The civil administration also used prisoners of war on building projects. Indeed the building that presently houses the parliament of independent Namibia was built partly with the aid of Herero prison labour.[248] However, the amount and quality of labour supplied continued to be insufficient. Civilian authorities regularly petitioned the military authorities for additional labour. The following partial transcript of a telegram sent on behalf of the Swakopmund chamber of commerce is a fine example of this petitioning:

> The civil economic community, excepting the Woermann line [shipping company], require 300 Natives fit for labour for the maintenance and continuance of their

---

[242] NNAW, BWI 406, *Akten E.V.8 Kriegsgefangene Eingeborene generalia begonnen 1/4/05–31/3/09. Rundverfügung Windhuk, 6 April 1905, der Kaiserliche Gouverneur in Vertretung Fecklenburg. Abkommen des Gouvernements mit der Militär-behörde betreffs Überweisung von Kriegsgefangenen.*
[243] NNAW, ZBU 454, D IV 1 3 Band 1, Bericht, Etappenkommando I b 7957, Windhuk 29/3/05. JBG's translation.
[244] ELCIN, VII 31.5 Swakopmund, H. Vedder in Swakopmund, 31/12/06, to K. Ritter, regarding the escape of Herero prisoners from the Woermann camp.
[245] Numerous letters written by various civilian companies for POW labour are to be found in NNAW, ZBU 454, Band 1–3.
[246] NNAW, ZBU 454 Band 1–3. For children one look at the various photographs in the Namibian National Archives will suffice to show the employment of minors by the German troops. See particularly the photographs in Acc. 109 which carry the following appellation: *Eingeborenen Kinder helfen Kraal bauen.*
[247] Ibid. & ELCIN II 9.1,7 Privatbrief von Missionar J.Bohm aus der Aufstandszeit 1904 ff aus Walfischbay.
[248] NNAW, ZBU 454, Leutwein in Windhoek, 12/2/05, to Bauamt.

companies . . . therefore we request your excellency that a big transport of native prisoners of war be handed over to the district administration for distribution by the civilian administration.[249]

Conditions in the camps were horrendous. Apart from the texts provided by the civilian and military authorities, there are also extremely detailed reports written by the missionaries, who were actively involved in the herding of Herero into the camps. The missionary chronicles for Swakopmund provide a clear image of conditions in these camps:

> When missionary Vedder arrived in Swakopmund in 1905 there were very few Herero present.[250] Shortly thereafter vast transports of prisoners of war arrived. They were placed behind double rows of barbed wire fencing, which surrounded all the buildings of the harbour department quarters [Hafenamtswerft], and housed in pathetic [jammerlichen] structures constructed out of simple sacking and planks, in such a manner that in one structure 30–50 people were forced to stay without distinction as to age and sex. From early morning until late at night, on weekdays as well as on Sundays and holidays, they had to work under the clubs of raw overseers [Knutteln roher Aufseher], until they broke down [zusammenbrachen]. Added to this the food was extremely scarce. Rice without any necessary additions was not enough to support their bodies, already weakened by life in the field [as refugees] and used to the hot sun of the interior, from the cold and restless exertion of all their powers in the prison conditions of Swakopmund. Like cattle hundreds were driven to death and like cattle they were buried. This opinion may appear hard or exaggerated, lots changed and became milder during the course of the imprisonment . . . but the chronicles are not permitted to suppress that such a remorseless rawness [rucksichtslose Roheit], randy sensuality [geile Sinnlichkeit], brutish overlordship [brutales Herrentum] was to be found amongst the troops and civilians here that a full description is hardly possible.[251]

The conditions in Swakopmund were bad. Vedder's presence in part ensured that the military authorities instituted an inquiry into the state of affairs, which concluded that, in the interests of labour, the prisoners 'be provisioned and strengthened in the interior before being sent here'.[252] In Lüderitz conditions were, if anything, worse than in Swakopmund. Initially missionaries were not present in Lüderitz. It was only later that, acting on reports of Herero evangelists

---

[249] NNAW, ZBU 454, Telegram Fuchs in Swakopmund, 13/2/05, to von Trotha. JBG's translation.
[250] With the outbreak of the war all Herero living in Swakopmund, and those captured along the railway-line towards Karibib, were placed onto the ship SS Eduard Bohlen, which at that stage was anchored off the coast at Swakopmund. Not really knowing what to do with the prisoners the authorities decided to offer the male prisoners to South African labour contractor A. Hewitt as labour for the mines. Hewitt gladly accepted these prisoners, but argued that, as the prisoners were already embarked as sea, he need not have to pay customs duty nor 20 mark per labourer as demanded by the German authorities. Hewitt did not have to pay and on 20 January 1904 the SS Eduard Bohlen, with 282 prisoners on board, set sail for Cape Town and the mines of the Rand. NNAW, BSW 7, folio 110, Letter from the Kaiserliches Bezirksamt Swakopmund to the Kaiserliche Gouvernement Windhuk dated 12/2/04.
[251] ELCIN, V. Ortschroniken Swakopmund. JBG's translation. The author of the text, Dr Heinrich Vedder, would later become an acclaimed national socialist, anthropologist and historian of Namibian affairs. After the Second World War Vedder was appointed to the South African senate as representative of the black population of Namibia. His election led in part to the majority of Herero leaving the Rhenish Mission church and establishing their own independent church.
[252] NNAW, ZBU 454, Dr Fuchs in Swakopmund, 29/5/05, to Kaiserliche Gouvernement. JBG's translation.

Photo 5.6: Christian Herero women prisoners of war, captured shortly after the outbreak of war, carrying crates at the harbour in Swakopmund in 1904
Source: Namibian National Archives, Windhoek

who had been sent there, they voiced their deep concern to the authorities.[253]

An aspect of the forced labour system was that the district authorities were ordered to submit monthly reports to the central government as to 'how many prisoners, categorized as men, women and children, found within the district authorities area, had been allocated to civilians or to the government itself'.[254] Because these lists were to provide the German authorities with an indication as to the labour available, they also included the categorization as to whether prisoners were fit or unfit [*Arbeitsfähig Unfähig*] for labour purposes.[255] In the case of Swakopmund, the district authorities' list was accompanied by a death register [*Totenregister*], which listed the cause of death as either exhaustion, heart failure, bronchitis or scurvy. Furthermore the list contained roneoed death certificates which already listed the cause of death as 'death by exhaustion following privation'. These only needed to be filled in for a tally to be kept of the daily dead.[256]

[253] ELCIN, VII 31 Swakopmund 1, Eich in Okahandja 14/6/05 to Vedder, acting on German military reports, mentions the death of 59 men, 59 women and 73 children in the Luderitz camp. Conditions in Luderitz were so bad that during the course of 1906 Major von Estorff who was in charge of the military authorities in Luderitz disobeyed the order of his commanding officers and had the camp moved to a healthier setting.
[254] NNAW, ZBU 454, Etappenkommando in Windhuk 30/3/05 to Kaiserliche Gouvernement. JBG's translation.
[255] See for instance NNAW, ZBU 454 D IV 1 3 Band 2 Kriegsgefangene, *Bestandsnachweisung über Eingeborene Kriegsgefangene*, Windhoek 18/8/1906.
[256] NNAW, Bezirksamt Swakopmund 107 (Old notation SD63–182) *Totenregister fur Eingeborene*. Another aspect that needs to be mentioned here is the conducting of medical experiments on POWs. Dr Carla Krieger Hinck, in her thesis *Über die Medizische Versorgung der ehemaligen Kolonie Deutsch Südwest Afrika*, DMed Uni München 1973, basing herself on the *Sanitätsbericht über die kaiserliche Schutztruppe für SWA während des Herero und Hottentottenaufstandes für die Zeit vom*

Herero prisoners of war not only died, they also resisted and fled. The files of the magistrate court in Lüderitz make ample mention of Herero prisoners of war, men as well as women, who had been put to work on the construction of a railway-line from Lüderitz to Aus, who actively resisted, often for naught, the mistreatment to which they were subjected.[257] Further to the north at Swakopmund, large numbers of refugees fled to the comparative safety of the British territory of Walvisbay. According to German intelligence reports, the postman, operating between Swakopmund and Walvisbay, acted as a go-between for labour recruiters of the South African mines. As a result of his activities, large numbers of Herero prisoners fled to Walvisbay and eventually the South African mines.[258] The extent of Herero flight from Swakopmund was such that the Woermann shipping company, a major recipient of the forced labour, was often short of harbour labour. As a missionary, who was working in Swakopmund at the time, noted:

> . . . Timotheus Hipangua, fled with wife and child and many others in the night of 4 Nov 1906 to Walvisbay. Many had preceded him and many would follow him, to swop their toiling existence here for an existence of tedium in the mines of South Africa.[259]

Finally in 1908 the camps were abolished.[260] Henceforth all Herero over the age of seven were expected to carry metal discs around their necks. These bore a number that corresponded with a number in a register that kept track of allocated 'free' labour.[261] Some registers which had been used to keep control

---

1/1/04–31/3/07, Band 1 Berlin 1909, pp. 105–6, refers to these activities and to the post-mortems conducted on POWs who had died in the camps. Interested in the medical aspects of death Krieger Hinck mentions that the 778 post-mortems conducted in 1906 provide a good record of the causes of their death. In later years these activities were followed up by the collection of skulls, which Herero women prisoners of war were forced to scrape clean with the aid of glass shards. NNAW, ZBU 2027. SAWW.II.d.8 *Eingeborenangelegenheiten Herero Alte Akte Generalia*. Der Staatssekretär des Reichs-Kolonialamts, Berlin 31/7/08, an den Herrn Gouverneur in Windhuk. Specifically deals with Prof. Klaatsch's (University of Breslau) request for Herero skulls. And *Meine Kriegs-Erlebnisse in Deutsch-Südwest-Afrika*, von einem Offizier der Schutztruppe, (Minden i. W. 1907), p. 114, which carries a photograph with the following text: 'A chest of Herero skulls was recently sent by troops from German South West Africa to the pathological institute in Berlin, where they will be subjected to scientific measurements. The Skulls, from which Herero women have removed the flesh with the aid of glass shards . . .' With thanks to Ms G. Krüger for this reference. Leonhard Schultze, *Zoologische und Anthropologische Ergebnisse einer Forschungsreise im westlichen und zentralen Südwestafrika* (Jena 1909), contains a detailed exposé of the anatomical details of a number of dead Herero and Nama POWs. Following their deaths, usually by hanging, their bodies had been placed in preservatives and shipped to Germany for dissection.
257 NNAW, BLU 220, SPS 49 Strafprozesssache gegen die Hererofrau Anna; NNAW, BLU 221, SPS 85 Strafprozessache gegen die Herero Kriegsgefangene Justine; SPS 81 Strafprozessache gegen die Hererofrau Johanna; SPS 80 against a number of runaways; NNAW, BLU 28, (Old notation ZD 96–523) Eingeborenenangelegenheiten E.1.K Eingeborenen Unruhen.
258 NNAW, BSW 107, (Old notation SD 68–204), Entlaufen von Eingeborenen nach Walfischbay, UA 10/2.
259 ELCIN, V. Ortschroniken, Swakopmund 1906.
260 NNAW, BWI 406, Akten E.V.8 Kriegsgefangene Eingeborene generalia begonnen 1/4/05–31/3/09. Windhoek 3 April 1908 Durch Verfügung des Kaiserlichen Gouvernements vom 26 Marz 1908 ist die Kriegsgefangenschaft der Hereros mit dem 1 April 1908 Aufgehoben.
261 For an overview of labour legislation see Tony Emmett, 'Popular Resistance in Namibia, 1920–1925' in *Resistance and Ideology in Settler Societies*, Southern African Studies Vol. 4, edited by Tom Lodge (Johannesburg 1986) p. 10. NNAW, Acc 508. The carrying of metal discs had initially been recommended by von Trotha three years earlier.

of the allocations of forced labour, were retained and used to list the allocation of labour according to the new pass and labour laws.[262]

Conclusion

The Herero–German war was not the result of a premeditated Herero insurrection against German colonial governance. Ideas of a nationwide insurrection existed solely in German colonial minds. Land shortage, on the part of the Herero, was not a cause of the war. Herero chiefs willingly sold land in the aftermath of the rinderpest. Instead, those opposed to the further sale of Herero land were the German governor Theodor Leutwein and the Rhenish Missionary Society. Once legislation was passed limiting the amount of Herero land available for sale, German settlers were cut off from land. The jingoistic attitudes of the settlers and their sympathizers that resulted from this legislation led to the creation of a climate wherein the outbreak of war became inevitable. Anxious to ensure sufficient land for future settlement a German officer consciously forged land treaties. It was this man's troubled conscience and panic that led to the first shots of the war being fired in Okahandja. The Herero–German war broke out as the result of settler paranoia coupled with the incompetence and panic of a German officer.

The letters, attributed to Samuel Maharero, which purport to show that the war was the result of a premeditated revolt against German rule on the part of the Herero, were post-dated and at least one of the letters was planted to deflect settler hostility away from missionary activities.

The manner in which chief Zacharias Zeraua and his subjects in Otjimbingwe became involved in the war illustrates how Herero chiefs and their followers, irrespective of their professed loyalties, were driven and drawn into the war against the Germans. As with the outbreak of the war in Okahandja, German paranoia inevitably drove the Herero to war.

Attempts at a negotiated settlement were consciously sabotaged and were frustrated by German metropolitan ideas on how the war was to be fought. But for German metropolitan interference, the Herero–German war could have been contained and the war brought to an early end. Instead conflict within German ranks led to opportunities to negotiate being studiously ignored and the war was allowed to continue and engulf the whole of the territory.

Though the Germans had effectively won the war, they were unable to expel all the Herero from the territory. However, the war did lead to the complete destruction of Herero society as it had existed prior to the war. As a result of the war, the Herero lost all their rights to land, cattle, chiefs and their own religion. How Herero society reestablished itself in the aftermath of the war is the subject of the following chapter.

---

[262] NNAW, BWI 440.SAW In the case of Windhoek the registers were retained into the period after South Africa's occupation of Namibia in 1915.

6

The Histories of the Old Testament Teach Us

1905–14

Introduction

By early 1905, Germany had won the Herero–German war. Herero society, as it had existed prior to 1904, had been destroyed. The Herero were left propertyless, landless and leaderless, and legislation was passed to ensure the eternity of this condition.[1] However, it was within the confines of this legislation that Herero society was able to reestablish itself, albeit in a different form, but independent of Germany. That is, Herero were able to maintain, reestablish, transform and recreate their own identity as Herero. The following chapter looks at the way in which, following Hamakari – and contrary to the hopes and aspirations of German colonial officials who had assigned the Herero to oblivion – Herero ensured that their identity as Herero came to be maintained.[2]

The chapter is divided into sections detailing social developments amongst the Herero people between 1905 and 1914. The first three sections detail the

---

[1] For the development of German legislation regarding the dispossession of all Herero property see BAP, RKA 1220, *Einziehung von Vermögen Eingeborener im Südwestafrikanischen Schutzgebiet. 9 Mai 1905–6 Februar 1914.* Von Lindequist in Windhoek, 17/7/05, to colonial office. In this letter von Lindequist echoed von Trotha's suggestion that Herero prisoners be indelibly marked, by noting that henceforth, 'The native will receive as legitimation a tin counter embossed with a number, magisterial district and the Kaisers crown.' Letter from the Reichs-Justizamt in Berlin, 31/10/05, to the colonial office & for a printed version of the legislation, which was passed into law on 26/12/05, see *Deutsches Kolonialblatt*, 1/1/06, pp. 1–3.

For copies of the legislation regarding the control of Herero see, NNAW, ZBU, 2023 *Verwaltung der Eingeborenen angelegenheiten*, WII a 4 – a 10. For published texts, see *Verordnung des Gouverneurs von Deutsch-Südwestafrika, betr. Dienst- und Arbeitsverträge mit Eingeborenen des südwestafrikanischen Schutzgebiets, Verordnung des Gouverneurs von Deutsch-Südwestafrika, betr. Maßregeln zur Kontrolle der Eingeborenen,* & *Verordnung des Gouverneurs von Deutsch-Südwestafrika, betr. die Paßpflicht der Eingeborenen,* all of 18/8/07, *DKB*, 15/12/07, pp. 1179–84. For a detailed discussion of this legislation, see Bley, *South West Africa*, pp. 170–17, and for African responses to this legislation see, P. Prein, 'Guns and Top Hats: African resistance in German South West Africa, 1907–1915' in *Journal of Southern African Studies*, Vol. 20, No. 1, 1994, pp. 99–121.

[2] In 1911 a colonial official in German South West Africa initiated a file on the Herero, which he captioned with the words, *aufgelösten Eingeborenenstämme,* 'dissolved Native Tribes', NNAW, ZBU 2027.

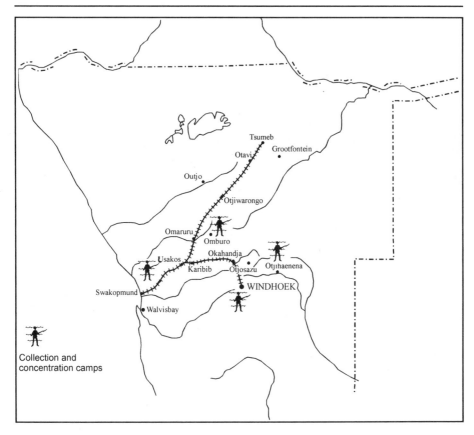

Map 6.1: The missionary collection camps for Herero war refugees at Omburo and Otjihaenena, 1905

survival of the Herero in POW camps, and their conversion to Christianity, the inclusion of Herero into the German army and its structures, and the existence of Herero in communities beyond direct colonial control. Following the abolition of the POW camps, there was an extreme shortage of labour in the territory, which facilitated the movement of Herero and the reestablishment of Herero society mediated by mission Christianity. The extensive process by which a Herero catechumen was initiated into becoming a Herero Christian, and thereby a member of a community which existed beyond the confines of German colonial control, came to replace the extensive process which had existed in the period prior to the war, by which a Herero youth was initiated into becoming a Herero adult. The chapter closes with a short discussion on relations between 'initiated' Herero Christian adults and uninitiated Herero youth.

Camps

At the end of the Herero–German war a majority of the Herero in GSWA were professed Christians and lived in POW camps. The following section examines

Photo 6.1: Herero children, captured after fighting at Omaruru, constructing a kraal near Omburo in 1904
Source: Namibian National Archives, Windhoek

Photo 6.2: Herero prisoner of war camp in Windhoek; in the background the German fort or Feste
Source: Namibian National Archives, Windhoek

the link that existed between Herero incarceration in POW camps, and Herero conversion to Christianity.

In late 1905, an estimated 8800 Herero were confined in military prison camps and put to work as forced labourers on various military and civilian projects scattered across German South West Africa.[3] Upon assuming office in late 1905, the new civilian governor of the territory, Friedrich von Lindequist, issued a proclamation to the Herero still hiding in the field. In it he urged the Herero to give themselves up, either to the military or at two collection points, Omburo and Otjihaenena, which were run solely by the Rhenish Missionary Society.[4] By 1908, when the camps were eventually abolished, a further estimated 15,000 Herero had been collected with the aid of the Rhenish Missionary Society.[5] The Herero POWs were put to work, as forced labourers, on various civilian and military projects. After an initial ban, the missionaries were also permitted to minister in the camps run by the military. In a period of great misery this was a fortuitous development; indeed had it not been for the activities of the missionaries it is likely that even more Herero prisoners would have died.

Missionary sources provide us with direct first-hand eye-witness accounts of conditions in the camps. In Karibib missionary Elger wrote:

> And then the scattered Herero returned from the Sandfeld. Everywhere they popped up – not in their original areas – to submit themselves as prisoners. What did the wretched people look like?! Some of them had been starved to skeletons with hollow eyes, powerless and hopeless, afflicted by serious diseases, particularly with dysentery. In the settlements they were placed in big *kraals*, and there they lay, without blankets and some without clothing, in the tropical rain on the marshlike ground. Here death reaped a harvest! Those who had some semblance of energy naturally had to work
> . . .
> It was a terrible misery with the people; they died in droves. Once 24 came together, some of them carried. In the next hour one died, in the evening the second, in the first week a total of ten – all to dysentery – the people had lost all their energy and all their will to live . . .
> Hardly cheering cases were those where people were handed in to be healed from the effects of extreme mistreatment [*schwerer Misshandlungen*]: there were bad cases amongst these.[6]

In Windhoek missionary Meier described the arrival of Herero from the field:

> In the beginning of 1905 the first arrived . . . back from the Sandfeld . . . Their condition mocked all manner of description. Dressed in rags or totally naked, starved to the bone, in the coming period one often saw them arriving in contingents of 150–200. Unfortunately many whose lives had been spared in the war later died of exhaustion and lack of proper care in the prisoner camp. Finally the mission could

---

[3] *BRMG*, 1906, p.10.
[4] Otto von Weber, *Geschichte des Schutzgebietes Deutsch-Südwest-Afrika*, p. 171. These two collection points were later increased to four.
[5] ELCIN, V. 33 Chroniken, Usakos 1907. For a detailed discussion on the number of Herero survivors and POWs, see Nuhn, *Stürm*, pp. 314–15.
[6] ELCIN, V. 12, Missions Chronieken, Karibib 1906, written by missionary Elger. See also *BRMG* 1906, pp. 11–12. That this mistreatment of Herero was not merely incidental but structural is indicated by a circular letter from military headquarters in Windhoek to the German officer commanding Karibib in late 1906. The letter noted '. . . due to the mishandling of Herero prisoners, who act as carriers, it is advisable to recruit Ovambo labour as carriers'. NNAW, STR 19 *1. und 4. Kompagnie Karibib*, Letter Windhuk 16/11/06.

no longer merely look on – on certain days often 10 or more corpses were carried out.[7]

Conditions in the camp did little to improve the lot of the Herero. Meier described the condition of Herero who came to the sick bay run by the mission, and his words provide some indication as to what happpened in the Windhoek camp:

> How often these poorest, those who deserved pity, came staggering! Many of them, who could no longer move, were brought on stretchers, most of them unconcious, however those who could still think, were glad that the hard supervision of the feelingless guards in the *Kraal* and their *Shambok* [rawhide whip] . . . had for the time being been left behind.[8]

During the period of time that the camps existed, there was a movement of mass conversion amongst the Herero. Missionary Meier, who in May 1905 ministered to approximately 500 prisoners in Windhoek, noted, 'Never again, before or thereafter, have I had such attentive audiences, as specifically in those days.'[9] Missionaries reported consistently high attendances and a hunger on the part of the Herero for Christian religious instruction. Those Herero with some form of religious training established themselves as Christian ministers. During the evenings or during work-breaks, Herero evangelists and missionaries preached to the prisoners. Herero sought out missionaries.[10] On the part of the Herero, there was a struggle for missionaries. At the same time, on the part of the Catholic and Lutheran missionaries, a struggle for Herero souls developed. In their eagerness to guide converts to the true faith, the missionaries of the two denominations engaged in a long-drawn-out struggle for a monopoly over the souls of the Herero. Eventually, following discussions between the missionaries and the military authorities, a decision was reached whereby Herero POWs were to be divided equally between the two denominations. Where this was not possible, the Herero prisoners were to be ministered to by the two denominations on alternate Sundays.[11]

On Monday I was in Windhoek, to whence Brother Meier had called me, in

[7] ELCIN, V. 37, Chronieken, Windhoek 1905, written by missionary Meier. JBG's translation.
[8] Ibid.
[9] Ibid.
[10] On high attendances, see ELCIN, V.31, Chroniken Swakopmund, 1905, p. 8.
   On Herero preachers, see NNAW, foto 417. VEMA, repro SW 5226–7, 'Andreas Kukuri hält Werftgottesdienst'.
   BRMG 1906, pp. 68–9, reported on the Herero evangelists working amongst Herero POWs working on the Otavi railway-line: Samuel Kutako, who was given 25 lashes by the military camp authorities in which he was working, had 87 in catechism classes and 103 children in school: Zachäus Hanari, whose wife and mother died in the camps, had 34 in catechism classes and 70 children in school; Julius Hindjou, who was a voluntary evangelist but recognized by the mission, had 60 in catechism classes and 24 children in school. All three evangelists were suffering from scurvy when they were visited by missionary Kuhlmann in 1906. Kuhlmann bought additional food for them and their flocks, p. 90. Former school teacher Gustav Kamatoto, preached at the Otjihaenena collection point.
   On Herero seeking missionaries see *BRMG*, 1906, p. 72. Herero POWs working on the Otavi railway-line flocked out to meet Rhenish mission inspector Spiecker once they had found out that he was associated with the mission.
[11] For conflict see ELCIN, *I 1.22 Konferenz Protokoll Karibib 15–17 Januar 1906 & Otjimbingwe 15–26 Sept 1906*. During the September sitting the conference even carried its struggle beyond the borders of GSWA; when referring to the Herero around lake Ngami the missionaries stressed that all should be done to prevent them 'from falling into the hands of the Romans'.

connection with the military command's intention to distribute the captured Herero to the Catholic and our Mission. The division is to be as follows, 5 rows of huts in the prisoner *Kraal* are to be allocated to us and 5 rows to the Romans . . . The missionaries are requested not to enter the territory of the different denomination.[12]

But why did the Herero become Christians?[13] To argue that the Herero became Christians solely for personal cynical secular gain would not do justice either to the historical evidence or to the validity of the personal professions of faith expressed by Herero converts at the time. The Herero became Christians for a variety of reasons, which ranged from identity and solace to organization, protection and information. Indeed, during the course of time it came to be the case that to be Herero it was necessary to be Christian. The two became synonymous. Christianity provided the Herero with organization, protection, meaning – in what appeared to be a meaningless world – and allowed them to reestablish a society.

Missionary Meier, who ministered to the POWs in Windhoek, described in detail the case of a dying Herero woman prisoner. She told Meier how in a dream, laden with Christian symbolism, she had seen two spotlessly clean men who had come to her and asked her when she wanted to come to heaven. The dying woman had told the two men that they would have to wait a bit, as she wanted to take her child, of about one, with her into heaven. 'As she told me about her dream, I saw how her sunken face glowed with inner joy. "Muhonge," she called after me as I left, "please pray for me, so that I too may enter."' Meier noted that shortly afterwards her daughter died and 'her wish was granted' when she too died.[14]

In the camps Herero leaders and men of fighting age, allegedly involved in complicity in the war, were systematically sought out, tried in 'court martials' and executed, usually by hanging.[15] In some cases the missionaries were allowed to minister to some of these unfortunates. Missionary Meier, who was deeply

For copy of text of arrangement between RCs, RM and the military, for access to prisoners, see ELCIN VII 31.1. Swakopmund, 15/12/05.

For interdenominational struggles continuing at stations long after the war see particularly ELCIN, V. 8, Chroniken Gobabis, and as yet ELCIN uncatalogued folder entitled *Jahresberichte v. H. Pardey Grootfontein 1908–1924*, particularly the conference report for Grootfontein of 26/9/10.

For conflict with denominations other than the Catholics see ELCIN, *I 1.29 Beilagen und Protokolle 1913–1922*, which contains information on the London Missionary Society working among Herero refugees at Tsau in Bechuanaland.

[12] ELCIN, VII 31 Swakopmund 1, Eich in Okahandja, 22/11/05, to Vedder.

[13] For further discussions on why Herero became Christians following the war, see *BRMG*, 1910, p. 243; Oswin Köhler, 'The stage of acculturation in South West Africa', in *Sociologus*, 1956, Vol. 6, No. 2. pp. 138–53 & ELCIN manuscript by Theo Sundermeier, *Die Oruuano und ihre Spaltungen*, particularly p. 2, '*Doch nicht die niederlage und die hohe Verlustquote, sondern die Eingeborenenverordnungen von 1906 und 1907 waren es, die das Hererovolk, seine Sozial-ordnungen und religiosen Bindungen, endgultig zerschlugen. Die totale Landenteignung, das Verbot, Grossvieh zu halten und die zwangsweise Verteilung der Familien auf die Farmen der weissen kolonialherren machten die Herero orientierungslos. Ihre Stammesgefuge zerbrach, und traditionelle, auf der Rinderhaltung basierende Religionsausübung wurde verhindert. Ohne Landbesitz und ohne Rinder waren sie vater und ahnenlos.*'

[14] ELCIN, V. 37, Chroniken Windhoek, 1905.

[15] See Leonhard Schultze, *Zoologische und anthropologische Ergebnisse einer Forschungsreise im westlichen und zentralen Südwestafrika* (Jena 1909), which contains anatomical information on Herero and Nama gained from post-mortems conducted on POWs. In one instance, where the heads of 18 POWs were dissected for a study on brain size and form by an Italian pathologist, the cause of death for 14 of the 18 was given as death by hanging.

affected by the incident, described at great length the final days of Zacharias Kukuri, the former *Omuhona* of Otjosazu. On the basis of a fellow prisoner's testimony, Kukuri was sentenced to death. In the days leading up to his execution, Kukuri's arms were bound behind his back, even though he was suffering from smallpox. Ill from the disease and maltreatment, Kukuri was transported to his execution on the back of an ox cart. Meier, who accompanied Kukuri to his execution, described the events as follows:

> ... I did not see the slightest trace of fear on him, instead it was as if he were going to a wedding. *'Muhonge'*, he said at one stage, *'oami otja Elias mohamakuao na je otjinga me keende kejuru metemba,'* i.e. *'Muhonge*, like Elias, I too travel to heaven in a waggon.'
>
> Having arrived at the execution site, I noticed how he kept looking at the gallows, at which preparations were still taking place. I feared for his tranquillity and asked him to stop looking at it. *'Muhonge,'* he said to me, 'I hear everything, why should I not look at it? For is it not "my wood" [my cross]?'
>
> When we finally stood underneath the gallows, we prayed together that beautiful song: 'So then take my hand and lead me.' Possibly he noticed that I was worried about him. Anyway when I was finished he said, 'It would appear that you still fear that I am afraid, but have I not told you: "When a father calls his child, does that child then fear to go to him?", Give my wife, who is in Okahandja, my greetings and tell her that I have died in the faith of the lord Jesus, so too tell my children if you should ever see them.' I asked him again to be infatuated with the lord Jesus. 'Lord Jesus, you help me,' with this, after he had given me his hand, he climbed up the ladder. Soon the noose was laid around his neck. And then – never will I forget that moment – the unheard of happened, as he fell the noose slipped and the wretch fell to the ground. He lost consciousness for a moment, so too, the observers were dumbstruck [*allgemeine Bestürzung bemächtigte*]. Today I still see how his eyes sought me out. Soon however 2 soldiers were there, they lifted him up, and then a little to the side, on orders of the major who led the proceedings, he was shot.[16]

To large numbers of Herero in the camps, the missionaries, and the faith that they purveyed, brought true spiritual solace, and a way in which a seemingly unintelligeble world could be understood. Mission chronicles and missionary reports are scattered with reports on Herero converting to Christianity shortly before their deaths by execution or otherwise. These conversions were sincere and they brought a manner of solace and peace of mind to a large number of those killed. That is, people became true believers as it gave hope, understanding and meaning to their lives.

For those Herero who were not executed, the Christian faith and its texts provided a historical precedent which allowed them to contextualize their imprisonment and condition. The Bible, and particularly the Old Testament, provided an example of previous events, informed one on how to act in these conditions, and promised the inevitable absolution of those who persevered in their faith.[17] Inspired by the Old Testament, Herero elders in Swakopmund wrote a letter to the Rhenish mission inspector Dr Spiecker, in which they asked for the translation of the Old Testament into Herero. The reasons they gave, to substantiate their request, referred directly to their own imprisonment:

---

[16] ELCIN, V. 37, Chroniken Windhoek, 1905. The execution of Zacharias Kukuri, the *Omuhona* of Otjosazu.
[17] ELCIN, VII 31 Swakopmund 1, Eich in Okahandja 17/4/05 to all the missionaries, mentions that there has been an appeal for books by the Herero POWs.

Our dear great teacher! We, who belong to your community, have the need that you allow the words of the Old Testament to be written in our language by the missionaries who are in our country, so that the words begin with the first books of Moses through to those of the prophets and those of the Kings and to all those other books which until now have not been written in our language. All of the histories of the Old Testament teach us how we should act, about all the conditions that existed during the period of the first heathenism, the enemies and the imprisonments. Therefore it is essential that they be translated. Our greeting! Enough.[18]

But it was not only the Old Testament, it was also the teachings of Jesus Christ that brought faith and subsequent understanding. Shortly before his death, Leibhard Kutuziremumue of Omaruru wrote a letter to Asser Mutjinde, a church elder, formerly also of Omaruru. In the war Asser Mutjinde had fled to Nababes, and the copper mines of the northern Cape. Here he ministered to a group of fellow Herero exiles. Leibhard Kutuziremumue referred to his friend's letter and wrote:

I thank you heartily for rebuking me in your letter of 11th December and reminding me that in his love Jesus Christ has punished me. You called me by my name and asked: 'Leibhard do you now love the Lord Jesus or not?' As I thought about your question I said to myself, 'It is the Lord Jesus himself who is now aking me, as he once asked his servant: Simon Peter, do you love me?' I answer you as follows: I love him truly; for he loved me first. My dear friend there is absolutely nothing which is more blissful, as this our promised land; therefore I say to you, that I truly love him. Our missionaries are very diligent and true in their plea for the Herero with the beneficent Lord Jesus.[19]

The Bible provided the Herero with people with whom they could identify. It provided them with incidents that reminded them of their own predicament and allowed them to persevere. The case of Samuel Kariko, a church elder and evangelist of Omaruru, is a case in point. Acting upon the reports of the extremely harsh and deadly conditions in the POW camp in Lüderitz, the annual conference of the Rhenish mission decided to send Samuel Kariko to Lüderitz, to minister to the prisoners there. Missionary Vedder was ordered to make sure that Samuel Kariko was sufficiently fed and warmly dressed, before he was placed on one of the Woermann steamers that transported Herero POWs from Swakopmund to Lüderitz.[20] Drawing mental if not physical strength from the New Testament, Kariko likened himself to Jesus's apostles and wrote:

As a prisoner I travelled by sea to Lüderitzbucht, to do the Lord's work there. People wanted to make me similar to Paul, it was a pity though, that I, not like him, did not

[18] *BRMG*, 1906, p. 148. JBG's translation. The Old Testament was published in Otjiherero only in 1987.
[19] ELCIN, V. Chroniken Omaruru, 1906. Edited version of the letter is also to be found in *BRMG*, 1906, p. 147. JBG's translation.
[20] ELCIN, *I 1.22 Protokoll der Konferenz Rh. Missionare im Hererolande Gehalten zu Otjimbingwe vom 15–26 Septbr 1906*. In Lüderitz the Herero POWs were put to work on the railway-line to Aus. Up to 45 per cent of those transported to Lüderitz died. Samuel Kariko, too, did not last long in Lüderitz, and within six months he requested permission to return to Swakopmund along with eight of his family members. In September of 1906 Herero evangelist Victor Matirapi, formerly of Otjimbingwe, was dispatched to Lüderitz. VII 31 Swakopmund 1, Eich in Okahandja, 22/11/05 to Vedder, refers to Kariko's request to leave Lüderitz. Kariko was transferred to Usakos where he was expected to take over the position of Gottlieb, who had defected to the Roman Catholics. Eich in Okahandja, 8/12/05, to Vedder.

have the spirit of holiness in my heart.[21]

Apart from providing spiritual sustenance the Rhenish mission also provided direct physical aid in the form of food, clothing and a modicum of health care. These very direct physical contributions to Herero well-being greatly improved the standing of the missionaries and the acceptance of their teachings. Following reports of the dreadful conditions in the camps, particularly at the coast, the Rhenish mission set about collecting and buying clothing, bedding and food for the prisoners.

> I hear from returning Ovambo that the Herero are involved in quarry work and that many of them are dying, that they only get rice as food and that they cannot endure this. Please appeal to the authorities concerned that the Herero get a more mixed diet including milk at least until they are somewhat fattened up [*herausgefuttert*]. Secondly tell the Herero they have to cook their rice properly, thirdly get them pots to cook in.[22]

missionary publications in Germany called upon their supporters to supply them with all forms of clothing.[23] In camps where the missionaries were present rudimentary health-care facilities were established. The correspondence of missionary Heinrich Vedder, who was stationed in Swakopmund, provides us with a clear insight into the mission's direct physical contributions to the well-being of the Herero POWs.

> The Herero community consists primarily of Herero prisoners who were sent in numerous transports from the interior to work at the coast. For a period of time the need under them was very big . . . About 800 of them died during the course of the year. The many pieces of clothing, sent by friends of the mission in the motherland, served to alleviate some of the need, furthermore large sums of money could be paid out so that the exhausted and sick could be helped with sleeping blankets and sufficient nutrition. Following requests by the station missionary [Vedder], a sick bay and a provisional chapel were erected in the prisoner *Kraal*, in which often more than a 1000 prisoners were to be found. Fate's effect was to be noticed in the 'Word'. Nearly all the Herero prisoners have now reported for religious instruction. The Herero school is also being regularly and diligently attended by 124 pupils.[24]

During the course of 1906, Herero forced labourers began to be compensated for their work. However, those who were *arbeitsunfähig* were no longer given any sustenance by the military, though food and clothing for these people continued to be supplied by the mission.[25]

Herero prisoners were subjected to extreme forms of exploitation, abuse and mistreatment. To some extent the mission was able to provide the Herero prisoners with protection from this abuse. Through interceding with the military commanders, some of the missionaries were able to ensure that Herero were

---

[21] ELCIN, V. Chroniken 1906 Omaruru, for an edited version of Samuel's letter, see *BRMG*, 1906, p. 147. JBG's translation. Samuel was referring to St Paul's second letter to the Corinthians 16: 23–33.
[22] ELCIN, VII 31 Swakopmund 1, Dannert in Omaruru, 14/2/05, to Vedder.
[23] *BRMG*, 1905, 1906, p. 10 & 1907. ELCIN, VII 31 Swakopmund 1, Spiecker in Barmen, Germany, 11/3/05, to Vedder. Mentions that he has placed advertisements for clothing in the German papers.
[24] ELCIN, *VII 31.5 Evangel. Mission, Swakopmund Quartal und Jahresberichte. Conferenz Berichte Jahresabrechnungen 1906–1930*, Swakopmund 15/1/06 Jahresbericht 1905. JBG's translation.
[25] ELCIN, V. Chroniken Omaruru, 1906.

Photo 6.3: Captured Herero women; in the background the German fort or Feste *in Windhoek*
Source: Namibian National Archives, Windhoek

allowed off work on Sundays, that injured prisoners could be attended to, and that children were allowed time off to attend classes.[26] However, partly due to their own convictions, the missionaries were unable to prevent women and girls from being subjected to sexually degrading compulsory internal examinations. German troops raped Herero women and regularly made use of sexual services offered. When informed of these activities, missionary authorities, unwilling to understand the extent of Herero oppression, suffering and abuse, were unable to comprehend that people, in a vain attempt at alleviating their condition, could be forced into prostitution. Instead, they drafted hypocritical letters of condemnation:

> . . . I was appalled by what you reported on the disgusting activities of the Herero women. Of course one cannot really expect anything different from these people. Even if they have become Christians, we cannot allow ourselves to forget the deep immoral dirt out of which they have come, and again and again with our love and patience we must attempt to show them the disgusting and shameful [*verderbliche und schandliche*] aspects of their activities.[27]

[26] ELCIN, VII 31.5, *Evangel. Mission, Swakopmund Quartal und Jahresberichte. Conferenz Berichte Jahresabrechnungen 1906–1930*, Jahresbericht der Station Swakopmund für 1906 Swakopmund 27/12/06.

Die zahlreiche, aus Kriegsgefangenen bestehende Hererogemeinde litt andauernd unter dem Versetzungen an andere Platze, wie sie die Gefangenschaft mit sich bringt. Da die Gefangenen in der Regel auch Sonntags, sowohl Vormittags als auch nachmittags arbeiten mussten, musste der Gottesdiensts in die Zeit der Mittagspause von 1–2 Uhr verlegt werden. Trotz dieser unpassenden Zeit wurde er aber fleissig besucht. Aus der Zahl der Taufbewerber konnten in November 108 getauft werden. Die Schule, die zu Anfang des Jahres von mehr als hundert Kindern besucht wurde, konnte leider in den letzten wochen des Jahres nicht mehr gehalten worden, da die Kinder von der Kommandanteur zur Arbeit herangezogen wurden.

[27] ELCIN, VII 31 Swakopmund 1. Rhenish mission inspector Spiecker in Barmen, Germany, 26/4/05, to Vedder. JBG's translation.

Sexually transmitted diseases such as gonorrhoea and syphilis were rampant amongst German troops.[28] In early 1906, in an effort to curtail the spread of these diseases, the German military camp authorities began to force Herero women and girls to undergo internal examinations.[29] Though there was a storm of protest, this form of abuse was still common long after the camps had been abolished.[30] Missionary Elger noted in 1911:

> For many months periodical venereal disease examinations of the whole native population have been taking place. Without regard to the person's age (small children excluded), on the grounds of Police orders, the genitals and the activities [*Wandels*] of all natives are subjected to an investigation by a medical doctor in such a manner that the feelings of decency [*Schamgefuhl*] of the people are most deeply hurt . . . However, the *Wachtmeister* told me: 'I have no guilt, I only do what I have been ordered to do.'[31]

To what extent the missionaries reduced this abuse is debatable. However it seems probable that their mere presence served to limit abuse; if not by their mere presence then at least by their position as representatives of an institution that was able to influence public opinion in Germany.[32]

Apart from providing some measure of protection, the mission provided Herero prisoners with an identity that was outside and beyond the immediate control of their captors, and which endured beyond the camps. In a situation were the German military actively sought to destroy traditional kin and clan networks and ties, the identity and the affiliation provided by the mission came to replace those networks which were no longer permitted to exist.[33] Once one became a catechumen, one's identity came to be fixed in a realm which was independent of the German military. Herero became registered in baptismal records held by the mission; records which could be drawn upon at any time to confirm one's status and, most importantly, one's identity.[34] A frequent complaint of the missionaries was that those they were teaching were often removed and transferred to other camps depending on where labour was

---

[28] *Sanitätsbericht über die deutsche Truppe in Südwestafrika 1907/1909*, Vol. 1 (Berlin 1909) p. 2 and p. 161.

[29] ELCIN, V. Chroniken, Karibib 1906. Missionary Elger complained, but could not prevent the examinations from taking place. See also Bley, *South West Africa*, pp. 212–19, for a short discussion on prostitution, compulsory examination and German colonial race laws.

[30] *BRMG*, 1913, p. 100. Herero women into prostitution drawn in by white men.

[31] ELCIN, V. Chroniken Karibib, 1911.

[32] In this regard see particularly, ELCIN, VII 31 Swakopmund 1, *Abschrift Besprechung der beiden Inspektoren Hausleiter & Spiecker im Kolonialamt zu Berlin am 18 Sept. 1905*. Refers to a meeting held in Berlin between the missionary inspectors, *kolonialdirektor* dr. Stubel, *Gouverneur* von Lindequist, *Geheimrat* dr Golinelli and *Oberrichter* Richter. The meeting dealt specifically with the numerous deaths of prisoners in POW camps.

[33] Gunther Wagner, 'Aspects of conservatism and adaption in the economic life of the Herero', in *Sociologus*, 1952, Vol. 2, No. 1, pp. 1–25. P. 4 '. . . life histories collected by the present writer from a number of elderly Herero indicate that for many years after the war the majority of tribesmen were not able to maintain regular and close contacts with their kindred. It may therefore be assumed that the complex system of rights and duties which under traditional conditions had linked the individuals to both his patrilineal and matrilinel kin . . . was more or less completely suspended.'

[34] A case in point is that of Hulda Kahunda, who in 1914 was able to trace her antecedents and prove her virtue, through the letters and records kept by the Rhenish mission and the missionaries, Pardey and Bernsmann. ELCIN, as yet uncatalogued files entitled, *Grootfontein/Akten Parday Urkunden Tauf u. abmelde – Zeugnisse 1908–1940/48*, F. Bernsmann in Otjimbingwe, 8/6/14, to Pardey.

needed. These transferred initiates would often accost missionaries or evangelists working in the camp to which they had been transferred, and claim a certain degree of education. Being unable to keep track of these initiates, or verify the validity of their claims, the Rhenish mission society had special passes printed which were issued to Herero Christians and those undergoing religious instruction in the camps. If and when the need arose, these cards could be used to identify the newly transferred bearer as a Christian initiate in need of missionary attention.[35]

Registration as a Christian and the accoutrements attached to this status allowed one to tap into Christian networks elsewhere.[36] On the basis of their identity as Christians, Hereros could ask the missionaries to intercede on their behalf. Strictly speaking families in the camps could not be split up and sent to different camps. This did, however, occur. Herero who were married according to Christian rites could ask the missionary to intercede on their behalf, and, given that their bond was a Christian one, they had a greater chance that the missionary would support their case.[37]

Apart from solace, understanding, aid, protection and identity, association with the mission also supplied the Herero with a very important commodity, that of information. By associating with the missionaries and evangelists, Herero prisoners could come to know what had happened to their kin, what conditions were like in other camps, and what their prospects were. Missionaries and evangelists could, and were permitted, to read and write.[38] As such they could and did maintain correspondence on behalf of prisoners. Missionary correspondence of the time is littered with missionaries asking one another as to the whereabouts of various Herero. Furthermore missionaries and evangelists could move relatively freely through the territory; as such they carried and spread information of both an official and a personal nature across the territory. Herero prisoners of war refused to embark on ships to the work camps of Lüderitz because, due to the reports supplied by the mission, they were aware of the extreme conditions prevalent there.[39] Indeed in some instances missionaries were prohibited from telling Herero POWs where they were being sent to.[40]

> Today or tomorrow, another load of prisoners will leave from here [Okahandja] to there [Swakopmund]. They are to be sent for railway construction to Lüderitzbucht. I would gladly have spoken to the people before [they leave], however they are not

---

[35] ELCIN, V. Chroniken Omaruru, 1906.

[36] Christian Herero who had fled to Botswana and South Africa almost immediately made use of these networks and form of organization to establish themselves in their new host societies. See ELCIN, II 1.7a, *Inland Briefe 1905 (von Missionaren)*, British and Foreign Bible Society in Cape Town, 21/8/05, to Olpp asking for a Herero language bible.

[37] *BRMG*, 1906, p.73. Reports extensive Christian marriages on the part of the Herero POWs. Clearly a new form of authority was introduced in a situation where Herero kinship structures and society had been destroyed, thereby annihilating the immediate relevance of issues such as bridewealth, cross-cousin marriages and so forth. In effect the elders had lost their control.

[38] Something that the common Herero could not be seen to be doing if he or she valued their lives. In this regard see W. Hillebrecht, '*Habe keinerlei Papiere in deiner Kiste . . .*', in *Werkstatt-Geschichte* 1 (Hanover 1992).

[39] ELCIN, V. Chroniken 1906 Omaruru, see the reports of Samuel Kariko in Lüderitz. See Kol.Blatt 1906, p. 402, for report on Herero refusing to travel to the coast on a account of conditions there. See also *BRMG* 1906, p. 165.

[40] *BRMG*, 1906, p. 165.

to know where they are being sent to, that is why I am not allowed to. Perhaps you can do it.[41]

Herero became Christians not solely for cynical personal secular gain. Rather they converted to Christianity for a wide variety of reasons which, in essence, related to their identity as people seeking to reestablish a sense of society. By becoming Christians, or at the very least by associating with them, Herero prisoners could begin to rebuild a society. For apart from the benefits of information, aid, protection and identity, Christianity, and the predominantly Protestant lifestyle attached to this faith, provided a blue-print with which Herero prisoners could begin to rebuild a society. In a situation where all forms of traditional social governance and organization had been bankrupted or destroyed, Christianity provided a new form of social organization that appeared to work. This process of rebuilding, and the benefits of Christian association, continued after the camps were finally abolished in 1908.

Army

In 1908 Governor von Lindequist noted with obvious pleasure that Herero were being used to hunt Herero still in the field, and that, though Herero blood was being spilt, German blood was being spared.[42] The men referred to were Herero POWs. These men had been armed by the Germans and sent out to persuade Herero remaining in the field to come into the collection points or to hand themselves over to the German military. The following section deals with these and other Herero who served and fought in the German military, police and colonial forces in the aftermath of the Herero–German war.

The men referred to by Lindequist were not the first Herero to cooperate with the German military. Indeed, ever since the arrival of the *Schutztruppe*, Herero had been involved and associated with the German military. Prior to the war, three of Samuel Maharero's sons had fought alongside German troops and been involved in joint patrols with them.[43] From 1892 onwards, Herero soldiers associated with Samuel Maharero were involved in joint campaigns with the German army. Kajata, one of Samuel Maharero's eastern chiefs and a later Herero war hero, had even been decorated for bravery and presented with a ceremonial sword by the Germans, following the 1896 Ovambanderu campaign.[44] The extent of Herero involvement in the German military was such that, in early 1904, in the days immediately prior to the Herero–German war, Herero men in the Waterberg region believed that they were to be conscripted to fight alongside German troops against the Bondelswart Namas, who were involved in a war against the Germans. From the very beginning of its presence in the territory, substantial numbers of Herero men were employed by the German army, either as labourers, waggon drivers, herdsmen, batmen or soldiers.[45] When the Herero–German war broke out, a number of Herero

[41] ELCIN, VII 31 Swakopmund 1, Eich in Okahandja, 16/12/05, to Vedder.
[42] Kol. Blatt 1906, p. 402.
[43] Leutwein, *Elf Jahre*, p. 93.
[44] Leutwein, *Elf Jahre*, p. 103; Dr Felix Meyer, *Wirtschaft und Recht der Herero* (Berlin 1905), p. 21.
[45] Reports of Herero policemen and soldiers are to be found in ELCIN, V. 37 Chroniken Windhoek, which mentions 40–50 Herero in service of the police.

soldiers continued to serve in the German forces.[46] One of these men was Sepp, the *bambuse*, or batman, of Ludwig von Estorff. Sepp died during the battle for Omaruru in 1904. Estorff, one of the most intriguing of the *Schutztruppe* officers, had a tombstone erected in Sepp's memory and inscribed with words that tellingly referred to the book of Revelation chapter 2 verse 10:

> Do not be afraid of what you are about to suffer. I tell you, the devil will put some of you in prison to test you, and you will suffer persecution for ten days. Be faithful, even to the point of death, and I will give you the crown of life.[47]

Until at least the mid-1980s, the German military graveyard at the Waterberg contained a gravestone in remembrance of the Herero and Berg Damara soldiers who had fought alongside the Germans in the battle at Hamakari and the war as a whole. The gravestone bore the words *Hier ruhen treue Kaffernsoldaten der Kaisl. Schutztruppe.*[48]

After the war substantial numbers of orphans were taken into German military service as *bambusen*. It was so common for German officers to have *bambusen* that the Woerman line had special reduced transport prices for 'Boys' returning to Germany with their masters.[49] The German colonial administration, anxious to maintain its labour resources, expressly legislated against the export of these servants and labourers from the colony. Following the war, extensive numbers of Herero orphans, who had been *bambusen* in the army, now became regular soldiers. However, they were not alone in being associated with the army, women were also involved, as washerwomen and as prostitutes and concubines. Missionaries were most worried about this. An official German government report, published in 1912, noted that 'there were 650 Africans with regular jobs with the armed forces, and a further indefinite number lived in the army locations, without being in registered employment, usually working as servants'.[50] It is safe to assume that the 650 referred to were men; it is also safe to assume that these 650 men were accompanied by or associated with 650 women, and that they had at least 650 children between them.[51] In other

---

[46] Indeed, it could even be argued that one of the first shots of the Herero–German war was fired by a Herero in German service, for the arrested Herero who was executed on the night prior to the outbreak of the war in 1904 was shot by a Herero soldier.

[47] The translated text on the tombstone read as follows:

> Faithful unto death. In this way I want to give you the crown of life. Revelations John 2. 10.
> My dear faithful unto death servant the Herero Sepp, fell on 4 February 1904 in the battle for Omaruru.
> Von Estorff, Major.

Taken from photograph following p. 163 of Ludwig von Estorff, *Wanderungen und Kämpfe in Südwestafrika, Ostafrika und Südafrika: 1894–1910*, reprint by SWA scientific society (Windhoek 1979).

[48] A photograph of the rough sandstone marker appears in the *Windhoek Observer*, 18/8/1979, p. 8.

[49] Though the archives of the Woermann company remain closed to historians, one is allowed free access to the Woermann house in Hamburg. Photographs illustrating the company's history have been hung in the stairwell of the building. On an autumn afternoon in 1993 Dag Henrichsen and I visited the building and discovered a photograph of a price list for passenger services between Hamburg and the African continent. A 'Boy' could be transferred from Africa to Europe, in the accompaniment of his master, for a charge that was less than that of a child.

[50] Bley, *South West Africa*, p. 250.

[51] It is only fair to admit that unfortunately we do not know how many of these Africans saw themselves as being Herero. However given the number of *bambusen* collected during the war and missionary reports of the time it is safe to assume that most of them were Herero.

Photo 6.4: Herero women washing German soldiers' uniforms
Source: Namibian National Archives, Windhoek

words by 1912 nearly two thousand Herero, or no less than 13 per cent of the
total Herero population at the time, were directly associated with the German
military.[52]

By 1915, when Imperial German control of Namibia was replaced by that
of South Africa, the *bambusen* and their associates had spent a minimum of
ten years within the structures of the *Schutztruppe*. By 1915 the *bambusen*, who
had been taken into the army as juveniles, were all young men who had operated
independently from mainstream pass-carrying Christian Herero society. As
soldiers associated with the German colonial government, and charged with
implementing its laws, they had had power which extended way beyond their
uninitiated status as boys. In 1915, these young men and their following were
effectively robbed of their power, when the army that had supported them was
defeated. Not only were they robbed of their power, but they also appeared to
have been robbed of the structures whereby they had been able to define their
society. However, in the aftermath of the First World War, the Herero soldiers
continued to use the institutional structures of the German army to define
themselves and to arrange their society.

Beyond the colonial ambit

To put it crudely, the Herero in the camps became Christians and those in the
army became soldiers. It has been argued that in both instances the structures
and ideologies within their new environment were used to reestablish society.

[52] Nuhn, *Stürm*, p. 315. Refers to official census of 1911 which has a total of 15,130 Herero
living in GSWA.

In the following section we will deal with those Herero who remained beyond the ambit of German control and remained in the field. These Herero either became impoverished hunter-gatherers or tried to reestablish the structures of the past.

Immediately following the outbreak of the war, various Herero leaders attempted to maintain their positions of power. This they did by raiding other less fortunate groups of people, or by subduing these groups by force and exacting tribute from them. In some cases, the Herero elites who did this were able to rely on the positions of power which they had occupied prior to the war, that is, their positions of authority carried on into the new condition of war. Obviously their ability to exact tribute ensured that their power increased. Willy Maharero, Kahaka Seu and Friedrich Maharero were Herero elites who maintained their positions by operating amongst Herero refugees in Botswana and on the eastern fringes of the *Omaheke*, and exporting labour to the South African mines.

Another area which formed a refuge for Herero beyond German control was the Kaokoveld, in the north-west of the colony. Here incoming groups of Herero, fleeing the war in the centre of the colony, were able to subjugate the pastoralist and hunter-gatherer communities already living there. A number of the incoming Herero were well armed and soon established themselves as the new elite. Building upon pre-war relations that had existed between traders operating in southern Angola and Herero traders operating out of Omaruru, Herero related to the Omaruru elite were able to establish themselves as the dominant force in the Kaokoveld.

In the late nineteenth century, Vita Tom, or *Kaptein* Oorlog (war) as he was also known, had established himself as a war-lord in southern Angola. Vita Tom was the son of one of the daughters of a sister of Manasse Tjisiseta, the most powerful chief of Omaruru, and was brought up by one of Manasse's sisters; therefore he was extremely closely related to the Omaruru elite. With the outbreak of the Herero–German war, Vita Tom was joined in southern Angola by large numbers of refugees from Omaruru. During the early 1900s Vita Tom and his forces regularly fought alongside Portuguese and Angolan Boer forces in battles against the Ovambo kingdoms. During these expeditions large numbers of Herero who had fled to the Ovambo kingdoms were captured and absorbed into the following of Vita Tom. Amongst the better-known Herero who became followers of Vita Tom in this way were Salatiel Kambazembi, formerly of Waterberg, and Thomas Mutate, formerly of Omaruru.[53]

Prior to the Herero–German war, two men living in the Kaokoveld, Muhona Katiti (literally small chief) and Kasupi, led two communities consisting of Himba pastoralists and Ovatjimba hunter-gatherers. With the outbreak of the war both men were joined by substantial numbers of Herero refugees. Kasupi, who operated in the north-western sector of the Kaokoveld, was associated with Vita Tom, and as such was well armed.[54] Between 1904 and 1915 relations between Kasupi and Muhona Katiti deteriorated, as each chief attempted to achieve a dominant position in the area. In 1913 Christian Herero refugees associated with Kasupi and Vita Tom, who had been living in southern Angola,

[53] E.L.P. Stals and A. Otto-Reiner, *Oorlog en Vrede aan die Kunene; Die verhaal van Kaptein Vita Tom 1863–1937* (Windhoek 1990) p. 31.
[54] ELCIN, report by Heinrich Vedder on a trip to the Kaokoveld in 1914, p.6.

were settled at a number of strategic waterholes in the Kaokoveld.[55] These communities, which were visited by missionary Vedder in 1914, were described as consisting of people of Himba, Boer, Bushmen, Herero, Portuguese and Nama descent. They were led by literate Herero refugees, formerly of Omaruru, Okahandja and the Waterberg, who conducted church services and communicated with one another in Dutch and Herero. Due to the conflict between Muhona Katiti and Kasupi, most of the community's fairly substantial cattle herds were kept in southern Angola. Here a portion of these herds was used for the purchase of arms and ammunition. Vedder reported that guns could be bought from the Portuguese for six oxen and 100 rounds of ammunition for one ox.[56] Kasupi, well supplied and well connected to the most powerful warlord in southern Angola, did not need the German colony, let alone any of its representatives; it is therefore hardly surprising that he refused to meet Vedder. Instead he sent a messenger to Vedder, who let it be known that: 'he [Kasupi] was old, had a sick knee and could not come, furthermore he did not need the Whites in his country'.[57]

In 1909 Governor Schuckman noted in a letter to the German foreign office that the Herero living in the field were fast on their way to becoming 'Bushmen'. In a sense, he was quite correct, given that it has been argued that the term 'Bushmen' was introduced in the southern African context to refer to impoverished pastoralists who became bandits, 'struikrovers'.[58] In another sense though, Schuckman was also correct in noting that the Herero were becoming Bushmen, that is, they did become something similar to the stereotypical images that exist of Bushmen as pristine hunter-gatherers in the Kalahari. The Herero who had fled into the *Omaheke* sought to maintain their existence. This they did by hunting and gathering, and/or raiding others. As Schuckman noted, the Herero had been driven into the *Omaheke* and 'They already live the lives of Bushpeople, flee into the bush when they see whites, particularly patrols, and if pursued would probably flee across the English border [into Bechuanaland].'[59] It was a view echoed by an officer in charge of one of these patrols, Lieutenant von Gersdorff, who wrote:

> The Herero living in unbound freedom, consisting primarily of escaped prisoners and labourers, live in the Sandfeld like the poor Ovatjimba did in the past. From a pastoralist people they have become a hunting and gathering people, therefore, in their development, they have taken a step backwards.[60]

Gersdorff described how these people lived in the *Omaheke*. Temporary shelters were erected at an hour and a half's walk from waterholes; this to avoid two forms of predators, German patrols and lions, both of which preyed on game and people drawn to the waterholes. In an effort to reduce dependence on the waterholes, water-holding tubers were collected and reburied in the vicinity of settlements. Shelters were built in stands of thick 'wag 'n bietjie' acacia,

[55] Ibid., pp. 10–11.
[56] Ibid., pp. 11–12.
[57] Ibid., p. 12. Unfortunately for Kasupi, in 1915 his benefactor, Vita Tom, decided to move into the Kaokoveld directly, Muhona Katiti was destroyed, but so too was the power of Kasupi.
[58] This has been argued by R. Ross, in Ross, Vossen and Wilmsen (eds) *Language, History and Identity* in *Quellen zur Khoisanforschung*, forthcoming (Cologne 1998), on the basis of Richard Elphick, *Khoikhoi and the Founding of White South Africa* (Johannesburg 1985) p. 227.
[59] BAP, RKA 21001, Governor Schuckmann in Windhoek, ?/5/09, to foreign office Berlin.
[60] Kol. Blatt. 1909, p. 892.

which were virtually impregnable for mounted horsemen. Apart from collecting *veld* foods, game was trapped and hunted with slings, spears, bows and arrows with fire-hardened or metal heads. A picture thus emerges of a society that shied away from all forms of contact with the German military.[61] However, given the extreme labour shortage at the time, the colonial government sought to induce these people to return to areas under German control so that they could then be employed as labourers. With this in mind a ten-man Herero patrol, reminiscent of those sent out by the mission in the previous years, was sent into the Sandfeld with the following printed message:

> May 1909: I the Kaiser's Governor, let it hereby be known, that it is my will, that you now remain on the places upon which you are now settled, that you remain living in peace and do not walk around in the bush like wild animals.
>
> That is why I tell you via my messengers: Philemon, David, Willibald, Gabriel, Bartolomaus, Hugo, Isaac, Paulus, Hermann and Leonhard, that it is not necessary for you to run away when my police patrols approach. It is however necessary for you to carry my number.
>
> Therefore I will send police with the messengers who will hand out the numbers to you.
>
> The troops will leave you in peace as long as you remain peacefully on your places, upon which you are now settled, and those which will still be specifically allocated to you.
>
> If you Herero remain peacefully on those places which I will allocate to you, I will give you a couple of *bockis* [goats] again, so that you can get milk for your children.[62]

The patrol returned with reports of approximately 500 Herero living in the vicinity of Epata, the last major waterhole along the Eiseb river before the Bechuana border. A number of these people were resettled as farm labourers and horticulturalists at the Waterberg.[63] However, not all Herero living in the field as Bushmen could be induced to return.

At the outbreak of the Herero–German war in 1904, two Herero men, living in the Grootfontein district, Kandiapu and Kanjemi, joined in hostilities against the German military. In itself there was nothing surprising in their decision to fight against the Germans. However, at the outbreak of the war, both men were in the service of to the German military and police.[64] As such, possible surrender to the German military or to the missionaries, at the missionary collection points, was out of the question. Instead, making use of the weapons they had captured, they established a community in the Sandveld due east of Grootfontein. The community, which consisted of approximately 200 people, had a number of *Werften* at distances varying from twenty to 100 km to the east of the Omuramba Omatako, in the Otjituuo region. From these bases in the

---

[61] Ibid., pp. 892–4.

[62] BAP, RKA 2101, Proclamation Schuckmann to the Herero May 1909. JBG's translation.

[63] BAP, RKA 2101, Governor Schuckmann in Windhoek, 30/10/09 to foreign office Berlin. In a further letter of 3/12/09 Schuckmann reported that a further 145 Herero had been registered in the field.

[64] BAP, RKA 1492, Governor in Windhoek, 22/7/11, to foreign office Berlin. Refers to '*Der frühere eingeborene Soldat Kanjemi*'. Governor in Windhoek, 9/8/11, to foreign office Berlin. Refers to Kandiapu as '*Herero Polizeidiener*'.

NNAW, BSW 74, folio 70, charge sheet Windhoek 27/7/11. It would appear that at an earlier stage Kandiapu had been captured and placed on a farm as a farm labourer. One of the charges brought against him was that he had run away from a farm.

Sandveld, the followers of Kanjemi and Kandiapu raided the settler farms along the Omuramba Omatako and Otjituuo. Apart from raiding, the community also harmed the labour-hungry settlers by forming a refuge for large numbers of Herero who ran away from the farms.[65]

In due course Kanjemi became known amongst the farm labourers of the Grootfontein district as the 'Captain of the Sandveld'. Numerous armed patrols were sent out to eliminate Kanjemi and his followers. Due to the difficult terrain and absence of waterholes, these military patrols failed in their mission. As conventional patrols had failed, Herero policemen were sent out to discover the whereabouts of the 'Captain of the Sandveld'. In 1910 four of these policemen found the *Werft* of Kanjemi's associate, Kandiapu. Though the Herero policemen had discovered the *Werft*, they were not very successful in bringing its inhabitants to heel. Instead, they were attacked and robbed of their clothes and rifles.[66] In early 1911, it was decided to employ the services of undercover Herero policemen. These were placed as labourers on the farms known to be frequented by the followers of Kanjemi, or where the farmer's workforce had been or were in contact with the 'Captain of the Sandveld'. In this way enough information was gathered to ensure the success of an expedition sent into the Sandveld, and in July of 1911 Kanjemi, Kandiapu and a number of their followers were captured.

The existence of Herero beyond the immediate control of the German colonial authorities was something that the German colonial authorities could not tolerate. Herero communities independent of German colonial control challenged the legitimacy of the German colonial enterprise, and were treated as such. The extreme punishment meted out to Kandiapu and Kanjemi, along with the particular manner in which they were dealt with, gives us some indication as to the extent to which they were perceived of as a serious threat. In sentencing Kanjemi to death by hanging, Governor Seitz ordered that the sentence was to be carried out as soon as possible, but that the place and time of the execution were to be kept secret. This was to prevent a crowd from gathering, and particularly to prevent the taking of photographs.[67] Kandiapu was sentenced to five years' imprisonment with forced labour. However, this was not considered sufficiently safe for the colony and in August 1911 Governor Seitz ordered that Kandiapu be banished for ever to Cameroon. In motivating his banishment, Seitz wrote:

> After Kandiapu had associated for years with an armed group in the Sandveld, he forms a danger to the general peace, stability and security of this country. His continued presence in the colony can therefore no longer be accepted. To prevent his return to German South West Africa it is furthermore necessary that he be forced to reside in Cameroon.[68]

Kandiapu never made it to Cameroon – badly beaten and mishandled he died in prison in Swakopmund whilst waiting for the steamer which was to take him away. In a final injustice, the cause of Kandiapu's death was euphemistically given as 'madness'.[69]

[65] BAP, RKA 1492, Governor Seitz in Windhoek, 22/7/11, to the foreign office Berlin.
[66] BAP, RKA 1492, Governor Seitz in Windhoek, 9/8/11, to foreign office Berlin.
[67] NNAW, BSW 74, Governor Seitz in Windhoek, 31/7/11, to Magistrates office Windhoek.
[68] NNAW, BSW 74, folio 69, Banishment order signed by Governor Seitz in Windhoek, 9/8/11.
[69] NNAW, BSW 74, folio 72, Prison death certificate for Kandiapu, Swakopmund 13/11/11.

In a sense it could be argued that those who were in a position to raid attempted to reestablish the social structures that had existed prior to the war; however, there were also those groups which raided solely to survive. Immediately after the outbreak of the war rogue bands of Herero began operating in German South West Africa. Some of these were probably based upon bandit bands, such as the *Bloubergbende* which operated in the vicinity of Karibib, and which had been in existence prior to the outbreak of the war.[70] Others were formed by rogue elements during the war. Whilst missionary-led patrols were being sent into the field, to induce Herero living in the field to come to the collection camps, there were groups of Herero who refused to come in and actively attacked the mission patrols. These groups probably formed the basis for later raiding communities living in the Sandveld. One such group was the *Andreas bende* which operated to the north-west of Otjihaenena and attacked Herero sent out by the mission to collect Herero from the field.[71] Other groups are known to have operated in the eastern reaches of the *Omaheke*, far beyond the reach of the German military, but within striking distance of Herero and Tawana herds in Bechuanaland.[72]

Herero in Ngamiland and South Africa

From the mid-nineteenth century onwards, large numbers of Herero had lived in ethnically homogeneous communities, beyond the confines of central Namibia in what is now Botswana.[73] Here, at the beginning of the twentieth century they were subject to the authority of the Batawana *Kgosi* Sekgoma Letsholathebe. Sekgoma Letsholathebe's position as *Kgosi* of the Batawana was contested, and as such he devoted a large amount of his time and energy to extending his support base. Thus, through slave raiding, cattle loans, and other forms of patronage, he built up a large following of dependent commoners and immigrants, amongst whom were large numbers of Herero refugees.[74]

Between 1884 and 1904, Herero had moved into Botswana in three distinct

---

[70] NNAW, BloubergBande BSW 107.

[71] Kol. Blatt. 1906, p. 241 for reference to *Andreas bende* and Philemon, Konnjara, Hamana.

[72] NNAW, ACC.107, M. Schokke, *Schutztruppe* first company's report on expedition to Omaheke and Kaukaufeld; detailed description of the area, list of waterholes in Kaukaufeld, 1911. Notes on one such combined band,

> It is interesting that till a short time ago 18–20 Hereros with guns but without ammunition have been living near Garu. As long as there was open water in the bush. At last the lack of water compelled them to change the place to go to Garu. With the returning Bechuanas they crossed then the boundary. I inspected the empty werfts and I believe that the statement of the Bushmen is correct. It corresponds also with what Hauptmann Hollaender found out during his patrol, but large numbers of Hereros are not any more in the north of the Sandveldt'.

[73] C.J. Andersson, *Lake Ngami*, p. 218. & Josaphat Hahn, 'Das Land der Ovahererό', in *Zeitschrift der Gesellschaft für Erdkunde zu Berlin*, 1868 pp. 194 & 243. Theophilus Hahn, 'Ein Rassenkampf im nordwestlichen Theile der Cap-Region', in *Globus*, 14, 1869 pp. 270–1, details Herero attacks on the settlement of Gobabis and the capture of waggons loaded with ivory and ostrich feathers. These were sold to the missionary trader Carl Hugo Hahn at Otjimbingwe. The route east of Gobabis to the Lake was heavily contested, with Barolong, Boer, Batawana, Banderu and Herero all claiming jurisdiction. See also: Josephat Hahn, 'Die Ovaherero', in *Zeitschrift der Gesellschaft für Erdkunde zu Berlin*, 1869, p. 244.

[74] Thomas Tlou, *A History of Ngamiland 1750 to 1906: the Formation of an African State* (Gaborone 1985). Also Chapter 2 of Barry Morton, forthcoming Indiana University PhD thesis, *A Social and Economic History of a Southern African Native Reserve: Ngamiland, 1890–1966*.

waves. The first took place in 1884 when Imperial Germany declared a protectorate over most of present-day Namibia, and a number of Herero families crossed over the newly created border into the Bechuanaland Protectorate. The most important of these families was that of Samuel Shephard which was granted refuge by Sekgoma Letsholathebe.[75]

> When they returned from schooling to their *onganda* (family quarters) in their land, it so happened that there arose a question, should the chief get the throne from the Germans or the English? . . .
>
> The Herero were gathered at a place where they were to decide on the issue and Samuel Shephard came late and found out that the Hereros had decided to take the German throne. He then decided to leave for Botswana and came in that direction.[76]

The second wave of Herero into Botswana took place in 1896, with the outbreak of the Mbanderu Khauas-Khoi war.[77] This flight of people into the Bechuanaland Protectorate increased when raiding escalated after rinderpest, and Herero chiefs attempted to reestablish their depleted cattle herds and authority. With the outbreak of the Herero–German war in January 1904, the third wave of Herero began, as hundreds, if not thousands, sought refuge in the Bechuanaland Protectorate.[78] The first to enter generally retained access to their cattle.[79] As such they were, as long as they could find sufficient grazing and water, self-sufficient, and initially Sekgoma Letsholathebe (then still the Batawana regent) showed every desire to help the British authorities in the resettlement of these refugees in the Ghanzi reserve, an area that he claimed as his own.[80] Here they would provide a buffer against the Boers and the Germans, pay tax and provide a support base for his position vis-a-vis his Batawana rivals and his claims of jurisdiction to the area. Things were very different for the second group of Herero, those without cattle; of these, Williams, the resident magistrate in Tsau, Ngamiland, noted:

> The distribution of the men or other arrangements necessary to relieve this territory as speedily as may be of the burden of a large number of able bodied destitute refugees who must by some means be made to support themselves and as there is no demand here for labour the suggestion that they be transferred to Palapye as opportunity offers.[81]

[75] Tlou, *History Ngamiland*, p. 94.

[76] Interview conducted at Samedupi 23/12/92. Samuel Sheppard was the son of Saul Sheppard, who had been bought by Sir James Alexander in 1836 and educated at Woolwich in England. Upon his return Samuel acted as Maharero's secretary. In the 1970s the anthropologist Vivelo interviewed one of Samuel's descendants, and recorded the following:

> The Germans had brought a big, comfortable chair for Samuel. My father said that Samuel and the Germans were getting too friendly. Eventually, he predicted, there would be trouble and ultimately war. He advised that we leave before the trouble began.

Frank R. Vivelo, *The Herero of Western Botswana* (New York 1977), p. 168.

[77] Mbanderu under the leadership of Kandu Matundu, Kuneho Henguva and Kakopere Hange, and Herero under Kahaka Seu sought refuge in the Bechuanaland Protectorate. Kaendee Kandapaera, *War, Flight, Asylum: A brief history of the Ovambanderu of Ngamiland, Botswana, 1896–1961*, unpublished BEd research essay submitted to Department of History, University of Botswana, May 1992, p. 27. & Interviews conducted with Usiel Kandapaera 18–23/12/92.

[78] BNA, RC 11/1, Acting Resident Commissioner Mafeking 1 December 1904, Intructions for the Acting Magistrate Ngamiland.

[79] BNA, RC 11/1, Merry in Tsau, 27/4/05, to Resident Commissioner.

[80] BNA, RC 10/18, Williams at Tsau, 12/3/04 to RC.

[81] BNA, RC 11/1, M.G. Williams in Tsau, 31/10/04 to RC.

Though Sekgoma stated his willingness to provide temporary locations within the Batawana reserve for as many of Samuel's followers as might arrive, the British authorities were anxious to prevent the further expansion of Sekgoma's power base; as such they supported the move of these refugees away from Ngamiland and on to the mines in South Africa.[82]

Shortly after the arrival of the first Herero refugees in north-western Bechuanaland, the Witwatersrand Native Labour Agency (WNLA) applied to the British authorities to lift their ban on the export of labour from this area of the protectorate.[83] Not surprisingly the colonial authorities, faced with an unprecedented influx of refugees, immediately lifted the ban and during 1905 there were three labour recruiters operating in Ngamiland alone. Here they received complete cooperation from the British colonial officials.[84] Accompanied on their forays by members of the Bechuanaland Protectorate police the labour recruiters were extremely successful.[85]

In small batches of fifteen to twenty men, the recruits were sent down, on foot, to the Transvaal and the mines. The recruits passed along a number of staging posts, which were usually small trade stores working in alliance with the recruiters. The desperate condition in which these recruits found themselves is clearly indicated by the following example. In August 1905 a trader, who ran a staging post, notified the police that a number of labour recruiter Clarke's recruits appeared to be infected by smallpox. Accordingly the men would have to be placed in quarantine, which would effectively have meant that they could no longer work on the mines. Upon receiving the message police corporal Hatton and his men immediately hurried to the scene only to find that: 'the boys had gone as soon as they had heard that the police were sent for'.[86] The police did come across others who reported of the infected that 'their chests are bad and they have high fever'.[87]

Eighty years later, whilst conducting interviews in western Botswana, I came across the proverb Ekutu ra Sero. People would say, 'Do not immediatly accept what a person gives you for it might be the sack of the man called Sero.' My informants stated that, following their flight to the Bechuanaland Protectorate, most of the refugees had had no food and were starving. Then a man named Sero had arrived. Sero had had bags of rice and sugar with him and people had been allowed to eat as much as they wanted. However, once the food was finished Sero would say, 'You have eaten all my food, now you must pay me.' Of course the people had not been able pay as they had absolutely nothing. Whereupon Sero would threaten them and say that if the men did not go to work for him in the mines then he would have them imprisoned. As an informant stated: 'people . . . saw that eating this food was tantamount to tying together one's feet or killing a person and putting his or her head in a bag'.[88]

[82] BNA, RC 11/1, Williams in Tsau, 21/11/04, to RC.
[83] BNA, Resident Commissioner (RC).11/1 Hereros Correspondence No. 786 (A), High Commissioner in Johannesburg, 25/1/05, to Resident Commissioner Mafeking.
[84] BNA, HE Record Dept, WNLA, File 247, Witwatersrand Native Labour Association limited list of Employees 15 March 1905.
[85] BNA, R.C. 11/1 786 B. Resident Magistrate, Lt Merry in Tsau, 5/7/05, to Resident Commissioner at Mafeking.
[86] BNA, District Commissioner Serowe (DCS) 43/9, Cpl Hatton in Rakops, 13/8/05, to District Commissioner Serowe.
[87] Ibid.
[88] Interviews conducted with Mr Commissioner Ngate Hange in Maun on 23 and 24/12/92, and Mr Usiel Ketanga Kandapaera and Mr Katjikoro Kakero in Tororamuru 26 to 29/12/92.

Therefore never immediately accept what a stranger gives you, for it might be the sack of Sero.

Very little is known about the Herero communities that emerged at the mines in South Africa after the Herero-German war. Of particular importance though, for the maintenance and organization of a separate and specific Herero identity on the mines, was Christianity – more specifically the retention of belief in the tenets of Lutherian protestantism as taught by the missionaries of the Rhenish Missionary Society. This faith comes to the fore, even in the cynical descriptions of Loton Ridger, a labourer recruiter for the South African mines, who was operating in Ngamiland in 1905:

> After our *Indaba* [meeting] was finished some of the Damaras [Herero], now more cheerful at the prospect of soon reaching the lake and seeing their friends again, began to sing hymns, taught them in their young days by the German missionaries before they were expelled from their homes by the German soldiers. The irony of it! Taught the love of God by the German missionary, to be hunted down like rats by the German soldiers![89]

In 1992, one of my informants Mrs Magdelina Kanaimba told me of her childhood in Nigel in the Transvaal, where they had been the only Herero family present in the early 1920s. In Nigel, Mrs Kanaimba's father, who had been an evangelist for the Lutheran missionaries in German South West Africa, had worked at one of the mines as a first-aid orderly. Every Sunday her father used to travel by train from Nigel, via Springs to Mayfair station, from where he would then walk to the Crown Mines Herero Location where he would preach from German psalm books and Bibles.[90] Throughout the early 1900s the Rhenish Missionary Society received requests, from the various assorted preachers of the Transvaal, for Herero Bibles and hymn books as well as proof of baptism and confirmation for various Herero miners.[91] The existence of a specific Herero community on the Rand appears to have come to an end in the early 1930s.

As noted earlier, Sekgoma Letsholathebe was not the legitimate *Kgosi* of the Batawana. In 1906 he was arrested by Bechuanaland Protectorate forces as he returned to Ngamiland from Mafeking where he had travelled to receive medical treatment, and was incarcerated in the fort at Gaborone. Shortly thereafter Sekgoma was replaced as *Kgosi* of the Batawana by Mathiba in a coup which enjoyed the support of the Bechuanaland Protectorate colonial officials.[92] Never officially charged in a court of law, Sekgoma was eventually released from prison in 1912 and exiled to Kavimba on the south bank of the Chobe river. Here, during the coming years, he was joined by a substantial number of his followers and allies, Herero and Mbanderu refugees amongst them.

The deposition of Sekgoma Letsholathebe had major implications for Ovaherero society in Ngamiland. One of the first things to be brought up was the position of the Herero who had found sanctuary in Ngamiland.[93] Under Sekgoma's rule a number of Herero had been able to find more than just a

---

[89] Loton Ridger, *Wanderer*, p. 283.
[90] Interview conducted with Mrs Kanaimba in Gabane on 17/12/92.
[91] See for instance ELCIN, I1–17A Letter from British and Foreign Bible Society in Cape Town to Rhenish Missionary Society in Wuppertal asking for Herero Bibles 21/8/05.
[92] BNA, S.32/7, Ralph Williams in Tsau Lake Ngami, 10/7/06, to HC.
[93] BNA, RC 11/2, Williams in Tsau, 28/6/06, to RC.

temporary safe haven in Ngamiland, and had established themselves as chiefs, allied to Sekgoma, but with their own client base. Amongst those who had been able to remain in Ngamiland were the Mbanderu associated with Nicodemus Kavarure. In early 1907 the acting resident magistrate in Tsau began reviewing the grounds on which Herero had been permitted to stay in Ngamiland.[94] Life for the Herero and Mbanderu followers of the deposed *Kgosi* became increasingly more difficult in Ngamiland. Eventually in 1916 the Banderu chief Nicodemus Kavarure petitioned the Bechuanaland Protectorate government for permission to trek away from Ngamiland.[95] Messengers were sent, to the resident commissioner in Mafeking, 'to apply on his behalf for permission to leave the protectorate and settle their people at Nyae Nyae in the South West African protectorate'.[96] As reasons for applying for permission to move the two messengers stated that:

> ... Chief Mathibe, under whom they have been for several years is inclined to exact too much from the Damaras in his reserve. Making them weed lands, build houses, bury dead Batawana, make roads and hunt buffaloes etc.[97]

Though they were not permitted to return to Namibia, finally in early 1917 the Banderu and Herero followers of Sekgoma were given permission to trek to Sekgoma at Kavimba.[98]

In conclusion regarding the Herero in Botswana, they retained their identities as immigrants, but they became full members of Tswana society. Their communities were parts of Tswana wards, had loans from Batswana, and even had to work for them and sell them commodities to survive during bad times. Those who had passed on through Botswana to South Africa ended up as labourers on the farms and mines, on the latter of which they were able to establish homogeneous communities united by the tenets of Rhenish missionary Christianity.

Reestablishing a nation

When the Herero POW camps were abolished in 1908, there were effectively three separate Herero identities in Namibia: the Herero Christians of the camps; the Herero soldiers in the German army; and the Herero living beyond the ambit of the German colonial administration. In the war and in the camps the Herero had been systematically deprived and robbed of their possessions, society, religious beliefs, and political and economic leaders. The sole form of social organization that had been permitted and that had remained accessible to them was that provided by mission Christianity and its acolytes. When the camps closed, the supply of Herero POW labour was cut off and the already acute labour shortage was exacerbated. The conditions of extreme labour shortage provided the Herero with a certain amount of leeway, which allowed them to move, recoalesce and begin to reestablish their society within the

[94] BNA, S.30/4/1, Acting Magistrate Tsau Ngamiland 2/1/07 to Government Secretary in Mafeking.
[95] BNA, S.128/1.
[96] BNA, S 126/1, Acting Government Secretary in Mafeking, 1/7/16, to Resident Magistrate.
[97] Ibid.
[98] BNA, S.126/1, RM in Maun, 20/3/17, to RC.

confines of German colonial legislation. The following section describes this process and details the reestablishment, through the mediation of Christianity, of Herero society.

Labour demand

Once the war eventually ended in 1908, Leutwein's dire warnings, regarding the irreversible destruction of labour and impending labour shortage, were shown to be true.[99] As the economy of the territory picked up again, the demand for labour increased, particularly so following the discovery of diamonds in the vicinity of Lüderitzbucht in 1908. In an effort to alleviate the demand for labour, the colonial government was forced to start recruiting labour from Ovamboland and as far afield as the eastern Cape province in South Africa.[100] *Leutnant* Streitwolf was sent to Lake Ngami, to induce the Herero to return to GSWA, and trader Lenssen was sent to Ovamboland to urge the Herero living there to return.[101] In 1908 the Boer Oosthuisen, who lived in Grootfontein, was sent on a mission to recruit labour in Ovamboland.[102] Children were used as labourers.[103] Missionaries regularly complained that Herero children were often unable to attend religious instruction or school as they were employed by masters who refused to give them time off.[104] By 1914, even those people who had traditionally been regarded as being unable to perform menial labour, the Bushmen, were being rounded up and redistributed amongst farmers as forced labour.

Herero communities considered to be living idle lives, beyond the reach of settler employers, were broken up and redistributed amongst settlers who wanted labour.[105] This policy had been begun during the war. Even those Herero living under the protection of the mission were not excluded from this policy. In 1906, the military, contrary to its promise to the Rhenish Missionary Society, which had been given permission to maintain twenty families at the Omburo collection point, surrounded the families living there and drove them off to settler farmers who had demanded labour.[106] Once work on the Otavi railway-line had been completed, Herero who had been employed as forced labourers in its construction were forcefully redistributed amongst those farmers who

---

[99] Leutwein cited in Drechsler, *Fighting*, p. 148.

[100] William Beinart, 'Cape workers in German South-West Africa, 1904–1912: Patterns of migrancy and the closing of options on the Southern African labour market', in *The Societies of Southern Africa in the 19th and 20th Centuries*, collected seminar papers No. 27, Vol. 11, University of London, Institute of Commonwealth Studies, 1981.

[101] Lenssen, *Chronik*, p. 172.

[102] Kol. Blatt. 1908, p. 429.

[103] In this regard see particularly the excellent work done by Gesine Krüger on 'Little Norbert' in *A pass token in the archives. Traces of the history of every day life after the German–Herero war*, unpublished paper presented at the Symposium, 'Writing History. Identity and society in Namibia', held at the Department of History, University of Hanover, 5–7 May 1994.

[104] ELCIN, VII 31.5, *Evangel. Mission, Swakopmund Quartal und Jahresberichte*. Conferenz Berichte Jahresabrechnungen 1906–30. Another side-effect of this employment was that children were often taken to Germany.

[105] NNAW, STR Kaiserliche Schutztruppe für DSWA, STR 19 1.und 4. Kompagnie Karibib. Contains reports of patrols in the countryside and their coming across Herero in the field who are taken to farms as labourers.

[106] See ELCIN, V. Chroniken, Omaruru 1907. Drechsler, *Fighting*, pp. 209–10.

claimed to need labour.[107] Herero who were not employed by White settlers were considered to be idle and were rounded up to be distributed amongst settler farmers. In the Outjo district Ovambo chieftains who had left Ovamboland following succession disputes had established themselves, along with their followers, on the farm Otjeru. Here, assisted by Berg Damara and Herero clients, they grew crops and kept cattle. In 1910, 'to prevent Otjeru from becoming a settlement of workshy vagabonds' it was decided that 'natives of another tribal affiliation will not be permitted to settle there'. It was therefore decided to divide and allocate the Herero and Damara cattle herders and workers living there, along with their families, to those farmers in the district who had requested labour.[108] In an effort to secure labour for the settlers, legislation was passed which stated that all tribes with the exception of the Ovambo, who lived beyond direct German control, were to be exempted from work in the mines.[109]

It was in this context, of an extreme settler hunger for labour, that raids came to be systematically organized into the Sandfeld to capture 'Bushmen' who could then be used for labour.[110] Mission reports of the time make for illuminating reading, particularly with regard to missionary ideas and proselytization:

> On the farms to the east of Grootfontein there are nearly only bushmen, who are all still heathens . . . In Sandfeld there still appear to be many Bushmen and it would be good if they could all be made to settle here or on the farms. As it is well nigh impossible to missionise in the Sandfeld amongst the Bushpeople. The police are involved in getting the Bush people out of the Sandfeld. However how often do they not run away again, after they have been brought to a Farmer or somewhere else. It would appear that at the populated centres, where they must become accustomed to law [*Zucht*] and order and where they must also work, they do not feel well and appear to prefer the free life in the Sandfeld. Therefore I also do not know whether the police are not proceeding too severely, whereby they will most certainly not win the support of the people. A couple of days before I got to Naitsas, the police had fetched a *werft* of 52 people out of the field. They would not have gotten these people if they hadn't surprised them. Because a couple of days earlier, when they had attempted to capture another *werft*, they had to return without having completed their objective. The bush people had probably heard of the coming of the police, and therefore they had sent their women and children away, and attempted, as well as they could, to barricade themselves in their *werft*. Apparently they wanted to engage in battle with the police. However as a native policemen opened fire, because he believed his superior was in danger, they ran away. They were also unable to capture the wounded one, even though they shot him through the chest.[111]

[107] ELCIN, V. Chroniken, Omaruru 1907.

[108] NNAW, BOU. 8 S. 1 South West Company Limited 1/2/96–12/9/10 Band 1. O. III Ovamboreservat Otjeru 1/12/09. Outjo den 2 Marz 1910 letter to the Kaiserliche Gouvernement Windhuk, Die Wartung und Pflege der Viehbestande können die betreffenden Ovambo unter zuhilfenahme ihrer Familien selbst besorgen.

[109] NNAW, BSW 74, (Old notation SD 65–185) Bezirksamt Swakopmund E.2.a Eingeborenen Arbeiter Allgemeines.

[110] NNAW, DOK 28, Akten E.3.a. Eingeborenenstamme, Allgemeines, Band 1, Begonnen am 4 April 1907, Contains letter from Governor to Distriktsamt Okahandja regarding captured Bush people who can be utilized as stock keepers 11/11/14. Also contains a list of farmers who want bush people.

[111] ELCIN, Uncatalogued file entitled *Jahresberichte v. H. Pardey Grootfontein 1908–1924. Grootfontein den 28 Juni 1911 Zweiter Quartalbericht 1911. Grootfontein den 8 Jan 1914, Vierter Quartalbericht 1913.* Östlich und nördlich of Grootfontein . . . In diesem Gebiet wohnen oder

The colonial government urged the mission to assist in the sedentarization of these people as well as care for them.[112] In an effort to prevent their running away, it was decided to transfer captured Bushmen to Swakopmund. Here they died in great numbers until, following debates in the legislative council, it was decided to ensure that better care was taken of them.[113]

Movement

The POW camps were abolished in 1908. In the immediate aftermath of the abolition, people travelled throughout the territory as they sought their family, former homes, friends and society. This movement was exacerbated and facilitated by the extreme demand for labour that existed in the territory. This demand gave the Herero a measure of leeway in deciding to whom and where they could sell their labour. In effect the Herero regained an element of their liberty, however limited this may have been, in being able to influence the sale of their labour and consequently their area of residence.

During the war, to break the links that existed between Herero and their lands, large numbers of captured Herero were deported and put to work in the south of the territory. The deportation of Herero prisoners from their lands ensured that they became dependent on their captors and broke all links that may have existed with Herero still in the field. This policy of deportation was also applied to Nama prisoners. At the end of the war these two streams of people, Nama from the north and Herero from the south, sought to return to where they had originally come from.[114] Herero labourers were reluctant to engage in long-term labour contracts, as these would have limited their ability to move. Prein has argued that the institution of short-term labour contracts that came into being at the time reflected an attempted response to the tendency of labour to move. Such was the shortage of labour that Herero who abandoned contracts that were not to their liking could claim to have lost their passes and be confident that they would then be taken on under an assumed name in a new job closer to an area where they wanted to be.[115] The extent of Herero movement throughout the territory was so great that German settlers

---

vielmehr wohnten die Buschleute, die in letzter zeit durch Polizei und Militar eingehangen worden sind. Bekanntlich hatten leute dieses Stammes einen Farmer vergiftet und andere bedroht, so dass sich die Regierung veranlasst sah, jenes gebiet von den Buschleuten zu 'saubern'. Wie man hort ist eine ganze Anzahl leute, die sich widersetzten oder flohen von den Militar und Polizeipatrouillen niedergeschossen worden, andere sind hier im Gefangnis gestorben, obgleich sie gute Kost bekamen, so dass nicht allzuviel übrig geblieben sein durften. Hier im Gefangnis sind ungefähr noch 20 Männer, 10 Frauen und ein Kind. Die ubrigen Kinder (etwa 20) und einige Frauen (ungef. 10) sind bereits an die Farmer gegeben worden. 15 Manner sind schon seit Langerer Zeit in Swakopmund.

[112] ELCIN, VII Cupboard uncatalogued, in process of being catalogued by Pastor R. Weßler in March 1992. In a folder simply entitled *Grootfontein*, Rundschreiben No. 17 Karibib 5 Jan 1914 J. Olpp to various missionaries point 5. Auf dringende bitte des Gouverneurs werden wir den uns zugewiesenen Teil der gefangenen Buschleute des Grootfonteiner Bezirks in Gaub ansiedeln und seßhaft zu machen versuchen. Die Regierung zahlt das Kopfgeld.

[113] NNAW, Legislative assembly discussions. See foto-copy file 7, article 14, p. 13. See photocopy file 8, article 2.

[114] Bley, *South West Africa*, p. 256.

[115] For the process of losing passes and seeking employment elsewhere see Prein, 'Guns and Top Hats: African resistance in German South West Africa, 1907–1915' in *Journal of Southern African Studies*, Vol. 20, No. 1, 1994, pp. 99–121, & Bley, *South West Africa*, pp. 250–6.

became convinced that the Herero were recoalescing and that a new war was imminent.[116]

Though Herero had been ordered to report and surrender themselves to the missionary collection points and military stations, and though patrols were regularly sent out to seek Herero, many Herero continued to live in the field and roam from one area to the next.[117] These people were effectively beyond the control of the German authorities and provided an attractive alternative to Herero serving contracts that were not to their liking. German settlers and soldiers, partially constrained by the conditions of peace, could do little more than rant and rage at the Herero who had chosen to remain out of settler employment and in the field. The extreme frustration felt by the German troops and settlers at the that time is well illustrated in a letter written by the officer commanding the station at Waldau, approximately twenty kilometres to the north-west of Okahandja:

> As numerous unemployed [*beschäftungslose*] Herero, men as well as women, have recently been wandering about [*herumtreiben*], in the vicinity of Waldau and along the railway line, who, when hailed, flee into the bush and hide there, I request the *Kaiserliche Distriktsamt* to inform me whether it is permitted to shoot at these male Herero when they refuse to stand still when hailed, so that in this way they will be forced to stand still.
> Bauer[118]

Herero were distributed, as labourers, among the many settler farmers who requested them; this did not, however, prevent them from engaging in what the missionaries referred to as the 'dreadful practice' of *hartloop*, running away.[119] The number of people breaking contract increased during years in which there was good rainfall and a concomitant increase in the availability of field foods. The movement of Herero away from farms was not solely confined to the farms of the new 'inexperienced' settlers, but also affected the so-called *Alte Afrikaner* farmers.[120] In early 1909, at the height of an above-average rainy season, farmer Conrad Rust, an *Alte Afrikaner* who had written a 'settler's account of the war', reported from his farm, Monte Christo, that: Simon Katerna No. 5255; David Katerna No. 8593; Maria Karaspura No. 5258; Katarina Kamatwec No. 5257 and Zwanzig Kanjuwara No. 8570, had all fled from his farm and were believed to be headed in the direction of the Bechuanaland border.[121]

[116] NNAW, DOK 28, Three statements of early 1909 in which settlers express their belief that another rebellion is brewing.

[117] NNAW, STR Kaiserliche Schutztruppe für DSWA, STR 19 1. und 4. Kompagnie Karibib, Order on the 12/2/08 for patrols to be sent out along Kuiseb in an effort to apprehend 16 escaped Herero who are attempting to reach Khomas Hochland.

[118] NNAW, DOK 28, Bauer at Station Waldau, 12/5/07, to Kaiserliche Distriktsamt Okahandja. JBG's translation.

[119] ELCIN, V. Chroniken, Gobabis 1908.

[120] Prein, in his excellent article, blames the running away of Herero from farmers on the fact that farmers, though they claimed to be *Omuhona*, failed to realize that this entailed that they should also redistribute wealth to their clients/employees. This was particularly true amongst the new settlers. Prein, *JSAS*, pp. 110–11.

[121] NNAW, DOK 28, Akten: E. 3. b. Eingeborenenstamme betreffend: Hereros, Band 1. The Kaiserliche Bezirksamtmann in Windhuk, 6/2/09, to Kaizerliche Bezirksamt Okahandja. It is possible that these people hoped to be recruited in Bechuanaland for work on the mines. During 1908 and 1909 there were reports of an Englishman named Stanley or Stan operating in Hereroland attempting to recruit people for the South African mines.

Making use of the extreme demand for labour, Herero refugees living in
Ovamboland took the opportunity to return to northern Hereroland disguised
as Ovambo migrant labourers. In the period of one week, in 1908, more than
a thousand Ovambo migrant labourers were taken into service at the Guchab
and Tsumeb mines in northern Hereroland. Of these labourers, a number
turned out to be Herero, who had attempted to pass as Ovambo: 'Like them
they are dressed solely in a loincloth and, as is the Ovambo fashion, have shorn
their hair to a small bushel at the centre.' These Herero reported that they had
disguised themselves as Ovambo, as they had feared that they would have been
recognized as Herero and would have been punished.

> They further noted that there were still many Herero in Ovamboland, who eagerly
> wanted to return; however they feared that they would be punished for their alleged
> involvement in the revolt and that they would lose the remainder of their cattle
> stocks.[122]

Herero not only sought to return to the areas where they had originally come
from prior to the war, but large numbers of Herero also remained in the areas
in which they had been incarcerated, or moved to areas which they had not
previously occupied. Given that for many Herero their former homesteads and
settlements had been utterly destroyed, and that they had very few prospects
of being able to reestablish themselves in their former territories, it is no surprise
that a number of Herero decided to move or settle in areas where they had
previously not resided, but where their future prospects looked better. The
decision of Chief Zacharias Zeraua, formerly of Otjimbingwe, to settle in
Windhoek is a case in point. Following the war, Zeraua's former settlement,
Otjimbingwe, was but a shadow of its former self. Already in the 1870s, when
the trade routes shifted northwards, Otjimbingwe had gone into economic
decline. This was exacerbated in 1900 when the Windhoek to Swakopmund
railway- line bypassed the settlement. Added to this, the former Herero capital,
Okahandja, also lost its position in the Herero–German war. Instead, following
the war, Windhoek became the largest and most important settlement. Needless
to say, Zacharias, when released from imprisonment, chose, as the sole surviving
Herero chief in the territory, not to return to Otjimbingwe or Okahandja, but
asked for permission to remain in Windhoek.[123]

The recoalescence of Herero society through the mediation of Christianity

It was within the confines of stringent legislation, designed to control and mould
their lifes, that the Herero, through the mediation of Christianity, reestablished
themselves.

[122] Kol. Blatt. 1908, p. 429, 'Zur Arbeiterfrage'. At this stage it is only fair to note that these
Herero/Ovambo migrants were often not voluntary migrants. Ovambo chieftains controlled the
movement of migrant labourers to and from Ovamboland, and received increasingly greater control
of the wages earned by these migrants. See in this regard the work of Clarence Smith. Given that
the Herero had entered into Ovamboland as refugees, they were at the bottom of the social standing
in Ovamboland and as such could be and were easily ordered around by their Ovambo hosts. See
in this regard the work of Eirola on Herero migration in Ovamboland following the Herero–
German war.
[123] NNAW, DOK 28, Von Lindequist in Windhoek, 20/8/07, to Kaiserliche Bezirksamt Okahandja.

In an effort to control the movement and labour of the indigenous population of the territory, the German colonial administration instituted legislation which was designed to control and mould the Herero and Nama of Namibia into an anxiously awaited and dreamed-of tribeless black proletariat.[124] It was legislation which sought to ensure that:

> Every Tribal organization will cease. *Werfs* deep in the bush which try to avoid political supervision will not be tolerated. They would provide focal points for memories of tribal life and days when the Africans owned the land.[125]

Germany's colonial mission was 'to divest the Herero as far as possible of their national characteristics and gradually to merge them with the other native groups into a single coloured working-class'.[126] Helmut Bley has noted that German settler discussions at the time regarding native legislation:

> ... did not restrict themselves to a discussion of the economic and political pressures by which the labour laws could be enforced. Instead they aimed at totally changing the Africans' personality by recreating their feelings, wiping out their memories, and making their legal status dependent on their political attitudes. It was particularly true of the attempt to divest the Africans of their 'national characteristics' – this at a time when national identity was highly cultivated in Europe – and of the systematic denial of any freedom to the Africans, even within the limited sphere of the 'working-class'.[127]

Herero society, and the world it had created, had collapsed. The majority of educated Christian Herero had fled across the border. Initiation, even amongst the non-Christian Herero, had stopped. The Germans made sure that the Herero were widely dispersed, that all tribal connections, both political and cultural, were destroyed, and that their symbols, the oxen, the insignia, and chiefs were also destroyed.[128] Towns and settlements which had carried Herero names were renamed.[129] As the governor, Lindequist, noted on a journey in 1907: 'Omaruru, which used to be a highground of Herero identity, has completely become a German village.'[130]

In a later journey, through devastated land where the waterholes dug by Herero for their cattle were collapsing, the governor noted: 'Where the Herero have had 10 thousands of cattle we will too.'[131] A complete transformation was intended, and appeared to have taken place.

---

[124] On German attempts at creating a new tribeless black proletariat see H. Bley, *South West Africa*. NNAW, ZBU, 2023 *Verwaltung der Eingeborenen angelegenheiten*, WII a 4 – a 10. For copies of the legislation regarding the control of Herero, see *Verordnung des Gouverneurs von Deutsch-Südwestafrika, betr. Dienst- und Arbeitsverträge mit den südwestafrikanischen Schutzgebiets, Verordnung des Gouverneurs von Deutsch-Südwestafrika, betr. Maßregeln zur Kontrolle der Eingeborenen, & Verordnung des Gouverneurs von Deutsch-Südwestafrika, betr. die Paßflicht der Eingeborenen*, all of 18/8/07, *DKB*, 15/12/07, pp. 1179–84. For a detailed discussion of this legislation, see Bley, *South West Africa*, pp. 170–3, and for African responses to this legislation, see P. Prein, 'Guns and Top Hats: African resistance in German South West Africa, 1907–1915' in *Journal of Southern African Studies*, Vol. 20, No. 1, 1994, pp. 99–121.
[125] Deputy Governor Tecklenburg to the colonial office, 17/5/04, cited in Bley, *South West Africa*, p. 223.
[126] Ibid. p. 224.
[127] Ibid. p. 224.
[128] Bley, *South West Africa*, p. 255.
[129] Kol. Blatt. 1907, p. 826 & Kol. Blatt. 1908, p. 233.
[130] Kol. Blatt. 1906, p. 643.
[131] Kol. Blatt. 1908, p. 727.

A superficial look at the mass conversion of the Herero following the war might seem to lend credence to the idea that the Herero had indeed been divested of their personality, memories and 'national characteristics'. However the Herero as Christians still saw themselves as Herero. Indeed, the opportunities provided by being Christian allowed Herero to reestablish themselves as Herero, within the confines of totalitarian legislation. That is, the missionary brand of Christianity introduced to Namibia by the Rhenish mission, mediated in and allowed for the reestablishment of a new Herero nation.

Christian elites led the way in reestablishing the nation. This had already begun during the gathering, when Christian converts were sent out to gather the dispersed from the field. At this stage this was not without its dangers and some of the Christians sent out to gather those in the field were killed.[132]

> That people are coming in, is due to Nathaniel, whom I sent out with his companion from the Omatako, to collect the people. Unfortunately Nathaniel has become the offer of his peace mission, at the third *werft*, the *werft* owner Kandjenaua shot him along with his escort.[133]

Those in the field who refused to come in identified the mission, and consequently its message, with the German suppression. Thus one had a splitting between non-Christian leaders in the field who refused to come in, and the Christian leadership which developed in the camps, urging the dispersed to come in.

The twinning of Herero leadership, acceptable to those still in the field, with Christianity was a process that took place during the time that the collection points were maintained. Both missionary Kuhlmann and Diehl consciously took along Christian members of the old elite of the area in which the collection points were established. By 1904, all the elite Herero families of Hereroland had been in contact with the Rhenish mission and nearly all of them had allowed some of their male descendants to be educated by the mission, and in some cases even to become evangelists employed by the mission. The surviving Christian sons of the Herero elite, which had been destroyed and dispersed in the war, continued their Christian mission after the war and assisted the Rhenish mission in its activities. In turn, as the sole surviving free representatives of the previous elite, they found their status enhanced, a condition that the mission exploited in its collection activities. In late 1905 missionary Diehl established the mission collection point at Otjihaenena. He was accompanied by twelve armed Herero, the former school-teacher of Otjihaenena, Gustav Kamatoto, and the former evangelist of Otjihaenena, Erastus, who was closely related to Nikanor the former *Omuhona* of Otjihaenena.[134] Similarly, missionary Kuhlman established the Omburo collection point with the assistance of twenty armed Hereros and the former *Omuhona* of Omburo, the Christian Friedrich. Kuhlmann reported that people specifically came to the collection point to see if it was true that the *Omuhona* and *Muhonge* had returned.[135] Further Herero evangelists who were closely related to the former Herero elites, and who had survived the war to assist the mission in its activities, were Samuel

---

[132] Kol. Blatt. 1906, p. 241, & *BRMG*, 1906, pp. 91 & 161–5.
[133] ELCIN, VII 31 Swakopmund 31.1, letter Dannert in Omaruru, 17/1/05 to Vedder.
[134] *BRMG*, 1906, pp. 89–91.
[135] *BRMG*, 1906, p. 71.

Kariko, Asser Mutjinde – both of Omaruru – and Gustav Kandji. The presence of Christian elites at the collection points had a very direct effect on those in the field, and expedited the movement of people to the camps. By definition, those who refused to come to the collection points or actively resisted being led into the camps came to be defined non-Christian field-Hereros.

A problem faced by the Rhenish mission following the war was the total absence of large, stable congregations of Herero, such as had existed at the mission settlements prior to the war. To overcome this problem, the mission appointed *Wanderevangelisten*, wandering evangelists. These men were dispatched from farm to farm, where they would conduct farmwork for a number of weeks and preach to the farm labourers in their free hours. Their activities were backed up by the missionaries themselves, who also travelled from farm to farm preaching to the small groups of Herero employed on the farms. Referring to the changed circumstances Kuhlmann wrote:

> In the past we were the masters. We could determine the time of the day that the natives should gather. Now we have to take into account the conditions prevalent [on the farms], if we want to reach everyone.[136]

The same was true for the Herero leadership. No longer were there settlements which they could administer. Instead together with their erstwhile subjects they were labourers, subservient to the military, farmers, mine-owners and railway authorities who sought to control their every move.[137] At the slightest suspicion of something untoward, those unfortunates suspected of being involved were arrested and interrogated. The summary arrest of Barnabas Zeraua, the son of the former chief of Otjimbingwe, Zacharias Zeraua, by the settler farmer Rudno in January 1909, is a case in point. Rudno reported that he had observed that 'the natives of farmer Polle, particularly their *werft* elder Augustinus, had been maintaining regular contact with the natives of his [Rudno's] *werft*', therefore he had had Barnabas arrested. A police patrol was sent to the area to investigate the case. Though Barnabas was shown to be related by marriage to Augustinus, the patrol concluded that a revolt was not imminent and that nothing untoward had happened.[138]

In the German sphere of control, the only form of Herero leadership that was allowed to develop was that of missionary evangelists.[139] All other forms of Herero leadership had either been destroyed or lived beyond the reach of the German administration. Those Herero who were placed into positions of authority by the Germans as *voormanne* were often also affiliated to the mission as evangelists.[140] Though the new Herero leadership that developed in the territory in the years after the war was Christian, this did not mean that old feuds that had existed between the Herero elites prior to the war were not continued in renewed conditions of peace. In 1910 a number of elders of the Herero community in Swakopmund were relieved of their functions, because, 'on a Sunday following the church service a serious case of fisticuffs [*Prugelei*]

---

[136] *BRMG*, 1914, p. 160.
[137] As missionary Vedder, with his penchant for the euphemistic, put it: 'The chieftaincies were abolished. Now there were only Herero labourers, for the Herero nation existed no longer, and strict, but just, laws regulated native affairs', Hahn, et al., *Native Tribes*, p. 162.
[138] NNAW, DOK 28, E.3.B, Kaiserlichen Bezirksamt in Karibib, 13/1/09, to Kaiserliche Distriktsamt Okahandja.
[139] ELCIN, uncatalogued folder entitled *Jahresberichte v. H. Pardey Grootfontein 1908–1924*.
[140] ELCIN, V. 26 Ortschroniken, Otjimbingwe 1908.

developed in the house of an elder which resulted in the arrest and imprisonment of the leaders'. The reason given for the altercation was 'the continual
struggle for leadership [*Grossmannsucht*] and tribal feud that exists between
those who come from Omaruru on the one hand, and those who come from
Okahandja on the other hand'.[141]

Under the leadership of their evangelists and in line with the teachings of
Lutheran Christianity, the Herero began to reestablish themselves as a nation.
Anxious to maintain their Herero labourers, settler farmers invited and allowed
the evangelists to work on their farms.[142] Some settler farmers had small
churches built, organized white bread and tea at baptisms, and even presented
labourers with a complete new set of clothes upon their baptism.[143] Scattered
across the country, Herero communities living on the farms and mines, under
the command of their *omuhonge* [teacher], began to communicate to one
another. The evangelists, who travelled from farm to farm, from community
to community, at the invitation of the settler farmers, intent on a stable and
productive labour force, spread the word, and with it the information of their
fellow Herero.[144] The wandering evangelists were referred to in the settler press
as wandering weekly tabloids.[145] In a sense this description of the evangelists
was very apt, particularly when one realizes that these men were distributing a
monthly Herero-language magazine, which was published by missionary Lang
in Tsumeb.[146] In this way the family connections of the past could be
reestablished, fleshed out and continued. Another way in which farmers sought
to maintain Herero labourers on their farms, even though this was prohibited
by law, was by providing the Herero communities working on their farms with
cattle and stretches of land which could be cultivated. That the practice of
'leasing' cattle and land to the Herero communities resident on the settler farms
was effective is indicated by conditions on the farm Abakobib, in the
Grootfontein district, where:

> . . . numbers of Natives live, who are independent, i.e. they keep large stock and
> farm maize, for which they naturally have to pay rent. This results in there being
> many more Natives [on this farm] than on other farms, which all have their particular
> *Werften*. Since approximately one year Zacharias has been holding regular baptism
> classes on this farm.[147]

[141] ELCIN, VII 31.5, *Evangel. Mission, Swakopmund Quartal und Jahresberichte. Conferenz Berichte
Jahresabrechnungen 1906–1930*, Jahresbericht Swakopmund 1908.
[142] In Lüderitz whites protested against Herero becoming Christians, *BRMG*, 1912, p. 20. On
farmers inviting missionaries, see *BRMG*, 1914, p. 84 & 1913, p. 15.
[143] *BRMG*, 1914, p. 164.
[144] *BRMG*, 1913, p. 9, Mission evangelist Alfred working amongst farm labourers near Usakos,
not appointed by the mission. p. 14 Missionary Kühmist reports that in the Keetmanshoop area
20 Herero living on a farm had been taught to read by a Christian Herero, and that they had
built a *pontok* for instruction purposes; p. 15 Herero farm worker preaching and teaching in
Grootfontein area. *BRMG*, 1912, p. 184 Gotthard Hamambo evangelist on farms near Otjimbingwe. p. 185 Joseph evangelist amongst Herero in military service. ELCIN, New folder entitled
Jahresberichte v. H. Pardey Grootfontein 1908–24. Grootfontein den. 3. April 1911 erster
Quartalbericht 1911. Refers to Zacharias granted to the mission by his employer Kaufmann
Billholt.
[145] Prein, *JSAS*, p. 114.
[146] *BRMG*, 1914, p. 66; 1913, p. 11, at a monthly run of 550. The literacy which this entailed
was reflected in a hunger for all forms of literature. In 1912 the missionaries noted in alarm that
children were singing songs that had come out of *Schundliteratuur*, shameful literature. *BRMG*,
1912, p. 186.
[147] ELCIN, New folder entitled Jahresberichte v. H. Pardey Grootfontein 1908–24. Grootfontein
den. 3. April 1911 erster Quartalbericht 1911.

With the reestablishment of leadership and communication, a new specifically Herero identity began to develop, which was mediated by Herero understanding of Lutheran mission Christianity. This did not mean, though, that this new identity was always one which was necessarily appreciated by the mission. Mission reports are littered with accounts of sugar-beer drinking and schoolmasters who had fallen foul of drink.[148] Apart from the expected missionary dislike of sugar-beer drinking and moonlit nights of all-night dancing, the mission also turned against that which it saw as a return to heathen idol worship. The mission cards, initially issued during the period of the camps to POWs undergoing religious instruction, came to take on a meaning of their own. The cards, which had once provided Herero and Nama POWs with tangible physical proof of their existence and identity beyond the confines of German military administration, began to be distributed as amulets following the death of their bearers.[149]

An indication of the re-found stability in Herero social life, in German South West Africa, and the striving to complete this life in all its facets, was the contacts initiated by the Herero of the territory with those living in exile in Bechuanaland and elsewhere. By 1914 the Herero living in GSWA had reached a stage of stability and self-awareness in which they could begin to search for the missing pieces that would complete the puzzle of their social relations. In other words conditions were such that in GSWA Herero could begin attempting to reestablish the social relations which they believed had existed prior to the war. In this it was necessary for them to find the missing links in the chain of social relations that bound them. Some of these missing links were to be found in Bechuanaland. In the interests of worker stability and larger numbers of workers on their farms, some farmers actively encouraged the Herero to seek to reestablish contact with their kin in exile. Indeed these farmers petitioned the military authorities, urging them to desist from leading military patrols into areas where it was expected that Herero, living in Bechuanaland, but seeking to return to GSWA, communicated with their kin in GSWA and, it was hoped, would pass through.[150] The mere fact that settler farmers urged the military to allow the free passage of their workers, whom they openly admitted were communicating with their kin in Bechuanaland, is an indication of the extreme labour shortage suffered by the settlers, and their faith in their ability to control the social conditions existing in the territory to their own advantage. Had the farmers felt threatened by their subjected labour force, they would never have allowed them to communicate with those who were not subjected, much less urge them to do so.[151]

[148] BRMG, 1913, p. 8 Usakos, p. 9 Okahandja; p. 100 Keetmanshoop. 1914, p. 187 Swakopmund.
[149] ELCIN, VII Cupboard uncatalogued, in process of being catalogued by Pastor R. Weßler in March 1992. In folder simply entitled, *Grootfontein. Vertraulich! Rundschreiben Serie II No. 7*, Eich in Swakopmund, 9/2/12, to conference.
[150] NNAW, BOM 34, [GA.5] Grenzhereros 19/3/14, letter from farmer W. Eichhoff, farm Okamatangara, 19/3/14, to Bezirksamtmann Görgens, in Omaruru. In the letter Eichhoff mentioned that for the past six months he had maintained a Herero family, under the leadership of Otjirowi, who had come from the Lake Ngami area, and requested that all police patrols be stopped so that further families could be induced to cross over from Bechuanaland.
[151] NNAW, ZBU 2027, WII d 3 Band 1 Angelegenheiten der aufgelösten Eingeborenenstämme Herero, Angefangen 1911, Letter from Bezirksamtmann Görgens in Omaruru, ?/3/14, to Governor Windhoek, date stamped 4/4/14. The Governor followed up the advice and noted in a letter that, 'the area between Eiseb and Omuramba u Omatako east of the line Okauha police station Otjosondu Okawakuatjiwu is to be avoided by *Schutztruppen* patrols for the time being, it will be necessary to request my permission beforehand.'

The Herero, with their re-found identity and leadership, became ever more strident in their demands for access to land and cattle in the years immediately prior to the Fiirst World War. Settler farmers, desperate for labour and anxious to retain that which they had, began, contrary to strict interpretations of the law, to provide their Herero farm workers with cattle and plots of land which could be cultivated, in exchange for services rendered. Shortly after the camps had been abolished extensive discussion had taken place, on the part of the settlers and the colonial government, regarding the feasibility of establishing Herero reserves in Omburo and Otjihaenena. At that stage the ideas were turned down for a number of reasons. There was, as the settlers were always to remind the government, an extreme shortage of labour, added to this the creation of reserves in the middle of settler farms would lead to an increase in cattle rustling, besides the Herero cattle would form a source of infection for settler cattle, and the reserves would form a focal point for idlers and political ferment.[152] However, by 1914, settlers in the colony's legislative council had begun calling for a change in legislation so that Herero could be allowed their own cattle again and that they be granted access to land. Interesting in this context is the fact that it was the governor, Theodor Seitz, who at this stage was disinclined to allow Herero access to cattle on the grounds that: 'Natives, with their bad bulls, would then corrupt the highly bred farmer cattle.' It was up to the *Bezirksamtmann* of Omaruru, Görgens, to remind the governor that: 'In my district the farmers have decided by themselves, to allow the Natives to own large stock.'[153] In effect by 1914, the Herero were in a position where, in exchange for their labour, they could dictate to settler farmers that they be granted cattle and access to land. Failure to provide these two commodities led to the desertion of Herero labourers from their employers to the farms where cattle ownership was permitted, to the mines, or to the urban centres of the territory.[154]

Following the formal abolition of the camps in 1908, large numbers of Herero remained in the urban centres to which they had been transported. Here they formed the basis of a permanent urban population which made its living by working for a wage. In Windhoek, Karibib, Swakopmund, Keetmanshoop and, to a lesser extent, Lüderitz, permanent urban populations of Herero were formed. Initially these populations were based on the military POW camps and the forced labour camps to which these POWs had been transferred. Thus most centres had at least three distinct Herero locations, which had their origins in the former military, police and railway POW labour camps. As settler legislation in the territory became increasingly more racist, legislation was passed which called for the abolition of the locations in the urban centres, and the establishment of single 'Native locations' outside the urban centres.[155] Though these centres were undoubtedly a refuge for the youth and women, whom Prein referred to as escaping patriarchy, their activities in the urban centres did not extend beyond illegal beer-brewing, prostitution, etc. They did

---

[152] NNAW, ZBU 3032, *WII e3 Eingeborenen Reservate Hereroreservate Omburo und Otjihaenena Band 1 Angefangen 28/12/10*, Kaiserliches Distriktamt Omaruru, 23/11/10, to Kaiserliche Gouvernment Windhuk & Governor in Windhoek, 2/2/11, to Colonial Office Berlin.

[153] NNAW, BOM 1–5, Copy of legislative council meetings of 21–23 April 1914, p. 8.

[154] Prein, *JSAS*, pp. 110–11.

[155] See particularly Bley, *South West Africa*, pp. 263–7.

not relate directly to the reestablishment of Herero society, rather they related to the uninitiated youth serving in the army and the police.[156]

Initiates versus the uninitiated

In 1913, at the annual conference of the Rhenish mission in GSWA, missionary Kuhlmann entertained his audience with a paper, entitled 'Characterizing the Christianity of our Herero communities'. Kuhlmann opened his presentation by stating that, with Herero Christian converts, heathenism continued to stream underneath the Christian veneer.

> ... the old heathen perceptions [*Vorstellungen*] of the Herero, continue to operate, also with the Herero who have become christians, as an undercurrent.[157]

It was a view echoed forty years later by Oswin Köhler, who saw the conversion to Christendom as a mere 'rite de passage', in that the mission formed an institution where 'they could assemble again' but which 'for the Herero . . . was to a large extent of transitional institutional value'.[158] I disagree with Köhler's claim that the mission and its Christian message were merely of transitional value for the Herero. Instead I would argue that the Herero conversions were genuine and without guile. The converts, though, retained aspects of their cultural background that exasperated their northern European pedagogues, but which made conversion all the more acceptable to the Herero.[159] The movement into Christendom by the Herero was more than mere 'rite de passage'. It was sincere. The move into Christendom, with its extensive catechism, schooling and prescribed way of life, came to replace the extensive initiation practices that had existed previously. These traditional Herero initiation rites had ceased to be performed during the war and the time of the camps.[160] Missionaries were aware that the Christendom that had existed prior to the war on the stations was something very different to that which had now developed amongst the Herero; indeed the very language used and ideas expressed were different.[161] This discrepancy they explained away as being due to the changed conditions and the different class of Herero converts that they were now getting. There was, however, more at work than that.

Kuhlmann's words indicate that, within the mass conversions of the time, we can see the maintenance and transformation of Herero culture and its concomitant identity. That is, the underlying structures within Herero society

---

[156] ELCIN, V. Chroniken 31 Swakopmund, 1912. For events regarding beer drinking, township life and youth.

[157] *BRMG*, 1914, pp. 57–63.

[158] O. Köhler, 'The stage of acculturation in South West Africa', in *Sociologus*, 1956, Vol. 6, No. 2, p. 139.

[159] On the issue of exasperated northern European pedagogues, a fine example is that of Rhenish missionary Kuhlmann who in 1913 presented a paper to the *BRMG* annual conference entitled 'Characterizing Christianity in our Herero community'. In his presentation Kuhlmann referred to the 'heathen' ideas of the Herero which continued to affect the Christian Herero as an undercurrent. For a published and edited version of the presentation see *BRMG* 1914, pp. 57–63.

[160] Rudolf Lehmann, 'Einige Spannungs- und Ausgleichserscheinungen in der Sozialen Organisation Mittel- und SWA völker', in *Thurnwald Festschrift; Beiträge zur Geseuungs- und Völkerwissenschaft* (Berlin 1950).

[161] Mossolow, *Waterberg*, p. 5.; R. Ohly, *The Destabilization of the Herero Language* (Windhoek 1987).

were not destroyed but maintained and brought to the fore in a different form. It was particularly in the realm of kinship that one saw the maintenance of Herero identity. Peter Delius has noted for the Nzundza Ndebele that, following their defeat, dispersal and enslavement by Boer forces in the 1880s, it was out of expediency, in that nuclear marriages came to be the only ones accepted by the Boers. That is, the Boers consciously tried to tear Ndebele society asunder. The kinship structures that had existed within Ndebele society were systematically ignored and transgressed. Yet in spite of all this assault, Ndebele family kinship structures continued to exist, and were used to rebuild a specific Ndzundza ethnic identity.[162] Analagous processes occurred in Namibia. Following the Herero–German war, concepts of northern European mono-gamous Christian marriages were deemed to be the only ones acceptable by the German colonial administration. Herero POWs, for their part, used Christian marriages to prevent the splitting of families; the spate of marriages in the Okahandja POW camps are an example of this. However, other forms of marriage and kinship arrangement continued to exist and continued to be acceptable and relevant for Herero.[163] The terms relating to the importance of Herero kinship structures and the taboos associated therewith were clearly not destroyed. Though Herero society had collapsed, this did not mean that taboos had simply disappeared; obviously taboos associated with sexual relations, kinship, food and the like remained in the minds of Herero. Similarly, though the societal superstructure which had existed to enforce these regulations had been destroyed, sanction on specific relations continued to exist within the minds of surviving Herero. Though these Herero kinship structures were unacceptable in the eyes of the settlers, the settlers and the Herero continued to act upon them. Even though they denied it, the existence and importance of these structures was accepted by the German settlers, to such an extent that they acted upon it. That is, in the eyes of all those involved, the structures, whose existence was officially questioned, were still identifiably Herero and clearly made one Herero.

The Herero conversions after the war were different to those prior to the war, and the missionaries were aware of this discrepancy, but shifted it aside in the struggle for souls, and the belief that at least this was a step in the right direction.[164] For the Herero, however, there was a major difference. The converts prior to 1903 had accepted and internalized the ideas of morality, marriage, etc. within the missionary concept of northern European Lutheran-ism in the late nineteenth century. The Herero converts of the period 1904–14, though they were true believers, maintained their paradigm of kinship structures existing prior to the war. These structures were not destroyed.

Thus Herero maintained their identity; one way of doing this was by substituting the long and arduous physical and mental conversion into Christianity (with its name-giving, etc.) for the initiation that had existed prior to the war. That is, the long-drawn-out process of becoming Christian, with its concomitant taboos, etc., came to replace initiation into Herero adulthood

---

[162] Peter Delius, 'The Ndzundza Ndebele: Indenture and the making of ethnic identity, 1883–1914', in *Holding their Ground: Class, Locality and Culture in 19th and 20th Century South Africa*, edited by P. Bonner, I. Hofmeyr, D. James, T. Lodge (Johannesburg 1989), pp. 227–58.
[163] In this instance see the case of Diehl at Otjihaenena, where an evangelist is married by church law to a woman in the Windhoek camps, and by 'customary' law to a woman in the field.
[164] *BRMG*, 1914, p. 63.

with its concomitant taboos. Herero saw this transformation as being one which was very real, and refused to take on police- or settler-ascribed names when being baptized. At birth Herero were given a name by their *Mukuru*, that is, their father as the representative of his ancestors. This name was bound to one's soul, it was one's true name, by which one was known to one's siblings and *Mukuru*. Herero who were baptized after the war took on names that bound them to their fellow converts and to God. It was a name, and an identity, that could not be destroyed by mere mortals.[165]

Given that Christian conversion came to replace initiation, conflict arose between the Herero Christian converts and those whom, in their eyes, were the uninitiated youth. However, these uninitiated youths were very powerful, for they served in the army and the police. This is not to say that the *bambusen* who became soldiers were not initiated; all recruits are initiated into an army. It was, however, a form of initiation that was not acceptable to mainstream Herero society. They had power, but were uninitiated. Another factor that was unacceptable to mainstream Herero was the granting of power to Ovatjimba. From the beginning of its presence in GSWA the German army had employed Ovatjimba, people who previously had had no power, but now, due to their status as soldiers, were powerful. For the ageing orphans, who had been collected during the war, and those Tjimba who had joined the army prior to the war, the kinship structures open to the civilians did not apply. They were beyond society. Furthermore the morality of the Christians did not apply to them, they were a morality and a force unto themselves, a morality and force which became leaderless when their army was defeated in the First World War.

Conclusion

In essence, this chapter has sought to discover how, in the face of determined attempts at destroying their society, the Herero were able to survive and recreate their own society. In the aftermath of the war, there had been calls for the complete elimination of the Herero as a separate ethnic identity.[166] An attempt was made to take from the Herero all that defined them as such, and to mix them along with the other inhabitants of Namibia into a 'single coloured working-class'.[167] In line with these aims, a series of laws had been passed which 'aimed at totally changing the African's personality by recreating their feelings, wiping out their memories, and making their legal status dependent on their political attitudes'.[168] Yet the Herero did survive as a separate ethnic identity, and how this came about was the subject of this chapter.

The chapter commenced with an overview of the three groups of Herero that had survived the Herero–German war, those in the bush, those in the camps, and those in the German army. Of the three groups, the camp Herero were numerically the most significant. During the course of their incarceration, the camp Herero converted to Christianity. These people became Christians, not solely because of material improvements in their condition, but because

---

[165] For a discussion on the importance of names and the refusal to accept settler names, see *BRMG*, 1914, p. 58.
[166] Bley, *South West Africa*, p. 223.
[167] Ibid., p. 224.
[168] Ibid.

Christianity provided them with an identity that existed beyond the confines of German incarceration.

With the abolition of the POW camps there was an acute shortage of labour in the territory. The extreme shortage of labour facilitated the movement of Herero and allowed them to recoalesce and begin to reestablish a society. The society which came to be reestablished was based upon the structures found within the institution of mission Christianity. These structures came to replace and complement those that had existed in Herero society prior to 1904, some of which had never been destroyed.

7

This Land is not Yours
It is the Property of America & the Herero
1915–23

Introduction

In 1915 Herero soldiers, under the command of South African army officers and dispatched by their chief Samuel Maharero, assisted in the invasion of German South West Africa. Eight years later, in 1923, Herero soldiers, now under the command of their own officers, carried the remains of Samuel Maharero to his grave in a coffin covered by the Union Jack.

In the aftermath of the South African invasion and occupation of GSWA, the Herero established themselves with cattle in areas of their own choosing. As the new South African administration established itself, and sought to gain control over the territory and its inhabitants, the Herero made use of the divisions that existed within the new administration and organized themselves in ways that protected their own specific interests. It was not until the death and funeral of Samuel Maharero that the disparate groups of Herero came together to establish a single unitary Herero identity.

Herero new age

In 1915 two events occurred which drastically altered the course of Herero history. South African armies occupied Namibia and the grain harvests in Ovamboland, in northern Namibia, failed. These two events freed the Herero from German domination and service.

In 1915 armies commanded by the famous Boer war Afrikaner general and prime minister of South Africa, Louis Botha, invaded GSWA from the Union of South Africa. In a short sharp campaign, the once proud and seemingly invincible *Schutztruppe* were routed and defeated. In August of 1915, General Louis Botha accepted the surrender of German South West Africa, from Governor Seitz at Khorab, near to Grootfontein.[1]

At the outbreak of the First World War, Herero believed that better times

---

[1] Gerald Lange, *Imperial Service* (Johannesburg 1991).

were upon them and acted accordingly. The German authorities, aware of and frightened by these expectations, asked the missionaries to curb and control the passions of their Herero flocks.[2] This the missionaries attempted to do, by seeking to convince the Herero that war was a 'White Man's War', and that the Herero should remain loyal to the Germans. The Herero were not fooled, and some, with clear insight into their true position, replied to missionary pleas with the following telling answer: 'We have already been imprisoned for a long time, they can only wage a war with our masters.'[3]

Ideas as to the benefits of British rule had long been prevalent in Herero society. In the 1870s and 1880s Herero royals had regularly petitioned British authorities in the Cape Colony with requests for formal British protection. These beliefs were expanded upon in the run-up to, and in the immediate aftermath of, the Herero–German war, when thousands of Herero found refuge in Bechuanaland and South Africa under the protection of the British crown. These people provided first-hand reports on the superior conditions in the Cape Colony, Transvaal and Bechuanaland. Some of these optimistic reports may have been exaggerated, but they certainly helped to raise expectations amongst Herero in GSWA. As Rhenish missionary Pardey, whose Herero evangelist deserted him for the advancing South African troops, reported:

> Most Natives believed, that the golden age of *Omaere* drinking had dawned, an age in which they could, as they had in the past, live in the field and on cattleposts, without being drawn into labour . . . The heathendom resurfaced . . . The heathen dances once again became fashionable, even amongst the Herero who usually seldom indulged in dancing. Whole nights long one could hear the howling [*Gejohle*], it also happened that on Sundays they danced in church. My rebukes had little effect. As soon as the people saw me they walked away, only to return later to make things worse. Eventually I asked the native commissioner to take steps against the ever increasing dancing.[4]

As the South African forces advanced ever further into GSWA, Herero at all levels of society deserted their erstwhile employers. Farm labourers, domestic servants, church evangelists, police *bambusen*, army auxiliaries and missionary teachers, all abandoned their employers and returned to their former areas of residence, sought freedom in the field, or found employment with the advancing South African troops. Herero soldiers and policemen, who had previously fought with the German forces, now betrayed their erstwhile employers. A thoroughly shocked Rhenish missionary described what happened in Gobabis:

> On 14 June [1915] at 4 o'clock an English officer and 25 Boers, wearing stolen clothing and straw hats, entered and took Gobabis, the women of Gobabis moved to the German fort, now occupied by the South Africans, and started dancing. The next morning the natives showed the South Africans where the arms of the Gobabis *Schutzverein* [civil militia] were buried. Betrayal followed upon betrayal, and who were the traitors? Precisely those natives, who during their mastery had lived so exceedingly well, the police *bambusen*.[5]

All across the country the Herero left their employers and sought to establish themselves independently of their former masters. Herero who had been

[2] ELCIN, V. 31 & V. 10 1914.
[3] ELCIN, Uncatalogued document entitled *Vierter Quartalbericht der Gemeinde Grootfontein 1914.*
[4] Ibid.
[5] ELCIN, V. 8 1915.

scattered across the territory migrated to those areas where they had previously lived under their own leaders. Mission teachers and evangelists, often drawn from the chiefly families that had existed prior to 1904, abandoned their places of employment and returned to the sites of their former chieftaincies. In some instances these 'chiefly evangelists' were accompanied by new followers, whom they had acquired whilst working as evangelists in the aftermath of the Herero–German war. The new colonial administration was inundated with requests regarding the whereabouts of leaders known to be in South Africa. As the new colonial administration strengthened its grip on the country, the extent to which Herero were moving through the country started to become apparent. Throughout the territory and from far beyond, Herero abandoned areas to which they had been deported, assigned, moved or fled, and returned to areas of their own choosing.[6]

Not only did the Herero attempt to establish themselves at a physical distance from their former masters, they also attempted to establish themselves independently of the ideological institutions associated with the settlers. Missionaries reported a return to and dramatic increase in, what they termed, 'heathenism'. In the first years after the South African takeover, there was a dramatic increase in Herero divorces. In effect, some of the aspects of the church and its related institutions had outlived their usefulness to the Herero.[7]

Though the incoming administration was sympathetic to settler farmers, the virtually immediate release from detention of German settler soldiers being a case in point, there were two prime reasons why the new administration, in its initial years, did not take steps to prevent the desertion of Herero labourers from the German settler farms. The first reason was a logistical one. The South Africans were initially simply unable to enforce the continued residence of Herero on the farms of their former employers. South African troops were engaged in a bloody war in East Africa and could ill afford to become embroiled in a further conflict in SWA. The second reason why Herero were able to leave their former employers was directly related to the great Ovamboland famine of 1915.

During the course of 1915, the grain harvests of the kingdoms of Ovamboland in northern Namibia failed completely. Hordes of young men abandoned their homesteads in the north, and headed south in search of food and work.[8] At this stage there was a great demand for labour. Upon the cessation of hostilities, the diamond mines at Pomona, Elisabethbucht, Oranjemund, Kolmanskop and Lüderitz, and the copper mines at Tsumeb had resumed production. Similarly the recently released German settler farmers returned to their farms and sought to continue farming. The farms and the mines

---

[6] The extent of Herero migration can to some extent be gleaned from the new administration's professional interest in the matter and its appointing part of its bureacracy to deal specifically with the issue. NNAW ADM. 76. The return of *Kaptein* Oorlog from southern Angola can also be attributed to the recent South African takeover of Namibia; however, it is probable that the effects of the drought and his deteriorated relations with the Portuguese also induced him to return to Namibia.

[7] The aspect of Herero establishing independent churches is dealt with in greater detail in a further section of this chapter.

[8] See ADM 106 for reports on famine. See E.H.L. Schwarz, *The Kalahari or Thirstland Redemption* (Cape Town ?1920/28). Opposite page 65 has photograph taken by Lt C.H.L. Hahn which is entitled 'Skeletons of Ovambos who perished in the 1915–16 famine'; the collection of bones has been gathered together as it only shows femurs and skulls and no rib-cages.

urgently needed labour, and the Ovambo famine victims took up the positions vacated by the Herero.[9] The route south from Ovamboland was marked by the corpses and skeletons of those who had collapsed and died as they failed to make the journey south. In Karibib, in central Namibia, in a single week, in November 1915, fifty-one Ovambo migrants died. During the famine more than 1000 famine victims perished in Karibib alone.[10] The new authorities, who, towards the end of 1915 and early 1916, were having to deal with 'Ovambos dying at a rate of 10 to 15 per diem', established a labour depot in Karibib to facilitate the distribution of the Ovambo famine victims. Here the Ovambo were fed, selected and allocated to their future employers.[11] Commenting on the death-rate of the Ovambo famine victims in late 1916, the military magistrate for Karibib reported:

> . . . now the average is something like 2 or 3 per month. This, of course, may be partly accounted for by improved conditions in Ovamboland, and also to the lesser number of Ovambo on hand here now, but the improvement is so phenomenal that I feel convinced it must be largely due to the compound system.[12]

Not only did the Ovambo find employment in the mines or with settlers, they also found employment as cattle-herdsmen with Herero who had acquired stock. By early 1917 the new administration had begun implementing a policy that sought to withdraw Ovambo labour from the farms and place them with the railways and mines. This policy did not meet with much enthusiasm on the part of the farmers. The Officer in Charge of Native Affairs in the Windhoek district commented in his annual report for 1916:

> My office records show that there are still 361 male Ovambo in service in Windhoek and District, which figure may be regarded as representing the shortage of local labour. It is at present not possible, if one is to study the wellbeing of the farmer, to withdraw Ovambo labour from him by imperatively disallowing re-engagemnet of time-expired labourers and, while the policy of withdrawing Ovambo from farms and placing them with Railways and Mines is fully appreciated, the process must of necessity be a gradual one, and it is not anticipated that there will be an adequate supply of Herero and Damara to take their place before the end of 1917.[13]

The replacement of Herero by Ovambo labour was a process that bothered the new administration:

> . . . the introduction of Ovambo labour, which replaced hundreds of Herero who refused to work for Germans and are consequently out of employment. These Herero have gone to squat on Crown lands, in locations and wherever else it was possible for them, in the absence of police, to do so. There appears to be no doubt that as

[9] NNAW, ADM 76, Hereros General Migration, Draft letter, Secretary for the Protectorate in Windhoek, 14/3/16, to Military Magistrate in Otjiwarongo.
[10] ELCIN, V. 12 & V. 32 1915.
[11] NNAW, ADM 106 & ADM 77.
[12] NNAW, ADM 106, Annual report 1916, Vol. 1. In later years the South Africans introduced other aspects of the South African compound system, such as the brewing of 'kaffir beer' to prevent scurvy. See SWAA 1681 Letter Dec. 13 1916 to Magistrate Swakopmund from Sgt of Railways in Walvisbay stating that 'I beg to inform you that a large quantity of Kaffir beer is being brewed on the premises of the Native compound SARH Walvis bay. The brewery is under the strict supervision of compound overseer Swart, who rations out a limited quantity about twice a week to each of the natives.'
[13] NNAW, ADM 110, Native Affairs General, Annual Reports, Bowker, Officer in charge of Native Affairs, Windhoek, 31/12/16, to Secretary for the Protectorate, p.8.

long as the Ovambo retain the positions formerly occupied by the Herero, there will be a surplus of labour, which the local demand cannot absorb.[14]

The arrival of the new South African administration and the failure of the grain harvests in Ovamboland in 1915 freed the Herero from enforced employment at specific locations. Their former positions of employment were taken up by Ovambo employees, and henceforth the Herero labourers were free to move to areas of their own choosing. All over the territory, Herero reoccupied the farms and lands from which they had been driven in the Herero–German war.[15] Okahandja, formerly the most important Herero settlement in the country, which had been largely cleared of its original Herero inhabitants, was one of the centres to which Herero returned. During the course of 1915 two 'Native' locations sprang up in Okahandja, one on the site of the old location and another next to the railway.[16] Lands in the vicinity of Okahandja were similarly reoccupied by Herero, causing recently released settler farmers to complain of Herero 'squatting' on their farms.[17] Lands around Windhoek and Avis were also reoccupied and settlers reported that settlements of 'illegal squatters', engaged in horticulture and pastoralism, had sprung up.[18] All across the territory, as the new age dawned, Herero reoccupied their former lands.

Freed from enforced employment and in partial occupation of their former lands, the Herero sought to consolidate their new-found independence through the acquisition of cattle. It was in the fluid conditions of the South African invasion and its immediate aftermath that the Herero acquired the bulk of their cattle herds. During the German–South African hostilities, German settler farmers had enlisted in the *Schutztruppe* and abandoned their farms to the care of their wives and overseers. Prior to the war some of these Herero overseers had already illicitly received cattle from settler farmers in return for services rendered. In the unsettled circumstances of war extensive rustling took place and large numbers of settlers and Africans lost herds of large and small stock.[19] Often Herero herdsmen and overseers simply absconded with the cattle stocks of their former masters. Added to this, members of the incoming administration were involved in cattle dealing, and there was thus an extensive illicit trade in rustled, confiscated and captured cattle.[20] Due to the famine in Ovamboland, and the collapse of the German administration, which had previously prevented cattle from entering into central Namibia from Ovamboland, cattle could now easily be moved into northern Hereroland and traded with the Herero. Furthermore following the collapse of the German administration hundreds

[14] NNAW, ADM 76, Draft letter Secretary for the Protectorate in Windhoek, 14/3/16, to Military Magistrate in Grootfontein.
[15] NNAW, ADM 106, Annual Report 1916 Vol 1, Office of the military Magistrate Tsumeb 5/1/17. Following the war large numbers of farms, in the north of the territory, were abandoned on account of 'Bushmen raids'. It is probable that these farms, too, were occupied by the Herero.
[16] NNAW, ADM 83, Okahandja Native affairs.
[17] NNAW, ADM 83, July 1916, Indicative of the changed times, by 9 October the police moved in to round up all the 'vagrants'.
[18] NNAW, NAW 1. NAW 6. SAW, Census of Black population in Windhoek in 18/10/15, Berg Damaras men 471; women 700; children 1521; Hereros 721; 1001; 271; 1993; Hottentots 239; 329; 171; 739; Ovambos 45; 12; 4; 61; Bastards 24; 40; 26; 90; Cape Boys 52; 22; 12; 86. Grand Total 4490. This is excluding Klein Windhuk, Station, Race Course and Hospital locations.
[19] NNAW, ADM & OCT; ELCIN, V. 8 Ortschroniken Gobabis, 1915.
[20] NNAW, ADM 106, 1916 Annual report, Military Magistrate's Office Okahandja 2/1/17, refers to O.C. Native Affairs Lieutenant Ratttray and mentions that he was later dismissed for cattle speculation.

of Herero who had sought refuge in Ovamboland were able to return to Hereroland with their cattle herds.[21] In 1915 cases of lungsickness, which had previously been endemic in Ovamboland and southern Angola, were reported in northern Hereroland and were probably caused by infected cattle being imported from the north.[22]

The Herero made use of the incoming administration's inability to enforce its will on them, to acquire cattle and occupy territories free from the control of the incoming administration. Here the Herero reestablished themselves as cattle ranchers or horticulturalists. Life in some of these settlements appears to have been fairly prosperous. In some instances Ovambo famine victims were employed as herders.[23] In other instances the land tenancy relations, which had existed illicitly between Herero and settlers, continued under the new South African administration. This was particularly so in the Omaruru district where incoming administrators were warned against the dangers of allowing 'kaffir farming'.[24]

The Herero acquired cattle and reoccupied land to such an extent that to all intents and purposes the incoming South African administration was faced with a fait accompli. Herero with substantial cattle herds had reoccupied some of their former lands and had reestablished Herero leadership in the urban centres of Namibia. Partly due to a different perspective on colonial development, but primarily due to the existing state of affairs, the South African administration was forced to recognize, accept, deal and enforce legislation, with a reestablished Herero leadership, Herero possession of cattle and Herero occupation of land.[25] In early August 1916, the Administrator's office in Windhoek let it be known that:

> Under the German Law no native was allowed to possess any riding animals or large stock. Contrary to the provisions of this law the acquisition of Livestock is now sanctioned as it will tend to make the Native more contented and law abiding.[26]

Once Herero rights to the ownership of cattle had been granted, Herero access to land also had to be granted. The course of events in the Otjimbingwe reserve is a fine example of how the new administration was ill-prepared for its task and how, essentially, it was unable to influence the course of events in such a way that it achieved the initiative, but instead was forced to accept the new conditions as they arose. In early 1916 administrators in the Karibib district were informed that: 'Neubrun is now the only Government farm on which Natives in this district are allowed to run stock.' Within seven months the military magistrate in Karibib reported that: '2–300 natives [were] squatting on Neubrun', and that they were in possession of about three times as much stock, amongst which scab had broken out. In an effort to alleviate the problem the magistrate reported that he would be sending troops to round up the surplus

---

[21] The return of *Kaptein* Vita otherwise known as 'Oorlog' to Namibia in 1915 is a fine example of the changed conditions in Namibia.
[22] NNAW, ADM 60, Lungsickness general Okahandja.
[23] NNAW, SWAA 1129.
[24] NNAW, ADM 43, T.L. O'Reilly, Office of the Military Magistrate Omaruru, 20/11/1916, to the Secretary for the Protectorate; D.F. Herbst, Secretary for the Protectorate Windhoek, 16/2/17, to the military magistrate Omaruru, & ADM 85, Capt. P.J. Venter, Superintendent of Locations, in Windhuk, 8/3/17, to the Officer in Charge Native Affairs Windhuk.
[25] Correspondence in NNAW, ADM 43, Protectorate of South West Africa, Native Affairs.
[26] NNAW, ADM 43.

stock. Unfortunately for him, his activities were all to no avail. Within five months of his attempts to round up the surplus stock, the central administration in Windhoek, clearly unable to contain the situation and forced to accept Herero demands for more land, sent the following directive to the military magistrate in Karibib:

> ... I am directed to inform you that the indiscriminate placing of natives on farms cannot be sanctioned.
>
> When making your periodical trips in the district, *you should pick on some farm which you consider will make a suitable permanent reserve for natives and forward your application for authority to establish same with your recommendations.*[27]

The new colonial administration, having been forced to accept Herero possession of cattle and access to grazing, had to develop a system of control whereby it could seek to govern its new subjects. In the case of Hereroland, this entailed recognizing and working with Herero leadership. Thus in late 1916, Traugott Maharero and other Herero leaders were recognized as Herero headmen and retained on a government salary.[28]

Conflict with settlers

Not surprisingly the new-found independence of the Herero galled settler farmers in the territory. As the Herero reacquired stock and reoccupied territory, it was inevitable that they came into conflict with the settler farmers. These saw their livelihood threatened by the Herero, not only in terms of agricultural production, but also through the loss of what they saw as their land and labour. Associated with the improvement in the material well-being of the Herero was an increase in self-awareness and a sense of independence. In response to this greater independence and the perceived threat that the Herero now posed to settler interests, the settlers submitted a flood of complaints and allegations, some of which were patently false, to the new South African authorities.

> Various reports have, during the last two or three months, reached the office of the Native Commissioner, of a proposed rising of the Herero ... These reports emanated solely from the German farmers, and although it is not believed that a rising is contemplated or will occur, yet irresponsible talk and actions by Natives on this subject should be firmly dealt with. As herein before stated interdistrict removals of Natives are prohibited, and any tendency to a rising can best be obviated by keeping an eye on the movements of the Native and by discouraging, as much as possible, aimless travelling.[29]

These personal submissions were followed up by petitions from settlers organized in agricultural societies. In 1916, the Agricultural Society of South

---

[27] NNAW, SWAA 1134 A158/13 Otjimbingwe reserve 1916–1924. Correspondence between Military Magistrate Karibib and Secretary for the Protectorate, Windhoek, 9/5/16; 8/12/16 & 15/2/17. Emphasis added.

[28] In the case of Okahandja, Taugott Maharero was recognized as headman and retained on a government salary of £1. NNAW, ADM 106, Annual report 1916, Vol. 1, Military Magistrate's Office Okahandja 2/1/17.

[29] NNAW, ADM 43, Report issued by the office of Native Commissioner Windhuk 31/1/16 entitled *Reported unrest amongst the Hereros.*

West Africa submitted three resolutions to the new administration and
requested that a number of measures be taken. The resolutions submitted dealt
with the taxation of 'native dogs', the carrying of daggers or spears, and the
branding of cattle. The resolutions all dealt with issues that were directly related
to Herero attempts at achieving and maintaining independence from settler
control; that is, the right to hunt, and the control of cattle independent of settler
control. On behalf of the agricultural society, its president, Bohnstedt, 'begged'
to make the following requests:

> That the outlying (*im Felde*) native locations . . . be removed. That the keeping of
> large stock by natives be prohibited. That the squatting on Government farms by
> natives with their cattle, who do so in order to avoid labour, be prohibited. To limit
> the period of absence of Natives on leave.[30]

Some settlers did not wait to see whether the new administration would take
action on their behalf; instead, possibly in an attempt at forcing the
government's hand, they undertook action on their own behalf.

In August of 1916 Paul Ahnert, a fifty-one-year-old Hanoverian, who had
had the good fortune to be appointed farm manager by a more successful settler,
was charged with the crime of malicious injury to property. On an early winter's
morning in August 1916, Paul Ahnert had shot and killed two goats and
maimed a third. The goats had belonged to two Herero, Edward and Isaac,
who lived at Otjihaenena. Giving evidence Edward stated:

> I am a Herero and reside at Otjihenena in this district, I know the accused. I
> remember Thursday the 17th. inst, I came up to Grootfontein to work that day. I
> am on the Railway. I left my goats at my *werft* at Otjihenena that morning in charge
> of Otjikonko [an Ovambo who was employed by Herero in Otjihaenena as a herder].
> There were 12 goats when I left, all alive and well. I returned home at about 6 p.m.
> the same night and Otjikonko reported to me that some of the goats were dead and
> on arriving at my *werft* I saw two dead goats.[31]

The case highlights the problem existing within Hereroland at the time.
Relatively well-off and independent Herero could afford to employ herdsmen
and reinvest in livestock, but did not have sufficient access to land and grazing.
In his defence, Paul Ahnert, who pleaded guilty to the charge, indicated clearly
where the problem lay: 'The natives at Otjihenene always trespass, *they must of
necessity, as they have no land of their own.*'[32] The case brought to the fore the
shortage of grazing for Herero livestock and resulted in the secretary of the
protectorate, Major J.F. Herbst, writing the following to the military magistrate
in Grootfontein:

> It is extremely undesirable that natives working on the Railways should be allowed
> to graze their stock on the very limited areas in occupation of the railways. They
> must of necessity trespass on the adjoining farms in order to maintain their stock.
>   The administrator will be glad if you will consider the question of setting aside a
> suitable farm as native reserve in your district where the stock of natives who are
> not required to work and all those who are away at work may be kept.[33]

[30] NNAW, ADM 43, Bohnstedt in Karibib, 30/4/16, to Military Magistrate.
[31] NNAW, SWAA 1129 Otjitua Reserve A158/10 Grootfontein 1916–1924, which includes a
subfile on the trial Rex vs Paul Ahnert.
[32] Ibid.
[33] NNAW, SWAA 1129, Herbst in Windhoek, 19/9/19, to Military Magistrate Grootfontein.

In due course the farm 'Ovisume' was selected by the military magistrate and approved of by Herbst as a 'Native Reserve' subject to the following conditions:

> That only natives with exemption certificates, old men and women unfit for labour, the herds of men at work whose cattle will graze on the reserve, be allowed there.
>
> That the usual grazing fees be paid for all stock grazed on this reserve.
>
> It is of course understood that regulations may at any time be imposed by this administration governing the control of the community and its stock there. You will further make it clear to all natives in your district that the reserve is not intended to be a squatting place for natives who are fit for employment except for those under exemption certificates, but is primarily established with the object of securing a location for the old and infirm, and a grazing ground for the cattle of those persons who are in employment on the farms and elsewhere.
>
> You should now proceed to endeavour to collect on the reserve such persons as are entitled to reside there, carefully registering them and their stock and giving permits to them to protect them from molestation.[34]

Thus the unexpected outcome to the case was that, in response to the affair, the administration created a new 'Native Reserve' for the Herero. The granting of a reserve to the Herero in the Grootfontein district can hardly have been what the settlers had hoped for. The case highlights the conflict of interests that existed in the new administration and which influenced all the legislation that it passed: the conflict that existed between settler interests on the one hand, and forms of liberal native policy interests on the other.

Settlers and liberals

The legislation passed by the new incoming South African administration was mediated and bedevilled by the conflicts that existed between settler interests on the one hand, and a paternalistic liberal 'Native' policy on the other. In effect these conflicts were an echo of the conflicts being fought out in the legislature of the Union of South Africa. The incoming South African administrators came from the newly established Union of South Africa where the 1913 Natives Lands Act had only recently been passed. This piece of legislation severely limited and restricted the rights of Africans to purchase or own land in the Union. The land Act had been passed with great conflict between liberal interests, who wanted to maintain African rights to land, and settler and mining interests, who wanted land and cheap labour.[35] These conflicts were transferred into the Namibian context. Added to this, the various provinces that made up the Union had different forms of Native administration. Obviously the new administrators, who were drawn from the different provinces of the Union, represented differing forms of 'Native' administration. Similarly the South African troops, who came into Namibia and who were initially involved in 'Native' administration, came from different areas of the Union and represented differing attitudes towards the 'Natives'. It was within the margins of the conflict between liberal and settler interests that Herero were able to reestablish themselves between 1915 and 1923.

[34] NNAW, SWAA 1129 Otjitua Reserve, Administrator's office Windhoek, 27/3/19, to the Military Magistrate Grootfontein.

[35] Saul Dubow, *Racial Segregation and the Origins of Apartheid in South Africa: 1919–36* (Oxford 1989), pp. 29–39.

The South African invasion forces contained within them the contradictions that would later come to the fore in the new administration. The forces commanded by Botha consisted primarily of 'poor white' Boer soldiers commanded by English officers. Botha and many of his fellow Boer soldiers had fought against the English thirteen years previously in the Boer war. Some of them had even sought and found sanctuary in GSWA during the war in which Imperial Germany had supported the Boer republics. At the outbreak of the First World War Imperial Germany had armed and supported those Boer rebels who refused to fight with the English and who had crossed into GSWA and had once again taken up arms against the British. These Boers, who in GSWA were organized into a *Freiwilligen-Korps* under the leadership of Andries de Wet, were later joined by Boer rebels in South Africa under the command of General Maritz. The Boer soldiers who made up the bulk of the invading South African forces joined the invasion force not so much out of patriotism and belief in the British crown, but out of the need for a job and the belief that there was a profit to be made.

For many South African soldiers there was indeed a substantial profit to be made in the raiding of cattle. Though the incoming South Africans were officially opposed to stock theft, indeed the lashing of African stock thieves was to be permitted, theft took place under the auspices of the British crown, and a spate of claims were laid against the invading forces.[36] Events surrounding the occupation of the town of Gobabis by South African troops in 1915 were not unique. A few days prior to the occupation of Gobabis, Boer soldiers, who had deserted from the South African troops, drove about 1400 rustled cattle through the town en route to the Bechuanaland border and the Boer cattle ranches at Ghanzi. Shortly thereafter on 14 June at 4 p.m. a South African English officer and his force of twenty-five Boer soldiers, who were wearing stolen clothing and straw hats, entered and took the town. The contrast between the rule of law and looting, between liberal and settler interests, comes well to the fore. The difference between rustling cattle and looting clothing is only a matter of degree, albeit that the one was conducted under the auspices of the British crown. This form of commerce continued after the war and involved members of the South African army who had been detailed to deal with 'Native Affairs'.[37]

Settler interests

In 1903 General Louis Botha, defeated after three years of unremitting warfare, had returned to his farm in the eastern Transvaal. Far from being welcomed home by faithful servants, Botha was driven off his lands by a hostile group of tenants who informed Botha that he had no further business there; in effect they had reoccupied the lands which had been taken away from them twenty years previously.[38] Though Botha never did pursue his farming career, he never forgot his homecoming and henceforth, when he did become one of South Africa's leading politicians and later prime minister, his political decisions were always coloured by the events surrounding his homecoming in the eastern Transvaal. Anxious to spare his opponents the same experience, and a firm

---

[36] NNAW, ADM 78, Native claims for losses sustained during S.W.A. Campaign.
[37] NNAW, ADM 106, Annual report 1916. See particularly the sacking of Major Rattray, O.C. Native affairs and others in Okahandja.
[38] Peter Warwick, *Black People and the South African War: 1899–1902* (Johannesburg 1983), p. 165.

believer in the necessity of racial solidarity, Botha established extremely lenient terms of surrender with the German troops. Active service officers were allowed to retain their weapons and horses, and were allowed to choose their own places of residence. German soldiers were permitted to retain their weapons, albeit without ammunition, but were to be interned at Aus. Reservists, after having surrendered their military weapons, were permitted to return to their former places of residence and continue their occupations. In other words, German settler farmers, who had fought as reservists and had been defeated by the South Africans, were permitted to return to their farms and continue their occupation as if nothing had happened.

In a sense very little had changed. On the issues of labour and land, settler farmers could and did expect a sympathetic ear from the incoming South Africans. Settler farmers still felt perfectly within their rights when they called upon South African troops to re-capture labourers who had run away from their farms during the hostilities:

> To O.C. S.A.M.R Kalkfeld Native female Sara. Mr. R. Hacklander Omburo reports here, that the above native female is at present residing on Onjakava Farm (Mr. Keiser) near Kalkfeld. This native left him during hostilities, and *he now wants her back on the farm*. Please take the necessary action for her return, as Mr. Hacklander states that she wants to come back. Charge Office Omaruru, 17/11/15 W. Adams Sergt I/C.[39]

South African officers, contrary to the official condemnation of such German practices, found it perfectly reasonable that first-time African offenders be lashed for stock theft, and that African children be indentured to settler farmers who felt that they needed labour.[40] In the instance of Windhoek the *kriegsgefangenen Register*, the register of Herero POWs, which had listed their camp deaths and forced labour allocations, were simply maintained and continued by the incoming South African forces.[41] German settler farmers, who complained about 'Natives squatting' on their farms, could rest assured that the events that had befallen Louis Botha would not befall them. By October 1916, little more than a year after their defeat at the hands of South African troops in Namibia, German settlers could sit back and watch as South African police, acting on the basis of their complaints, moved in to round up 'African vagrants' living on farms in the Okahandja district.[42]

Liberals

When the South African troops invaded German South West Africa they brought along with them aspects of political thought current at the time in their own country. One of these aspects was a form of liberalism which has become known in history as the Cape Liberal tradition. The Cape Liberal tradition has many detractors, and there are many who maintain that the tradition only catered for those already in possession of wealth and power. This

[39] NNAW, Native Affairs Omaruru 2. JBG's emphasis.
[40] NNAW, ADM 110 Native affairs: annual reports 1915. Sub-file contains memorandum to military magistrates in 1917 that the secretary for the protectorate was not averse to the imposition of lashes on first-time stock theft offenders. Another sub-file in the same batch contains information on the indentureship of children as labourers to various soldiers and farmers.
[41] NNAW, BWI 440, C III, *Register für Kriegsgefangene.*
[42] NNAW, ADM 83, Okahandja Native affairs, Settler complaints of natives squatting on the farm Oviakondua.

much may be true, but the truth is also that, in comparison to the other provinces of South Africa, the Cape Liberal tradition was the most colour-blind and racially tolerant (in the nineteenth-century sense of Afrikaner vs English) political tradition in the sub-continent. One of the tradition's prime spokesmen was Senator Theo L. Schreiner who, like his more illustrious sister, believed in the equality and rights of all women and men. Speaking in the South African senate in Cape Town, shortly after the South African invasion, Schreiner informed his honourable colleagues that, merely because Germany had defeated the Herero and taken their land, this did not mean that they, as the new victors, need do the same:

> The Hereros are not an agricultural people but a pastoral people living by cattle raising, and they need sufficient grazing ground. I think that is only right and just. We are out to do justice to all nations, regardless, as the Right Honourable Prime Minister said in London before leaving, of colour or race, therefore do not let us think that because the German nation destroyed 70,000 of these Hereros, that it is right that we should take the land which was really theirs and give it out in farms to white people.[43]

Similarly, within the South African armed forces that invaded the territory, there were those who genuinely wanted to improve the lot of their fellow men. Associated with this, there was a genuine horror at what had occurred in the Herero–German war, a horror which became all the more manifest when files of the German administration, which extensively detailed all manner of abuses, were captured by the incoming troops.[44] Similarly the incoming administrators were influenced by what they came across in their new positions. The awe at what had happened comes across in some of the archival texts. The new magistrate of Okahandja noted that the town had been 'the great place of the Herero people', yet 'nothing remains of their great stadt'. In Windhoek the Officer in Charge of Native Affairs stumbled upon the unmarked mass graves of Herero POWs to the north-east of the railway station. 'This burial ground is unfenced and a common traffic ground for persons and animals; a golf green has been built on a portion of it . . . would it be possible to have this site enclosed with a wire fence please?'[45] Furthermore during the South African invasion, African transport riders and scouts who were captured by German troops were tortured, mutilated and summarily executed: 'Some had one eye scooped out, some had their ears cut off, and others were castrated.'[46] The treatment meted

[43] NNAW, ADM 156, Native Reserves, Speech of Senator Theo L. Schreiner in the senate in the debate on the question of the second reading of the treaty of peace and South West Africa mandate bill, 17 September 1919. Schreiner followed up his pleas with personal letters to the then administrator of SWA, Sir Howard Gorges.

[44] Of late it has been claimed that the infamous 'Blue Book' which detailed the treatment of Africans in GSWA was little more than a piece of propaganda put about to further South Africa's territorial ambitions and Britain's position at the negotiating table. Granted that the book was used to strengthen Britain's position vis-a-vis Germany, it must however be borne in mind that the bulk of the evidence contained in the 'Blue Book' is little more than the literal translation of German texts published at the time which were the findings of a German commission of inquiry into the effects of corporal punishment. NNAW, ADM 255, *Report on the Natives of SWA and their treatment by Germany, Prepared in the Administrator's office Windhuk South-west Africa January 1918.*

[45] NNAW, NAW 15, O.C. Native Affairs in Windhuk, 25/3/19, to the Secretary for the Protectorate. The eventual outcome of the case was that the graves were allowed to be forgotten and to this day have been abandoned.

[46] Albert Grundlingh, *Fighting Their Own War: South African Blacks and the First World War* (Johannesburg 1987), p. 87.

out by the German military to all South African non-white prisoners of war undoubtedly did little to alleviate the horror felt by the incoming forces.[47]

With the example of what had existed before and with the hope and belief that they could create a more just administration, liberal elements in the new colonial government of Namibia attempted to develop a new 'Native' policy. In April of 1916 some of the German laws regarding the Native population were amended. Henceforth the compulsory registration of all Africans above the age of seven was scrapped, as was the enforced carrying of the brass pass badges bearing a registration number and embossed with the Imperial German crown. Instead, a new pass system was introduced for all males above the age of fourteen and women living in urban areas. The new system of passes also allowed for the exemption of Africans from compulsory employment, and implicitly accepted the ownership of stock by Africans.[48] In August 1916, a year after the German surrender, the new administration issued a memorandum which dealt with Native affairs. The memorandum dealt with:

(a) the laws affecting the Native Population in the Protectorate of South West Africa;

(b) the practice followed by the present Administration in carrying out the provisions of these laws; and

(c) the Native Policy, generally, of the Protectorate Administration.

The memorandum noted that during the German administration,

> The right or authority delegated to certain officials to flog or chain Natives for certain offences were indulged in to the extreme by practically every member of the Police Force in the most trivial cases of complaint by Masters, whilst assaults upon women by these very guardians of the peace, and by members of the European population, were numerous, and as a rule went unpunished.

The memorandum continued by noting that Africans had had no form of redress, and that it was this that had made them 'disinclined to work for German masters'. Instead a new series of Master and Servant laws were to be introduced, and

> The Master should be made to realize that a Native, as much as a European, is entitled to the protection of the Laws of the country from assaults upon his person, and attempts to defraud him of his just dues under his contract, and that no individual whatsoever, except a Magistrate, is allowed to mete out punishment.

However well intentioned this may have sounded, the object was still the same, the African was to be a labourer, and a suitably submissive well-mannered one at that:

> It should be impressed on the Native that while our officers give protection to all, and will assist every Native to secure for him fair treatment and fair wages, it is incumbent upon him to carry out his service in proper manner to the best of his ability, *and to be obedient and respectful.*[49]

---

[47] H.E. Lenssen, *Chronik von Deutsch-Südwestafrika, 1883–1915*, fourth edition (Windhoek 1994), pp. 218–19.

[48] NNAW, ADM 43, Draft of 'Protectorate Laws in regard to Registration and Control of Natives' sent by J.F. Herbst, Deputy Secretary for the Protectorate, to the Secretary for Native Affairs in Cape Town, 26/4/16.

[49] NNAW, ADM 43, Native Affairs Memorandum, Administrator's office, Windhoek, 3/8/16.

Police officers were encouraged to 'acquaint themselves with the conditions of the labour market in their districts so as to be able to advise Natives where employment can be found', but, 'on no account can Natives be forced to take service with masters indicated by the police, against their will. They must be allowed to select their own masters.'[50]

However well-intentioned the new paternalistic legislation may have been, the implementation of the new rule of law was hampered by bureaucratic ineptitude, and the attitudes of those employed to enforce it.[51] As the new military magistrate in Okahandja put it: 'When I assumed duty here at the latter end of 1915 the position was chaotic. NO records of any value had been kept since our occupation. The German records were lying about in sheds and outbuildings and had been tossed about at the will of anyone who chanced to pass.'[52] Added to the chaotic condition of his new administration's records, the military magistrate of Okahandja had to rely on soldiers, to enforce his legislation, who had not the slightest inkling as to the rights of the people they were supposed to be administering. The assault on the Herero chief, Traugott Maharero, in Okahandja in 1918, by members of the new administration illustrated the need for adequate administrators.

In 1916 Traugott Maharero, one of the few direct family members of Samuel Maharero still resident in Namibia, had been officially recognized by the new South African administration as a headman in Okohandja.[53] Others clearly believed that the native, irrespective of his standing, should know his place to be subservient to theirs. On a winter's afternoon in 1918, troopers Labuschagnie and van Rensburg entered the Okahandja location, ostensibly 'to see if there were any natives without passes'. The troopers came upon Traugott Maharero and his councillors. In a statement Traugott described what happened:

> I was lying down on the ground at the time next to my hut talking to some people. As the policeman asked me for my pass he kicked me with his booted foot and said I must shew him my pass. He said: 'Stan op [sic], where is your pass'. Headman Goddard of Ovitoto who was with me at once said to the policeman that that [sic] is Traugott, he does not carry a pass. I then told the policeman he must go to the Magistrate and see him about me as I did not have a pass. The policeman kicked me from behind when I was lying down. I at once assumed a sitting position and he then kicked me again.[54]

For his part, a rather surprised, not to say indignant, trooper Labuschagnie stated:

> I did not kick this boy [at this stage Traugott was at least forty years of age] at all, he did not even get up when I asked him for his pass, and was very impertinent. Most of the natives here show some respect towards the Police, they stand up when they are spoken to, this native did not even trouble to get up when I spoke to him and simply ignored me. This is the first time a native reported me. I never had trouble in dealing with natives. This native had no reason for reporting me as I did not kick or do him an injustice in any way.[55]

[50] Ibid., p. 6.
[51] In a sense events in Namibia forshadowed the collapse of 'sympathetic paternalism' in South Africa. Dubow, *Racial Segregation*, pp. 107–8.
[52] NNAW, ADM 106, Annual report 1916, military magistrate's Office Okahandja 2/1/17.
[53] NNAW, SWAA 2082, Native Chiefs and Headmen Okahandja, 22/6/16.
[54] NNAW, ADM 44, Statement by Traugott Maharero, Okahandja 8/8/18. Transcribed as is.
[55] NNAW, ADM 44, Statement by Caspar Hendrik Labuschagnie, 9/8/18. Transcribed as is.

Not surprisingly fellow trooper, Hendrik Jacobus Uys Janse van Rensburg, supported Labuschagnie's statement. According to van Rensburg, trooper Labuschagnie merely 'went up to him [Traugott] and stirred him with his foot', and besides Traugott had 'replied in a very sullen and disrespectful manner' clearly not becoming of a 'Boy'.[56] With hindsight one is hardly surprised that trooper Labuschagnie was not disciplined. However, one is surprised to learn that the incident was used to villify Traugott. Lieutenant Liebenberg, the trooper's commanding officer, in dealing with the case concluded:

> It is quite clear that Traugott is hardly fit to be respected as [a headman]. By his behaviour (according to his own statement) he plainly shows that he does not respect a white man, and did not even think it necessary to get up when he was spoken to by the Police. As native chief he should be more respectful towards white people and at all times be an example to other natives.[57]

Following the assault on Traugott, and others like it, Gorges, as administrator of SWA, and Swart, the magistrate in Okahandja, complained about the quality of the men that they had in their employ.[58] Though true concern for the human condition may have influenced their position, it is more likely that their fear that SWA would not be incorporated into the Union of South Africa played a major part in determining Native policy. Gorges, in a letter to the South African prime minister, touched on the abuses of South African soldiers and also disclosed the prime reason why these abuses had to be stopped:

> The present state of affairs cannot continue without involving the Union in difficulties in the future over the administration of this country.
> My fear is that responsible officers of police including also I regret to say Col. de Jager, do not yet realize the need for the closest adherence to my standing instructions on the treatment of natives in this country despite the fact that the need for improvement in that respect is being constantly placed before them. Only within the last few weeks has the almost unbelievable argument been placed officially before me by that officer [Col. de Jager], in entering a plea on behalf of a policeman here who punished a native by chaining him up with German punishment chains for a day.
> Nearly a year and a half ago [in] the Sandveld [a] series of assaults on natives was reported by Major Thomas, Magistrate at Okahandja (Magistrate of Britstown in the Union). The reply of the superiors of the men concerned (in order to divert attention from the main issue) was a wholly unfounded personal attack on Major Thomas . . . the attack was unwarranted, and to this day nothing has been done to bring the offenders to book. With this sort of thing going on it is not to be wondered at that such conduct is repeated in out of the way places like Witvlei. Stoop is not an isolated offender. Cases have also occurred recently at Gibeon and Kalkfeld.
> I am unfortunately yet without precise information as to the disposal and form of government to be provided for this country when peace is signed. I do, however, assume that the speeches delivered at the Allied Conference in Paris give a very fair indication of what the intentions of the British and Allied governments are in respect both of the country and its native inhabitants. Great use was made in Paris of the Blue Book compiled here under my directions dealing with the ill-treatment of the Hereros and other tribes of this country by the Germans and the solemn declaration

---

[56] NNAW, ADM 44, Statement by Hendrik Jacobus Uys Janse van Rensburg, 9/8/18, Okahandja.
[57] NNAW, ADM 44, Liebenburg, O.C. Det 2nd M.C. Police District No. 3, Okahandja, 9/8/18, to Military Magistrate Okahandja.
[58] NNAW, ADM 44, Swart, Magistrate Okahandja, 9/3/20, to the Secretary for the Protectorate, Windhuk.

was made that the care of these helpless and undeveloped peoples is to be one of the primary duties of the League of Nations and that the custody and tutelage of these peoples is to be given to a state which has shewn that it can exercise a conscience in the matter.

It is our sincere desire that the control of this country will for all time shortly pass completely into the hands of the Union but whether the transfer will be effected without dissentient voices amongst the natives will depend entirely on the quality of the officials sent here to represent the Union. Chains and the liberal use of the *sjambok* [rawhide whip] by the Police will clearly not secure that clean sheet which I am so anxious to present when the existing Military occupation of this country comes to an end.[59]

Though the new administration used the issue of German native policy to further its own ends, there were, following the South African invasion, concrete improvements in the standard of living of Herero in the territory.[60] In theory, Africans now had access to the rule of law, were allowed to own cattle, seek their own employers, be exempted from employment and live on crown lands. As a whole the differing strands of thought, between paternalistic liberals and settler interests, which made up the new administration's approach to Native affairs, formed the field within which Herero had to operate and settlers could hope to find a sympathetic ear for their complaints. One specific aspect of this new policy was the creation of Native Reserves.

New reserves

When South African armies invaded Namibia in 1915, the Herero had no rights to land or cattle. By the time South Africa was granted Namibia as a mandated territory in 1921, the Herero lived in reserves and had extensive cattle herds. This section, by paying particular attention to developments in the former polities of Omaruru and Okahandja, details the process by which Herero reacquired rights to the land, albeit in the form of reserves, and seeks to show how Herero politics and society developed during this period of time.

The granting of reserves to the Herero by the new administration was a victory for the liberals and the Herero, who had forced the administration to accept the fait accompli of Herero in occupation of land and cattle. The new administration had certainly not intended granting reserves to the Herero, neither had it intended that the Herero regroup as an independent polity. Indeed in a personal letter to senator Theo L. Schreiner, Sir Howard Gorges, the South African administrator of SWA, had said as much:

Seeing that the whole of Hereroland was confiscated by the Germans and cut up into farms and is now settled by Europeans it would be an impossible project, much as one feels for this unfortunate tribe, to place them back on their tribal lands. The effect of the German action has been to break up the Hereros into families and they

---

[59] NNAW, ADM 44, Administrator Gorges in Windhoek, 8/4/19, to Prime Minister, Union of South Africa.
[60] In a letter to Smuts, 9/6/18, Gorges wrote that he had ordered his magistrates 'to do their utmost to suppress any attempts of the ill-treatment of the natives pointing out that a clean record in this matter was essential if we wanted to use the German maltreatment of the natives as a reason for keeping this country'. Cited in S.J. Schoeman, *Suidwes-Afrika onder militêre bestuur 1915–1920*, MA UNISA 1975, p. 86.

now occupy broadly, in the local scheme of things, much the same place economically as do the natives one finds all over the non-native districts of the Cape Province. They work now where they find the conditions suit them best and are under no form of tribal jurisdiction or control. *To restore the Herero Chiefs to the positions they used to hold or to collect the tribe (assuming that the individual members would be willing to submit to such a process) in a reserve would, I fear, completely disorganise industry in this country and have gravely unsettling effects.*[61]

However, in a process that developed from illegal squatting, to squatting and grazing licences, through to grazing reserves, a series of African reserves were established in the territory prior to 1921.

Immediately following the invasion of South African forces into Namibia, Herero left their former employers and settled on unoccupied land in the vicinity of their former settlements. Here they commenced farming and a life independent of the settlers. The extent of this resettlement was such that the new administration, in attempting to keep track of its subjects, and in the interests of its revenues, began selling squatting licences to Herero thus settled. An aspect of squatting was 'Kaffir-farming', that is, the leasing of farms to Africans living there, and/or allowing farms to be managed by Africans. This appears to have been particularly prevalent in the Omaruru district. In December of 1916 the military magistrate in Omaruru suggested that action be taken against the practice and that he be allowed to 'insist on all absentee farmers or lessees having responsible white managers living on their farms'. This, it was felt, would assist in alleviation of the poor white problem.[62] Squatters were blamed for rustling and poaching, and it was felt that on government reserves better control could be maintained on the activities of the Herero.[63]

In September 1916 the first grazing reserves were established on the crown lands at Orumba, Okatumba, Fürstenwalde and Aukaigas in the Windhoek district, not only because this was an area of Herero concentration, but because this was also an area, near to Windhoek, where the new administration could exercise its authority. Reserves were also established for the benefit of large commercial companies, such as the Deutsche Farm Gesellschaft. For the DFG a grazing reserve of 12,000 hectares was set aside at Neuheusis in 1916.[64] In 1917 further grazing reserves were created in the districts of Omaruru, Karibib and Keetmanshoop.

Officially the grazing reserves 'produced a marked impression on the native mind, rendering them more settled and inclined to take up voluntary service, feeling that in their absence their sole possession stock will be cared for and protected'.[65] It was with these considerations in mind that, in 1920, it was decided to allocate crown lands for Native Reserves in a more deliberate manner. The Transvaal Crown Land Disposal Ordinances of 1903 and 1906

[61] NNAW, ADM 156, File No. W. 36, Native Reserves, letter Gorges in Windhoek, 25/11/19, to Theo L. Schreiner.

[62] NNAW, ADM 43, T.L. O'Reilly, Military Magistrate, Omaruru, 20/11/16, to Secretary for the Protectorate, Windhoek. The writings in the margin of this letter indicate that Herbst, as Secretary for the Protectorate, was sympathetic to O'Reilly's suggestions and asked for the existing legislation to be checked for possible implementation of this plan.

[63] NNAW, ADM 43, T.L. O'Reilly, Military Magistrate, Omaruru, 20/11/16, to Secretary for the Protectorate, Windhoek.

[64] NNAW, ADM 43, Bowker in Windhoek, 15/1/17, to Secretary for the Protectorate.

[65] S.J. Schoeman, *Militêre*, p. 96, citing Report on Native administration, 1916, p. 4.

were implemented in Namibia as proclamations 13 and 54 of 1920. This allowed the administrator greater freedom of action in allocating crownlands for Native Reserves.[66]

Otjohorongo Herero Reserve

The case of the establishment of Otjohorongo Herero Reserve near Omaruru clearly illustrates that the incoming South African administration, in attempting to gain the initiative and control of Herero affairs, found itself, in the face of pressure from the Herero, forced to accede to Herero demands for land.

In early 1917, Major T.L. O'Reilly, the magistrate for Omaruru, referred to the 'astonishing' amounts of stock held by Africans in the district. Indeed in 1916 no less than forty exemptions from labour had been granted in the district.[67] A short while previously he had written to his superiors complaining that Herero were squatting on unoccupied farms and engaged in poaching, theft and the practice of 'Kaffir-Farming'. In reply, O'Reilly's superiors ordered him to 'have the Native squatters . . . removed to the Native reserve or place them in employment'.[68] O'Reilly was a cautious man. He did not embarrass his superiors by informing them that there was no reserve to remove the Herero to. A short while later, though, O'Reilly was approached by a Herero delegation, which counted Daniel Kariko, who had returned to Namibia at the time of the South African invasion, Moses Mbandjo, Christof Katjiume, Gerhard Zeraua – that is surviving members of the former Herero elite of the Omaruru polity – and others amongst its ranks. The delegation came 'asking for farms, where we can stay to live, with our Children, for the blind and crippled people and people in work'. The Herero were well acquainted with the fears, entertained by the Magistrate, settlers and administration alike, of the Herero as parasitic, work-shy slackers, and they clearly sought to allay these fears by including the following requests in their text:

> We want to take all our stock to the farm appointed by you, also the stock of the people in the service of the whites, so that we need not trouble the white people on their farms with our stock. Our stock will stay on the farm, it is not to say that we want to leave our services [employment] and stay on the farm.

Daniel Kariko and his colleagues knew exactly what it was that the new administration expected of the 'Native' – obedient stock-free labour – and in their text they included the key to this treasure. After having named a number of possible farms, and having in passing informed on a German settler illegally occupying a farm, the delegation concluded:

> We have all come to agreement, that is why we are asking the big chief for this permission, and the big chief to assist us in this matter, so that if we go to farms searching for work that we need not take all our stock with us. When we go searching for work with all our stock it is very difficult. That is the reason why plenty of us cannot obtain work from the white people on farms because they say we cannot

---

[66] S.J. Schoeman, *Militêre*, p. 96.
[67] NNAW, ADM 106, Annual report 1916.
[68] ADM 43, Herbst Secretary for the Protectorate in Windhoek, 16/2/17, to the Military Magistrate Omaruru.

engage people with plenty of stock in our service. Therefore most of the people that can work has [*sic*] a lot of stock.[69]

Kariko and his colleagues succeeded in their plan. Within a day of having received their petition, O'Reilly completed and sent off a detailed four-page letter to the secretary of the Protectorate. O'Reilly was sympathetic to the request and fully endorsed the petition, even going to the extent of including a little piece of historical justification:

> The Berg Damaras here have a very large Reserve on the Omaruru river at Okombahe. As you are aware, this area was allotted to the Berg Damaras in former times, by the Herero Chiefs, who were then masters here. The fortunes of war have now left the Hereros without any ground at all, while their former slaves and subjects, the Berg Damaras, still retain the excellent Reserve. This fact is a source of much heartburning and envy on the part of the proud Hereros who still regard the Berg Damaras with contempt.[70]

It is clear that Daniel Kariko, the former *Omuhona* of Okombahe, who had been removed from power by Theodor Leutwein twenty years previously, had got through to Major O'Reilly. After having touched on the Union government's commitment to segregation in South Africa, the near certainty that SWA would become part of the Union, and thus that segregation would be implemented in SWA, O'Reilly referred once more to the petition:

> To come to the petition itself, there is nothing unreasonable in it . . . When one considers their past history and treatment, it will, I think, be readily conceded that common justice necessitates the granting to them of some small corner of our vast area which they call their own, and fairness likewise suggests that they, a prouder and an infinitely more superior tribe, should, at any rate, not be allowed to remain in a worse position than the Berg Damaras.
>
> It is also obvious that a Reserve of this kind will conduce towards better Police control, less friction with white farmers over private stock grazing, less indigency, and that sense of having been treated fairly which, in the Native mind, always tends to make better and more honest servants. At the present time, the Herero with stock of his own is in an unenviable position; he is dependent entirely on the tender mercies of the German farmer, who takes advantage of him as far as he can. At Okombahe the Berg Damaras keep all their stock. The old men and women and the children tend the stock and cultivate the gardens while the young men go to work on the farms. They work better and are on the average more willing than the Herero, simply because there is behind that labour a feeling of quasi independence, the knowledge of a 'Home' to return to occasionally for a rest, where the 'old folks' are living and where the German master cannot dictate and domineer.[71]

O'Reilly was impressed by the petition, and realized that he may have seemed a little too enthusiastic: 'You will pardon me for somewhat getting off the point, but I feel rather strongly on the native question as a whole and think we, in

---

[69] NNAW, SWAA 1140, Native Reserves Omaruru, petition, 17/4/17, presented by Moses Mbuaandjou; Daniel Kariko; Christof Katjimuine; Kavikunino Turitjo; Elia Riatjama; Gebhard Katjimuine; Gottlieb Uapuruapi; Gerhard Zeraua; Gottfrid Ndjiharine [Tjiharine]; Samuel Kariko; Alexander Kakara; Jacobus Nguazireko; Josua Kaumbi; Paulus Tjiseua; Erastus Katjizenkosengo; Alfred Katjimuine; Tjeepi Kaiminia; Simeon Kuzeeko.
[70] NNAW, SWAA 1140, O'Reilly in Omaruru, 18/4/17, to Secretary for the Protectorate, Windhuk.
[71] NNAW, SWAA 1140, O'Reilly in Omaruru, 18/4/17, to Secretary for the Protectorate, Windhuk. O'Reilly's view regarding the creation of reserves reflected the ideas of J.H. Pim, a well-known liberal thinker on 'Native Affairs' at the time in South Africa. See, Dubow, *Racial Segregation*, pp. 23–7.

this protectorate, can do much towards helping to solve some of its difficulties owing to the very novel conditions of the country.'[72] The magistrate need not have worried about his enthusiasm for J.F. Herbst, the Secretary for the Protectorate, had no hesitation in granting permission to O'Reilly and 'a few of the leading Hereros' to seek out a suitable locality.[73]

Initially O'Reilly and his companions had hoped to establish a reserve on the banks of the Ugab river. For a variety of reasons though, this plan was rejected, one of the prime reasons being 'the fact that the Hereros who accompanied me . . . were terrified at the idea of being placed on neighbourly terms with lions'. However, a suitable stretch of land was found in the vicinity of the old German police station at Otjihorongo. One of the prime motivations for choosing this locality was the fact that it was surrounded by 'unsurveyed Government ground, and it [was] far enough away from the nearest farmers to obviate friction with the natives'. Furthermore, 'the Herero headmen who accompanied [O'Reilly] were very satisfied with this area, and consider[ed] the veld good and the water sufficient'.[74]

In early September 1917 J.F. Herbst, the secretary for the protectorate, wrote to O'Reilly to inform him that the administrator had 'approved of the selection of the site inspected and recommended by you'. Permission was granted to create a Herero reserve subject to the following conditions:

1. That only natives with exemption certificates, old men and women unfit for labour, the herds of men at work whose cattle will graze on the reserve, be allowed a residence there.

2. That the usual grazing fees be paid for all cattle grazed on this reserve.[75]

O'Reilly's ideas on solving the poor white problem involved ensuring the compulsory appointment of white farm managers on all farms; in keeping with this policy he recommended that his former interpreter, Dixon, a son of the trading family who had first arrived in the 1840s, be offered the position of 'Superintendent' of the reserve. It was envisaged that 'in addition to his duties as Superintendent' Dixon 'could act as a Game warden, and probably surreptitious hunting . . . will then be discovered'.[76] In early 1918, less than a year after Kariko and his colleagues had submitted their petition, the administrator of SWA appointed Dixon, as the superintendent, and Christof Katjiume (one of the petitioners), as the headman of the Otjohorongo Native Reserve, the first official Native Reserve to be established under the new administration in SWA.[77]

The establishment of the Otjohorongo Reserve details a number of aspects that need to be looked at in turn. Through sheer force of numbers and presence

---

[72] NNAW, SWAA 1140, O'Reilly in Omaruru, 18/4/17, to Secretary for the Protectorate, Windhuk.
[73] NNAW, SWAA 1140, Herbst in Windhoek, 4/5/17, to Military Magistrate Omaruru.
[74] NNAW, SWAA 1140, O'Reilly in Omaruru, 23/8/17, to Secretary for the Protectorate.
[75] NNAW, SWAA 1140, J.F. Herbst, Secretary for the Protectorate in Windhoek, 7/9/17, to Military Magistrate Omaruru.
[76] NNAW, SWAA 1140, Military Magistrate in Omaruru, 29/12/17, to Secretary for the Protectorate.
[77] NNAW, SWAA 1142, A.158/21 Native Reserves Otjohorongo Omaruru, Administrator's office in Windhoek, 22/2/18, to Military Magistrate Omaruru. Even though Dixon was to be appointed superintendent of Otjohorongo and Christof Katsimune was to be appointed headman of the reserve, it is not surprising that in oral testimony Daniel Kariko is credited with having established the reserve.

on the land, the gathered Herero were able to force the administration to change. Failure on the part of the administration would merely have led to an increase in the number of squatters, herding stock and 'Kaffir-farming' on settler farms. The Herero were able to influence the manner in which the administration brought about its change in policy. The Herero were able to do this for the simple reason that they knew how to approach and manipulate the administration. This was particularly true of Daniel Kariko, who, through his extensive sojourn in South Africa, was well-acquainted with the whims of South African administrators. The case of Otjohorongo also indicates the extent to which decisions regarding 'Native Affairs' were heavily dependent on the personal views of the new administrators. Once the Herero were able to convince O'Reilly of the validity of their needs, they were effectively assured of their reserve. In the aftermath of the German administration, the Herero made use of the inconsistent approach of the new administration, with regard to 'Native Afairs', to improve their well-being.

Orumbo

The establishment of Herero reserves was an attempt by the new South African administration to contain and control the Herero. In the event they were simply overwhelmed by the sheer number of Herero who flocked into the newly established reserves. The hard-handed reaction of the South African administrators served only to further radicalize the situation and aid the further development of centralized Herero leadership. This process is well illustrated by events in the Orumbo Reserve near Windhoek.

Immediately following the South African invasion, African stock keepers began acquiring cattle and 'squatting' on the lands surrounding Windhoek. Stock returns for August 1916 show that, in little more than a year after the German defeat, Africans living in the Windhoek district had acquired more than a thousand head of cattle, 14,000 goats, 3000 sheep, and a fair number of horses and donkeys.[78] Though grazing and squatting fees were collected for this stock, it was clear the new administration had no intention of allowing the situation to persist:

> It is however felt . . . that were it possible to in some degree concentrate this stock at centralised points two useful purposes would be served: I. Large areas of Government Grazing ground would be reserved for Government stock which at present are being overrun by native stock. Secondly there would be less difficulty in controlling the movement of native stock and the collection of fees payable would in large measure be simplified and a closer check kept on squatting generally.[79]

South African officers, accompanied by three 'headmen' drawn from the Damara, Herero and Nama communities of Windhoek, were sent to investigate lands to the east and west of Windhoek, with the intention of finding territory suitable for the establishment of reserves.[80] In September of 1916, partly in

[78] NNAW, ADM 85, Native Reserves, General Windhoek District, Native Stock Census Windhoek Cattle Posts, August 1916.
[79] NNAW, NAW 12, Officer Commanding Native Affairs in Windhuk, 26/5/16, to Deputy Secretary for the Protectorate.
[80] NNAW, ADM 85, Native Reserves General, Windhoek district, Bowker, Report on general conditions of section of country inspected, Windhoek 10/7/16.

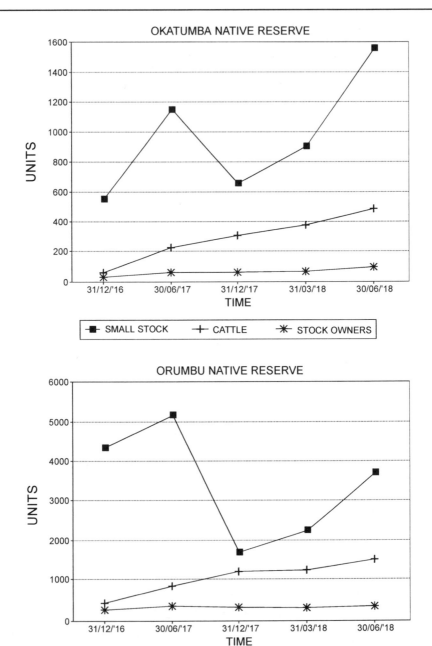

Figure 7.1: Graphs showing the relationship between stock and stock owners over time in Okatumba and Orumbo reserves

response to settler complaints and African realities, the new administration reserved the farms Orumbo, Okatumba, Aukaigas and Fürstenwalde as Native grazing reserves.[81]

Due to the crowded conditions and the constant harassment of stock, serious diseases had broken out amongst Herero livestock, prior to the establishment of the reserves. In the last seven months of 1916, no less than 1500 head of small stock were lost to 'scab' alone. Following the reservation of the farms, stock was rounded up and dipped at Aukeigas before being allocated to one of the four reserves. The new administration was intent on pursuing a policy of segregation. In line with this, Herero and Damara were to be separated. Aukeigas and Fürstenwalde were earmarked for Damara settlement and Orumbo for Herero settlement.[82] By the end of 1916 5867 small stock belonging to Herero, which had been ranging on the Windhoek commonage and the farms Oneama and Aukeigas, had been dipped and were being concentrated at Orumbo. Apart from the small stock no less than 500 head of cattle had also been concentrated at Orumba and Okatumba. Concomitant to the establishment of the grazing reserves, grazing licences were sold at 3d for ten small stock and 3d per head of horned cattle, horses, mules and donkeys. The charges levied were considerably less than those which had been charged by farmers on whose land Herero stock had previously grazed. The grazing licences were introduced to counter squatting, encourage settlement on the reserves and, more importantly, to force people to enter into wage labour. In a year and a half 1616 licences were sold. It is necessary to bear in mind that the reserves were also constructed to facilitate the removal of indigents from the urban centres. Or as the budget-conscious annual report on Native Affairs for Windhoek in 1916 put it:

> There are at present 50 indigents in the location being fed at a monthly cost of £14. This expenditure could be reduced considerably by settling these people at Orumbo where they would have use of the milk from the 'Community Cattle' and where they could make gardens, the water supply in the Nosab River being sufficient for that purpose.[83]

Along with the introduction of grazing reserves all manner of measures were introduced to regulate the acquisition and possession of cattle and to ensure the steady supply of labour. A headman was appointed at Orumbo. Branding irons were bought on government loans, thereby facilitating rights to ownership and state taxation purposes. Those men in possession of more than fifty head of small stock, or ten head of cattle, could, upon payment of 10/-, be granted labour-exemption certificates.[84] In order to further reduce squatting, as well

---

[81] In the 1950s people living at Aukeigas were forced to leave in terms of the Group Areas Act. The inhabitants were deported to Damaraland. Their former home was transformed into the Daan Viljoen game park. Following Namibian independence the former inhabitants of Aukeigas and their descendants returned to reclaim their land. Throughout 1992 and 1993 they, along with their herds, squatted along the road that leads from Windhoek to the game park.

[82] NNAW, NAW 10, Capt. Venter, Superintendent of Reserves, in Windhoek, 5/1/19, to the Officer in Charge Native Affairs Windhoek District.

[83] NNAW, ADM 110, Native Affairs General, Annual Reports, Bowker, Officer in charge of Native Affairs, Windhoek, 31/12/16, to Secretary for the Protectorate.

[84] By early March Bowker, who was faced with an influx of no less than 400 pieces of stock a week, was recommending that the exemption certificates be increased up to 100 small stock and 20 large stock. In the interests of fulfilling labour requirements Bowker also advised that 'all able bodied male natives be called upon to give six months of the year to labour independently of their stock possession'. ADM 85, Bowker in Windhoek, 20/3/17, to Secretary for the Protectorate.

as ensure an adequate supply of labour, it was made obligatory that 'a herd be responsible for not less than 100 head of small stock'.[85] Be that as it may, conditions at Omburo were vastly superior to that at Windhoek itself: 'The mortality since arrival at Orumbo is practically nil.'[86] The water supply on the eastern and southern reaches of Orumbo was 'excellent'. It was suggested that boreholes be sunk in the northern sector of the farm, and that if this were to be successful, the farm could carry approximately 12,000 head of small stock.[87] Furthermore, the annual report for 1916 reported that the establishment of Native Grazing Reserves had produced a marked impression on the 'Native mind'. An impression, according to the report, which, most importantly, rendered the African more settled and inclined to take up voluntary service. For, stated the report, the African would know that in his absence his sole possession, stock, would be cared for and protected: 'stimulating their fast expiring ambition to acquire more stock with obvious attendant advantages to the labour market. Money they must have and they realize that through labour alone can they get it.'[88]

In March of 1917 Native Affairs officers were clearly overwhelmed by the number of people and stock flooding into the reserves:

> In many cases where a farm labourer has a large number of stock the farmer either refuses to allow the native to graze his stock on his farm or else charges extortionate fees for grazing which compels the native to resort to the reserves. As a result of this we have stock coming on to the reserves from all parts of the district at the rate of about 400 a week.[89]

A cursory glance at the stock figures for the grazing reserve at Orumbo between December 1916 and June 1918 shows that, though the average number of stock-owners remained constant, the rise in the number of cattle was simply phenomenal. It is clear that small stock were being traded for cattle, and the inverse relationship between small stock sales and cattle acquisition is clearly shown. From the moment the reserve was established Herero exchanged their small stock for cattle. If, for the sake of argument, we accept that a single head of cattle consumes the equivalent of ten head of small stock – they were taxed accordingly – it will be noticed that within a year of the grazing reserves opening, the number of cattle, 1212, or the equivalent of 12,120 head of small stock, had already exceeded the land's grazing capacity, which had been estimated to be at 12,000 head of small stock. The exchange of small stock for cattle and the overall accumulation of stock are mirrored in the grazing reserve at Okatumba. Here, however, the number of stock-owners in the reserve grew four-fold, and this reflects the continued growth of small stock in the reserve. The graphs also reflect that the Herero moved their stock during the rainy season and purchased new stock immediately after the rains.

Already in early 1917, once the true extent of Herero stock ownership had

[85] NNAW, ADM 110, Native Affairs General, Annual Reports, Bowker, Officer in Charge of Native Affairs, Windhoek, 31/12/16, to Secretary for the Protectorate.
[86] Ibid.
[87] Bowker referred to this as the 'Orumbo Water Scheme' and came to determine a major part in the reserves development.
[88] NNAW, ADM 110, Native Affairs General, Annual Reports, Bowker, Officer in charge of Native Affairs, Windhoek, 31/12/16, to Secretary for the Protectorate.
[89] NNAW, ADM 85, Capt. P.J. Venter, Superintendent of Locations, in Windhoek, 8/3/17, to the Officer in Charge Native Affairs, Windhoek.

started to become apparent, Captain Bowker, the officer in charge of Native Affairs in the Windhoek district, had written to the secretary for the Protectorate:

> There are important issues connected with the reserves which it is felt should be brought before you at this juncture and not left in abeyance until a European land settlement scheme may be introduced. It will be apparent . . . that there is not sufficient grazing to accommodate all the native stock possessions of the district. When we arrive at normal weather conditions and the present unusual grass supply is reduced to its average complications will arise and it will again be necessary to revert to the old unsatisfactory condition of affairs by distributing native stock over various Government farms in order to prevent their death by starvation . . . there is only one lasting solution . . . earmark a block of ground sufficient in extent to accommodate native stock for the next 20 years.[90]

Bowker recommended that a further block of farms be reserved for Native grazing. In response to Bowker's request, Captain P.J. Venter, the superintendent of reserves, was dispatched, in true Western style in a tent waggon drawn by fourteen mules, to investigate a series of ten farms to the east of Windhoek.[91] In the conclusion to his report Venter described what had already occurred at Orumbo and Okatumba, the two reserves which had been opened less than a year previously:

> I found the small stock in such poor condition that they are dying off in large numbers daily, dried carcasses can be seen in large numbers on stacks at almost every hut . . . . The farms Orumbo and Okatumba are sadly overstocked, and consequently the grazing is well nigh exhausted and the large stock in poor condition.[92]

To alleviate the stock problems the ten additional farms, investigated by Venter, were reserved for grazing and in September of 1918 a water-boring programme was started. Perhaps a little optimistically Bowker commented on Venter's water-boring programme, 'if he succeeds in finding adequate water at 5 points I think the question of grazing of native stock will be solved for many years to come so far as the Windhuk district is concerned'.[93]

Initially Venter, who was accompanied by ten Herero labourers employed at 10/- per month, attempted to drill for water with hand drills. Within the first week of operations the drilling tower, not having been anchored, fell over. After three months, with a lot of ingenuity, broken screws and borrowed food, Venter reached a depth of 95 feet but no water,[94] added to which the hole had to be abandoned as it was too crooked and bent to allow for further drilling. Not surprisingly Bowker came to the conclusion that, 'looked at in the brightest light I fear the prospect of finding sufficient water on the new proposed reserves

[90] NNAW, ADM 85, Bowker in Windhoek, 19/3/17, to Secretary for the Protectorate.
[91] NNAW, NAW 12, Officer in Charge of Native Affairs in Windhoek, 19/4/17, to the Deputy Assistant Quartermaster-General. At this stage there was a tussle going on between Native Affairs and the Quartermaster-General with regard to the farms Aukeigas and Furstenwalde. In March of 1917 the Deputy Assistant Quartermaster-General had written to the Secretary for the Protectorate suggesting that the farms be used for the grazing of Transport and Remount animals and that the farms be placed under his jurisdiction. Not surprisingly Native Affairs, who were already faced with a severe land shortage, protested vehemently against the suggestion.
[92] NNAW, ADM 85, Venter in Orumbo North, 21/8/17, to the Officer in charge Native Affairs, Windhoek district.
[93] NNAW, ADM 85, Bowker in Windhoek, 15/10/18, to Secretary for the Protectorate.
[94] NNAW, ADM 85, Venter in Windhoek, 3/1/19, to Bowker.

with hand boring machines within a reasonable period of time is poor'.[95] Consequently a request was submitted for a 'steam boring plant' for operation on the reserve. Bowker believed 'that Capt. Venter has a natural aptitude for working with machinery and I have no doubt that with a few days training under an experienced mechanic he will be able to undertake the boring operations'.[96]

Until Venter started working on the drilling machines, Bowker had commented that his work was 'most thorough [and] accurate and reflects much credit on that officer'.[97] Elsewhere Bowker had noted, 'it is with much pleasure that I can report to you that all his work is most thorough . . . his attitude of mind to the native is good, if anything it errs on the side of kindness'.[98] However once the man, with a natural aptitude for machines, began working on the water-drilling programme, his other work collapsed.

From the very beginning of the South African invasion, Herero had begun reacquiring cattle and with that the need for land. Along with the increase in economic power and independence, there was a change in Herero conscious-ness, a willingness, on the part of the Herero, to stand up for their rights. In March 1919, shortly after the steam drilling had begun, a delegation of Herero approached Venter to complain about his orders. Venter had ordered a number of Herero living on the northern boundary of Orumbo to cease watering their stock and planting their crops on the neighbouring farm of Otjivero. The Herero stated that they had already planted and that they would remain where they were. Furthermore they demanded that 'the Government *must* give them additional farms to graze and water their cattle on'. Venter was clearly out of his depth. In a report on the affair, touched by pathos and reflective of his firm paternalistic belief in the civilizing mission, Venter wrote of the affair:

> I . . . explained to them that we are doing our best to get water on their proposed Native Reserve and that if they would only give a helping hand we shall soon have enough water and grazing for their cattle.
>
> Their answer to this was that we shall never get water on the new proposed native reserve, and therefore the Government must make some other arrangements.[99]

Venter granted the delegation permission to lodge their complaints at a higher bureaucratic level, and with that ensured that he would come to bear the brunt of his superior's wrath. For though, strictly speaking, all people were to have access to the rule of law, Venter was meant to act as a doorstop. That is, Venter's role was to prevent the 'Natives from being restless'. Bowker's response, as the officer in charge of Native Affairs in the Windhoek district, was quick, and his retribution merciless and brutal.

In Namibia in 1919, the trees of Orumbo were to be the 'big stick' that Bowker wielded in his 'soft-talking' approach to the Herero of Orumbo. Shortly after the opening of the Orumbo grazing reserve in 1916, Bowker had written:

> Orumbo is a richly wooded farm and the indiscriminate cutting of trees has been

---

[95] NNAW, ADM 85, Bowker in Windhoek, 19/3/19, to Director of Works, Windhoek.
[96] Ibid.
[97] NNAW, ADM 43, Bowker at Okatumba, 15/9/18, to the Secretary for the Protectorate.
[98] NNAW, ADM 85, Bowker in Windhoek, 15/10/18, to Secretary for the Protectorate, Audit of Books and General Inspection of Native Stock Reserves.
[99] NNAW, NAW 12, Superintendent of Reserves, Venter, in Orumbo, 13/3/19, to Officer in Charge Native Affairs. This piece of text was written in Niger, where my wife was employed in a Dutch development project. The sentiments expressed by Venter clearly echo the sentiments expressed in the present by equally paternalistic believers.

strictly forbidden, they may only be cut for building purposes; there is a sufficient quantity of dry wood to meet the cooking requirements of the Natives for a long period.[100]

On the farm Orumbo there was a white thorn forest, probably consisting of camel thorn trees, approximately four to five hundred metres wide and about three kilometres long. When the reserve was opened 'the most explicit orders were issued that this forest was not to be cut'.[101] At the opening of the reserve, special meetings were held to inform the inhabitants of the prohibition. The administration believed that there was sufficient 'hakkies' timber for the construction of buildings, kraals and garden fences, and reserve inhabitants were given permission to cut as much 'hakkies' timber as they needed. However, in 1917, contrary to what Bowker and Venter had ordered, it was observed that some white thorn trees had been cut. Meetings were held to remind the reserve inhabitants of the ban. In April 1919, following the Herero delegation to Venter, which had demanded more land and water, Bowker seized upon the issue of the trees of Orumbo, as an instrument with which to castigate the Herero.

Bowker, irritated by the Herero delegation that had approached Venter, called every man on the reserve to a meeting. There, as he noted in his own words:

> I issued a final warning and told them that if any further cutting took place, I would burn their kraals and garden fences and cause all persons residing in the forest to remove to the main location, and destroy their huts.[102]

Two months later, in July 1919, on a blustery winter's afternoon, Bowker returned to Orumbo and addressed a 'meeting of natives on Orumbo on the subject of their cattle trespassing on neighbouring farms'. It was an address, spoken in true colonial 'nativespeak', laden with the paternalistic ideas of the civilizing mission, and chilling in its implications. In it Bowker reminded his audience of the threats that he had issued two months previously.

> Once I give an order, that order must be carried out. The sooner they understand that the better it will be for their own interests. I am going to show the people today how strong the law is and how far it can reach. It seems to me that you have got the impression that all the strength of the law in the land today lies in the tongue – in talk. You seem to think because there is a change in the law and because the *jambok* [rawhide whip] has been taken away that you can do as you like. There is a stronger law than that of the *jambok* and that law I will show you today. So far as I understand the cattle that were found across the boundary yesterday belong to the people who live near the boundary in the forest . . . since you are such children that you cannot look after yourselves, I must see that there is someone who can look after you – Now – All the natives who are living by the river must come and live in the main location . . . if they wish to build new houses they can get a permit to cut wood from the hak doorns but not wood from the forest by the river. Today is Monday. On Sunday week I shall burn every hut on the river bank – that is 13 days from today. You must move and everything left in your huts on the Sunday appointed will be burnt. I shall not wait for you to finish your new huts, you can live on the veld or visit your friends in the main location . . .
> I dislike punishing. I dislike it so much that I have held back from punishing you

---

[100] NNAW, ADM 110, Native Affairs General, Annual Reports, Bowker, Officer in charge of Native Affairs, Windhoek, 31/12/16, to Secretary for the Protectorate, p. 6.
[101] NNAW, NAW 12, Report on inspection of reserves, 1919.
[102] Ibid.

this long time but you have forced me to punish you. I have no alternative . . . If you will not listen to kindness I shall use cruelty.[103]

Bowker carried out his threat, the huts and gardens were destroyed and burnt. Added to this, Bowker sacked the Herero foreman at Orumbo, Bartholomeus. In sacking Bartholomeus, who until then had been on a government salary, Bowker stated: 'Apparently the man who was foreman here was afraid of you and did as you told him.'[104] This was not what Bowker expected of a headman, and as he later stated: 'Your former headman did as you told him, he did not make you do as he told you. That is no good to me.'[105] In his stead Bowker appointed a Tswana policeman, Cornelius Izaak, 'because I know that he would not be afraid to report them if they did wrong'.[106] What Bowker wanted was grateful, docile Hereros. The forms of representation which were contained in the promise of British rule were a lie. Herero were expected to do as they were told.

The lies, inherent in the language of colonial control, were well illustrated by events surrounding the celebration in Orumbo of Britain's victory in the war against Imperial Germany. Less than a month after Bowker had effectively destroyed the livelihood of a number of people in Orumbo, he once again addressed the inhabitants of Orumbo, this time on the occasion of the signing of the treaty of Versailles. The speech, coming less than a month after Bowker had ordered their gardens and huts to be destroyed, must have sounded hollow, cruel and insulting in the extreme. Dealing with the ending of the war and referring to the Union Jack, Bowker stated:

> This flag now flies in this country in place of the German flag . . . I shall now ask Captain Venter to hoist the flag and as you see it reach the top of the pole you must stand, remove your hats and while Capt. Venter and I stand at the salute, you will give three cheers.[107]

After the raising of the flag (whether or not the audience cheered is not recorded) Bowker informed his audience that they were now all British subjects and subject to British laws.

> I may tell you now while speaking on this subject that you have a great deal to learn, that is all you natives of this protectorate . . . It is the greatest work which men such as Capt. Venter and I have to do in this land – to teach you the meaning of the law. We have both been born and brought up and worked among natives since we were children and *you are without exception the most ill-mannered, worst disciplined and most ungrateful we have ever known.*[108]

Having informed his audience what he thought of them, Bowker proceeded to fulfil his civilizing mission.

> The natives of the Union regard it as a duty when an officer leaves his house in the morning and goes to his office that they stand up and take off their hats. In this country you seem to expect a white officer to walk around you, to get out of your

[103] NNAW, NAW 12, Orumbo 21/7/19, Meeting of Natives on Orumbo on the subject of their cattle trespassing on neighbouring farms.
[104] NNAW, NAW 12, Address of Bowker to Orumbo 21/7/19.
[105] NNAW, NAW 12, Address of Bowker to Orumbo, 1/8/19.
[106] NNAW, ADM 85, Bowker's address to Orumbo delegation in Windhoek, 2/9/19.
[107] NNAW, NAW 12, Text of speech delivered by Bowker at Orumbo, 1/8/19.
[108] Ibid. Emphasis added.

way rather than disturb you. Now on this first day of the new government this is the first lesson I will have you learn. When your officer leaves his house to open his office you will rise and greet him. It is not a great thing to ask. I ask you to respect your superiors, if you do not do so how can you expect your superiors to respect you.[109]

It is hardly surprising that, after their huts had been burnt down, their gardens destroyed and their fences demolished, the Herero of Orumbo had no further faith in Bowker. Less than a month after Bowker's address, a ten-man Herero delegation from Orumbo sought an audience directly with the secretary for the protectorate in Windhoek. The delegation protested against Bowker's actions, and demanded further access to land and water. The delegation was allowed to speak and were spoken to by Bowker, but returned empty-handed. Instead Bowker chose to harangue the delegation as to the correct procedure to be followed when submitting complaints:

> Had Captain Venter . . . refused to issue . . . a pass you were at liberty to come to Windhuk without a pass, he may not refuse you a pass to see the Secretary if you have a complaint against any officer of Native affairs. You should then have come to my office and asked me to arrange an interview with the Secretary. Had I refused you an audience with the Secretary you would have been at liberty to go to him direct. That is the course of procedure in all cases, and you know it.[110]

In his harangue Bowker conveniently forgot that this was exactly the procedure that the Herero had followed. The delegation had gone via the 'chain of command'. They had approached Venter in March at the water-drilling site to seek permission to travel to Windhoek, in April they had spoken to Bowker – who had reacted by burning down their houses and gardens in July – and they had come direct to the secretary for the protectorate in August. By closing off this route of protest, and by the actions he had taken, Bowker had effectively radicalized the relations between the administration and Herero in Orumbo.

Though the secretary for the protectorate supported Bowker's actions, Bowker must have realized how drastic his actions had been. In seeking to deflect blame from himself, Bowker argued that Venter was to blame. Venter, who in March of 1919 had first been approached by a Herero delegation seeking land and water, and who had granted the delegation permission to lay their demands before Bowker, now became the scapegoat, the cause of all the trouble. In a report to the secretary for the protectorate, Bowker wrote:

> I desire here to draw particular attention to the blame attaching to the Superintendent of Reserves in the matter of tree cutting and trespassing. In 1916 I demarcated the location boundaries and instructed the Superintendent to allow building on no other portion of the farm. In 1917 he had allowed several small locations to be built on various other sites, explaining that this was necessary as scab infected stock had to be quarantined. He undertook to remove the quarantine locations as soon as the disease had been eradicated. This however he failed to do and allowed a location as large as the main location to spring up in the white thorn forest. I frankly admit that most of the damage was done while Capt. Venter was away boring for water; but where I consider he is very much to blame and should be severely censured is that firstly he failed on his return to Orumbo to take any steps whatever to prevent a continuance of that most beautiful and valuable forest, and secondly in that he failed to carry out my instructions to remove the natives to the main location after the

[109] NNAW, NAW 12, Text of speech delivered by Bowker at Orumbo, 1/8/19.
[110] NNAW, NAW 85, Bowker address to Orumbo natives in Windhoek, 2/9/19.

eradication of scab. He did not even report the position in respect of tree cutting . . . It is obvious that had Capt. Venter exercised a reasonably strong control there would have been no need for the drastic measures taken by me in July last.[111]

Looking back at Bowker's actions, it would seem that he was consciously intent on worsening the relations that existed between the Herero and the administration. Clearly this was not the case. Bowker had specific ideas as to how 'Natives' and the administration should interact, and when this failed to occur he sought to transform the situation to his ideal. In so doing Bowker unintentionally radicalized the situation. The new-found self-consciousness that the Herero had acquired and the radicalized situation that had emerged are well illustrated by an incident that took place in the winter of 1920. George Baas, a tenant farmer on the farm Okahna near Orumbo Native Reserve, reported that 'the Natives of Orumbo graze and water their cattle day for day month for month at my dams; I have often told those people to keep their cattle away, but it was of no avail'. Finally Baas decided to take the law into his own hands and, as he himself with unintended understatement put it, 'now something more serious has happened'. Together with two labourers Baas 'seized about 600 head of cattle' and drove them towards his homestead. Here they were met by three men and 'some women' who 'drove those cattle away by force'. Baas's labourers had run away and all Baas could do was look on and be confronted by 'those 3 men armed with knob kirries and stones' who told him that if he should 'seize their cattle again they would kill [him]'. On the following day the same herd of cattle, now under the guard of four mounted men and three on foot, were once again driven to Baas's dam.[112]

The Herero reserves were established in an attempt to contain and control the Herero. The resources available to the Herero in the reserves, however, were inadequate. When Herero, acting within the framework of the promises of British rule, approached the new colonial administration to seek improvements and later, following Bowker's actions, redress, they were rebuffed. This rebuff led directly to the further radicalization of Herero vis-a-vis the administration, and an increase in the self-awareness of Herero regarding their true position in the colonial scheme of things.

New ideas and changed attitudes

In 1921 Namibia was granted as a mandated territory to South Africa by the League of Nations. Two years previously, at the signing of the treaty of Versailles, it had already become clear that the country would to all intents and purposes become part of the Union of South Africa. The initial superficial alleviation of oppression had been instituted solely to assure South Africa's rights as a mandatory power. In the years following the South African invasion, the Herero had been able to rebuild a modicum of autonomy vis-a-vis the settlers and the new administration. The realization that the new administration intended continuing a policy supportive of racial inequality and settler interests led to a marked change in the attitude of the Herero, and other Africans, towards South

[111] NNAW, NAW 12, Report on inspection of reserves, 1919.
[112] NNAW, ADM 44, George Baas, Farm Okahna, 19/7/20, to the commissioner of police, Windhoek.

Africa. Once they came to realize that the South African occupation was not to entail the return of their land, they began to organize in opposition to the South African administration.

After 1919, Herero sought ways to express their new-found power and identity within what was becoming an increasingly restrictive atmosphere of a territory governed by settler interests. Indicative of the changed attitudes were the spate of complaints lodged against the police in 1919 and 1920.[113] Magistrates began sending in reports that referred to the changed attitudes to be found amongst the Herero, changed attitudes that did not necessarily imply opposition to the administration, but did imply a sense of growing self-awareness independent of the administration and its activities. The military magistrate of Otjiwarongo summed up the atmosphere in his district at the time in the following manner:

> So far as this district is concerned, cases of absolute refusal to work for masters have been few indeed. I have of late months remarked an increasing sullenness on the part of the Hereros, and an increasing disinclination to accept orders given by the Native affairs Officer, and orders given by myself. This is particularly noticeable in natives who have acquired cattle, but are still in employment. From a fairly close observation of the natives on the farms it is becoming increasingly evident that the Herero has set before him some definite idea of again becoming the dominant native race, and to that end he is straining every nerve to acquire large and small stock, in order that he may again become independent, and relieved of the necessity of working. In the meantime a sort of passive resistance movement, at present confined to doing work as badly as possible, is being initiated. Some of the Exempted natives in this area have lately acquired other natives to work for them as cattle herds.[114]

Similar reports emanated from other districts of the country. Though one must not lose sight of the fact that the magistrates were intent on ensuring a sufficient supply of labour, it is clear that a fairly substantial proportion of the Herero were becoming increasingly able to withdraw themselves out of the labour market, much to the chagrin of the magistrates. With Namibia now to all intents and purposes an integral part of the Union, the excesses of the German period were being conveniently forgotten or not fully comprehended by the officials in the new administration. The proclaimed adherence to the rule of law, irrespective of race, was soon being forgotten in the interests of settler demands for labour. The Native Affairs reports at the time clearly indicate the changed attitudes amongst the colonial officials who were now faced with increasingly self-aware Herero. The Herero had ceased to be victims in need of British protection; instead they had become protagonists in the struggle for labour:

> Klein Windhuk Location too, is a general rendezvous for slackers, as there is no system of control there . . . During the German occupation, I believe natives were not allowed to acquire stock, today we have large numbers who are stock-owners on a big scale, and naturally, they have a very independent spirit. The native with just a few head of cattle considers it infra dig to work. I would suggest that all natives be made to work irrespective of number of stock owned.[115]

[113] See particularly NNAW, ADM 44, *Complaints by Natives Against Police 1919, 567/6*. Report by Administrator Gorges on police violence.
[114] NNAW, ADM 44, Military Magistrate in Otjiwarongo, 9/6/20, to Secretary for the Protectorate.
[115] NNAW, NAW 7, Sub-file Complaints. Native Affairs Windhoek 23/7/20 to magistrate Windhoek.

The initially charitable Herero perceptions of the new South African administration were influenced by the return and reestablishment of Herero chieftains in the territory, some of whom had already lived under South African administration in South Africa. Following the South African occupation of Namibia, Herero living in exile had begun seeking contact with their family members, friends and colleagues living in Namibia. As forms of overt Herero political leadership came to be tolerated by the South African administration, so Herero leadership living in exile sought to influence the course of events in Namibia. In the case of the Omaruru polity, and the Herero who had previously lived around Otjozondjupa, events were influenced in a very direct manner by the immediate return of the Herero chiefs Daniel Kariko and Salatiel Kambazembi from exile in South Africa and southern Angola. In the case of Okahandja, things were different. At the war's end in 1915, Samuel Maharero was living in the northern Transvaal in South Africa. Samuel did not immediately seek to return to Namibia. It is possible that the experiences of exile taught Samuel Maharero that he could not take for granted the support of people he might claim to be his. Indeed, it is probable that Samuel believed that he could not depend on a power base in Namibia, in the way that Daniel Kariko or Salatiel Kambazembi could, because in terms of popular perception he had led his people into a disastrous war. Added to this were the issues of Samuel's age, debts to the Anglo-French company, pride and the knowledge that he would return to Namibia as a poor man. Instead, he sought to influence events by sending his son Friedrich to Namibia. Friedrich's visit was to have profound effects on the further development of Herero history in Namibia.[116]

In July 1920, Friedrich Maharero and eight of his followers, from South Africa and Bechuanaland, requested permission to visit Namibia for a period of nine months.[117] Permission was granted and Friedrich spent the final months of 1920 visiting Keetmanshoop, Windhoek and Okahandja. Missionaries reported that Friedrich was collecting money from his father's followers, so that a farm could be bought for Samuel Maharero in Namibia, to which he could then return.[118] In February 1921 Friedrich Maharero and Hoseah Kutako

---

[116] Friedrich's trip to Namibia was to have a profound impact upon the further development of Herero history in the territory. Friedrich must have been overwhelmed during this trip, in which he was asked to rekindle Maharero's *Okuruo*; to appoint Hosea Kutako as provisional paramount and to provide information as to the whereabouts of countless missing relatives. Mbanderu oral histories report that it was during this time that the green flag of the Mbanderu was started. Sources report that when Mbanderu asked Friedrich as to the whereabouts of their relatives Friedrich replied that they had all disappeared and that as a result they should join forces with the red flag of the Okahandja Herero. The leadership disputes going on in the present between the various Herero leaders are partly due to the fact that, via Friedrich Maharero's legitimation of Hoseah Kutako as Herero chief, people other than those of the house of Tjamuaha have been able to claim rights to the throne. The case of the South African appointee Chief Riaruako is a fine example of this.
[117] NNAW, SWAA 2085, E.H. Goddard Office of the Native Commissioner Nylstroom, 20/7/20, to Secretary for Native Affairs Pretoria.
[118] NNAW, SWAA 432, Translation of letter sent by Irle in Germany in May 1921 to Halbich in Karibib. Irle seems to have been a fairly pessimistic person. Regarding the collection of money by Friedrich Maharero for a farm, his letter continued:

If this is so, then woe to the German farmers, woe to the Germans of those parts in general. There will be bloodshed once more, as in 1904, resulting from the secret rogueries of Samuel Maharero. All of you including the Administrator, know nought of the vengeance (vendettas) of the Hereros. Refer to my book: 'The Hereros'. 'An eye for an eye, a tooth for a tooth' is the duty of retribution, the neglect of which will bring death even to progeny.

appeared in the offices of the officer commanding Native Affairs, Captain Bowker. They requested permission to visit Orumbo Reserve and invited Bowker to be present. Bowker, because he did not have access to a motor-car, claimed to be unable to travel to Orumbo and declined the invitation.[119] If he had, he would have witnessed the ceremony whereby Friedrich Maharero laid his hand on Hoseah Kutako's head and in the name of his father, Samuel Maharero, proclaimed Hoseah Kutako to be his father's regent in Namibia.[120] No colonial officials or missionaries were present at the ceremony in Orumbo. Indeed it was not until after the death of Samuel Maharero that the archival documents began referring to Hoseah as Samuel's regent in the territory. However, henceforth Hoseah Kutako would take a leading role in Namibian politics, a role way in excess of his nominal position as a headman of Windhoek location.

An indication of the changes at hand were provided by events surrounding the visit of Prince Arthur Frederick Patrick Albert of Connaught, Governor-General of the Union of South Africa, to the territory in August of 1922. The protectorate administration, anxious to create a good impression, had arranged for the prince to be greeted by the headmen of the various communities in the territory. In order to ensure that nothing untoward would occur, Native Affairs officers and magistrates scampered across the country to collect and edit the 'addresses' of the various communities. All went well, with the exception of Orumbo Reserve, where Hoseah Kutako had assumed his regency, and Windhoek, where he was headman. The Herero at Orumbo informed the authorities that 'they did not wish to [submit an address] . . . as they relied on the Hereros of Windhoek to do all that was necessary for them'.[121] Though the Herero in Windhoek had submitted a suitably innocuously worded address to the administration, the Native commissioner was warned, by his subordinates, that the Herero of the district intended submitting an as yet unseen petition to the prince during his address. Commenting on the petitioners, the official noted:

> . . . they seem to have lost confidence in the authorities and will not tell anything of their intentions. I am afraid that a lot of trouble emanates from the Negro Improvement Society.[122]

Truppenspieler

As early as 1916 the new administration had begun receiving reports from worried settlers across the country of young men gathering together and marching to and fro. These military men would later become known, condescendingly, as the *Truppenspieler*, or those that play at being soldiers.[123]

---

[119] NNAW, SWAA 2085, OC Native Affairs in Windhoek, 25/2/21, to the secretary. Surprisingly no documents could be found in the archives which detailed the ascendancy of Hoseah to the regency. It would appear that no colonial officials were present during the ceremony in Orumbo.
[120] Werner, *Herero*, pp. 130–1.
[121] NNAW, ADM 156, Addresses Cape Coloured Community, Herero and Ovambanderus, Damaras, Hottentots. R.L. Cope, OC Native Affairs in Windhoek, 3/8/22, to Native Commissioner SWA.
[122] NNAW, ADM 156, R.L. Cope in Windhoek, 22/7/22, to Native Commissioner.
[123] NNAW, SWAA 432 A 50/59 Vol. 1 *Truppenspielers* 1917–38.

*Photo 7.1: Herero honour guard drawn up to meet the train bearing Samuel
Maharero's coffin in Okahandja in 1923*
Source: Archives of the Basler Afrika Bibliographien; Fritz Gaerdes collection

Herero society was highly militarized. From the 1860s onwards, Herero men had been organized into European-style, highly armed, uniformed and mounted military units. The military commanders of these units were generally a chief's principal adviser, and formed an integral part of the polities' *Otjira*. These military units were usually only mobilized in times of trouble. The exception though was Manasse Tjisiseta, the chief of Omaruru, who had fielded a permanent standing army.[124] With the advent of German colonialism in Namibia, numerous Herero were employed as auxiliaries in the German army, and Herero military units fought alongside German forces.[125] Following the Herero–German war, numerous Herero orphans and children were captured and adopted, initially as mascots and servants, later as soldiers, into the German army. These young men grew up and were socialized in the confines of the military. With the defeat of the German forces in 1915, these young men were left leaderless. Their structures of social organization had collapsed. From being powerful functionaries of the colonial state, they became young uninitiated society-less men. In the aftermath of the German defeat, these young men sought to maintain and recreate the structures that had given their lives meaning, power and standing. As propertyless uninitiated young men, employed as wage labourers in the towns and farms of Namibia, they came together to recreate their power. They appropriated the names and titles of their former commanders. They sent hand-written telegrams in German to one another. They issued military passes, pay books, and commands to one another. And, on moonlit nights, they gathered together, to march, talk and dream of the power that could be theirs.

The *Otruppe* were organized into regiments that corresponded with magisterial districts. Regiments were characterized by specific uniforms, designations and names. Thus, the *Otruppe* of Windhoek wore a khaki uniform, those of Keetmanshoop wore whites and those of Lüderitz, khaki tunics and white trousers.[126] The regiments also had different designations. Thus, *Otruppe* of Okahandja were known as an infantry regiment, and those of Windhoek as a machine-gun regiment. The areas under the control of the various *Otruppe* regiments were given new names. Significantly Okahandja was named *Paradies* (paradise) and was headed by the *Kaiser*, a.k.a. Eduard Maharero, the brother of Traugott Maharero.[127]

An initial glance at the documents captured from the *Otruppe* by the South African colonial administration in 1917, presents one with an image of a surreal world, a world in which His Excellency Governor von Deimling, State Secretary Heighler, Treasurer von Ministermann, *Oberstleutnants* Leutwein, Franke and von Estorff; Major Muller and *Hauptmann und Adjudant* Schmetterling von Preusen – i.e. Butterfly of Prussia – correspond with one another in a mixture of German and Herero. Patrol reports, military passes, pay slips, notices of promotion and regimental transfer, written on music paper and the discarded stationery of the German colonial administration, litter the archives. On closer inspection, it becomes clear that the messages refer to collected contribution dues, letters of attestation to other regiments and the payment of fines

---

[124] Otjimbingwe volunteer auxiliaries of Andersson.
[125] See the war against Kahimemua, the installation of Samuel Maharero as paramount chief.
[126] Werner, *Herero*, p. 129.
[127] NNAW, SWAA 432, *Truppenspieler* 1917–18 Vol. 1.

and assistance, out of regimental funds on behalf of regimental members. Information that was of importance to regimental members, such as a magisterial ban on marching, were passed on by circular telegrams.[128] A member of a regiment, travelling through the district of another regiment, and who was able to produce a letter of attestation, *Reisepaß*, from his regiment commander, was guaranteed the support of the regiment he was visiting. Thus in May 1917 a telegram was sent to Lt Col Franke (a.k.a. Erastus) requesting him to pay *Oberleutnant* von Mausbach, who had travelled from Omaruru, the sum of 3/- so that he could continue on his journey to Windhoek. The telegram was sent by Schmetterling von Preusen, *Hauptmann und Adjudant der Ettapenkommando* (a.k.a. Fritz).[129] Effectively, by copying the structures and images of the German military, young Herero men had set up a countrywide support and information network for themselves. A network that extended from Lüderitz and Keetmanshoop in the south, to Gobabis in the east, Tsumeb, Grootfontein and Otjiwarongo in the north, Swakopmund and Omaruru in the west and Okahandja and Windhoek in the centre of the territory.[130] The regiments formed an organization which looked after the welfare of its members, a social structure to replace the society which they did not have or were only marginally part of.

Ideas within the administration were divided with regard to the *Otruppe*, and ranged from outright rejection and demands for the outright banning of the movement to benevolent mocking. Hans Joel, an *Otruppe* commander in Lüderitz, who had asked if he and his colleagues could be 'allowed to play as soldiers i.e. to drill as soldiers in the military', was informed that his application was refused and that 'there are other forms of sport such as football and cricket in which you can indulge without being interfered with'.[131] However apart from these light-hearted exchanges, the administration was clearly worried by the sight of blacks in uniforms. In 1919 shopkeepers wrote to the administration asking whether they were permitted to sell military-style tunics to Africans. At the time there was a debate raging in the administration as to exactly what constituted resistance or opposition to the administration. After much deliberation it was decided that Africans could wear military tunics as long as they did not sport red flashes on their tunics, red flashes being the symbol of *Otjiserandu*, the red flag and the colour of the troops of Maharero.[132] Already at this stage the fear of communist-inspired agitation had developed in Namibia; the outright rejection of the administration of the socialist red flag can only have served to legitimate it further in the eyes of the Herero. It is possible that the idea of the red flag was given greater impetus by Herero who had returned from the mines in South Africa where the socialist movement was gaining

[128] NNAW, SWAA 432, enclosure 11, circular telegram 1/7/16.

[129] NNAW, SWAA 432, See enclosure 4, telegram 5/5/17.

[130] Dag Henrichsen & Gesine Krüger, '"We have been captives long enough, we want to be free": Land, uniforms and politics in the history of Herero during the interwar period', in: *Namibia Under South African Rule* (Windhoek, Oxford 1998) ed. P. Hayes, M. Wallace, J. Silvester & W. Hartmann; & Wolfgang Werner, '"Playing Soldiers": The Truppenspieler Movement among the Herero of Namibia, 1915 to ca. 1945', *Journal of Southern African Studies*, Vol. 16, No. 3, September 1990, pp. 485–502.

[131] NNAW, SWAA 432, Hans Joel in Luderitzbucht, 2/1/24, to the administrator Windhoek, & Harry Drew, for the secretary for SWA in Windhoek, 12/2/24, to Hans Joel.

[132] NNAW, SWAA 1421, Unauthorized use of Uniforms 1919–45, Messrs Binnes and Newman write to the military authorities in 1919 asking if they can sell military-style tunics to blacks.

ground.[133] That is, the power inherent in the symbolism of the socialist revolution was also transferred to the red flag of the *Otjiserandu*, thereby giving it an even greater appeal to legitimacy and universalism.[134] Be that as it may, the militarism inherent in the *Otruppe*, its liberal use of universalistic symbols and its creation of a world that operated independently of the colonial administration, mirrored that of the movement created by Marcus Garvey – the Universal Negro Improvement Association, which swept across southern Africa in the early 1920s.

UNIA

In early 1922, a rather flustered missionary Kuhlmann explained to his superiors that the following words had appeared emblazoned in indelible tar paint on rocks at the side of a road leading into Omaruru:

> Omaruru 5th February 1922. This land belongs to Michael [Tjisiseta]. This land is not yours, it is the property of America and the Herero.[135]

As if this was not dramatic enough, one of the rocks was also adorned with a mural which depicted a hand gripping a flaming heart. The Universal Negro Improvement Association had arrived in Namibia. The conflation of historical claims to the land with images and ideas of the UNIA clearly showed that the millenarian ideas engendered by the UNIA elsewhere in Africa had caught on here as well. The missionaries were quick to claim that the Herero were being 'communistically manipulated' by outside forces operating from within the Herero reserves.[136] But, though the movement had developed amongst immigrant communities in the south of Namibia, by 1922 UNIA had become the main unifying organization amongst the African communities of the territory, and would remain as such until the death of Samuel Maharero in 1923.

In October of 1920, the Universal Negro Improvement Association was introduced to Namibia, when a number of West Africans and West Indians, working in Lüderitz, set about establishing division number 294 of the UNIA. Initially the movement was confined solely to West Africans and West Indians, and reflected their interests.[137] Thus, in articles that appeared in the *Negro World*,

[133] With the red flag of *Otjiserandu* in mind, van Onselen in *New Nineveh* refers to the following particularly tantalizing set of events:

> . . . workers on the Witwatersrand . . . constantly added new symbols, ideas and attitudes to their store of conceptual baggage which they then carried back to the rural areas and redistributed amongst their kinsmen. (p. 40)

With this in mind van Onselen refers to a Morolong 'Kitchen boy' who called himself John Whitesun and was allied to a man named Jesus Christ in Vryburg. In their preaching they 'remembered the rinderpest', and their increasingly radical millenarian message attracted a growing number of supporters who were distinguished by the red cloth badges they wore (p. 40).
[134] On the fear of communist agitators, see the ELCIN, V. 32 Chroniken, Karibib 1922.
[135] ELCIN, VII 23.2, Berichte ans Missionshaus 1910–30, Kuhlmann in Omaruru 20/4/22 to ?. Missionary Kuhlmann devoted most of his letter trying to work out who might have painted the murals.
[136] ELCIN, V. 32 Karibib 1922.
[137] Office bearers in the UNIA had to be able to read and write, and in the context of the UNIA this meant being able to read and write English. The office bearers in Lüderitz were nearly all West Africans or West Indians, the only exceptions being South Africans.

'German Jews' were lambasted for controlling the trade in the black location in Lüderitz.[138] Before long, though, the movement spread amongst the Nama, Damara and Herero communities of the territory.[139]

The driving force behind the UNIA, and its spread into Namibia society as a whole, was Fitzherbert Headly, a West Indian employed as a Chief Stevedore in Lüderitz harbour.[140] In December 1921, whilst on a month's long leave, Headly travelled to Windhoek. Here Headly held meetings with Herero, Nama and Damara leaders. He was a charismatic man and extremely successful in his meetings with the Herero leadership of Windhoek. Consequently, a branch office of the UNIA was established in Windhoek. Hosea Kutako who, a few months previously had been appointed by Samuel Maharero as his successor and representative in Namibia, John Aaron Simon Mungunda – Hosea's brother who had fought for the South Africans in German East Africa – Nikanoor Hoveka – the Ovambanderu headman in Windhoek – along with Headly and a number of other men submitted a new year's greeting to the mayor of Windhoek in January 1922. In it, they announced the establishment of their organization and demanded that the municipality assign them a stand to 'erect a suitable Hall for conducting our meetings in an orderly Manner'.[141]

With its red membership cards, red, green and black rosettes, newspapers, calendars and the promise of far more, the UNIA attracted the attention of the territory's African inhabitants. Needless to say, this attraction was enhanced by the fact that the Herero leaders had granted their allegiance to the movement. Furthermore UNIA members believed that their contribution money would be used to purchase land for Africans.[142] This linked up with Friedrich Maharero's earlier visit to Namibia, during which he had collected money for the purposes of purchasing a farm for his father who wished to return to Namibia.[143] By January 1922 it was claimed that an estimated 500 had become members of the movement in Windhoek.[144] In April 1922 a branch was opened in Swakopmund, and in October 1922 meetings were held in Karibib and Usakos, with the aim of opening further UNIA offices.[145] However,

[138] Fitzherbert Headly, 'A Voice from Lüderitz, Dutch South Africa', in *The Negro World*, 8 October 1921.

[139] NNAW, SWAA 421, Letter written in Nama and translated into Dutch. By the middle of 1921 letters written in Nama urged people to send money to UNIA's head office in New York, this so that Africa could be bought and liberated from slavery, and an African government established in Africa. These letters provide one with some insights into the way in which people believed the world operated.

[140] Fitzherbert Headly arrived in SWA during the German occupation. He spent some time working as a clerk for the Woermann company. Following the South African occupation Headly became employed on the railways. Initially Headly confined himself to promoting the position of his fellow educated UNIA members. However, following mid-1921 Headly became involved in nationalist politics. After the collapse of UNIA he became involved in a trade union. In later life he had a run-in with authorities on account of fish size caught. He remained involved until his death in the early 1950s.

[141] NNAW, SWAA 421, Headly and others in Windhoek, 2/1/22, to His worship the Mayor in council.

[142] NNAW, SWAA 421, Letter in Nama.

[143] NNAW, SWAA 421, translation of letter by missionary Irle in Germany, May 1921, to Halbich.

[144] NNAW, SWAA 421, Scotland[?], manager of Liebig's Extract of Meat Co., Neuheusis, 20/1/22, to Secretary SWA Protectorate.

[145] NNAW, SWAA 421, J.D. Abraham in Swakopmund, 14/4/22, to magistrate in Swakopmund. The magistrate, in response to Abraham's notification, noted that he thought Abraham would 'be best dealt with by being deported'. Schulz in Swakopmund, 18/5/22, to Secretary for

not everybody appears to have been bitten by the bug. Upon his return to Lüderitz in January 1922, Headly addressed a four-page missive to Barnabas, a Herero headman in Windhoek, urging him to:

Fall into line with the UNIA and so do something for yourself get a move on we are awaiting on Africa our Brothers across the Seas are awaiting on you all, now is your time to make a bid for freedom and liberty before it is too late for if we lose this opportunity we are doomed fo another thousand years and that is for life everlasting 'Amen'. So therefore I am making this appeal to you as a reputed Leader of our race to get yourself and that great race of ours the Herrero [sic] Nation to join up into the UNIA and let us go forward and get our freedom.[146]

Similarly the Swartboois, clearly intimidated by what they saw occurring around them and conscious of the wrath of a colonial state scorned, wrote:

During the past years the Monrovia people have gone to Windhoek with their Congress . . . They first of all held discussions with the foremen of the location. Then they called the whole of the people together and spoke to them . . . numbers of people, black as well as yellow, have had themselves entered in the Congress book and pay money for this. Almost all the natives of Windhoek and also of the farms of the district have done this.

Only we men of the Zwartbooi tribe have not registered in this congress book.

And now we pray the Government that we may be freed from the affairs of this congress and to give us a written reply stating the reason why the Government keeps aloof . . . For we do not know whether this congress law is for or against the English [South African] Government and whether the badges these people wear, are Government badges. We therefore approach you so that we may understand all these things, for we do not want to do anything against the Government.

But, by approaching you and asking for information we are guilty in the eyes of the Congress. And we have been threatened that we shall lose the blessings which the advent of the Congress Government will pour out on Africa.[147]

For the Herero, however, UNIA continued to be the vehicle for their ideas and demands. By October of 1922, UNIA in central SWA had become dominated by Herero.[148] When UNIA sought to open offices in Karibib and Usakos, those sent to initiate the movement were Herero, John Hungunda [probably John Mungunda] and Theodor Hanbanue. A month later West Africans, who had initially dominated the movement, lost control of the Windhoek branch of the UNIA to the Herero royals.[149] John Aaron Simon Mungunda, the brother of Hoseah Kutako who had fought in Tanganyika, became president, and Clemens Kapuuo, the man who would succeed Kutako as chief of the Herero in Namibia, became secretary of the Windhoek branch.

Protectorate. It would appear that Abraham's premises were raided by the police in late May 1922, for a number of internal UNIA documents relating to the establishment of a UNIA branch have been filled along with Abraham's papers and stamped 'South-West Africa Police 23 May 1922 Swakopmund'. For Karibib and Usakos see SWAA 421, Letters adressed to the Magistrate Karibib October 1922 by Post commanders in Usakos and Karibib. Interestingly the UNIA members who initiated the establishment of UNIA offices in these two towns were not West African and at least one of them was Herero.

[146] NNAW, SWAA 421, Fitzherbert Headly in Lüderitz, 25/1/22, to Barnabas.
[147] NNAW, SWAA 421, Letter from David Zwartbooi, Izaak Zwartbooi, Petrus Bois, Hieser Hendrik and Timotheus Richter to SWA Protectorate administration. Dated by the Administration Translation Bureau as 20/11/22.
[148] BRMG, 1923, p. 72.
[149] NNAW, SWAA 421, Harry Drew Windhoek, 10/11/22, to Secretary for the Protectorate. Drew refers to the falling out between the West Africans and the Herero.

At the same time the branch was closely linked to Traugott Maharero of Okahandja, who for his part was an officer of the *Otruppe* in Okahandja.[150] To the horror of Rhenish missionaries, Herero graves were visited by UNIA members who poured libation in the name of Marcus Garvey.[151] Thus by late 1922 the UNIA had become integrated into Herero socio-political activity, closely linked to the *Otruppe* and indistinguishable from the Okahandja Herero royals.

UNIA, which was indeed universal, provided structures whereby the Herero could link up with societies and structures beyond the confines of Namibia.[152] In this manner links with the exiled Herero in Bechuanaland and South Africa were strengthened with the aid of UNIA's structures, imagery and rhetoric. The eastern districts of Namibia were influenced by UNIA coming out of western Bechuanaland. Thus in 1922 the Magistrate of Gobabis questioned his colleague in Ghanzi, Bechuanaland:

> At present time there is also some form of agitation going on amongst the Hereros & some of the Bechuanas. On one or two occasions recently these agitators have come over from Bechuanaland, but we have not heard of them until too late to prevent their departure. They wear rosettes of red, blue and green at their native meetings, and have been explaining how war should be made against the Europeans . . . are members of any socialistic or other political society I would be glad if you could advise me.[153]

Similarly, Samuel Sheppard, the son of Saul Sheppard who had settled in Bechuanaland following the German occupation of Namibia, spent most of 1922 and the first half of 1923 travelling through Bechuanaland, South Africa and Namibia on behalf of UNIA.[154]

In the 1950s Herero society would collect money to finance the journeys of their representatives to the United Nations in New York. In effect these trips were but an echo of what the Herero had already tried to do in 1922. Then, John Aaron Mungundu and Johannes Tyirimunye, as representatives of the UNIA, requested permission for Mungundu and Izaak Jantje to travel to the UNIA head offices in New York.[155] Effectively UNIA allowed the Herero to place their predicament, their loss of independence and land, on the world's stage. UNIA provided the means whereby they could link into power structures capable of influencing the policies and activities of their colonizers.

---

[150] NNAW, SWAA 421, R.L. Cope, OC Native Affairs in Windhoek, 22/11/22, to Secretary for South West Africa. NNAW, SWAA 432, enclosure 11, circular telegram 1/7/16. Traugott carried the rank of *Wachtvorsteher*, in the regiment stationed in *Paradies*, Okahandja.

[151] *BRMG*, 1923, pp. 71–2.

[152] In late 1922 the Industrial and Commercial Workers Union, ICU, set up by Clements Kadalie, started operating in southern Namibia. No reference has been found to the ICU being active amongst the Herero, though it is probable that amongst the 70 new members recruited by the ICU in Keetmanshoop following their first meeting, there were a few Herero. *BRMG*, 1923, p. 23.

[153] BNA, Damara S.5/1, Bushmen crossing from South West Africa into Bechuanaland Protectorate. Reported unrest and murder of Capt. van Ryneveld, Magistrate of Gobabis.

[154] BNA, S.5/1, Office of the Magistrate Gobabis, 4/4/23, to the Magistrate Ghanzi & Resident Magistrate in Ghanzi, 2/5/23, to Resident Commissioner:

> Samuel Sheppard is a native who travelled from Maun to Ghanzi, held meetings at Kakfontein, then proceeded to Lehututu and towards the Upington district eventually reaching Windhuk after months of travel. I endeavoured to trace him and have now received the attached letter.

[155] NNAW, SWAA 421, Native Commissioner in Windhoek, 11/7/22, to the Secretary.

Church

Associated with the development of Herero self-awareness, manifested in the UNIA and *Truppenspieler*, was the growing independence on the part of the Herero with regard to the Christian faith. No longer were the missionaries seen or accepted as the sole interpreters of and final authorities on the Christian faith. As a Herero put it:

> You teachers of today are not like the old teachers. You serve God and the Kaiser (the government); the old missionaries only served God.[156]

Tired of being informed of the woes being suffered by Germany and the German people in the aftermath of Versailles, the Herero started demanding what the German people and the missionaries had done for them in their hour of need. Typical of these attitudes were the events surrounding the visit of General Jan Smuts, the South African Prime Minister, to Grootfontein in September 1920. There representatives of the Herero community submitted a petition to Smuts and demanded that the German missionaries be removed. As Nafbali, a Herero spokesman and missionary evangelist, put it:

> . . . in the past the German missionaries had been like fathers to them, however they had betrayed them in the Herero war, furthermore they had to pay church contributions, even though they had been poor since the Herero war.[157]

The Herero felt betrayed by the mission, and for its part the mission felt similarly betrayed, particularly given the role of Nafbali in the affair. Needless to say, the missionaries fired Nafbali.[158]

As the true condition of South African occupation became ever more apparent, Herero, building forth on the ideas propagated by UNIA, began voicing their discontent specifically in terms of race. The role of whites as colonial oppressors irrespective of nationality came to be understood by the Herero. Responding to missionary demands for church contributions, Herero stated:

> We are of course your servants; because until now we have brought you our money. We do not make any distinction as to whether you are Germans, Englishmen or Boers. Because, for us, you are all White, just as we are for you all Black, irrespective of whether we are Herero, Bergdama or Ovambo.[159]

Associated with Herero development of ideas regarding Christianity and race is the development of independent Ethiopian churches in the territory.[160] Initially these churches had been brought into the country by Xhosa contract workers working on the diamond mines near Lüderitz.[161] With the South African invasion many Herero who had been living in the Union returned influenced by the ideas of independent churches operating on the Rand. Furthermore the 40000 Africans who accompanied the South African invasion also brought along Ethiopianist ideas and beliefs. Already prior to the South African invasion

[156] *BRMG*, 1924, p. 116. JBG's translation.
[157] ELCIN, V. 10 Grootfontein, 1920.
[158] Ibid.
[159] *BRMG*, 1924, p. 116.
[160] It is perhaps indicative that the documents detailing the rise of the independent Watch-tower church were catalogued along with the materials on the *Truppenspieler*. NNAW, SWAA 432 A 50/59 Vol. 2 *Truppenspielers* 1917–1938.
[161] Beinart, 'Cape workers in GSWA', p. 59.

Photo 7.2: Herero evangelist Andreas Kukuri conducting a church service
Source: United evangelical mission archives, Wuppertal

settlers had viewed African Christians with distrust.[162] Following the invasion, this position did not change and nominally God-fearing colonial officials and settlers sought to prescribe and curtail African religious activity.[163] Ethiopianist churches that sought permission to begin proselytizing in the territory were fobbed off with a wide variety of excuses, ranging from the need for peace to the already converted nature of the African.[164]

In late 1922 a 'Native Churches Inquiry Commission' was set up and questionnaires dealing with the issue were sent to all magistrates, missionaries and Native Affairs officers in the Union of South Africa and SWA. Indicative of the attitudes existing in Namibia, not a single questionnaire was filled in or sent to the commission, even though franked and addressed envelopes had been enclosed. A full nine months after the questionnaires were distributed, the magistrate of Swakopmund wrote that he had spoken to Rev. Eich of the Rhenish Mission:

> Eich has had a very long experience of native mission work in SWA. He tells me nothing is known to him about separate churches amongst the natives of this country. He says a certain amount of 'seditious' propaganda has been circulating at times amongst the natives here from the Union & from Monrovia [UNIA] with a view to

[162] Settlers in Lüderitz sought to prevent Herero from becoming Christians.
[163] NNAW, NAW 12, *Kapitein* Venter in Windhuk, 15/5/17, to Konst. Venter, Aris. In the letter, entitled 'Kaffir Kerk te Schaaprevier', Captain Venter noted *'het spreekt van zelf dat veraf wonende kaffirs niet toegelaten kan worden iedere avond naar kerk te gaan, twee maal per week zyn voor de zulke hoogst voldoende'*. It is probable that the meetings were not Church services but meetings of the *Otruppe*.
[164] NNAW, ADM 128, Ethiopian catholic church in Zion.

their having their own churches & ministers but the movement has made no headway. In some of the Herero communities the attendance at divine service has decreased in consequence of what he terms 'foreign agitation' but no founding of a separate church has as yet taken place.[165]

Missionaries noted that increasingly the Herero were becoming the trouble-makers [*Unruhstifter*] in their church communities and were active in inciting other communities. Holy communion, an aspect of crucial importance in Lutheran protestantism, started being boycotted by the Herero. Herero voiced their disillusionment with missionary schooling: 'The children learn nothing in the school; by staying with the mission we have remained dumb.'[166] Of particular concern to the Herero was that the mission did not take stock of the realities in which they were living. The Herero wanted to move forward, and wanted their children and themselves to be trained accordingly. 'What does it help to continually hear God's word. We should be learning English, or the missionaries should teach us other skills.'[167] In Karibib missionaries were informed in writing that they had no 'heart for the poor, the old and the children'. God-fearing at the best of times, the missionaries did not resort to Satan but now blamed communist agitators, whom they claimed were operating out of the newly established Native Reserves, for having manipulated their communities.[168] That the Herero were capable of independent thought was apparently beyond them.

Bondelswarts

A further factor that influenced the thinking of all of the territory's inhabitants was the crushing, by the South African army, police and air force, of a revolt initiated by the Bondelswarts against the South African administration in 1922. The Bondelswarts were a small Nama polity in southern Namibia. At the outbreak of the First World War the majority of them had been deported and interned in camps in the north of the territory. During the course of this deportation the polity lost all of its stock. From the beginning of the South African occupation of Namibia, the Bondelswarts had petitioned the South African administration for restitution of their stock, land and leaders. In what seemed like a conscious policy of neglect the new administration systematically negated the demands of the polity. Deprived of stock the Bondelswarts were forced to resort to hunting or working in the most abominable conditions on settler farms in the area. Children were pawned to farmers.[169] Throughout 1919,

[165] NNAW, SWAA 2060, Native Churches, Magistrate of Swakopmund, 24/8/23, to Native Commissioner. Regarding the questionnaire the magistrate noted that, though he had received them the previous year, he did not 'reply to it as the questions hardly seemed applicable to the situation up here'.
[166] *BRMG*, 1924, p. 116.
[167] Ibid.
[168] ELCIN, V. 32 Ortschroniken, 1922.
[169] NNAW, ADM 43, Military Magistrate in Maltahohe, 11/2/19, to the Secretary for the Protectorate: '. . . in the course of my recent visit to certain farms in this district en route to the farm Duwisib . . . I ascertained that several farmers had native minors in their possession which they stated had been given to them by the parents of the said children'. The military magistrate, sensitive as always to local conditions concluded his missive by stating that he personally saw no objection to the 'little ones . . . remain[ing] in the possession of their present masters', particularly 'as in some cases the children have been callously deserted by their parents'.

1920 and 1921 the Rhenish missionaries sought to draw the administration's attention to the deteriorating conditions in the polity.[170] In 1922, undaunted, and in the interests of settler demands for labour, the administration introduced a staggered system of dog tax, whereby the tax to be paid increased exponentially to the amount of dogs owned. To a society which depended on its hunting dogs for survival, this proved to be the final straw. They detained the police officer who had come to collect the tax. Thereupon the administrator ordered in the army, police and air force. Following the crushing of the polity, the German Consul-General in South Africa noted:

> The success the administration of the protectorate has achieved is chiefly attributed to the use of modern means of warfare, notably motor vehicles and three aeroplanes sent from Pretoria into the area where the revolt was taking place. It appears to me that the planes, in particular, have rendered good service in reconnoitring the positions of the bands of natives, in maintaining liaison between the different police patrols, and in supplying them with water. Through the lavish use of bombs they have speeded up the process of wiping out the bands.[171]

Following the bombing of the Bondelswarts, there could be no doubt in the minds of the territory's African inhabitants as to the true position of the new administration. The sjambok may have been officially dispelled but the conditions remained unchanged. Africans were to be the labourers of the settlers on African land.

To all intents and purposes, by 1923 the Herero had reestablished themselves. They had regained cattle and some land; they had reinstated some of their leaders; they had established structures which linked them to one another and the wider world; and, perhaps most importantly, they had begun to understand the true nature of South African occupation.

Death of Samuel

In Okahandja, on a cold winter's day in 1923, an honour guard of Herero soldiers, dressed in German uniforms, wearing German military ranks, and marching to German commands, carried a coffin to the grave. A military brass band, which played a German funeral march, and 170 mounted Herero soldiers, riding four abreast, preceded the coffin. No less than 2500 uniformed Herero soldiers, and an unspecified number of Herero women and onlookers, followed the coffin to its final resting place on the banks of the Okahandja river. Samuel Maharero, the first paramount chief of the Herero, who had died in exile, was thus laid to rest in the grave of his father, Kamaharero, and his grandfather, Tjamuaha. This section details Samuel's death and funeral, and seeks to examine what the implications of this were for Herero society.

During the South African invasion of Namibia, Samuel Maharero supplied the Union troops with soldiers of his own, in the hope that, as his son put it, 'if the country was taken back from the Germans it would be given back to Samuel

---

[170] NNAW, ADM 110, Annual Reports, contains scores of requests for drought relief in the years leading up to 1922. *BRMG*, 1923, p. 78.
[171] Quoted in Drechsler, *Fighting*, p. 248.

Photo 7.3: Part of the funeral cortège of Samuel Maharero in Okahandja in 1923.
Wearing sashes in the front are Hoseah Kutako and Friedrich Maharero
Source: Namibian National Archives, Windhoek

and his people'.[172] This, as we have seen, was not to be, and, though Samuel Maharero was initially given permission to return to the land of his birth, this permission was later withdrawn and he was doomed to die in exile, far from the support and comfort of the graves of his fathers.[173] On 14 March 1923,

[172] Frida Troup, *In the Face of Fear* (London 1950) p. 57. For snippets on Africans and Herero in the South West African war, see Albert Grundlingh, *Fighting Their Own War: South African Blacks and the First World War*, Ravan Press (Johannesburg 1987) p.59. On black involvement in 'white' wars in southern Africa, see Melvin E. Page, *Africa and the First World War*, Macmillan Press (London 1987); B.D. Willan, 'The South African Native Labour Contingent, 1916–1918', *JAH*, 19 (1978) pp. 61–86; P. Warwick, *Black People and the South African War: 1899–1902*, Ravan Press (Johannesburg 1983). There were even two Herero, known only as Adam no. 7646 and August no. 7649, who served with the South African Native Labour contingent in France. NNAW, NAW 1.

[173] NNAW, SWAA 2085, Maharero Vol. 1, Letter from Samuel Maharero, in Nylstroom, 25/2/1920, to Resident Commissioner in Mafeking. Unfortunately the files relating to Samuel Maharero's application for permission to move to the Bechuanaland Protectorate from the Transvaal are missing from the Botswana National Archives. According to BNA archivists in March 1992 the files: Damara S.24/4

> Samuel Maherero [*sic*]. Proposal to settle him and his followers in the Bechuanaland Protectorate, (removal from Transvaal to Bamangwato Reserve, death of Chief Samuel, and move of other Maherero from the Bakwena reserve). (J) 786 D 1919–24;

were missing and they stated that they had been 'stolen about 20 years ago, the whole box is missing'. After the war the Union authorities sought to invite Samuel to Windhoek to attend a concessions commission in South West Africa. Though permission was granted by the Department of Native Affairs in Pretoria, Samuel was at this stage too sick to travel to SWA. NNAW, SWAA 2085, Department of Native Affairs in Pretoria, 6/9/20. NNAW, SWAA 2085, Swakopmund 11th Jan 1923 Herbst wrote to the resident commisioner of British Bechuanaland Protectorate in Mafeking to tell him that at no stage was Samuel Maharero to be allowed into Namibia and to inform if he intends coming. Interestingly, the department of Native Affairs in Pretoria was at this stage still prepared to allow Samuel to travel to SWA.

Samuel Maharero died in exile in Serowe, the capital of the Bamangwato kingdom, in what is now Botswana.[174]

Samuel Maharero had cancer of the stomach. Prior to his death he had been bed-ridden and had suffered greatly from a great deal of pain for a number of months. Samuel did not die directly of cancer. The immediate cause of his death was exhaustion and resultant heart failure. His last days were filled with pain and agony. Lying in a hut in exile, Samuel must have pondered on the events of his life. In a sense Samuel's death was similar to that of his father. Kamaharero's last days had also been spent in pain. Like Samuel, Kamaharero had spent the last days of his life musing on life and suffering from stomach cramps, though these were caused not by cancer but by dysentery or poison. But, unlike Samuel, Kamaharero spent the last days of his life in the land of his birth and next to the grave of his father, Tjamuaha. On the morning of his death Samuel requested that he be buried along with his fathers in Okahandja.[175] In his final days Samuel Maharero was visited by his friends and relatives, some of whom had died thirty years previously.[176] Though his mental faculties would not have been affected by the cancer, it is probable that his physician, A. Worrall, prescribed him morphine, the painkiller of the day. And if this is the case it would certainly go some way towards explaining some of Samuel's more esoteric final words to his people, which were dictated on the day prior to his death.

Samuel Maharero's testament to his people consisted of a series of transcriptions of dictations, conversations and visions, steeped in Christian symbolism, and clearly shows the extent to which Christian teachings had become part and parcel of Herero society.[177] In essence Samuel Maharero urged the remaining Herero to be humble before God, regroup, trust in one another,

---

[174] BNA, DCS, RM in Serowe, 14/3/23, to RC. Following his residence in the Transvaal Samuel had moved to the Bechuanaland Protectorate and settled at Serowe under the chieftaincy of Khama, *Kgosi* of Bamangwato district. Khama provided the Herero with tracts of land near Mahalapye in his district. Following the granting of land by Khama, and the establishment of Herero leadership as *Bakgosi* of Khama, Herero flocked to the area and a period of centralizing took place as Herero, scattered in the southern districts of the protectorate, began moving to Mahalapye in the Bamangwato district. For further information on this process see Manasse, Kebonang, and BNA, DCMOL 2/3, DCS 2/15.

[175] DCS 2/9 District Commissioner Serowe, Death of Chief Samuel Maharero and removal of remains for burial at Okahandja in South West Africa. 1923, Telegram: 'RM Serowe 14th March regret report Chief SM is dying I saw him this morning with MO and he asked me to greet his honour and say that he wishes to be buried at Okahandja in Damaraland next to his father. Please telegraph if S's wishes can be carried out.'

[176] In Samuel Maharero's final message to his people, he detailed one such visit as follows:

I was awake and was visited by three of my elder brothers Wilhelm, Elias (Kandirikira) and Kamatjikuria (Kandirikira) as ghosts. They said: 'Do not be afraid, we have come to see your illness, we are the children of Tjamuaha, there is not much time, we are going to wait for you at the grave.' I then called for Tjikune through his children and the tribe, and asked for the arrangements for the journey, he (Tjikune) called for Murauria, through the tribe, and wanted to see if the master of this country would give me a place. I will arrange for the dwellings to be in the order they used to be in. (NNAW, ACC 200)

[177] NNAW, ACC 200. Friedrich Maharero read the message to the Herero councillors and headmen at Okahandja at the funeral. The message was probably passed on to Courtney Clarke by Vedder who discussed the message in the *BRMG* 1923, pp. 117–22. Unfortunately we do not have a Herero-language original of the message, added to which there are major differences between the ACC 200 document and the message presented by Vedder in the *BRMG*. It would appear that the *BRMG* message has been somewhat edited by Vedder.

maintain their identity as Herero and seek to regain their land:

> When the big flood of water came God kept 8 people and they multiplied over the whole earth.[178] I have no news to tell you, but what must I say to you the leaders of the Nation. You are my children. You know all my troubles. God has worked for you.

Samuel's message articulated the message that, in God's hands, the Herero would find succour and shelter. As with the descendants of Noah, the Herero, if they were willing to submit to God, would once again regain their former numbers and position. Samuel Maharero's message resonated strongly with passages taken from the book of Isaiah, which was a favourite text among Herero congregants at the time.[179] In other words, though God had punished the Herero for their sins, God in His mercy had left survivors, which had prevented the Herero from being completely exterminated, and provided them with the chance to reestablish themselves in keeping with God's law.

> . . . You may be oppressed or treated with contempt, do not get cross, be loyal to your authorities and the church and keep the peace amongst yourselves and love one another and mourn together.
>
> My son Frederick [Friedrich], please for the sake of your grandfather, if there is anyone who does wrong he must be punished according to the law. If first to the nation and your country you do good, then you will please God. God has punished me rightly, when he punished my children, that is you.
>
> You have no trust in one another. A person who has not the trust of his people cannot be their head and be a father to his people.
>
> My children work for God, my sickness is due to your evils and that of my people, but if you trust in God he will forgive you your sins. If you do evil it will not benefit you.[180]

The transcription was directed primarily at Samuel's successor, his son Friedrich Maharero, and it called upon Friedrich to do all in his power to ensure the reunification of the Herero. The section, with its call on Herero to submit

---

[178] Reference to Noah, I find the longevity of certain images incredible, that an image that started out in the Epic of Gilgamesh 4000 years ago in Babylon should come to be used in Namibia in the twentieth century is astounding. However, perhaps this is not as strange as it seems as Chief Riaruako claimed in 1991, at the book launch of Gerhardus Pool's *Samuel Maharero*, that the Herero had migrated southwards from Babylon leaving all others behind.

[179] *BRMG*, 1923, pp. 109–10.

> Why should you be beaten anymore?
> Why do you persist in rebellion?
> Your whole head is injured, your whole heart is afflicted.
> From the sole of your foot to the top of your head there is no soundness – only wounds and welts and open sores, not cleansed or bandaged or soothed with oil.
> Your country is desolate, your cities burned with fire; your fields are being stripped by foreigners right before you, laid waste as when overthrown by strangers.
> The Daughter of Zion is left like a shelter in a vineyard, like a hut in a field of melons, like a city under siege.
> Unless the Lord Almighty had left us some survivors, we would have become like Sodom, we would have been like Gomorrah. (Isaiah 1: 5–9)

Missionary Werner, who was stationed in Okahandja at the time, wryly commented that as a missionary working amongst the Herero he often felt that Isaiah 1: 4 best described his experiences:

> Ah, sinful nation, a people loaded with guilt, a brood of evildoers, children given to corruption! They have forsaken the Lord; they have spurned the Holy One of Israel and turned their backs on him.

[180] NNAW, ACC 200.

to the law and care for one another, echoed the teachings of Jesus Christ as portrayed by Matthew.[181] Samuel Maharero's claim that he was suffering on account of his people echoes the idea of Jesus Christ dying for the sins of mankind. This image of Samuel Maharero as the Christ is reinforced by the final section of Samuel Maharero's message to his people. This was not delivered through the mouth of Samuel Maharero, but after his death through the medium of Diana Riarua, the daughter of Assa Riarua. After his death in Botswana, Samuel Maharero appeared to Diana and informed her that he had risen from the dead.[182] Samuel's words echoed those of Jesus to Mary Magdalene, when he told Diana:

> You will not die, you will go and tell the people, who will wear mourning for me – they are not mine – mine are those who will do my will.[183]

Friedrich Maharero, who had been at his father's side when he died, succeeded Samuel as chief of the Herero in Botswana. Friedrich conducted his father's funeral arrangements. Three days after Samuel's death, an empty lead-lined coffin to the value of £120 was ordered and delivered to Mafeking. From Mafeking it travelled by rail to Palapye Road, where it was met by waggon and taken to Serowe, where Samuel's body had been temporarily buried. Immediately after Samuel's death, a flurry of correspondence ensued between the authorities of the Bechuanaland Protectorate, the Union of South Africa, the South West African Protectorate, the South African Railways and Herero representatives in Bechuanaland and SWA.[184] Finally after months of wrangling, Friedrich Maharero and forty-nine compatriots were granted three-month passes and permitted to accompany Samuel's body to Okahandja.[185] Two hundred pounds, which had been kept on fixed deposit at the South African National Bank in Nylstrom, were withdrawn to pay for part of the funeral and travelling costs.[186] Finally in August of 1923 the lead-lined coffin, accompanied by its funeral entourage, departed by train for Okahandja.[187]

A uniformed Herero honour guard of 150 mounted men and 1500 footmen met Samuel's body as his train steamed into Okahandja station on Thursday morning, 23 August 1923. The honour guard, led by Hoseah Kutako, Traugott Maharero, Friedrich Maharero and Mr Warner, the magistrate of Okahandja, escorted the coffin to the house of Traugott Maharero. Here it was placed in state in a 'mourning chamber' which men were barred from entering.

In the weeks prior to the funeral, Herero from all over the country had begun converging on Okahandja. Special rail tariffs were introduced to facilitate

---

[181] See particularly Matthew 5–8.
[182] Matthew 28: 1–10; Mark 16: 1–20 & John 20: 1–18.
[183] See Matthew 12: 49–50 & Mark 3: 34–35.
[184] See, in particular, BNA, DCS 2/9 District Commissioner Serowe, 'Death of Chief Samuel Maharero and removal of remains for burial at Okahandja in South West Africa. 1923'.
[185] BNA, DCS 2/9, J. Ellenberger Government Secretary in Mafeking, 13/7/23, to Resident Magistrate in Serowe.
[186] BNA, DCS 2/9, Acting Resident Magistrate Serowe 16/3/23 to Acting Government Secretary, Mafeking. It is probable that this was money which Samuel had earned through acting as a labour tout for the Transvaal mines. What is particularly interesting is that the money was placed on a five-year fixed deposit, in other words it could not be got hold of by anyone bar in the case of death. It is possible that Samuel had already intended that this money be used for his funeral costs.
[187] Ovambanderu histories collected indicate that the coffin that travelled to Okahandja was either empty, or filled with stones, a donkey or a goat, but not with the remains of Samuel Maharero.

Herero travel and ensure the speedy return of Herero employees. Thus on the third day, Sunday 26 August 1923, when Samuel's coffin was taken from Traugott's house and placed on trestles, it was flanked by no less than 2500 uniformed Herero men, 170 uniformed and mounted Herero, and an unspecified amount of Herero women. Given that the total Herero population at the time was in the region of 20000, the number of Herero who attended the funeral was phenomenal.

Courtney-Clarke, secretary for the protectorate, Mr Cope, Native Affairs officer, and Mr Warner, magistrate of Okahandja, attended the ceremony on behalf of the settler administration. Courtney-Clarke and his administrative colleagues were clearly impressed:

> On arrival at the Location we were led into a hollow square formed by the Natives in front of the Chief's house, the women being massed on one side with the men formed up on the other sides. Practically all of them, with the exception of the Chief's sons and Headmen, were in uniform, either old German or British. No pains had apparently been spared to obtain this form of clothing for the occasion. The funeral was well organized by the Natives responsible and unlike Native functions was well up to the timetable throughout . . . I have attended a number of Native functions in the Union but I must frankly say I have never seen one better conducted.[188]

In effect the funeral, in its outward appearances, was identical to those which had been given to high-ranking German officials who had died in the territory – full of pomp and ceremony, marching brass bands, mounted soldiers, and massed ranks of soldiers. The outer paraphernalia of Samuel's funeral was identical to the state funeral which had been given to the commander of German forces in GSWA, *Oberstleutnant* von Heydebreck, in 1914. The Damara brass band and a number of the Herero who now marched at the funeral of Samuel Maharero had marched at the funeral of Heydebreck nine years previously, and it was they who undoubtedly provided information as to the hows and possibly whys of a state funeral.[189] Referring to the German commands, uniforms and the like, missionary Vedder commented that the Herero wanted to bury Samuel Maharero with the greatest possible honour, 'and for that, they had until now only had German examples'.[190]

Hosea Kutako, who two years previously had been appointed by Samuel Maharero as his representative in SWA, led the proceedings and acted as master of ceremonies. After Samuel's coffin had been placed on trestles in front of Traugott's house, Hoseah stepped forward and called out, 'He has come, he is going, the Sun.'[191] Whereafter Rudolf Kondio, a Rhenish missionary evangelist, stepped forward and read from the book of John, chapter 2. Unfortunately we do not know precisely what it was that Rudolf Kondio read. Chapter 2 of the

---

[188] NNAW, ACC. 200.

[189] *Oberstleutnant* von Heydebreck was the commander of German forces till his death in the first months of the First World War. He was fatally wounded in November 1914 whilst testing artillery shells in Kalkfontein. He was buried with full military honours in Windhoek.

[190] *BRMG* 1924, p. 118.

[191] What the exact meaning of Hoseah's words were we cannot be certain. Unfortunately we do not have a Herero-language rendition of the funeral and we thus have to rely on the text of Courtney-Clarke. However, sun can be translated into Otjiherero as 'ejuva' which can carry two meanings, 'sun' or 'day'. It is probable that the words were spoken in 'Deep Herero' and that the words were loaded with extra meaning relating to the dawning of a new age. This is at least what Vedder also seemed to believe, and would fit in nicely with the passages read from the Bible by the Herero evangelists.

book of John contains two sections. The first deals with Jesus changing water into wine and the second deals with Jesus clearing the temple of the merchants and the money-lenders. The first section deals with the first miracle performed by Jesus, and ends with the words, 'He thus revealed his glory, and his disciples put their faith in him.' Though this could well be the section read, my personal choice is for Chapter 2, verses 20–2:

> The Jews replied, 'It has taken forty-six years to build this temple, and you are going to raise it in three days?' But the temple he had spoken of was his body. After he was raised from the dead, his disciples recalled what he had said. Then they believed the Scripture and the words that Jesus had spoken.[192]

The reading finished, the mourners set off towards the mission church, where Samuel's coffin was placed before the altar. Samuel's sons, Hoseah Kutako and the colonial officials sat in the front row on opposite sides of the aisle. Heinrich Vedder, assisted by Werner, conducted the funeral service in Otjiherero. Prior to the funeral the organizers had approached the missionaries to determine the manner in which the funeral service was to be conducted. They had requested that a full funeral service be conducted in the church, even to the extent that the handfuls of soil be tossed onto the coffin inside the church and not at the graveside. The Herero wanted the funeral to be conducted in this manner so that the ceremony at the graveside could take place strictly according to Herero custom. Initially it had been intended that Werner should conduct the service. However, Werner was so upset by the requests that he refused to conduct the funeral.[193] His position was undoubtedly further strengthened by a Herero prohibition on the holding of a Damara church service in the church on the morning of the funeral.[194] However, given that the church had been built, maintained and financed by the Herero congregation of Okahandja prior to 1904, it is hardly surprising that the Herero saw the church as falling within their jurisdiction.[195] Vedder conducted the service, which lasted for about three-quarters of an hour. His sermon was based on the first book of Peter 1: 24, 25:

> All men are like grass, and all their glory is like the flowers of the field; the grass withers and the flowers fall, but the word of the Lord stands for ever.[196]

Following the service the procession made its way to the site of Samuel's former house. Here further ceremonies, described only as 'licking the dust', took place.[197]

---

[192] NNAW, ACC 200.

[193] Pool, *Samuel*, p. 299.

[194] It must be borne in mind that until the outbreak of the Herero–German war in 1904, the church was built, maintained and financed by the Herero congregation living in Okahandja. Furthermore it must not be forgotten that a number of Damara leaders took part in the funeral celebrations for Samuel Maharero.

[195] See the earlier arguments between Kamaharero and the missionaries regarding the church in the 1880s.

[196] See Isiah 40: 6, 8.

[197] NNAW, SWAA 2025, Courtney-Clarke, Windhoek, 28/8/23, report on the funeral of Samuel Maharero entitled, *Visit to Okahandja*. In a letter from Lewis Warner, the magistrate of Okahandja, 9/8/23, to Courtney-Clarke prior to the funeral, Warner outlined the planned funeral proceedings and noted, 'Frederick and his followers, also Traugott and his followers then lick the dust (We don't do this).'

In the shade of casuarinas and eucalypti, the graves of Tjamuaha and Maharero lay within the grounds of a forestry station, which had been established by the German administration on the banks of the Okahandja river following the Herero–German war.[198] It was to these graves that the funeral procession and Samuel's coffin draped in the Union Jack proceeded:

On the arrival of the procession the mounted men took up their position on one side of the square, the women on the other and the men and band on the third. The coffin and bearers however halted on the furthest corner of the square and one of the oldest men Tjorovi knelt down on the ground with the bearers and announced the arrival of the dead man to his ancestors, calling out –

'Father I have brought your child and all your people (giving the names of all his descendants) open the road for your son.'

After some delay and repetition he announced the road was open and the cortege crossed the square and took up its position at the grave side, the male members of the family kneeling round the grave. Tjorovi again proceeded to call on the departed, saying –

'Father I have brought your child Samuel, I have brought all, Frederick [Friedrich] is here, all his brothers are here, I have brought them all to you. Can't you hear I speak to you.'

This was repeated several times followed by –

'Don't you know who is speaking. I am speaking Tjorovi your sister's son. Have you no sense, why don't you listen, I have brought your child who was away a long time, I can't tell you why but you know yourself. Take him to your breast.'

Suddenly he displayed great signs of joy and announced the departed had heard and had replied saying 'he wanted Samuel'. This was greeted by a great shout from all assembled of 'Yes! Yes! He wants him.'[199]

Courtney-Clarke, speaking through an interpreter, presented a speech on behalf of the administrator. In keeping with colonial ideas on the behaviour of the ideal native, the speech urged the Herero to work, keep the peace, be industrious, respect the law, follow the example of Khama, avoid the example of Cetswayo, Dinizulu or Lobengula and generally efface themselves. Even the few words which might have struck a chord, those related to the issue of land, were smothered in the admonition that 'these Reserves are not to be regarded as places where your young men can live idle and lazy lives. They will have to go out to work and earn money to improve them.'[200] In a final show of magnanimity Courtney-Clarke agreed to allow a Herero guard of honour of

[198] In 1915, following the South African invasion, the station was transferred to the municipality, who wished to build a swimming pool on the grounds. The swimming pool was constructed in 1932, and still exists.
[199] NNAW, ACC 200, pp. 4–5. It is interesting to note that the same procedure is followed at the annual commemorations at the graves, where an elder calls on the ancestors and waits for a reply before proceeding further.
[200] NNAW, ACC 200, p. 7. The words spoken on behalf of Hofmeyr would come to have a bitter ring to them following the Herero rebellion and the forced removal of Herero to the reserves.

I am setting apart reserves for your people . . . as soon as these reserves have been marked off and water has been found on them you will be able to move into them with your wives.

ten men to keep watch over the grave for one night.[201] After all, Samuel Maharero's new grave lay in what was, according to the law at the time, European municipal land; i.e. it was off-limits to all Africans after sunset. The Europeans left and the Herero continued with their funeral. Samuel was buried next to his fathers.

For the Herero the funeral of Samuel Maharero was the largest socio-political event since the Herero–German war. It was an event that brought to the fore a number of issues which showed that the funeral was indeed, as in the final words of Courtney-Clarke's speech, 'the beginning of a new era for the Herero Nation'.[202] The funeral demonstrated to the Herero and the outside world that they were once again a self-aware self-regulating political entity, with their own unique identity, a socio-political entity that had its own command structures that did not 'do under' for the regulated order and symbolism of the colonial state, either in time management, uniforms or marching. The funeral showed their continued faith in the British empire at the time, even though this was a faith which would soon come to an end. It showed their growing independence from the Rhenish church. The Herero determined the way in which the funeral was to be conducted, who was to attend and to a large extent what was to be said. Christian Herero evangelists and *Ovandangere* spoke on behalf of Samuel's soul. Herero soldiers paraded in honour of Samuel. Samuel's foes, descendants, followers and successors marched and prayed at his grave. In effect Samuel's funeral brought together for the first time the Herero who had survived the Herero–German war. Herero who had fled to Bechuanaland and South Africa; Herero who had become indentured labourers on the settler farms; and the young Herero men who had become German soldiers, now marched together for the first time as a single unit. Samuel's funeral was the catalyst that reunited the Herero. The uninitiated youths, who had become the soldiers of the Kaiser and Marcus Garvey, now became, once again, the soldiers of the Herero, reunited with the missionary evangelists, and their indentured flocks. The reading of the Bible, by the missionary evangelists, the marching of the youth, the prayers of the *Ovandangere*, and the awe of the whites all served to ensure that the funeral of Samuel Maharero heralded the reunification of the Herero. At the funeral of Samuel Maharero the various strands of Herero society that had emerged in the aftermath of the war came together and, through the process and ceremony of burying Samuel Maharero, were woven and drawn together to make up, for the first time in history, a unitary Herero society.

Postscript

Following the funeral of his father, Friedrich Maharero appealed to the South African administration to be permitted to stay in SWA. His appeal was backed by the signatures of Hosea Kutako, Traugott Maharero, Alfried Maharero, Salatiel Kambazembi, Joel Kasetura, Asser Kamusuvise, Silphanus Mungunda and Wilfried Kazondonga; i.e. all the eastern and central Herero leaders in the territory.[203] Conspicuously absent was the support of the Herero of

---

[201] NNAW, ACC 200, p. 8.
[202] Ibid.
[203] NNAW, SWAA 1/1/3 cc 4, document to the administrator of South West Africa requesting that Friedrich be allowed to remain in the territory.

Omaruru. Clearly the differences that had existed between Omaruru and Okahandja prior to the Herero–German war were to be continued into the future.

Friedrich was not to remain in SWA and in December 1924 he was escorted to the Union border by a policeman, who provided his superiors with a detailed report on Friedrich's meeting with Baster representatives in Rehoboth.[204] The inhabitants of the Rehoboth district, Basters as well as Herero, were soon to take part in an armed revolt against the enforced branding and removal of stock from the Rehoboth district. Significantly this confrontation was to become known as 'the war of Garvey's button'. It appears that Friedrich's presence in SWA has come to be conflated, in popular histories, with the alleged presence of Marcus Garvey in the territory. Following Friedrich's departure he was not permitted to return to the territory again until shortly before his death in 1952.

At the time of Friedrich's death grand apartheid was flourishing in SWA. As a condition to allowing Friedrich to be buried along with his fathers, the Okahandja municipality demanded that Hoseah Kutako sign an undertaking stating that henceforth 'any other descendants of Maharero will be buried at other places'.[205] Or, as the major of Okahandja told Hoseah Kutako, 'he did not wish Kaffirs to be buried there'.[206] Even for some members of the Bantu affairs department at the time, this was going a bit far and the municipality was asked to explain why this course of action had been taken. Two months later the following reply was received:

> You are most certainly aware that the graveyard referred to is in the immediate vicinity of the village's water installations, and the possibility of water contamination cannot be left beyond consideration. You will certainly admit that, during years of good rains, impure [water] will filter through the porous river bed to the water sources of the village. In the interests of the health of the village, and the public of Okahandja, my council considered it advisable to submit such a request to the Herero tribe.
>
> I also accept that you are conscious of the fact that the late Frederik [Friedrich] Maharero was brought from Bechuanaland to be buried here, without the local authorities being previously informed or consulted. Is it then uncharitable of the council to wish that arrangements be established in anticipation of future events? Or are the Herero to retain free rights to exercise their tribal traditions within the town area, without the council being permitted to demand or request specific conditions?
>
> Either way sooner or later the limited area will force the Herero to find another graveyard, and why should the public interests of whites be left behind in the interests of native traditions which will inevitably die out?[207]

As if this was not enough the Okahandja municipality commissioned a geological enquiry into the issue headed by Dr Henno Martin.[208] Henceforth Herero leaders were no longer to be buried alongside Tjamuaha, Maharero,

204 NNAW, SWAA 1/1/2 Intelligence Natives SWA, Report by David Ngiki, Okahandja 29/12/24.

205 NNAW, SWAA 2086, Hoofnaturellekommissaris in Windhoek, 20/9/52, to Die Stadklerk Okahandja.

206 NNAW, SWAA 2086, Notule van die Kwartaalikse Vergadering Gehou te Aminuis op 28 April 1953. During the course of this meeting Hoseah Kutako reminded the 'Welfare officer' that white children had used the cross, placed on Samuel's grave, as a target for their pellet guns.

207 NNAW, SWAA 2086, Stadsklerk Okahandja, 14/11/52, to Die Hoofnaturellekommissaris. JBG's translation.

208 Henno Martin is well known for his two-year sojourn in the Namib desert during the Second World War to escape internment, *The Sheltering Desert* (Windhoek 1957).

Samuel and Friedrich. Thus Hoseah Kutako and Clemens Kapuuo were buried elsewhere. However, in the early 1980s, when the South African administration was heavily dependent on the support of the Herero population of Namibia, the burial of Herero chiefs alongside Tjamuaha was permitted once again. Apparently 'native traditions' do not inevitably die out.

Conclusion

When the South African invasion of Namibia began in 1915, Herero believed that a new age, which would entail the restoration of Herero independence and land, was dawning. The Herero acted in accordance with this belief. Herero abandoned their erstwhile German employers and sought to rebuild a new life independent of settler control. They were aided in this by the famine in Ovamboland which forced thousands of Ovambo on to the territory's labour market, effectively freeing the Herero from employment. Herero occupied abandoned farms, established new herds and began converting acquired small stock into large stock. As the Herero prospered, they came into increasing conflict with the settlers. In response to this the new South African administration passed legislation which was continually mediated by the conflict that existed between liberal and settler tendencies within the South African administration. It was within the ever-changing parameters of this conflict that the Herero came to reestablish themselves, largely beyond the bounds of settler control. That is, the Herero were able to make use of the leeway provided by this conflict to reestablish Herero society. One of the unintentional outcomes of this conflict was the creation of Herero reserves. The Herero reserve established at Otjohorongo is a fine example of how Herero were able to make use of conflict within the settler administration to further their own aims.

The establishment of Orumbo Reserve was an attempt by the administration to contain and control the Herero living in the vicinity of Windhoek. In the event, the administration was simply overwhelmed by the sheer numbers of Herero and herds involved. Caught between attempting to appease settler interests and fulfilling Herero demands, the administration reacted hard-handedly against the Herero. This, coupled to the inadequacy of the reserves, led to the further radicalization and growing self-awareness on the part of the Herero vis-a-vis the South African administration. The administration's actions allowed for the development of a new centralized and ever more radicalized Herero leadership associated with Hoseah Kutako.

Within Herero society new ideas and attitudes, with regard to the manner in which the world was organized, and their place within it, came to be ever more widespread in Herero society. The development of the *Truppenspieler*, which provided Herero youth with social support and status, the development of UNIA, which provided the catalyst and means for the reestablishment of Herero chiefly authority, the development of Herero discontent vis-a-vis the mission church, and the suppression of the Bondelswarts rebellion, all served to emphasize to the Herero what their true status as subjects of the South African administration in Namibia was. These events served to educate the Herero as to their position as a colonized black population. Samuel Maharero's funeral brought together, for the first time, the Herero royals of Botswana and

Namibia, the Herero soldiers, and the Herero Christians, newly converted and otherwise. The funeral of Samuel Maharero not only served to bring together the various strands that went to make up the Herero, but also served to emphasize to the Herero their specific identity as Herero with a specific history of having come through the hellfire of war.

Conclusion

Between 1890 and 1923 Herero society was destroyed and rebuilt. The politics of this society prior to its destruction in 1904 and the manner in which Herero society reestablished itself after 1904 are the subject-matter of this thesis.

When research for this work was started, the author's ideas on Herero history were largely determined by childhood recollections of Herero celebrations and the works of Bridgman, Drechsler, Bley and Pool.[1] This book has attempted to go beyond these observations which saw the war as the 'be all and end all' of Herero history, the year zero upon which all that is Herero is based and in terms of which all that is Herero is to be understood. Indeed, rather much of what it argues is totally unrelated to the war, and in that sense uncharted. Consequently it has been necessary to revise considerably the accepted views on central Namibian history. Most notably, it has become clear that Herero society was much less monolithic than originally thought. Ethnic divisions were far from clear-cut, and very porous. Herero society, if such can be defined, was riven by tensions and splits which extended beyond the Herero as conventionally defined, so that the incoming Germans were able to play off one leader against another, thereby facilitating their conquest. The nineteenth century in central Namibia was characterized by evolution and disintegration of polities and ethnicities. This process was partially arrested and frozen with the establishment of German colonial control in Namibia.[2]

---

[1] As a child the author attended Herero day celebrations in Okahandja. These celebrations, along with the works of J.M. Bridgman, *The Revolt of the Hereros*, H. Drechsler, '*Let Us Die Fighting*', and G. Pool, *Die Herero-Opstand*, all concentrated on the Herero–German war to the detriment of a further analysis of Herero history. The work of H. Bley, *South-West Africa under German Rule*, too, dealt with the war but was more concerned with an analysis of German colonial involvement in Namibia than with Herero history.

[2] Charles Ambler's excellent *Kenyan Communities in the Age of Imperialism* (Yale 1988) brought to the fore that:

> In contemporary Africa, ethnic boundaries are often the site of intensely bitter and violent conflict; and to many people – Africans and outsiders alike – tribalism represents an atavistic, seemingly insurmountable obstacle to progress. Yet the history of central Kenya makes clear that in Kenya at least the roots of ethnicity are twisted and shallow. (p. 157)

Through the astute manipulation of Herero kinship structures and missionary and German administrator ideas of succession and governance, Samuel Maharero ensured that Imperial Germany supported him in his struggle against the other Herero chiefs, and recognized and supported him in the newly created position of paramount chief of all the Herero. In exchange for land, cattle and labour, taken from his newly acquired subjects, Samuel Maharero was able to purchase and rely on the support of Imperial Germany.[3] The dispossession and enforced land clearances which resulted from this alliance led to increased social tension and pressure on the land remaining in Herero hands. The Ovambanderu Khauas-Khoi war of 1895 was a direct result of Samuel Maharero's alliance with the German colonial administration.[4]

The rinderpest epidemic which struck Namibia in 1896 spread with extreme rapidity, because Herero herds, on account of the land clearances and boundary enforcements, had been forced into an ever smaller range, thereby ensuring that the quarantining of herds had become well-nigh impossible. Herero society, which had already been substantially weakened by the activities of Samuel Maharero and his German allies, was further weakened as the powers of Herero chiefs were usurped by German vaccinating and culling teams. Added to this, the power of chiefs was undercut as they lost not only their means of acquiring capital, but also their means of patronage. In the aftermath of the epidemic, crop failures, diseases, droughts, and the breakdown of power structures that had existed beforehand served to destabilize Herero society even further.[5] Rinderpest ensured that pressure on the land was reduced, and that large numbers of Herero were forced onto the labour market. New war-lords, such as Kajata and Willy Kain, made use of the turmoil to improve their position through the export of labour. Samuel Maharero, too, sought to retain his power by exporting labour and selling land.[6]

Frightened by the extent of Herero land sales, Rhenish missionaries, in

The findings of this thesis indicate that the development of ethnic identities in central Namibia in the nineteenth century mirrored what happened in central Kenya at the same time. Ambler's words regarding central Kenyan communities are equally relevant to the communities of central Namibia. Along with Ambler's work, the influential work edited by Leroy Vail, *The Creation of Tribalism in Southern Africa* (London 1989), on the development and entrenchment of ethnic identities in southern Africa, greatly influenced the author's thinking.

[3] Similar alliances between incoming colonialists and African chiefs were made throughout Africa. Elsewhere in southern Africa P. Bonner, *Kings, Commoners and Concessionaires: The Evolution and Dissolution of the nineteenth-century Swazi State* (Cambridge 1983), and P. Delius, *The Land Belongs to Us: The Pedi Polity, the Boers and the British in the Nineteenth Century Transvaal* (Braamfontein 1983), have detailed the development and ultimate dissolution of similar alliances.

[4] Events in southern Tswanaland in the 1870s and 1880s foreshadowed what happened in Namibia. Here too people were driven off their lands, forced onto ever smaller stretches of land until eventually war and further dispossession became the outcome. For a detailed overview of events in southern Tswanaland, see Kevin Shillington, *The Colonisation of the Southern Tswana, 1870–1900* (Braamfontein 1985).

[5] Jeff Peires has described in great detail what can happen to a society when it is struck by such natural disasters as befell the Herero. To some extent events in central Namibia following the rinderpest appear to reflect similar conditions to what occurred in the eastern Cape following the lungsickness epidemics of the 1850s. J. Peires, *The Dead Will Arise: Nongqawuse and the Great Xhosa Cattle-killing Movement 1856–7* (Johannesburg 1989).

[6] The turmoil that emerged in central Namibia following the Ovambanderu Khauas-Khoi war and the rinderpest was in many ways similar to the unstable situation that emerged in Zululand following the Anglo-Zulu war of 1879, and which is described by Jeff Guy, *The Destruction of the Zulu Kingdom* (London 1979). In both instances new warlords sought to improve their positions through raiding and labour export.

conjunction with the German governor, Theodor Leutwein, sought to create reserves of inalienable Herero land. A substantial proportion of the colony's settlers, soldiers and administrators were opposed to the creation of reserves and agitated against the new legislation. In the climate of opposition to Herero reserves and the belief in settler rights to the land, war between the Herero and Imperial Germany became a self-fulfilling prophecy.[7] During the war, Herero attempts at reaching a negotiated settlement were studiously ignored, as elements of the Imperial German army followed a policy of genocide.

Between 1905 and 1908 the majority of the Herero survivors were incarcerated in concentration camps and allocated as forced labourers to civilian, administrative and military enterprises alike. The majority of the camp inhabitants were women. In the aftermath of the war, Imperial Germany sought to transform the Herero and the survivors of the Nama–German war into a single amorphous black working class.[8] The bulk of Herero society came to be organized around Herero mission evangelists, who were effectively the only Herero who were permitted to travel and read and write. A large number of Herero orphans were taken, as servants, into the German army. Here they found employment and social structure. By 1915 there were primarily two groups of Herero in Namibia, Christians and soldiers.

In 1915 the German occupation of Namibia was replaced by South African occupation. On account of the South African invasion, the young Herero who had become German soldiers were left leaderless and without the social structure that had given them status and identity. Left in limbo these young men created a new social structure, based on that which they knew best, the German army. These newly created *Otruppe* provided the young men with identity, social support, contacts and standing.[9] The new South African administration was characterized by conflicts between paternalistic liberal interests and settler interests. Making use of the margins, created in the South African administration by these settler and liberal conflicts, the Herero reacquired cattle herds and demanded the restitution of land rights. The reacquisition of cattle, and the granting of reserves led to a growing independence on the part of the Herero vis-a-vis the new colonial administration. Overwhelmed by the sheer numbers of Herero demanding land rights,

[7] Shula Marks, in her *Reluctant Rebellion: the 1906–8 Disturbances in Natal* (Oxford 1970), has described how, in a similar series of misunderstandings and conscious deceit to those which led to the outbreak of the Herero-German war, the war against Bambatha became a self-fulfilling prophecy.

[8] The work of Peter Delius, 'The Nzundza Ndebele: Indenture and the making of ethnic identity, 1883–1914', in: *Holding their Ground: Class, Locality and Culture in 19th and 20th Century South Africa*, edited by P. Bonner, I. Hofmeyr, D. James, T. Lodge (Johannesburg 1989), pp. 227–58, on the Ndzundza Ndebele details how, following their defeat by the Transvaal Boers, the Ndebele were able to retain and reestablish their identity as Ndzundza Ndebele contrary to the wishes of their victors who wished to see them reduced to an amorphous mass of labour power. The manner in which the Ndzundza Ndebele were able to overcome their subjugation mirrors that of the Herero.

[9] The development of the *Otruppe* is a fascinating aspect of Namibian history and is sure to occupy the work of future academics dealing with Namibia. Suffice is to say that in many regions of the colonized world in the twentieth century people have engaged in activities that appear to mimic those of the colonizer. For interesting views on this phenomenon, see Terence Ranger, *Dance and Society in Eastern Africa, 1890–1970: The Beni Ngoma* (Berkeley 1975), Paul Stoller, *Embodying Colonial Memories: Spirit Possession, Power, and the Hauka in West Africa* (London 1995), Michael Taussig, *Mimesis and Alterity: A Particular History of the Senses* (New York 1993) and Peter Worsley, *The Trumpet Shall Sound: A Study of 'Cargo Cults' in Melanesia* (London 1957).

the administration overreacted and ensured the further radicalization of the Herero vis-a-vis the administration. This radicalization and opposition to colonial rule was reflected in the growth of independent churches, the development of new political groupings, such as the UNIA, and the emergence of a new Herero leadership. Though UNIA was initiated in Namibia by West Indians and Africans, its organizational structures soon passed over into the hands of Herero. The millenarian and militaristic messages purveyed by UNIA in Namibia ensured that UNIA was a catalyst in bringing together the two strands of Herero society existing at the time.[10] The universalistic pan-African identity of UNIA was soon discarded for a narrower, specific Herero identity which was first manifested, and therefore probably born, at the funeral of Samuel Maharero. The funeral not only brought together the two strands, Christians and soldiers, but also brought Herero in Namibia back into contact with Herero living in exile following the war of 1904. Herero society was refounded at the funeral of Samuel Maharero in 1923, when all the various splintered historical strands of Herero society came together to create that which had not existed beforehand, a single Herero identity.

This book, it is hoped, will provide a historical framework and basis for further research that is to be conducted on Herero society and history. It is, unashamedly, a history of the male elite. In particular it revolves around and concentrates on the activities of one man, Samuel Maharero. As such it calls for further research to be conducted on those who have been referred to in passing in this work, the other Herero chiefs, chiefdoms, councillors, evangelists, women and children.

In conclusion thus, the first half of this book dealt with the ways in which the political structures of Hereroland developed, in the last quarter of the nineteenth century, but could not cope with German imperialism. Indeed, even before the outbreak of the Herero–German war, Herero society was falling apart. The second half of this book dealt with Herero society in the aftermath of the Herero–German war when, on the basis of German militarism and missionary endeavour, Herero society reestablished itself. By 1923, and the funeral of Samuel Maharero, Herero society had redeveloped structures which could and were used to attempt to cope with the new colonial administration which the South Africans were creating, and further the struggle of the Herero towards redemption.

[10] Helen Bradford, in her *A Taste of Freedom: The ICU in Rural South Africa, 1924–1930*, has documented the impact of mass organizations on the rural communities in South Africa. That this impact was far greater than initially anticipated mirrors the case of the UNIA in Namibia between 1920 and 1923.

Sources & Bibliography

ARCHIVES

Namibia
Namibian National Archives Windhoek (NNAW)

This extensive and extremely well-organized institution provided the basis for this work.

1. Archives
1.1. Government departments and offices

ZBU	Zentralbureau des kaiserlichen Gouvernements 1884–1915
GSW	Kaiserliches Gericht Otjimbingwe und Bezirksgericht Swakopmund 1885–1915
GWI	Kaiserliches Bezirksgericht Windhoek 1890–1915
BSW	Kaiserliches Bezirksamt Swakopmund 1892–1915
BWI	Kaiserliches Bezirksamt Windhoek 1893–1915
BOM	Kaiserliches Bezirksamt Omaruru 1894–1915
BKA	Kaiserliches Bezirksmat Karibib 1894–1915
DOK	Kaiserliches Distriktsamt Okahandja 1894–1915
HBS	Kaiserliches Hafenbauamt Swakopmund 1896–1914
BLU	Kaiserliches Bezirksamt Lüderitzbucht 1896–1915
STR	Kaiserliche Schutztruppe für D.S.W.A. 1896–1915
BOU	Kaiserliches Bezirksamt Outjo 1897–1915
DGO	Kaiserliches Distriktsamt Gobabis 1898–1915
EKW	Eingeborenenkommissariat Windhoek 1900–14
DZE	Kaiserliches Distriktsamt Zessfontein 1901–12
GLU	Kaiserliches Bezirksgericht Lüderitzbucht 1906–14
GOM	Kaiserliches Bezirksgericht Omaruru 1909–15
ADM	Secretary of the Protectorate 1915–20
OCT	Officer Commanding Union Troops 1915–19
NOM	Native Affairs Omaruru 1915–33
NAW	Native Affairs Windhoek 1916–40
SWAA	SWA Administration: Secretariat, A-series 1920–60

1.2 Magistrates
>   LLU   Lüderitz 1914–
>   LGR   Grootfontein 1915–
>   LOK   Okahandja 1915–
>   LOM   Omaruru 1915–
>   LSW   Swakopmund 1915–
>   LTS   Tsumeb 1915–
>   LWI   Windhoek 1915-
>   LOU   Outjo 1915–
>   LGO   Gobabis 1919–
>   LUS   Usakos 1927–

1.4 Commissions and Committees of Enquiry
>   KCO   Concessions 1919–
>   KWL   War Losses 1920–

1.5 Boards
>   RLA   Land Board 1919–47

2.Accessions
>   A.3   Maharero 1860–87
>   A.37   R. Duncan 1888–91
>   A.100   J. von Moltke 1883–1922

3. Microforms
3.1. Government departments and offices
>   ZBU   Zentralbureau 1884–1914
>   ADM   Secretary for the Protectorate 1915–20

Archives of the Evangelical Lutheran Church in Namibia (ELCIN), Windhoek, Namibia

At the time of my visit to these archives in 1992 and 1993 they were being reorganized by Pastor Weßler who, during the course of his work, helped me extensively and gave me access to files which had not yet been catalogued. Amongst these were a number of files dealing with the Grootfontein district. Where I have cited these files in the text I have indicated that they were uncatalogued. Unfortunately, as Weßler continued his work, and I continued my research, it became apparent that a number of files had gone missing at some stage in the late 1980s when parts of the archive were micro-filmed. Particularly galling is the loss of *Stationsakten* relating to Okahandja.

I. Konferenzprotokolle und Beilagen
>   1.11   Beilagen zum Konferenz Protokoll 1898
>   1.13   Antwortschreiben an die Herero und Namakonferenz 1863–
>   86 und Beilagen
>   1.14   1889–1904 Gouvernement Korrespondenz (Gesetze Zoll
>   Reservate)
>   1.16   Briefe von Nama u. Hererohauptlingen 1864–72
>   1.17   Politisches Briefe 1879–92
>   1.18   Briefe Maharero u.a. 1885–1904
>   1.21   1888–90 Besondere Angelegenheiten
>   1.22   Konferenz Protokoll Karibib 15–17 Januar 1906
>   Konferenz Protokoll Otjimbingwe 15–26 Sept 1906

1.29	Beilagen und Protokolle 1913–22
1.3	1873–1905 Protokollbuch der Konferenzen im Hereroland
1.4	1887–99 1906/1909 Protokolle der Nama und Herero Konferenzen

II. Innere Verwaltung

1.1	1888–1904 Korrespondenz Viehe
	Abschriften ausgegangenen Briefe 1888–1904
	Verschiedene eingegangene Briefe 1892–1903
1.2	Korrespondenz zwischen Missionar Brockmann und Praeses Eich 1905–8
1.3	Verschiedenes 1900–8
1.7a	Inland Briefe 1905 (von Missionaren)
	Verschiedene Inland Briefe 1905
	Briefe betreffend Industrieschule 1905
	Rundbriefe von Eich 1905
9.1,7	Privatbrief von Missionar J. Bohm aus der Auffstandszeit 1904 ff aus Walfischbay

V. Chroniken

13.2	Keetmanshoop Herero
20.2	Okahandja Ortsgeschichte
22.2	Okombahe
23.1 & 2	Omaruru
25.	Otjimbingwe
27.	Outjo
31.	Swakopmund
32.	Karibib
33.	Usakos
6.2	Gaub
8.	Gobabis
10.	Grootfontein
12.	Karibib
37.	Windhoek (Herero/Ovambo)

VII. Einzelne Stationen

12 Karibib
12.1	1902–8 Copierbuch
12.2	Korrespondenz 1906–7
12.3	Rheinische Mission Otjimbingwe Amtliche Briefe des Inlandes außer Schreiben v.u. an die Regierung 1908–20

22 Okombahe
| 22.1 | Brief des Kapitan Cornelius 1894 |
| 22.2 | Schriftstucke vom Distriktsamt und Korrespondenzen mit demselben 1900–15 |

23 Omaruru
| 23.2 | Berichte ans Missionshaus 1910–30 |
| 23.3 | Berichte 1895–1964 Auszuge aus der Ortschronik uber u. von Frau Kuhlmann |

27 Franzfontein
27.1	Alte Akten aus der Franzfontein Gemeinde 1895–1904 Missionar Reichmann
27.2	Alte Akten Fragmente *ca.* 1895–1904
27.3	Gemeinde Glieder Franzfontein

31 Swakopmund

Botswana
Botswana National Archives (BNA), Gaborone

1) 'HC' Series – Papers of the High Commissioner, Cape Town, including Administrator/Deputy Commissioner Vryburg, 1884–99
2) 'RC' Series – Papers of Resident Commissioner, Mafekeng, *ca.* 1895–1930
3) 'DC' Series – Papers of Resident Magistrate/District Commissioner Offices to 1958
4) 'AC' Series – Papers of Assistant Commissioners North and South, *ca.* 1890–1924
5) PP series – Misc. Private Papers
6) BNB – Misc. holdings of Archives library including books, manuscripts, microfilms and audio tapes

South Africa
Barlow Rand Archives, Johannesburg

These archives contain the files of H. Eckstein & Co. who had a controlling share in the now defunct Anglo-French company, which recruited Samuel Maharero and his followers and settled them on land in the northern Transvaal following their flight from Namibia.

Box HE 208 F 12
    HE Record Dept. 24 April 1903–4 February 1907
Box HE 221 F 47C
    HE Record Dept. Chamber of Mines Labour importation agency Ltd. 18 April 1904
Box HE 290 F251W
    HE Record Dept. WNLA & CMLIA Amalgamation 31 Aug. 1905–30 Dec. 1909

Cape Archives Depot (CAD), Cape Town

Government House (GH)
    Vol. 23 General despatches
        /40   Raising among the Natives in German Territory of Damaraland 1896
        /82   Herero natives from German South West Africa crossing into Cape Colony 1904
        /120   Regarding extradition of Bondels Paul and Abraham Herero 1908

Attorney General (AG)
    Vol. 1733 Jacko and Hans, Damara Boys. Brought from West coast for indentureship to Farmers. Walfish Bay 1906–1907
    Vol. 1847 Damara Men, Women and Children. Deportation of certain. Gordonia 1908
    Vol. 1931 Blouboeke en Wetboeke in Verband met Damaraland en Walfisch Bay 1880–1906

Native Affairs (NA)
    Vol. 166–9

Letters received from Special Magistrate Northern Border. 1874–87
Vol. 170–271
Letters received from Civil Commissioners and resident Magistrates. 1873–1904
Vol. 285–293
Letters received from Damaraland and Walvisbay. 1876–91
Vol. 398–477
Letters received from private individuals, institutions and local bodies. 1865–1907
Vol. 1128–35
Papers of Labour agents. 1897–1903
Vol. 1136–42
Papers of W. Coates Palgrave. 1876–84

Public Works Department (PWD)
Vol. 2/70
Memorandum on the collection of Berg Damaras in the vicinity of Walwich Bay, 21/1/81
Vol. 2/8/20
Aided Immigration. Introduction of Natives from Damaraland and St Helena. 1891–3

Zimbabwe
Zimbabwe National Archives (ZNA), Harare

In April 1993 I was given permission to do one day of research in these archives. I spent most of the day trying to track down Herero who may possibly have ended up in Zimbabwe as labourers following the Herero–German war, particularly as the labour recruiter 'Matabele' Wilson was active amongst Herero refugees in the aftermath of the war. In the event I only found one possible tenuous source:

A 11 2/8/22, Wankie Mine Labour

Germany
Bundesarchiv Potsdam (BAP)

Reichskolonialamt, 10.01 (RKA)

Allgemeine Angelegenheiten in Deutsch-Südwestafrika
Expeditionen und Reisen Goering, Gouverneuren, Offizieren, Missionaren und Kaufleuten, in die verschiedene teilen der Kolonie. Abschluss von Schutzvertragen mit Stammeshauptlingen. Lageberichte und Vorschläge für die weitere Entwicklung der Kolonie.

2078 B	Band 1 Jan 1886–Juli 1886
2079 B	Band 2 Juli 1886–Juli 1887
2080 B	Band 3 Juli 1887–Jan 1892
2081	Band 4 Jan 1892–Mai 1894
2082 B	Band 5 Juni 1894–Marz 1896
2083	Band 6 Apr 1896–Sep 1902

Das Herero-Land (Damara-land) und Namaqua land. Sept 1880–Feb
1881
2098–102
Aufstand der Hereros 3 Bänder (1890s)
2103-5
Entsendung einer bewaffneten Expedition gegen die Hereros unter
Führung des Hauptmanns von Francois. 5 Bänder; Marz 1889–Sept
1892
2106-10
Das Gebiet des Hererohauptlings von Omaruru (1885) Okt 1894–Okt
1898
2150
Hinrichtung des Herero Kanjemi Aug 1911- Sept 1911
1492
Expeditionen der SWA Company 2 Bänder; Sept 1892–Juli 1896
1480–1
Berichte des Mr. Matthew Rogers an die SWAC Nov 1892–Okt 1893
1482
2 Bänder Kronland und Eingeborenenreservate in SWA Jan 1893–
Jan 1903; – Aug 1921
1218–19
Auswanderung von Afrikanern aus Südwestafrika, Aug 1901–Febr
1902
1225
Sklavenhandel in DSWA Sept 1889–Sept 1895
1959
3 Bänder Robert Lewis (Minenrechte) 1886–1895
1574–6
4 Bänder Rindvieh in DSWA Juli 1893–Mai 1920
8417–20
Aufenthalt von Robert Koch und Stabsarzt Kohlstock in Südafrika und
Südwestafrika zur Bekampfung der Viehseuchen 3. Bänder. Okt 1896–
1908
6089–91

Vereinigte Evangelischen Missionsarchiv (VEMA), Wuppertal

C Feldakten
C/g Allgemeines
C/h Stationen und Farmen
C/k Missionarskonferenzen
C/s Prädides und Inspektoren in SWA, Inspektionsreisen

UNPUBLISHED THESES & PAPERS

Durham, Deborah, *Greetings in Another Key: Playing with Language and Identity in Botswana*, Paper read at 1994 annual meeting of the African Studies Association, Toronto.
Gewald, Jan-Bart, *The Creation of Damaraland: The Creation of a new Ethnicity?*, paper presented at conference on 'Ethnicity and Nationalism in Southern Africa', held in Grahamstown, South Africa, April 1993.
— *Bakgalagadi ethnic formation in post independence Namibia*, presented at the annual

RUL ISS Africa seminar, The Hague, 8 June 1993.
— *The Road of the Man called Love and the Sack of Sero: The export of Herero labour to the South African Rand, 1890–1914*, presented at the Annual meeting of the African Studies Association, Boston, 4–7 December 1993.
— *The Return of Herero Refugees to Namibia post 1914*, presented at "'Trees never meet, but people do'": Mobility and containment in Namibia, 1915–1945', Workshop, Cambridge University, Cambridge, 10–11 December 1993.
— *Death by Camel: the Herero Succession Dispute of 1890–1894*, presented at the PhD seminar RUL, Leiden, 29 April 1994.
— *The Curse of Kahimemua: the impact of rinderpest in Hereroland*, presented at the Namibian history conference, *'Geschichte Schreiben: Konstruktion von Gesellschaft und Identität in Namibia'*, Hanover, 5 May 1994.
— *Seeking to return?, Herero exiles 1904–1923*, presented at the Annual meeting of the African Studies Association, Toronto, 3–6 November 1994.
— *The life and times of Mbadamassi, a soldier for King and Kaiser*, presented at the CNWS Seminar 'Ethnic Soldiering and its Impact', held in Leiden on 13–14 January 1995.
— *Unburdening myself of Herero history*, presented at the African studies PhD seminar RUL, Leiden, 8 March 1995.
Gibson, Gordon D., *The Social Organization of the Southwestern Bantu*, DPhil Thesis, University of Chicago (Chicago 1952).
Hagolani, Elhanan, *Das Kulturmodell der Bantu-sprechenden Rindernomaden Südwestafrikas*, DPhil Thesis, Universität zu Köln (New York 1968).
Hayes, Patricia, *A History of the Ovambo of Namibia, ca. 1880–1930*, PhD, Cambridge University, 1992.
Hendrickson, Anne Alfhild Bell, *Historical Idioms of Identity: Representation among the Ovaherero in Southern Africa*, PhD Thesis (New York 1992).
— *Women, Dolls and Herero Identity in Urban Namibia and Botswana*, paper presented at ASA conference Toronto 1994.
Henrichsen, Dag, *Herrschaft und Identität im vorkolonialen Zentralnamibia. Das Damaraland im 19. Jahrhundert*, PhD, University of Hamburg, 1998.
Kandapaera, Kaendee, *War, Flight, Asylum: A brief history of the Ovambanderu of Ngamiland, Botswana, 1896–1961*, unpublished BEd research essay submitted to Department of History, University of Botswana, May 1992.
Kinahan, John, *Pastoral Nomads of the Central Namib Desert*, PhD, University of the Witwatersrand, 1989.
Krieger Hinck, Carla, *Über die Medizische Versorgung der ehemaligen Kolonie Deutsch Südwest Afrika*, DMed, Uni München, 1973.
Krüger, Gesine, *A pass token in the archives. Traces of the history of every day life after the German–Herero war*, unpublished paper presented at the Symposium, 'Writing History. Identity and society in Namibia', held at the Department of History, University of Hanover, 5–7 May 1994.
— *'He has come. He is going. The sun.' Aspekte von Kriegsbewältigung, Identität und Rekonstruktion in der Hererogesellschaft*, Vortrag Humboldt-Universität 26/10/94 – Colloquium Peripherie–Zentrum Universität Hannover 14/11/94.
— *'. . . so schicke uns jemanden mit einem Brief von Dir.' Alltagsgeschichtliche Quellen zur Nachkriegszeit des Deutsch-Hererokriegs 1904–1907*, working paper No. 1: 1995, presented in Basle, 27/9/1995, Basler Afrika Bibliographien.
— *Kriegsbewältigung und Geschichtsbewusstsein. Zur Realität, Deutung und Verarbeitung des deutschen Kolonialkriegs 1904–1907*, PhD, University of Hanover, 1995.
Malan, J.S., *Dubbele afkomsberekening by die Himba, 'n Herero-sprekende volk in Suidwes-Afrika*, unpublished DLitt et Phil dissertation, Rand Afrikaans University (Johannesburg 1971).
Morton, Barry, *A Social and Economic History of a Southern African Native Reserve: Ngamiland, 1890–1966*, PhD, Indiana University, 1996.
Rooyen, J.W.F. van, *A sociological study of ideology among the Herero in central Namibia*,

MA, UNISA, Pretoria, 1984.

Schoeman, S.J., *Suidwes-Afrika onder militêre bestuur 1915–1920*, MA, UNISA (Pretoria 1975).

Schrank, G., *German South West Africa: Social and Economic Aspects of its History, 1884–1915*, New York University, PhD, 1974.

Silvester, Jeremy Gale, *Black Pastoralists, White Farmers: The dynamics of land dispossession and labour recruitment in southern Namibia 1915–1955*, PhD, School of Oriental and African Studies, 1993.

Stals, E.L.P. and A. Otto-Reiner, *Oorlog en Vrede aan die Kunene; Die verhaal van Kaptein Vita Tom 1863–1937* (Windhoek 1990).

Steyn, H.P., *Pastoralisme by die Himba van Suidwes-Afrika*, PhD, University of Stellenbosch, 1978.

Sundermeier, Theo, *Die Oruuano und ihre Spaltungen* (Windhoek n.d.).

Werner, Wolfgang, *An economic and social history of the Herero of Namibia, 1915–1946*, PhD, University of Cape Town, 1989.

NEWSPAPERS & PERIODICALS

Berichte der Rheinischen Missionsgesellschaft, 1884–1923.

Deutsches Kolonialblatt: Amtsblatt für die Schutzgebiete des Deutschen Reichs, herausgegeben in der Kolonial-Abteilung des auswärtigen Amts, 1903–14.

Deutsche Kolonialzeitung: Organ des deutschen Kolonialvereins, 1903–4, 1906.

The Namibian, 1986–1996.

The Negro World, 8 October 1921.

Onze Wereld, December 1995.

Die Republikein, 28/8/95; 15/9/95 & 20/9/95

The South African Review of Books, Feb/March, June/July, Aug/Oct 1990.

Windhoek Observer, 18/8/1979.

PUBLISHED SOURCE MATERIALS & BOOKS

Alexander, J.E., *Expedition of Discovery into the Interior of Africa*, 2 volumes (London 1838).

Almagor, Uri, 'Pastoral Identity and Reluctance to Change; the Mbanderu of Ngamiland', in *The Journal of African Law*, 24 (1980), 1, pp. 35–61.

Alnaes, K., 'Oral Tradition and Identity; the Herero in Botswana', in *The Societies of Southern Africa in the 19th and 20th Centuries*, Vol. 11 (1981), pp. 15–23.

— 'Living with the past: The songs of the Herero in Botswana', in *Africa*, 59.3 (1989), pp. 267–99.

Ambler, Charles, *Kenyan Communities in the Age of Imperialism* (Yale 1988).

Anderson, Benedict, *Imagined Communities: Reflections on the Origin and Spread of Nationalism*, Revised and extended edition (London 1991).

Anderson, David M. and Douglas H. Johnson (eds), *Revealing Prophets* (London 1995).

Andersson, Charles John, *Lake Ngami: or, exploration and discoveries during four years' wanderings in the wilds of South Western Africa* (London 1856) (Cape Town 1967 reprint).

— *The Matchless Copper Mine in 1857: Correspondence*, Charles John Andersson Papers edited by Brigitte Lau, Vol. I (Windhoek 1987).

— *Trade and Politics in Central Namibia 1860–1864*, Charles John Andersson Papers, Vol. II (Windhoek 1989).

Auer, G., *In Südwestafrika gegen die Hereros: Nach den Kriegs-Tagebüchern des Obermatrosen G. Auer*, bearbeitet von M. Unterbeck, Zweite Auflage (Berlin 1911).

Baines, Thomas, *Explorations in South-West Africa* (Salisbury [Harare] 1973 reprint).

Ballard, C., 'The repercussions of Rinderpest: Cattle plague and peasant decline in colonial Natal', in *The International Journal of African Historical Studies*, 19, 3 (1986).

Beinart, William, 'Cape workers in German South-West Africa, 1904–1912: Patterns of migrancy and the closing of options on the Southern African labour market', in *The Societies of Southern Africa in the 19th and 20th Centuries*, collected seminar papers No. 27, Vol. 11, University of London, Institute of Commonwealth Studies, 1981.

Bley, Helmut, *South West Africa under German Rule, 1894-1914*, translated and edited by Hugh Ridley (London 1971), first published in German (Hamburg 1968).

Bonner, P., *Kings, Commoners and Concessionaires: The Evolution and Dissolution of the nineteenth-century Swazi State* (Cambridge 1983).

Brauer, Dr Erich, *Züge aus der Religion der Herero: Ein Beitrag zur Hamitenfrage* (Leipzig 1925).

Bridgman, J.M. *The Revolt of the Hereros* (Berkeley 1981).

Brincker, H., *Wörterbuch und kurzgefasste Grammatik des Otji-Hérero mit Befügung verwandter Ausdrücke und Formen des Oshi-Ndonga – Otj-Ambo* (Leipzig 1886) reprint 1964.

Calvert, Albert, *South West Africa during the German Occupation, 1884-1915* (London 1915).

Cawthra, Gavin. *Brutal Force: The Apartheid War Machine* (London 1986).

Chapman, James, *Travels in the interior of South Africa, comprising fifteen years hunting and trading, with journeys across the continent from Natal to Walvisch Bay and visits to Lake Ngami and the Victoria Falls* (London 1868).

Clarence Smith, W.G. and R. Moorsom, 'Underdevelopment and class formation in Ovamboland, 1845–1915', in *Journal of African History*, XVI, 3 (1975) pp. 365–81.

Cohen, David William, *The Combing of History* (Chicago 1994).

Cooke, H.J., 'The Physical Environment of Botswana', in *Proceedings of the Symposium on Settlement in Botswana: the historical development of a human landscape*, edited by R. Renée Hitchcock and Mary R. Smith, Botswana Society (Gaborone 1982).

Dammann, E., '100 Jahre wissenschaftlicher arbeit am Herero', in *Uebersee Rundschau*, 9 (1957) No.4 (July) p. 65.

Dannert, Eduard, *Zum Rechte der Herero insbesondere über ihr Familien- und Erbrecht* (Berlin 1906).

Dedering, Tilman, 'The German–Herero-War of 1904: Revisionism of genocide or imaginary historiography? *The Journal of Southern African Studies*, Vol. 19, No. 1, 1993, pp. 80–8

De Josselin De Jong, J.P.B., *De Maleische Archipel als Ethnologisch Studieveld* (Leiden 1935).

Delius, Peter, *The Land Belongs to Us: The Pedi Polity, the Boers and the British in the Nineteenth Century Transvaal* (Braamfontein 1983).

— 'The Ndzundza Ndebele: Indenture and the making of ethnic identity, 1883–1914', in *Holding their Ground: Class, Locality and Culture in 19th and 20th Century South Africa*, edited by P. Bonner, I. Hofmeyr, D. James, T. Lodge (Johannesburg 1989), pp. 227–58.

Denbow, James, 'A new look at the later prehistory of the Kalahari', in *Journal of African History*, 27 (1986), pp. 3–28.

Drechsler, H., *'Let us Die Fighting': The Struggle of the Herero and Nama against German Imperialism (1884-1915)* (London 1980), first published in German (Berlin 1966).

Dubow, Saul, *Racial Segregation and the Origins of Apartheid in South Africa: 1919–36* (Oxford 1989).

Eirola, Marti, *The Ovambogefahr: The Ovamboland Reservation in the Making* (Rovaniemi 1992).

Elbourne, Elizabeth and Robert Ross, 'Combatting Spiritual and Social Bondage: Early missions in the Cape Colony', in Richard Elphick and Rodney Davenport (eds), *A History of Christianity in Southern Africa* (Cape Town, Berkeley and Oxford 1998) pp. 31–50.

Elphick, Richard, *Khoikhoi and the Founding of White South Africa* (Johannesburg 1985).

Emmett, Tony, 'Popular Resistance in Namibia, 1920–1925', in *Resistance and Ideology in Settler Societies*, Southern African Studies Vol. 4, edited by Tom Lodge (Johannesburg 1986).

Erkkilä, Antti and Harri Siiskonen, *Forestry in Namibia 1850–1990*, University of Joensuu (Joensuu 1992).

Esterhuyse, J.H., *South West Africa, 1880–1894: the Establishment of German Authority in South West Africa* (Cape Town 1968).

Estorff, Ludwig von, *Wanderungen und Kämpfe in Südwestafrika, Ostafrika und Südafrika: 1894–1910* (Windhoek 1979).

Farson, Negley, *Behind God's Back* (London and New York 1941).

Ferguson, R. Brian, 'Tribal Warfare', *Scientific American*, pp. 90–5, January 1992.

— *War in the Tribal Zone: Expanding States and Indigenous Warfare*, edited by R. Brian Ferguson and Neil L. Whitehead (Santa Fe 1992).

Francois, Curt von, *Deutsch Südwestafrika* (Berlin 1899).

Francois, Hugo von, *Nama und Damara* (Magdeburg 1895).

Galaty, John G. and Pierre Bonte, *Herders, Warriors, and Traders: Pastoralism in Africa*, Westview Press (Oxford, Boulder 1991).

Galton, Francis, *The Narrative of an Explorer in Tropical South Africa, being an account of a visit to Damaraland in 1851* (London 1853 & 1890).

Generalstabes, *Kämpfe der deutschen Truppen in Südwestafrika, bearbeitet nach Angaben der Kriegsgeschichtlichen Abteilung I des Großen Generalstabes. Erster Band. Der Feldzug gegen die Hereros* (Berlin 1906–8).

Gewald, Jan-Bart, 'The Great General of the Kaiser', in *Botswana Notes and Records*, Vol. 26, 1994, pp. 67–76.

— 'Untapped Sources: Slave exports from southern and central Namibia up to the mid-nineteenth century', in *The Mfecane Aftermath*, edited by C. Hamilton (Johannesburg 1995).

— 'Forced Labour in the *Onjembo*, the Herero German war of 1904–1908', *Itinirario*, Vol. XIX (1995) number 1.

— 'History in the making: Commemorations of the dead and Herero identity in the 20th century', in *Proceedings CERES/CNWS Summer School 1994*, edited by J. van der Klei (Utrecht 1995).

— 'On being Damara between 1893 and 1993', forthcoming *Quellen zur Khoisan-Forschung/Research in Khoisan Studies* (Cologne 1998).

Gibson, Alan G.S., *Between Cape Town and Loanda: a Record of Two Journeys in South West Africa* (London 1905).

Gibson, Gordon D., 'Double Descent and its Correlates among the Herero of Ngamiland', *American Anthropologist*, Vol. 58, No. 1, February 1956, pp. 109–39.

Godee Molsbergen, Dr E.C., *Reizen in Zuid Afrika in de Hollandsche Tijd*, tweede deel, de Linschoten vereeniging (The Hague 1916).

Gordon, Robert J., *The Bushman Myth: the Making of a Namibian Underclass* (Boulder, San Francisco, Oxford 1992).

— 'The Impact of the Second World War on Namibia', in *Journal of Southern African Studies*, 1993, Vol. 19, no. 1, pp. 147–65.

Grundlingh, Albert, *Fighting Their Own War: South African Blacks and the First World War*, Ravan Press (Johannesburg 1987).

Guy, Jeff, *The Destruction of the Zulu Kingdom* (London 1979).

Haacke, Wulf D., 'The Kalahari Expedition March 1908. The Forgotten Story of the

Final Battle of the Nama War', in *Botswana Notes and Records*, Vol. 24, 1992, pp. 1–18

Hahn, Carl Hugo, *Tagebücher 1837–1860; Diaries Parts I–V, A Missionary in Nama- and Damaraland*, edited and compiled by B. Lau (Windhoek 1985).

Hahn, Carl Hugo (Cocky) with L. Fourie and H. Vedder, *The Native Tribes of South West Africa* (Cape Town 1928).

Hahn, Josaphat, 'Das Land der Ovahereró', in *Zeitschrift der Gesellschaft für Erdkunde zu Berlin*, 1868, pp. 194–243.

— 'Die Ovaherero', in *Zeitschrift der Gesellschaft für Erdkunde zu Berlin*, Verlag von Dietrich Reimer (Berlin 1869).

Hahn, Theophilus, 'Ein Rassenkampf im nordwestlichen Theile der Cap-Region', in *Globus*, 14, 1869 pp. 270–1.

Hall, Justice, *Hall Report 1960, Report of the commission of enquiry into the occurrences in the Windhoek location on the night of the 10th to the 11th December, 1959* (Pretoria 1960).

Hamilton, Caroline and John Wright, 'The Making of the Amalala: ethnicity, ideology and relations of subordination in a precolonial context', *South African Historical Journal*, 22, November 1990.

Hendrickson, Anne Alfhild Bell, 'The "Long" Dress and the Construction of Herero Identities in Southern Africa', *African Studies*, Vol. 53, No. 2, 1994, pp. 25–54.

— 'Bodies and Flags: The representation of Herero identity in colonial Namibia', in *Clothing and Difference: Embodied Identities in Colonial and Post-Colonial Africa*, Duke University Press (Durham 1996) H. Hendrickson ed.

Henrichsen, Dag, '"Ehi rOvaherero". Mündliche Überlieferungen von Herero zu ihrer Geschichte im vorkolonialen Namibia', *Werkstatt Geschichte* No. 9: Afrika – Europa, Hamburg December 1994.

Henrichsen, Dag, and Gesine Krüger, '"We have been captives long enough, we want to be free": Land, uniforms and politics in the history of Herero during the interwar period', in *Namibia Under South African Rule: Mobility & containment 1915–46*, ed. P. Hayes, M. Wallace, J. Silvester and W. Hartmann (Windhoek, Oxford and Athens 1998).

Herero-Texte, *Herero-Texte; erzahlt von A. Kukuri*, übers. und hrsg. von E. Dammann (Berlin 1983).

Heywood, A., Lau, B. and Ohly, R. (eds), *Warriors, Leaders, Sages and Outcasts in the Namibian Past* (Windhoek 1992).

Hillebrecht, W., 'Habe keinerlei Papiere in deiner Kiste . . .', *Werkstatt Geschichte*, No. 1 (Hanover 1992).

Hintrager, Oskar, *Südwestafrika in der deustchen Zeit* (Munich 1955).

Hofmeyr, Isabel, *'We Spend our Years as a Tale That is Told': Oral Historical Narrative in a South African Chiefdom* (Johannesburg 1993).

Irle, J., *Die Herero: Ein Beitrag zur Landes-, Volks- und Missionskunde* (Gütersloh 1906) (Nendeln, Kraus reprint, 1973).

Kinahan, Jill, 'Heinrich Vedder's sources for his account of the exploration of the Namib coast', *Cimbebasia*, 11, pp. 33–9, 1989.

Kinahan, John, *Pastoral Nomads of the Central Namib Desert: The People History Forgot*, Namibia Archaeological Trust, New Namibia Books (Windhoek 1990).

Kjekshus, H., *Ecology Control and Economic Development in East African History: The Case of Tanganyika, 1850–1950* (London 1977).

Klopper, Sandra, 'Mobilising Cultural Symbols in Twentieth Century Zululand' in R. Hill, M. Muller and M. Trump, *African Studies Forum I* (Pretoria 1991) pp. 193–226.

Köhler, Oswin, 'The stage of acculturation in South West Africa', *Sociologus*, 1956, Vol. 6, No. 2, pp. 138–53.

Kühne, Horst, 'Die Ausrottungsfeldzüge der "Kaiserlichen Schutztruppen in Afrika" und die sozialdemokratische Reichstagsfraktion', *Militärgeschichte*, Band 18, 1979.

Lamphear, John, 'The People of the Grey Bull: The origin and expansion of the

Turkana', *JAH*, 1988, Vol. 29, No. 1, pp. 27–39.
— *The Scattering Time: Turkana Responses to Colonial Rule* (Oxford 1992).
Lange, Gerald, *Imperial Service* (Jonannesburg 1991).
Lau, Brigitte, '"Thank God the Germans came": Vedder and Namibian historiography', in *Africa Seminar Collected Papers*, Centre for African Studies, University of Cape Town, Vol. 2, pp. 24–53, edited by K. Gottschalk and C. Saunders (Cape Town 1981).
— 'The Kommando in southern Namibia, 1800-1870', in *Perspectives on Namibia: Past and Present*, edited by C. Saunders, Centre for African Studies, University of Cape Town (Cape Town 1983), pp. 25–44.
— 'Conflict and power in nineteenth-century Namibia', *Journal of African History*, 27 (1986).
— *Southern and Central Namibia in Jonker Afrikaner's Time* (Windhoek 1987).
— 'Uncertain Certainties: The Herero–German war of 1904', *Mibagus*, No. 2, Windhoek April 1989, pp. 4–8. Republished in B. Lau, *History and Historiography*, edited by A. Heywood (Windhoek 1995) pp. 39–52.
Lebzelter, Viktor, *Eingeborenenkulturen in Südwest- und Südafrika* (Leipzig 1934).
Legassick, M., 'The Northern Frontier to 1820: The emergence of the Griqua people', in *The Shaping of South African Society, 1652–1820*, edited by Richard Elphick and Hermann Giliomee, Maskew Miller Longman (Cape Town 1984) pp. 243–90.
Lehmann, Rudolf, 'Einige Spannungs- und Ausgleichserscheinungen in der Sozialen Organisation Mittel- und SWA völker', in *Thurnwald Festschrift; Beiträge zur Gesehungs- und Völkerwissenschaft* (Berlin 1950).
— 'Die Häuptlings-Erbfolgeordnung der Herero', *Zeitschrift für Ethnologie*, Band 76, 1951, pp. 94–102.
Lenssen, H.E., *Chronik von Deutsch-Südwestafrika* (Windhoek 1994).
Leutwein, Theodor, *Elf Jahre Gouverneur in Deutsch-Südwestafrika* (Berlin 1906).
Lonsdale, John, 'The Prayers of Waiyaki: Political uses of the Kikuyu past', in David Anderson and Douglas Johnson (eds), *Revealing Prophets: Prophecy in Eastern African history* (London 1995).
Loth, H., *Die Christliche Mission in Südwestafrika* (Berlin 1963).
Loton Ridger, A., *A Wanderer's Trail: Being a faithful record of travel in many lands* (New York 1914).
Luttig, Hendrik Gerhardus, *The Religious System and Social Organisation of the Herero* (Utrecht 1933).
Malan, J.S., 'Double Descent among the Himba of South West Africa', *Cimbebasia*, Ser. B, Vol. 2, No. 3, 1973, pp. 81–112.
— 'The Herero-speaking people of Kaokoland', *Cimbebasia*, Ser. B, Vol. 2, No. 4 (1974), pp. 113-29.
— *Peoples of South West Africa/Namibia* (Pretoria 1980).
Marais, Eugene N., *Sketse uit die Lewe van Mens en Dier* (Kaapstad 1928).
Marks, Shula, *Reluctant Rebellion: The 1906–8 Disturbances in Natal* (Oxford 1970).
Martin, Henno, *The Sheltering Desert* (Windhoek 1983) originally published in German. First English edition 1957, reprinted 1974.
Mbanderu, *The Mbanderu: Their History until 1914 as told to Theo Sundermeier in 1966*, translated from German by Annemarie Heywood and annotated by Brigitte Lau (Windhoek 1986).
McKiernan, Gerald, *The Narrative and Journal of Gerald McKiernan in South West Africa, 1874–1879*, edited by P. Serton (Cape Town 1954).
Medeiros, Carlos Laranjo, *Vakwandu: History, Kinship and Systems of Production of an Herero People of South-West Angola* (Lisbon 1981).
Mertens, Alice, *South West Africa and its Indigenous Peoples* (London 1966).
Meyer, Felix, *Wirtschaft und Recht der Herero* (Berlin 1905).
Mossolow, N., *Waterberg: Beitrag zur Geschichte der Missionsstation Otjozondjupa des Kambazembi-Stammes und des Hererolandes*, John Meinert (Windhoek 1980?).

Mudimbe, V.Y. *The Invention of Africa: Gnosis, Philosophy, and the Order of Knowledge* (Bloomington and London 1988).

Noyes, John Kenneth, *Colonial Space, Spatiality, Subjectivity and Society in the Colonial Discourse of German South West Africa 1884–1915* (Philadelphia 1992).

Nuhn, Walter, *Sturm über Südwest: Der Hereroaufstande von 1904 – Ein düsteres Kapitel der deutschen kolonialen Vergangenheit Namibias* (Koblenz 1989).

Nurse, G.T., 'Population movement around the Northern Kalahari', in *African Studies*, 42 (1983), 2, pp. 153, 163.

Ohly, R., *The Destabilization of the Herero Language* (Windhoek 1987).

Onselen, Charles van, 'Reactions to Rinderpest in South Africa 1896–97', *Journal of African History* XIII 3 (1972), pp. 473–88.

Page, Melvin E., *Africa and the First World War*, Macmillan Press (London 1987).

Pager, H., *The Rock Paintings of the Upper Brandberg. Part 1: Amis Gorge*, Heinrich Barth Institute (Cologne 1989).

Palgrave, W.C., *The Commissions of W.C. Palgrave: Special Emissary to South West Africa 1876–1885*, edited and introduced by E.L.P. Stals (Cape Town 1991), Second Series No. 21, Van Riebeeck Society.

Paul, C., *Die Mission in unseren Kolonien* (Dresden 1905).

Peires, J.B., *The Dead Will Arise: Nongqawuse and the Great Xhosa Cattle-killing Movement 1856–7*, Ravan Press (Johannesburg and London 1989).

Penn, N.G., 'Pastoralists and pastoralism in the northern Cape frontier zone during the eighteenth century', in *The South African Archeological Society, Goodwin Series: Prehistoric Pastoralism in Southern Africa*, Vol. 5, June 1986, pp. 63–98.

— 'The Frontier in the Western Cape, 1700–1740', *Papers in the Prehistory of the Western Cape, South Africa*, edited by J. Parkington and M. Hall, BAR International Series 332 (Cape Town 1987) pp. 464–5.

Phoofolo, Pule, 'Epidemics and Revolutions: The rinderpest epidemic in late nineteenth-century southern Africa', in *Past and Present*, No. 138, 1993, pp. 112–43.

Poewe, K., *The Namibian Herero* (Lewiston and Queenston 1983).

Pool, Gerhardus, *Die Herero-Opstand 1904–1907* (Cape Town 1979).

— *Samuel Maharero* (Windhoek 1991).

Prein, Philipp, 'Guns and Top Hats: African resistance in German South West Africa, 1907–1915', *Journal of Southern African Studies*, Vol. 20, No. 1, 1994, pp. 99–121.

Ranger, Terence, *Dance and Society in Eastern Africa, 1890–1970: The Beni Ngoma* (Berkeley 1975).

— 'European Attitudes and African Realities: The rise and fall of the Matola chiefs of south-east Tanzania', *Journal of African History*, 20, I, 1979, pp. 63–82.

— 'The invention of tradition in colonial Africa', in E. Hobsbawm and T. Ranger (eds), *The Invention of Tradition* (Cambridge 1983).

— *Peasant Consciousness and Guerilla War in Zimbabwe* (Harare 1985).

— 'The Invention of Tradition Revisited: The case of colonial Africa', in T. Ranger and O. Vaughan (eds), *Legitimacy and the State in Twentieth Century Africa: Essays in Honour of A.H.M. Kirk-Greene* (London 1993), pp. 62–111.

Report, *Report on the Natives of South West Africa and Their Treatment by Germany* Cd 9146, prepared in the Administration Office, Windhoek, January 1918 (London 1918).

Rohrbach, P., *Deutsche Kolonialwirtschaft* (Berlin-Schöneberg 1907).

Ross, Robert, 'The destruction and reconstruction of Khoisan society in the Cape Colony', forthcoming in R. Ross, R. Vossen and E. Wilmsen (eds) *Language History and Identity: Papers from the First Khoisan Conference, Tutzing 1994* (Cologne 1998) in *Quellen zur Khoisanforschung*/Research in Khoisan Studies.

Rust, C., *Krieg und Frieden im Hererolande: Aufzeichnungen aus dem Kriegsjahre 1904* (Berlin 1905).

Sanitätsbericht, *Sanitätsbericht über die kaiserliche Schütztruppe für SWA während des Herero und Hottentottenaufstandes für die Zeit vom 1/1/04–31/3/07*, Band 1 (Berlin

1909).

Schapera, Isaac, *Notes on some Herero Genealogies* (Cape Town 1945 [Johannesburg 1979]).

Schlosser, K., 'Die Herero in Britisch-Betschuanaland-Protektorat und ein Besuch in einer ihrer Siedlungen Ncwe-le-tau', *Zeitschrift für Ethnologie*, Vol. 80 (Berlin 1955), pp. 200–58.

Schoeman, S. and E. Schoeman, *Namibia* (Oxford 1984).

Schultze, Leonhard, *Zoologische und anthropologische Ergebnisse einer For-schungsreise im westlichen und zentralen Südwestafrika* (Jena 1909).

Schwarz, E.H.L., *The Kalahari or Thirstland Redemption* (Cape Town ?1920/28).

Scott, M., *A Time to Speak* (London 1958).

Shillington, Kevin, *The Colonisation of the Southern Tswana, 1870–1900* (Braamfontein 1985).

Siiskonen, Harri, *Trade and Socioeconomic Change in Ovamboland, 1850–1906*, Studio Historica 35 (Helsinki 1990).

Smith, A.B., *Pastoralism in Africa: Origins and Development Ecology*, Witwatersrand University Press (Johannesburg 1992).

Spear, Thomas, 'Oral Traditions: whose history?', *History in Africa*, 8 (1981), pp. 165–83.

Spraul, Gunter, 'Der "Völkermord" an den Herero: Untersuchungen zu einer neuen Kontinuitätsthese', *Geschichte in Wissenschaft und Unterricht*, 1988/12, pp. 713-39.

Steenkamp, W.P., *Is the South-West African Herero Committing Race Suicide?* (Cape Town 1922).

Stoller, Paul, *Embodying Colonial Memories: Spirit Possession, Power and the Hauka in West Africa* (London 1995).

Strassberger, Elfriede, *The Rhenish Mission Society in South Africa 1830–1950* (Cape Town 1969).

Sudholt, Gert, *Die deutsche Eingeborenenpolitik in Südwestafrika. Von den Anfängen bis 1904* (Hildesheim, 1975).

Sundermeier, T. and S. Kuvare, *Die Mbanderu; Studien zu ihrer Geschichte und Kultur* (St Augustin, 1977); English translation Windhoek, 1986.

Taussig, M, *Shamanism, Colonialism and the Wild Man: A Study in Terror and Healing* University of Chicago Press (Chicago 1986, 1987).

— *Mimesis and Alterity: A Particular History of the Senses* (New York 1993).

Thompson, G., *Travels and Adventures in Southern Africa* (London 1827).

Tindall, B.A. (ed.), *The Journal of Joseph Tindall: Missionary in South West Africa 1839–55* (Cape Town 1959).

Tlou, Thomas, *A History of Ngamiland 1750 to 1906: the Formation of an African State* (Gaborone 1985).

Tonkin, Elizabeth, 'Investigating Oral Tradition', *Journal of African History*, 27 (1986), pp. 203–15.

Troup, Frida, *In the Face of Fear* (London 1950).

Truschel, L.W., 'German South West Africa', *Journal of Africana*, Vol. 14, No. 4 (1983), pp. 277-91.

Vail, Leroy (ed.), *The Creation of Tribalism in Southern Africa* (London 1989).

Van Onselen, Charles, *New Nineveh: Studies in the Social and Economic History of the Witwatersrand, 1886–1914* (Johannesburg 1982).

Vansina, Jan, *Oral Tradition as History* (Madison and London 1985).

— *Paths in the Rainforests: Towards a History of Political Tradition in Equatorial Africa* (Madison and London 1990).

Vedder, Heinrich, *South West Africa in early times, being the story of South West Africa up to the date of Maharero's death in 1890* (London 1938). Originally published in German in 1934, *Das Alte Südwestafrika: Südwestafrikas Geschichte bis zum Tode Mahareros 1890* (Windhoek reprint 1981).

Vivelo, F.R., *The Herero of Western Botswana* (New York 1977).

Vries, J.L. de., *Mission and Colonialism in Namibia* (Johannesburg 1978).

Wagner, Gunther, 'Aspects of conservatism and adaption in the economic life of the Herero', in *Sociologus*, 1952, Vol. 2, No. 1, pp. 1–25.

Walker, E.A., *A History of Southern Africa* (London 1965).

Warwick, Peter, *Black People and the South African War: 1899–1902* (Johannesburg 1983).

Weber, Otto von, *Geschichte des Schutzgebietes Deutsch-Südwest-Afrika*, second edition (Windhoek 1979).

Werner, Wolfgang, '"Playing Soldiers": The Truppenspieler Movement among the Herero of Namibia, 1915 to *ca.* 1945', *Journal of Southern African Studies*, Vol. 16, No. 3, September 1990, pp. 485–502.

Wesseling, H.L., *Verdeel en Heers. De Deling van Afrika, 1880–1914* (Amsterdam 1992).

Willan, B.D., 'The South African Native Labour Contingent, 1916–1918', *JAH*, 19 (1978) pp. 61–86.

Williams, Frieda-Nela, *Precolonial Communities in Southwestern Africa. A History of Ovambo Kingdoms 1600–1920* (Windhoek 1991).

Wilmsen, E.N., *Exchange Interaction and Settlement in North Western Botswana* (Boston 1980).

— *Land Filled with Flies* (Chicago 1989).

Witbooi, H., *Die dagboek van Hendrik Witbooi* (Cape Town 1929).

— *The Hendrik Witbooi Papers*, edited and translated by Eben Maasdorp (Windhoek 1991).

Worger, William, *South Africa's City of Diamonds, Mine Workers and Monopoly Capitalism in Kimberley, 1867–1895* (New Haven 1987).

Worsley, Peter, *The Trumpet Shall Sound: A Study of 'Cargo Cults' in Melanesia* (London 1957).

Wright, John, 'Politics, Ideology and the Invention of "Nguni"', in Tom Lodge (ed.), *Resistance and Ideology in Settler Societies* (Johannesburg 1986), pp. 96–118.

Yellen, J.E., and A.S. Brooks, 'The Late Stone Age Archaeology in the /Xai /Xai Region: a response to Wilmsen', *Botswana Notes and Records*, Vol. 22, Botswana Society (Gaborone 1990).

Index